Discover California

Experience the best of California

This edition written and researched by

Sara Benson,
Andrew Bender, Alison Bing, Celeste Brash,
Tienlon Ho, Beth Kohn,
Adam Skolnick, John A Vlahides

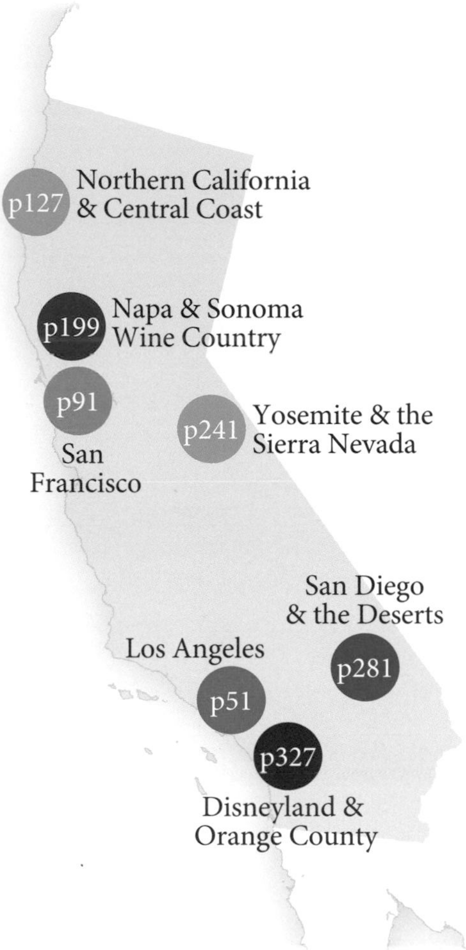

Northern California & Central Coast p127

Napa & Sonoma Wine Country p199

San Francisco p91

Yosemite & the Sierra Nevada p241

San Diego & the Deserts p281

Los Angeles p51

Disneyland & Orange County p327

Northern California & Central Coast

- Redwoods
- Santa Barbara
- Point Reyes
- Mendocino
- Lassen Volcanic National Park

Napa & Sonoma Wine Country

- Napa Valley
- Wine Tasting
- Historic Sonoma
- Old Faithful Geyser
- Culinary Institute of America at Greystone

Los Angeles

- Hollywood
- South Bay Bicycle Trail
- Getty Center & Getty Villa
- Griffith Observatory
- Venice Boardwalk

San Francisco

- Golden Gate Park
- Alcatraz Island
- Vintage Streetcars & Cable Cars
- North Beach
- Mission District

Yosemite & the Sierra Nevada

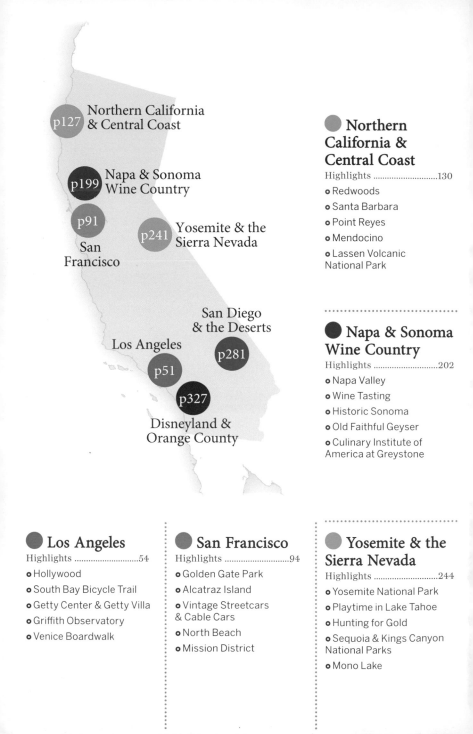

- Yosemite National Park
- Playtime in Lake Tahoe
- Hunting for Gold
- Sequoia & Kings Canyon National Parks
- Mono Lake

Contents

Plan Your Trip

Discover

Contents

Discover California

Disneyland & Orange County 327

In Focus

Survival Guide

This Is California

Everyone heads to the Golden State to find fame and fortune – but you can do better. Come for the landscape, stay for sensational food, and glimpse the future in the making on America's creative coast.

California is older than it seems. Coastal bluffs and snow-capped peaks created over millennia of tectonic upheavals threatened to shake California right off the continent. And after unchecked 19th-century mining, logging and oil drilling threatened to undermine its ancient natural splendors, California's pioneering environmentalists rescued about 2.5 million acres of old-growth trees. Conservation initiatives by John Muir and his Sierra Club created Yosemite National Park and Redwood National & State Parks, and though Unesco named them World Heritage sites, visitors call them simply breathtaking.

Every time they sit down to eat, Californians have nationwide impact. Since California produces most US fresh produce and specialty meats, minor menu decisions go a long way. Californians are taking trendsetting stands on mealtime moral dilemmas: certified organic versus spray-free, grass-fed versus grain-finished, farm-to-table versus urban-garden grown, veganism versus humanely raised meats. But no matter what you order, it's likely to be local and creative, and it better be good – Californians compulsively share their dining experiences via social-media platforms like Facebook, Twitter and Yelp, all created here. For a chaser, try a stiff drink: California produces the nation's most prestigious wines, and has more breweries than any other state.

Californians are once again getting by on their wits. From the Gold Rush to the dot-com bubble, California has survived booms and busts – and the recent US recession was no different. Trends are started here not by moguls in offices, but by a motley crowd of surfers, artists and dreamers concocting the out-there ideas behind skateboarding, interactive art and biotechnology. California always seems to have the talent and technology to stage another economic comeback – and if you linger long enough in art galleries, cafes and bars here, you may actually see the future coming.

> “Trends are kick-started here by a motley crowd of surfers, artists and dreamers.”

Cable car (p124), San Francisco

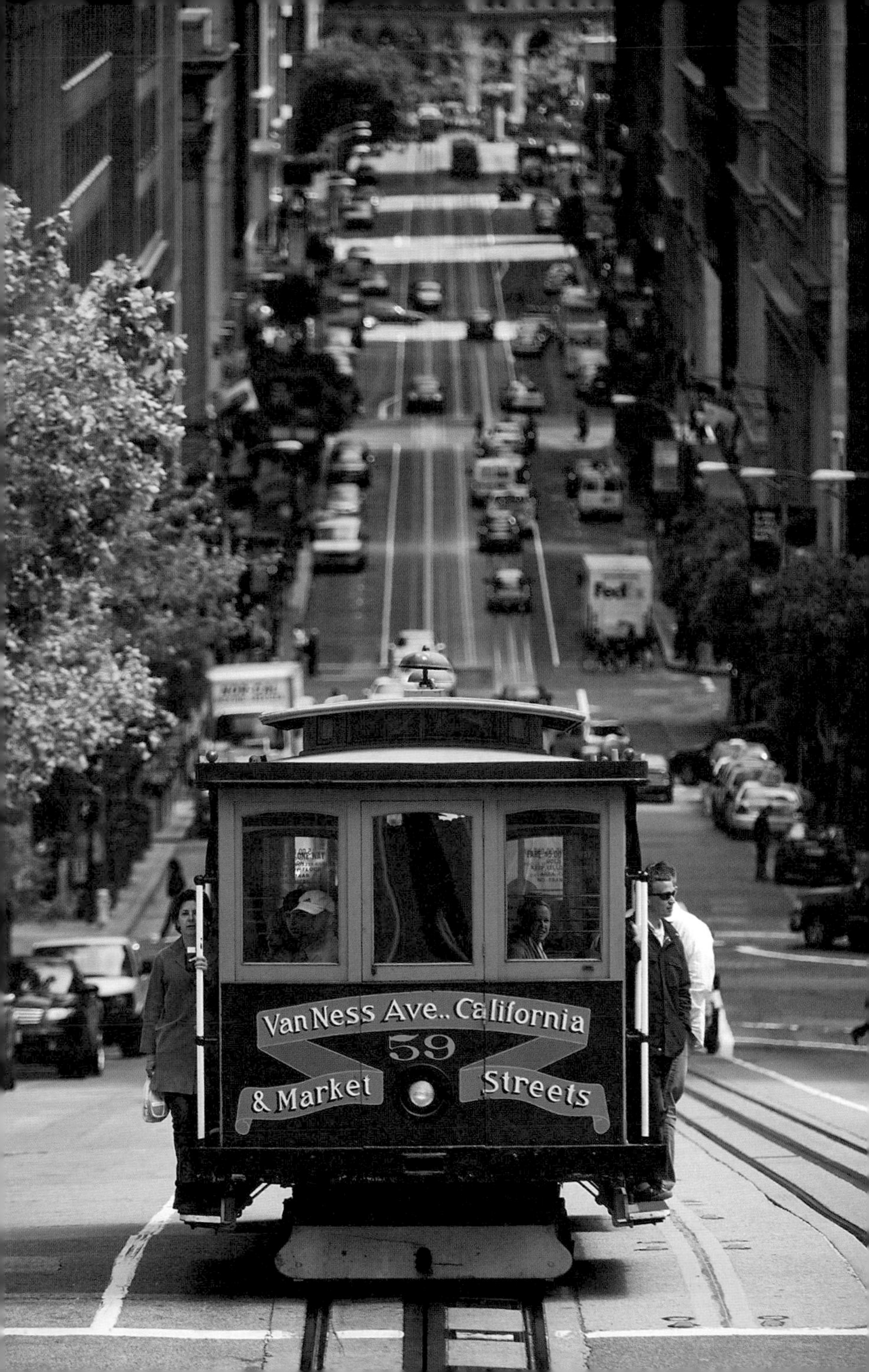
VanNess Ave.. California
59
& Market
Streets

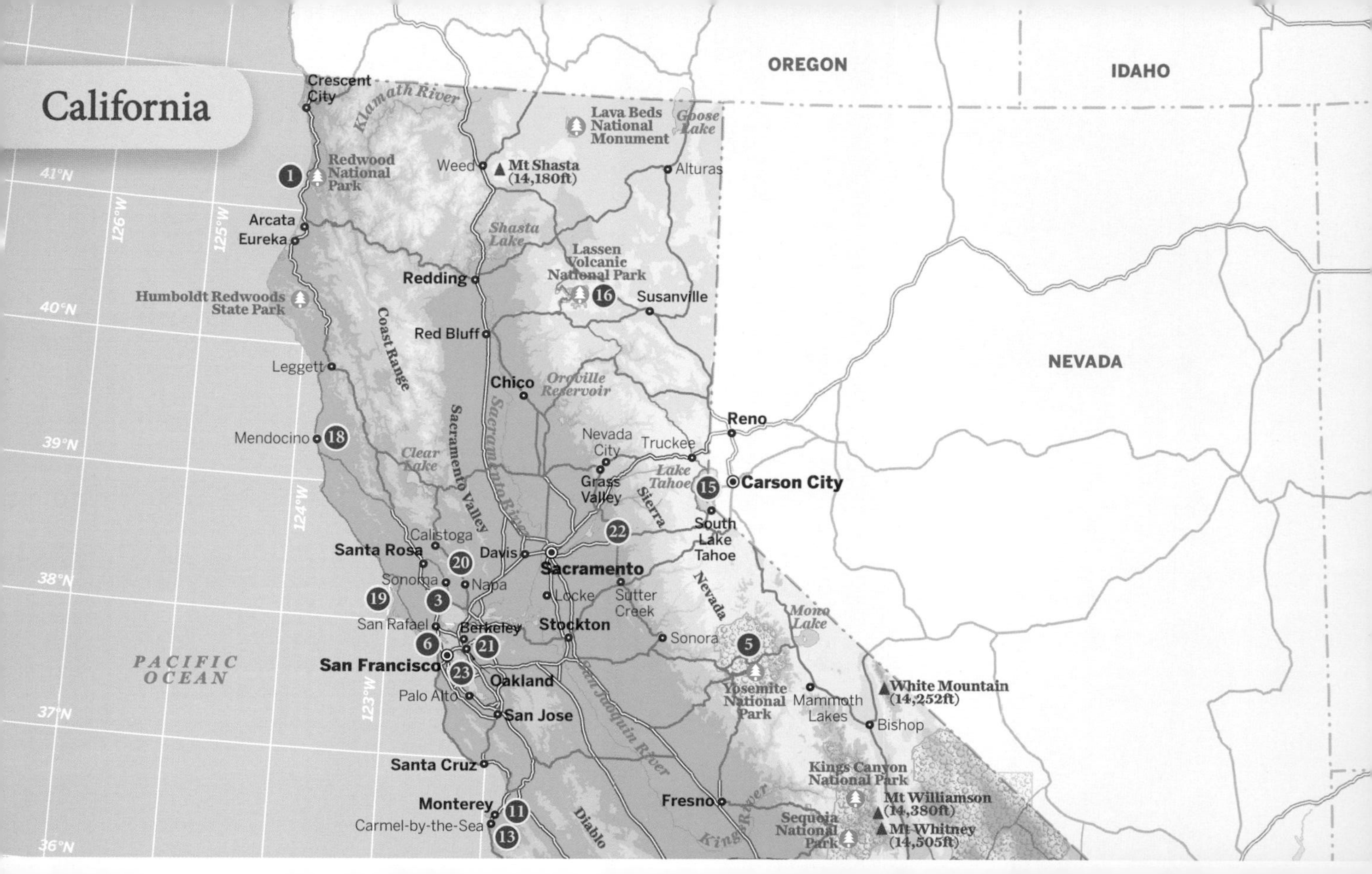
California
OREGON
IDAHO
NEVADA
PACIFIC OCEAN
Crescent City
Klamath River
Redwood National Park
Lava Beds National Monument
Goose Lake
Weed
Mt Shasta (14,180ft)
Alturas
Arcata
Eureka
Shasta Lake
Lassen Volcanic National Park
Redding
Humboldt Redwoods State Park
Susanville
Coast Range
Red Bluff
Leggett
Chico
Oroville Reservoir
Sacramento Valley
Sacramento River
Reno
Mendocino
Nevada City
Truckee
Clear Lake
Grass Valley
Lake Tahoe
Carson City
Sierra
South Lake Tahoe
Calistoga
Santa Rosa
Davis
Sacramento
Sonoma
Napa
Locke
Sutter Creek
Nevada
Mono Lake
San Rafael
Berkeley
Stockton
Sonora
San Francisco
Oakland
Yosemite National Park
Mammoth Lakes
White Mountain (14,252ft)
Palo Alto
San Jose
San Joaquin River
Bishop
Santa Cruz
Kings Canyon National Park
Fresno
Mt Williamson (14,380ft)
Monterey
Carmel-by-the-Sea
Diablo
Kings River
Sequoia National Park
Mt Whitney (14,505ft)
41°N
40°N
39°N
38°N
37°N
36°N
126°W
125°W
124°W
123°W
1
3
5
6
11
13
15
16
18
19
20
21
22
23

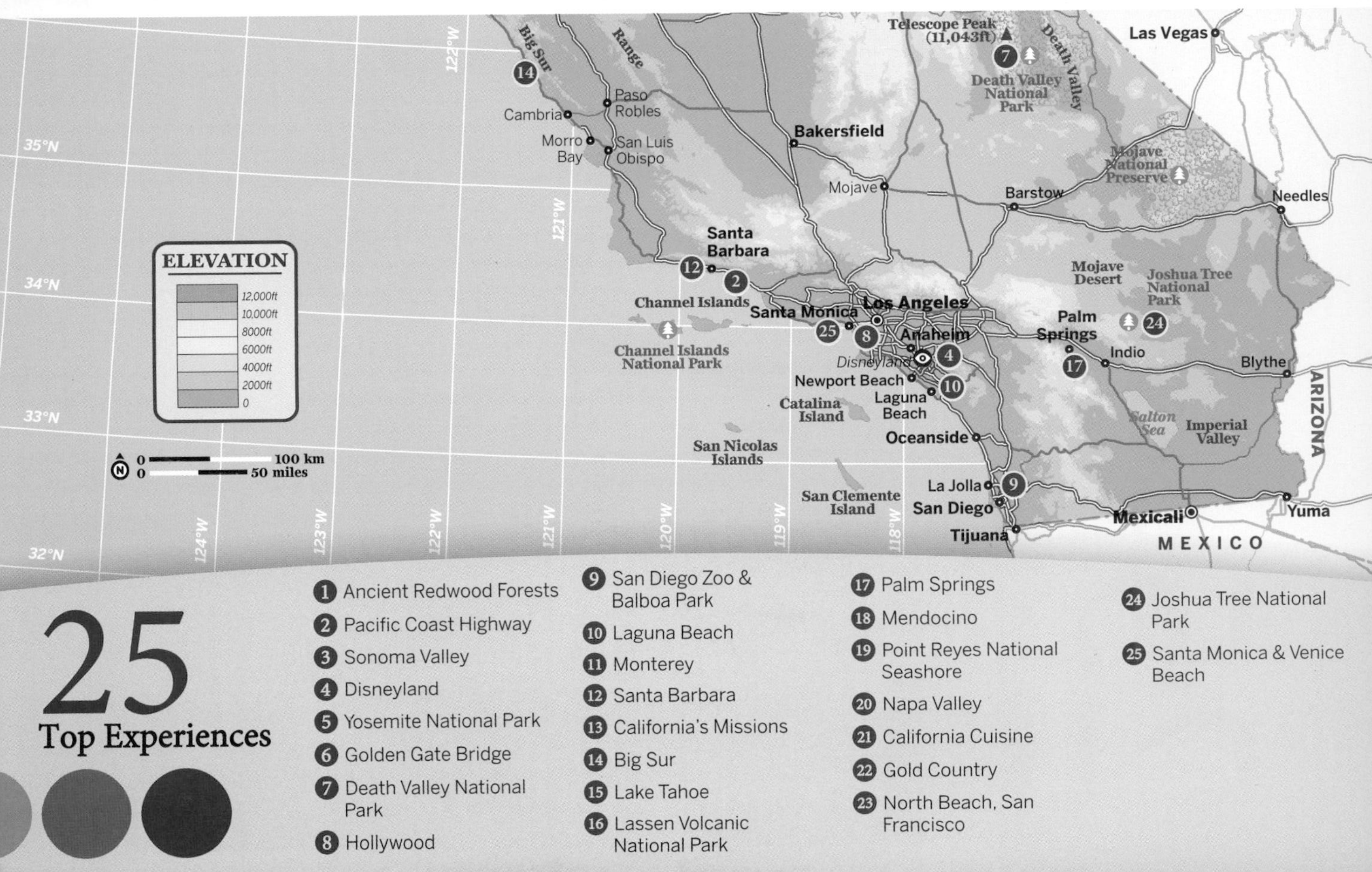

25 Top Experiences

1. Ancient Redwood Forests
2. Pacific Coast Highway
3. Sonoma Valley
4. Disneyland
5. Yosemite National Park
6. Golden Gate Bridge
7. Death Valley National Park
8. Hollywood
9. San Diego Zoo & Balboa Park
10. Laguna Beach
11. Monterey
12. Santa Barbara
13. California's Missions
14. Big Sur
15. Lake Tahoe
16. Lassen Volcanic National Park
17. Palm Springs
18. Mendocino
19. Point Reyes National Seashore
20. Napa Valley
21. California Cuisine
22. Gold Country
23. North Beach, San Francisco
24. Joshua Tree National Park
25. Santa Monica & Venice Beach

25 California's Top Experiences

Ancient Redwood Forests

Ditch the cell phone and hug a tree, man. And why not start with the world's tallest trees, the redwoods of Northern California? The state's towering giants grow along much of the coast, from Big Sur north to the Oregon border. It's possible to cruise past these trees – or even drive right through them at old-fashioned tourist traps – but nothing compares to the awe you'll feel while walking underneath them. Meditate at Muir Woods National Monument (p141), the Avenue of the Giants (p155) or Redwood National & State Parks (p163). Stout Grove (p167), Jedediah Smith Redwoods State Park

1

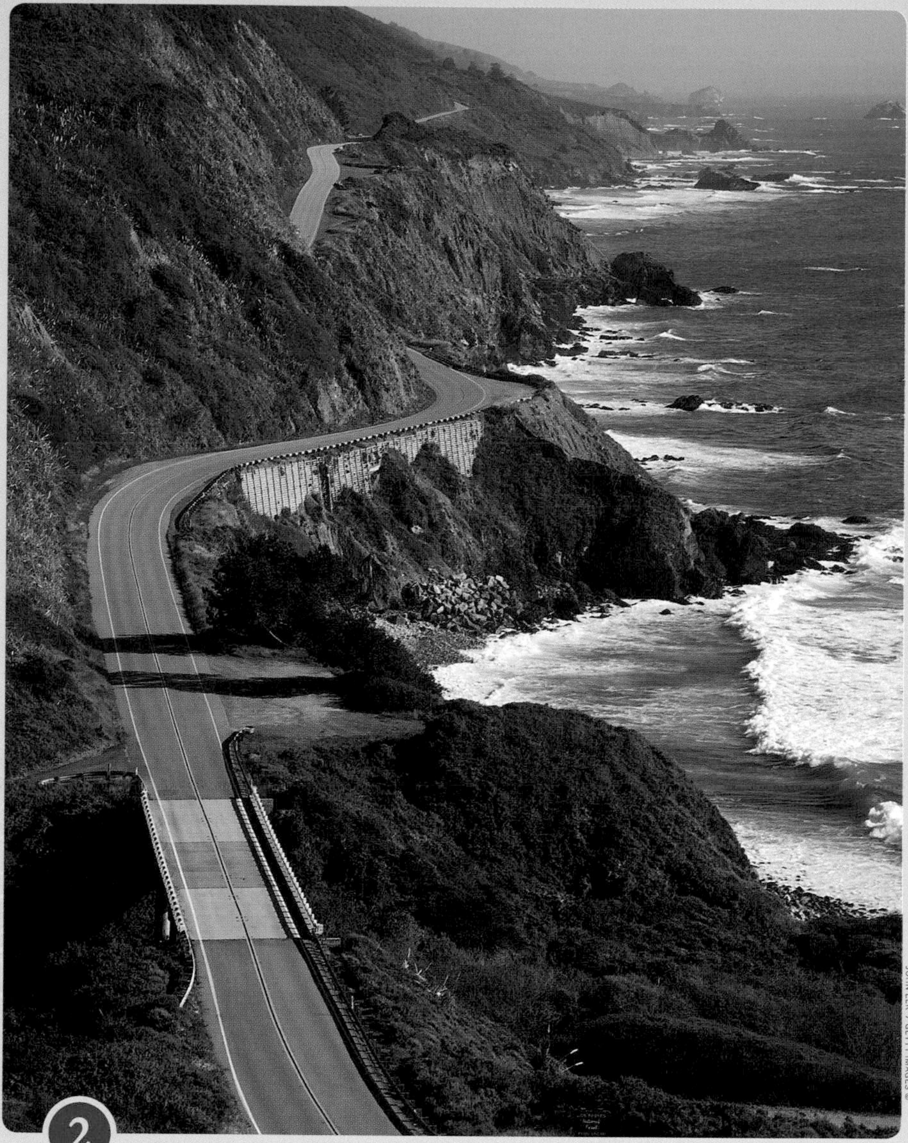

JOHN ELK / GETTY IMAGES ©

2

Pacific Coast Highways

Make your escape from traffic-jammed freeways and cruise the coast in the slow lane. PCH (the generic term for the route) snakes past sea cliffs and beach towns, and connects the dots between major coastal cities, too: surfin' San Diego, rocking LA and beatnik San Francisco. In between, you'll uncover hidden beaches, rustic seafood shacks, and wooden seaside piers for catching sunsets over the Pacific. Hwy 1

Sonoma Valley

As winemaking in the neighboring Napa Valley grows ever more dizzyingly upscale, in Sonoma Valley (p227) sun-dappled vineyards are surrounded by pastoral ranchlands. The uniqueness of *terroir* is valued most in this down-to-earth wine country, where you may taste new vintages straight from the barrel inside a tin-roofed shed while playing with the winemaker's pet dog. Who cares if it's not noon yet? Relax and enjoy your late-harvest zinfandel with a scoop of white-chocolate ice cream drizzled with organic olive oil. This is Sonoma; conventions need not apply. Barriques at a Healdsburg vineyard

3

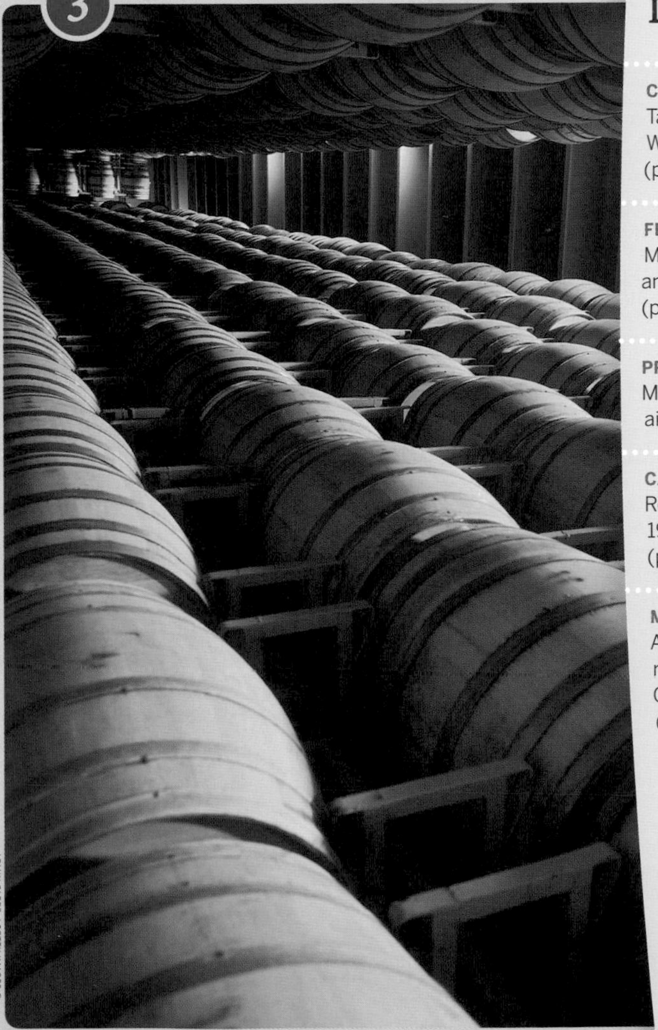

The Best... Dining Spots

CHEZ PANISSE
Taste the revolution Alice Waters started in Berkeley. (p148)

FERRY BUILDING
Mind-blowing restaurants and a farmers market. (p100)

PRADO
Mediterranean cuisine in airy Balboa Park. (p307)

CAFÉ BEAUJOLAIS
Romantic Cal-French in 19th-century surrounds. (p154)

MADRONA MANOR
A retro-formal Victorian mansion with artful California haute cuisine. (p219)

The Best...
Day Hikes

HALF DOME
Super-strenuous hike but worth every second. (p263)

GRIFFITH PARK
For spectacular views of LA and the Hollywood sign. (p65)

BUMPASS HELL
Traipse along a wooden boardwalk through geothermal wonders. (p168)

POINT LOBOS STATE NATURAL RESERVE
Watch as the wildflowers come out in April and May. (p180)

MUIR WOODS NATIONAL MONUMENT
The closest redwoods to San Francisco. (p141)

JUAN CAMILO BERNAL / SHUTTERSTOCK ©

4 Theme Parks

Disneyland (p336) is SoCal's most-visited tourist attraction. Inside Anaheim's mega-popular theme parks, beloved cartoon characters waltz arm-in-arm down Main Street, U.S.A., and fireworks explode over Sleeping Beauty Castle on hot summer nights. The state's theme-park fun doesn't stop there: Disney California Adventure (p338), Legoland (p305) and Knott's Berry Farm (p340) also draw huge crowds of the young and young-at-heart. Knott's Berry Farm

DOUGLAS STEAKLEY / GETTY IMAGES ©

5 Yosemite National Park

At Yosemite National Park (p258), meander through wildflower-strewn meadows in valleys carved by glaciers, avalanches and earthquakes. Everything looks bigger here, whether you're getting splashed by thunderous waterfalls that tumble over sheer cliffs, staring up at granite domes or walking in ancient groves of giant sequoias. Perch at Glacier Point during a full moon or drive the high country's dizzying Tioga Rd in summer.

Golden Gate Bridge

Sashay out onto San Francisco's iconic bridge (p100) to spy on cargo ships threading through pylons painted 'International Orange,' then take in 360-degree views of the rugged Marin Headlands, far-off downtown skyscrapers, and Alcatraz Island. Watch the boats with billowing sails tack across the bay, and the chilly surfers wipe out near Fort Point.

6

ORIEN HARVEY / GETTY IMAGES ©

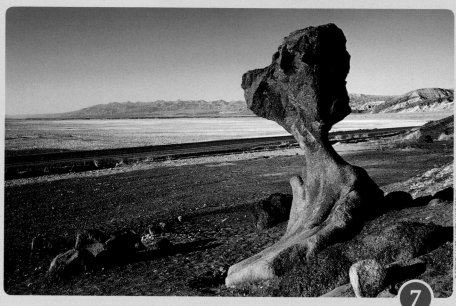

WITOLD SKRYPCZAK / GETTY IMAGES ©

7

Death Valley National Park

Just uttering the name brings up visions of broken-down pioneer wagon trains and parched lost souls crawling across desert sand dunes. But the most surprising thing about Death Valley (p322) is how full of life it really is. Spring wildflower blooms explode with a painter's palette of hues across camel-colored hillsides. Feeling adventurous? Twist your way up narrow canyons cluttered with geological oddities, stand atop volcanic craters formed by violent prehistoric explosions, or explore Wild West mining ghost towns where fortunes have been lost – and found. Mushroom Rock, Death Valley National Park

Hollywood

The studios have moved, but Hollywood (p62) and its pink-starred Walk of Fame still attracts millions of wide-eyed visitors every year. Like an aging starlet making a comeback, this once-gritty urban neighborhood in LA is undergoing a rebirth of cool, blossoming with hip hotels, restored movie palaces and glitzy bars. Snap a photo outside Grauman's Chinese Theatre or inside Hollywood & Highland's Babylon Court with the Hollywood sign as a backdrop – go ahead, we know you can't resist. Hollywood Walk of Fame (p62)

8

The Best... Beaches

SOUTH LAKE TAHOE
Try your sand with a panoramic dose of mountain vistas. (p251)

SANTA BARBARA
Sandy swimming beaches line the city tip to toe. (p193)

LAGUNA BEACH
You can't go wrong with volleyball and basketball courts, and excellent swimming. (p349)

HUNTINGTON BEACH
Ogle the surfers, and drop in if you dare. (p345)

CORONADO
Cycle down San Diego's Silver Strand and take a dip. (p301)

San Diego Zoo & Balboa Park

A rare SoCal urban green space, Balboa Park (p293) is where San Diegans come to play (when they're not at the beach, naturally). Bring the family and spend the day immersed in more than a dozen art, cultural and science museums, or just marveling at the Spanish revival architecture while sunning yourself along El Prado promenade. Glimpse exotic wildlife and ride the 'Skyfari' cable car at San Diego's world-famous zoo (p299), or see a show at the Old Globe Theater (p310), a reconstruction of the Shakespearean original. Balboa Park

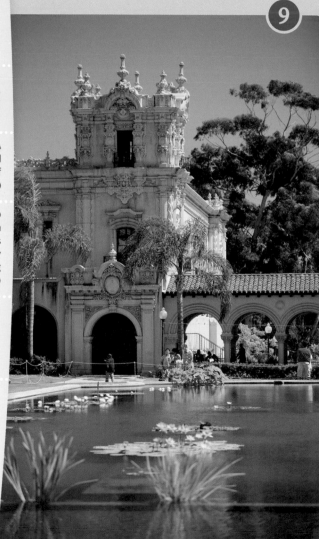

9

The Best... Drives

FOXEN CANYON WINE TRAIL
Hidden wineries among oak-covered hills. (p196)

MT SHASTA
Take the Everitt Memorial Hwy almost to the top of the mountain. (p169)

TIOGA ROAD
Highway 120 goes through the best of Yosemite's epic high country; it's only passable from late spring through early fall. (p260)

17-MILE DRIVE
A scenic journey around Pebble Beach, between Pacific Grove and Carmel. (p183)

AVENUE OF THE GIANTS
A 32-mile detour through the heart of redwood country. (p155)

RICHARD CUMMINS / GETTY IMAGES ©

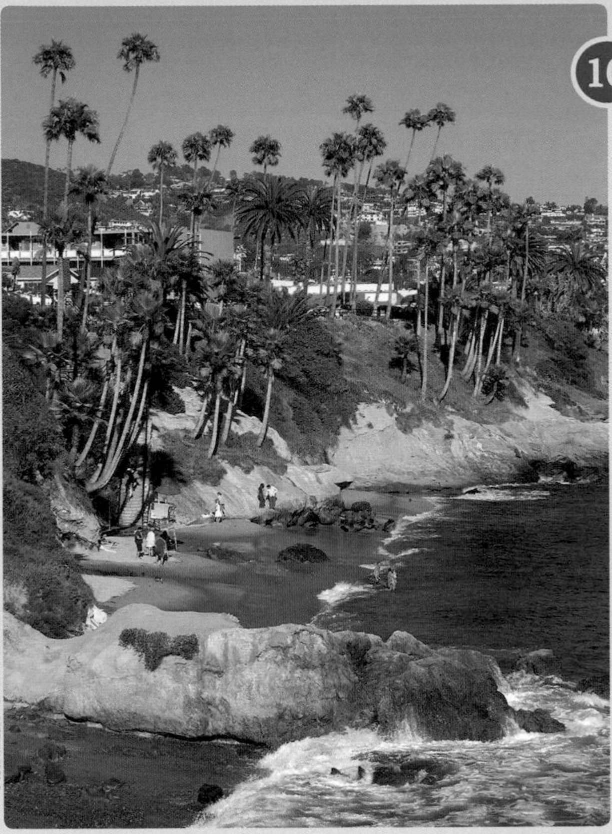

10 Laguna Beach

In Orange County, Huntington Beach draws the hang-loose trust-fund surfer crowd, while teens and yachties play in the soap-opera fantasyland of Newport Beach. But further south, Laguna Beach (p349) beckons, with its sophisticated blend of money and SoCal culture. Oh, and natural beauty: startlingly beautiful seascapes led an early-20th-century artists' colony to take root here. Laguna's bohemian past still peeks out in downtown's art galleries, historic arts-and-crafts bungalows tucked among multimillion-dollar mansions, and the annual Festival of Arts & Pageant of the Masters (p44).

11 Monterey

Forget those hypnotizing Hollywood visions of sun-soaked SoCal beaches. Northern California's hurly-burly fishing villages are made for heartier outdoors lovers. Hop aboard a whale-watching cruise out into Monterey Bay National Marine Sanctuary (p177), some of whose denizens of the deep also swim in Cannery Row's ecologically sound aquarium (p181). Soak up the authentic maritime atmosphere on the coast, or head downtown to Monterey State Historic Park (p176) to wander among flowering gardens and adobe-walled buildings from California's Mexican past. Jellyfish, Monterey Bay Aquarium

DOUGLAS STEAKLEY / GETTY IMAGES ©

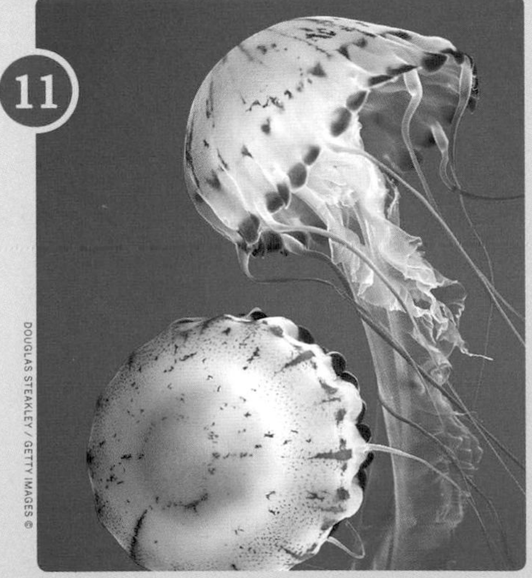

JOHN ELK III / GETTY IMAGES ©

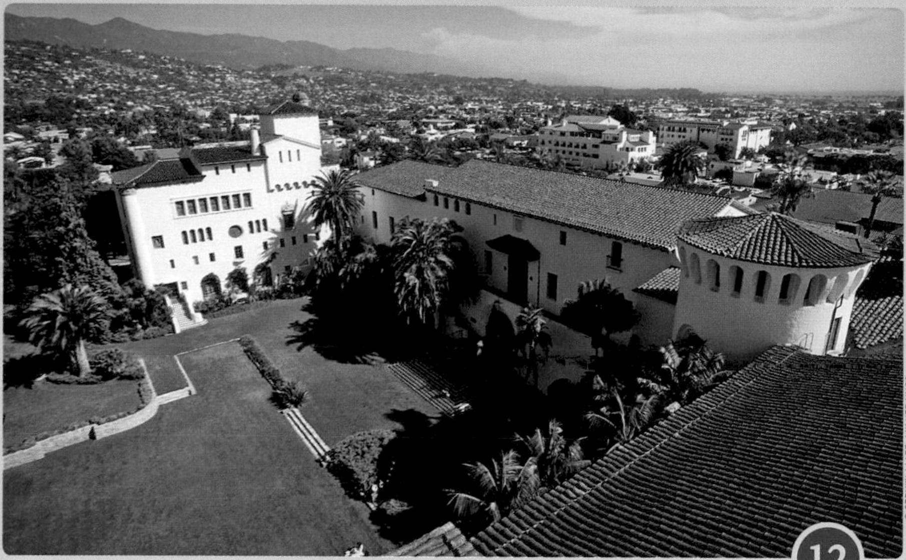

12

Santa Barbara

Egotistically calling itself the 'American Riviera,' – but that's not such a stretch – Santa Barbara (p190) is so idyllic, you just have to sigh. Waving palm trees, sugar-sand beaches, boats bobbing by the harbor – it'd be a travel cliche if it wasn't the truth. California's 'Queen of the Missions' is a beauty, as are downtown's red-roofed, whitewashed adobe buildings all rebuilt in harmonious historical style after a devastating 1925 earthquake. Come escape just for the day, or maybe a wine-drenched weekend in the country. Santa Barbara County Courthouse (p191)

EDDIE BRADY / GETTY IMAGES ©

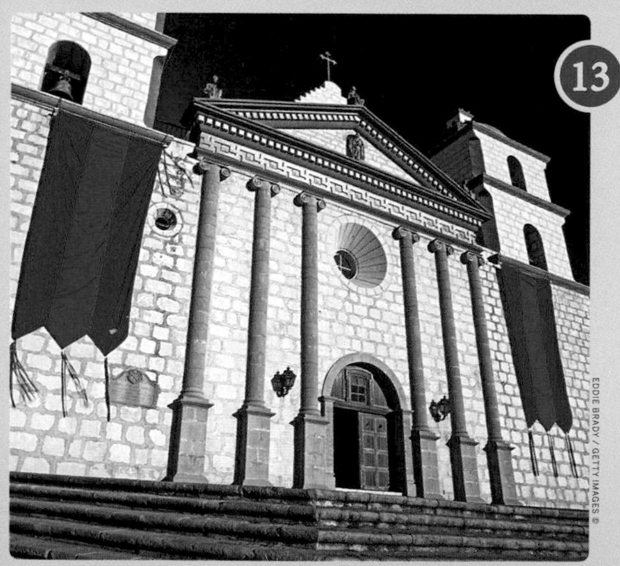

13

California's Missions

If you road-trip anywhere along the coast between San Diego (p290) and Sonoma (p231), you can't help but follow in the footsteps of early Spanish conquistadors and Catholic priests. Foremost among those colonists was peripatetic Padre Junípero Serra, who founded many of California's 21 historical missions in the late 18th century. Some have been authentically restored; others are just the ruins of an era long past. Mission Santa Barbara (p191)

Big Sur

Nestled up against mossy, mysterious-looking redwood forests, the rocky Big Sur (p182) coast is a secretive place. Get to know it like the locals do – find hidden hot springs and beaches where the sand is tinged purple. Time your visit for May, when waterfalls peak, or after summer-vacation crowds have left but sunny skies still rule. Look skyward to catch sight of endangered California condors taking wing above the cliffs.

14

THOMAS WINZ / GETTY IMAGES ©

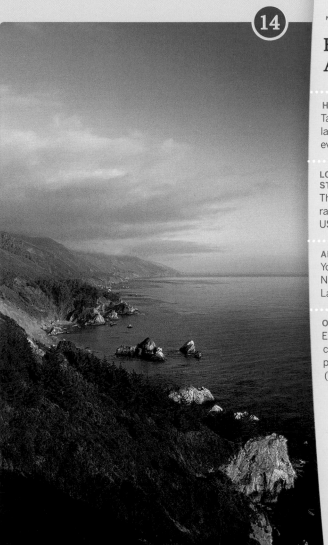

The Best... Historic Architecture

HEARST CASTLE
Take a tour of one of the largest private residences ever built in the US. (p189)

LOS ANGELES UNION STATION
The last of the grand railroad stations built in the USA. (p61)

AHWAHNEE HOTEL
Yosemite's swank lodge is a National Historic Landmark. (p265)

OLD TOWN
Explore San Diego's Mexican and early American past near Downtown. (p298)

The Best...
Maritime Museums

MONTEREY
Hundreds of artifacts spanning California's history. (p177)

SAN DIEGO
Step aboard the 1863 *Star of India* (p293) and the USS *Midway* aircraft carrier (p292).

SANTA BARBARA
Hands-on and virtual reality exhibits make this a fabulous destination for kids. (p192)

POINT ARENA LIGHTHOUSE
One of the only lighthouses on the West Coast where you can climb right to the top. (p152)

USS PAMPANITO
Tall folks will want to watch their heads on this WWII submarine. (p105)

RICHARD CUMMINS / GETTY IMAGES ©

RICHARD STOCKTON / GETTY IMAGES ©

Lake Tahoe

Tucked high in the Sierra Nevada mountains, this all-seasons adventure base camp revolves around the USA's second-deepest lake (p250). In summer, startlingly clear blue waters are perfect for splashing, kayaking or even scuba diving. Meanwhile, mountain-bikers careen down epic single-track and hikers stride along trails that thread through thick forests. After fun in the sun, you can retreat to a cozy lakefront cottage and toasts s'mores in the firepit. When the lake turns into a winter wonderland, gold-medal ski resorts keep downhill fanatics, punk snowboarders and Nordic traditionalists more than satisfied.

16 Lassen Volcanic National Park

This alien landscape bubbles over with roiling mud pots, noxious sulfur vents and steamy fumaroles, not to mention its colorful cinder cones and crater lakes. You won't find the engulfing crowds of more famous national parks at this off-the-beaten-path destination, but Lassen (p167) still offers peaks to be conquered, azure waters, forested campsites, and boardwalks through Bumpass Hell that will leave you awestruck by the terrible beauty.

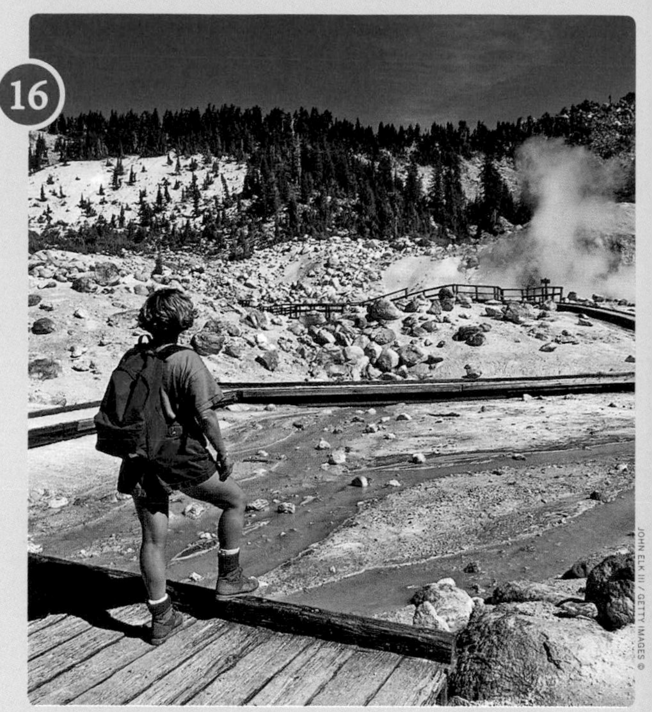

Fumaroles, Bumpass Hell (p168)

JOHN ELK III / GETTY IMAGES ©

17 Palm Springs

A star-studded oasis (p311) in the Mojave since the days of Frank Sinatra's Rat Pack, 'PS' is a chic desert resort getaway. Lounge by your Mid-Century Modern hotel's swimming pool; go art-golfing, gallery hopping or vintage shopping; and then drink cocktails from sunset till dawn. Feeling less loungey? Break a sweat on hiking trails through desert canyons on Native American tribal lands, or scramble to a summit in the San Jacinto Mountains, reached via an aerial tramway.

Palm Springs Aerial Tramway (p311)

BRIAN D CRUICKSHANK / GETTY IMAGES ©

Mendocino

Mendocino (p151) is the North Coast's sandcastle. Nothing restores the soul like a ramble out onto craggy headland cliffs and among berry brambles. In summer, fragrant bursts of lavender and jasmine drift along fog-laden winds. Year-round surf is never out of earshot, and driftwood-littered beaches are reminders of the sea's power. Originally a 19th-century port built by New Englanders, Mendocino today belongs to bohemians who would scoff at puritanical virtues, favoring art and nature's outdoor temple for their religions instead. Point Cabrillo Lighthouse (p152), Mendocino

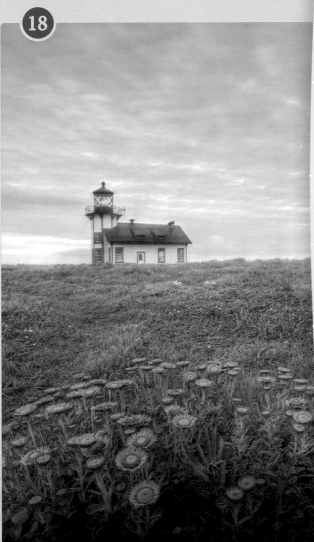

18

The Best... Unique Experiences

KINETIC SCULPTURE MUSEUM
If you miss the race in May, check out some of its former champion kinetic contraption entries. (p158)

MYSTERY SPOT
Travel back in time for optical illusions and campy good fun. (p176)

MADONNA INN
Fantastically bizarre theme rooms – check out the 'Caveman' or 'Yahoo' (p188)

ALCATRAZ
Sure, everyone goes, but it's a prison. On an island. In the middle of the bay. (p101)

The Best... Wildlife Watching

POINT REYES NATIONAL SEASHORE
Whales, elk and marine mammals galore. (p146)

ANŌ NUEVO STATE PARK
A beach crowded with noisy elephant seals. (p172)

YOSEMITE NATIONAL PARK
Keep your eyes peeled for bears and mule deer. (p258)

MOJAVE NATIONAL PRESERVE
Scan the Joshua tree landscape for desert tortoises, coyotes and jackrabbits. (p321)

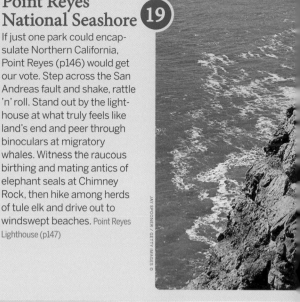

Point Reyes National Seashore 19

If just one park could encapsulate Northern California, Point Reyes (p146) would get our vote. Step across the San Andreas fault and shake, rattle 'n' roll. Stand out by the lighthouse at what truly feels like land's end and peer through binoculars at migratory whales. Witness the raucous birthing and mating antics of elephant seals at Chimney Rock, then hike among herds of tule elk and drive out to windswept beaches. Point Reyes Lighthouse (p147)

JAY SPOONER / GETTY IMAGES ©

WES WALKER / GETTY IMAGES ©

20 Napa Valley

A trip to Napa Valley (p210) lives up to the lore: visitors cruise the Silverado Trail on bicycles in search of the perfect cabernet, soak in the region's luxuriant spas and order dinner off the visionary menus of celebrity chefs. Among the endless fields of grapes and rolling, oak-dotted hills, this is a beautiful place to get pampered. Book a limo to transport you to your wine-tasting appointments, or dodge that pesky traffic in a hot-air balloon.

California Cuisine

The Golden State has seen more than its fair share of boom times and busts, and Hollywood starlets come and go, but for epicures, the prize remains the same: California's food and wine (p372). As you travel up and down the coast, tasting everything from fish tacos at seafood shacks to farm-to-table feasts on chefs' seasonal menus, you'll have just cause to pat your belly blissfully more than once.

Bowl of cioppino

21

LISA HUBBARD / GETTY IMAGES ©

RICHARD CUMMINS / GETTY IMAGES ©

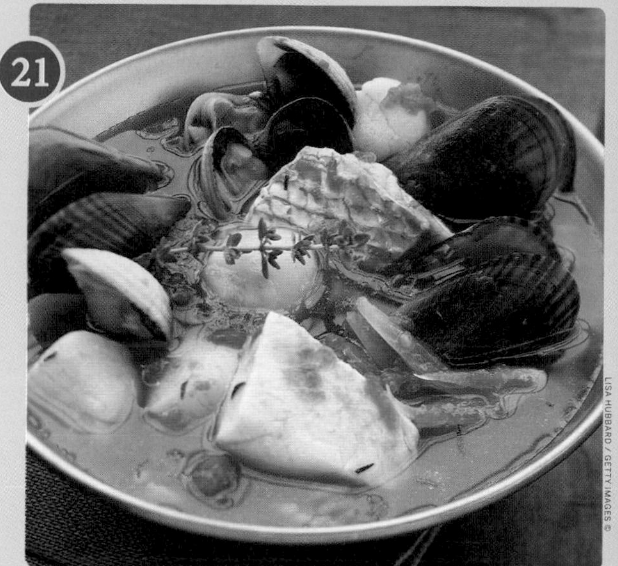

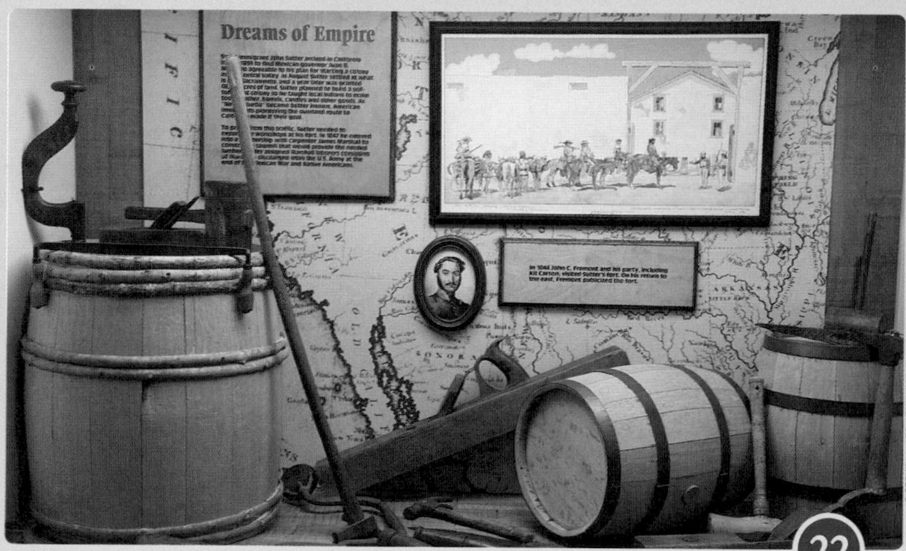

22

Gold Country

'Go west, young man!' could have been the rallying cry of tens of thousands of immigrants who arrived during California's Gold Rush. Today, the Sierra Nevada foothills (p277) are a stronghold of Golden State history, tainted by banditry, bordellos and bloodlust. Hwy 49, which winds past sleepy townships and abandoned mines, is a gateway to swimming holes and rafting, and the fruits of some of California's oldest vines. Marshall Gold Discovery State Historic Park

23

North Beach, San Francisco

Scale the heart-stopping stairway streets in a neighborhood that has attracted bebop jazz musicians, Civil Rights agitators, topless dancers and Beat poets. With its tough climbs and giddy vistas, North Beach (p98) is a place with more sky than ground, an area that was civilized but never entirely tamed. Seek out clouds of green parrots as they shriek and flutter over bohemian hillside cottages, before you descend back to earth for a perfect frothy espresso or a scoop of gelato. Coit Tower (p99) & Columbus statue, Telegraph Hill, North Beach

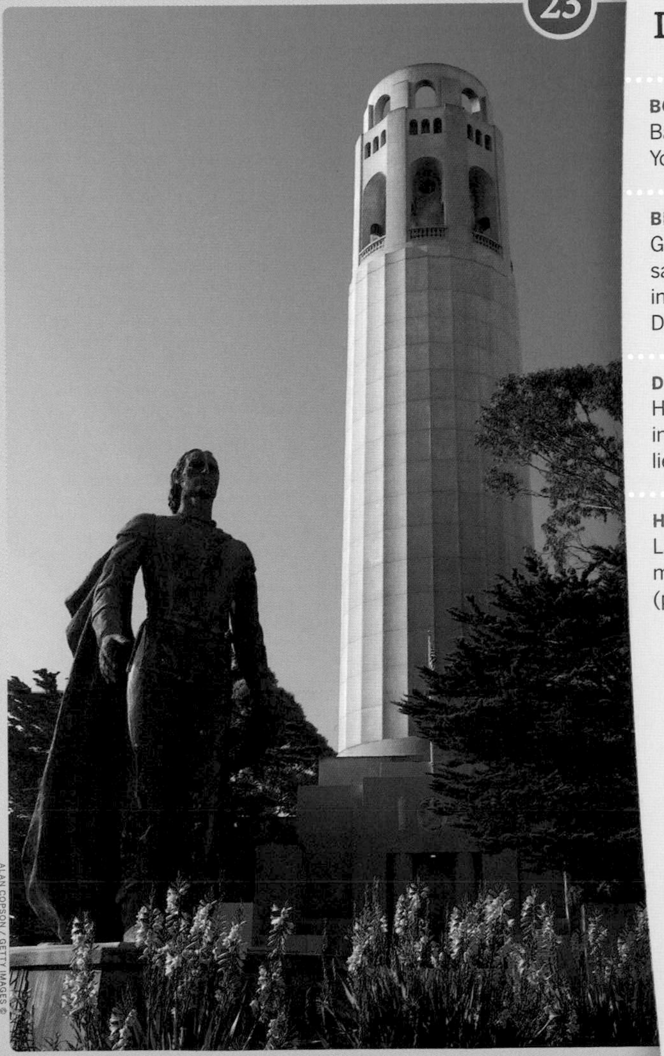

The Best... Desserts

BOUCHON BAKERY
Baked goods to die for in Yountville. (p219)

BI-RITE CREAMERY
Get in line for the fresh salted-caramel ice cream in San Francisco's Mission District. (p117)

DUARTE'S TAVERN
Homemade fruit pies, including a luscious olallieberry version. (p172)

HOMEWOOD
Late-harvest dessert wines made in Sonoma County. (p229)

The Best... Geology

LA BREA TAR PITS
Ancient fossils excavated from the bubbling ooze. (p68)

LAVA BEDS NATIONAL MONUMENT
Go underground to crawl through lava tubes and claustrophobic passageways. (p168)

DEATH VALLEY NATIONAL PARK
Salt flats, mineral-painted hills and saw-toothed miniature mountains. (p322)

SEQUOIA & KINGS CANYON NATIONAL PARKS
Explore caves with trippy stalactites and stalagmites. (p268)

Joshua Tree National Park

Chalk up your hands and try not to look down as you tackle the boulders of Joshua Tree National Park (p318). The longest climbs are not much more than 100ft or so, but there are many challenging technical routes, and most can be easily top-roped for training. Not a rock hound? Hike its landscape of desert-fan-palm oases or kick up some trail dust with a mountain-bike exploration of its 4WD roads. Or just drive to Keys View for vistas of the Coachella Valley and the Salton Sea.

24

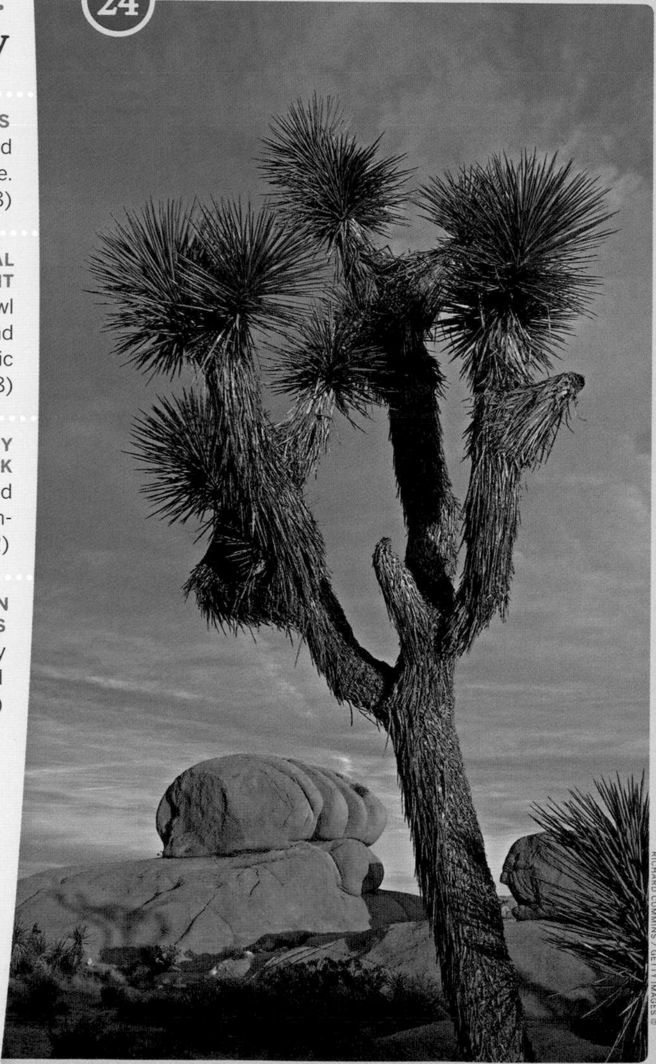

DENISE TAYLOR / GETTY IMAGES ©

25

Santa Monica & Venice

Who needs LA traffic? Hit the beach instead. Posh Santa Monica (p69) grants instant happiness. Learn to surf, ride a solar-powered Ferris wheel, dance under the stars on an old-fashioned pier, let the kids explore the aquarium's tidal touch pools or dip your toes in the water and let your troubles float away. Did we mention jaw-dropping sunsets? Afterwards join the parade of new-agers, muscled bodybuilders, goth punks and hippie tribal drummers at nearby Venice (p70), where everyone lets their freak flag fly. Santa Monica Beach

California's Top Itineraries

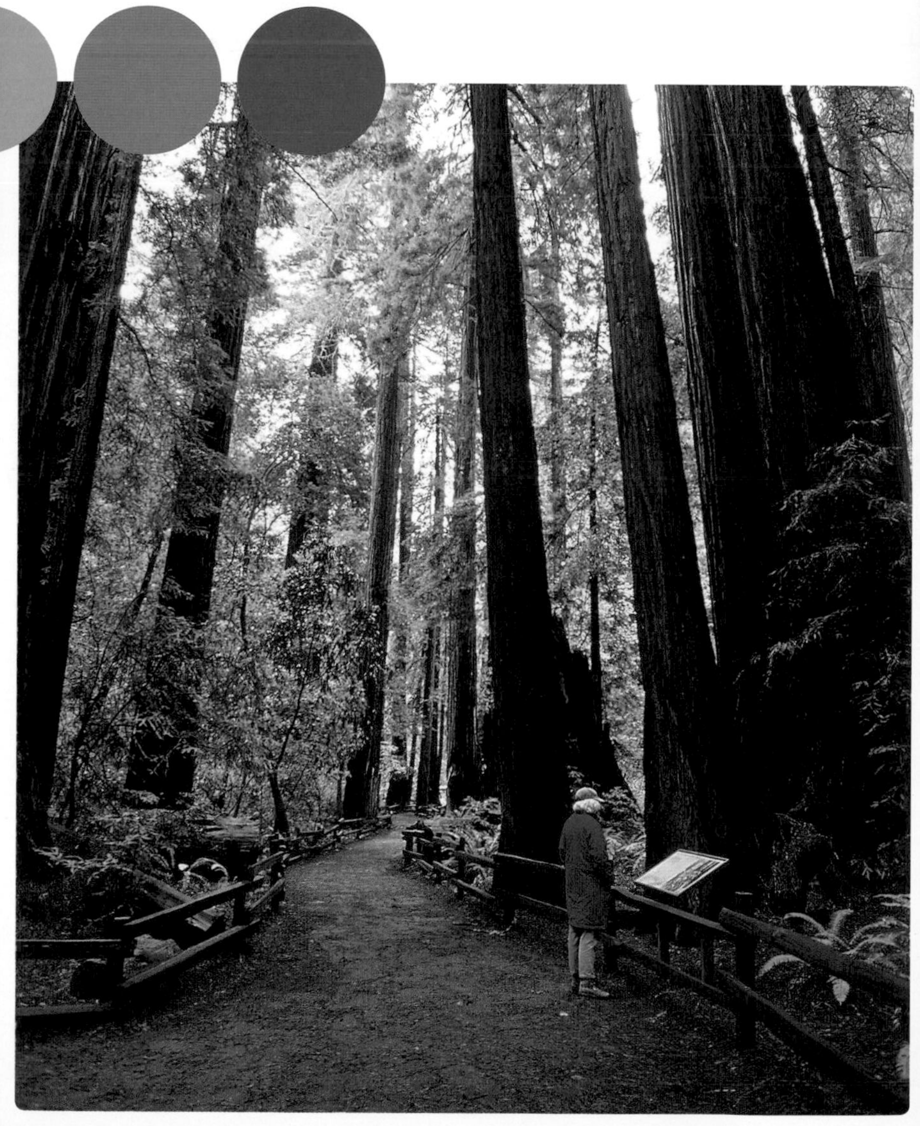

San Francisco to Wine Country Bay Area Roundup

5 DAYS

Explore San Francisco then head north to visit the natural attractions and famed grape-growing regions just beyond. Budget two nights in the city, and the rest in the wilds of Marin and chic Wine Country.

1 San Francisco (p100)

In the hilly 7-sq-mile peninsula that is dashing, innovative and ever-evolving San Francisco, uncover the alleyways of **Chinatown** and wander the mural-adorned **Mission District**. Then brave the fog on a cruise over to evocative **Alcatraz** and visit a colony of blubbery sea lions sunning themselves on the floating docks at **Fisherman's Wharf**. Lose yourself on a sunny day in **Golden Gate Park**, stopping to smell the flowers where hippies danced during 1967's Summer of Love, and gawking at the rare critters and marine beasts on display at the **Academy of Sciences**.

SAN FRANCISCO ➔ MARIN COUNTY

20 minutes From downtown over Hwy 101. **30 minutes** From San Francisco Ferry Building to Sausalito.

2 Marin County (p136)

Escape the city via the landmark **Golden Gate Bridge**, stopping for photographs of San Francisco from the viewpoints in Marin. Choose from hiking across the **Marin Headlands**, taking the ferry from **Tiburon** over to Angel Island to go kayaking, hiking and mountain-biking, or kicking back and letting the little ones run wild at the play structures of the **Bay Area Discovery Museum**. Meander north along the Marin County coast, passing the tall redwood trees of **Muir Woods National Monument**. Pause to bury your toes in the sand at small-town **Stinson Beach** on your way to view elk and elephant seals on the bluffs of wildly beautiful **Point Reyes National Seashore**.

Muir Woods National Monument (p141)
PHOTOGRAPHER: STEPHEN SAKS / GETTY IMAGES ©

MARIN COUNTY ➔ WINE COUNTRY

One hour Point Reyes Station to Sonoma via Hwy 116.

3 Wine Country (p210)

Beyond the quaint Hitchcock-movie location of Bodega Bay, country roads wind through **Russian River Valley** vineyards. Truck east across Hwy 101 to tipple in the heart of Northern California's renowned Wine Country, orbiting stylish **Napa** and its countrified, still-chic cousin **Sonoma**. Taste your way through the cabernets and chardonnays and reserve ahead for dinner at one of the chichi eateries in **Yountville**. Soak your road-weary bones in a mud bath in **Calistoga** and swim some laps in a spring-fed pool before looping back to San Francisco.

Los Angeles to Orange County Beaches SoCal Dreaming

Get a taste of Southern California life with an infusion of big-city sophistication, a romp through some fabulous beaches and some theme parks the kids will never forget. If you visit in summertime, plan to spend more time at the beach.

1 Los Angeles (p60)

Kick things off in Los Angeles, where top-notch attractions, beaches and tasty food form an irresistible trifecta. After you've traipsed along the star-studded sidewalks of clubby **Hollywood**, dived into the arts and cultural scenes **Downtown** or **Mid-City**, and snapped photos of the Hollywood sign from Griffith Observatory, you'll be ready to party on **Sunset Blvd**. On your next day, **Santa Monica** beckons with a carnival pier, creative restaurants and boutiques. Move on to nearby Venice for primo people-watching on the **Venice Boardwalk**. If you have time, dig deeper into LA culture on a literary or city history tour with **Esotouric**, or visit the hilltop **Getty Center**. Good shopping can be found across the city; stars frequent **Robertson Blvd**.

LOS ANGELES ➔ DISNEYLAND

45 minutes Via I-5.

2 Disneyland (p336)

In Anaheim, make a date with a mouse named Mickey at perfectly 'imagineered' Disneyland, and try to hold on as the **Space Mountain** roller coaster attempts to whirl you into an alternate universe. Stick around until the sun goes down for the nightly **fireworks** that burst over Sleeping Beauty Castle and the artificial snow that falls in winter. Next door, **Disney California Adventure** celebrates the Golden State, with thrill rides and night-time spectaculars. Both parks are not far from **Knott's Berry Farm**, which has an Old West theme and frighteningly fun rides.

DISNEYLAND ➔ ORANGE COUNTY BEACHES

30 minutes To Huntington Beach via Hwy 22 and Hwy 39.

Venice Beach (p70), Los Angeles

3 Orange County Beaches (p345)

Take a day off in **Huntington Beach**, aka Surf City, USA. Rent a board, play beach volleyball, build a bonfire at day's end – whatever – just kick back and chill. Make a stop in **Newport Beach** for soap-opera-worthy people-watching by the piers, and consider taking the ferry to car-free **Balboa Island** for a ramble around its promenade. Then roll south to **Laguna Beach**, a former artists' colony with over two dozen public beaches to spoil you, and a protected inlet frequented by divers and snorkelers.

San Francisco to Los Angeles A Tale of Two Cities

With 10 days, you can compare and contrast California's two rival cities and savor everything in between. Spend a few days roaming the famously foggy hills of San Francisco before puttering south along the coast to take the pulse of eclectic LA.

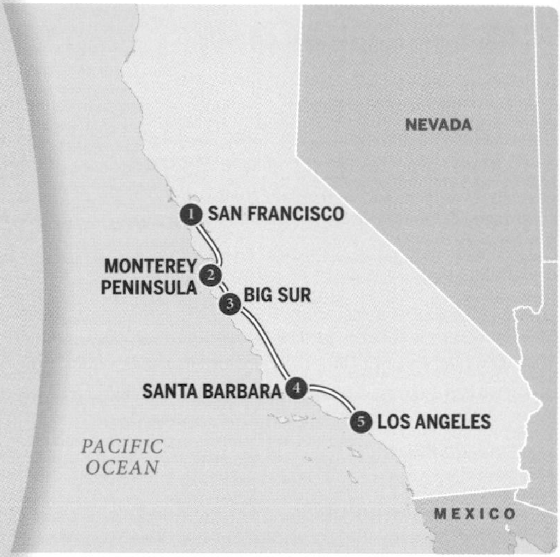

❶ San Francisco (p100)

Start with a taste test through the **Ferry Building** and a stroll along the bay. Hop a cable car to **Fisherman's Wharf** to ogle the sea lions at Pier 39, and set sail for the former prison and thriving bird habitat at **Alcatraz**. Cap off the day with a ramble across the **Golden Gate Bridge**. The following day, check out the city's biggest green space and some of its best museums in **Golden Gate Park**, and do some shopping in the nearby **Haight** or in downtown's **Union Square**. Swim the tide of humanity in **Chinatown** and then settle in for a quiet coffee in **North Beach**. Book dinner at one of the city's destination restaurants, and shake it 'til dawn at a **SoMa** club.

SAN FRANCISCO ➲ MONTEREY PENINSULA

Two hours Via Hwy 101.

❷ Monterey Peninsula (p176)

Stop by **Carmel-by-the-Sea** to tour its exquisite Spanish mission and for coastal views of dramatic Monterey pines. Visit John Steinbeck country at Monterey's restored **Cannery Row**, and allow a few hours to marvel at the marine life of the **Monterey Bay Aquarium**.

MONTEREY PENINSULA ➲ BIG SUR

One hour Hwy 1.

❸ Big Sur (p182)

At the fabled stretch of shoreline called Big Sur, stroll **Pfeiffer Beach** and stay at a nearby inn or campground. Continuing south, take a gander at the opulent hilltop pleasure dome of **Hearst Castle**.

View of Golden Gate Bridge from Baker Beach (p107), San Francisco

BIG SUR ➲ SANTA BARBARA

4 hours and 40 minutes Via Hwy 1 and Hwy 101.

❹ Santa Barbara (p190)

Vying for the coveted Southern California beauty prize is Santa Barbara, where you should meander along **Stearns Wharf** and take a dip in one of its many beaches. Visit the **Mission Santa Barbara** on your way into town, and spend the night in the Mediterranean-style downtown.

SANTA BARBARA ➲ LOS ANGELES

Two hours Hwy 101. **Three hours**

❺ Los Angeles (p60)

It's unlikely you'll see a celebrity (head to Malibu or Robertson Blvd for that), but the **Hollywood Walk of Fame** and **Grauman's Chinese Theatre** are a nod to Hollywood's yesteryear. For a backstage look at what's being filmed today, catch a **Universal Studios** tour. Check out **Griffith Park**, America's largest urban park, for views of the **Hollywood sign** and the zoo. Just south of the park, **Los Feliz** and **Silverlake** are non-touristy neighborhoods good for strolling. The next day, go **Downtown**, tour the Walt Disney Concert Hall and get a cocktail at the rooftop bar at the Standard hotel. Or spend the day cruising the beach towns from **Malibu** to **Manhattan Beach**.

San Diego to Avenue of the Giants Pacific Coast & Tall Trees

Can't avert your eyes from the Pacific Ocean? Harbor a secret desire to hug some stratospheric trees? Take this classic road trip from San Diego, tracing the coast north until the road ducks through sky-high redwoods.

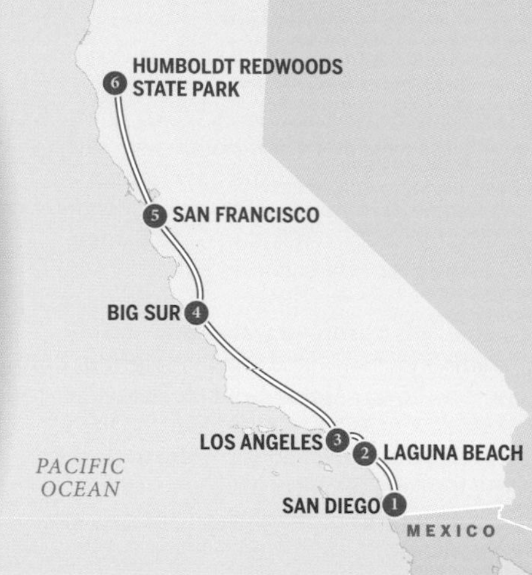

❶ San Diego (p290)

Give yourself two days to soak up the sun and sights in this pleasant SoCal city. Start with some animal spectaculars and rides at **SeaWorld San Diego**, and let the kids go nuts at the petting pools. Then go wiggle your toes around in the hot sand at **Mission Beach** and try to stay standing during a surfing lesson. Budget most of the following day for the museums, gardens and the overall atmosphere of **Balboa Park**, making certain to see some of the 3000 animals at its world-famous **zoo**. Pass the evening enjoying the nightlife in downtown's **Gaslamp Quarter**.

SAN DIEGO ➔ LAGUNA BEACH

90 minutes Via I-5.

❷ Laguna Beach (p349)

Continue north to artsy **Laguna Beach**, the quintessential California beach town. Stop by the **Laguna Art Museum** and peruse the galleries on S Coast Hwy. For swimming, **Main Beach** is your best bet.

LAGUNA BEACH ➔ LOS ANGELES

One hour Via I-5.

❸ Los Angeles (p60)

Ditch the car to ramble along the **South Bay Bicycle Trail**, then gawk at LA's prehistoric past at the gooey **La Brea Tar Pits**. In Downtown LA, Frank Gehry's **Walt Disney Concert Hall** and the collection at the **Museum of Contemporary Art** are highlights.

LOS ANGELES ➔ BIG SUR

5½ hours Via Hwy 101 and Hwy 1.

❹ Big Sur (p182)

Navigate the soupy fog clinging to the coast and bask in the region's bohemian history with an overnight stay in an oceanside yurt at **Treebones Resort**, and a browse in the welcoming **Henry Miller Memorial Library**. Keep the camera handy to snap the postcard views from **Julia Pfeiffer Burns State Park**.

BIG SUR ➔ SAN FRANCISCO

Three hours Via Hwy 1 and Hwy 101.

❺ San Francisco (p100)

Bite into inspiring California cooking at the **Ferry Building**, then hop a boat over to infamous **Alcatraz** prison, aka 'The Rock.' For panoramic bay views, it's all aboard a **cable car** between **Downtown** and **North Beach** or **Fisherman's Wharf**.

SAN FRANCISCO ➔ HUMBOLDT REDWOODS STATE PARK

3½ hours Via Hwy 101.

❻ Humboldt Redwoods State Park (p155)

Work your way north on Hwy 101 to **Leggett**, where your magical mystery tour of the Redwood Coast really begins. In **Humboldt Redwoods State Park**, encounter some of the tallest trees on Earth along the **Avenue of the Giants**.

Marina, San Diego (p290)

San Francisco to Los Angeles California's Greatest Hits

Jump off for a whirlwind tour of the state. You'll experience its two most exciting cities, wildlife-rich coastline, high granite mountains, a patchwork quilt of vineyards, and a desiccated desert wilderness.

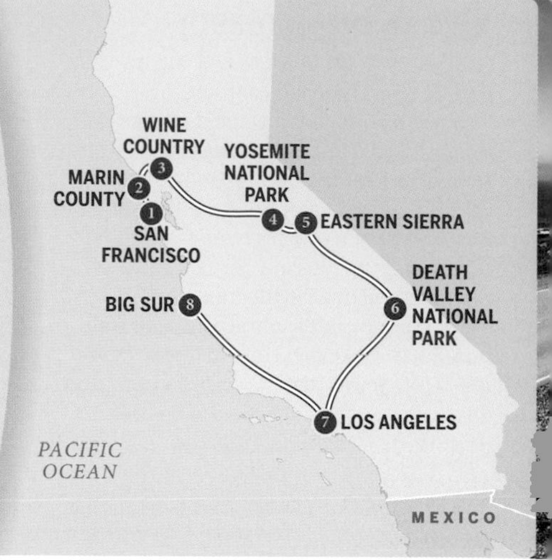

❶ San Francisco (p100)

Take a bell-clanging trip aboard the city's fabled **cable cars** and traipse the creaky wooden floors at **City Lights** bookstore. Wander through the **Ferry Building** and grab lunch, then check out the latest show at the spacious **Asian Art Museum**. Explore **Golden Gate Park** and take a stroll at sunset along **Ocean Beach**.

SAN FRANCISCO ➔ MARIN COUNTY

20 minutes From downtown over Hwy 101.

30 minutes From San Francisco Ferry Building to Sausalito.

❷ Marin County (p136)

Head north over the Golden Gate Bridge into the heart-stopping hills of Marin, calling at the headlands viewpoint of **Point Bonita Lighthouse** and the hushed redwood grove at **Muir Woods**. Continue north to the animal-spotting bonanza of **Point Reyes National Seashore**.

MARIN COUNTY ➔ WINE COUNTRY

One hour Point Reyes Station to Sonoma via Hwy 116.

❸ Wine Country (p210)

Put all your senses into play with a seaweed wrap and a hot-spring bath in the spa town of **Calistoga** and book a meal to remember at one of the destination restaurants in **Yountville** or **Healdsburg**. Naturally, don't think of missing the opportunity to go wine tasting in **Napa Valley** and at other regional wineries.

WINE COUNTRY ➔ YOSEMITE NATIONAL PARK

Four hours Via Hwy 120.

❹ Yosemite National Park (p258)

Descend into **Yosemite Valley**, and you'll understand the lure of this landscape. Give yourself at least two days to explore Yosemite's trails, splash in the **Merced River** and romp through soaring groves of **giant sequoias**. Splurge for an overnight stay or a meal at the historic **Ahwahnee Hotel** to experience its classic grandeur.

YOSEMITE NATIONAL PARK ➔ EASTERN SIERRA

Two hours Yosemite Valley to Mono Lake via Hwy 120 (closed late fall through late spring). **3½ hours**

Wildflowers, Big Sur (p182)
PHOTOGRAPHER: JAN STROMME / GETTY IMAGES ©

5 Eastern Sierra (p271)

Continue to the Eastern Sierra along Hwy 120, losing elevation to reach the haunting vista of **Mono Lake**, then head south on the mountain-hemmed Eastern Sierra Scenic Byway, with a stop at the geological curiosity of **Devils Postpile National Monument**. Complete the day in the **Alabama Hills**, watching the sunset seep into steely silver mountains and ginger-orange hills.

EASTERN SIERRA ➔ DEATH VALLEY NATIONAL PARK

Two hours Alabama Hills to Furnace Creek via Hwy 190.

6 Death Valley National Park (p322)

Detour east to feel a wall of heat and witness the unusual geology of Death Valley National Park. Drive around its odd array of mineral deposits, learn about the area's mining history and then overnight at one of the accommodation options in **Furnace Creek** to cool off in a spring-fed pool.

DEATH VALLEY NATIONAL PARK ➔ LOS ANGELES

Five hours Via Hwy 395 and I-15 Fwy.

7 Los Angeles (p60)

Spend one day inland, looking for your favorite star on the **Hollywood Walk of Fame** and admiring historic theaters and architecture **Downtown**. Head to the beaches the next day, including shopping Abbot Kinney Blvd in **Venice** and Third Street Promenade in **Santa Monica**.

LOS ANGELES ➔ BIG SUR

5½ hours Via Hwy 101 and Hwy 1.

8 Big Sur (p182)

Four hours from LA, stop in to gawk at the grandeur of **Hearst Castle**. Once you arrive at the stretch of coast called Big Sur, take a stroll on the purplish sand at **Pfeiffer Beach**. End the adventure with a cliffside dinner at **Nepenthe**.

California Month by Month

Top Events

- **Tournament of Roses**, January
- **Festival of Arts & Pageant of the Masters**, July
- **Pride Month**, June
- **Coachella Music & Arts Festival**, April
- **Cinco de Mayo**, May

January

Tournament of Roses

Before the Rose Bowl college football game, this famous New Year's parade of flower-festooned floats, marching bands and prancing equestrians draws over 100,000 spectators to Pasadena, a Los Angeles suburb.

Chinese New Year

Firecrackers, parades, lion dances and street food celebrate the lunar new year, falling in late January or early February. Some of California's biggest celebrations happen in San Francisco and LA.

February

Modernism Week

Do you dig Palm Springs' retro vibe, baby? Join other Mid-Century Modern aficionados in mid-February for more than a week of architectural tours, art shows, film screenings, expert lectures and swingin' cocktail parties.

Wildlife Watching

Don't let winter storms drive you away from the coast! February is prime time for spotting migratory whales offshore, colonies of birthing and mating elephant seals, roosting monarch butterflies and hundreds of bird species along the Pacific Flyway.

March

Festival of the Swallows

After wintering in South America, the swallows famously return to Mission San Juan Capistrano in Orange County around March 19. The historic mission town cel-

May Kinetic Grand Championship
PHOTOGRAPHER: JUDY BELLAH / GETTY IMAGES ©

ebrates its Spanish and Mexican heritage all month.

Mendocino Coast Whale Festivals

As the northbound winter migration of gray whales peaks, Mendocino and nearby towns celebrate with food and wine tasting, art shows and naturalist-guided walks and talks over three weekends in March..

April

Coachella Music & Arts Festival

Indie no-name rock bands, cult DJs and superstar rappers and pop divas all converge outside Palm Springs for a musical extravaganza in mid-April. Bring lots of sunscreen and drink tons of water.

San Francisco International Film Festival

Forget about seeing stars in Hollywood. One of the country's longest-running film festivals has been lighting up San Francisco since 1957, with a slate of over 150 independent-minded films, including provocative premieres from around the globe in late April and early May.

May

Cinco de Mayo

¡Viva México! Margaritas, music and merriment commemorate the victory of Mexican forces over the French army at the Battle of Puebla on May 5, 1862. LA and San Diego really do it up in style.

Calaveras County Fair & Jumping Frog Jubilee

Taking inspiration from Mark Twain's famous short story, the Gold Rush–era pioneer settlement of Angels Camp offers old-fashioned family fun over a long weekend in mid-May, with country-and-western musicians, rodeo cowboys and a celebrated frog-jumping contest.

Bay to Breakers

Jog costumed (although no longer naked or intoxicated) during San Francisco's annual pilgrimage from the Embarcadero to Ocean Beach on the third Sunday in May. Watch out for those participants dressed as salmon, who run 'upstream' from the finish line!

Kinetic Grand Championship

Over Memorial Day weekend, this 'triathlon of the art world' merits a three-day, 42-mile race from Arcata to Ferndale on the North Coast. Competitors outdo each other in inventing human-powered, self-propelled and sculptural contraptions to make the journey.

June

Pride Month

Out and proud since 1970, California's LGBTQ pride celebrations take place throughout June, with costumed parades, coming-out parties, live music, DJs and more. The biggest, bawdiest celebrations are in San Francisco and LA; San Diego celebrates in mid-July.

July

Reggae on the River

Come party with the 'Humboldt Nation' of hippies, Rastafarians, tree huggers and other beloved NorCal freaks for two days of live reggae bands, arts and crafts, barbecue, juggling, unicycling, camping and swimming in late July and early August.

August

Old Spanish Days Fiesta

Santa Barbara celebrates its early Spanish, Mexican and American *rancho* culture with parades, rodeo events, crafts exhibits and live music and dance shows, all happening in early August.

Perseids

Peaking in mid-August, these annual meteor showers are the best time to catch shooting stars with your naked eye or a digital camera. Head away from urban light pollution to places like Joshua Tree and Death Valley National Parks in SoCal's deserts.

Festival of Arts & Pageant of the Masters

Exhibits by hundreds of working artists and a pageant of masterpiece paintings 're-created' by actors keep Orange County's Laguna Beach plenty busy during July and August.

California State Fair

A million people come to ride the giant Ferris wheel, cheer on pie-eating contestants and horseback jockeys, browse the blue-ribbon agricultural and arts-and-crafts exhibits, taste California wines and microbrews, and listen to live bands for two weeks in late July.

Comic-Con International

Affectionately known as 'Nerd Prom,' the alt-nation's biggest annual convention of comic-book geeks, sci-fi and animation lovers, and pop-culture memorabilia collectors brings out-of-this-world costumed madness to San Diego in late July.

September

Monterey Jazz Festival

Cool trad-jazz cats, fusion magicians and world-beat drummers all line up to play at one of the world's longest-running jazz festivals, featuring outdoor concerts and more intimate shows on the Central Coast over a long weekend in mid-September.

October

Vineyard Festivals

All month long under sunny skies, California's wine counties celebrate bringing in the harvest from the vineyards with gourmet food-and-wine shindigs, grape-stomping 'crush' parties and barrel tastings, with some events starting earlier in September.

November

Día de los Muertos

Mexican communities honor dead ancestors on November 2 with costumed parades, sugar skulls, graveyard picnics, candlelight processions and fabulous altars. Join the colorful festivities in San Francisco, LA and San Diego.

Death Valley '49ers

Take a trip back to California's hardy 19th-century Gold Rush days during this annual encampment at Furnace Creek, with old-timey campfire singalongs, cowboy poetry readings, horseshoe tournaments and a Western art show in early November.

December

Mavericks

South of San Francisco, Half Moon Bay's monster big-wave surfing competition only takes place when winter swells top 50ft, usually between December and March. When the surf's up, invited pro surfers have 24 hours to fly in from around the globe.

Parade of Lights

Spicing up the Christmas holiday season with nautical cheer, brightly bedecked and illuminated boats float through many harbors, notably Orange County's Newport Beach and San Diego. San Francisco and LA host winter-wonderland parades on land.

New Year's Eve

Out with the old, in with the new: millions get drunk, resolve to do better, and the next day nurse hangovers while watching college football. Some cities and towns put on alternative, alcohol-free First Night street festivals.

Far left: July Festival of Arts & Pageant of the Masters exhibit **Left: November** Toys and decorations, Día de los Muertos

What's New

For this new edition of Discover California, our authors hunted down the fresh, the transformed, the hot and the happening. Here are a few of our favorites. For up-to-the-minute recommendations, see lonelyplanet.com/usa/california.

1 **BAY BRIDGE & TRAIL**
After years of costly construction delays, the graceful new span of San Francisco's Bay Bridge (www.baybridgeinfo.org; toll 5-10am & 3-7pm Mon-Fri $6, other times Mon-Fri $4, Sat & Sun $5) between Oakland and Yerba Buena Island is finally open – you can drive across it, of course. But more adventurous types will want to cycle or walk atop it on the sky-high Bay Bridge Trail (www.baybridgeinfo.org/path), which is definitely not for anyone with an unnerving fear of heights.

2 **SUNNYLANDS**
Near Palm Springs, step inside a mid-century modern estate where heads of state, royalty and Hollywood celebrities once stayed, surrounded by desert gardens and a fine-art collection. (p317)

3 **ACE HOTEL, DOWNTOWN LOS ANGELES**
Portland's hip hotel chain wows with new Downtown LA digs and the restored United Artists Theatre, a glittering 1920s movie palace now showcasing live music and dance. (p76)

4 **EXPLORATORIUM**
Newly expanded and relocated to the waterfront, San Francisco's Exploratorium – an interactive science museum that delights kids and adults alike – is better than ever. (p106)

5 **SFJAZZ CENTER**
See legendary performers on stage in Hayes Valley at the country's only purpose-built, stand-alone jazz center. (p120)

6 **SANTA BARBARA'S FUNK ZONE**
It's just what this sometimes stuffy seaside city needed: an edgy, creative neighborhood space for art, food, craft beer and regional wines, all just a short walk from the beach. (p196)

7 **YOSEMITE NATIONAL PARK**
In 2014, California's most beloved national park celebrated the 150th anniversary of its original grant, which jump-started the USA's entire national park system. (p258)

8 **LEGOLAND HOTEL**
Let your kids pretend to be pirates or rule their own castle inside this northern San Diego theme park's super-fun lodgings, a quick drive from the ocean in Carlsbad. (p305)

9 **ANAHEIM PACKING DISTRICT**
Only a couple of miles from Disneyland, downtown Anaheim's early-20th-century citrus-packing house and car dealership have been transformed into a dining, drinking and shopping hot spot. (p344)

Get Inspired

 Books

- **Cannery Row** (1945) Before you visit Monterey, read John Steinbeck's true-to-life account.
- **LA Confidential** (1990) James Ellroy's novel about the seedy world of 1950s Los Angeles.
- **My First Summer in the Sierra** (1911) Find out why John Muir felt passionate enough to found the Sierra Club.
- **Slouching Towards Bethlehem** (1968) Musings by Joan Didion.
- **Tripmaster Monkey** (1989) Maxine Hong Kingston on the Chinese American community in San Fran's turbulent '60s.

 Films

- **Dirty Harry** Do you feel lucky enough to see San Francisco on the big screen? Do you, punk?
- **The Graduate** Love and lies in Southern California suburbs.
- **LA Story** Steve Martin drives 25ft to his neighbor's house.
- **Vertigo** The quintessential 'San Francisco meets Hitchcock' classic.
- **Chinatown** Roman Polanski's version of the LA water wars.

Music

- **California Love** (2Pac and Dr Dre) The rappers' ode to California, from Long Beach to Sactown.
- **Californication** (Red Hot Chili Peppers) Anthony Kiedis' journey to the dark side of Hollywood.
- **Los Angeles** (X) Exene Cervenka and John Doe's post-punk homage to their city.
- **Surfin' USA** (Beach Boys) Like a page out of a Southern California beach-town atlas.

 Websites

- **Discover LA** (www.discoverlosangeles.com) Where to surf, dine and sun.
- **San Francisco Travel** (www.sanfrancisco.travel) Official info about the city's unique offerings.
- **San Diego Convention & Visitors Bureau** (www.sandiego.org) Amusement parks, historic neighborhoods and microbreweries.
- **California Department of Parks & Recreation** (www.parks.ca.gov) California's state parks.
- **National Park Service** (www.nps.gov/state/ca) National parks and monuments in California.

This list will give you an instant insight into the state.

Read *My California: Journeys by Great Writers* offers a memorable romp through California with contemporary authors from Pico Iyer to Michael Chabon.

Watch *Sideways* shows a bachelors' journey through the Santa Barbara wine country, maligning merlot and scoring points for pinot.

Listen *(Sittin' On) The Dock of the Bay* by Otis Redding might make you seek out a houseboat hideaway.

Log on www.visitcalifornia.com is the official state tourism site.

Poppies, San Diego County
PHOTOGRAPHER: RICHARD CUMMINS / GETTY IMAGES ©

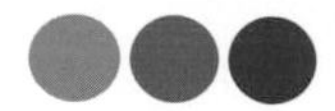

Need to Know

Currency
US dollars ($)

Language
English

Visas
Generally not required for citizens of Visa Waiver Program (VWP) countries, but only with ESTA approval (apply online at least 72 hours in advance).

Money
ATMs widely available. Credit cards usually required for reservations. Traveler's checks rarely accepted.

Cell Phones
The only foreign phones that work in the USA are GSM multiband models. Buy prepaid SIM cards locally.

Wi-Fi
In most lodgings (daily surcharge may apply) and coffee shops (free for customers).

Internet Access
Internet cafes are common (average $6 to $12 per hour). Most libraries and some accommodations have free computers offering online access.

Tipping
18% to 20% in restaurants, 10% to 15% for taxis, bars $1 per drink, porters $2 per bag.

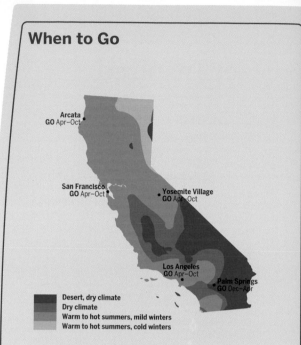

When to Go

High Season (Jun–Aug)

- Accommodation prices up 50% to 100% on average
- Major holidays even busier and more expensive
- Summer is low season in the desert, where temperatures exceed 100°F (38°C)

Shoulder Season (Apr–May & Sep–Oct)

- Crowds and prices drop off, especially along the coast and in the mountains
- Mild temperatures; many sunny days
- Weather typically wetter in spring, drier in autumn

Low Season (Nov–Mar)

- Accommodation rates drop by the coast, not always in cities
- Chilly temperatures, frequent rainstorms and heavy snowfalls in the mountains
- Winter is peak season in SoCal's desert regions

Advance Planning

- **Two months before** Shop for airfares online; book accommodations in popular areas.
- **One month before** Set up special tours of film studios; make reservations at in-demand restaurants.
- **One week before** Buy Disneyland tickets if you don't want to stand in line; choose from a mountain of options and plan a rough itinerary.

Your Daily Budget

Budget Less than $75

- Hostel dorm beds: $25–$40
- Take-out meal $6–$12
- Find farmers markets for cheap eats

Midrange $75–200

- Two-star motel or hotel double room: $75–150
- Rental car per day, excluding insurance and gas: $30–$75

Top End More than $200

- Three-star hotel or beach resort room: $150–$300
- Three-course meal in top restaurant, excluding drinks: $75–$100

Exchange Rates

Australia	A$1	$0.83
Canada	C$1	$0.87
Euro zone	€1	$1.25
China	Y10	$1.62
Japan	¥100	$0.85
Mexico	MXN10	$0.69
New Zealand	NZ$1	$0.78
UK	£1	$1.57

For current exchange rates see www.xe.com.

What to Bring

- **Clothing** Pack good walking shoes. Dress to impress in LA. Bring a jacket for summer in San Francisco.
- **Photo ID** Required to rent cars, drink alcohol, buy cigarettes or enter bars and clubs.
- **Insurance** Buy adequate travel insurance that covers any medical care you might need.

Arriving in California

- **Los Angeles International Airport**

Taxis to most destinations ($30 to $50) take 30 minutes to one hour. Door-to-door shuttles ($16 to $27) operate 24 hours a day. FlyAway bus ($8) runs to downtown LA. Free shuttles will get you to LAX City Bus Center & Metro Rail station.

- **San Francisco International Airport**

Taxis into the city ($35 to $55) take 25 to 50 minutes. Door-to-door shuttles ($16 to $20) operate 24 hours a day. BART trains ($8.65, 30 minutes) serve the airport from 5:30am to 11:45pm.

Getting Around

- **Car** Often necessary away from major cities, especially along the coast and in the mountains and deserts.
- **Train** Fastest way to get around LA and SF Bay Area. Long-distance and regional routes connect some cities and bigger towns.
- **Boat** Ferries ply San Francisco Bay.
- **Bus** Greyhound and Amtrak run inexpensive (but time-consuming) options between major cities and some larger towns.
- **Air** Flights between LA and San Francisco save time.

Sleeping

- **Resorts** From swish lodges to casual outdoorsy spots.
- **Hotels** Usually the higher the overnight rate, the more amenities.
- **Motels** Ubiquitous along highways and in heavily visited areas.
- **Camping** Very popular, from luxury tents to bare-bones primitive wilderness.
- **Hostels** Independent and HI hostels are popular, especially along the coast in larger cities.
- **B&Bs** Every coastal town has at least a few; quaint and romantic but can be pricey.

Be Forewarned

- **Driving distances** LA to San Francisco is at least 5½ hours, and it's another five or six hours north of SF to Redwood National & State Parks.
- **Earthquakes** Small tremors happen daily, but are rarely felt.
- **Smog** Smog and heat can make an unhealthy combination. Watch weather and air-quality reports for advice on staying inside.

Pacific Park
RIZES
DANGER
DANGER

Los Angeles

Ah, Los Angeles: land of star-struck dreams and Tinseltown magic. You may think you know what to expect from LA: celebrity worship, plastic-surgery junkies, endless traffic, earthquakes, wildfires...

True, your waitress today might be tomorrow's starlet and you may well encounter artificially enhanced blondes and phone-clutching honchos weaving lanes at 80mph, but LA is intensely diverse and brimming with fascinating neighborhoods and characters that have nothing to do with the 'Industry' (entertainment, to the rest of us). Its UN of cooking has pushed the boundaries of American cuisine for generations. Arts and architecture? Frank Lloyd Wright to Frank Gehry. Music? The Doors to Dr Dre and Dudamel.

So do yourself a favor and leave your preconceptions in the suitcase. LA's truths are not doled out on the silver screen or gossip rags: rather, you will discover them in everyday interactions. Chances are, the more you explore, the more you'll enjoy.

Amusement rides, Santa Monica Pier (p70)

Los Angeles

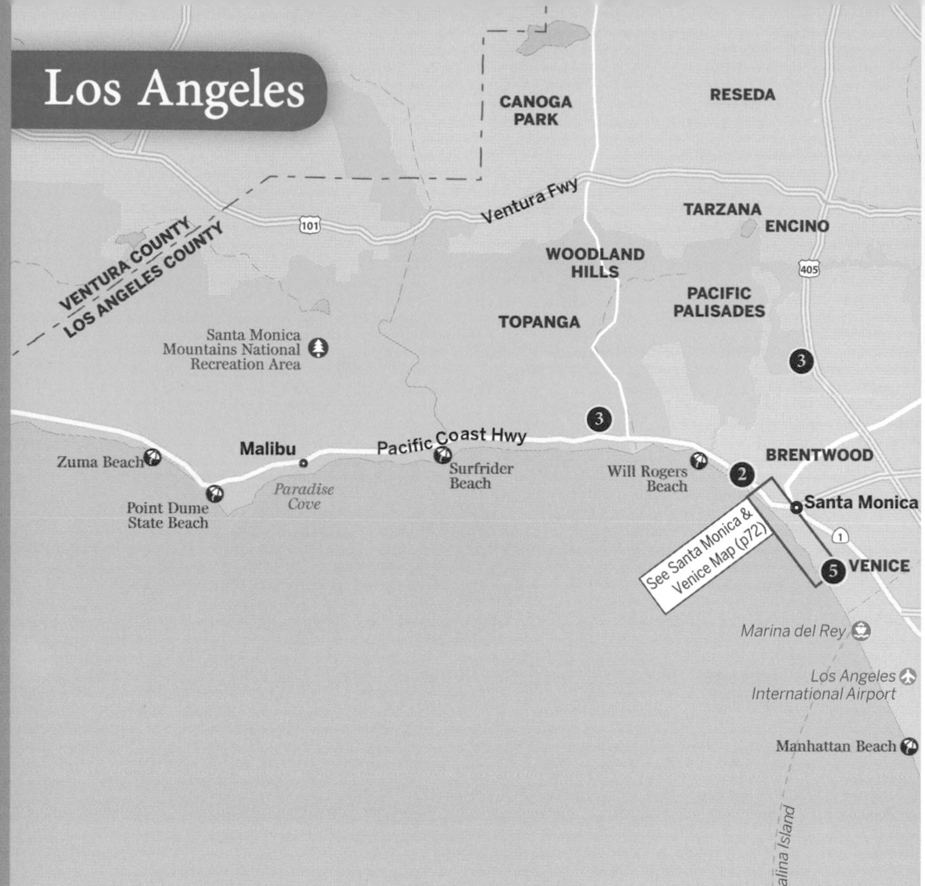
CANOGA PARK
RESEDA
Ventura Fwy
101
TARZANA
ENCINO
VENTURA COUNTY
LOS ANGELES COUNTY
WOODLAND HILLS
405
PACIFIC PALISADES
TOPANGA
Santa Monica Mountains National Recreation Area
3
3
Malibu
Pacific Coast Hwy
Zuma Beach
Surfrider Beach
Will Rogers Beach
2
BRENTWOOD
Point Dume State Beach
Paradise Cove
Santa Monica
1
See Santa Monica & Venice Map (p72)
5
VENICE
Marina del Rey
Los Angeles International Airport
Manhattan Beach
PACIFIC OCEAN
Catamaran to Catalina Island
0
10 km
0
4 miles

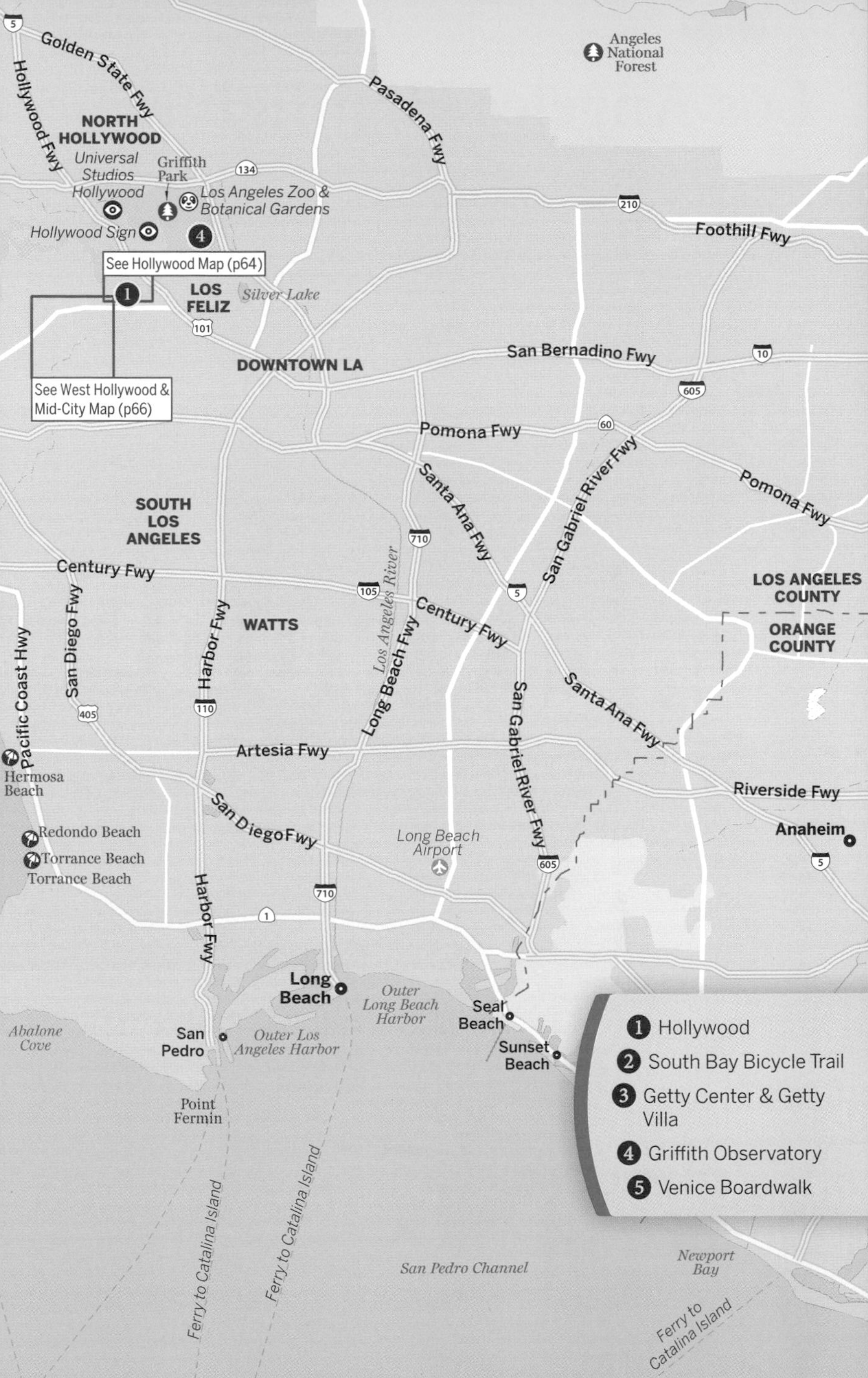
Angeles National Forest
Golden State Fwy
Hollywood Fwy
NORTH HOLLYWOOD
Universal Studios Hollywood
Griffith Park
Los Angeles Zoo & Botanical Gardens
Hollywood Sign
Pasadena Fwy
Foothill Fwy
See Hollywood Map (p64)
LOS FELIZ
Silver Lake
DOWNTOWN LA
See West Hollywood & Mid-City Map (p66)
San Bernadino Fwy
Pomona Fwy
Santa Ana Fwy
San Gabriel River Fwy
SOUTH LOS ANGELES
Century Fwy
San Diego Fwy
Harbor Fwy
WATTS
Los Angeles River
Long Beach Fwy
LOS ANGELES COUNTY
ORANGE COUNTY
Pacific Coast Hwy
Hermosa Beach
Artesia Fwy
Riverside Fwy
Redondo Beach
Torrance Beach
Long Beach Airport
Anaheim
Long Beach
Outer Long Beach Harbor
Seal Beach
Sunset Beach
Abalone Cove
San Pedro
Outer Los Angeles Harbor
Point Fermin
Ferry to Catalina Island
San Pedro Channel
Newport Bay
1 Hollywood
2 South Bay Bicycle Trail
3 Getty Center & Getty Villa
4 Griffith Observatory
5 Venice Boardwalk

Los Angeles Highlights

Hollywood

Hollywood (p62) has been synonymous with motion pictures since Cecil B DeMille shot one of the world's first full-length feature films in a Hollywoodland barn in 1914. LA took center stage in the world of popular culture and has been there ever since. Celebrity-spotting tip: keep an eye out for packs of paparazzi photographers. Technically, it's illegal to hike up to the Hollywood sign, but viewing spots are plentiful.

1

CHRISTIAN ADAMS / GETTY IMAGES ©

2 South Bay Bicycle Trail

This two-lane beach thoroughfare (p70), known in LA as 'The Strand,' mixes LA's two favorite things: freeways and looking good. Hundreds of bikini-clad bicyclists and oiled-up in-line skaters glide along a flat, pothole-free 'street,' which runs along the beach from Will Rogers State Beach to Torrance Beach. Go ahead, just try to make the 22-mile-long journey without singing Randy Newman's 'I Love LA.'

WENDY CONNETT / ALAMY ©

SERGIO PITAMITZ / GETTY IMAGES ©

Getty Center & Getty Villa

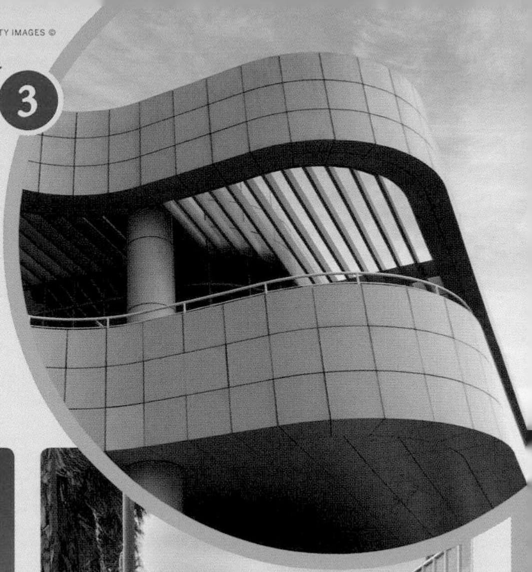

3

One of the top museums for European art in the US, the Getty Center (p69, pictured right) isn't just about the art. Plan on spending a day soaking up the sun on the lawn, wandering the garden maze or enjoying one of the special events. If you can't get to this postmodernist edifice, you can make it to the Getty Villa (p69), an ancient art-filled treasure trove.

IZZET KERIBAR / GETTY IMAGES ©

4

Griffith Observatory

Cosmically informing Angelenos since 1935, this observatory (p65), located in gigantic Griffith Park, underwent a $100-million refurbishment last decade. Check out its out-of-this-world astronomical exhibits and its calendar of viewings on clear evenings. For the best views in all of Griffith Park (including of the Hollywood sign), ramble the 2-mile trail from the Fern Dell area to the observatory.

5

Venice Boardwalk

Dodgy glass-pipe vendors, thong bikinis, steroid-laden muscle men with their pit bulls...what isn't there to love about Venice Beach (p73)? Perhaps nowhere on Earth are folks more inclined to let their freak flag fly high. If you're looking for stereotypical California wingnuts, this is certainly the place. Venice's namesake canals are just two blocks east of the beach.

Los Angeles' Best...

Street Markets

- **Original Farmers Market** Started in 1934, this Mid-City market sports a dozen inexpensive eateries. (p79)
- **Grand Central Market** Packed and lively, with permanent restaurants and booths in Downtown LA. (p78)
- **Santa Monica Farmers Markets** The Wednesday market is the biggest and best, and often patrolled by local chefs. (p80)
- **Olvera St** Mexican market at LA's original non-indigenous settlement site. (p60)

Places to Take Kids

- **Santa Monica Pier** Rides, games, souvenirs, all along a fabulous beach. (p70)
- **La Brea Tar Pits** Kids will love this giant fossil sandbox. (p68)
- **Griffith Park** Hiking trails, picnic spots and a kid-friendly observatory and zoo. (p65)
- **Hollywood & Highland** Redeveloped mall replaces grit with campiness on Hollywood Blvd. (p62)

Beaches

- **Zuma Beach** Stunningly gorgeous Malibu's even more stunningly gorgeous beach. (p68)
- **Santa Monica** Extra-wide, hugely popular beach that's packed on weekends with families escaping the inland heat. (p69)
- **Manhattan Beach** Glamorous condos, swank shops and surfers. (p74)
- **Venice** An amusing sideshow of beachside bodybuilders, fire dancers, assorted fabulous freaks and people-watching galore. (p73)

Places to See Art

- **Los Angeles County Museum of Art** Ancient art through to David Hockney, with Friday evening jazz. (p62)
- **Getty Center** A billion-dollar architecturally impressive art museum with equally impressive gardens and city views. (p69)
- **Getty Villa** Head back in artistic time 2000 years for Roman, Greek and Etruscan antiquities. (p69)
- **Museum of Contemporary Art** Art as cutting-edge as LA. (p61)

Left: Pony rides, Griffith Park (p65);
Above: Grand Central Market (p78), Los Angeles

Need to Know

ADVANCE PLANNING

- **Two months before** See which TV shows are taping; call or book online for free audience tickets.
- **One month before** Book your hotels. Sign up for VIP movie and TV studio tours.
- **Two weeks before** Make restaurant reservations.

RESOURCES

- **Discover Los Angeles** (www.discoverlosangeles.com) Official tourist information.
- **LA.com** (www.la.com) Clued-in guide to shopping, dining, nightlife and events.
- **LA Weekly** (www.laweekly.com) Free alternative news and arts-and-entertainment listings tabloid.
- **Los Angeles Times** (www.latimes.com) Southern California's leading daily newspaper.
- **LAist** (www.laist.com) Hip lists of the city's bests from dive bars to trails to french fries to spas.
- **KCRW** (www.kcrw.com) LA's public-radio beacon of good taste, real news and great music.
- **ExperienceLA** (www.experiencela.com) Excellent cultural calendar.
- **US Geological Survey** (earthquake.usgs.gov) Up-to-the-minute earthquake updates.
- **South Coast Air Quality Management District** (www.aqmd.gov) Air-quality forecasts and advisories.

GETTING AROUND

- **Bus** LA buses: not just for the pre-teen or desperate anymore.
- **Car** An extension of your very existence in LA; Santa Monica to Hollywood can take 30 minutes to an hour or more.
- **Metro Rail** Not nearly comprehensive enough but an impressive effort.
- **Walking** Best within neighborhoods: Santa Monica, Hollywood, West Hollywood and Silver Lake.

BE FOREWARNED

- **Drugs** Venice Beach, Hollywood and Downtown LA see their fair share of shady behavior.
- **Freeways** Traffic is ubiquitous during rush 'hour,' which runs from 5am to 9am and 3pm to 7pm.

Los Angeles Walking Tour

Downtown LA is the most historical, fascinating part of the city. There's great architecture, world-class music, top-notch art, superb dining and innovative fashion. Downtown is both a power nexus and an ethnic mosaic.

WALK FACTS

- **Start** LA Live
- **Finish** Union Station
- **Distance** 3 miles
- **Duration** Four hours

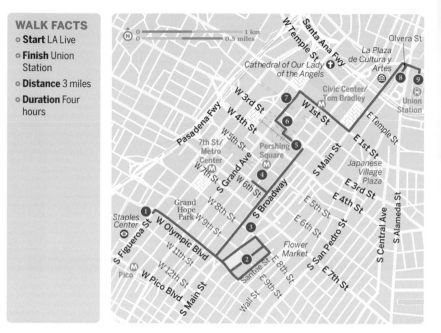

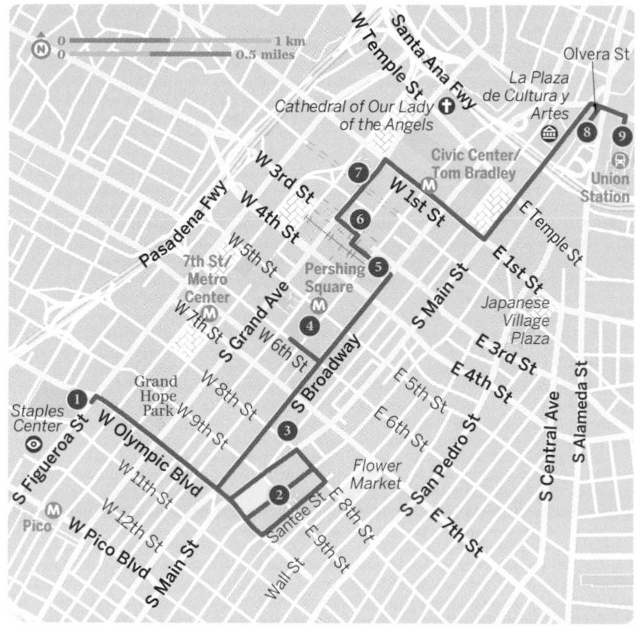

❶ Grammy Museum & LA Live

The Grammy Museum is easily the highlight of LA Live. Learn about different musical genres through the interactive exhibits, watch live footage and see Michael Jackson's glove.

❷ Fashion District

The axis of the Fashion District, this 90-block nirvana for shopaholics is at the intersection of 9th and Los Angeles Streets, where the fashionistas and designers congregate.

❸ Broadway Theatre District

Highlighted by the still-running Orpheum Theatre (built in 1926), Broadway was LA's historic entertainment hub with no fewer than a dozen theaters built in a riot of styles, from beaux arts to East Indian to Spanish Gothic.

❹ Pershing Square

The hub of Downtown LA's historic core, Pershing Square became the city's first public park in 1866. It is now enlivened by public art, summer concerts and a holiday-season ice rink.

❺ Grand Central Market

On the ground floor of a 1905 beaux-arts building where architect Frank Lloyd Wright once kept an office, stroll along the sawdust-sprinkled aisles beneath old-timey ceiling fans, past stalls piled high with mangoes, peppers and jicamas.

6 Museum of Contemporary Art

A collection that arcs from the 1940s to the present, and includes works by Mark Rothko, Dan Flavin, Joseph Cornell and other big-shot contemporary artists, is housed in a postmodern building by Arata Isozaki.

7 Walt Disney Concert Hall

Frank Gehry pulled out all the stops when designing this iconic concert venue, a molten blend of steel, music and psychedelic architecture.

8 El Pueblo de Los Angeles

Here's where LA's first non-indigenous colonists settled in 1781. El Pueblo preserves the city's oldest buildings, some dating back to its days as a dusty, lawless outpost.

9 Union Station

A glamorous Mission Revival-style landmark with art-deco accents, Union Station opened in 1939 as America's last grand rail station. The marble-floored main hall, with cathedral ceilings, original leather chairs and grand chandeliers, is breathtaking. Charles Bukowski worked at the Terminal Annex post office just north of the station, inspiring his 1971 novel *Post Office*.

Los Angeles in...

ONE DAY

Go star-searching on the **Hollywood Walk of Fame** (p62) along revitalized Hollywood Blvd. Up your chances of spotting actual celebs by hitting the boutiques on paparazzi-infested **Robertson Blvd** (p85). Then drive to the lofty **Getty Center** (p69) before heading west to the **Venice Boardwalk** (p73) to see the seaside sideshow. Watch the sunset over the ocean in **Santa Monica** (p69).

TWO DAYS

Take our walking tour around Downtown LA. Stop for lunch at the **Grand Central Market** (p78) or **Bar Amá** (p78). Head to **Griffith Park** (p65) to snap a photo of the Hollywood sign, then meander around the **Griffith Observatory** (p65), the **Autry National Center** (p65) or LA's **zoo** (p65). If there's time, check out the shops and restaurants in **Los Feliz** (p79) and **Silver Lake** (p85). Top off the day with cocktails at the rooftop bar at the **Ace Hotel** (p76) in Downtown LA.

Diners in a Los Feliz cafe

Discover Los Angeles

At a Glance

- **Downtown LA** (p60) Cultural institutions, entertainment venues and fabulous architecture.
- **Hollywood** (p62) Movie-industry flash and a marvelous urban park.
- **West Hollywood** (p66) LA's gay ground zero, plus chic shopping and nightclubs galore.
- **Mid-City** (p68) Museum Row and a classic farmers market.
- **Santa Monica** (p69) Beachside, laid-back and pedestrian friendly.

Olvera St markets, El Pueblo de Los Angeles
MITCH DIAMOND / GETTY IMAGES ©

Sights

Los Angeles may be vast and amorphous, but the areas of visitor interest are fairly well defined. About 15 miles inland, Downtown LA is the region's hub, combining great architecture and culture with global-village pizzazz. Northwest of Downtown, there's sprawling Hollywood and nearby hip 'hoods Los Feliz and Silver Lake. West Hollywood is LA's center of urban chic and the gay and lesbian community, while Long Beach, at six o'clock from Downtown LA, is a bustling port with big-city sophistication.

South of Hollywood, Mid-City's main draw is Museum Row, while further west are ritzy Beverly Hills and the Westside communities of Westwood and Brentwood. Santa Monica is the most tourist- and pedestrian-friendly beach town; others include swish-but-low-key Malibu and bohemian Venice.

DOWNTOWN LA & AROUND

Crowds fill Downtown LA's performance and entertainment venues, and young professionals and artists have moved by the thousands into new lofts, attracting bars, restaurants and galleries.

El Pueblo de Los Angeles

Compact, colorful and car-free, this historic district is an immersion in LA's Spanish–Mexican roots. Its spine is **Olvera Street**, a festive tack-o-rama where you can chomp on tacos and stock up on handmade candy and folkloric trinkets.

Avila Adobe Museum
(☎213-628-1274; http://elpueblo.lacity.org; Olvera St; ⏰9am-4pm) FREE The oldest surviving house in LA was built in 1818 by a wealthy ranchero and one-time LA mayor, and later became a boarding house and restaurant. Restored and furnished in heavy oak, it's open for self-guided tours and provides a look at life in the early 19th century.

La Plaza de Cultura y Artes Museum
(☎213-542-6200; www.lapca.org; 501 N Main St; ⏰noon-5pm Mon, Wed & Thu, to 6pm Fri-Sun) FREE This museum chronicles the Mexican-American experience in Los Angeles, from the Mexican–American War when the border crossed the original pueblo, to the Zoot Suit Riots to Cesar Chavez and the Chicana movement.

Union Station Landmark
(www.amtrak.com; 800 N Alameda St; P) Built on the site of LA's original Chinatown, the station opened in 1939 as America's last grand rail station. It's a glamorous exercise in Mission Revival with art-deco accents. The marble-floored main hall, with cathedral ceilings, original leather chairs and grand chandeliers, is breathtaking.

Grand Ave & Around

Under construction at research time, the forthcoming museum, the **Broad** (www.thebroad.org; 221 S Grand Ave) FREE promises to be both an architectural marvel and a deep and nourishing well of modern art.

Walt Disney Concert Hall Building
(☎info 213-972-7211, tickets 323-850-2000; www.laphil.org; 111 S Grand Ave; ⏰guided tours usually noon & 1pm Tue-Sat; P) FREE A molten blend of steel, music and psychedelic architecture, this iconic concert venue is the home base of the Los Angeles Philharmonic, but has also hosted contemporary bands such as Phoenix and classic jazz men like Sonny Rollins. Frank Gehry pulled out all the stops: the building is a gravity-defying sculpture of heaving and billowing stainless-steel.

Museum of Contemporary Art Museum
(MOCA; ☎213-626-6222; www.moca.org; 250 S Grand Ave; adult/child $12/free, 5-8pm Thu free; ⏰11am-5pm Mon & Fri, to 8pm Thu, to 6pm Sat & Sun) A collection that arcs from the 1940s to the present and includes works by Mark Rothko, Dan Flavin, Joseph Cornell and other big-shot contemporary artists is housed in a postmodern building by Arata Isozaki. Galleries are below ground, yet sky-lit bright.

Cathedral of Our Lady of the Angels Church
(☎213-680-5200; www.olacathedral.org; 555 W Temple St; ⏰6:30am-6pm Mon-Fri, from 9am Sat, from 7am Sun; P) FREE José Rafael Moneo mixed Gothic proportions with contemporary design for his 2002 Cathedral of Our Lady of the Angels, which exudes a calming serenity achieved by soft light filtering through its alabaster panes. Wall-sized tapestries as detailed as a Michelangelo fresco festoon the main nave.

South Park

The southwestern corner of Downtown LA, South Park isn't a park but an emerging neighborhood, including Staples Center arena, LA's convention center and LA Live, which includes a dozen restaurants, live-music venues, a 54-story hotel tower and the 7100-seat Nokia Theatre, home to the *American Idol* finals.

Grammy Museum Museum
(www.grammymuseum.org; 800 W Olympic Blvd; adult/child $13/11, after 6pm $8; ⏰11:30am-7:30pm Mon-Fri, from 10am Sat & Sun; 👪) The highlight of LA Live. Music lovers will get lost in interactive exhibits, which define, differentiate and link musical genres, while live footage strobes. You can glimpse such things as Guns N' Roses' bass drum, Lester Young's tenor, Yo Yo Ma's cello and Michael's glove (though exhibits and collections do rotate).

RICHARD CUMMINS / GETTY IMAGES ©

Don't Miss
Los Angeles County Museum of Art

LACMA is one of the country's top art museums and the largest in the western USA. The collection in the Renzo Piano–designed **Broad Contemporary Art Museum** (BCAM) includes seminal pieces by Jasper Johns, Roy Lichtenstein and Andy Warhol. (Pictured above is *Urban Light* by Chris Burden.)

Other LACMA pavilions brim with paintings, sculpture and decorative arts: Rembrandt, Cézanne and Magritte; ancient pottery from China, Turkey and Iran; photographs by Ansel Adams and Henri Cartier-Bresson; and a jewel box of a Japanese pavilion. There are often headline-grabbing touring exhibits. Parking is $10.

NEED TO KNOW

LACMA; Map p66; ☎323-857-6000; www.lacma.org; 5905 Wilshire Blvd; adult/child $15/free; 🕒11am-5pm Mon, Tue & Thu, to 9pm Fri, 10am-7pm Sat & Sun; P

HOLLYWOOD, LOS FELIZ & SILVER LAKE

Aging movie stars know that a facelift can quickly pump up a drooping career, and the same has been done with the legendary **Hollywood Blvd**, preened and spruced up in recent years. Though it still hasn't recaptured its Golden Age (1920s–1960s) glamour, much of its late-20th-century seediness is gone.

Historic movie palaces bask in restored glory, Metro Rail's Red Line makes access easy, some of LA's hottest bars and nightclubs have sprung up here, and even 'Oscar' has found a permanent home in the Dolby Theatre, part of the vast shopping and entertainment complex called Hollywood & Highland.

The most interesting mile runs between La Brea Ave and Vine St, along the **Hollywood Walk of Fame**, which

Detour: Universal Studios Hollywood

One of the world's oldest and largest continuously operating movie studios, **Universal** (www.universalstudioshollywood.com; 100 Universal City Plaza, Universal City; admission from $87, under 3yr free; open daily, hours vary; P) first opened to the public in 1915, when studio head Carl Laemmle invited visitors at a quaint 25¢ each (including a boxed lunch) to watch silent films being made.

Your chances of seeing an actual movie shoot are approximately nil at Universal's current theme-park incarnation, yet generations of visitors have had a ball here. Start with the 45-minute narrated **Studio Tour** aboard a giant, multicar tram that takes you past working soundstages and outdoor sets. Also prepare to survive a shark attack à la *Jaws* and an 8.3-magnitude earthquake. It's hokey but fun.

Among the dozens of other attractions, **King Kong 360 3-D** scares the living daylights, **The Simpsons Ride** is a motion-simulated romp 'designed' by Krusty the Klown, and you can splash down among the dinos of **Jurassic Park – The Ride**, while the **Special Effects Stage** illuminates the craft of movie-making. You can also get a thrill on the brand new **Transformers: The Ride 3-D**. **WaterWorld** may have bombed as a movie, but the live-action show is a runaway hit, with stunts including giant fireballs and a crash-landing seaplane. Note: kids may be too short or too easily spooked for many attractions.

Parking costs $10 to $16, or arrive via Metro Rail's Red Line.

honors more than 2400 celebrities with brass stars embedded in the sidewalk. For interesting historical tidbits about local landmarks, keep an eye out for the sign markers along here, or join a guided walking tour.

Following Hollywood Blvd east beyond Hwy 101 (Hollywood Fwy) takes you to the neighborhoods of **Los Feliz** (los *fee*-liss) and **Silver Lake**, both boho-chic enclaves with offbeat shopping, funky bars and a hopping cuisine scene.

The Metro Red Line serves central Hollywood (Hollywood/Highland and Hollywood/Vine stations) and Los Feliz (Vermont/Sunset station) from Downtown LA and the San Fernando Valley.

Grauman's Chinese Theatre — Landmark

(Map p64; 323-463-9576; www.tclchinesetheatres.com; 6925 Hollywood Blvd; tours & movie tickets adult/child/senior $13.50/6.50/11.50) Ever wondered what it's like to be in George Clooney's shoes? Just find his footprints in the forecourt of this world-famous movie palace. The exotic pagoda theater – complete with temple bells and stone heaven dogs from China – has shown movies since 1927 when Cecil B DeMille's *The King of Kings* first flickered across the screen.

Dolby Theatre — Theater

(Map p64; www.dolbytheatre.com; 6801 Hollywood Blvd; tours adult/child, senior & student $17/12; 10:30am-4pm) The Academy Awards are handed out at the Dolby Theatre, which has also hosted the American Idol finale, the ESPY awards, the Miss USA pageant and a recent Neil Young residency. On the tour you get to sniff around the auditorium, admire a VIP room and see Oscar up close.

Hollywood Sign — Landmark

LA's most famous landmark first appeared in the hills in 1923 as an advertising gimmick for a real-estate development called 'Hollywoodland'. Each letter is 50ft tall and made of sheet metal. Once

Hollywood

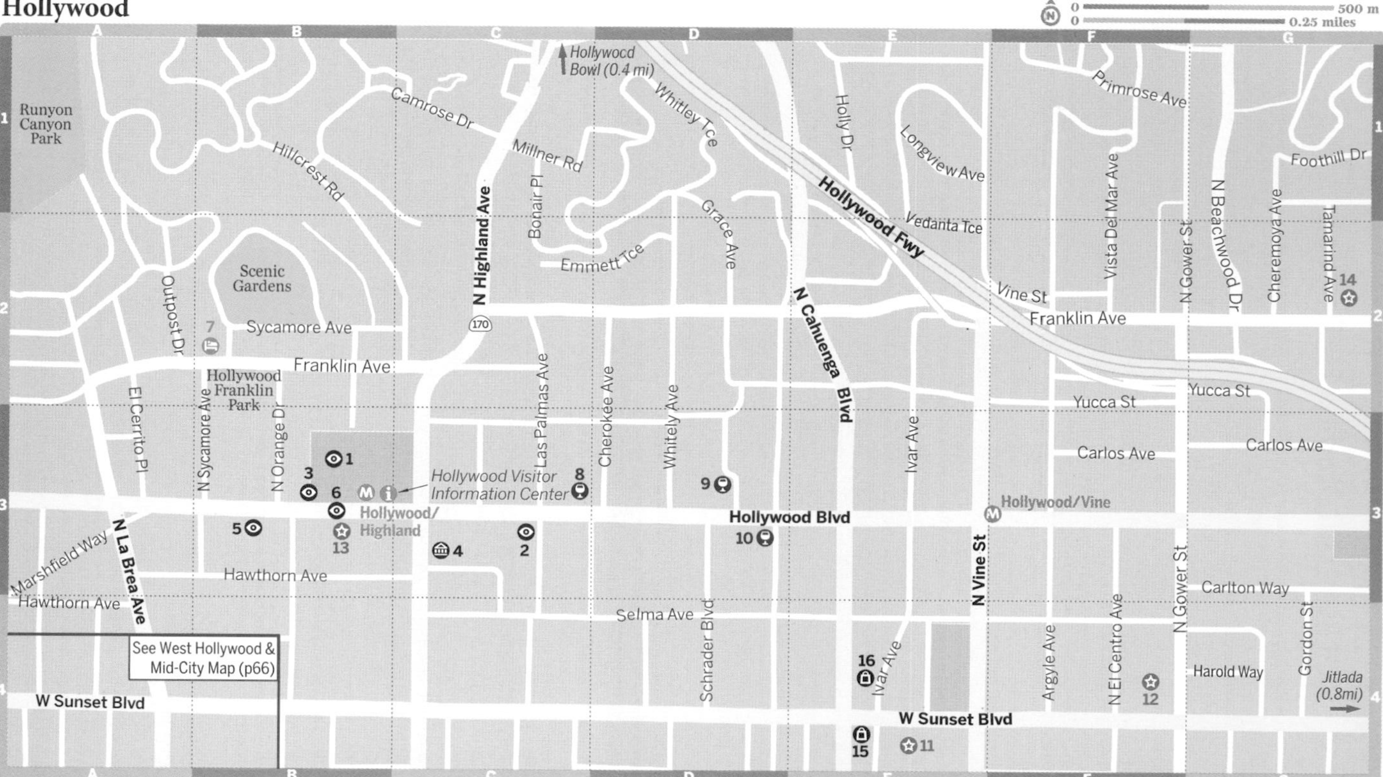
0 500 m
0 0.25 miles
Runyon Canyon Park
Scenic Gardens
Hollywood Franklin Park
Hollywood Bowl (0.4 mi)
Jitlada (0.8mi)
See West Hollywood & Mid-City Map (p66)
Hollywood Visitor Information Center
Hollywood/Highland
Hollywood/Vine
Hollywood Blvd
Hollywood Fwy
N Highland Ave
N Cahuenga Blvd
N Vine St
N La Brea Ave
W Sunset Blvd
Franklin Ave
Camrose Dr
Millner Rd
Hillcrest Rd
Whitley Tce
Grace Ave
Emmett Tce
Bonair Pl
Holly Dr
Longview Ave
Vedanta Tce
Vine St
Primrose Ave
Vista Del Mar Ave
N Gower St
N Beachwood Dr
Cheremoya Ave
Tamarind Ave
Foothill Dr
Outpost Dr
Sycamore Ave
El Cerrito Pl
N Sycamore Ave
N Orange Dr
Las Palmas Ave
Cherokee Ave
Whitely Ave
Ivar Ave
Yucca St
Carlos Ave
Marshfield Way
Hawthorn Ave
Selma Ave
Schrader Blvd
Carlton Way
Argyle Ave
N El Centro Ave
Harold Way
Gordon St
170
1
2
3
4
5
6
7
8
9
10
11
12
13
14
15
16

Hollywood

Sights
1 Dolby Theatre........B3
2 Egyptian Theatre........C3
3 Grauman's Chinese Theatre........B3
4 Hollywood Museum........C3
5 Hollywood Roosevelt Hotel........B3
6 Hollywood Walk of Fame........B3

Activities, Courses & Tours
TMZ Tours........(see 3)

Sleeping
Hollywood Roosevelt Hotel........(see 5)
7 Magic Castle Hotel........B2

Drinking & Nightlife
8 Musso & Frank Grill........C3
9 No Vacancy........D3
10 Sayers Club........D3

Entertainment
American Cinematheque........(see 2)
11 Arclight Cinemas........E4
12 CBS........F4
13 El Capitan Theatre........B3
Grauman's Chinese Theatre........(see 3)
14 Upright Citizens Brigade Theatre........G2

Shopping
15 Amoeba Music........E4
16 Space 1520........E4

aglow with 4000 light bulbs, the sign even had its own caretaker who lived behind the 'L' until 1939.

Hollywood Museum — Museum

(Map p64; ☎323-464-7776; www.thehollywoodmuseum.com; 1660 N Highland Ave; adult/child $15/5; ⊙10am-5pm Wed-Sun) We quite like this musty temple to the stars, crammed with kitsch posters, costumes and rotating props. The museum is housed inside the handsome 1914 art-deco Max Factor Building, where the make-up pioneer once worked his magic on Marilyn Monroe and Judy Garland.

Hollywood Bowl — Landmark

(www.hollywoodbowl.com; 2301 Highland Ave; rehearsals free, performance costs vary; ⊙Apr-Sep; P) Summers in LA just wouldn't be the same without this chill spot for music under the stars, from symphonies to big-name acts such as Baaba Maal, Sigur Rós, Radiohead and Paul McCartney. A huge natural amphitheater, the Hollywood Bowl has been around since 1922 and has great sound.

Griffith Park — Park

(☎323-913-4688; www.laparks.org/dos/parks/griffithpk; 4730 Crystal Springs Dr; ⊙5am-10:30pm, trails sunrise-sunset; P 👪) FREE A gift to the city in 1896 by mining mogul Griffith J Griffith, and five times the size of New York's Central Park, Griffith Park is one of the country's largest urban green spaces. It contains a major outdoor theater, the city zoo, an observatory, two museums, golf courses, playgrounds, 53 miles of hiking trails, Batman's caves and the Hollywood sign.

Griffith Observatory — Museum

(☎213-473-0800; www.griffithobservatory.org; 2800 E Observatory Rd; planetarium shows adult/child $7/3; ⊙noon-10pm Tue-Fri, from 10am Sat & Sun; P 👪) FREE This landmark 1935 observatory opens a window onto the universe from its perch on the southern slopes of Mt Hollywood. Its planetarium boasts the world's most advanced star projector, and astronomical touch displays on the evolution of the telescope, and the ultraviolet x-rays used to map our solar system. We loved the camera obscura on the main floor.

Autry National Center — Museum

(☎323-667-2000; www.autrynationalcenter.org; 4700 Western Heritage Way; adult/seniors & students/child $10/6/4, 2nd Tue each month free; ⊙10am-4pm Tue-Fri, to 5pm Sat & Sun; P) Want to know how the West was really won? Then mosey over to this excellent museum – its exhibits on the good, the bad and the ugly of America's westward expansion rope in even the most reluctant cowpokes. Kids can pan for gold and explore a stagecoach. Year-round gallery talks, symposia, film screenings and other cultural events spur the intellect.

Los Angeles Zoo & Botanical Gardens — Zoo

(☎323-644-4200; www.lazoo.org; 5333 Zoo Dr; adult/senior/child $18/15/13; ⊙10am-5pm, closed Christmas; P 👪) The Los Angeles

West Hollywood & Mid-City

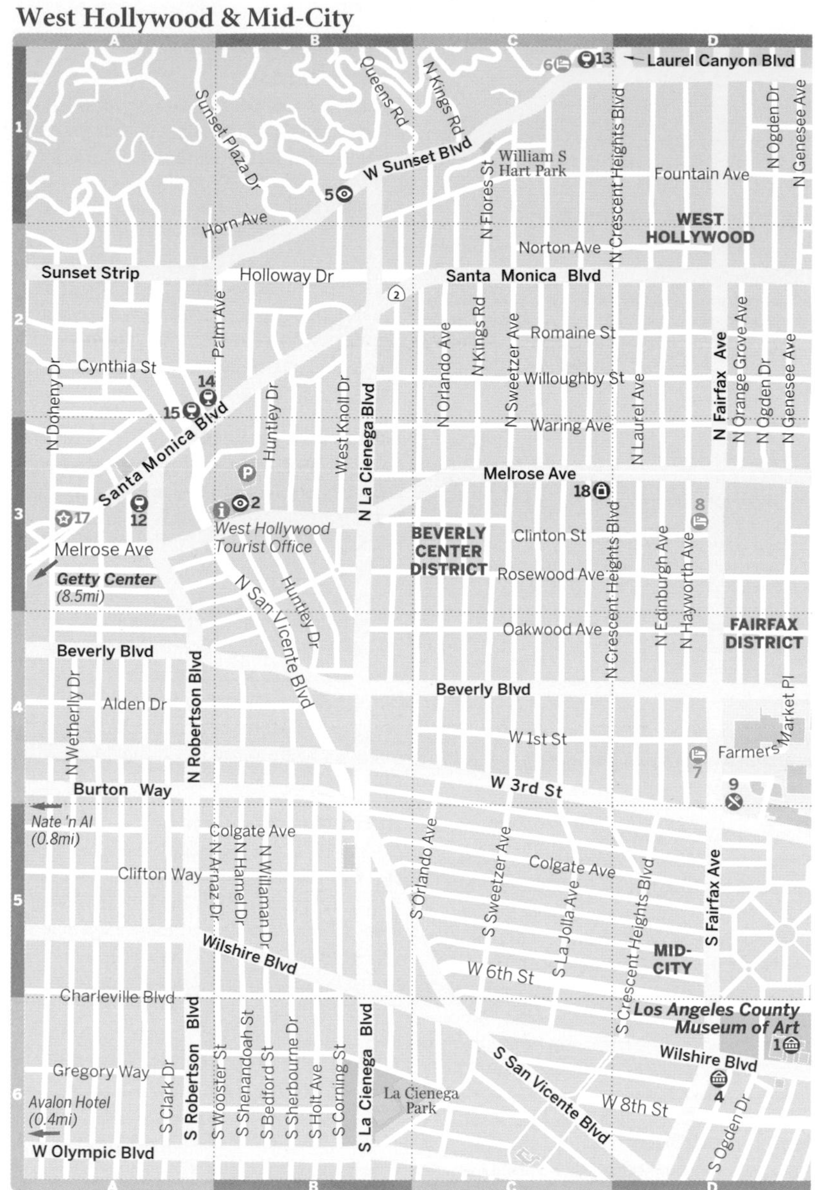

Zoo, with its 1100 finned, feathered and furry friends from over 250 species, rarely fails to enthrall the little ones. What began in 1912 as a refuge for retired circus animals now brings in over a million visitors each year.

WEST HOLLYWOOD

Rainbow flags fly proudly over Santa Monica Blvd. Celebs keep gossip rags happy by misbehaving at clubs on the fabled Sunset Strip. Welcome to the city

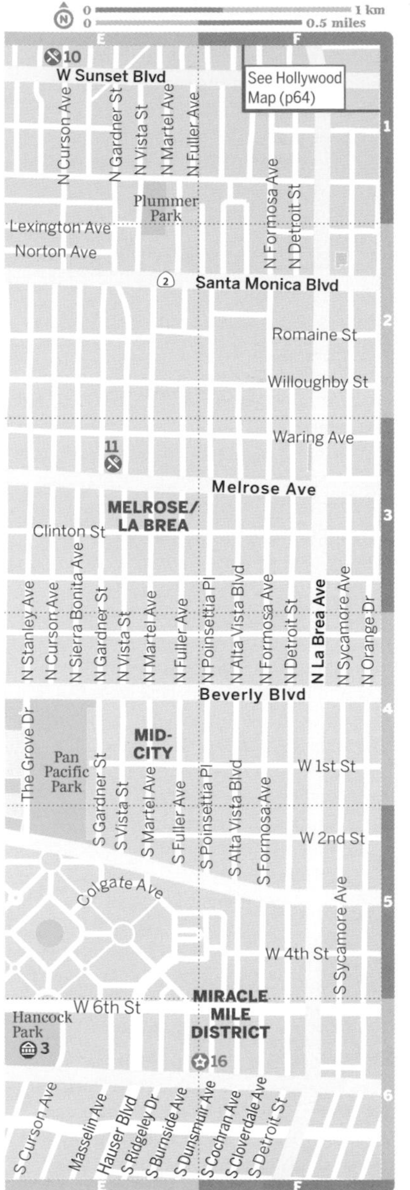

West Hollywood & Mid-City

Don't Miss Sights
1 Los Angeles County Museum of Art . D6

Sights
2 Pacific Design Center B3
3 Page Museum & La Brea Tar Pits E6
4 Petersen Automotive Museum D6
5 Sunset Strip B1

Sleeping
6 Chateau Marmont C1
7 Farmer's Daughter Hotel D4
8 Orbit D3

Eating
9 Original Farmers Market D4
10 Pikey E1
11 Pingtung E3

Drinking & Nightlife
12 Abbey A3
13 Bar Marmont C1
14 Eleven A2
15 Micky's A2

Entertainment
16 El Rey F6
17 Troubadour A3

Shopping
18 Fred Segal C3

of West Hollywood (WeHo), 1.9 sq miles of pure personality.

Boutiques on Robertson Blvd and Melrose Ave purvey the sassy and chic for Hollywood royalty, Santa Monica Blvd is gay central, WeHo's eastern precincts are filled with Russian speaking émigrés, and Sunset Blvd bursts with clubs, chichi hotels and views across LA.

Pacific Design Center — Landmark

(PDC; Map p66; www.pacificdesigncenter.com; 8687 Melrose Ave; 9am-5pm Mon-Fri) Interior design is big in WeHo, with over 120 trade-only showrooms at the Pacific Design Center and dozens more in the surrounding **Avenues of Art & Design** (Beverly Blvd, Robertson Blvd & Melrose Ave). PDC showrooms generally sell only to design pros, but often you can get items at a mark-up through the Buying Program.

Sunset Strip — Street

(Map p66; Sunset Blvd) A visual cacophony of billboards, giant ad banners and neon signs, the sinuous stretch of Sunset Blvd running between Laurel Canyon and Doheny Dr has been nightlife central since the 1920s.

MID-CITY

Mid-City encompasses an amorphous area east of West Hollywood, south of Hollywood, west of Koreatown and north of I-10 (Santa Monica Fwy). There's plenty of street parking and validated parking at the Original Farmers Market and the adjacent Grove shopping mall.

Page Museum & La Brea Tar Pits — Museum

(Map p66; www.tarpits.org; 5801 Wilshire Blvd; adult/child/student & senior $7/2/4.50; 9:30am-5pm; P) Mammoths and saber-toothed cats used to roam LA's savannah in prehistoric times. We know this because of an archaeological trove of skulls and bones unearthed at La Brea Tar Pits, one of the world's most fecund and famous fossil sites.

Petersen Automotive Museum — Museum

(Map p66; www.petersen.org; 6060 Wilshire Blvd; adult/seniors & students/child $15/10/5; 10am-6pm Tue-Sun; P) A four-story ode to the auto, the Petersen Automotive Museum is a treat even for those who can't tell a piston from a carburetor. Start by ambling along a fun streetscape that reveals LA as the birthplace of gas stations, billboards, strip malls, drive-in restaurants and drive-in movie theaters. Then head upstairs to the hot rods, movie cars, and celebrity-owned rarities, presented in rotating exhibits.

BEVERLY HILLS & WESTSIDE

The mere mention of Beverly Hills conjures up images of fame and wealth, reinforced by film and TV. Opulent mansions flank manicured grounds on palm-lined avenues, especially north of **Sunset Boulevard**, while legendary **Rodeo Drive** is three solid blocks of style for the Prada and Gucci brigade.

Several city-owned parking lots and garages offer up to two hours free parking.

MALIBU

Malibu has been synonymous with celebrities since the early 1930s. Clara Bow and Barbara Stanwyck were the first to stake out their turf in what became known as the **Malibu Colony** and the earliest Hollywood elite to Barbra and Leo have lived here ever since.

Along Malibu's spectacular 27-mile stretch of the Pacific Coast Hwy, where the Santa Monica Mountains plunge into the ocean, are some fine beaches, including **Point Dume**, **Zuma** and the world-famous surfing spot **Surfrider**. Rising behind Malibu is **Malibu Creek State Park**, part of the Santa Monica Mountains National Recreation Area and laced with hiking trails. Malibu has no real center, but you'll find the greatest concentration of restaurants and

Ducks at Los Angeles Zoo (p65)
GARY VESTAL / GETTY IMAGES ©

SERGIO PITAMITZ / GETTY IMAGES ©

Don't Miss Getty Center

In its billion-dollar, in-the-clouds perch, high above the city grit and grime, the Getty Center presents triple delights: stellar art collection (Renaissance to David Hockney), Richard Meier's soaring architecture and Robert Irwin's ever-evolving gardens. On clear days, add breathtaking views of the city and ocean to the list. Visit in the late afternoon after the crowds have thinned. Parking is $15 ($10 after 5pm), or Metro bus 761 stops here.

NEED TO KNOW

☎310-440-7300; www.getty.edu; 1200 Getty Center Dr, off I-405 Fwy; 🕐10am-5:30pm Tue-Fri & Sun, to 9pm Sat; P

shops near the century-old **Malibu Pier**. The most likely star-spotting venue is the **Malibu Country Mart** (**www.malibucountrymart.com; 3835 Cross Creek Rd**) shopping center.

Getty Villa — Museum

(**☎310-430-7300; www.getty.edu; 17985 Pacific Coast Hwy; 🕐10am-5pm Wed-Mon; P**) **FREE** Although self-described as the Getty Villa Malibu, this famous museum in a replica 1st-century Roman villa is actually in Pacific Palisades. It's a stunning 64-acre showcase for exquisite Greek, Roman and Etruscan antiquities amassed by oil tycoon J Paul Getty.

SANTA MONICA

Santa Monica is the belle by the beach, mixing urban cool with a laid-back vibe.

Tourists, teens and street performers make car-free, chain-store-lined **Third Street Promenade** the most action-packed zone. For more local flavor, shop celeb-favored **Montana Avenue** or down-homey **Main Street**, backbone of the

neighborhood once nicknamed 'Dogtown' as birthplace of skateboard culture. Rent bikes or in-line skates from many outlets along the beach.

Santa Monica Pier Landmark

(Map p72; ☎310-458-8900; www.santamonicapier.org; 👪) Once the very end of the mythical Route 66, and still the object of a tourist love affair, the Santa Monica Pier dates back to 1908, and is the city's most compelling landmark. There are arcades, carnival games, a vintage carousel, a Ferris wheel, a roller coaster, and an aquarium, and the pier comes alive with free concerts (Twilight Dance Series) and outdoor movies in the summertime.

Bergamot Station Arts Center Art Gallery

(www.bergamotstation.com; 2525 Michigan Ave; ⏰10am-6pm Tue-Fri, 11am-5:30pm Sat; P) Art fans gravitate inland toward this avant-garde center, a former trolley stop that now houses 35 galleries and the progressive **Santa Monica Museum of Art (www.smmoa.org; 2525 Michigan Ave; donation adult/seniors & students $5/3; ⏰11am-6pm Tue-Sat).**

VENICE

Venice was created in 1905 by eccentric tobacco heir Abbot Kinney as an amusement park, called 'Venice of America,' complete with Italian *gondolieri* who poled visitors around canals. Most of the waterways have since been paved over, but those that remain are flanked by flower-festooned villas, easily accessed from either Venice or Washington Blvds.

Activities

CYCLING & IN-LINE SKATING

Anyone who's ever watched tourism footage of LA (or the opening of *Three's Company*) knows about skating or riding on the **South Bay Bicycle Trail**. This paved path parallels the beach for 22 miles, from just north of Santa Monica to

Left: Santa Monica Pier; **Below:** Rollerbladers at Venice Beach
(LEFT) GLENN VAN DER KNIJFF / GETTY IMAGES ©; (BELOW) WALTER BIBIKOW / GETTY IMAGES ©

the South Bay, with a detour around the yacht harbor at Marina del Rey. Mountain-bikers will find the **Santa Monica Mountains** a suitably challenging playground. You'll find lots of good information at www.labikepaths.com.

There are numerous bike-rental shops, especially along the beaches.

Perry's Café & Rentals Bicycle Rental, Skating

(Map p72; ☎310-939-0000; www.perryscafe.com; Ocean Front Walk; mountain bikes & in-line skates per hour/day $10/30, bodyboards per hour/day $7/17; ⏰9:30am-5:30pm) With several locations on the bike path, it rents bikes and skates – or perhaps you'll grab a body board and ride the foaming rollers in the wide Santa Monica Bay? It offers a unique beach butler service, too, but only accepts cash.

HIKING

For a quick ramble, head to **Griffith Park** or **Runyon Canyon**, both just a hop, skip and jump from frenzied Hollywood Blvd. The latter is a favorite playground of hip and fitness-obsessed locals and their dogs, which roam mostly off-leash. You'll have fine views of the Hollywood Sign, the city and, on clear days, all the way to the beach. Runyon's southern trailhead is at the end of N Fuller Ave, off Franklin Ave.

Runyon Canyon is on the eastern edge of the 150,000-acre **Santa Monica Mountains National Recreation Area** (www.nps/gov/samo). This hilly, tree- and chaparral-covered park follows the outline of Santa Monica Bay from just north of Santa Monica all the way north across the Ventura County line to Point Mugu.

Santa Monica & Venice

Santa Monica & Venice

Don't Miss Sights
1 Venice Boardwalk A6

Sights
2 Santa Monica Pier A3

Activities, Courses & Tours
3 Perry's Café & Rentals A2

Sleeping
4 Palihouse B1
5 Venice Beach Inn & Suites A6

Eating
6 Gjelina B7
7 Santa Monica Farmers Markets B2

Drinking & Nightlife
8 Copa d'Oro B2

SWIMMING & SURFING

LA pretty much defines beach culture, yet be prepared: the Pacific is generally chilly; in colder months you'll want a wet suit. Water temperatures peak at about 67°F (20°C) in September. Water quality varies; for updated conditions check the 'Beach Report Card' at www.healthebay.org.

Surfing novices can expect to pay up to $125 for an up to two-hour private lesson or $75 to $90 for a group lesson, including board and wet suit. Contact these surfing schools for details:

Learn to Surf LA Surfing
(☎310-663-2479; www.learntosurfla.com; per lesson per person $90-120) Great for beginners, Learn to Surf LA guarantees you'll get up on the board on your first lesson. Lessons last one hour and 45 minutes.

Malibu Surf Shack Surfing
(www.malibusurfshack.com; 22935 Pacific Coast Hwy; kayaks per day $30, surf boards per day $20-35, SUP per hour/day $45/75, wetsuits per day $10-15, surf/SUP lessons per person $125/100; ⏰10am-6pm) This barefoot surf shop rents (and sells) kayaks, SUP (stand-up paddleboard) kits and surfboards. Surf and SUP lessons take place on Surfrider beach, last 90 minutes and include a full day's rental of the board and wetsuit. The paddling between here and Point Dume is excellent, with frequent dolphin and sea-lion sightings.

DANITA DELIMONT / GETTY IMAGES ©

Don't Miss Venice Boardwalk

Freak show, human zoo and wacky carnival, the Venice Boardwalk is an essential LA experience. This cauldron of counter-culture is the place to get your hair braided or a *qi gong* back massage, or pick up cheap sunglasses or a woven bracelet. Encounters with bodybuilders, hoop dreamers, a Speedo-clad snake charmer or an in-line-skating Sikh minstrel are pretty much guaranteed, especially on hot summer afternoons. Alas, the vibe gets a bit creepy after dark.

NEED TO KNOW

Ocean Front Walk; Map p72; Venice Pier to Rose Ave; 24hr

Tours

Los Angeles Conservancy Walking Tour
(**info 213-430-4219, reservations 213-623-2489; www.laconservancy.org; adult/child $10/5**) Downtown LA's intriguing historical and architectural gems – from an art-deco penthouse to a beaux-arts ballroom and a dazzling silent-movie theater – are revealed on 2½-hour walking tours operated by this nonprofit group. To see some of LA's grand historic movie theaters from the inside, the conservancy also offers the Last Remaining Seats film series, screening classic movies in gilded theater. Check the schedule and book tickets online.

TMZ Tours Hollywood Tour
(**Map p64; 855-4TMZ-TOUR; www.tmz.com/tour; 6925 Hollywood Blvd; adult/child $55/45; approx 10 tours daily**) Cut the shame: do you really want to spot celebrities, glimpse their homes, and gawk and laugh at their dirt? Join this branded tour imagined by the papparazzi made famous. Tours are two hours long, and

LA's Best Beaches

If you like digging your toes in the sand or riding the Pacific's waves, the LA area has plenty of places to indulge your California dreaming.

El Matador Small beach hideaway, about 2.5 miles northwest of Zuma Beach, hemmed in by battered rock cliffs and strewn with giant boulders. Wild surf; not suitable for children. Clothing optional (unofficially).

Venice Beach LA's most outlandish beach, with a nonstop parade of friends and freaks. Drum circle in the sand on Sundays.

Manhattan Beach The most upmarket of the South Bay beach cities (Redondo, Hermosa and Manhattan), where surfers still rule the waves.

Malibu Lagoon/Surfrider Beach Legendary surf beach with superb swells and extended rides. Water quality is only so-so. The lagoon is great for bird-watching.

Santa Monica Along the South Bay Bicycle Trail, this spacious stretch of sand lures volleyball players and families.

you will likely meet some of the TMZ stars and perhaps even celebrity guests on the bus!

Esotouric Bus Tour

(☎323-223-2767; www.esotouric.com; tours $58) Discover LA's lurid and fascinating underbelly on these offbeat, insightful and entertaining walking and bus tours themed around famous crime sites (Black Dahlia anyone?), literary lions (Chandler to Bukowski) and more.

STUDIO TOURS

Did you know it takes a week to shoot a half-hour sitcom? Or that you rarely see ceilings on TV because the space is filled with lights and lamps? You'll learn these and other fascinating nuggets while touring a working studio. Action is slowest during 'hiatus' (May to August). Reservations recommended; bring photo ID.

Parade float, Tournament of Roses

Warner Bros Studios Guided Tour
(☎818-972-8687, 877-492-8687; www.wbstudiotour.com; 3400 W Riverside Dr, Burbank; tours from $54; 8:15am-4pm Mon-Sat, hours vary Sun) For an authentic behind-the-scenes look, take a small-group tour by open-sided shuttle at **Warner Bros Studios**. This will show you around sound stages and backlots (outdoor sets), and into such departments as wardrobe and make-up. Reservations are required; bring photo ID. No children under eight years.

Sony Pictures Studios Guided Tour
(☎310-244-8687; www.sonypicturesstudiostours.com; 10202 W Washington Blvd; tour $38; tours usually 9:30am, 10:30am, 1:30pm & 2:30pm Mon-Fri) For an authentic behind-the-scenes look, take a small-group tour by open-sided shuttle at Sony Pictures Studios which will show you around sound stages and backlots (outdoor sets), and into such departments as wardrobe and make-up. Reservations are required; bring photo ID. Minimum age 12 years.

Paramount Pictures Guided Tour
(☎323-956-1777; www.paramountstudiotour.com; 5555 Melrose Ave; tours from $53; tours 9:30am-2pm Mon-Fri, hours vary Sat & Sun) For an authentic behind-the-scenes look, take a small-group tour by open-sided shuttle at **Paramount Pictures**. This will show you around sound stages and backlots (outdoor sets), and into such departments as wardrobe and make-up. Reservations are required; bring photo ID. No children under 12 years.

Festivals & Events

Tournament of Roses Parade
(www.tournamentofroses.com) This cavalcade of flower-festooned floats snakes through Pasadena on New Year's Day. Get close-ups during postparade viewing at Victory Park. Avoid traffic and take the Metro Rail Gold Line to Memorial Park.

Academy Awards Hollywood
(www.oscars.org) Ogle your favorite film stars from the Dolby Theatre's red-carpet-adjacent bleachers. Apply in September for one of 600 lucky spots. Held in late February or early March.

Toyota Grand Prix of Long Beach Sports
(www.gplb.com) World-class drivers tear up city streets at this weeklong racing spectacle by the sea.

Long Beach

Long Beach is the other half of the port of Los Angeles, with an industrial edge that has been worn smooth in its humming downtown and restyled waterfront.

Long Beach's 'flagship' is the **Queen Mary** (www.queenmary.com; 1126 Queens Hwy, Long Beach; tours adult/child from $26/15; 10am-6:30pm; P), a grand (and supposedly haunted!) British ocean liner, permanently moored here. Larger and fancier than the *Titanic,* it transported royals, dignitaries, immigrants and troops during its 1001 Atlantic crossings between 1936 and 1964. Parking is $17 to $20.

Kids will probably have a better time at the **Aquarium of the Pacific** (☎tickets 562-590-3100; www.aquariumofpacific.org; 100 Aquarium Way, Long Beach; adult/senior/child $29/26/15; 9am-6pm;) – a high-tech romp through an underwater world in which sharks dart, jellyfish dance and sea lions frolic. Imagine the thrill of petting a shark! Parking is $8 to $15.

Queen Mary and aquarium combination tickets cost $42/19 per adult/child aged four to 11 years.

Los Angeles for Children

Keeping the rug rats happy is child's play in LA.

The sprawling Los Angeles Zoo & Botanical Gardens (p65) in family-friendly Griffith Park (p65) is a sure bet. Dino fans dig the Page Museum & La Brea Tar Pits (p68). For live sea creatures, head to the Aquarium of the Pacific (p75); teens might get a kick out of the ghost tours of the *Queen Mary* (p75).

Among LA's amusement parks, Santa Monica Pier (p70) is meant for kids of all ages. Activities for younger children are more limited at Universal Studios Hollywood (p63).

Fiesta Broadway Carnival

(http://fiestabroadway.la) One of the world's largest Cinco de Mayo parties brings half a million folks to Downtown LA, although in 2014 they held it in late April. Check the website for details.

Sleeping

For seaside life, base yourself in Santa Monica, Venice or Long Beach. Cool-hunters and party people will be happiest in Hollywood or WeHo; culture-vultures, in Downtown LA.

DOWNTOWN

Figueroa Hotel Historic Hotel **$$**

(☎800-421-9092, 213-627-8971; www.figueroahotel.com; 939 S Figueroa St; r $148-184, ste $225-265; P ❄ @ ≋ 🐾) It's hard not to be charmed by this rambling owner-operated oasis a basketball toss from LA Live. Global-chic rooms blend Moroccan mirrors, Iraqi quilts, and Kurdish grain-sack floor cushions with paper lanterns from Chinatown. Prince (he's got an all-purple room named for him) is a repeat visitor. Parking costs $8.

Ace Hotel Hotel **$$$**

(☎213-623-3233; www.acehotel.com/losangeles; 929 S Broadway Ave; r from $250, stes from $400) Either lovingly cool, a bit too hip or a touch self-conscious depending upon your purview, there is no denying that Downtown's newest hotel opened to universal acclaim. And the minds behind it care deeply about their product. Some rooms are cubby-box small, but the 'medium' rooms are doable.

HOLLYWOOD

Magic Castle Hotel Hotel **$$**

(Map p64; ☎323-851-0800; http://magiccastlehotel.com; 7025 Franklin Ave; r incl breakfast from $174; P ❄ @ ≋) Walls at this perennial pleaser are a bit thin, but otherwise it's a charming base of operation with large, modern rooms, exceptional staff and a petite courtyard pool where days start with fresh pastries and gourmet coffee. Enquire about access to the Magic Castle, a fabled members-only magic club in an adjacent Victorian mansion. Parking costs $10.

Hollywood Roosevelt Hotel Hotel **$$$**

(Map p64; ☎800-950-7667, 323-466-7000; www.hollywoodroosevelt.com; 7000 Hollywood Blvd; r from $339; P ❄ @ ≋) The pool still draws plenty of eye-candy with attitude, and the cabanas are the way to go if you're looking for a splurge. Parking costs $30.

WEST HOLLYWOOD & MID-CITY

Orbit Hostel **$**

(Banana Bungalow; Map p66; ☎323-655-1510; www.orbithotels.com; 603 N Fairfax Ave; dm $22-25, r $69-79) This popular, well-run hostel occupies a converted art-deco nursing home. Translation: the local bubbies are gone and the global hipsters have moved in. Private rooms all have their own baths, TV and mini-fridge and there are six- to 12-bed dorms, which may only be booked online via the Hostel World website.

Chateau Marmont Hotel **$$$**
(Map p66; ☎323-656-1010; www.chateaumarmont.com; 8221 W Sunset Blvd; r $435, ste from $550; P 📶 🏊) The French-flavored indulgence may look dated, but this faux castle has long lured A-listers with its five-star mystique and legendary discretion. Howard Hughes used to spy on bikini beauties from the same balcony suite that became the favorite of U2's Bono.

Farmer's Daughter Hotel Motel **$$$**
(Map p66; ☎800-334-1658, 323-937-3930; www.farmersdaughterhotel.com; 115 S Fairfax Ave; r from $209; P ❄ @ 📶 🏊) Denim bedspreads and rocking chairs lend this flirty motel a farmhouse vibe. Long before the renovation, a young Charlize Theron stayed here with mom when they were hunting for a Hollywood career. Adventurous lovers should ask about the No Tell Room, which has mirrored headboards and another on the ceiling.

BEVERLY HILLS

Beverly Hills Hotel Luxury Hotel **$$$**
(☎310-276-2251; www.beverlyhillshotel.com; 9641 Sunset Blvd; r from $395; P ❄ @ 📶 🏊 🐾) If the powdery pink walls of this belle hotel could talk, the tales would make you laugh, blush, cry and cringe. Staying here means dwelling in the utmost, old-school luxury.

Avalon Hotel Hotel **$$$**
(☎800-670-6183, 310-277-5221; www.viceroyhotelgroup.com/avalon; 9400 W Olympic Blvd; r from $200; ❄ @ 📶 🏊 🐾) Mid-century modern gets a 21st-century spin at this fashion-crowd fave, which was Marilyn Monroe's old pad in its days as an apartment building. Funky retro rooms are all unique, but most have arced walls, marble slab desks and night stands, and fun art and sculpture. There's also a sexy hourglass-shaped pool. Call it affordable glamour.

SANTA MONICA & VENICE

Venice Beach Inn & Suites Boutique Hotel **$$**
(Map p72; ☎310-396-4559; www.venicebeachsuites.com; 1305 Ocean Front Walk; r from $159;

Aquarium of the Pacific (p75)

P) This good-value place right on the Boardwalk scores big for its bend-over-backwards staff, and bevy of beach toys for rent. There are exposed-brick walls, kitchenettes, wood floors and built-in closets. It's ideal for long stays. Kitchen suites are big enough for dinner parties.

Palihouse Boutique Hotel **$$$**
(Map p72; 310-394-1279; www.palihousesantamonica.com; 1001 3rd St; r $279-319, studios $319-379; P @) LA's grooviest new hotel brand (not named Ace) has taken over the 36 rooms, studios and one-bedroom apartments of the historic Embassy Hotel (c 1927). Expect a lobby with terracotta floors, beamed ceilings and coffee bar, plus booths and leather sofas.

LONG BEACH

Queen Mary Hotel Ship **$$**
(562-435-3511; www.queenmary.com; 1126 Queens Hwy, Long Beach; r from $99; @) There's an irresistible romance to ocean liners such as the *Queen Mary*, a nostalgic retreat that time-warps you to a long-gone, slower-paced era. Yes, the rooms are small, but the 1st-class staterooms are nicely refurbished with original art-deco details. Avoid the cheapest cabins on the inside – claustrophobic!

Eating

DOWNTOWN

For browsing, try the food stalls of the **Grand Central Market (www.grandcentralsquare.com; 317 S Broadway; 9am-6pm)**.

Sushi Gen Japanese **$$**
(213-617-0552; www.sushigen.org; 422 E 2nd St; sushi $11-21; 11:15am-2pm & 5:30-9:45pm) Come early to grab a table, and know that the folks here don't do the uber-creative 'look at me' kind of rolls. In this Japanese classic sushi spot, seven chefs stand behind the blonde wood bar, carving thick slabs of melt-in-your-mouth salmon, buttery toro, and a wonderful Japanese snapper, among other staples. The sashimi special at lunch ($18) is a steal.

Bar Amá Mexican, Fusion **$$$**
(213-687-8002; www.bar-ama.com; 118 W 4th St; dishes $8-25, dinner mains $32-36; 11:30am-2:30pm & 5:30-11pm Mon-Thu,

Queen Mary (p75 & p78), Long Beach

11:30am-3pm & 5:30pm-midnight Fri, 11:30am-midnight Sat, to 10pm Sun) One of three exquisite Downtown restaurants with profound Mexican influences offered by Josef Centeno. This one fries pig ears, braises short rib, and smothers enchiladas with mole sauce. Brussel sprouts are garnished with pickled red onions, and the roasted cauliflower and cilantro pesto, served with cashews and pine nuts, is a tremendous veggie choice.

If it's a family-style dinner you crave, order the lamb birria, two pounds of chicken mole or the whole roasted dorado which come with sides and are served family style. Oh, and the drinks list is sublime.

HOLLYWOOD, LOS FELIZ & SILVER LAKE

Elf Cafe — Vegetarian $$

(☎213-484-6829; www.elfcafe.com; 2135 Sunset Blvd; mains $12-20; 🌶) One of the best – if not the very best – vegetarian (not vegan) restaurants in LA. Start with feta wrapped in grape leaves and some spiced olives and almonds, then move onto a kale salad dressed with citrus, wild mushroom risotto and a fantastic kebab of seared oyster mushrooms.

Jitlada — Thai $$

(☎323-667-9809; jitladala.com; 5233 W Sunset Blvd; appetizers $5-10, mains $11-30; ⏲lunch & dinner; P) A transporting taste of southern Thailand. The crab curry and *fried som tum* (fried papaya salad) are fantastic, regulars dream about the Thai-style burger between visits, and the vivacious owner-operator counts Ryan Gosling and Natalie Portman among her loyal, mostly *farang* (European American) customers. Look for the wall of fame near the bathrooms.

Mess Hall — Pub Food $$

(☎323-660-6377; www.messhallkitchen.com; 4500 Los Feliz Blvd; mains $15-31; ⏲11:30am-3pm & 4-11pm Mon-Thu, to midnight Fri, 10am-3pm & 5pm-midnight Sat, 10am-3pm & 4-11pm Sun) Formerly The Derby, a swing dance spot made famous by the film *Swingers,* which was shot in the area, it is now a gastropub where you'll find $1 oysters and $5 beers on Tuesdays. It's been written up for having one of the best burgers in LA, and they also do a pulled-pork sandwich and a kale Caesar.

WEST HOLLYWOOD, MID-CITY & BEVERLY HILLS

Pingtung — Asian $

(Map p66; ☎323-866-1866; www.pingtungla.com; 7455 Melrose Ave; dishes $6-12; ⏲11:30am-10:30pm; 📶) Our new favorite place to eat on Melrose is this Pan-Asian market cafe where the dim sum (wild crab dumplings), seaweed and green papaya salads, and rice bowls piled with curried chicken and BBQ beef are all worthy of praise. It has an inviting back patio with ample seating, wi-fi and good beer on tap.

Original Farmers Market — Market $

(Map p66; www.farmersmarketla.com; 6333 W 3rd St; mains $6-12; ⏲9am-9pm Mon-Fri, to 8pm Sat, 10am-7pm Sun; P 👪) The Farmers Market is a great spot for a casual meal any time of day, especially if the rug rats are tagging along. There are lots of options here, from gumbo to Singapore-style noodles to tacos.

Pikey — Pub Food $$

(Map p66; ☎323-850-5400; www.thepikeyla.com; 7617 W Sunset Blvd; dishes $12-28; ⏲noon-2am Mon-Fri, from 11am Sat & Sun) A tasteful kitchen that began life as Coach & Horses, one of Hollywood's favorite dives before it was reimagined into a place where you can get broccoli roasted with bacon, arctic char crudo with grapefruit and jalapenos, seared squid with curried chickpeas, and a slow roasted duck leg. The cocktails rock.

Nate 'n Al — Deli $$

(☎310-274-0101; www.natenal.com; 414 N Beverly Dr; dishes $6.50-13; ⏲7am-9pm; 👪) Dapper seniors, chatty girlfriends, busy execs and even Larry King have kept this New York–style nosh spot busy since 1945. The huge menu brims with corned beef, lox and other old-school favorites, but we're partial to the pastrami, made fresh on-site.

MALIBU

Nobu Malibu Japanese **$$$**
(☎310-317-9140; www.noburestaurants.com; 22706 Pacific Coast Hwy; dishes $8-46; ⏰11am-3pm & 5:30pm-late; P) South of the pier and born again in landmark quality digs, Nobu Malibu is a cavernous, modern wood chalet with a long sushi bar on the back wall and a dining room that spills onto a patio overlooking the swirling sea. Remember, it's the cooked food that built the brand.

SANTA MONICA & VENICE

Santa Monica Farmers Markets Market **$**
(Map p72; www.smgov.net/portals/farmersmarket; Arizona Ave, btwn 2nd & 3rd Sts; ⏰8:30am-1:30pm Wed, to 1pm Sat; 👪) You haven't really experienced Santa Monica until you've explored one of its weekly outdoor farmers markets stocked with organic fruits, vegetables, flowers, baked goods and freshly shucked oysters.

Milo & Olive Italian **$$**
(☎310-453-6776; www.miloandolive.com; 2723 Wilshire Blvd; dishes $7-20; ⏰7am-11pm) We love this place for its small-batch wines, incredible pizzas, terrific breakfasts (creamy polenta and poached eggs anyone?), breads and pastries, all of which you may enjoy at the marble bar or shoulder to shoulder with new friends at one of two common tables. It's a cozy, neighborhood joint so they don't take reservations.

Gjelina Italian **$$**
(Map p72; ☎310-450-1429; www.gjelina.com; 1429 Abbot Kinney Blvd; dishes $8-26; ⏰11:30am-midnight Mon-Fri, from 9am Sat & Sun; 👪) Carve out a slip on the communal table between the hipsters and yuppies, or get your own slab of wood on the elegant, tented, stone terrace, and dine on imaginative small plates (raw yellowtail spiced with chili and mint and drenched in olive oil and blood orange) and sensational thin-crust, wood-fired pizza. They serve food until midnight.

Drinking & Nightlife

No Vacancy Bar
(Map p64; ☎323-465-1902; www.novacancyla.com; 1727 N Hudson Ave; ⏰8pm-2am) An old, shingled Victorian has been converted into LA's hottest night out. Even the entrance is theatrical: you'll follow a rickety staircase into a narrow hall and enter the room of a would-be madame, dressed in fishnet and hospitality who will soon press a button to reveal another staircase down into the living room and out into a courtyard.

Grocer, Santa Monica Farmers Markets
DAVID YOUNG-WOLFF / GETTY IMAGES ©

Gay & Lesbian LA

The rainbow flag flies especially proudly in 'Boystown,' along Santa Monica Blvd in West Hollywood, which is lined with dozens of bars, cafes, restaurants, gyms and clubs. Most places cater to gay men. Silver Lake, LA's original gay enclave, has evolved from largely leather and Levi's to encompass both cute hipsters of all ethnicities to leather-and-Levi's and an older contingent. Venice and Long Beach have the most relaxed, neighborly scenes.

If nightlife isn't your scene, the gay community has plenty of other ways to meet. **Will Rogers State Beach** ('Ginger Rogers' to her friends) in Santa Monica is LA's unofficial gay beach. **Long Beach Pride Celebration** (www.longbeachpride.com) is a warm-up for **LA Pride** (www.lapride.org), a weekend of nonstop partying and a parade down Santa Monica Blvd.

LA's essential gay bar and restaurant is **The Abbey** (Map p66; www.abbeyfoodandbar.com; 692 N Robertson Blvd; mains $9-13; 11am-2am Mon-Thu, from 10am Fri, from 9am Sat & Sun). Take your pick of preening and partying spaces spanning a leafy patio to a slick lounge, and enjoy flavored martinis and upscale pub grub. Other venues include **Eleven** (Map p66; www.eleven.la; 8811 Santa Monica Blvd; 5pm-2am Mon-Thu, to 3am Fri, noon-3am Sat, 11am-2am Sun), a glam spot that occupies a historic building, serves decent food and offers different theme nights; **Akbar** (www.akbarsilverlake.com; 4356 W Sunset Blvd; 4pm-2am), which has the best jukebox in town, a casbah atmosphere, and a crowd that's been known to change from hour to hour; and **Micky's** (Map p66; www.mickys.com; 8857 Santa Monica Blvd; 5pm-2am Sun-Thu, to 4am Fri & Sat), a two-story, quintessential WeHo dance club, with go-go boys, expensive drinks, attitude and plenty of eye-candy.

Sayers Club — Club

(Map p64; 323-871-8416; www.sbe.com/nightlife/locations/thesayersclub-hollywood; 1645 Wilcox Ave; cover varies; 8pm-2am Tue, Thu & Fri) When rock royalty such as Prince, established stars such as the Black Keys, and even movie stars such as Joseph Gordon-Levitt decide to play secret shows in intimate environs, they come to the back room at this brick-house Hollywood nightspot, where the booths are leather, the lighting moody and the music always satisfies.

Las Perlas — Bar

(107 E 6th St; 7pm-2am Mon-Sat, 8pm-2am Sun) With an Old Mexico whimsy, a chalkboard menu of over 80 tequilas and mescals, and friendly barkeeps who mix ingredients such as egg whites, blackberries and port syrup into new-school takes on the classic margarita, there's a reason we love Downtown's best tequila bar. But if you truly want to dig tequila, select a highland variety and sip it neat.

Bar Marmont — Bar

(Map p66; 323-650-0575323-650-0575; www.chateaumarmont.com/barmarmont.php; 8171 Sunset Blvd; 6pm-2am) Elegant, but not stuck up; been around, yet still cherished. With high ceilings, molded walls and terrific martinis, the famous, and wish-they-weres, still flock here. If you time it right you might see Tom Yorke, or perhaps Lindsay Lohan? Come midweek. Weekends are for amateurs.

Copa d'Oro — Bar

(Map p72; www.copadoro.com; 217 Broadway Ave; 5:30pm-midnight Mon-Wed, to 2am Thu-Sat) The cocktail menu was created by the talented Vincenzo Marianella – a man who knows his spirits, and has trained his

Below: Arclight Cinemas; **Right:** Grauman's Chinese Theatre
(BELOW) BRENT WINEBRENNER / GETTY IMAGES ©; (RIGHT) GAVIN HELLIER / GETTY IMAGES ©

team to concoct addictive cocktails from a well of top-end spirits and a produce bin of fresh herbs, fruits, juices, and a few veggies too. The rock tunes and the smooth, dark ambience don't hurt.

Angel City Brewery Brewery
(**213-622-1261; www.angelcitybrewery.com; 216 S Alameda St; 4-10pm Mon-Thu, to midnight Fri, noon-midnight Sat, noon-10pm Sun**) This wonderful microbrewer of fine beers and ales is the only one of its kind in Downtown LA. Located on the edge of the Arts District, tours are available on weekends, but you can always stop by their Public House to drink beer, listen to occasional live music, and patronize the food trucks that descend with welcome flavor.

Polo Lounge Lounge
(**www.beverlyhillshotel.com; 9641 Sunset Blvd; 7am-1:30am**) With its mix of tennis whites, business suits and chichi dresses, this swanky, wood-paneled watering hole has the feel of a Hollywood country club. From Isaac Mizrahi to George Hamilton to David Arquette, you never know who you'll see murmuring in the perpetually reserved, dark booths. It's part of the Beverly Hills Hotel.

Musso & Frank Grill Bar
(**Map p64; www.mussoandfrankgrill.com; 6667 Hollywood Blvd**) Hollywood history hangs in the thick air at Musso & Frank Grill, Tinseltown's oldest eatery (since 1919). Charlie Chaplin used to knock back vodka gimlets at the bar and Raymond Chandler penned scripts in the high-backed booths.

Entertainment

The freebie **LA Weekly** (**www.laweekly.com**) and the **Los Angeles Times** (**www.latimes.com**) daily newspaper are your best sources for plugging into the local scene.

CINEMAS

Movie-going is serious business in LA; it's not uncommon for viewers to sit through the end credits, out of respect for friends and neighbors.

Arclight Cinemas Cinema

(Map p64; ☎323-464-1478; www.arclightcinemas.com; 6360 W Sunset Blvd; tickets $14-16) Assigned seats and exceptional celeb-sighting potential make this 14-screen multiplex the best around. If your taste dovetails with its schedule, the awesome 1963 geodesic Cinerama Dome is a must. Bonuses: age 21-plus screenings where you can booze it up, and Q&As with directors, writers and actors. Parking is $3 for four hours.

Grauman's Chinese Theatre Cinema

(Map p64; www.manntheatres.com/chinese; 6925 Hollywood Blvd; adult $11.75-15.75, child & senior $9-12) Nowhere in the world are movie premieres as glitzy as at this industry favorite. Make sure you buy tickets for the glam historic theater, not the ho-hum Mann Chinese six-multiplex next door.

PERFORMING ARTS

Red Cat Theater

(www.redcat.org; 631 W 2nd St) Downtown's most avant-garde performance laboratory where theater, dance, music, poetry and film merge into impressive exhibitions presented in their own theater and gallery within the Walt Disney Concert Hall complex. The curious name is an acronym for Roy and Edna Disney/Cal Arts Theater. Admission to the gallery is free, theater ticket prices vary.

Upright Citizens Brigade Theatre Comedy

(Map p64; ☎323-908-8702; www.losangeles.ucbtheatre.com; 5919 Franklin Ave; tickets $5-10) Founded in New York by *SNL* alums Amy Poehler and Ian Roberts along with Matt Besser and Matt Walsh, this sketch-comedy group cloned itself in Hollywood

Historic Movie Palaces

If you like Grauman's Chinese Theatre (p63), take a gander at these spectacular shrines to film.

El Capitan Theatre (Map p64; ☎800-347-6396; elcapitan.go.com; 6838 Hollywood Blvd; VIP $25, general admission adult/senior & child $15/12; 👪) Disney rolls out family-friendly blockbusters at this movie palace, often with costumed characters putting on the Ritz in live preshow routines. The best seats are on the balcony in the middle of the front row. VIP tickets ($20) allow you to reserve a seat and include popcorn and a beverage.

American Cinematheque (Map p64; www.americancinematheque.com; 6712 Hollywood Blvd; adult/senior & student $11/9) A non-profit screening tributes, retrospectives and foreign films in the **Egyptian Theatre** (Map p64; www.egyptiantheatre.com; 6712 Hollywood Blvd). Directors, screenwriters and actors often swing by for post show Q&As.

Los Angeles Theatre (☎213-629-2939; www.losangelestheatre.com; 615 S Broadway) This 1931 theater is the most lavish movie palace on the strip. The soaring lobby is a sparkling hall of mirrors with a three-tiered fountain, crystal chandeliers and a grand central staircase leading to an auditorium where Albert Einstein and other luminaries enjoyed the premiere of Charlie Chaplin's *City Lights*. Restored, it presents special events and screenings.

Orpheum Theatre (www.laorpheum.com; 842 S Broadway) This 1926 theater was built for vaudeville and has hosted such entertainers as Judy Garland, George Burns and Nat King Cole. It's a truly sumptuous place with silk tapestries, a gilded, coffered ceiling, still-functioning Wurlitzer organ and an old brass box office. Fully restored, it offers a rich entertainment calendar. See a show here if you can.

United Artists Theatre (☎213-623-3233; www.acehotel.com/losangeles/theatre; 929 S Broadway) A historic gem of a theater restored by the Ace Hotel, who curates the calendar. It's homebase for LA's best modern dance company, and stages indie and up-and-coming bands as well.

in 2005 and is arguably the best improv theater in town. Most shows are $5 or $8 but Sunday's 'Asssscat' is freeeee.

Actors' Gang Theater Theater
(www.theactorsgang.com; 9070 Venice Blvd, Culver City) The 'Gang' was founded in 1981 by Tim Robbins and other renegade UCLA acting-school grads. Its daring and offbeat reinterpretations of classics have a loyal following.

LIVE MUSIC

Troubadour Live Music
(Map p66; www.troubadour.com; 9081 Santa Monica Blvd) The celebrated 1957 rock hall launched a thousand careers, including those of James Taylor and Tom Waits, and was central to John Lennon's "Lost Weekend in 1973". It's still a great spot for catching tomorrow's headliners and appeals to beer-drinking music aficionados who keep attitude to a minimum. Come early to snag a seat on the balcony. No age limit.

El Rey
Live Music

(Map p66; www.theelrey.com; 5515 Wilshire Blvd; cover varies) An old art-deco dance hall decked out in red velvet and chandeliers and flaunting an awesome sound system and excellent sightlines. Although it can hold 800 people, it feels quite small. Performance-wise, it's popular with indie acts such as Black Joe Lewis and the Honeybears, and the rockers who love them.

Echo
Live Music

(www.attheecho.com; 1822 W Sunset Blvd; cover varies) Eastsiders hungry for an eclectic alchemy of sounds pack this funky-town dive that's basically a sweaty bar with a stage and a smoking patio. It books indie bands, and also has regular club nights. Their Funky Sole party every Saturday is always a blast.

SPORTS

Dodger Stadium
Baseball

(☎866-363-4377; www.dodgers.com; 1000 Elysian Park Ave; ⏲Apr-Sep) Few clubs can match the Dodgers when it comes to history (Jackie Robinson, Sandy Koufax, Kirk Gibson, and Vin Scully), success and fan loyalty. The club's newest owners bought the organization for roughly two billion dollars, an American team sports record.

Staples Center
Sports Arena

(☎213-742-7340; www.staples-center.com; 1111 S Figueroa St; 👪) The **LA Lakers** **(☎213-742-7340; www.nba.com/lakers; tickets $50-250)** were down on their luck as of this writing, but the NBA's most successful organization still packs all 19,000 seats on a regular basis. Floor seats, like those filled by the ubiquitous Jack Nicholson, cost in excess of $5000 per game.

Shopping

Fashion-forward fashionistas (and paparazzi) flock to Robertson Blvd (between Beverly Blvd and W 3rd St) or Melrose Ave (between San Vicente Blvd and La Brea Ave) in West Hollywood, while bargain hunters haunt Downtown's **Fashion District (www.fashiondistrict.org)**, a frantic, 90-block trove of stores, stalls and showrooms where discount shopping is an Olympian sport. If money is no object, Beverly Hills beckons with international couture, jewelry and antiques, especially along Rodeo Dr. East of Hollywood, Silver Lake has cool kitsch and collectibles, especially around Sunset Junction (Hollywood and Sunset Blvds). Santa Monica has good boutique shopping on high-toned Montana Ave and eclectic Main St, while the chain store brigade (H&M to Banana Republic) has taken over Third Street Promenade. In nearby Venice, you'll find

Union Station (p88)

STEVE LEWIS STOCK / GETTY IMAGES ©

cheap and crazy knickknacks along the Venice Boardwalk, although locals prefer Abbot Kinney Blvd with its fun mix of art, fashion and bohemian emporiums.

Fred Segal Fashion

(Map p66; ☎323-651-4129; www.fredsegal.com; 8100 Melrose Ave; ⏰10am-7pm Mon-Sat, noon-6pm Sun) Celebs and beautiful people circle for the very latest from Babakul, Aviator Nation and Robbi & Nikki at this warren of high-end boutiques under one impossibly chic but slightly snooty roof. The only time you'll see bargains (sort of) is during the two-week blowout sale in September.

It's a Wrap! Vintage

(www.itsawraphollywood.com; 3315 W Magnolia Blvd, Burbank; ⏰10am-8pm Mon-Fri, 11am-6pm Sat & Sun) It's a Wrap boasts fashionable, post-production wares worn by TV and film stars. What that means for you is great prices on mainstream designer labels, including racks of casual and formal gear worn on such shows as *Nurse Jackie*, *The Office* and *Scandal*. The suits are a steal, and so is the denim. New arrivals are displayed by show affiliation.

Amoeba Music Music

(Map p64; ☎323-245-6400; www.amoeba.com; 6400 W Sunset Blvd; ⏰10:30am-11pm Mon-Sat, 11am-9pm Sun) When a record store not only survives but thrives in this techno age, you know it's doing something right. Flip through half-a-million new and used CDs, DVDs, videos and vinyl at this granddaddy of music stores. Handy listening stations and its outstanding *Music We Like* booklet keep you from buying lemons.

Rose Bowl Flea Market Market

(www.rgcshows.com; 1001 Rose Bowl Dr, Pasadena; admission from $8; ⏰9am-4:30pm 2nd Sun each month, last entry 3pm) California's Marketplace of Unusual Items descends upon the Rose Bowl football field bringing forth the rummaging hordes. There are over 2500 vendors and 15,000 buyers here every month, and it's always a great time.

Space 1520 Mall

(Map p64; www.space1520.com; 1520 N Cahuenga Blvd; ⏰11am-9pm Mon-Fri, 10am-10pm Sat, to 9pm Sun) The hippest minimall in Hollywood, this designer construct of

Amoeba Music

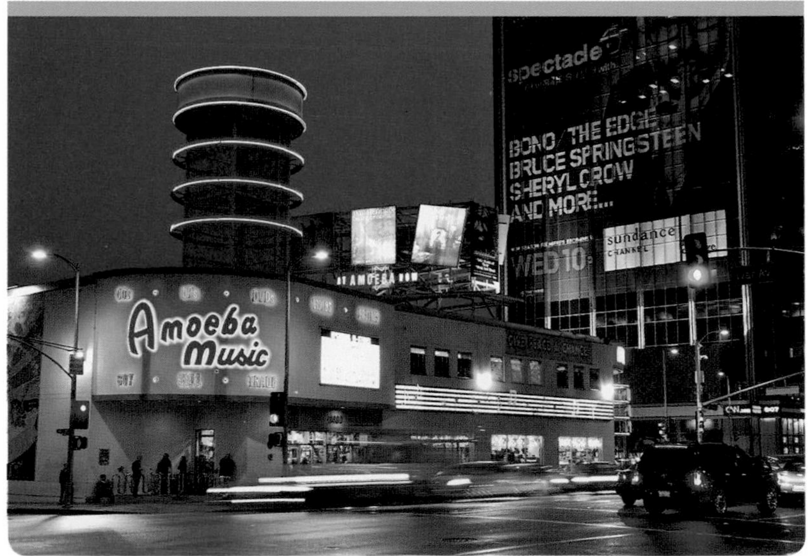

JAMES KIRKIKIS / GETTY IMAGES ©

Your 15 Minutes of Fame

Come on, haven't you always dreamed of seeing your silly mug on TV? Well, LA has a way of making dreams come true, but you have to do your homework before coming to town. Here are some leads to get you started.

Sitcoms and game shows usually tape between August and March before live audiences. To nab free tickets, check with **TV Tickets** (www.tvtix.com) or **Audiences Unlimited** (818-260-0041; www.tvtickets.com). Tickets to Jimmy Kimmel Live, which conveniently tapes at its namesake theater, are available via 1iota.com.

If you'd like to see yourself on screen, check with **Be In a Movie** (www.beinamovie.com) on how to become an extra in a big crowd scene at major film shoots. Although many game shows tape in LA, the chances of becoming a contestant are greatest on *The Price is Right,* taped at **CBS** (Map p64; 323-575-2624; www.cbs.com; 7800 Beverly Blvd; 9am-5pm Mon-Fri).

brick, wood, concrete and glass is home to classic and trend-setting mini-chains such as Umami Burger, Hennesy & Ingalls and Free People.

Information

Dangers & Annoyances

Despite what you see in the movies, walking around LA is generally safe. Downtown's Skid Row, an area roughly bounded by 3rd, Alameda, 7th and Main Sts, has plenty of homeless folks, as does Santa Monica.

Money

Travelex Santa Monica (310-260-9219; www.travelex.com; 201 Santa Monica Blvd, Suite 101, Santa Monica; 9am-5pm Mon-Thu, to 6pm Fri); West Hollywood (310-659-6093; www.travelex.com; US Bank, 8901 Santa Monica Blvd, West Hollywood; 9:30am-5pm Mon-Thu, 9am-6pm Fri, to 1pm Sat).

Tourist Information

Downtown LA Visitor Center (www.discoverlosangeles.com; 800 N Alameda St, Downtown; 8:30am-5pm Mon-Fri)

Hollywood Visitor Information Center (Map p64; 323-467-6412; http://discoverlosangeles.com; Hollywood & Highland complex, 6801 Hollywood Blvd, Hollywood; 10am-10pm Mon-Sat, to 7pm Sun) In the Dolby Theatre walkway.

Santa Monica (Map p72; 800-544-5319; www.santamonica.com; 2427 Main St, Santa Monica) Roving information officers patrol the promenade on Segways!

Getting There & Away

Air

Los Angeles International Airport (p397) is one of the world's busiest, located on the coast between Venice and the South Bay city of Manhattan Beach.

Locals love Bob Hope Airport, commonly called Burbank Airport, in the San Fernando Valley. It has easy-to-use terminals and proximity to Hollywood, Downtown LA and Pasadena.

To the south, on the border with Orange County, Long Beach Airport (Map p53) is convenient for Disneyland.

Bus

LA's hub for **Greyhound** (213-629-8401; www.greyhound.com; 1716 E 7th St) is in an unsavory part of Downtown LA, so avoid arriving after dark. Some buses go directly to the terminal in Hollywood and a few also pass through Pasadena and Long Beach.

Car & Motorcycle

All the major international car-rental agencies have branches at airports and throughout Los Angeles. If you haven't booked, use the courtesy phones in airport arrival areas at LAX.

Train

Amtrak trains roll into Downtown LA's historic **Union Station** (☎800-872-7245; www.amtrak.com; 800 N Alameda St) from across California and the country. The *Pacific Surfliner* travels daily to San Diego ($37, 2¾ hours), Santa Barbara ($29, 2¾ hours) and San Luis Obispo ($41, 5½ hours).

ℹ Getting Around

To/From the Airport

All services mentioned below leave from the lower terminal level of Los Angeles International Airport. Practically all airport-area hotels have arrangements with shuttle companies for free or discounted pick-ups. Door-to-door shuttles, such as those operated by **Prime Time** (☎800-733-8267; www.primetimeshuttle.com) and **Super Shuttle** (☎800-258-3826; www.supershuttle.com) charge $21, $27 and $16 for trips to Santa Monica, Hollywood or Downtown LA, respectively.

Curbside dispatchers will be on hand to summon a taxi for you. The flat rate to Downtown LA is $47, while going to Santa Monica costs $30 to $35, to West Hollywood around $40, to Hollywood to $50 and to Disneyland $90. Cabs leaving from LAX charge a $4 airport fee.

Public transportation has become a lot easier since the arrival of **LAX FlyAway** (☎866-435-9529; www.lawa.org; one-way $8). These buses travel nonstop to Downtown's Union Station ($8, 45 minutes) and Westwood Village near UCLA ($10, 30 minutes).

For Santa Monica or Venice, catch the free Shuttle C bus to the **LAX City Bus Center & MetroRail Station** (96th St & Sepulveda Blvd), then change to the Santa Monica Rapid 3 ($1, one hour). The center is the hub for buses serving all of LA.

The **Disneyland Resort Express** (☎714-978-8855; http://graylineanaheim.com; ⌚7:30am-10:30pm) travels hourly or half-hourly from LAX to the main Disneyland resorts (adult/child one way $30/20, round-trip $48/35).

Bicycle

Most buses have bike racks and bikes ride for free, although you must securely load and unload them yourself. Bikes are also allowed on Metro Rail trains except during rush hour (6:30am to 8:30am and 4:30pm to 6:30pm on weekdays).

Car & Motorcycle

Driving in LA doesn't need to be a hassle (a GPS device helps), but be prepared for some of the worst traffic in the country. Avoid rush hour (7am to 9am and 3:30pm to 6pm).

Parking at motels and cheaper hotels is usually free, while fancier ones charge from $8 to $40. Valet parking at nicer restaurants, hotels and nightspots is commonplace, with rates ranging from $3.50 to $10.

Public Transportation

Trip-planning help is available via LA's **Metro** (☎323-466-3876; www.metro.net), which operates about 200 bus lines and six light-rail and two subway lines:

Red Line Union Station to North Hollywood, via Downtown LA, Hollywood and Universal City.

Blue Line Downtown LA to Long Beach.

Gold Line Union Station, Tokyo and Chinatown in Downtown LA to Pasadena and East LA.

Expo Line Downtown LA to USC, Exposition Park and Culver City.

Green Line Norwalk to Redondo Beach, with local bus connection to LAX.

Purple Line Downtown to Koreatown.

The regular base fare is $1.75 per boarding or $7 for a day pass with unlimited rides. Single tickets and day passes are available from bus drivers and vending machines at each train station.

Local **DASH minibuses** (☎323-808-2273, 213-808-2273; www.ladottransit.com; per ride 50¢; ⌚6am-7pm) serve Downtown LA, Hollywood and other neighborhood routes. Santa Monica–based **Big Blue Bus** (☎310-451-5444; www.bigbluebus.com; fares from $1) serves much of western LA, including Santa Monica, Westwood and LAX. Its express bus 10 connects Santa Monica to Downtown LA ($2, one hour).

Taxi

Except for taxis lined up outside airports, train stations, bus stations and major hotels, it's best to phone for a cab. Fares are metered and vary depending upon the company and the city they're registered in. In the city of LA, rates are $2.85 at flagfall plus about $2.70 per mile.

Troubadour (p84)

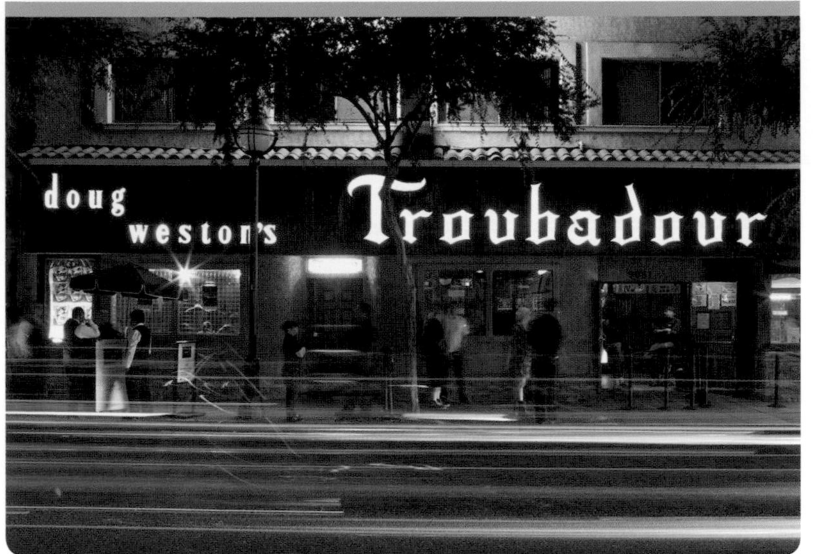

BRENT WINEBRENNER / GETTY IMAGES ©

Beverly Hills Cab (☎800-273-6611; www.beverlyhillscabco.com) A solid, dependable company, with good rates to the airport and a wide service area.

Taxi Taxi (☎310-444-4444; www.santamonicataxi.com) Easily the best and most professional fleet available. They'll drive you anywhere, but can only pick up in Santa Monica.

Yellow Cab (☎877-733-3305; www.layellowcab.com) If all else fails.

San Francisco

Get to know the world capital of weird from the inside out, from mural-lined alleyways named after poets to clothing-optional beaches on a former military base. But don't be too quick to dismiss San Francisco's wild ideas. Biotech, gay rights, personal computers, cable cars and organic fine dining were once considered outlandish too, before San Francisco introduced these underground ideas into the mainstream decades ago. San Francisco's morning fog erases the boundaries between land and ocean, reality and infinite possibility.

Rules are never strictly followed here, but bliss is. Golden Gate Bridge and Alcatraz are entirely optional – San Franciscans mostly admire them from afar – leaving you free to pursue inspiration in the beauty of Golden Gate Park, the city's flamboyantly painted Victorians and its funky Mission galleries. Just don't be late for your sensational, sustainable dinner: in San Francisco, you can find happiness and eat it too.

Golden Gate Bridge (p100)

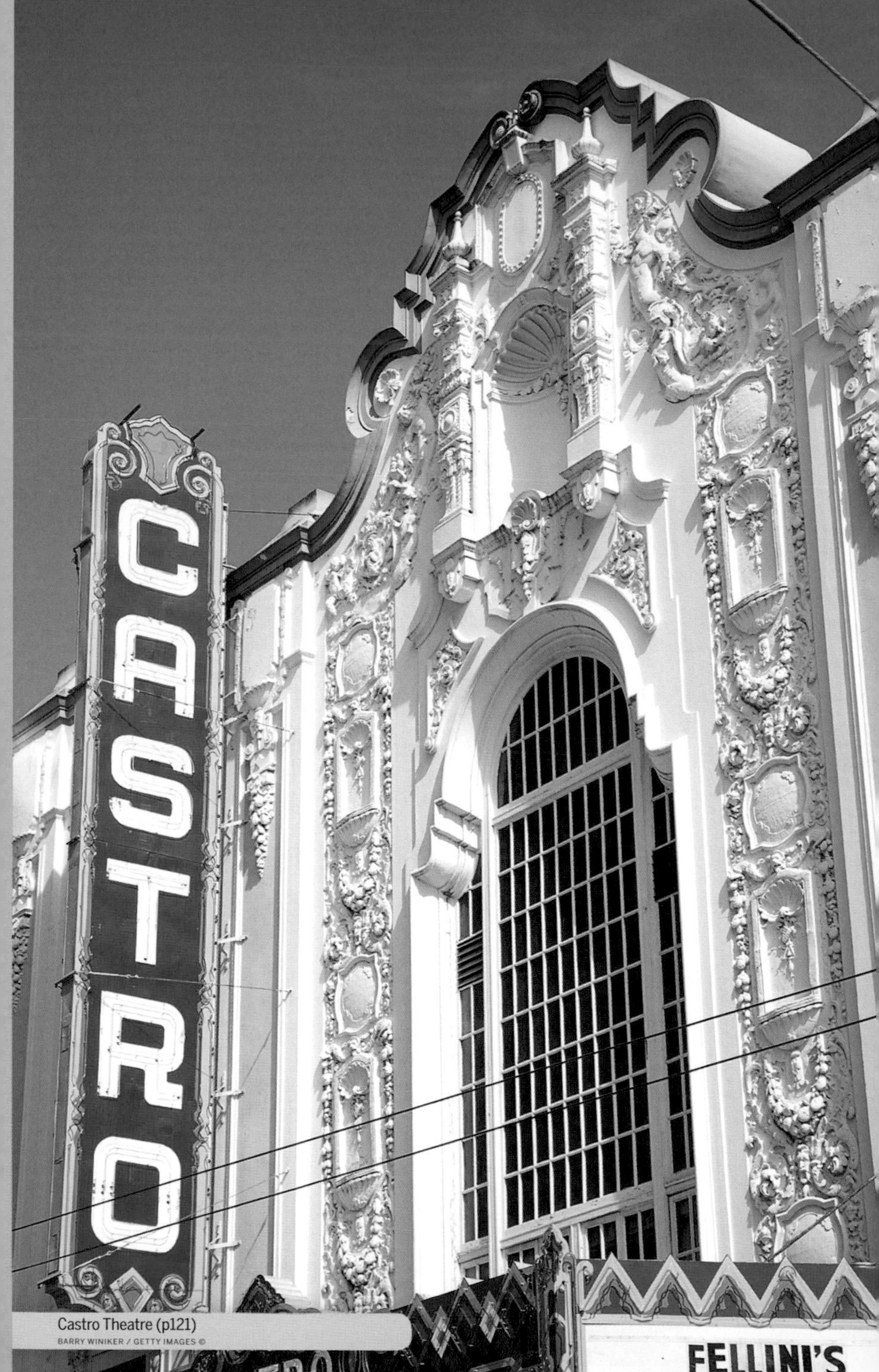

Castro Theatre (p121)

San Francisco

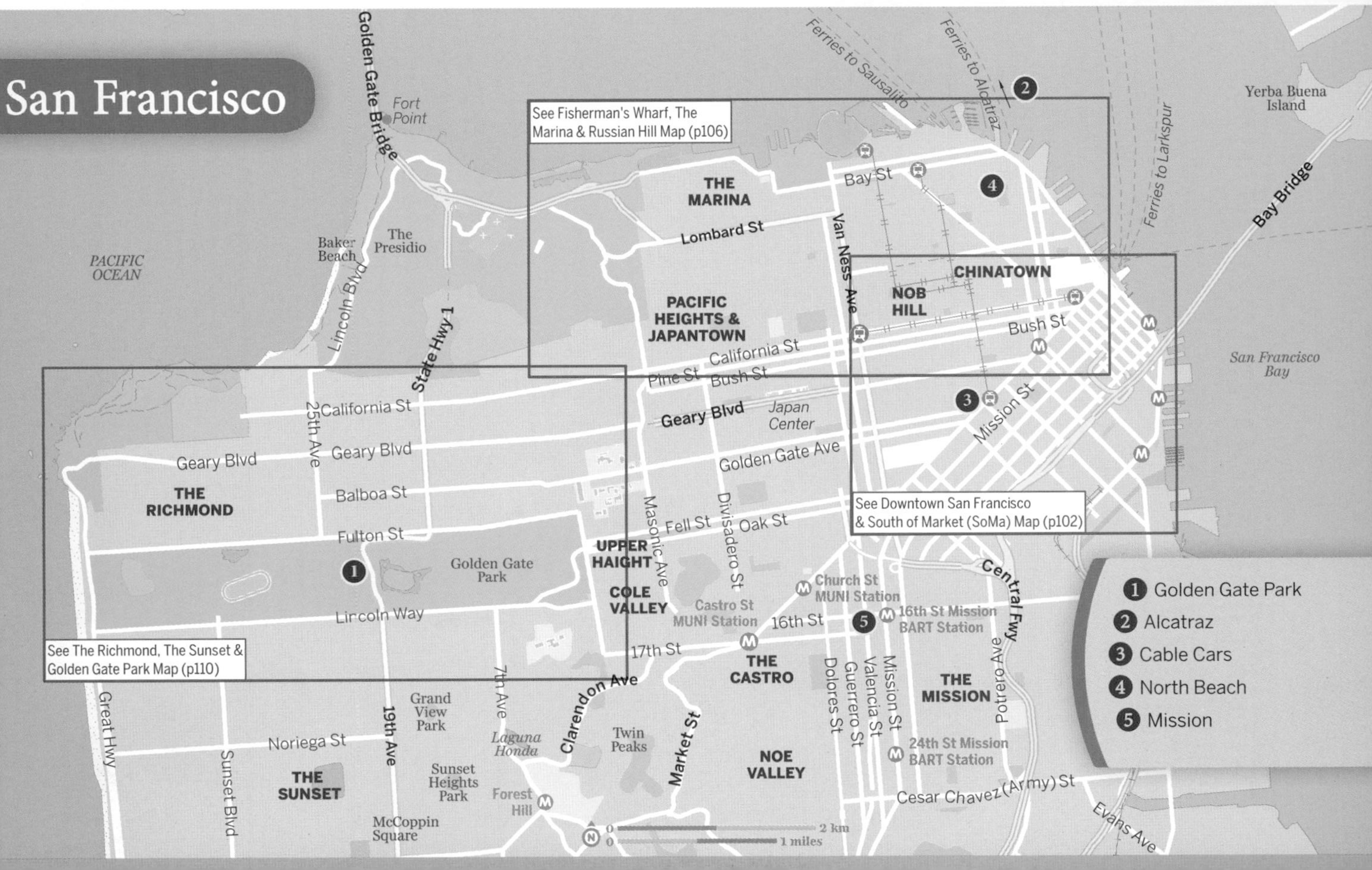

San Francisco Highlights

Golden Gate Park

When San Franciscans refer to 'the park,' there's only one that gets the definite article. Everything that San Franciscans hold dear is in Golden Gate Park (p107): free spirits, free music, redwoods, Frisbee, protests, fine art, bonsai and buffalo. Remember that eastern JFK Drive closes to cars on weekends and holidays; both of the park's museums give discounts to Muni riders. Below: Japanese Tea Garden (p108), Golden Gate Park

1

2

Alcatraz Island

Once housing infamous criminals such as Al Capone, the lighthouse-topped bay island of Alcatraz (p101) later became the site of an American Indian occupation. Pace the stark prison via a self-guided audio tour, as inmates recount their stories of life on 'The Rock.' Named by Spanish explorers for its bird colonies ('alcatraz' means pelican in Spanish), the island is still a sanctuary and breeding ground for seabirds.

Vintage Streetcars & Cable Cars 3

To see the city sights in old-fashioned style, board a historic F-line streetcar to cruise down Market St and skim along the Embarcadero piers. Feeling more adventurous? Nab a spot on a cable-car (p124) running board and cling to the pole as it crests Nob Hill then plummets and clangs its bell as it heads toward the bay.

4 North Beach

Shrill, green parrots streak through the skies of North Beach (p98), a longtime Italian and literary neighborhood with sidewalk cafes, scrumptious restaurants, scores of nightclubs and boozy watering holes, and one of the San Francisco's best bookshops, City Lights. Score a scoop of gelato or a bracing espresso and loaf around the green, grassy lawns of Washington Sq. Above: City Lights (p122)

5 Mission District

If the sun's to be found anywhere on a foggy San Francisco day, there's a good chance it's beaming in Mission (p108). Join a mural tour (p109) for an overview of expressive neighborhood art and then feast on the best burritos in town. At night, cross paths with mariachis for hire as you bar hop along Mission and Valencia Sts. Above: Detail of altar, Mission Dolores (p108)

San Francisco's Best...

Cheap Thrills

- **Golden Gate Bridge** Ramble the city's iconic gateway. (p100)
- **Ferry Plaza Farmers Market** Sample fresh fruit and snacks. (p100)
- **TIX Bay Area** Half-price, same-day theater tickets. (p120)
- **Lombard Street** Not truly the world's crookedest street, but darn close. (p106)
- **Ferries** Set sail across the bay at sunset. (p124)

Places for People-Watching

- **Caffe Trieste** North Beach's most evocative cafe. (p118)
- **Crissy Field** A nonstop parade of joggers, kite flyers and dog walkers. (p106)
- **Dolores Park** The site for soccer games, political protests, competitive tanning and other favorite local sports. (p109)
- **Baker Beach** San Francisco's chilly, partly clothing-optional strand. (p107)

Kid Magnets

- **California Academy of Sciences** Attractions include a butterfly-filled Rainforest Dome, a walk-through aquarium and lots of exotic creepy crawlies. (p112)
- **Pier 39** Blubbery sea lions push, shove and bark. (p105)
- **Musée Mecanique** An antique arcade housing old-fashioned musical and mechanical curiosities. (p105)
- **Exploratorium** A hands-on science museum. (p106)

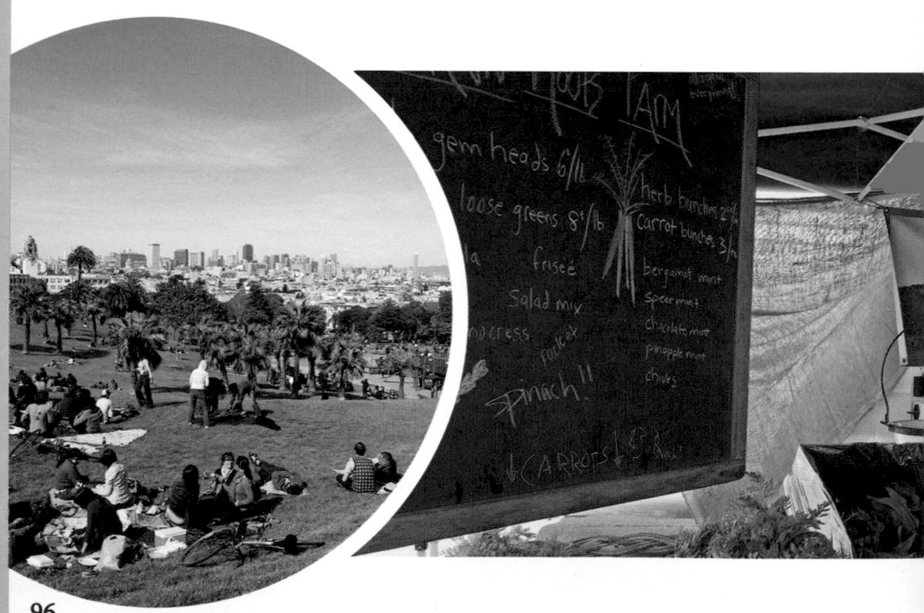

Foggy-Day Treats

- **USS Pampanito** You won't notice gray weather aboard this restored WWII submarine. (p105)
- **Castro Theatre** A chandelier-lit movie palace featuring Wurlitzer preludes. (p121)
- **Warming Hut** Curl up with a cappuccino and gaze out at the Golden Gate Bridge. (p116)
- **Precita Eyes Mural Tours** Vibrant murals are the perfect antidote to a monochrome day. (p109)

Left: Dolores Park (p109); **Above:** Ferry Plaza Farmers Market (p100)

(LEFT) THOMAS WINZ / GETTY IMAGES ©; (ABOVE) LONELY PLANET / GETTY IMAGES ©

Need to Know

ADVANCE PLANNING

- **One month before** Make dinner reservations for top restaurants.
- **Two weeks before** Buy tickets for Alcatraz, especially if you plan to visit on a weekend or in summer.

RESOURCES

- **Craig's List** (http://sfbay.craigslist.org) The Bay Area's definitive community bulletin board.
- **San Francisco Chronicle** (www.sfgate.com) Northern California's largest daily newspaper.
- **San Francisco Visitors Information Center** (http://www.sanfrancisco.travel) Lots of city maps and information.
- **511** (www.511.org) Website and phone number for public transportation and traffic information.
- **SF Eater** (http://sf.eater.com) The latest on SF food, nightlife and bars.
- **Open Table** (www.opentable.com) Make reservations at restaurants.
- **The Bold Italic** (www.thebolditalic.com) SF trends, openings and opinions.
- **UrbanDaddy** (www.urbandaddy.com) Bars, shops, restaurants and events.
- **Flavorpill** (www.flavorpill.com/sanfrancisco) Live music, lectures, art openings and movie premieres.
- **Bay Area Reporter** (www.ebar.com) Free GLBT community paper.
- **Bay Times** (www.sfbaytimes.com) Another free GLBT community paper.

GETTING AROUND

- **Bus** MUNI buses provide extensive coverage of the city, but can be slow.
- **Cable car** A perennial favorite, but limited to a few lines in the northeast part of the city.
- **Taxi** Easy to hail downtown.
- **Train** BART trains run from SFO airport to downtown with a few stops in between, and MUNI streetcars radiate south and west from there.

BE FOREWARNED

- **Weather** Pack warm clothes: it can get chilly any time of the year.

San Francisco Walking Tour

Conquer some of San Francisco's famous hills with this itinerary. Along the way, you'll pass through cinematic alleyways in Chinatown, savor the flavors of Italian North Beach, meet wild parrots and take in beautiful views.

WALK FACTS

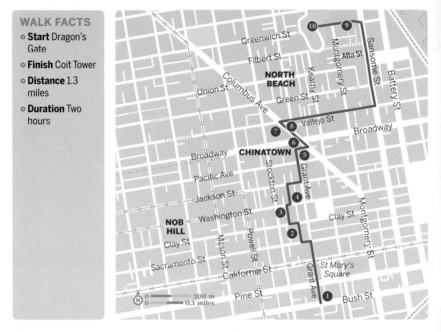

- **Start** Dragon's Gate
- **Finish** Coit Tower
- **Distance** 1.3 miles
- **Duration** Two hours

1 Dragon's Gate

Enter this ornate archway – donated by Taiwan in 1970 – and walk up Grant Ave past dragon lamps and pagoda-topped souvenir shops. The attractions here were created as a signature 'Chinatown Deco' look by forward-thinking Chinatown business leaders in the 1920s.

2 Waverly Place

This is the namesake for one of the main characters in Amy Tan's bestselling *The Joy Luck Club*. Look up from this alley street to admire prayer flags and red lanterns gracing ornamentally painted temple balconies.

3 Spofford Alley

Sun Yat-sen plotted the overthrow of China's last emperor at No 36, and the 1920s saw bootleggers' gun battles in this alley, but Spofford has mellowed with age. In the evenings you'll hear the shuffling of mah-jong tiles and *erhu* (a two-stringed Chinese fiddle) players warming up at local senior centers.

4 Ross Alley

Alternately known as Manila, Spanish and Mexico St after the working girls who once worked this block, mural-lined Ross Alley is occasionally pimped out for Hollywood productions, including *Karate Kid II* and *Indiana Jones & the Temple of Doom*.

5 Jack Kerouac Alley

Follow the aroma of tea shops and roast duck to another evocative alley, where the pavement is embedded with a Kerouac ode to San Francisco: 'The air was soft, the stars so fine, and the promise of every cobbled alley so great...'.

6 City Lights

Enter past the Dante-inspired sign warning 'Abandon All Despair, Ye Who Enter Here' to get into this literary landmark. Head upstairs to the Poetry section, open a book at random and read one poem. (If it's Allen Ginsberg's epic *Howl*, you could be here awhile.)

7 Molinari

After your food for thought, address that growling belly. Get your dream panini sandwich to go (house-cured salami highly recommended) for a picnic atop Telegraph Hill.

8 Caffe Trieste

But first, fuel up for the altitude gain with a shot of espresso at the back table where Francis Ford Coppola drafted his script for *The Godfather*. Play some opera on the jukebox and keep your eyes peeled for Poet Laureate Lawrence Ferlinghetti.

9 Greenwich Street Steps

Reach the top of Telegraph Hill on a passageway lined with cottages and terraced gardens. Choose your spot for a picnic in the company of wild parrots.

10 Coit Tower

This iconic tower was financed by the firefighter-obsessed heiress Lillie Hitchcock Coit, who rarely missed a fire or a firefighter's funeral. She even had the firehouse emblem embroidered on her bedsheets. Check out the once-controversial, newly restored murals and ascend the elevator for panoramic views of the bay.

San Francisco In...

ONE DAY

Grab a leather strap on the Powell-Hyde cable car and hold on: you're in for hills and thrills. Hop off at **Lombard St** (p106) and George Sterling Park for photo ops and views of the **Golden Gate Bridge** (p100). Next explore the waterfront: check out the vintage arcade at **Musée Mechanique** (p105) and watch sea lions at **Pier 39** (p105). End the evening with shivers on a night tour of **Alcatraz** (p101). Afterwards head to the Ferry Building and celebrate your great San Francisco escape with bubbly and oysters at **Hog Island Oyster Company** (p113) or Dungeness crab noodles at **Slanted Door** (p113).

TWO DAYS

Spend the morning on our San Francisco walking tour, then take BART to the **Mission** (p108) and view the mural-covered walls of this arty neighborhood. Break for burritos, then hoof it to the **Haight** (p105) for flashbacks at the Summer of Love site: **Golden Gate Park** (p107). Glimpse Golden Gate Bridge views atop the **MH de Young Museum** (p107), then take a walk on the wild side in the **California Academy of Sciences** (p112) rainforest dome.

'Painted ladies' houses, The Haight (p105)

Discover San Francisco

At a Glance

- **The Bay & The Embarcadero** (p100) A landmark bridge, a foodie heaven and an island prison.
- **South of Market (SoMa)** (p104) Art galleries, museums and nightclubs near downtown.
- **Fisherman's Wharf** (p105) Gawk at sea lions and play in an old-time arcade.
- **Golden Gate Park** (p107) More museums and gardens in the city's green space.

Exhibits at the Asian Art Museum
RICK GEHARTER / GETTY IMAGES ©

Sights

THE BAY & THE EMBARCADERO

Golden Gate Bridge Bridge

(Map p139; www.goldengatebridge.org/visitors; off Lincoln Blvd; northbound free, southbound toll $6, billed electronically to vehicle's license plate; for details, see www.goldengate.org/tolls; 28, all Golden Gate Transit buses) San Franciscans have passionate perspectives on every subject, especially their signature landmark, though everyone agrees that it's a good thing that the navy didn't get its way over the bridge's design – naval officials preferred a hulking concrete span, painted with caution-yellow stripes, over the soaring art deco design of architects Gertrude and Irving Murrow and engineer Joseph B Strauss, which, luckily, won the day.

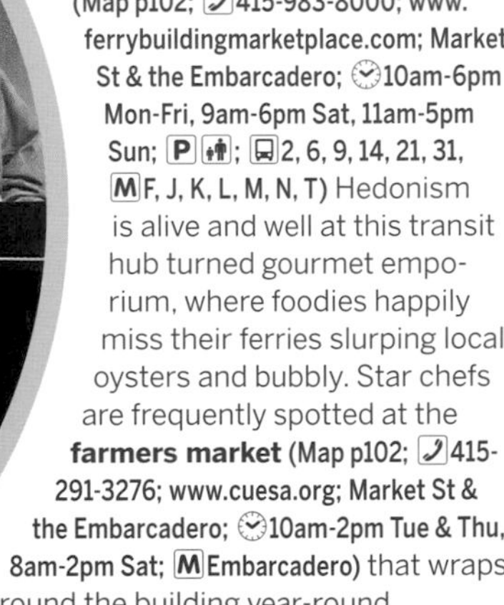

Ferry Building Landmark

(Map p102; 415-983-8000; www.ferrybuildingmarketplace.com; Market St & the Embarcadero; 10am-6pm Mon-Fri, 9am-6pm Sat, 11am-5pm Sun; P; 2, 6, 9, 14, 21, 31, M F, J, K, L, M, N, T) Hedonism is alive and well at this transit hub turned gourmet emporium, where foodies happily miss their ferries slurping local oysters and bubbly. Star chefs are frequently spotted at the **farmers market (Map p102; 415-291-3276; www.cuesa.org; Market St & the Embarcadero; 10am-2pm Tue & Thu, 8am-2pm Sat; M Embarcadero)** that wraps around the building year-round.

CIVIC CENTER

Asian Art Museum Museum

(Map p102; 415-581-3500; www.asianart.org; 200 Larkin St; adult/student/child $12/8/free, 1st Sun of month free; 10am-5pm Tue-Sun, to 9pm Thu; M Civic Center, B Civic Center) Imagi-

DAVID CLAPP / GETTY IMAGES ©

Don't Miss Alcatraz

Almost 150 years before Guantanamo came into existence, a rocky island in the middle of San Francisco Bay became the nation's first military prison: Alcatraz. Civil War deserters were kept in wooden pens along with Native American 'unfriendlies.'

In 1934 the Federal Bureau of Prisons took over Alcatraz to make a public example of bootleggers and other gangsters. 'The Rock' only averaged 264 inmates at one time, but its A-list criminals included Chicago crime boss Al 'Scarface' Capone. Though Alcatraz was considered escape-proof, in 1962 the Anglin brothers and Frank Morris floated away on a makeshift raft and were never seen again. Security and upkeep proved prohibitively expensive, and finally the island prison was abandoned to the birds in 1963.

Book tickets online at least two weeks ahead in summer. Day visits include captivating audio tours, with prisoners and guards recalling cell house life, while popular, creepy evening tours are partly guided.

NEED TO KNOW

Alcatraz Cruises 415-981-7625; www.alcatrazcruises.com; day tours adult/child/family $30/18/92, night tours adult/child $37/22; call center 8am-7pm, ferries depart Pier 33 half-hourly 9am-3:55pm, night tours 6:10pm & 6:45pm

nations race from ancient Persian miniatures to cutting-edge Japanese fashion through three floors spanning 6000 years of Asian arts. Besides the largest collection outside Asia – 18,000 works – the Asian offers excellent programs for all ages, from shadow-puppet shows and yoga for kids to mixers with cross-cultural DJ mashups.

Downtown San Francisco & SoMa

SAN FRANCISCO

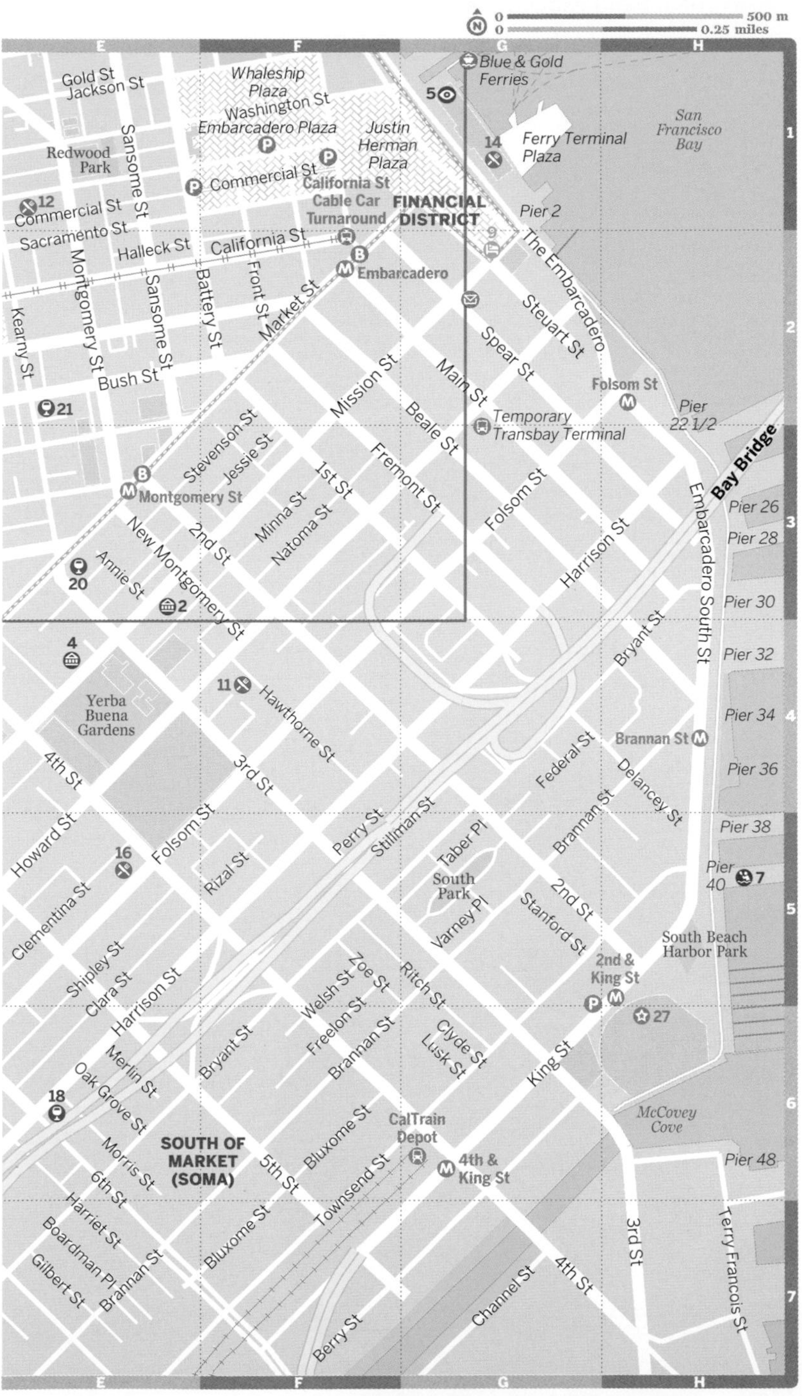
0 500 m
0 0.25 miles
Blue & Gold Ferries
Whaleship Plaza
Gold St
Jackson St
Washington St
Embarcadero Plaza
Justin Herman Plaza
Ferry Terminal Plaza
San Francisco Bay
Redwood Park
Commercial St
California St Cable Car Turnaround
FINANCIAL DISTRICT
Pier 2
Sacramento St
Halleck St
California St
Embarcadero
The Embarcadero
Steuart St
Spear St
Main St
Kearny St
Montgomery St
Sansome St
Battery St
Front St
Market St
Bush St
Mission St
Beale St
Folsom St
Pier 22 1/2
Temporary Transbay Terminal
Bay Bridge
Stevenson St
Jessie St
1st St
Fremont St
Montgomery St
Minna St
Natoma St
2nd St
New Montgomery St
Annie St
Folsom St
Harrison St
Embarcadero South St
Pier 26
Pier 28
Pier 30
Pier 32
Pier 34
Pier 36
Pier 38
Pier 40
Bryant St
Yerba Buena Gardens
Hawthorne St
Brannan St
Federal St
Delancey St
4th St
3rd St
Howard St
Folsom St
Rizal St
Perry St
Stillman St
Taber Pl
South Park
Varney Pl
Brannan St
2nd St
Stanford St
South Beach Harbor Park
Clementina St
Shipley St
Clara St
Harrison St
Welsh St
Zoe St
Freelon St
Ritch St
2nd & King St
Merlin St
Oak Grove St
Bryant St
Brannan St
Clyde St
Lusk St
King St
McCovey Cove
Morris St
SOUTH OF MARKET (SOMA)
5th St
Bluxome St
CalTrain Depot
4th & King St
Pier 48
6th St
Harriet St
Boardman Pl
Gilbert St
Brannan St
Bluxome St
Townsend St
3rd St
Terry Francois St
Channel St
4th St
Berry St
SAN FRANCISCO

Downtown San Francisco & SoMa

Sights
1 Asian Art Museum B5
2 Cartoon Art Museum E3
3 City Hall A6
4 Contemporary Jewish Museum E4
5 Ferry Building G1
6 Union Square D3

Activities, Courses & Tours
7 City Kayak H5

Sleeping
8 Hotel Rex C3
9 Hotel Vitale G2
10 Orchard Garden Hotel D2

Eating
11 Benu F4
12 City View E1
13 farm:table B3
14 Ferry Plaza Farmers Market G1
Hog Island Oyster Company .... (see 5)
Slanted Door .... (see 5)
15 Z & Y D1
16 Zero Zero E5

Drinking & Nightlife
17 Comstock Saloon D1
18 EndUp E6
19 Li Po D1
20 Local Edition E3
21 Rickhouse E2
22 Stud C7
23 Top of the Mark C2

Entertainment
24 American Conservatory Theater C3
25 Davies Symphony Hall A6
26 Great American Music Hall A4
27 San Francisco Giants H6
28 San Francisco Opera A6
29 SFJAZZ Center A6
30 TIX Bay Area D3

Shopping
31 Golden Gate Fortune Cookie Company D1
32 Macy's D3
33 Westfield San Francisco Centre D4

City Hall Historic Building
(Map p102; ☎ art exhibit line 415-554-6080, tour info 415-554-6139; www.sfgsa.org; 400 Van Ness Ave; ⏰ 8am-8pm Mon-Fri, tours 10am, noon & 2pm; 👪; M Civic Center, B Civic Center) FREE That mighty beaux arts dome pretty much covers San Francisco's grandest ambitions and fundamental flaws. Designed in 1915 to outdo Paris for flair and outsize the capitol in Washington, DC, the dome – the world's fifth largest – was unsteady until its retrofit after the 1989 earthquake, when ingenious technology enabled it to swing on its base without raising alarm.

SOUTH OF MARKET (SOMA)

Contemporary Jewish Museum Museum
(Map p102; ☎ 415-344-8800; www.thecjm.org; 736 Mission St; adult/child $12/free, after 5pm Thu $5, 1st Tue of month free; ⏰ 11am-5pm Mon, Tue & Fri-Sun, to 8pm Thu; M Montgomery, B Montgomery) That up-ended brushed-steel box

Pier 39
DAVID CLAPP / GETTY IMAGES ©

balancing improbably on one corner isn't a sculpture, but a gallery for the Contemporary Jewish Museum, a major new SF landmark derived from a former power substation. Exhibits are thoughtfully curated, heavy-hitting and compelling, investigating ideas and ideals through the lens of artists and social figures as diverse as Andy Warhol, Gertrude Stein and Harry Houdini.

Cartoon Art Museum Museum

(Map p102; ☎415-227-8666; www.cartoonart.org; 655 Mission St; adult/student $8/6, 1st Tue of month free; ⏰11am-5pm Tue-Sun; 👪; 🚌14, 15, 30, 45, Ⓜ Montgomery, Ⓑ Montgomery) Founded on a grant from Bay Area cartoon legend Charles M Schultz of *Peanuts* fame, this bold museum isn't afraid of the dark, racy or political, including R Crumb drawings from the '70s and a retrospective of political cartoons from the *Economist* by Kevin 'Kal' Kallaugher. Lectures and openings are rare opportunities to mingle with comic legends, Pixar studio heads, and obsessive collectors.

FISHERMAN'S WHARF

Pier 39 Pier

(Map p106; www.pier39.com; Beach St & the Embarcadero; Ⓟ 👪; 🚌47, 🚋Powell-Mason, Ⓜ F) The focal point of Fisherman's Wharf isn't the waning fishing fleet, but the carousel, carnival-like attractions, shops and restaurants of Pier 39 – and, of course, the famous sea lions. Developed in the 1970s to revitalize tourism, the pier draws thousands of tourists daily, but it's really just a big outdoor shopping mall. On the plus side, its visitors center rents strollers, stores luggage, and has free phone-charging stations.

Musée Mécanique Amusement Park

(Map p106; ☎415-346-2000; www.museemechanique.org; Pier 45, Shed A; ⏰10am-7pm Mon-Fri, to 8pm Sat & Sun; 👪; 🚌47, 🚋Powell-Mason, Powell-Hyde, Ⓜ F) Where else can you guillotine a man for a quarter? Creepy 19th-century arcade games such as the macabre French Execution compete for your spare change with the diabolical Ms Pac-Man.

If You Like... San Francisco's Neighborhoods

If you like touring the city's eclectic enclaves, we think you'll like exploring these historic and happening areas.

1 NORTH BEACH
Boutiques outnumber bohemians in the neighborhood where the Beat poets once howled, and tough stairway climbs lead to giddy vistas with wild parrots squawking overhead.

2 CHINATOWN
Stroll beneath the pagoda-style roofs and dragon lanterns of the shopping streets, and listen for the clack of mah jong tiles in quiet alleyways.

3 THE CASTRO
The heart of San Francisco's queer community, where you'll find scores of restaurants and bars and one of the city's most ornate arthouse cinemas.

4 THE MISSION
Visit the oldest building in the city, tour colorful alley murals, devour a chunky burrito, and then kick back with the hipsters at a buzzing outdoor bar.

5 THE HAIGHT
The legendary intersection of Haight and Ashbury Sts was the place to be in the psychedelic '60s; now vintage boutiques comingle with head shops at this gateway to Golden Gate Park.

USS Pampanito Historic Site

(Map p106; ☎415-775-1943; www.maritime.org/pamphome.htm; Pier 45; adult/child $12/6; ⏰9am-8pm Thu-Tue, to 6pm Wed; 👪; 🚌19, 30, 47, 🚋Powell-Hyde, Ⓜ F) Explore a restored WWII submarine that survived six tours of duty, while listening to sub-mariners' tales of stealth mode and sudden attacks in a riveting audio tour ($2) that makes surfacing afterwards a relief (caution claustrophobes).

Fisherman's Wharf, The Marina & Russian Hill

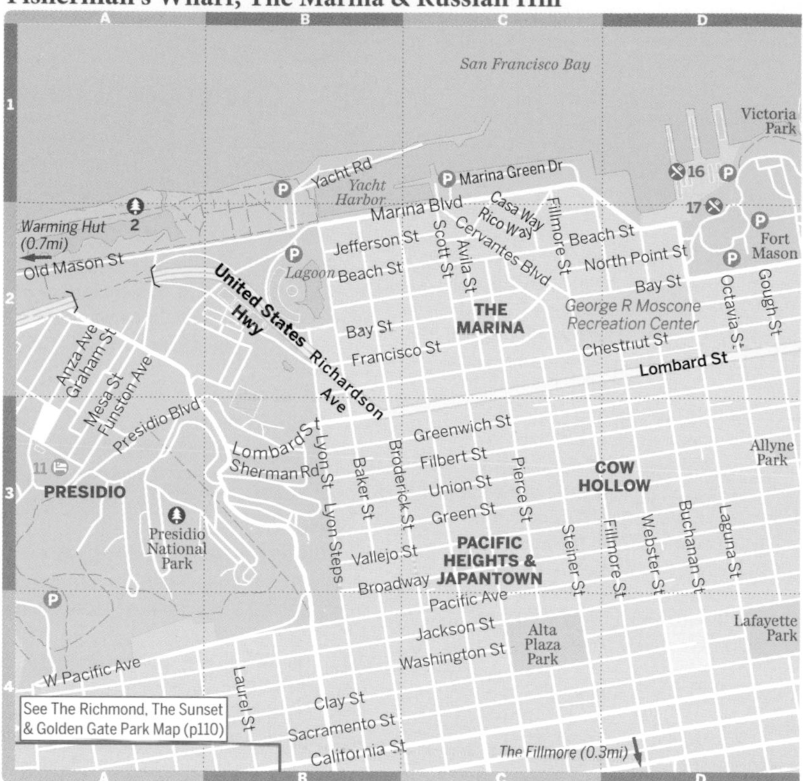

THE MARINA & RUSSIAN HILL

Exploratorium Museum

(Map p106; ☎415-528-4444; www.exploratorium.edu; Pier 15; adult/child $25/19, Thu evening $15; ⏲10am-5pm Tue-Sun, over 18yr only Thu 6-10pm; P 👪; M F) Is there a science to skateboarding? Do toilets really flush counterclockwise in Australia? Find answers to questions you wished you'd learned in school, at San Francisco's thrilling hands-on science museum. Combining science with art, and investigating human perception, the Exploratorium nudges you to question how you perceive the world around you. As thrilling as the exhibits is the setting: a nine-acre, glass-walled pier jutting straight into San Francisco Bay, with large outdoor portions you can explore free of charge, twenty-four hours a day.

Lombard Street Street

(Map p106; 900 block of Lombard St; Powell-Hyde) You've seen its eight switchbacks in a thousand photographs. The tourist board has dubbed this 'the world's crookedest street, ' which is factually incorrect. Vermont St in Potrero Hill deserves that award, but Lombard is much more scenic, with its red-brick pavement and lovingly tended flowerbeds. It wasn't always so bent; before the arrival of the automobile it lunged straight down the hill.

THE PRESIDIO

Crissy Field Park

(Map p106; www.crissyfield.org; 1199 East Beach; P; 30, PresidioGo Shuttle) The Presidio's army airstrip has been stripped of asphalt and reinvented as a haven for coastal

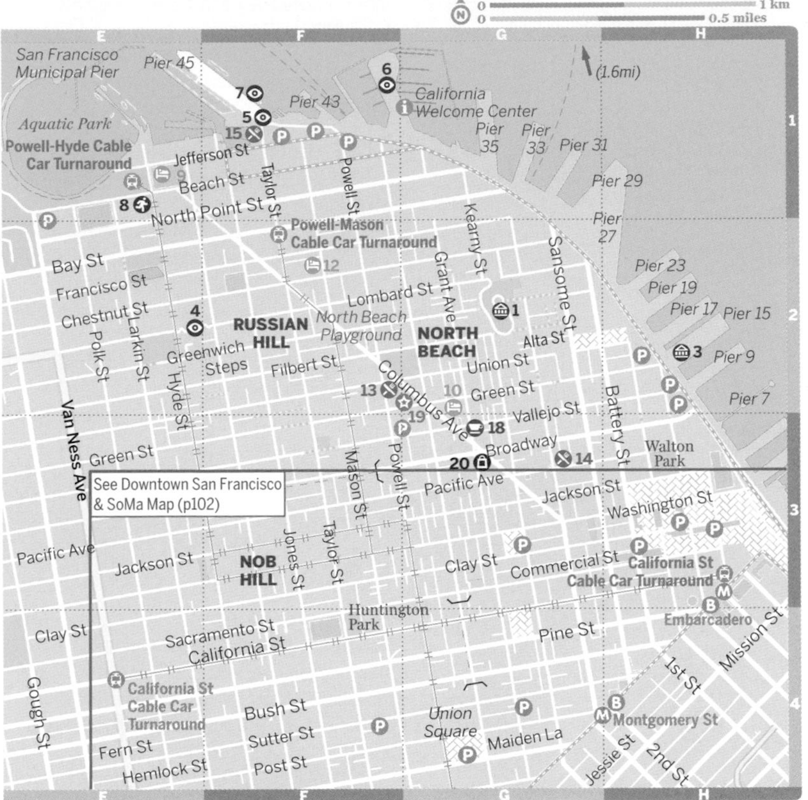

birds, kite-fliers and windsurfers enjoying sweeping views of Golden Gate Bridge.

Fort Point Historic Site
(Map p139; ☎415-556-1693; www.nps.gov/fopo; Marine Dr; ⏰10am-5pm Fri-Sun; P; 🚌28)
FREE Despite its impressive guns, this Civil War fort saw no action – at least until Alfred Hitchcock shot scenes from *Vertigo* here, with stunning views of the Golden Gate Bridge from below.

Baker Beach Beach
(⏰sunrise-sunset; P; 🚌29, PresidiGo Shuttle)
Unswimmable waters (except when the tide's coming in) but unbeatable views of the Golden Gate make this former Army beachhead SF's tanning location of choice, especially the clothing-optional north end – at least until the afternoon fog rolls in.

GOLDEN GATE PARK & AROUND

MH de Young Museum Museum
(Map p110; ☎415-750-3600; http://deyoung.famsf.org/; 50 Hagiwara Tea Garden Dr; adult/child $10/6, discount with Muni ticket $2, 1st Tue of month free, online booking fee $1 per ticket; ⏰9:30am-5:15pm Tue-Sun, to 8:45pm Fri Apr–Nov; 🚌5, 44, 71, MN) Follow sculptor Andy Goldsworthy's artificial fault line in the sidewalk into Herzog & de Meuron's sleek, copper-clad building that's oxidizing green to blend into the park. Don't be fooled by the de Young's camouflaged exterior: shows here boldly broaden artistic horizons from Oceanic ceremonial masks and Balenciaga gowns to sculptor Al Farrow's cathedrals built from bullets.

Fisherman's Wharf, The Marina & Russian Hill

Sights
1 Coit Tower G2
2 Crissy Field A2
3 Exploratorium H2
4 Lombard Street E2
5 Musée Mécanique F1
6 Pier 39 .... F1
7 USS Pampanito F1

Activities, Courses & Tours
8 Blazing Saddles E1

Sleeping
9 Argonaut Hotel E1
10 Hotel Bohème G2
11 Inn at the Presidio A3
12 San Remo Hotel F2

Eating
13 Cinecittà F2
14 Cotogna G3
15 Fisherman's Wharf Crab Stands F1
16 Greens D1
17 Off the Grid D2

Drinking & Nightlife
18 Caffe Trieste G3

Entertainment
19 Beach Blanket Babylon G2

Shopping
20 City Lights G3

Japanese Tea Garden Gardens

(Map p110; ☎tea ceremony reservations 415-752-1171; www.japaneseteagardensf.com; 75 Hagiwara Tea Garden Dr; adult/child $7/2, before 10am Mon, Wed & Fri free; ⏰9am-6pm Mar-Oct, to 4:45pm Nov-Feb; P 👪; 🚌5, 44, 71, M N) Since 1894, this picturesque 5-acre garden and bonsai grove has blushed with cherry blossoms in spring, turned flaming red with maple leaves in fall, and lost all track of time in the meditative Zen Garden.

THE MISSION & THE CASTRO

Mission Dolores Church

(Misión San Francisco de Asís; ☎415-621-8203; www.missiondolores.org; 3321 16th St; adult/child $5/3; ⏰9am-4pm Nov-Apr, to 4:30pm May-Oct; 🚌22, 33, B 16th St Mission, M J) The city's oldest building and its namesake, whitewashed adobe Misión San Francisco de Asís was founded in 1776 and rebuilt in 1782 with conscripted Ohlone and Miwok labor – note the ceiling patterned after native baskets. Recent restorations revealed a hidden mural behind the altar painted by Ohlone artisans: a sacred heart, pierced by a sword and dripping with blood.

GLBT History Museum Museum

(☎415-621-1107; www.glbthistory.org/museum; 4127 18th St; admission $5, 1st Wed of month free; ⏰11am-7pm Mon, Wed-Sat, noon-5pm Sun; M Castro) America's first gay-history museum cobbles ephemera from the community – Harvey Milk's campaign literature, matchbooks from long-gone bathhouses, the dress Laura Linney wore as Mary Anne Singleton in the TV adaptation of *Tales of the City* – together with harder-hitting installations, such as audiovisual interviews with Gore Vidal and pages of the 1950s penal code banning homosexuality.

Activities

Blazing Saddles Cycling

(Map p106; ☎415-202-8888; www.blazingsaddles.com/san-francisco; 2715 Hyde St; cycle hire per hour $8-15, per day $32-88; electric bikes per day $48-88; ⏰8am-7:30pm; 👪; 🚋Powell-Hyde) Blazing Saddles is tailored to visitors, with a main shop on Hyde St and seven rental stands around Fisherman's Wharf, convenient for biking the Embarcadero or to the Golden Gate Bridge. It also rents electric bikes and offers 24-hour return service – a big plus. Reserve online for a 10% discount; rental includes all extras (bungee cords, packs etc).

City Kayak Kayaking

(Map p102; ☎415-294-1050; www.citykayak.com; Pier 40, South Beach Harbor; kayak rentals per hr $35-65, 3hr lesson & rental $59, tours $58-98; M Brannan) You haven't seen San Francisco until you've seen it from the water. Newbies to kayaking can take lessons and venture into calm waters near the Bay Bridge, alone or escorted; experienced paddlers can brave choppy currents beneath the Golden Gate (conditions permitting; get advice first). We especially love the romantic, calm-water moonlight tours. Check website for details.

Tours

Precita Eyes Mission Mural Tours Tour
(415-285-2287; www.precitaeyes.org; adult $15-20, child $3; see website calendar for tour dates;) Muralists lead two-hour tours on foot or bike covering 60 to 70 murals in a six- to 10-block radius of mural-bedecked Balmy Alley; proceeds fund mural upkeep at this community arts nonprofit.

Chinatown Alleyway Tours Tour
(415-984-1478; www.chinatownalleywaytours.org; adult/student $18/12; 11am Sat; ; 8X, 8AX, 8BX) Neighborhood teens lead two-hour community nonprofit tours for up-close-and-personal peeks into Chinatown's past (weather permitting). Book five days ahead or pay double for Saturday walk-ins; cash only.

Festivals & Events

Lunar New Year Cultural
(www.chineseparade.com) Firecrackers, legions of tiny-tot martial artists and a 200ft-long dancing dragon make this parade at the end of February the highlight of San Francisco winters.

Bay to Breakers Sport
(www.baytobreakers.com; race registration $58-89.50; May) Run costumed or naked from Embarcadero to Ocean Beach the third Sunday in May, while joggers dressed as salmon run upstream.

SF Pride Celebration Cultural
(Jun) A day isn't enough to do SF proud: June begins with **International LGBT Film Festival** (www.frameline.org; mid-Jun), and goes out in style the last weekend with Pink Saturday's **Dyke March** (www.dykemarch.org) and the frisky, million-strong **Pride Parade** (www.sfpride.org).

Hardly Strictly Bluegrass Music
(www.strictlybluegrass.com; Oct) San Fran celebrates Western roots with three days of free Golden Gate Park concerts and headliners ranging from Elvis Costello to Gillian Welch in early October.

If You Like... Views

If you're wowed by the bay views from Lombard St, spend a fog-free day scaling some of the city's best vantage points.

1 **COIT TOWER**
(Map p106; 415-362-0808; www.sfrecpark.org; Telegraph Hill Blvd; elevator entry (nonresident) adult/child $7/5; 10am-5:30pm Mar-Sep, 9am-4:30pm Oct-Feb; 39) Up the Filbert St steps at Coit Tower, you'll find 360-degree views of downtown and wrap-around 1930s murals glorifying SF workers – once denounced as Communist, but now a landmark.

2 **TOP OF THE MARK**
(Map p102; www.topofthemark.com; 999 California St; cover $10-15; 5pm-11:30pm Sun-Thu, 4.30pm-12:30am Fri & Sat; 1, California St) So what if it's touristy? Nothing beats twirling in the clouds in your best cocktail dress to a full jazz orchestra on the city's highest dance floor. Call ahead to ensure a band is playing the night you're coming. Expect $15 drinks.

3 **DOLORES PARK**
(www.doloresparkworks.org; Dolores St, btwn 18th & 20th Sts; ; 14, 33, 49, B 16th St Mission, M J) Semiprofessional tanning, taco picnics and a Hunky Jesus Contest every Easter: welcome to San Francisco's sunny side. Dolores Park has something for everyone, from street ball and tennis to the Mayan pyramid playground (sorry kids: no human sacrifice allowed). Political protests and other favorite local sports happen year-round and there are free movie nights and Mime Troupe performances in summer.

Sleeping

UNION SQUARE

Orchard Garden Hotel Boutique Hotel **$$$**
(Map p102; 415-399-9807, 888-717-2881; www.theorchardgardenhotel.com; 466 Bush St; r $295-370; ; 2, 3, 30, 45, B Montgomery) San Francisco's first

The Richmond, The Sunset & Golden Gate Park

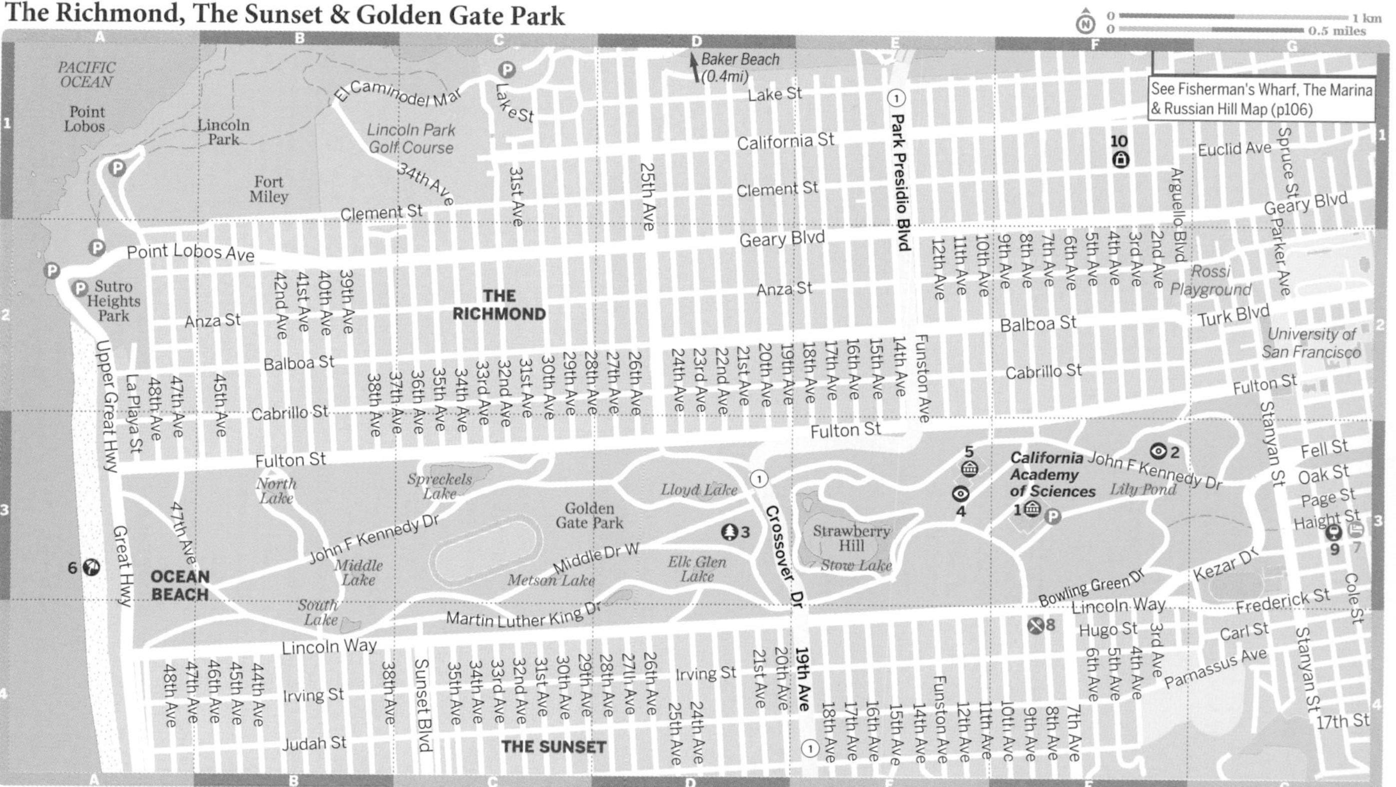

The Richmond, The Sunset & Golden Gate Park

all-green-practices hotel uses sustainably grown wood, chemical-free cleaning products and recycled fabrics in its soothingly quiet rooms. Don't think you'll be trading comfort for conscience: rooms have unexpectedly luxe touches such as high-end down pillows and Egyptian-cotton sheets. Don't miss the sunny rooftop terrace – a lovely spot at day's end.

Hotel Rex Boutique Hotel **$$$**
(Map p102; 415-433-4434, 800-433-4434; www.thehotelrex.com; 562 Sutter St; r $287-309; ; Powell-Hyde, Powell-Mason, M Powell, B Powell) French gramophone music fills the intimate lobby and lounge, conjuring New York's Algonquin in the 1920s. Rooms likewise feel inviting (despite compact size) with their traditional masculine aesthetic, hand-painted lampshades and local art. Beds are particularly great, with crisp linens and down pillows. Caveats: rear-facing rooms lack sunlight but are quiet; street-facing rooms are bright, but noisy. Request air-con.

SOUTH OF MARKET (SOMA)

Hotel Vitale Boutique Hotel **$$$**
(Map p102; 415-278-3700, 888-890-8688; www.hotelvitale.com; 8 Mission St; r $419-509; ; M Embarcadero, B Embarcadero) The ugly exterior disguises a fashion-forward shagadelic hotel, with echoes of mid-century-modern design, enhanced by up-to-the-minute luxuries. Beds are dressed with silky-soft, 450-thread-count sheets. There is an excellent on-site spa with two rooftop hot tubs. Best rooms face the bay and have spectacular bridge views.

NORTH BEACH

San Remo Hotel Hotel **$$**
(Map p106; 415-776-8688, 800-352-7366; www.sanremohotel.com; 2237 Mason St; r with shared bath $99-139; ; 30, 47, Powell-Mason) One of the city's best-value stays, the San Remo dates to 1906 and is long on old-fashioned charm. Rooms are simply done with mismatched turn-of-the-century furnishings and all rooms share baths. Think reputable, vintage boarding house. Note: least-expensive rooms have windows onto the corridor, not the outdoors. Family suites accommodate up to five. No elevator.

Hotel Bohème Boutique Hotel **$$$**
(Map p106; 415-433-9111; www.hotelboheme.com; 444 Columbus Ave; r $214-275; ; 10, 12, 30, 41, 45) Our favorite boutique hotel is a love letter to the Beat era, with moody orange, black and sage-green color schemes nodding to the 1950s, inverted Chinese umbrellas hanging from the ceiling and photos from the Beat years on the walls. Rooms are smallish, some front on noisy Columbus Ave (quieter rooms are in back) and baths are teensy, but it's smack in the middle of North Beach's vibrant street scene. No elevator.

FISHERMAN'S WHARF

Argonaut Hotel Boutique Hotel **$$$**
(Map p106; 415-563-0800, 800-790-1415; www.argonauthotel.com; 495 Jefferson St; r $389-449, with view $489-529; ; 19, 47, 49, Powell-Hyde) Fisherman's Wharf's top hotel was built as a cannery in 1908 and has century-old wooden beams and exposed brick walls. Rooms sport an over-the-top nautical theme, with porthole-shaped mirrors and plush, deep-blue carpets. Though all have the amenities of an upper-end hotel – ultra-comfy beds, iPod docks – some rooms are tiny with limited sunlight.

LONELY PLANET / GETTY IMAGES ©

Don't Miss California Academy of Sciences

Architect Renzo Piano's landmark LEED-certified green building houses 38,000 weird and wonderful animals in a four-story rainforest and split-level aquarium, all under a 'living roof' of California wildflowers. After dark, the wild rumpus starts at kids-only Academy Sleepovers, and over-21 NightLife Thursdays, when rainforest-themed cocktails encourage strange mating rituals among shy internet daters.

NEED TO KNOW

Map p110; ☎415-379-8000; www.calacademy.org; 55 Music Concourse Dr; adult/child $34.95/24.95, discount with Muni ticket $3; ⏲9:30am-5pm Mon-Sat, 11am-5pm Sun; P 👪; 🚌5, 6, 31, 33, 44, 71, M N

THE PRESIDIO

Inn at the Presidio Hotel **$$$**

(Map p106; ☎415-800-7356; www.innatthepresidio.com; 42 Moraga Ave; r incl breakfast $195-300; P @ 📶 🐾; 🚌43; PresidiGo Shuttle) 🍃 Built in 1903 as bachelor quarters for army officers, this three-story red-brick building in the Presidio was transformed in 2012 into a spiffy national-park lodge, styled with leather, linen and wood. Oversized rooms are plush, including feather beds with Egyptian-cotton sheets. Suites have fireplaces. Nature surrounds you, with hiking trailheads out back, but taxis downtown cost $25.

THE MISSION

Inn San Francisco B&B **$$**

(☎800-359-0913, 415-641-0188; www.innsf.com; 943 S Van Ness Ave; r incl breakfast $185-310, with shared bath $135-200; P @ 📶; 🚌14, 49) 🍃 The stately Inn San Francisco occupies an elegant 1872 Italianate-Victorian mansion, impeccably maintained and packed with period antiques. All rooms have fresh-cut flowers and sumptuous beds with fluffy featherbeds; some have Jacuzzi tubs. There's also a freestanding garden cottage that sleeps up to six. Outside there's an English garden and redwood hot tub open 24 hours (a rarity). Limited parking: reserve ahead. No elevator.

THE HAIGHT

Red Victorian Bed, Breakfast & Art B&B **$$**
(Map p110; 415-864-1978; www.redvic.net; 1665 Haight St; r incl breakfast $179-189, without bath $119-149; ; 33, 43, 71) The year 1967 lives on at the tripped-out Red Vic. Each individually decorated room in the 1904 landmark building pays tribute to peace, ecology and global friendship, with themes like Sunshine, Flower Children and, of course, the Summer of Love. Only four of 18 rooms have baths; all include breakfast in the organic **Peace Café**. Reduced rates for longer stays. No elevator.

Eating

THE EMBARCADERO

Hog Island Oyster Company Seafood **$$**
(Map p102; 415-391-7117; www.hogislandoysters.com; 1 Ferry Bldg; 4 oysters $13; 11:30am-9pm Mon-Thu, to 10pm Fri, 11am-10pm Sat, to 9pm Sun; M Embarcadero, B Embarcadero) Slurp the bounty of the North Bay, with a view of the East Bay, at this Ferry Building favorite for sustainably farmed oysters. Take yours au naturel, with caper *beurre blanc*, spiked with bacon and paprika or perhaps classic-style, with lemon and shallots. Mondays and Thursdays between 5pm and 7pm are happy hours indeed for shellfish fans, with half-price oysters and $4 pints.

Slanted Door Vietnamese **$$$**
(Map p102; 415-861-8032; www.slanteddoor.com; 1 Ferry Bldg; mains lunch $16-36, dinner

Ocean Beach

Golden Gate Park ends at the blustery **Ocean Beach (Map p110; 415-561-4323; www.parksconservancy.org; Great Hwy; sunrise-sunset; 5, 18, 31, M N)**, too chilly for bikini-clad clambakes but ideal for wet-suited pro surfers braving riptides (casual swimmers beware). Bonfires are permitted in designated fire-pits only; no alcohol allowed.

Ocean Beach

$18-45; ⌚11am-4:30pm & 5:30-10pm Mon-Sat, 11:30am-4:30pm & 5:30-10pm Sun; M Embarcadero, B Embarcadero) San Francisco's most effortlessly elegant restaurant harmonizes California ingredients, continental influences and Vietnamese flair. Owner-chef Charles Phan enhances top-notch ingredients with bright flavors, heaping local Dungeness crab atop cellophane noodles, and garlicky Meyer Ranch 'shaking beef' on watercress. And oh, the views. Book two weeks ahead for lunch, a month for dinner – or call at 5:30pm for last-minute cancellations.

UNION SQUARE

farm:table American **$**

(Map p102; ☎415-292-7089; www.farmtablesf.com; 754 Post St; dishes $6-9; ⌚7:30am-2pm Tue-Fri, 8am-3pm Sat & Sun; 🚌2, 3, 27, 38) A tiny storefront with one wooden communal table inside, two tables and a stand-up counter outside, farm:table uses seasonal, regional organics in its foodie-smart breakfasts and lunches, posting the daily-changing menu on Twitter (@farmtable). Good place to chill with locals. Great coffee. Cash only.

SOUTH OF MARKET (SOMA)

Zero Zero Pizza **$$**

(Map p102; ☎415-348-8800; www.zerozerosf.com; 826 Folsom St; pizzas $12-19; ⌚11:30am-2:30pm & 4-10pm Mon-Thu, to 11pm Fri, 11:30am-11pm Sat, to 10pm Sun; M Powell, B Powell) The name is a throw-down of Neapolitan pizza credentials – '00' flour is used exclusively for Naples' famous puffy-edged crust – and these pies deliver on that promise, with inspired SF-themes toppings. The Geary is an exciting offering involving Manila clams, bacon and chilies, but the real crowd-pleaser is the Castro, which, as you might guess, is turbo-loaded with housemade sausage.

Benu Californian, Fusion **$$$**

(Map p102; ☎415-685-4860; www.benusf.com; 22 Hawthorne St; tasting menu $195; ⌚5:30-8:30pm seatings Tue-Sat; 🚌10, 12, 14, 30, 45) SF has refined fusion cuisine over 150 years, but no one rocks it quite like chef/

Left: Fisherman's Wharf Crab Stands (p116); **Below:** Warming Hut (p116)
(LEFT) NEIL FARRIN / GETTY IMAGES ©; (BELOW) ROBERTO SONCIN GEROMETTA/ GETTY IMAGES ©

owner Corey Lee (formerly of Napa's French Laundry), who remixes local, sustainable fine-dining staples and Pacific Rim flavors with a SoMa DJ's finesse. This is contemporary California dining at its highest echelon. Its only flaw is the pretentiously casual room, which doesn't match the stupendously regal cooking.

CHINATOWN

City View — Chinese $

(Map p106; 415-398-2838; 662 Commercial St; dishes $3-8; 11am-2:30pm Mon-Fri, from 10am Sat & Sun; 8X, 10, 12, 30, 45, California St) Take your seat in the sunny dining room and your pick from carts loaded with delicate shrimp and leek dumplings, garlicky Chinese broccoli, tangy spare ribs, coconut-dusted custard tarts and other tantalizing dim sum. Arrive before or after the midday lunch rush, so you don't have to flag down speeding carts to peek inside those fragrant bamboo steamers.

Z & Y — Chinese $$

(Map p106; 415-981-8988; www.zandyrestaurant.com; 655 Jackson St; mains $9-20; 11am-9:30pm Mon-Thu, to 10:30pm Fri-Sun; 8X, Powell-Mason, Powell-Hyde) Graduate from ho-hum sweet-and-sour and middling mu shu to sensational Szechuan dishes that go down in a blaze of glory. Warm up with spicy pork dumplings and heat-blistered string beans, take on the house-made tantan noodles with peanut-chili sauce, and leave lips buzzing with fish poached in flaming chili oil and buried under red Szechuan chili-peppers. Go early; expect a wait.

NORTH BEACH

Cinecittà — Pizza $$

(Map p106; 415-291-8830; www.cinecittarestaurant.com; 663 Union St; pizza $12-15; noon-10pm Sun-Thu, to 11pm Fri & Sat; ; 8X, 30, 39, 41, 45, Powell-Mason) Follow tantalizing aromas into this 22-seat

Off the Grid

Some 30 **food trucks** (Map p106; www.offthegridsf.com; 2 Marina Blvd; dishes $5-10; 5-11pm Fri; ; 22, 28) circle their wagons at SF's largest mobile-gourmet hootenanny (other nights/locations attract less than a dozen trucks; see website). Arrive before 6:30pm or expect a 20-minute wait for Chairman Bao's clamshell buns stuffed with duck and mango, Roli Roti's free-range herbed roast chicken, or dessert from the Crème Brûlée Man. Cash only; take dinner to nearby docks for Golden Gate Bridge sunsets.

eatery for thin-crust Roman pizza, made from scratch and served with sass by Roman owner Romina. Local loyalties are divided between the Roman Travestere (fresh mozzarella, arugula and prosciutto) and Neapolitan O Sole Mio (capers, olives, mozzarella and anchovies). Local brews are on tap, house wine is $5 from 3pm to 7pm and Romina's tiramisu is San Francisco's best.

Cotogna Italian **$$**
(Map p106; 415-775-8508; www.cotognasf.com; 490 Pacific Ave; mains $17-29; 11:30am-11pm Mon-Thu, to midnight Fri & Sat, 5-9:30pm Sun; ; 10, 12) Chef-owner Michael Tusk won the 2011 James Beard Award for best chef. Ever since, it's been hard to book a table at Cotogna (and its fancier big sister Quince next door), but it's worth planning ahead to be rewarded with authentic, wood-fired rustica Italian cooking that magically balances a few pristine flavors in pastas, tender-to-the-tooth pizzas and rotisserie meats.

FISHERMAN'S WHARF

Fisherman's Wharf Crab Stands Seafood **$**
(Map p106; Taylor St; mains $5-15; MF) Brawny-armed men stir steaming cauldrons of Dungeness crab at several side-by-side take-away crab stands at the foot of Taylor St, the epicenter of Fisherman's Wharf. Crab season typically runs winter through spring, but you'll find shrimp and other seafood year-round.

THE MARINA

Warming Hut Cafe, Sandwiches **$**
(415-561-3040; 983 Marine Dr, Presidio; dishes $4-6; 9am-5pm; P; PresidiGo Shuttle) Wetsuited windsurfers and Crissy Field kite-fliers recharge with fair-trade coffee, organic pastries and organic hot dogs at the Warming Hut while browsing field guides and sampling honey from Presidio honeybees. Ingeniously insulated with recycled denim, this eco-shack below the Golden Gate Bridge evolved from a heartwarming concept: all purchases fund Crissy Field's ongoing conversion from US army airstrip to wildlife preserve.

Greens Vegetarian, Californian **$$**
(Map p106; 415-771-6222; www.greensrestaurant.com; Bldg A, Fort Mason Center, cnr Marina Blvd & Laguna St; lunch $15-18, dinner $18-25; 11:45am-2:30pm & 5:30-9pm Tue-Fri, from 11am Sat, 10:30am-2pm & 5:30-9pm Sun, 5:30-9pm Mon; ; 28) Career carnivores won't realize there's zero meat in the hearty black-bean chili with crème fraîche and pickled jalapeños, or in that roasted eggplant *panino* (sandwich) packed with hearty flavor from ingredients mostly grown on a Zen farm in Marin. On sunny days, get yours to go and enjoy it on a wharf-side bench, but if you're planning on proper weekend dinner or Sunday brunch, make reservations.

GOLDEN GATE PARK

Nopalito Mexican **$$**
(Map p110; 415-233-9966; www.nopalitosf.com; 1224 9th Ave; 11:30am-10pm; ; 6, 43, 44, 71, MN) Head south of Golden Gate Park's border for upscale, sustainably sourced Cal-Mex, including tasty *tortas* (sandwiches on round Mexican flatbread), tender *carnitas* (slow-braised pork) tacos and cinnamon-laced Mexican hot chocolate. Reservations aren't accepted, but on sunny weekends when

every Park dawdler craves margaritas and tangy fish ceviche, call one to two hours ahead to join the wait list.

THE MISSION

Bi-Rite Creamery Ice Cream **$**
(**☎415-626-5600; www.biritecreamery.com; 3692 18th St; ice cream $3-7; ⏰11am-10pm Sun-Thu, to 11pm Fri & Sat; 👪; 🚌33, Ⓑ16th St Mission, ⓂJ**) 🍃 Velvet ropes at clubs seem pretentious in laid-back San Francisco, but at organic Bi-Rite Creamery they make perfect sense: once temperatures pass 70 degrees, the line wraps around the corner for organic salted caramel ice cream with housemade hot fudge, or Sonoma honey-lavender ice cream packed into organic waffle cones. For a quicker fix, get balsamic strawberry soft-serve at the window (1pm to 9pm).

La Taqueria Mexican **$**
(**☎415-285-7117; 2889 Mission St; burritos $6-8; ⏰11am-9pm Mon-Sat, to 8pm Sun; 👪; 🚌12, 14, 48, 49, Ⓑ24th St Mission**) The definitive burrito at La Taqueria has no debatable saffron rice, spinach tortilla or mango salsa – just perfectly grilled meats, slow-cooked beans and classic tomatillo or mesquite salsa wrapped in a flour tortilla. If you skip the beans, you'll pay extra, because they pack in more meat – but spicy pickles and *crema* (Mexican sour cream) bring complete burrito bliss.

THE HAIGHT

Second Act Food Artisans **$**
(**www.secondactsf.com; 1727 Haight St; dishes $5-12; ⏰8am-6pm, to 8pm Fri**) When the collectively-run Red Vic movie house ended its 30-year run, neighbors demanded an encore – so now Second Act Marketplace houses local food makers and a neighborhood events space. Stop by for dumplings at **Anda Piroshki**, **High Cotton Kitchen** soul food, and **Eatwell Farm** cherry-lavender ice cream – and stick around for Friday happy hours and indie-movie premieres (see website).

Drinking & Nightlife

SOUTH OF MARKET (SOMA)

Local Edition Bar
(**☎415-795-1375; www.localeditionsf.com; 691 Market St; ⏰5pm-2am Mon-Fri, from 7pm Sat**) Get the scoop on the SF cocktail scene at this new speakeasy in the basement of

Chef preparing tacos at La Taqueria

the historic Hearst newspaper building. Lighting is so dim you might bump into typewriters, but all is forgiven when you get the Pulitzer – a scotch-sherry cocktail that goes straight to your head.

DNA Lounge Club

(www.dnalounge.com; 375 11th St; admission $3-25; ⏲9pm-3am Fri & Sat, other nights vary; 🚌12, 27, 47) One of SF's last mega clubs hosts live bands and big-name DJs, with two floors of late-night dance action just seedy enough to be interesting. Saturdays bring Bootie, the kick-ass original mash-up party (now franchised worldwide) and sometimes epic drag at Trannyshack; Monday's 18-and-over Goth dance party is (naturally) called Death Guild. Check the online calendar. Early arrivals may hear crickets.

UNION SQUARE

Rickhouse Bar

(Map p102; ☎415-398-2827; www.rickhousebar.com; 246 Kearny St; ⏲5pm-2am Mon, 3pm-2am Tue-Fri, 6pm-2am Sat; Ⓜ Montgomery, Ⓑ Montgomery) Like a shotgun shack plunked downtown, Rickhouse is lined floor-to-ceiling with repurposed whisky casks imported from Kentucky and backbar shelving from an Ozark Mountains nunnery that once secretly brewed hooch. The emphasis is (naturally) on whiskey, specifically hard-to-find bourbons. Come with a posse and order Pisco Punch, served vintage-style in a garage-sale punch bowl, with cups dangling off the side.

CHINATOWN

Li Po Bar

(Map p106; ☎415-982-0072; www.lipolounge.com; 916 Grant Ave; ⏲2pm-2am; 🚌8X, 30, 45, 🚋Powell-Mason, Powell-Hyde) Beat a hasty retreat to red vinyl booths where Allen Ginsberg and Jack Kerouac debated the meaning of life alongside a bemused golden Buddha. Enter the vintage 1937 faux-grotto doorway and dodge red lanterns to place your order: Tsing Tao beer or sweet, sneaky-strong Chinese mai tai made with *baiju* (rice liquor). Bathrooms and random DJ appearances are in the basement.

NORTH BEACH

Caffe Trieste Cafe

(Map p106; ☎415-392-6739; www.caffetrieste.com; 601 Vallejo St; ⏲6:30am-11pm Sun-

Caffe Trieste

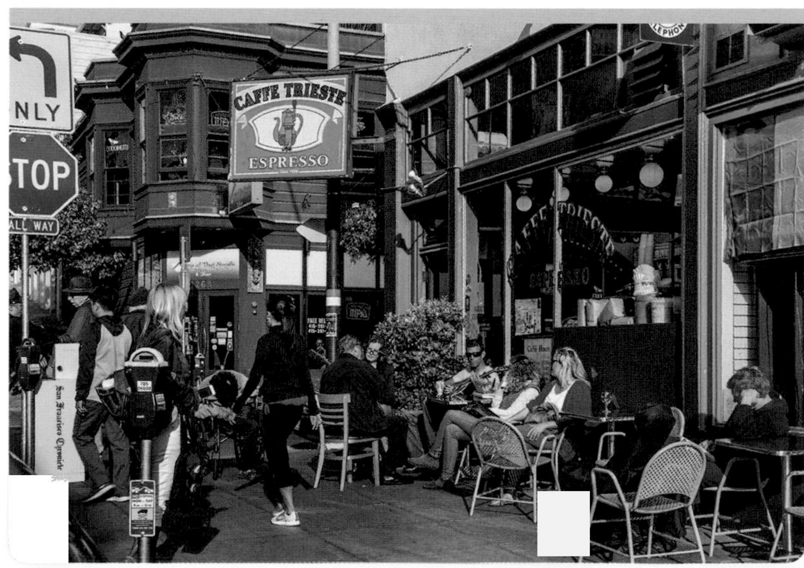

IZZET KERIBAR / GETTY IMAGES ©

Gay/Lesbian/Bi/Trans San Francisco

Singling out the best places to be queer in San Francisco is almost redundant. Though the Castro is a gay hub and the Mission is a magnet for lesbians, the entire city is gay-friendly. Top GLBT venues include the following:

Stud (Map p102; www.studsf.com; 399 9th St; admission $5-8; noon-2am Tue, from 5pm Wed & Sat, 5pm-3am Thu & Fri, 5pm to midnight Sun; 12, 19, 27, 47) Rocking the gay scene since 1966, and branching out beyond leather daddies with rocker-grrrl Mondays, Tuesday drag variety shows, raunchy comedy/karaoke Wednesdays, Friday art-drag dance parties, and performance-art cabaret whenever hostess-DJ Anna Conda gets it together.

Lexington Club (415-863-2052; www.lexingtonclub.com; 3464 19th St; 5pm-2am Mon-Thu, from 3pm Fri-Sun; 14, 33, 49, B 16th St Mission) Odds are eerily high you'll develop a crush on your ex-girlfriend's hot new girlfriend here over strong drink, pinball and tattoo comparisons – go on, live dangerously at SF's most famous/notorious full-time lesbian bar.

EndUp (Map p102; 415-646-0999; www.theendup.com; 401 6th St; admission $5-20; 10pm Thu-4am Fri, 11pm Fri-11am Sat, 10pm Sat-4am Mon, 10pm Mon-4am Tue; 12, 27, 47) Home of Sunday 'tea dances' (gay dance parties) since 1973, though technically the party starts Saturday. Bring a change of clothes and EndUp watching the sunrise on Monday over the freeway on-ramp.

Thu, to midnight Fri & Sat; ; 8X, 10, 12, 30, 41, 45) Poetry on bathroom walls, opera on the jukebox, live accordion jams weekly and sightings of Beat poet laureate Lawrence Ferlinghetti: this is North Beach at its best, since the 1950s. Linger over a legendary espresso and scribble your screenplay under the Sicilian mural just as young Francis Ford Coppola did. Perhaps you've heard of the movie: it was called *The Godfather*.

Comstock Saloon — Bar

(Map p106; 415-617-0071; www.comstocksaloon.com; 155 Columbus Ave; noon to 2am Mon-Fri, from 4pm Sat, 4pm to midnight Sun; 8X, 10, 12, 30, 45, Powell-Mason) Welcome to the Barbary Coast, where cocktails at this Victorian saloon remain period-perfect: Pisco Punch is made with pineapple gum and martini-precursor Martinez features gin, vermouth, bitters and maraschino liqueur. Call ahead to claim booths or tufted-velvet parlor seating, so you can hear dates when mezzanine ragtime-jazz bands play. Daytime drinking is rewarded Fridays, when lunch is free with two-drink purchase.

THE MISSION

Ritual Coffee Roasters — Cafe

(415-641-1011; www.ritualroasters.com; 1026 Valencia St; 6am-8pm Mon-Thu, to 10pm Fri, 7am-10pm Sat, to 8pm Sun; ; 14, 49, B 24th St Mission) Cults wish they inspired the same devotion as Ritual, where regulars solemnly queue for house-roasted cappuccino with ferns drawn in foam and specialty drip coffees with some genuinely bizarre flavor profiles – descriptions comparing roasts to grapefruit peel or hazelnut aren't exaggerating. Electrical outlets are limited to encourage conversation, so you can eavesdrop on dates, art debates and political protest plans.

El Rio — Club

(415-282-3325; www.elriosf.com; 3158 Mission St; admission $3-8; 1pm-2am; 12, 14, 27, 49, B 24th St Mission) The DJ mix at El Rio takes its cue from the patrons: eclectic, fearless, funky and sexy, no matter your orientation. Come for shuffleboard and free oysters on the half shell on Fridays at 5:30pm, and powerful margaritas will soon get you bopping to disco-post-punk mashups and flirting shamelessly in the back garden. Cash only.

THE HAIGHT & HAYES VALLEY

Toronado Pub
(415-863-2276; www.toronado.com; 547 Haight St; 11:30am-2am; 6, 22, 71, M N) Glory hallelujah, beer lovers: your prayers have been answered. Be humbled before the chalkboard altar that lists 50-plus beers on tap and hundreds more bottled, including spectacular seasonal microbrews. Bring cash and order sausages from **Rosamunde** (415-437-6851; http://rosamundesausagegrill.com; 545 Haight St; sausages $6.50-7; 11:30am-10pm Sun-Wed, to 11pm Thu-Sat; 6, 22, 71, M N) next door to accompany ale made by Trappist monks. It may get too loud to hear your date talk, but you'll hear the angels sing.

Alembic Bar
(Map p110; 415-666-0822; www.alembicbar.com; 1725 Haight St; 4pm-2am Mon-Fri, from noon Sat & Sun; 6, 33, 37, 43, 71, M N) The tin ceilings are hammered and floors well-stomped, but drinks expertly crafted from 250 specialty spirits are not made for pounding – hence the 'No Red Bull/No Jägermeister' sign and duck-heart bar snacks. Toast the Haight with a Lava Lamp (rosé bubbly with walnut bitters) or be rendered speechless by Charlie Chaplin, a sloe gin, lime and apricot liqueur concoction.

Entertainment

Scan the free weekly *San Francisco Bay Guardian,* and see what half-price and last-minute tickets you can find at **TIX Bay Area** (Map p102; www.tixbayarea.org), where tickets are sold on the day of the performance for cash only. For advance tickets to theater shows and big-name concerts, check **Ticketmaster** (www.ticketmaster.com) and **SHN** (www.shnsf.com).

LIVE MUSIC

SFJAZZ Center Jazz
(Map p102; 866-920-5299; www.sfjazz.org; 201 Franklin St; showtimes vary; 5, 7, 21, M Van Ness) Jazz greats coast-to-coast and from Argentina to Yemen are showcased at America's newest, largest jazz center. The SF Jazz Festival takes place here in July, but year-round the calendar features legends such as McCoy Tyner, Regina Carter, Béla Fleck and Tony Bennett (who left his heart here, after all). Upper-tier cheap seats are more like stools, but offer clear stage views.

Fillmore Concert Venue
(415-346-3000; www.thefillmore.com; 1805 Geary Blvd; tickets from $20; shows nightly) Hendrix, Zeppelin, Janis – they all played the Fillmore. The legendary venue that

Poster room, Fillmore
ANTHONY PIDGEON / GETTY IMAGES ©

launched the psychedelic era has the posters to prove it upstairs, and hosts arena acts in a 1250-seat venue where you can squeeze in next to the stage.

Great American Music Hall Live Music

(Map p102; ☎415-885-0750; www.gamh.com; 859 O'Farrell St; admission $12-35; ⏲box office 10:30am-6pm Mon-Fri & on show nights; 🚌19, 38, 47, 49) Once a bordello, the rococo Great American Music Hall is one of SF's coolest places for shows. A balcony with table seating rims the main standing-room floor area, the sound system is top-notch and there are food and drinks. Music ranges from rock, alt-rock and country to jazz and blues.

THEATER

Musicals and Broadway spectaculars play at a number of downtown theaters. But the pride of SF is its many indie theaters that host original, solo and experimental shows.

American Conservatory Theater Theater

(ACT; Map p102; ☎415-749-2228; www.act-sf.org; 415 Geary St; ⏲box office noon-6pm Mon, to curtain Tue-Sun; 🚌38, 🚋Powell-Mason, Powell-Hyde) Breakthrough shows destined for London or New York sometimes pass muster at the turn-of-the-century Geary Theater, which has hosted ACT's landmark productions of Tony Kushner's *Angels in America* and Robert Wilson's *Black Rider*, with a libretto by William S Burroughs and music by the Bay Area's own Tom Waits.

Beach Blanket Babylon Cabaret

(BBB; Map p106; ☎415-421-4222; www.beachblanketbabylon.com; 678 Green St; admission $25-100; ⏲shows 8pm Wed, Thu & Fri, 6:30pm & 9:30pm Sat, 2pm & 5pm Sun; 🚌8X, 🚋Powell-Mason) Snow White searches for Prince Charming in San Francisco: what could possibly go wrong? The Disney-spoof musical-comedy cabaret has been running since 1974, but topical jokes keep it outrageous and production numbers involving wigs big as parade floats are gasp-worthy. Pop icons and heads of state are spoofed by actors in campy costumes – even when President Obama, Queen Elizabeth and SF Giants attended.

CLASSICAL MUSIC, OPERA & DANCE

San Francisco Opera Opera

(Map p102; ☎415-864-3330; www.sfopera.com; War Memorial Opera House, 301 Van Ness Ave; tickets $10-350; Ⓑ Civic Center, Ⓜ Van Ness) SF has been obsessed with opera since the Gold Rush and it remains a staple on the social calendar. Blue bloods like Ann Getty *always* book the Tuesday A-series – the best nights to spot fabulous gowns and tuxedos. If you're walking by during a performance, wander into the box-office lobby and watch the stage monitors for a teaser.

Davies Symphony Hall Classical Music

(Map p102; ☎rush tickets 415-503-5577, 415-864-6000; www.sfsymphony.org; 201 Van Ness Ave; Ⓜ Van Ness, Ⓑ Civic Center) Home of nine-time Grammy-winning SF Symphony, conducted with verve by Michael Tilson Thomas. The season runs September to July.

ODC Theater Dance

(☎415-863-9834; www.odctheater.org; 3153 17th Street; ⏲box office noon-3pm Mon-Fri) For 40 years, redefining dance with risky, raw performances and the sheer joy of movement with performances September through December, and 200 dance classes a week.

CINEMAS

Castro Theatre Cinema

(☎415-621-6120; www.castrotheatre.com; 429 Castro St; adult/child $11/8.50; ⏲showtimes vary; Ⓜ Castro) The Mighty Wurlitzer organ rises from the orchestra pit before evening performances and the audience cheers for classics from the Great American Songbook, ending with (sing along, now): 'San Francisco open your Golden Gate/You let no stranger wait outside your door...' If there's a cult classic on the bill, say, *Whatever Happened to Baby*

Below: Hog Island Oyster Company (p113); **Right:** Cable car (p124) going down Hyde St
(BELOW) THOMAS WINZ / GETTY IMAGES ©; (RIGHT) MITCHELL FUNK / GETTY IMAGES ©

Jane?, expect participation. Otherwise, crowd are well-behaved and rapt.

Roxie Cinema Cinema
(415-863-1087; www.roxie.com; 3117 16th St; regular screening/matinee $10/7; 14, 22, 33, 49, B 16th St Mission) A little neighborhood nonprofit cinema with major international clout for distributing indie films and showing controversial films and documentaries banned elsewhere. Tickets to film festival premieres, rare revivals and raucous annual Oscars telecasts sell out fast – but if the main show is packed, check out documentaries in teensy next-door Little Roxy instead. No ads, plus personal introductions to every film.

SPORTS

San Francisco Giants Baseball
(Map p102; 415-972-2000; www.sfgiants.com; AT&T Park, 24 Willie Mays Plaza; tickets $5-135) Watch and learn how the World Series is won – bushy beards, women's underwear and all.

Shopping

San Francisco has big department stores and name-brand boutiques around Union Sq, including **Macy's** (Map p102; www.macys.com; 170 O'Farrell St; 10am-9pm Mon-Sat, 11am-7pm Sun; Powell-Mason, Powell-Hyde, M Powell, B Powell) and the sprawling **Westfield San Francisco Centre** (Map p102; www.westfield.com/sanfrancisco; 865 Market St; 10am-8:30pm Mon-Sat, to 7pm Sun; ; Powell-Mason, Powell-Hyde, M Powell, B Powell), but special, only-in-SF stores are found in the Haight, the Castro, the Mission and Hayes Valley (west of Civic Center).

City Lights Books
(Map p106; 415-362-8193; www.citylights.com; 261 Columbus Ave; 10am-midnight; 8X, 10, 12, 30, 41, 45, Powell-Mason, Powell-Hyde) 'Abandon all despair, all ye who enter,' orders the sign by the door to City Lights bookstore by founder and San Francisco

poet laureate Lawrence Ferlinghetti. This commandment is easy to follow upstairs in the sunny **Poetry Room**, with its piles of freshly published verse, a designated **Poet's Chair** and literary views of laundry strung across Jack Kerouac Alley.

Park Life Art, Gifts

(Map p110; ☎415-386-7275; www.parklifestore.com; 220 Clement St; ⏰noon-8pm Mon-Thu, from 11am Fri & Sat, 11am-7pm Sun; 🚌1, 2, 33, 38, 44) The Swiss Army knife of hip SF stores: design store, indie publisher and art gallery, all in one. Park Life is exceptionally gifted with presents too good to wait for birthdays, including Golden State pendants, Sutro Sam otter tees, Park Life's catalog of utopian visions by Shaun O'Dell and Ian Johnson's portrait of John Coltrane radiating prismatic thought waves.

Golden Gate Fortune Cookie Company Food & Drink

(Map p106; ☎415-781-3956; 56 Ross Alley; ⏰8am-6pm; 🚌30, 45, 🚋Powell-Mason, Powell-Hyde) Make a fortune in San Francisco at this bakery, where cookies are stamped from vintage presses and folded while hot – much as they were in 1909, when fortune cookies were invented for SF's Japanese Tea Garden (p108). Write your own fortunes for custom cookies (50¢ each) or get bags of regular or risqué cookies. Cash only; 50¢ tip per photo.

Information

Dangers & Annoyances

Keep your city smarts and wits about you, especially at night in SoMa, the Mission and the Haight. Unless you know where you're going, avoid the sketchy, depressing Tenderloin (bordered east–west by Powell and Polk Sts and north–south by O'Farrell and Market Sts), Skid Row (6th St between Market and Folsom Sts) and Bayview-Hunters Point. Panhandlers and homeless people are a fact of life in the city. People will probably ask you for spare change, but donations to local nonprofits stretch further. For safety, don't engage with panhandlers at night or around ATMs. Otherwise, a simple 'I'm sorry,' is a polite response.

Tourist Information

San Francisco Visitor Information Center (Map p102; 415-391-2000, events hotline 415-391-2001; www.onlyinsanfrancisco.com; lower level, Hallidie Plaza, Market & Powell Sts; 9am-5pm Mon-Fri, to 3pm Sat & Sun; Powell-Mason, Powell-Hyde, M Powell St, B Powell St) Provides practical information for tourists, publishes glossy tourist-oriented booklets and runs a 24-hour events hotline.

California Welcome Center (Map p106; 415-981-1280; www.visitcwc.com; Pier 39, Bldg P, Suite 241b; 9am-7pm)

Getting There & Away

Air

The Bay Area has three major airports: San Francisco International Airport (p397), 14 miles south of downtown SF, off Hwy 101; Oakland International Airport (p397), a few miles across the bay; and Mineta San José International Airport (p397), at the southern end of the bay. The majority of international flights use SFO.

Bus

Until the new terminal is complete in 2017, SF's intercity hub remains the **Temporary Transbay Terminal** (Map p102; Howard & Main Sts), where you can catch buses on **AC Transit** (www.actransit.org) to the East Bay, **Golden Gate Transit** (www.goldengatetransit.org) north to Marin and Sonoma Counties, and **SamTrans** (www.samtrans.com; one way $5) south to Palo Alto and the Pacific coast. **Greyhound** (800-231-2222; www.greyhound.com) buses leave daily for Los Angeles ($59, eight to 12 hours), Truckee near Lake Tahoe ($31, 5½ hours), and other destinations.

Car & Motorcycle

All major car-rental operators are represented at the airports, and many have downtown offices.

Ferry

Blue & Gold Ferries (Map p102; 415-705-8200; www.blueandgoldfleet.com; $6.25 one-way) **Blue & Gold Ferries** runs the Alameda–Oakland ferry from Pier 41 and the Ferry Building.

Golden Gate Ferry (415-455-2000; www.goldengateferry.org; adult/child $9.75/4.75; 6am-9:30pm Mon-Fri, 10am-6pm Sat & Sun) Ferry service from the Ferry Building to Sausalito and Larkspur.

Train

Caltrain (www.caltrain.com; cnr 4th & King Sts) Caltrain connects San Francisco with Silicon Valley hubs and San Jose.

Cable Cars

Andrew Hallidie's 1873 contraptions have held up miraculously well on San Francisco's slopes, and groaning brakes and clanging brass bells only add to the carnival-ride thrills. Cable cars stop almost every block on the California and Powell-Mason lines, and every block on north–south stretches of the Powell-Hyde line. To board on hills, act fast: leap onto the baseboard and grab the closest leather hand-strap. Here are route highlights:

Powell-Hyde Cable Car Golden Gate Bridge pops in and out of view, and you can hop off at the zig-zagging Lombard St or go straight to Ghirardelli Square.

Powell-Mason Cable Car Route cuts through North Beach and ends at Fisherman's Wharf.

California St Cable Car History buffs and crowd-shy visitors prefer this line, in operation since 1878. Heads west through Chinatown and climbs Nob Hill. The Van Ness terminus is a few blocks from Japantown.

Muni (p125) operates the lines, which run from about 6am to 1am daily, with scheduled departures every three to 12 minutes.

War Memorial Opera House, home to the San Francisco Opera (p121)

RICK GEHARTER / GETTY IMAGES ©

Amtrak (☎800-872-7245; www.amtrakcalifornia.com) Amtrak serves San Francisco via its stations in Oakland and Emeryville (near Oakland). Amtrak offers rail passes good for seven days of travel in California within a 21-day period (from $159). It also runs free shuttle buses from its stations in Emeryville and Oakland's Jack London Sq to San Francisco's Ferry Building and Caltrain station.

Getting Around

For Bay Area transit options, departures and arrivals, check ☎511 or www.511.org.

To/From the Airport

Taxis to downtown San Francisco costs $35 to $50. BART trains take 30 minutes to downtown SF (one-way $8.65). **SuperShuttle** (☎800-258-3826; www.supershuttle.com) door-to-door shared ride vans depart outside the baggage-claim areas, taking 45 minutes to most SF locations ($17).

Car & Motorcycle

If you can, avoid driving in San Francisco: street parking is harder to find than true love, and meter readers are ruthless. Convenient downtown parking lots are at 5th and Mission Sts, Union Sq, and Sutter and Stockton Sts. Daily rates run $25 to $50.

BART

Bay Area Rapid Transit (Bay Area Rapid Transit; www.bart.gov; one way $8.25) is a subway system linking SFO, the Mission District, downtown San Francisco and the East Bay.

Muni

Muni (Municipal Transit Agency; ☎511; www.sfmta.com) operates bus, streetcar and cable-car lines. Standard fare for buses or streetcars is $2, and tickets are good on buses or streetcars (not BART or cable cars) for 90 minutes; cable-car fare is $6 for a single ride. Tickets are available on board, but you'll need exact change.

Muni's **Visitor Passport** (1/3/7 days $15/23/29) allows unlimited travel on all Muni transport, including cable cars; it's sold at San Francisco's Visitor Information Center and many hotels.

Taxi

Fares run about $2.25 per mile, plus 10% tip ($1 minimum); meters start at $3.50.

Northern California & Central Coast

Northern California and the state's central coastline encompass a bonanza of natural vistas and bountiful wildlife. In Marin, you'll see wizened ancient redwoods blocking the sun, herds of elegant tule elk, plus leaping gray whales off the cape of wind-scoured Point Reyes.

Continuing north, craggy cliffs, towering redwoods and windswept bluffs define the wild, scenic and even slightly foreboding coast, where spectral fog has fostered the world's tallest trees and a maverick spirit. The Northern Mountains, including the snowcapped peaks of Mt Shasta and Lassen Volcanic National Park, contain California's remote frontier, where vast expanses of wilderness are divided by rivers and streams, and dotted with cobalt lakes, horse ranches, and alpine pinnacles. South of San Francisco, flower-power Santa Cruz and the historic port town of Monterey are gateways to the rugged lands of bohemian Big Sur and the coastal cities of laid-back San Luis Obispo and idyllic Santa Barbara.

Hiker at Mt Shasta (p169)
FEARGUS COONEY / GETTY IMAGES ©

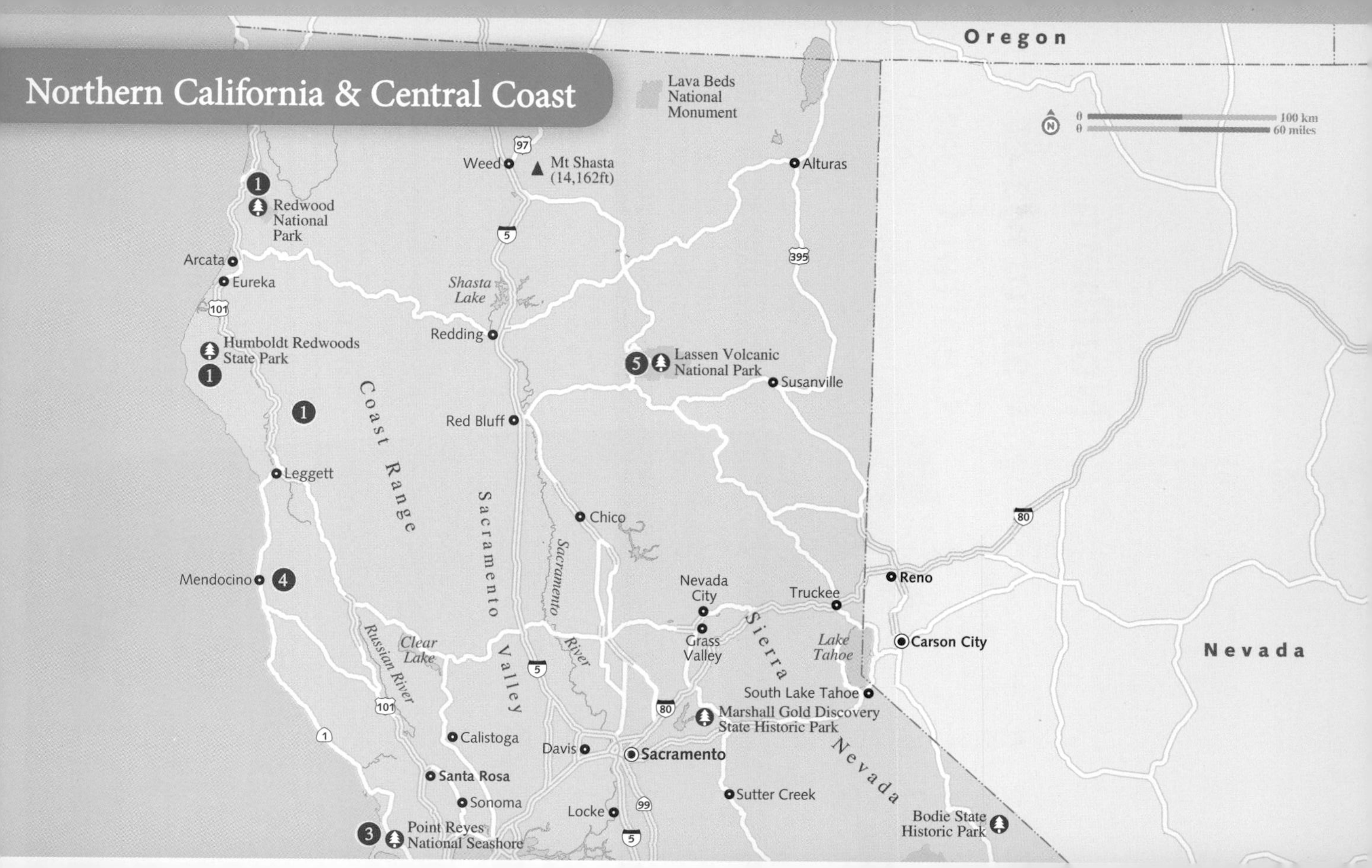
Northern California & Central Coast
Oregon
Nevada
Lava Beds National Monument
0 100 km
0 60 miles
Weed
Mt Shasta (14,162ft)
Alturas
Redwood National Park
Arcata
Eureka
Shasta Lake
Redding
Humboldt Redwoods State Park
Lassen Volcanic National Park
Susanville
Red Bluff
Coast Range
Leggett
Sacramento Valley
Chico
Sacramento River
Mendocino
Nevada City
Grass Valley
Truckee
Reno
Carson City
Sierra Nevada
Lake Tahoe
South Lake Tahoe
Clear Lake
Russian River
Marshall Gold Discovery State Historic Park
Calistoga
Davis
Sacramento
Santa Rosa
Sonoma
Sutter Creek
Locke
Bodie State Historic Park
Point Reyes National Seashore

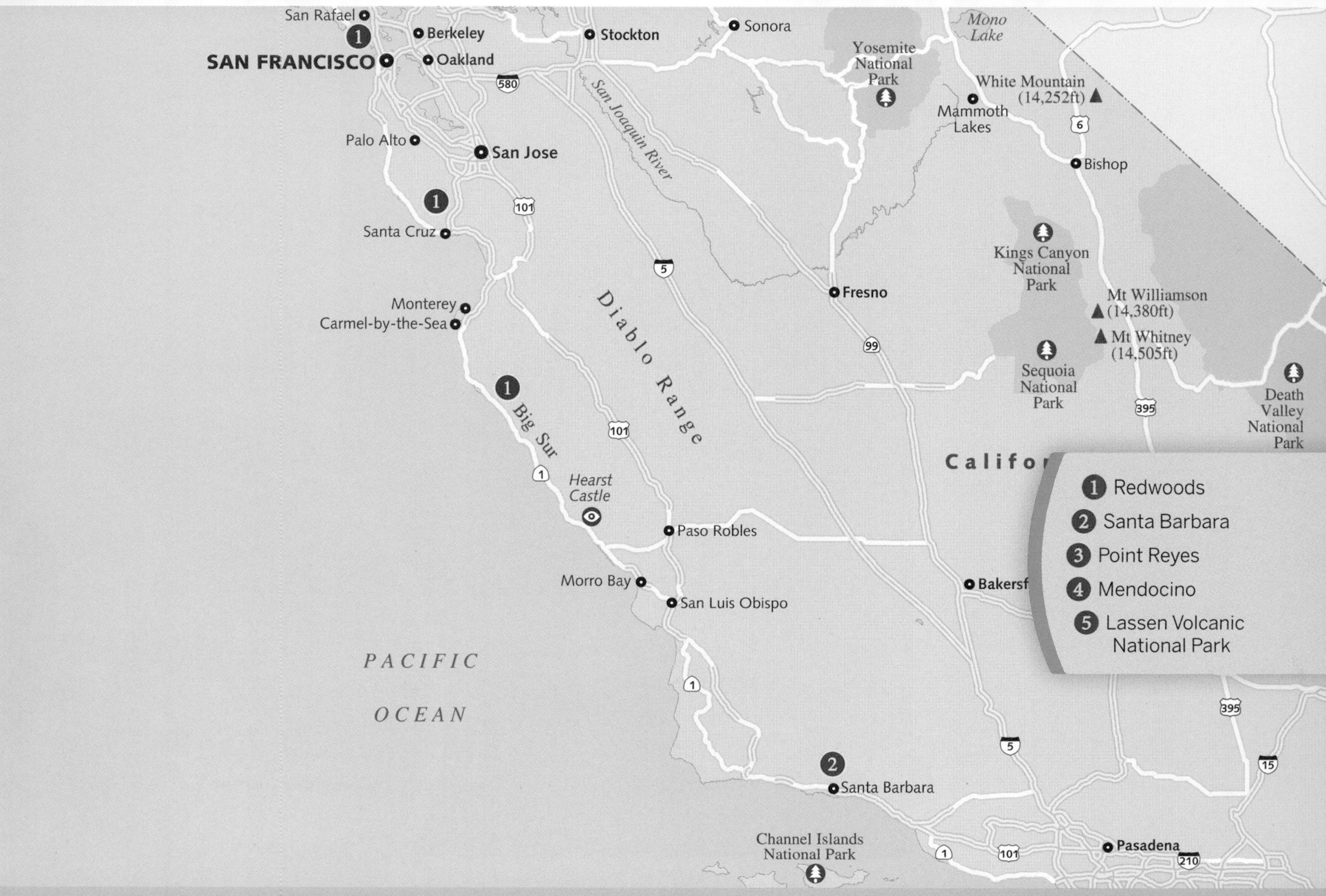
San Rafael
SAN FRANCISCO
Berkeley
Oakland
Stockton
Sonora
Mono Lake
Yosemite National Park
White Mountain (14,252ft)
Mammoth Lakes
Bishop
Palo Alto
San Jose
San Joaquin River
Santa Cruz
Kings Canyon National Park
Fresno
Mt Williamson (14,380ft)
Mt Whitney (14,505ft)
Monterey
Carmel-by-the-Sea
Diablo Range
Sequoia National Park
Death Valley National Park
Big Sur
Hearst Castle
Paso Robles
Morro Bay
San Luis Obispo
Bakersf
Califor
Redwoods
Santa Barbara
Point Reyes
Mendocino
Lassen Volcanic National Park
PACIFIC
OCEAN
Santa Barbara
Channel Islands National Park
Pasadena

Northern California & Central Coast Highlights

Redwoods

Coast redwoods, the tallest living things on earth, are found in a narrow, 450-mile-long strip along California's coast between Big Sur and southern Oregon. They can live for 2200 years, grow up to 379ft tall and achieve a diameter of 22ft at the base, with bark up to 12in thick. Redwoods thrive on fog. The driest time to visit is between May and September. Below: Avenue of the Giants (p155)

1

2 Santa Barbara

Just a 90-minute drive north of LA, Santa Barbara (p190) basks smugly in its near-perfection. Tucked between the Santa Ynez Mountains and the ocean, the city's red-tiled roofs, white-stucco buildings, Spanish mission, and Mediterranean vibe have long given credence to its claim to the title of the American Riviera. Its mild weather and bevy of surfing and swimming beaches don't hurt either.

ALAN MAJCHROWICZ / GETTY IMAGES ©

3 Point Reyes

Wander through the town of Point Reyes Station (p145) for a stroll and to pick up some cheese and picnic supplies at Tomales Bay Foods & Cowgirl Creamery before heading out to the Point Reyes National Seashore (p146; pictured right) to watch whales blow by in winter. Spend an afternoon kayaking in nearby Tomales Bay. Then ask yourself: Am I really only 1½ hours from San Francisco?

FEARGUS COONEY / GETTY IMAGES ©

4 Mendocino

The coastal headland town of Mendocino (p151) is beloved for weekend getaways. Browse the charming upscale shops and art galleries, then explore the lighthouse and wildlife preserve north of its picket-fence-lined core. Dramatic cypress trees stand watch over the booming ocean surf and solitary coves, and you can canoe through the largest tidal estuary in the northern half of the state here.

5 Lassen Volcanic National Park

Lassen (p167) is the state's ultimate geology lesson, with crunchy cinder cones, bubbling mud pots and steaming vents that stink like eggs months past their sell-by date. Though it last erupted in 1915, towering 10,463ft Lassen Peak is still considered an active volcano, though you might not want to ponder that as you survey its hard-won summit views. Above: Bumpass Hell (p168)

Northern California & Central Coast's Best...

Beaches

- **Pfeiffer Beach** Big Sur's most dramatic beach, where the sand is tinged purple. (p184)
- **East Beach** Santa Barbara's downtown, kid-friendly beach by the wharf. (p193)
- **Point Piedras Blancas** Come for the historic lighthouse, stay for the elephant seals and sea otters. (p187)
- **Stinson Beach** Good for long strolls and sunset views toward distant Point Reyes. (p144)

Charming Downtowns

- **Carmel-by-the-Sea** Galleries, upscale boutiques and fairy-tale cottages attract shoppers, art collectors and dog owners. (p180)
- **Sausalito** Take the ferry to the Bay Area's sunny vacation village. (p140)
- **Mendocino** One-of-a-kind shops line downtown's quaint streets. (p151)
- **Ferndale** Handmade ironworks and a general store in a darling town. (p158)

Places to Take Kids

- **Bay Area Discovery Museum** Parents will enjoy the cove's view of the bay; preschoolers will love the hands-on exhibits. (p140)
- **Santa Cruz Beach Boardwalk** A beachfront amusement park with carnival rides. (p173)
- **Monterey Bay Aquarium** Ogle the psychedelic jellyfish and touch tidepool animals. (p181)
- **Lassen Volcanic National Park** For an illustrative example of what you learned in science class. (p167)

Outdoor Adventures

- **Salt Point State Park** Rough-and-tumble coastline and wildlife galore. (p151)
- **Lava Beds National Monument** Stark, moonlike landscapes, cave tours, and 6,000-year-old rock paintings and petroglyphs. (p168)
- **Mt Shasta** Worth the haul, if you're into that whole stunningly gorgeous mountain wilderness thing. (p169)
- **Point Reyes National Seashore** Just watch out for tule elk in rutting season. (p146)

Left: Lava Beds National Monument (p168); **Above:** Stinson Beach (p144)

Need to Know

ADVANCE PLANNING

- **Two months before** Research outdoor activities and buy whatever gear you need.
- **One month before** Make reservations for Chez Panisse.
- **Two months before** Look up regional festivals and events.
- **Two weeks before** Break in your boots for all of the hiking you'll do.

RESOURCES

- **Redwood National & State Parks** (www.nps.gov/redw) Official information.
- **Muir Woods National Monument** (www.nps.gov/muwo) Plan your visit in advance.
- **Golden Gate National Recreation Area** (www.nps.gov/goga) Includes the Marin Headlands.
- **Big Sur California** (www.bigsurcalifornia.org) Information on lodging, restaurants, beaches and parks.
- **West Marin Chamber of Commerce** (www.pointreyes.org) Links to lodging near Point Reyes.

GETTING AROUND

- **Walking** The best way to explore compact downtown areas including San Luis Obispo, Monterey and Santa Barbara.
- **Ferry** From San Francisco, the best way to visit Sausalito or Tiburon.
- **Bus** Not convenient for the further reaches, but a great way to reach Muir Woods.
- **Car** Will allow you the most freedom to explore the redwoods and coast.
- **Train** Amtrak's *Coast Starlight* route runs between Los Angeles, Santa Barbara, San Luis Obispo and Oakland.

BE FOREWARNED

- **Safety** Watch your step while hiking, and keep an eye out for riptides, sharks and storms.
- **Tidepools** Read posted information or online guides to ensure you don't hurt the fragile ecosystem.
- **Costs** Accommodations on the coast can be quite expensive.
- **Climate** Redwoods thrive in fog, so bring warm clothes, nonslip shoes and rain gear for hikes.

Northern California & Central Coast Itineraries

Take your time as you tour miles of evocative coastline and forests of giant redwoods, contemplating the rhythm of the crashing Pacific surf and the fortitude of the sky-high trees.

5 DAYS

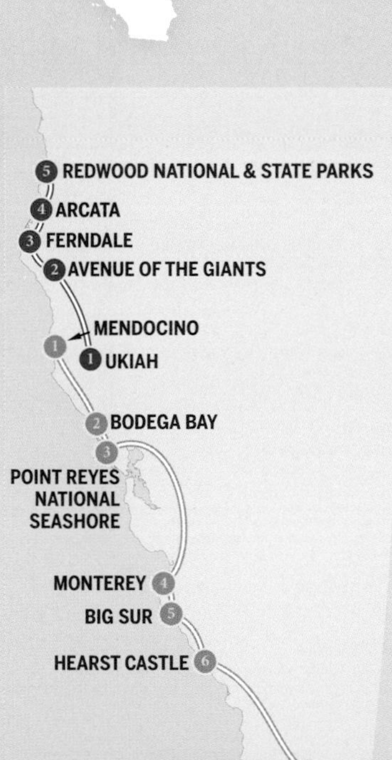

UKIAH TO REDWOOD NATIONAL & STATE PARKS
REDWOOD COUNTRY

Don't let the distance scare you off; visiting the redwoods is an easy trip from the Bay Area in five days (or even less). To save time, take Hwy 101 instead of the coast. Stop first in ❶ **Ukiah** (p156) for a stress-relieving soak in one of the local hot-spring resorts and a visit to the tranquil old-growth redwood stand at Montgomery Woods State Reserve. The next day you'll enter the southern Redwood Coast with a drive along the ❷ **Avenue of the Giants** (p155). You can spend an entire day hiking the area and craning your neck to see the tops of the ancient trees, but be sure to reach ❸ **Ferndale** (p158) by nightfall to stay in one of the adorable town's 'butterfat mansion' B&Bs. Spend the next day in ❹ **Arcata** (p161), a university town where the smell of biodiesel fuel and patchouli hangs in the air. Take a walk along the wildlife sanctuary on Humboldt Bay to spot scores of water birds. Spend the rest of your time in ❺ **Redwood National & State Parks** (p163), hiking the moss-covered Fern Canyon or admiring the giant redwoods in Lady Bird Johnson Grove.

Top Left: Humboldt Redwoods State Park (p155); **Top Right:** Neptune Pool, Hearst Castle (p189)

1 WEEK

REDWOOD NATIONAL PARK TO SANTA BARBARA

CRUISING THE COAST

Start a lazy road trip that follows the water's edge, leaving Redwood National Park and retracing forested Hwy 101 south until you join coastal Hwy 1. Pass the afternoon and evening in the North Coast jewel of 1 **Mendocino** (p151), exploring its rocky headlands and cozying up for the night at one of its picturesque lodgings. The next day, call in at 2 **Bodega Bay** (p149) to relive *The Birds* and scan the water for breaching whales at Bodega Head. For a wildlife bonanza of tule elk, elephant seals and even more whales, wind your way to the stark shoreline bluffs of the 3 **Point Reyes National Seashore** (p146). After seeing what lives above the water, venture on to the world-famous aquarium in 4 **Monterey** (p176) to see the slippery creatures that thrive underneath the waves. You could spend a lifetime pondering the wild and solitary 5 **Big Sur** (p182) – the most dazzling section of California coastline – but reserve a place to stay so you can linger for the sunset. Book advance tickets for a tour of opulent 6 **Hearst Castle** (p189), then plant yourself in the warm sand in 7 **Santa Barbara** (p190).

Discover Northern California & Central Coast

At a Glance

- **Marin County** (p136) Rugged headlands, wild beaches and organic local agriculture, all just across the bridge from San Francisco.
- **North Coast** (p149) Soaring redwood forests cluster close to quaint towns.
- **Northern Mountains** (p167) Remote and impressive mountain peaks.
- **Central Coast** (p171) A personality-packed stretch of coastline with dazzling beaches.

Rodeo Beach, Marin Headlands
MICHAEL MARFELL / GETTY IMAGES ©

MARIN COUNTY

If there's a part of the Bay Area that consciously attempts to live up to the California dream, it's Marin County. Just across the Golden Gate Bridge from San Francisco, the region has a wealthy population that cultivates a seemingly laid-back lifestyle. Towns may look like idyllic rural hamlets, but the shops cater to cosmopolitan and expensive tastes. The 'common' folk here eat organic, vote Democrat and drive hybrids.

Nature is what makes Marin County such an excellent day trip or weekend escape from San Francisco.

Marin Headlands

The headlands rise majestically out of the water at the north end of the Golden Gate Bridge, their rugged beauty all the more striking given the fact that they're only a few miles from San Francisco's urban core. As trails wind through the headlands, they afford stunning views of the sea, the Golden Gate Bridge and San Francisco, leading to isolated beaches and secluded spots for picnics.

Sights

After crossing the Golden Gate Bridge, exit immediately at Alexander Ave, then dip left under the highway and head out west for the expansive views and hiking trailheads. Conzelman Rd snakes up into the hills, where it eventually forks. Conzelman Rd continues west, becoming a steep, one-lane road as it descends to Point Bonita. From here it continues to Rodeo Beach and Fort Barry. McCullough Rd heads inland, joining Bunker Rd toward Rodeo Beach.

Hiking & Cycling the Golden Gate Bridge

Walking or cycling across the Golden Gate Bridge to Sausalito is a fun way to avoid traffic, get some great ocean views and bask in that refreshing Marin County air. It's a fairly easy journey, mostly flat or downhill when heading north from San Francisco (cycling back to the city involves one big climb out of Sausalito). You can also simply hop on a ferry back to SF.

Point Bonita Lighthouse Lighthouse
(**www.nps.gov/goga/pobo.htm; off Field Rd; 12:30-3:30pm Sat-Mon**) FREE At the end of Conzelman Rd, this lighthouse is a breathtaking half-mile walk from a small parking area. From the tip of Point Bonita, you can see the distant Golden Gate Bridge and beyond it the San Francisco skyline. It's an uncommon vantage point of the bay-centric city, and harbor seals haul out nearby in season. To reserve a spot on one of the free monthly full-moon tours of the promontory, call 415-331-1540.

Nike Missile Site SF-88 Historic Site
(**415-331-1453; www.nps.gov/goga/nike-missile-site.htm; off Field Rd; 12:30pm-3:30pm Thu-Sat**) FREE File past guard shacks with uniformed mannequins to witness the area's not-too-distant military history at this fascinating Cold War museum staffed by veterans. Watch them place a now-warhead-free missile into position, then ride a missile elevator to the cavernous underground silo to see the multikeyed launch controls that were thankfully never set in motion.

Marine Mammal Center Animal Rescue Center
(**415-289-7325; www.marinemammalcenter.org; 10am-5pm;**) FREE Set on the hill above Rodeo Lagoon, the Marine Mammal Center rehabilitates injured, sick and orphaned sea mammals before returning them to the wild, and has educational exhibits about these animals and the dangers they face. During the spring pupping season the center can have up to several dozen orphaned seal pups on site and you can often see them before they're set free.

Activities

HIKING

At the end of Bunker Rd sits Rodeo Beach, protected from wind by high cliffs. From here the **Coastal Trail** meanders 3.5 miles inland, past abandoned military bunkers, to the **Tennessee Valley Trail**. It then continues 6 miles along the blustery headlands all the way to Muir Beach.

Sleeping

HI Marin Headlands Hostel Hostel $
(**415-331-2777; www.norcalhostels.org/marin; Fort Barry, Bldg 941; dm $26-30, r $72-92, all with shared bath; @**) Wake up to grazing deer and dew on the ground at this spartan

Golden Gate Bridge Toll

The bridge toll ($7) crossing from Marin to San Francisco is now all electronic; drivers can no longer stop to pay. Rental-car drivers may use their car company's toll program or pay in advance online, and motorists in private vehicles are billed by mail if they haven't prepaid online. See www.goldengate.org/tolls/tolltipsforvisitors.php for payment information.

Marin County

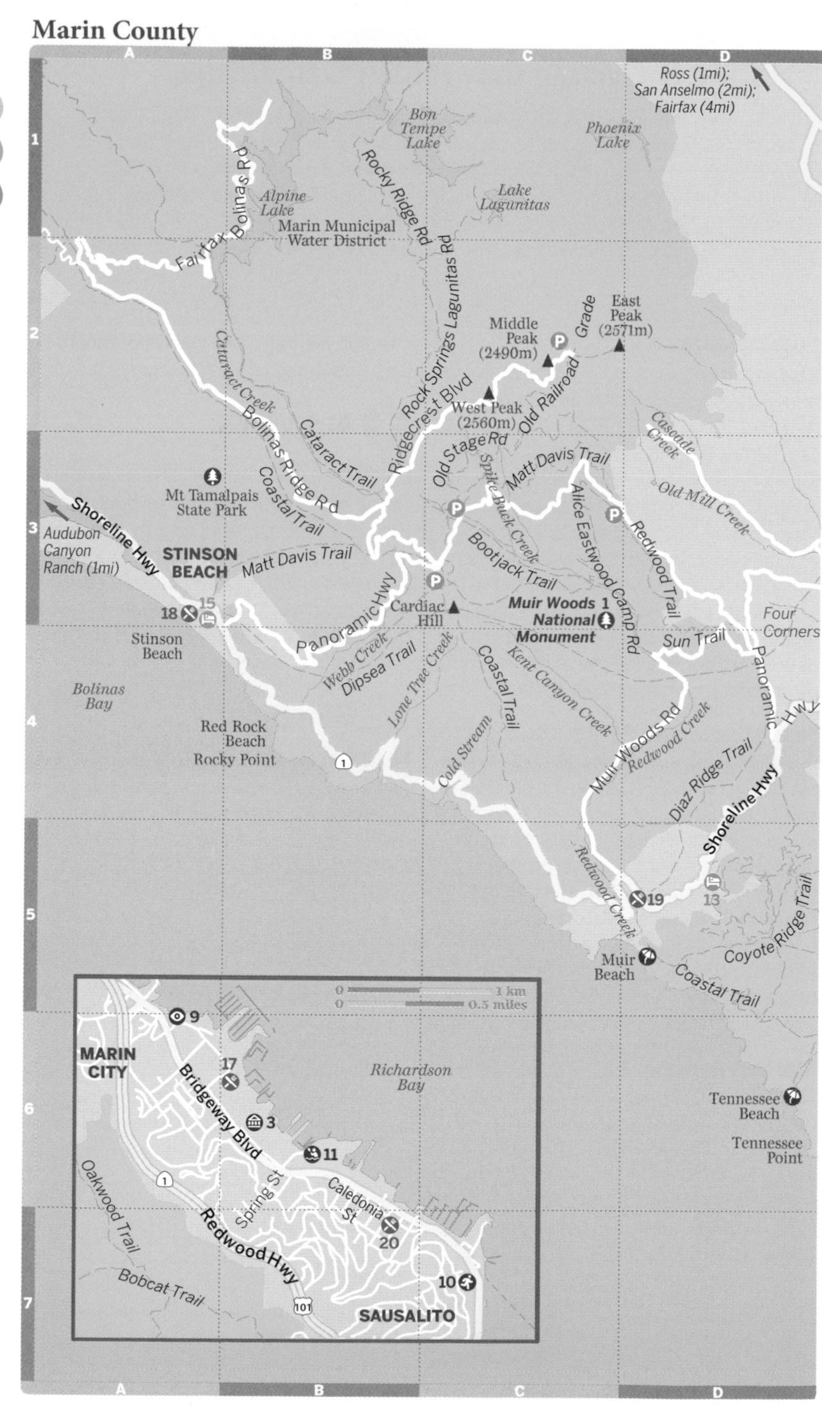

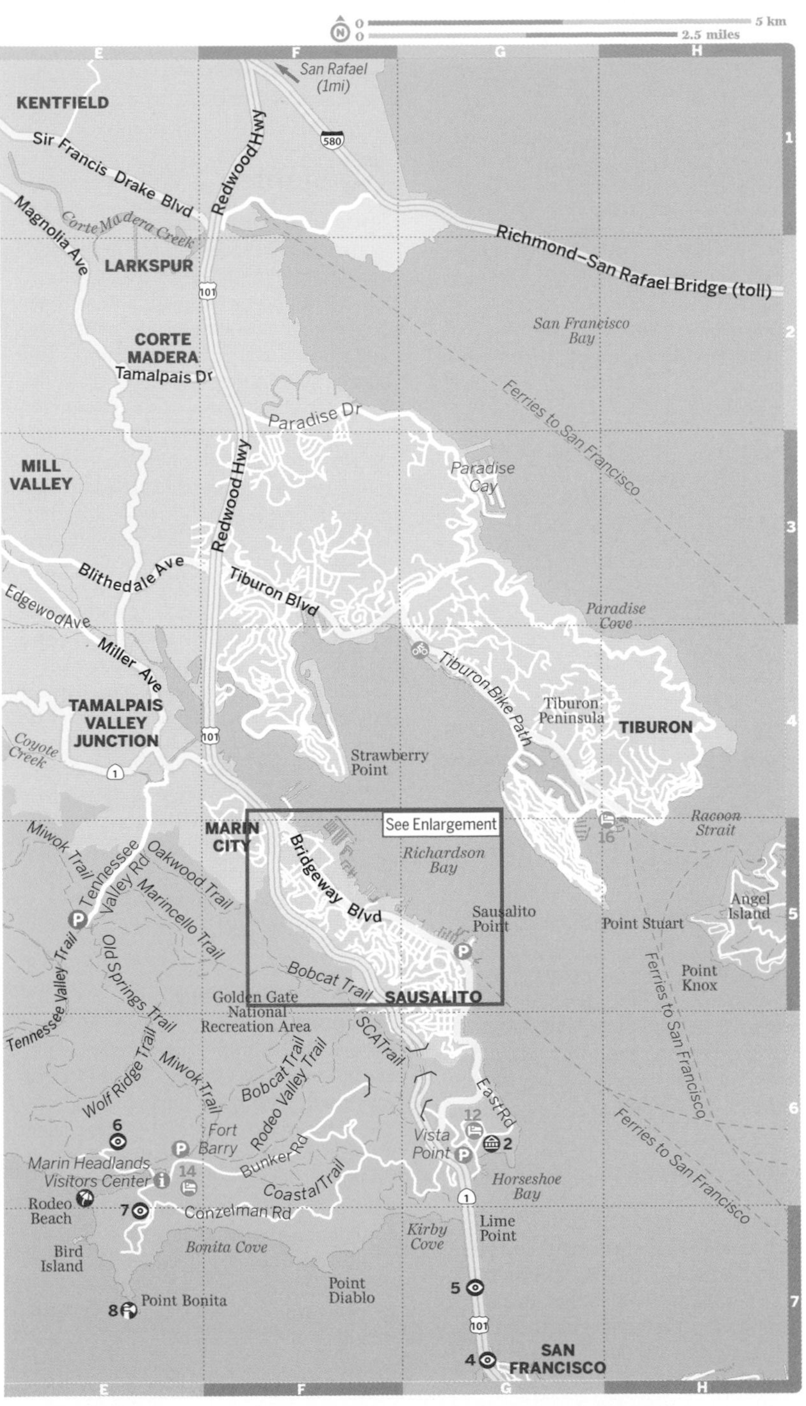

NORTHERN CALIFORNIA & CENTRAL COAST

Marin County

Don't Miss Sights

1 Muir Woods National Monument C3

Sights

2 Bay Area Discovery Museum............ G6
3 Bay Model Visitors Center..................B6
4 Fort Point G7
5 Golden Gate Bridge G7
6 Marine Mammal Center......................E6
7 Nike Missile Site SF-88 .... E7
8 Point Bonita Lighthouse E7
9 Sausalito Houseboats A6

Activities, Courses & Tours

10 Sausalito Bike Rentals C7
11 Sea Trek Kayak & SUP........................B6

Sleeping

12 Cavallo Point....................................... G6
13 Green Gulch Farm & Zen Center D5
14 HI Marin Headlands Hostel.................E6
15 Sandpiper A3
16 Water's Edge Hotel............................. H5

Eating

17 Fish B6
18 Parkside Cafe A3
19 Pelican Inn D5
Sam's Anchor Cafe.................... (see 16)
20 Sushi Ran B7

1907 military compound snuggled in the woods. It has comfortable beds and two well-stocked kitchens, and guests can gather round a fireplace in the common room, shoot pool or play ping-pong. Hiking trails beckon outside.

Information

Information is available from **Golden Gate National Recreation Area** (GGNRA; 415-561-4700; www.nps.gov/goga) and the **Marin Headlands Visitors Center** (415-331-1540; www.nps.gov/goga/marin-headlands.htm; Fort Barry; 9:30am-4:30pm), in an old chapel off Bunker Rd near Fort Barry.

Sausalito

Perfectly arranged on a secure little harbor on the bay, Sausalito is undeniably lovely. Named for the tiny willows that once populated the banks of its creeks, it's a small settlement of pretty houses that tumble neatly down a green hillside into a well-heeled downtown. Much of the town affords the visitor uninterrupted views of San Francisco and Angel Island, and due to the ridgeline at its back, fog generally skips past it.

Sights

Sausalito Houseboats Architecture
Bohemia still thrives along the shoreline of Richardson Bay, where free spirits inhabit hundreds of quirky homes that bobble in the waves among the seabirds and seals. Structures range from psychedelic mural-splashed castles to dilapidated salt-sprayed shacks and immaculate three-story floating mansions. It's a tight-knit community, where residents tend sprawling dockside gardens and stop to chat on the creaky wooden boardwalks as they wheel their groceries home.

Bay Model Visitors Center Museum
(415-332-3871; www.spn.usace.army.mil; 2100 Bridgeway Blvd; 9am-4pm Tue-Sat, plus 10am-5pm Sat & Sun in summer;) One of the coolest things in town, fascinating to both kids and adults, is the Army Corps of Engineers' solar-powered visitor center. Housed in one of the old (and cold!) Marinship warehouses, it's a 1.5-acre hydraulic model of San Francisco Bay and the delta region. Self-guided tours take you over and around it as the water flows.

Bay Area Discovery Museum Museum
(415-339-3900; www.baykidsmuseum.org; 557 McReynolds Rd; admission $11, free 1st Wed each month; 9am-5pm Tue-Sun;) Just under the north tower of the Golden Gate Bridge, at East Fort Baker, this excellent hands-on activity museum is specifically designed for children. Permanent (multilingual) exhibits include a wave workshop, a small underwater tunnel and a large outdoor play area with a shipwreck to romp around. A small cafe has healthy nibbles.

THOMAS WINZ / GETTY IMAGES ©

Don't Miss
Muir Woods National Monument

Walking through an awesome stand of the world's tallest trees is an experience to be had only in Northern California and a small part of southern Oregon. The old-growth redwoods at Muir Woods, just 12 miles north of the Golden Gate Bridge, is the closest redwood stand to San Francisco. The trees were initially eyed by loggers, and Redwood Creek, as the area was known, seemed ideal for a dam. Those plans were halted by congressman and naturalist William Kent, who donated 295 acres to the federal government. President Theodore Roosevelt made the site a national monument in 1908, the name honoring John Muir, naturalist and founder the Sierra Club.

Muir Woods can become quite crowded, especially on weekends. Try to come midweek, early in the morning or late in the afternoon, when tour buses are less of a problem. Even at busy times, a short hike will get you out of the densest crowds and onto trails with huge trees and stunning vistas. A lovely cafe serves local and organic goodies and hot drinks that hit the spot on foggy days.

The 1-mile **Main Trail Loop** is a gentle walk alongside Redwood Creek to the 1000-year-old trees at **Cathedral Grove**; it returns via **Bohemian Grove**, where the tallest tree in the park stands 254ft high. The **Dipsea Trail** is a good 2-mile hike up to the top of aptly named **Cardiac Hill**.

The parking lot fills up during busy periods, so consider taking the seasonal **Muir Woods Shuttle** (Route 66F; www.marintransit.org; round trip adult/child $5/free; ⌚weekends & holidays late-Mar–Oct). The 40-minute shuttle connects with Sausalito ferries arriving from San Francisco before 3pm.

NEED TO KNOW

☎415-388-2595; www.nps.gov/muwo; Muir Woods Rd, Mill Valley; adult/child $7/free; ⌚8am-sunset

Activities

Sausalito is great for **bicycling**, whether for a leisurely ride around town, a trip across the Golden Gate Bridge or a longer-haul journey.

Sea Trek Kayak & SUP Kayaking
(**415-332-8494; www.seatrek.com; Schoonmaker Point Marina; single/double kayaks per hour $20/35**) On a nice day, Richardson Bay is irresistible. Kayaks and stand-up paddleboards (SUP) can be rented here, near the Bay Model Visitor Center. No experience is necessary, and lessons and group outings are also available.

Sausalito Bike Rentals Bicycle Rental
(**415-331-2453; www.sausalitobikerentals.com; 34a Princess St; bicycle per hour $10; 10am-6pm**) Rent road, mountain, tandems ($25 per hour) and electric ($20 per hour) bicycles to explore the area.

Sleeping & Eating

Cavallo Point Hotel **$$$**
(**888-651-2003, 415-339-4700; www.cavallopoint.com; 601 Murray Circle; r from $359;**) Spread out over 45 acres of the Bay Area's most scenic parkland, Cavallo Point is a buzz-worthy lodge that flaunts a green focus, a full-service spa and easy access to outdoor activities. Choose from richly renovated rooms in the landmark Fort Baker officers' quarters or more contemporary solar-powered accommodations with exquisite bay views (including a turret of the Golden Gate Bridge).

Fish Seafood **$$**
(**415-331-3474; www.fish311.com; 350 Harbor Dr; mains $14-28; 11:30am-8:30pm;**) Chow down on seafood sandwiches, oysters and Dungeness crab roll with organic local butter at redwood picnic tables facing Richardson Bay. A local leader in promoting fresh and sustainably caught fish, this place has wonderful wild salmon in

Left: Sausalito houseboats (p140); **Below:** Muir Beach (p144)
(LEFT) RICHARD CUMMINS / GETTY IMAGES ©; (BELOW) MASON CUMMINGS / GETTY IMAGES ©

season, and refuses to serve the farmed stuff. Cash only.

Sushi Ran Japanese **$$$**
(☎415-332-3620; www.sushiran.com; 107 Caledonia St; sushi $4-33; ⏰11:45am-2:30pm Mon-Fri, 5-10pm Sun-Thu, to 11pm Fri & Sat; ✎) Many Bay Area residents claim this place is the best sushi spot around. If you didn't reserve ahead, the wine and sake bar next door eases the pain of the long wait for a table.

Getting There & Away

Driving to Sausalito from San Francisco, take the Alexander Ave exit (the first exit after the Golden Gate Bridge) and follow the signs into Sausalito. There are five municipal parking lots in town, and street parking is difficult to find.

The ferry is a fun and easy way to travel to Sausalito. **Golden Gate Ferry** (☎415-455-2000; www.goldengateferry.org; one-way $10.25) operates to and from the San Francisco Ferry Building six to nine times daily and takes 30 minutes. The **Blue & Gold Fleet** (☎415-705-8200; www.blueandgoldfleet.com; Pier 41, Fisherman's Wharf; one-way $11) sails to Sausalito four to five times daily from the Fisherman's Wharf area in San Francisco. Both ferries operate year-round and transport bicycles for free.

Tiburon

At the end of a small peninsula pointing out into the center of the bay, Tiburon is blessed with gorgeous views. The name comes from the Spanish *Punta de Tiburon* (Shark Point). Take the ferry from San Francisco, browse the shops on Main St, grab a bite to eat and you've seen Tiburon. The town is also a jumping-off point for nearby **Angel Island**, a pleasant spot for hiking and cycling and the site of a historic immigration station.

Sleeping & Eating

Water's Edge Hotel Hotel **$$$**
(☎415-789-5999; www.watersedgehotel.com; 25 Main St; r incl breakfast $249-539; ❄@📶)

This hotel, with its deck extending over the bay, is exemplary for its tasteful modernity. Rooms have an elegant minimalism that combines comfort and style, and all afford an immediate view of the bay. The rooms with rustic, high wood ceilings are quite romantic. Perks include complimentary bicycles and evening wine and cheese.

Sam's Anchor Cafe Seafood **$$**
(415-435-4527; www.samscafe.com; 27 Main St; mains $14-32; 11am-9:30pm Mon-Fri, 9:30am-10pm Sat & Sun;) Sam's has been slinging seafood and burgers since 1920, and though the entrance looks like a shambling little shack, the area out back has unbeatable views. On a warm afternoon, you can't beat a cocktail or a tasty plate of sautéed prawns on the deck.

Getting There & Away

Blue & Gold Fleet (415-705-8200; one-way $11) sails daily from either Pier 41 or the Ferry Building in San Francisco to Tiburon. You can transport bicycles for free. From Tiburon, ferries also connect regularly to Angel Island.

Muir Beach

The turnoff to Muir Beach from Hwy 1 is marked by the longest row of mailboxes on the coast. Muir Beach is a quiet little town with a nice beach, but it has no direct bus service. Just north of Muir Beach there are superb views up and down the coast from the **Muir Beach Overlook**; during WWII, watch was kept from the surrounding concrete lookouts for invading Japanese ships.

Sleeping & Eating

Green Gulch Farm & Zen Center Lodge **$$**
(415-383-3134; www.sfzc.org; 1601 Shoreline Hwy; s $90-155, d $160-225, d cottage $350-400, all with 3 meals;) Green Gulch Farm & Zen Center is a Buddhist retreat in the hills above Muir Beach. The center's accommodations are elegant, restful and modern, and delicious buffet-style vegetarian meals are included. A hilltop retreat cottage is 25 minutes away by foot.

Pelican Inn Pub Food **$$$**
(415-383-6000; www.pelicaninn.com; 10 Pacific Way; mains $14-34;) The oh-so-English Tudor-style Pelican Inn is Muir Beach's only commercial establishment. Hikers, cyclists and families come for pub lunches inside its timbered restaurant and cozy bar, perfect for a pint, a game of darts and warming up beside the open fire. The British fare is respectable, but nothing mind-blowing – it's the setting that's magical. Upstairs are seven luxe rooms (from $206) with cushy half-canopy beds.

Stinson Beach

Positively buzzing on warm weekends, Stinson Beach is 5 miles north of Muir Beach. The town flanks Hwy 1 for about three blocks and is densely packed with galleries, shops, eateries and B&Bs. The beach itself is often blanketed with fog, and when the sun's shining it's blanketed with surfers, families and gawkers. There are views of Point Reyes and San Francisco on clear days, and the beach is long enough for a vigorous stroll. From San Francisco it's nearly an hour's drive, though on weekends plan for toe-tapping traffic delays.

Sights & Activities

Three-mile-long **Stinson Beach** is a popular surf spot, but swimming is advised from late May to mid-September only; for updated weather and surf conditions call 415-868-1922. The beach is one block west of Hwy 1.

Audubon Canyon Ranch Wildlife Reserve
(415-868-9244; www.egret.org; donations requested; usually 10am-4pm Sat, Sun & holidays mid-Mar–mid-Jul) Audubon Canyon Ranch is about 3.5 miles north of Stinson Beach on Hwy 1, in the hills above the Bolinas Lagoon. A major nesting ground for great blue herons and great egrets, viewing scopes are set up on hillside blinds where you can watch these magnificent birds congregate to nest and

hatch their chicks in tall redwoods. At low tide, harbor seals often doze on sand bars in the lagoon. Confirm hours, as a recent nesting failure may alter future public access.

Sleeping & Eating

Sandpiper Motel, Cabin **$$**
(☎415-868-1632; www.sandpiperstinsonbeach.com; 1 Marine Way; r $145-225; 📶) Just off Hwy 1 and a quick stroll to the beach, the ten comfortable rooms and cabins of the Sandpiper have gas fireplaces and kitchenettes, and are ensconced in a lush garden and picnic area. Prices dip from November through March; two-night minimum stay on weekends.

Parkside Cafe American **$$**
(☎415-868-1272; www.parksidecafe.com; 43 Arenal Ave; mains $9-25; ⏰7:30am-9pm, coffee from 6am) Parkside Cafe is famous for its hearty breakfasts and lunches, and noted far and wide for its excellent coastal cuisine. Reservations are recommended for dinner.

Point Reyes Station

Though the railroad stopped coming through in 1933 and the town is small, Point Reyes Station is nevertheless the hub of West Marin. Dominated by dairies and ranches, the region was invaded by artists in the 1960s. Today it's an interesting blend of art galleries and tourist shops.

Sleeping & Eating

Cute little cottages, cabins and B&Bs are plentiful in and around Point Reyes. The **West Marin Chamber of Commerce** (☎415-663-9232; www.pointreyes.org) has numerous listings, as does the **Point Reyes Lodging Association** (www.ptreyes.com).

Windsong Cottage Guest Yurt Yurt **$$**
(☎415-663-9695; www.windsongcottage.com; 25 McDonald Ln; d yurt $185-210; 📶) A wood-burning stove, private outdoor hot tub, comfy king bed and kitchen stocked with breakfast supplies make this round sky-lighted abode a cozy slice of heaven.

Tomales Bay Foods & Cowgirl Creamery Deli, Market **$**
(www.cowgirlcreamery.com; 80 4th St; sandwiches $6-12; ⏰10am-6pm Wed-Sun; 🥕) A market in an old barn selling picnic items, including gourmet cheeses and organic produce. Reserve a spot in advance for the small-scale artisanal cheesemaker's demonstration and tasting ($5); watch the curd-making and cutting, then sample a half dozen of the fresh and aged cheeses. All of the milk is local and organic, with vegetarian rennet in the soft cheeses.

Waterfront houses, Tiburon
RICHARD CUMMINS / GETTY IMAGES ©

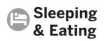

Bovine Bakery Bakery **$**
(www.thebovinebakery.com; 11315 Hwy 1; pastry $3; ⌚6:30am-5pm Mon-Fri, 7am-5pm Sat & Sun) Don't leave town without sampling something buttery from possibly the best bakery in Marin. A sweet bear-claw pastry and an organic coffee are a good way to kick off your morning.

Osteria Stellina Italian **$$**
(☎415-663-9988; www.osteriastellina.com; 11285 Hwy 1; mains $15-24; ⌚11:30am-2:30pm & 5-9pm;) This place specializes in rustic Italian cuisine made from locally sourced produce, including pizza and pasta dishes and Niman Ranch meats. For dessert, the water-buffalo-milk gelato is the way to go.

Point Reyes National Seashore

The windswept peninsula Point Reyes is a rough-hewn beauty that has always lured marine mammals and migratory birds as well as scores of shipwrecks.

Point Reyes National Seashore has 110 sq miles of pristine ocean beaches, and the peninsula offers excellent hiking and camping opportunities. Be sure to bring warm clothing, as even the sunniest days can quickly turn cold and foggy.

Sights & Activities

For an awe-inspiring view, follow the **Earthquake Trail** from the park headquarters at Bear Valley. The trail reaches a 16ft gap between the two halves of a once-connected fence line, a lasting testimonial to the power of the 1906 earthquake that was centered in this area. Another trail leads from the visitors center a short way to **Kule Loklo**, a reproduction of a Miwok village.

Limantour Rd, off Bear Valley Rd about 1 mile north of Bear Valley Visitor Center, leads to the Point Reyes Hostel and **Limantour Beach**, where a trail runs along Limantour Spit with Estero de Limantour on one side and Drakes Bay on the other. The **Inverness Ridge Trail** heads from Limantour Rd up to Mt Vision (1282ft), from where there are spectacular views of the entire national seashore. You can drive almost to the top of Mt Vision from the other side.

Replica Miwok bark huts, Kule Loklo, Point Reyes National Seashore

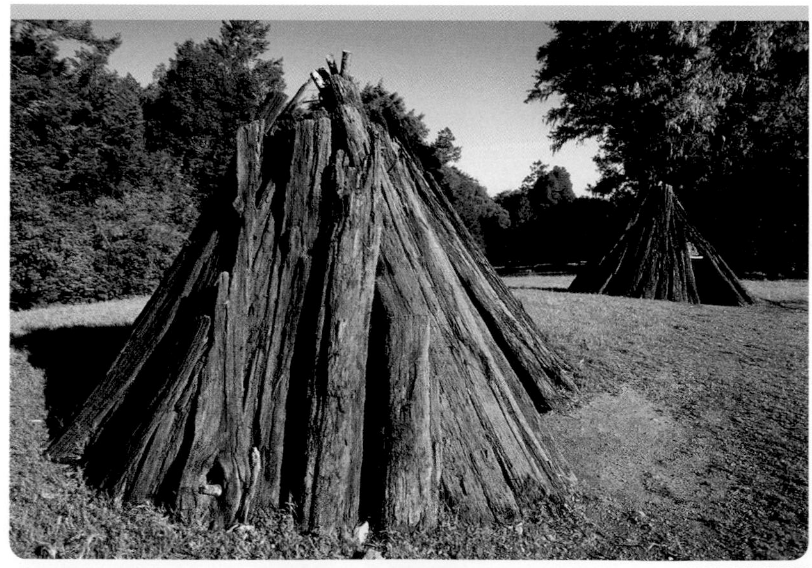

RSCHNAIBLE / GETTY IMAGES ©

Don't Miss
Point Reyes Lighthouse

At the very end of Sir Francis Drake Blvd, with wild terrain and ferocious winds, this spot feels like the ends of the earth and offers the best **whale-watching** along the coast. The lighthouse sits below the headlands; to reach it requires descending over 300 stairs. Nearby **Chimney Rock** is a fine short hike, especially in spring when the wildflowers are blossoming. A nearby viewing area allows you to spy on the park's **elephant seal colony**.

On good-weather weekends and holidays from late December through mid-April, the road to Chimney Rock and the lighthouse is closed to private vehicles. Instead you must take a shuttle ($5, children under 17 free) from Drakes Beach.

NEED TO KNOW

lighthouse 10am-4:30pm Fri-Mon, lens room 2:30-4pm Fri-Mon

In Inverness and across the bay in Marshall (on Hwy 1, 8 miles north of Point Reyes Station), **Blue Waters Kayaking** (**415-669-2600; www.bluewaterskayaking.com; rentals/tours from $50/68;**) has Tomales Bay tours, or rent a kayak and paddle around secluded beaches and rocky crevices solo; no experience necessary.

Pierce Point Rd continues to the huge windswept sand dunes at **Abbotts Lagoon**, full of peeping killdeer and other shorebirds. At the end of the road is Pierce Point Ranch, the trailhead for the 3.5-mile **Tomales Point Trail** through the **Tule Elk Reserve**. The plentiful elk are an amazing sight, standing with their big horns against the backdrop of Tomales Point, with Bodega Bay to the north, Tomales Bay to the east and the Pacific Ocean to the west.

Detour: Berkeley

As the birthplace of the Free Speech and disability-rights movements, and the home of the hallowed halls of the University of California, Berkeley is no bashful wallflower. A national hot spot of (mostly left-of-center) intellectual discourse and one of the most vocal activist populations in the country, this East Bay college town has a mix of graying progressives and idealistic undergrads.

UNIVERSITY OF CALIFORNIA, BERKELEY

The Berkeley campus of the University of California (called 'Cal') is the oldest university in the state. The **UC Berkeley Art Museum** (510-642-0808; www.bampfa.berkeley.edu; 2626 Bancroft Way; adult/child $10/7; 11am-5pm Wed-Sun) has 11 galleries showcasing a huge range of works, from ancient Chinese to cutting-edge contemporary. The complex also houses a sculpture garden.

The **Campanile** (Sather Tower; adult/child $3/2; 10am-3:45pm Mon-Fri, to 4:45pm Sat, 10am-1:30pm & 3-4:45pm Sun;) was modeled on St Mark's Basilica in Venice. The 328ft spire offers fine views of the Bay Area. At the top you can stare up into the carillon of 61 bells, ranging from the size of a cereal bowl to that of a Volkswagen.

GOURMET GHETTO

The section of Shattuck Ave north of University Ave is the 'Gourmet Ghetto,' home to lots of excellent eating establishments, including California cuisine landmark **Chez Panisse** (cafe 510-548-5049, restaurant 510-548-5525; www.chezpanisse.com; 1517 Shattuck Ave; cafe dinner mains $22-30, restaurant prix-fixe dinner $65-100; cafe 11:30am-2:45pm & 5-10:30pm Mon-Thu, to 3pm & to 11:30pm Fri & Sat; restaurant seatings 5:30-6pm & 8-8:45pm Mon-Thu & half hour later Fri & Sat) .

Sleeping & Eating

HI Point Reyes Hostel Hostel **$**
(415-663-8811; www.norcalhostels.org/reyes; 1390 Limantour Spit Rd; dm $25, r $82-120, all with shared bath;) Just off Limantour Rd, this rustic HI property has bunkhouses with warm and cozy front rooms, big-view windows and outdoor areas with hill vistas, and a newer LEED-certified building with four private rooms (two-night minimum stay on weekends) and a stunning modern kitchen. It's in a beautiful secluded valley 2 miles from the ocean and surrounded by lovely hiking trails.

Dancing Coyote Beach Cottages Bungalow **$$$**
(415-669-7200; www.dancingcoyotebeach.com; 12794 Sir Francis Drake Blvd; cottages $200-260;) Serene and comfortable, these four modern cottages back right onto Tomales Bay, with skylights and decks extending the views in all directions. Full kitchens contain tasty breakfast foods and fireplaces are stocked with firewood for foggy nights.

Sir & Star Restaurant **$$$**
(415-663-1034; www.sirandstar.com; cnr Sir Francis Drake Blvd & Hwy 1; mains $20, prix fixe Sat/other nights $75/48; 5-9pm Wed-Sun, plus earlier hours in summer;) In the former Olema Inn, a creaky 1876 building, hyper-local Sir & Star delights with Marin-sourced seasonal bounty like Tomales Bay oysters, Dungeness crab and duck 'faux' gras. Reservations recommended.

Information

The park headquarters, **Bear Valley Visitor Center** (☎415-464-5100; www.nps.gov/pore; ⏰10am-5pm Mon-Fri, from 9am Sat & Sun), is near Olema and has information and maps. You can also get information at the Point Reyes Lighthouse and the **Ken Patrick Center** (☎415-669-1250; ⏰9:30am-4:30pm Sat, Sun & holidays) at Drakes Beach. All visitor centers have slightly longer hours in summer.

Getting There & Away

By car you can get to Point Reyes a few different ways. The curviest is along Hwy 1, through Stinson Beach and Olema. More direct is to exit Hwy 101 in San Rafael and follow Sir Francis Drake Blvd all the way to the tip of Point Reyes. For the latter route, take the Central San Rafael exit and head west on 4th St, which turns into Sir Francis Drake Blvd. By either route, it's about 1½ hours to Olema from San Francisco.

Just north of Olema, where Hwy 1 and Sir Francis Drake Blvd come together, is Bear Valley Rd; turn left to reach the Bear Valley Visitor Center. If you're heading to the further reaches of Point Reyes, follow Sir Francis Drake Blvd through Point Reyes Station and out onto the peninsula (about an hour's drive).

NORTH COAST & THE REDWOODS

Get ready for a fabulous coastal drive, which cuts a winding course on isolated cliffs high above the crashing surf. Compared to the famous Big Sur coast, the serpentine stretch of Hwy 1 up the North Coast is more challenging, more remote and more real: passing farms, fishing towns and hidden beaches. North of Fort Bragg, Bay Area weekenders and antique-stuffed B&Bs give way to lumber wars, pot farmers and an army of carved bears. Last but not least, the route goes through a number of pristine, ancient redwood forests.

Bodega Bay

Bodega Bay is the first pearl in a string of sleepy fishing towns that line the North Coast and was the setting of Hitchcock's terrifying 1963 avian psycho-horror flick *The Birds*. The skies are free from bloodthirsty gulls today (though you best keep an eye on the picnic); it's Bay Area weekenders who descend en masse for extraordinary beaches, tide pools, whale-watching, fishing, surfing and seafood.

Bodega Bay

MITCH DIAMOND / GETTY IMAGES ©

Sights & Activities

Surfing, beachcombing and sportfishing are the main activities here, the last of which requires advance booking. From December to April, the fishing boats host whale-watching trips, which are also good to book ahead.

Bodega Head Lookout

At the peninsula's tip, Bodega Head rises 265ft above sea level. To get there (and see the open ocean), head west from Hwy 1 onto Eastshore Rd, then turn right at the stop sign onto Bay Flat Rd. It's great for **whale-watching**. Landlubbers enjoy **hiking** above the surf, where several good trails include a 3.75-mile trek to Bodega Dunes Campground and a 2.2-mile walk to Salmon Creek Ranch.

Chanslor Ranch Horseback Riding

(**707-785-8849; www.chanslorranch.com; 2660 N Hwy 1; rides from $40**) Just north of town, this friendly outfit leads horseback expeditions along the coastline and the rolling inland hills. Ron, the trip leader, is an amiable, sun-weathered cowboy straight from central casting; he recommends taking the Salmon Creek ride or calling ahead for weather-permitting moonlight rides. The 90-minute beach rides are donation based, and support a horse-rescue program.

Bodega Bay Sportfishing Center Fishing, Whale-Watching

(**707-875-3344; www.bodegacharters.com; 1410 Bay Flat Rd**) Beside the Sandpiper Cafe, this outfit organizes full-day fishing trips ($135) and whale-watching excursions (three hours adult/child $50/35). It also sells bait, tackle and fishing licenses. Call ahead to ask about recent sightings.

Sleeping

Bodega Harbor Inn Motel **$$**

(**707-875-3594; www.bodegaharborinn.com; 1345 Bodega Ave; r $80-155, cottages $135-175;**) Half a block inland from Hwy 1, surrounded by grassy lawns and furnished with both real and faux antiques, this modest yet adorable blue-and-white shingled motel is the town's most economical option. Pets are allowed in some rooms for a fee of $15 plus a security deposit of $50. It also offers a variety of cottages and rentals around town.

Bay Hill Mansion B&B **$$$**

(**877-468-1588; www.bayhillmansion.com; 3919 Bay Hill Rd; d $279-299;**) A luxe B&B in a spacious, modern mansion. The decor is tasteful without much imagination but the cleanliness and comfort standards here are some of the best we've ever seen. Get a private yoga class or massage then the helpful hosts can direct you to the area's best spots. Views overlook trees with just a peek at the bay.

Gerstle Cove, Salt Point State Park

WILLIAM SMITHEY JR / GETTY IMAGES ©

Eating

Spud Point Crab Company Seafood $
(www.spudpointcrab.com; 1910 Westshore Rd; dishes $4-11; ⏲9am-5pm; 👪) In the classic tradition of dockside crab shacks, Spud Point serves salty-sweet crab cocktails and *real* clam chowder, served at picnic tables overlooking the marina. Take Bay Flat Rd to get here.

Terrapin Creek Cafe & Restaurant Californian $$
(☎707-875-2700; www.terrapincreekcafe.com; 1580 Eastshore Dr; lunch mains $12-19, dinner mains $23-30; ⏲11am-2:30pm & 4:30-9pm Thu-Sun; 🍴) Bodega Bay's most exciting upscale restaurant is run by a husband-wife team who espouse the Slow Food movement and serve local dishes sourced from the surrounding area. Comfort-food offerings like black cod roasted in lemon grass and coconut broth are artfully executed, while the Dungeness crab salad is fresh, briny and perfect. Jazz and warm light complete the atmosphere.

Sonoma Coast State Beach

Stretching 17 miles north from Bodega Head to Vista Trail, the glorious **Sonoma Coast State Beach** (☎707-875-3483) is actually a series of beaches separated by several beautiful rocky headlands. Some beaches are tiny, hidden in little coves, while others stretch far and wide. Most of the beaches are connected by vista-studded coastal hiking trails that wind along the bluffs. Exploring this area makes an excellent day-long adventure, so bring a picnic. Be advised however: the surf is often too treacherous to wade, so keep an eye on children.

Sights & Activities

Salmon Creek Beach Beach
Situated around a lagoon, this beach has 2 miles of hiking and good waves for surfing.

Portuguese Beach & Schoolhouse Beach Beaches
Both beaches are very easy to access and have sheltered coves between rocky outcroppings.

Duncan's Landing Beach
Small boats unload near this rocky headland in the morning. A good place to spot wildflowers in the spring.

Shell Beach Beach
A boardwalk and trail leads out to a stretch perfect for tide-pooling and beachcombing.

Goat Rock Beach
Famous for its colony of harbor seals, lazing in the sun at the mouth of the Russian River.

Salt Point State Park

If you stop at only one park along the Sonoma Coast, make it 6000-acre **Salt Point State Park** (☎707-847-3321; per car $8; ⏲visitor center 10am-3pm Sat & Sun Apr-Oct), where sandstone cliffs drop dramatically into the kelp-strewn sea and hiking trails crisscross windswept prairies and wooded hills, connecting pygmy forests and coastal coves rich with tidepools. The 6-mile-wide park is bisected by the San Andreas Fault – the rock on the east side is vastly different from that on the west. Check out the eerily beautiful tafonis, honeycombed-sandstone formations, near Gerstle Cove.

Mendocino

Leading out to a gorgeous headland, Mendocino is the North Coast's salt-washed gem, with B&Bs surrounded by rose gardens, white-picket fences and New England–style redwood water towers. Bay Area weekenders walk along the headland among berry bramble and wildflowers, where cypress trees stand over dizzying cliffs. Nature's power is evident everywhere; from driftwood-littered fields and cave tunnels to the raging surf.

If You Like… Beach Towns

If you like coastal towns such as Bodega Bay, explore these Pacific settlements with a dash of salt spray:

1 GUALALA & ANCHOR BAY
Gualala sits square in the middle of the 'Banana Belt,' a stretch of coast known for unusually sunny weather. Founded as a lumber town in the 1860s, the downtown stretches along Hwy 1 and has a bustling commercial district with cute, slightly upscale shops. Just north, quiet Anchor Bay has several inns and, heading north, a string of secluded, hard-to-find beaches.

2 POINT ARENA
This laid-back little town combines creature comforts with relaxed, eclectic California living. Sit by the docks a mile west of town at Arena Cove and watch surfers mingle with fishermen and hippies. Two miles north of town, the 10-story, 1908 **Point Arena Lighthouse** (707-882-2777; www.pointarenalighthouse.com; 45500 Lighthouse Rd; adult/child $7.50/1; 10am-3:30pm, to 4:30pm late May-early Sep) is the only lighthouse in California you can ascend.

3 ELK
Thirty minutes north of Point Arena, itty-bitty Elk is famous for its stunning cliff-top views of 'sea stacks,' towering rock formations jutting out of the water.

4 MORRO BAY
Morro Bay is about 12 miles northwest of San Luis Obispo. Its biggest claim to fame is Morro Rock, a volcanic peak jutting dramatically from the ocean floor.

5 CAPITOLA
Six miles east of Santa Cruz is the little seaside town of Capitola, nestled quaintly between ocean bluffs and attracting affluent crowds. Downtown is laid out for strolling, with arty shops and touristy restaurants inside seaside houses.

Sights

Mendocino Art Center — Gallery

(707 937 5818, 800 653 3328; www.mendocinoartcenter.org; 45200 Little Lake St; 10am-5pm Apr-Oct, to 4pm Tue-Sat Nov-Mar) Behind a yard of twisting iron sculpture, the city's art center takes up a whole tree-filled block, hosting exhibitions, the 81-seat **Helen Schonei Theatre** and nationally renowned art classes. This is also where to pick up the *Mendocino Arts Showcase* brochure, a quarterly publication listing all the happenings and festivals in town.

Point Cabrillo Lighthouse — Lighthouse

(www.pointcabrillo.org; Point Cabrillo Dr; 11am-4pm Sat & Sun Jan & Feb, daily Mar-Oct, Fri-Mon Nov & Dec) FREE Restored in 1909, this stout lighthouse stands on a 300-acre wildlife preserve north of town, between Russian Gulch and Caspar Beach. **Guided walks** of the preserve leave at 11am on Sundays from May to September. You can also stay in the lighthouse keeper's house and cottages which are now **vacation rentals** (707-937-6124, 866-937-6124; www.pointcabrillo.org; Point Cabrillo Dr; lightkeeper's house from $461, cottages from $132;).

Activities

Catch A Canoe & Bicycles Too! — Canoeing, Kayaking

(707-937-0273; www.catchacanoe.com; Stanford Inn by the Sea, 44850 Comptche-Ukiah Rd; kayak & canoe rental adult/child from $28/14; 9am-5pm) This friendly outfit at the Stanford Inn (p154) south of town rents bikes, kayaks and stable outrigger canoes for trips up the 8-mile Big River tidal estuary, the longest undeveloped estuary in Northern California. No highways or buildings, only beaches, forests, marshes, streams, abundant wildlife and historic logging sites. Bring a picnic and a camera to enjoy the ramshackle remnants of century-old train trestles and majestic blue herons.

Mendocino

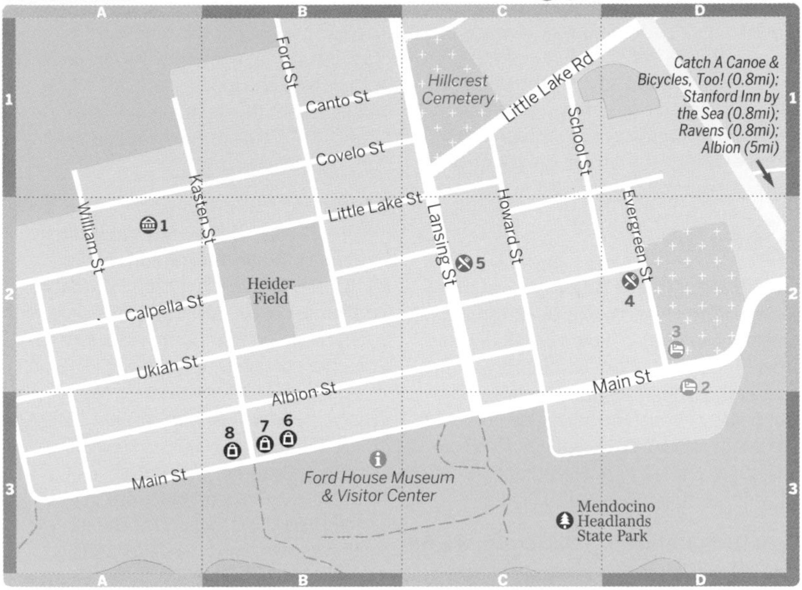

Catch A Canoe & Bicycles, Too! (0.8mi); Stanford Inn by the Sea (0.8mi); Ravens (0.8mi); Albion (5mi)

Hillcrest Cemetery

Heider Field

Ford House Museum & Visitor Center

Mendocino Headlands State Park

Mendocino

Sights

1 Mendocino Art Center A2

Sleeping

2 Alegria D2
3 Raku House D2

Eating

4 Café Beaujolais D2
5 GoodLife Cafe & Bakery C2

Shopping

6 Compass Rose Leather B3
7 Gallery Bookshop B3
8 Out Of This World B3

Mendocino Headlands State Park Outdoors

A spectacular park surrounds the village, with trails crisscrossing the bluffs and rocky coves. Ask at the visitor center about guided weekend walks, including **spring wildflower walks** and **whale-watching**.

Sleeping

Andiron Cabin **$$**

(707-937-1543, 800-955-6478; www.theandiron.com; 6051 N Hwy 1, Little River; most cabins $109-299;) Styled with hip vintage decor, this cluster of 1950s roadside cottages is a refreshingly playful option amid the cabbage-rose and lace aesthetic of Mendocino. Each cabin houses two rooms with complementing themes: 'Read' has old books, comfy vintage chairs and hip retro eyeglasses, while the adjoining 'Write' features a huge chalk board and a ribbon typewriter.

Glendeven B&B **$$$**

(707-937-0083; www.glendeven.com; 8205 N Hwy 1; r $165-320;) This elegant estate 2 miles south of town has organic gardens, grazing llamas (with daily feedings at dusk), forest and oceanside trails and a wine bar serving only Mendocino wines – and that's just the start. Romantic rooms have neutral-toned, soothing decor, fireplaces and top-notch linens. Farm-to-table dinners are available at the bistro.

Alegria B&B **$$$**

(800-780-7905, 707-937-5150; www.oceanfrontmagic.com; 44781 Main St; r $239-299;) A perfect romantic hideaway, beds have views over the coast, decks have ocean view and all rooms have wood-burning fireplaces; outside a gorgeous path leads to a big, amber-grey beach. Ever-so-friendly innkeepers whip up amazing breakfasts served in the sea-view dining area. Less expensive rooms are available across the street at bright and simple **Raku House** (www.rakuhouse.com; r from $159).

Eating

GoodLife Cafe & Bakery Cafe **$**
(www.goodlifecafemendo.com; 10485 Lansing St; light meals $6-10; 8am-4pm) Here's where locals and tourists mingle in an unpretentious, noisy and cozy cafe setting. Get bakery goods and fair-trade coffee for breakfast and comfort food such as mac and cheese or curry bowls at lunch. Lots of gluten-free options are available.

Café Beaujolais Californian **$$$**
(707-937-5614; www.cafebeaujolais.com; 961 Ukiah St; dinner mains $23-35; 11:30am-2:30pm Wed-Sun, dinner from 5:30pm daily) Mendocino's iconic, beloved country-Cal–French restaurant occupies an 1896 house restyled into a monochromatic urban-chic dining room, perfect for holding hands by candlelight. The refined, inspired cooking draws diners from San Francisco, who make this the centerpiece of their trip. The locally sourced menu changes with the seasons, but the Petaluma duck breast served with crispy skin is a gourmand's delight.

Ravens Californian **$$$**
(707-937-5615; www.ravensrestaurant.com; Stanford Inn, Comptche-Ukiah Rd; breakfast $11-15, mains $24-30; 8-10:30am Mon-Sat, to noon Sun, dinner 5:30-10pm;) Ravens brings haute-contemporary concepts to a completely vegetarian and vegan menu. Produce comes from the idyllic organic gardens of the **Stanford Inn** (800-331-8884, 707-937-5615; www.stanfordinn.com; cnr Hwy 1 & Comptche-Ukiah Rd; r $211-299; @), and the bold menu takes on everything from sea-palm strudel and portabella sliders to decadent (guilt-free) desserts.

Shopping

Mendocino's walkable streets are full of cute shops, and the ban on chain stores ensures unique, often upscale gifts. There

Cross-section of redwood tree, Humboldt Redwoods State Park

are many small galleries in town where one-of-a-kind artwork is for sale.

Compass Rose Leather Leather Goods

(45150 Main St) From hand-tooled belts and leather-bound journals to purses and peg-secured storage boxes, the craftsmanship here is unquestionable.

Out Of This World Outdoor Equipment

(45100 Main St) Birders, astronomy buffs and science geeks head directly to this telescope, binocular and science-toy shop.

Gallery Bookshop Books

(www.gallerybookshop.com; 319 Kasten St) Stocks a great selection of books on local topics, titles from California's small presses and specialized outdoor guides.

Information

Ford House Museum & Visitor Center Tourist Information

(707-537-5397; www.mendoparks.org; 735 Main St; 11am-4pm) Maps, books, information and exhibits, including a scale model of 1890 Mendocino.

Humboldt Redwoods State Park & Avenue of the Giants

Don't miss this magical drive through California's largest redwood park, **Humboldt Redwoods State Park** (www.humboldtredwoods.org), which covers 53,000 acres – 17,000 of which are old-growth – and contains some of the world's most magnificent trees. It also boasts three-quarters of the world's tallest 100 trees. Tree huggers take note: these groves rival (and many say surpass) those in Redwood National Park, which is a long drive further north.

Exit Hwy 101 when you see the 'Avenue of the Giants' sign, take this smaller alternative to the interstate; it's an incredible, 32-mile, two-lane stretch. You'll find free driving guides at roadside signboards at both the avenue's southern entrance, 6 miles north of Garberville, near Phillipsville, and at the northern entrance, south of Scotia, at Pepperwood; there are access points off Hwy 101.

South of Weott, a volunteer-staffed **visitor center (707-946-2263; 9am-5pm Apr-Oct, 10am-4pm Nov-Mar)** shows videos and sells maps.

Three miles north, the **California Federation of Women's Clubs Grove** is home to an interesting four-sided hearth designed by renowned San Franciscan architect Julia Morgan in 1931 to commemorate 'the untouched nature of the forest.'

Primeval **Rockefeller Forest**, 4.5 miles west of the avenue via Mattole Rd, appears as it did a century ago. You quickly walk out of sight of cars and feel like you have fallen into the time of dinosaurs. It's the world's largest contiguous old-growth redwood forest, and contains about 20% of all such remaining trees. Check out the subtly variegated rings (count one for each year) on the cross sections of some of the downed giants that are left to mulch back into the earth over the next few hundred years.

In **Founders Grove**, north of the visitor center, the **Dyerville Giant** was knocked over in 1991 by another falling tree. A walk along its gargantuan 370ft length, with its wide trunk towering above, helps you appreciate how huge these ancient trees really are.

The park has over 100 miles of trails for hiking, mountain-biking and horseback riding. Easy walks include short nature trails in Founders Grove and Rockefeller Forest and **Drury-Chaney Loop Trail** (with berry picking in summer). Challenging treks include popular **Grasshopper Peak Trail**, south of the visitor center, which climbs to the 3379ft fire lookout.

Sleeping & Eating

Miranda Gardens Resort Resort **$$**

(707-943-3011; www.mirandagardens.com; 6766 Avenue of the Giants, Miranda; cottages with kitchen $165-300, without kitchen $115-200;) The best indoor stay along the avenue. The

Detour: Ukiah: Hot Springs & Ancient Trees

Opened in 1854, **Vichy** (707-462-9515; www.vichysprings.com; 2605 Vichy Springs Rd, Ukiah; lodge s/d $145/205, creekside r $205/255, cottages from $295;) is the oldest continuously operating mineral-springs spa in California and the only warm-water, naturally carbonated mineral baths in North America. A century ago, Mark Twain, Jack London and Robert Louis Stevenson traveled here for the water's restorative properties. Day use costs $30 for two hours and $50 for a full day.

A clothing-optional resort that's beloved by locals, back-to-the-land hipsters, backpackers and liberal-minded tourists, **Orr Hot Springs** (707-462-6277; tent sites $50-60, d $150-180, cottages $215-250;) has private tubs, a sauna, spring-fed rock-bottomed swimming pool, steam, massage and magical gardens. Day use costs $30. Accommodation includes use of the spa and communal kitchen; some cottages have kitchens. Reservations are essential. To get there from Hwy 101, take N State St exit, go north a quarter of a mile to Orr Springs Rd, then 9 miles west. The steep, winding mountain road takes 30 minutes to drive.

Two miles west of Orr, 1140-acre **Montgomery Woods State Reserve** (Orr Springs Rd) protects five old-growth redwood groves, and some of the best groves within a day's drive from San Francisco. A 2-mile loop trail crosses the creek, winding through the serene forest.

cozy, dark, slightly rustic cottages have redwood paneling, some with fireplaces, and are spotlessly clean. The grounds – replete with outdoor ping pong and a play area for kids and swaying redwoods – have wholesome appeal for families.

Benbow Inn Historic Hotel **$$$**
(707-923-2124, 800-355-3301; www.benbowinn.com; 445 Lake Benbow Dr, Garberville; r $99-315, cottage $230-315;) This inn is a monument to 1920s rustic elegance; the Redwood Empire's first luxury resort is a national historic landmark. Hollywood's elite once frolicked in the Tudor-style resort's lobby, where you can play chess by the crackling fire, and enjoy complimentary afternoon tea and evening hors d'oeuvres.

Point Arena (p152)
KENNAN HARVEY / GETTY IMAGES ©

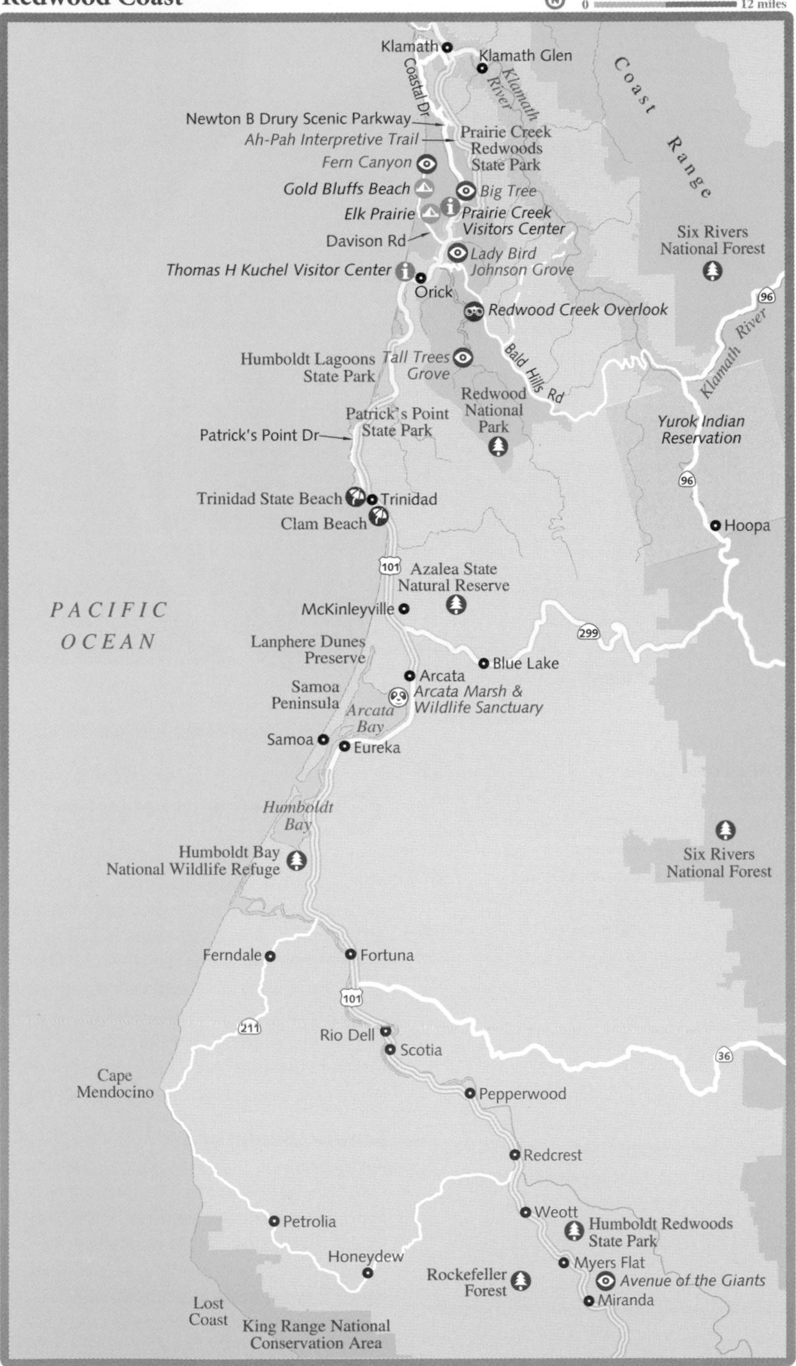

0 20 km
0 12 miles
Klamath
Klamath Glen
Coastal Dr
Klamath River
Coast Range
Newton B Drury Scenic Parkway
Ah-Pah Interpretive Trail
Prairie Creek Redwoods State Park
Fern Canyon
Gold Bluffs Beach
Big Tree
Elk Prairie
Prairie Creek Visitors Center
Davison Rd
Lady Bird Johnson Grove
Thomas H Kuchel Visitor Center
Orick
Six Rivers National Forest
96
Redwood Creek Overlook
Klamath River
Bald Hills Rd
Humboldt Lagoons State Park
Tall Trees Grove
Redwood National Park
Patrick's Point State Park
Patrick's Point Dr
Yurok Indian Reservation
96
Trinidad State Beach
Trinidad
Clam Beach
Hoopa
101
Azalea State Natural Reserve
PACIFIC OCEAN
McKinleyville
299
Lanphere Dunes Preserve
Blue Lake
Arcata
Samoa Peninsula
Arcata Marsh & Wildlife Sanctuary
Arcata Bay
Samoa
Eureka
Humboldt Bay
Humboldt Bay National Wildlife Refuge
Six Rivers National Forest
Ferndale
Fortuna
101
211
Rio Dell
Scotia
36
Cape Mendocino
Pepperwood
Redcrest
Weott
Humboldt Redwoods State Park
Petrolia
Honeydew
Myers Flat
Rockefeller Forest
Avenue of the Giants
Miranda
Lost Coast
King Range National Conservation Area

Below: Victorian-era building, Ferndale; **Right:** Competitors in the annual Kinetic Grand Championship
(BELOW) WITOLD SKRYPCZAK / GETTY IMAGES ©; (RIGHT) JUDY BELLAH / GETTY IMAGES ©

Woodrose Café Breakfast **$$**
(www.woodrosecafe.com; 911 Redwood Dr; meals $9-16; 8am-12pm;) Garberville's beloved cafe serves organic omelets, veggie scrambles and buckwheat pancakes with *real* maple syrup in a cozy room. Lunch brings crunchy salads, sandwiches with all-natural meats and good burritos. Plenty of gluten-free options.

Ferndale

The North Coast's most charming town is stuffed with impeccable Victorians – known locally as 'butterfat mansions' because of the dairy wealth that built them. There are so many, in fact, that the entire place is a state and federal historical landmark. Dairy farmers built the town in the 19th century and it's still run by the 'milk mafia': you're not a local till you've lived here 40 years. A stroll down Main St offers galleries, old-world emporiums and soda fountains.

Sights & Activities

Half a mile from downtown via Bluff St, enjoy short tramps through fields of wildflowers, beside ponds, past redwood groves and eucalyptus trees at 110-acre **Russ Park**. The **cemetery**, also on Bluff St, is amazingly cool with graves dating to the 1800s and expansive views to the ocean. Five miles down Centerville Rd, **Centerville Beach** is one of the few off-leash dog beaches in Humboldt County.

Kinetic Sculpture Museum Museum
(580 Main St; 10am-5pm Mon-Sat, noon-4pm Sun;) This warehouse holds the fanciful, astounding, human-powered contraptions used in the town's annual **Kinetic Grand Championship (www.kineticgrandchampionship.com)**. Shaped like giant fish and UFOs, these colorful piles

of junk propel racers over roads, water and marsh in the May event.

Fern Cottage Historic Building
(☎707-786-4835; www.ferncottage.org; Centerville Rd; group tours per person $10; ⏰by appointment) This 1866 Carpenter Gothic grew to a 32-room mansion. Only one family ever lived here, so the interior is completely preserved.

Sleeping

Shaw House B&B **$$**
(☎800-557-7429, 707-786-9958; www.shawhouse.com; 703 Main St; r $110-159, ste $200-250; 📶🐾) Shaw House, an emblematic 'butterfat palace,' was the first permanent structure in Ferndale, completed by founding father Seth Shaw in 1866. Today, it's California's oldest B&B, set back on extensive grounds. Original details remain, including painted wooden ceilings. Most of the rooms have private entrances, and three have private balconies over a large garden.

Hotel Ivanhoe Historic Hotel **$$**
(☎707-786-9000; www.ivanhoe-hotel.com; 315 Main St; r $95-145; 📶) Ferndale's oldest hostelry opened in 1875. It has four antique-laden rooms and an Old West–style, 2nd-floor gallery, perfect for morning coffee. The adjoining saloon, with dark wood and lots of brass, is an atmospheric place for a nightcap.

Gingerbread Mansion Historic B&B **$$$**
(☎707-786-4000; www.gingerbread-mansion.com; 400 Berding St; r $175-495; 📶) This is the cream of dairyland elegance, an 1898 Queen Anne–Eastlake that's unsurprisingly the town's most photographed building. And the inside is no less extravagant with each room having its own unique (and complex) mix of floral wallpaper, patterned carpeting, grand antique furniture and perhaps a fireplace, wall fresco, stained glass window or Greek statue thrown in for kicks.

Eating

Mario's Lost Coast Cafe Vegetarian, Vegan **$**
(468 Main St; sandwiches $7.25; 10am-3:30pm;) Step into Mario's homey kitchen and be blown away. This guy mills his own flour, bakes his own bread and is so passionate and well-versed in all things food that it's no wonder the soups, sandwiches, salads and baked goods are easily the best vegetarian choices north of Fort Bragg. Coffee is on the house. Cash only.

Poppa Joe's American **$**
(409 Main St; mains $5-7; 11am-8:30pm Mon-Fri, 6am-noon Sat & Sun) You can't beat the atmosphere at this diner, where trophy heads hang from the wall, the floors slant at a precarious angle and old men play poker all day. The American-style breakfasts are good, too – especially the pancakes.

Shopping

Blacksmith Shop & Gallery Metal Goods
(707-786-4216; www.ferndaleblacksmith.com; 455 & 491 Main St) From wrought-iron art to hand-forged furniture, this is the largest collection of contemporary blacksmithing in America.

Eureka

One hour north of Garberville, on the edge of the giant Humboldt Bay, lies Eureka, the largest bay north of San Francisco. With strip-mall sprawl surrounding a lovely historic downtown, it wears its role as the county seat a bit clumsily. Despite a diverse and interesting community of artists, writers, pagans and other free-thinkers, Eureka's wild side slips out only occasionally – but mostly, it goes to bed early. Make for Old Town, a small district with colorful Victorians, good shopping and a revitalized waterfront. For nightlife, head to Eureka's trippy sister up the road, Arcata.

Sights

The free *Eureka Visitors Map*, available at tourist offices, details walking tours and scenic drives, focusing on architecture and history. **Old Town**, along 2nd and 3rd Sts from C St to M St, was once down-and-out, but has been refurbished into a buzzing pedestrian district.

Carson Mansion Historic Building
(143 M St) Of Eureka's fine Victorian buildings the most famous is the ornate 1880s home of lumber baron William Carson. It took 100 men a full year to build. Today it's a private men's club. The **pink house** opposite, at 202 M St, is an 1884 Queen Anne Victorian designed by the same architects and built as a wedding gift for Carson's son.

Sequoia Park Park
(www.sequoiaparkzoo.net; 3414 W St; park free, zoo adult/child $5/3; zoo 10am-5pm May-Sep, Tue-Sun Oct-Apr;) A 77-acre old-growth redwood grove is a surprising green gem in the middle of a residential neighborhood. It has biking and hiking trails, a children's playground and picnic areas, and a small **zoo**.

Morris Graves Museum of Art Museum
(www.humboldtarts.org; 636 F St; admission $5; noon-5pm Thu-Sun) Across Hwy 101, the excellent museum shows rotating Californian artists and hosts performances inside the 1904 **Carnegie library**, the state's first public library.

Sleeping

Abigail's Elegant Victorian Mansion Inn **$$**
(707-444-3144; www.eureka-california.com; 1406 C St; r $115-145;) Inside this National Historic Landmark that's practically a living-history museum, the sweet-as-could-be innkeepers lavish guests with warm hospitality.

Eagle House Inn Historic Inn **$$**
(707-444-3344; www.eaglehouseinn.com; 139 2nd St; r $105-250;) This hulking Victorian

hotel in Old Town has 24 rooms above a turn-of-the-century ballroom that's used for everything from theater and movie performances to special events. Rooms and common areas are tastefully done with precious period decor. The coolest rooms are in the corner and have sitting areas in turrets looking over the street.

Carter House Inns B&B **$$$**
(**800-404-1390, 707-444-8062; www.carterhouse.com; 301 L St, Eureka; r incl breakfast $179-385;**) Recently constructed in period style, this hotel is a Victorian lookalike, holding rooms with top-quality linens and modern amenities; suites have in-room whirlpools and marble fireplaces. The same owners operate three sumptuously decorated houses: a single-level 1900 house, a honeymoon-hideaway cottage and a replica of an 1880s San Francisco mansion, which the owner built himself, entirely by hand.

Eating & Drinking

Brick & Fire Californian **$$**
(**707-268-8959; 1630 F St; pizzas from $14, mains $15-25; 11:30am-8:30pm Mon, Wed & Thu, to 9pm Fri, 5-9pm Sat & Sun**) Eureka's best restaurant is in an intimate, warm-hued, bohemian-tinged setting that is almost always busy. Choose from thin-crust pizzas, delicious salads (try the pear and blue cheese) and an ever-changing selection of appetizers and mains that highlight local produce and wild mushrooms. There's a weighty wine list and servers are well-versed in pairings.

Waterfront Café Oyster Bar
Seafood **$$**
(**102 F St; mains lunch $8-17, dinner $15-24; 9am-9pm**) With a nice bay view and baskets of steamed clams, fish and chips, oysters and chowder, this is a solid bayside lunch for the atmosphere more than anything. A top spot for Sunday brunch, with jazz and Ramos fizzes.

Lost Coast Brewery Brewery
(**707-445-4480; 617 4th St; 10 tasters for $12; 11am-10pm Sun-Thu, to 11pm Fri & Sat;**) The roster of the regular brews at Eureka's colorful brewery might not knock the socks off a serious beer snob (and can't hold a candle to some of the others on the coast), but highlights include the Downtown Brown Ale, Great White and Lost Coast Pale Ale. After downing a few pints, the fried pub grub starts to look pretty tasty.

Arcata

The North Coast's most progressive town, Arcata surrounds a tidy central square that fills with college students, campers, transients and tourists. Sure, it occasionally reeks of patchouli and

Carson Mansion

its politics lean far left, but its earnest embrace of sustainability has fostered some of the most progressive civic action in America. Here, garbage trucks run on biodiesel, recycling gets picked up by tandem bicycle, wastewater gets filtered clean in marshlands and almost every street has a bike lane.

 Sights & Activities

Humboldt State University — University

(HSU; www.humboldt.edu; 1 Harpst St) The University on the northeastern side of town holds the Campus Center for Appropriate Technology (CCAT), a world leader in developing sustainable technologies; on Fridays at 2pm you can take a self-guided tour of the **CCAT House,** a converted residence that uses only 4% of the energy of a comparably sized dwelling.

Arcata Marsh & Wildlife Sanctuary — Wildlife Reserve

On the shores of Humboldt Bay, this has 5 miles of walking trails and outstanding birding. The **Redwood Region Audubon Society (☎826 7031; www.rras.org; donation welcome)** offers guided walks Saturdays at 8:30am, rain or shine, from the parking lot at I St's south end. Friends of Arcata Marsh offer guided tours Saturdays at 2pm from the **Arcata Marsh Interpretive Center (☎707-826-2359; 569 South G St; tours free; ⏰9am-5pm).**

Finnish Country Sauna & Tubs — Day Spa, Massage

(☎707-822-2228; www.cafemokkaarcata.com; cnr 5th & J Sts; 30min per adult/child $9.50/2; ⏰noon-11pm Sun-Thu, to 1am Fri & Sat) Like some kind of Euro-crunchy bohemian dream, these private, open-air redwood hot tubs (half-hour/hour $9/17) and sauna are situated around a small frog pond. The staff is easygoing, and the facility is relaxing, simple and clean. Reserve ahead, especially on weekends.

 Sleeping

Hotel Arcata — Historic Hotel $$

(☎707-826-0217; www.hotelarcata.com; 708 9th St; r $89-156; 📶) Anchoring the plaza, this renovated 1915 brick landmark has friendly staff, high ceilings and comfort-

Redwood National Park

Drive-Thru Trees

Three carved-out (but alive!) redwoods await along Hwy 101, a bizarre holdover from a yesteryear road trip.

Chandelier Drive-Thru Tree (www.drivethrutree.com; 67402 Drive Thru Tree Road, Leggett; per car $5; 8:30am-9pm;) Fold in your mirrors and inch forward, then cool off in the uberkitschy gift shop. In Leggett, and arguably the best one.

Shrine Drive-Thru Tree (13078 Avenue of the Giants, Myers Flat; walk/drive through $3/6; sunrise-sunset;) Look up to the sky as you roll through, on the Avenue of the Giants in Myers Flat. The least impressive of the three.

Tour Thru Tree (430 Highway 169, Klamath; sunrise-sunset;) Take exit 769 in Klamath, squeeze through a tree and check out an emu.

able, old-world rooms of mixed quality. The rooms in front are an excellent perch for people-watching on the square, but the quietest face the back.

Arcata Stay Vacation Rentals **$$**
(877-822-0935, 707-822-0935; www.arcatastay.com; apt from $169) A network of excellent apartment and cottage rentals. There is a two-night minimum and prices go down the longer you stay.

Eating & Drinking

Wildberries Marketplace Market, Deli **$**
(www.wildberries.com; 747 13th St, Arcata; sandwiches $4-10; 6am-midnight;) Wildberries Marketplace is Arcata's best grocery, with natural foods, a good deli, bakery and juice bar.

Japhy's Soup & Noodles Noodles **$**
(1563 G St; mains $5-9; 11:30am-8pm Mon-Fri) Big salads, tasty coconut curry, cold noodle salads and homemade soups – and cheap!

3 Foods Cafe Fusion **$$**
(www.cafeattheendoftheuniverse.com; 835 J St; dishes $4-14; 5:30am-10pm Tue-Thu, to 11pm Fri & Sat, to 9pm Sun;) A perfect fit with the Arcata dining scene: whimsical, creative, worldly small plates (think Thai-style tacos or buttermilk fried chicken) at moderate prices (a prix fixe is sometimes available for $20). The lavender-infused cocktails start things off on the right foot. The 'uber' mac and cheese is the crowd favorite.

Redwood Curtain Brewery Brewery
(550 S G St, suite 6; 3-11pm Mon-Fri, 12-11pm Sat & Sun) A newer brewery (started in 2010), this tiny gem has a varied collection of rave-worthy craft ales and live music most Thursdays and Saturdays. Plus they offer free wheat thins and goldfish crackers to munch on.

Getting Around

Only in Arcata: borrow a bike from **Library Bike** (www.arcata.com/greenbikes; 865 8th St) for a $20 deposit, which gets refunded when you return the bike – up to six months later!

Redwood National Park

A patchwork of public lands jointly administered by the state and federal governments, **Redwood National & State Parks** are a string of state and federally managed land that starts in the south at Redwood National Park and continues north through Prairie Creek Redwoods State Park, by Del Norte Coast Redwoods State Park and ends with Jedediah Smith Redwoods State Park. A smattering of small towns break up the forested area, making it a bit confusing to get a sense of

If You Like... Wildlife-Watching

If you like the grazing elk at Prairie Creek Redwoods State Park and Point Reyes National Seashore, detour to these spots to view animals that squawk, fly or swim:

1 **POINT PIEDRAS BLANCAS**
North of Hearst Castle on the Central Coast, you'll find a bigger colony of northern elephant seals than the corpulent layabouts at Año Nuevo State Park.

2 **PINNACLES NATIONAL PARK**
(**831-389-4486; www.nps.gov/pinn; per car $5**) Explore talus caves of napping bats and witness the spectacle of enormous (and endangered) California condors taking wing at this craggy, out-of-the-way park inland from the Central Coast.

3 **KLAMATH BASIN NATIONAL WILDLIFE REFUGES**
(**530-667-2231; http://klamathbasinrefuges.fws.gov; 4009 Hill Rd, Tulelake; 8am-4:30pm Mon-Fri, 10am-4pm Sat & Sun**) These Northern California refuges provide habitat for a stunning array of bird migrating along the Pacific Flyway. When spring and fall migrations peak, more than a million birds can fill the skies.

the parks as a whole. Prairie Creek and Jedediah Smith parks were originally land slated for clear-cutting, but in the 1960s activists successfully protected them and today all these parks are an International Biosphere Reserve and World Heritage site.

Little-visited compared to their southern brethren, the world's tallest living trees have been standing here for time immemorial, predating the Roman Empire by over 500 years. Prepare to be impressed.

Sights & Activities

Just north of the southern visitor center, turn east onto Bald Hills Rd and travel 2 miles to **Lady Bird Johnson Grove**, one of the park's most spectacular groves, accessible via a gentle 1-mile loop trail. Continue for another 5 miles up Bald Hills to **Redwood Creek Overlook**. On the top of the ridgeline at 2100ft get views over the forest and the entire watershed – provided it's not foggy. Just past the overlook lies the gated turnoff for **Tall Trees Grove**, the location of several of the world's tallest trees. Rangers issue only 50 vehicle permits per day, but they rarely run out. Pick one up, along with the gate-lock combination, from the visitor centers. Allow four hours for the round-trip, which includes a 6-mile drive down a rough dirt road (speed limit 15mph) and a steep 1.3-mile one-way hike, which descends 800ft to the grove.

Information

Unlike most national parks, there are no fees and no highway entrance stations at Redwood National Park, so it's imperative to pick up a free map at the **park headquarters** (**707-464-6101; 1111 2nd St; 9am-5pm Oct-May, to 6pm Jun-Sep**) in Crescent City or at the **Redwood Information Center** (**Thomas H Kuchel Visitor Center; 707-464-6101; www.nps.gov/redw; Hwy 101; 9am-6pm Jun-Aug, to 5pm Sep-Oct & Mar-May, to 4pm Nov-Feb**) in Orick.

Prairie Creek Redwoods State Park

Famous for virgin redwood and unspoiled coastline, this 14,000-acre section of Redwood National & State Parks has spectacular scenic drives and 70 miles of hiking trails, many of which are excellent for children. Pick up maps and information and sit by the river-rock fireplace at **Prairie Creek Visitor Center** (**707-464-6101; 9am-5pm Mar-Oct, 10am-4pm Nov-Feb;**). Kids will love the taxidermy dioramas with push-button, light-up displays. Outside, Roosevelt elk roam grassy flats.

Sights & Activities

Newton B Drury Scenic Parkway Driving

Just north of Orick is the turn off for the 8-mile parkway, which runs parallel to Hwy 101 through untouched ancient redwood forests. This is a not-to-miss short detour off the freeway where you can view the magnificence of these trees. Numerous trails branch off from roadside pullouts, including family-friendly options and trails that fit ADA (American Disabilities Act) requirements, including Big Tree and Revelation Trail.

HIKING & MOUNTAIN BIKING

There are 28 mountain-biking and hiking trails through the park, from simple to strenuous. Those tight on time or with mobility challenges should stop at **Big Tree**, an easy 100yd walk from the car park. Several other easy nature trails start near the visitor center, including the **Revelation Trail** and **Elk Prairie Trail**. Stroll the recently reforested logging road on the **Ah-Pah Interpretive Trail** at the park's north end. The most challenging hike in this corner of the park is the truly spectacular 11.5-mile **Coastal Trail**, which goes through primordial redwoods.

Just past **Gold Bluffs Beach Campground** the road dead ends at **Fern Canyon**, where 60ft fern-covered sheer-rock walls can be seen from Steven Spielberg's *Jurassic Park 2: The Lost World*. This is one of the most photographed spots on the North Coast – damp and lush, all emerald green – and *totally* worth getting your toes wet to see.

Klamath

Giant metal-cast golden bears stand sentry at the bridge across the Klamath River announcing Klamath, one of the tiny settlements that break up Redwood National & State Parks. With a gas station/market, a diner and a casino, Klamath is basically a wide spot in the road. The Yurok Tribal Headquarters is here and the entire town and much of the surrounding area is the tribe's ancestral land. Klamath is roughly an hour north of Eureka.

Pinnacles National Park

Sights & Activities

The mouth of the **Klamath River** is a dramatic sight. Marine, riparian, forest and meadow ecological zones all converge: the birding is exceptional! For the best views, head north of town to Requa Rd and the **Klamath River Overlook** and picnic on high bluffs above driftwood-strewn beaches. On a clear day, this is one of the most spectacular viewpoints on the North Coast, and one of the best whale-watching spots in California. For a good hike, head north along the Coastal Trail. You'll have the sand to yourself at **Hidden Beach**; access the trail at the northern end of Motel Trees.

Just south of the river, on Hwy 101, follow signs for the scenic **Coastal Drive**, a narrow, winding country road (unsuitable for RVs and trailers) atop extremely high cliffs over the ocean. Come when it's not foggy, and mind your driving. Sections of the drive may be closed due to erosion.

Del Norte Coast Redwoods State Park

Marked by steep canyons and dense woods, half the 6400 acres of this **park** (☎707-464-6101, ext 5120; per car day-use $8) are virgin redwood forest, crisscrossed by 15 miles of hiking trails. Even the most cynical of redwood-watchers can't help but be moved.

Pick up maps and inquire about guided hikes at the Redwood National & State Parks Headquarters in Crescent City or the Redwood Information Center in Orick.

Hwy 1 winds in from the coast at rugged, dramatic **Wilson Beach**, and traverses the dense forest, with groves stretching off as far as you can see.

Picnic on the sand at **False Klamath Cove**. Heading north, tall trees cling precipitously to canyon walls that drop to the rocky, timber-strewn coastline, and it's almost impossible to get to the water, except via gorgeous but steep **Damnation Creek Trail** or **Footsteps Rock Trail**.

Between these two, serious hikers will be most greatly rewarded by the Damnation Creek Trail. It's only 4 miles long, but the 1100ft elevation change and cliffside redwoods make it the park's best hike. The unmarked trailhead starts from a parking area off Hwy 101 at mile marker 16.

Crescent Beach Overlook and picnic area has superb wintertime whale-watching. At the park's north end, watch the surf pound at **Crescent Beach**, south of Crescent City via Enderts Beach Rd.

Jedediah Smith Redwoods State Park

The northernmost park in the system of Redwood National & State Parks, the

Klamath River Overlook
STEPHEN SAKS / GETTY IMAGES ©

Trees of Mystery

It's hard to miss the giant statues of Paul Bunyan and Babe the Blue Ox towering over the parking lot at **Trees of Mystery** (707-482-2251; www.treesofmystery.net; 15500 Hwy 101, Klamath; adult/child & senior $14/7; 8am-7pm Jun-Aug, 9am-4pm Sep-May;), a shameless tourist trap with a gondola running through the redwood canopy. The **End of the Trail Museum** located behind the Trees of Mystery gift shop has an outstanding collection of Native American arts and artifacts, and it's *free*.

dense stands at **Jedediah Smith** (707-464-6101, ext 5112; day use $8) are 10 miles northeast of Crescent City (via Hwy 101 east to Hwy 197). The redwood stands are so thick that few trails penetrate the park, but the outstanding 11-mile **Howland Hill scenic drive** cuts through otherwise inaccessible areas (take Hwy 199 to South Fork Rd; turn right after crossing two bridges). It's a rough road, impassable for RVs, but if you can't hike, it's the best way to see the forest.

Stop for a stroll under enormous trees in **Simpson-Reed Grove**. If it's foggy at the coast it may be sunny here. There's a **swimming hole** and picnic area near the park entrance. An easy half-mile trail, departing from the far side of the campground, crosses the **Smith River** via a summer-only footbridge, leading to **Stout Grove**, the park's most famous grove. The **visitor center** (707-464-6101; 10am-4pm daily Jun-Aug, Sat & Sun Sep-Oct & Apr-May) sells hiking maps and nature guides. If you wade in the river, be careful in the spring when currents are swift and the water cold.

NORTHERN MOUNTAINS

The northeast corner is the remote, rugged, refreshingly pristine backyard of a state better known for sunny cities, sandy beaches and foggy groves of redwoods. Don't come here for the company (the towns are hospitable but tiny, with virtually no urban comforts); come to get lost in vast remoteness. Even the two principal attractions, Mt Shasta and Lassen Volcanic National Park, remain uncrowded (and sometimes snow-covered) at the peak of the summer.

Lassen Volcanic National Park

The dry, smoldering, treeless terrain within this 106,000-acre national park stands in stunning contrast to the cool, green conifer forest that surrounds it. That's the summer; in winter tons of snow ensures you won't get too far inside its borders. Still, entering the park from the southwest entrance is to suddenly step into another world. The lavascape offers a fascinating glimpse into the earth's fiery core. In a fuming display, the terrain is marked by roiling hot springs, steamy mud pots, noxious sulfur vents, fumaroles, lava flows, cinder cones, craters and crater lakes.

Sights & Activities

Lassen Peak, the world's largest plug-dome volcano, rises 2000ft over the surrounding landscape to 10,463ft above sea level. Classified as an active volcano, its most recent eruption was in 1917, when it spewed a giant cloud of smoke, steam and ash 7 miles into the atmosphere. The national park was created the following year to protect the newly formed landscape. Some areas destroyed by the blast, including the aptly named

Lava Beds National Monument

A wild landscape of charred volcanic rock and rolling hills, this remote **national monument** (☎530-667-8113; www.nps.gov/labe; 7-day entry per car $10) is reason enough to visit the region. Off Hwy 139, immediately south of Tule Lake National Wildlife Refuge, it's a truly remarkable 72-sq-mile landscape of volcanic features – lava flows, craters, cinder cones, spatter cones, shield volcanoes and amazing lava tubes.

Lava tubes are formed when hot, spreading lava cools and hardens when the surfaces get exposed to the cold air. The lava inside is thus insulated and stays molten, flowing away to leave an empty tube of solidified lava. Nearly 400 such tubular caves have been found in the monument, and many more are expected to be discovered. About two dozen or so are currently open for exploration by visitors.

On the south side of the park, the **visitor center** (☎530-667-2282, ext 230; ⌚8am-6pm, shorter hours in winter) has free maps, activity books for kids and information about the monument and its volcanic features and history. Rangers loan flashlights, rent helmets and kneepads for cave exploration and lead summer interpretive programs, including campfire talks and guided cave walks. To explore the caves it's essential you use a high-powered flashlight, wear good shoes and long sleeves (lava is sharp), and not go alone.

The weathered Modoc **petroglyphs** at the base of a high cliff at the far northeastern end of the monument, called Petroglyph Point, are thousands of years old.

Devastated Area, northeast of the peak, are recovering impressively.

Hwy 89, the road through the park, wraps around Lassen Peak on three sides and provides access to dramatic geothermal formations, pure lakes, gorgeous picnic areas and remote hiking trails.

In total, the park has 150 miles of **hiking trails**, including a 17-mile section of the Pacific Crest Trail. Experienced hikers can attack the **Lassen Peak Trail**; it takes at least 4½ hours to make the 5-mile round trip. Early in the season you'll need snow- and ice-climbing equipment to reach the summit. An easy 1.3 mile hike partway up, to the Grandview viewpoint, is suitable for families. The 360-degree view from the top is stunning, even if the weather is a bit hazy

Near the Kom Yah-mah-nee visitor facility, a gentler 2.3-mile trail leads through meadows and forest to **Mill Creek Falls**. Further north on Hwy 89 you'll recognize the roadside **sulfur works** by its bubbling mud pots, hissing steam vent, fountains and fumaroles. At **Bumpass Hell** a moderate 1.5-mile trail and boardwalk lead to an active geothermal area, with bizarrely colored pools and billowing clouds of steam.

Sleeping

Manzanita Lake Camping Cabins Cabin, Campground **$**
(☎summer 530-335-7557, winter 530-200-4578; www.lassenrecreation.com; Hwy 89, near Manzanita Lake; cabins $63-89; 📶) These recently built log cabins enjoy a lovely position on one of Lassen's lakes, and they come in one- and two-bedroom options and slightly more basic eight-bunk configurations, which are a bargain for groups. They all have bear boxes, propane heaters and fire rings, but no bedding, electricity or running water.

Information

Due to snow, the road through the park is usually only open from June to October. Call ahead or check the park website (www.nps.gov/lavo) to get current weather conditions.

Kom Yah-mah-nee Visitor Facility (530-595-4480; 9am-6pm Jun-Sep, hours vary Oct-May) About half a mile north of the park's southwest entrance, this handsome center is certified at the highest standard by the US Green Building Council. Inside there are educational exhibits (including a cool topographical volcano), a bookstore, an auditorium, a gift shop and a restaurant. Visitor information and maps available.

Mt Shasta

'Lonely as God, and white as a winter moon,' wrote poet Joaquin Miller. Mt Shasta's beauty is certainly intoxicating, and the closer you get the headier you begin to feel. Dominating the landscape, the mountain is visible for more than 100 miles from many parts of Northern California and southern Oregon. Though not California's highest peak (at 14,162ft it ranks fifth), Mt Shasta is especially magnificent because it rises alone on the horizon, unrivaled by other mountains.

The mountain and surrounding **Shasta-Trinity National Forest** (www.fs.usda.gov/stnf/) are crisscrossed by trails and dotted with alpine lakes. It's easy to spend days or weeks camping, hiking, river rafting, skiing, mountain-biking and boating.

Sights & Activities

You can drive almost the whole way up the mountain via the Everitt Memorial Hwy (Hwy A10) and see exquisite views at any time of year. Simply head east on Lake St from downtown Mt Shasta City, then turn left onto Washington Dr and keep going. **Bunny Flat** (6860ft), which has a trailhead for Horse Camp and the Avalanche Gulch summit route, is a busy place with parking spaces, information signboards and a toilet. The section of highway beyond Bunny Flat is only open from about mid-June to October, depending on snow, but if it's clear, it's worth the trouble. This road leads to **Lower Panther Meadow**, where trails

Mt Shasta, seen from Bunny Flat

connect the campground to a Wintu sacred spring, in the upper meadows near the **Old Ski Bowl** (7800ft) parking area. Shortly thereafter is the highlight of the drive, **Everitt Vista Point** (7900ft), where a short interpretive walk from the parking lot leads to a stone-walled outcrop affording exceptional views of Lassen Peak to the south, Mt Eddy and Marble Mountains to the west and the whole Strawberry Valley below.

Mt Shasta Board & Ski Park Snow Sports
(**snow reports 530-926-8686; www.skipark.com; full-day lift tickets adult/child $44/25; 9am-9pm Thu-Sat, to 4pm Sun-Tue)** On the south slope of Mt Shasta, off Hwy 89 heading toward McCloud, this winter skiing and snowboarding park opens depending on snowfall. The park has a 1435ft vertical drop, 32 alpine runs and 18 miles of cross-country trails. These are all good for beginner and intermediate skiers, and are a less-crowded alternative to the slopes around Lake Tahoe.

Mt Shasta City & McCloud

No town, no matter how lovely – and Mt Shasta City (population 3330) is lovely – could compete with the surrounding natural beauty here. Still, downtown itself is charming; you can spend hours poking around bookstores, galleries and boutiques. Orienting yourself is easy with Mt Shasta looming over the east side of town. The tiny, historic mill town of McCloud sits at the foot of the south slope of Mt Shasta, and is a quieter alternative to staying in Mt Shasta City. It's also the closest settlement to Mt Shasta Board & Ski Park.

Sleeping

Historic Lookout & Cabin Rentals Cabin **$**
(**530-994-2184; www.fs.fed.us/r5/shastatrinity; up to 4 people from $75)** What better way to rough it in style than to bunk down in a fire lookout on forested slopes? Built from the 1920s to '40s, cabins come with cots, tables and chairs, have panoramic views and can accommodate four people. Details about Hirz Mountain, Little Mt

Lone Cypress (p183), 17-Mile Drive

ROBERTO SONCIN GEROMETTA / GETTY IMAGES ©

Hoffman and Post Creek Lookouts can all be found on the national forest website.

Shasta MountInn B&B **$$**
(☎530-926-1810; www.shastamountinn.com; 203 Birch St; r without/with fireplace $135/185; 📶) Only antique on the outside, this bright Victorian 1904 farmhouse on the inside is all relaxed minimalism, bold colors and graceful decor. Each airy room has a great bed and exquisite views of the luminous mountain. Enjoy the expansive garden, wraparound deck, outdoor sauna and a complimentary foot massage. Not relaxed enough yet? Chill on the perfectly placed porch swings.

McCloud River Mercantile Hotel Inn **$$**
(☎530-964-2330; www.mccloudmercantile.com; 241 Main St; r incl breakfast $129-250 ; 📶) Stoll up the stairs to the 2nd floor of McCloud's central Mercantile and try not to fall in love; it's all high ceilings, exposed brick and a perfect marriage of preservationist class and modern panache. The rooms with antique furnishings are situated within open floor plans.

Eating

Mount Shasta Pastry Bakery **$**
(610 S Mt Shasta Blvd; pastries from $1.95; ⏰6am-2:30pm Mon-Sat, 7am-1pm Sun) Walk in hungry and you'll be plagued with an existential breakfast crisis: the feta spinach quiche, or the Tuscan scramble? The flaky croissants or a divine apricot turnover? It also serves terrific sandwiches, gourmet pizza and Peet's Coffee.

Trinity Café Californian **$$**
(☎530-926-6200; 622 N Mt Shasta Blvd; mains $17-28; ⏰5-9pm Tue-Sat) Trinity has long rivaled the Bay Area's best. The owners, who hail from Napa, infuse the bistro with a Wine Country feel and an extensive, excellent wine selection. The organic menu ranges from delectable, perfectly cooked steaks, savory roast game hen to creamy-on-the-inside, crispy-on-the-outside polenta. The warm, mellow mood makes for an overall delicious experience.

Mountain Star Cafe Vegetarian **$**
(241 Main St; mains $7-9; ⏰8am-3pm; 🖉) Deep within the creaking Mercantile, this sweet lunch counter is a surprise, serving vegetarian specials made from locally sourced, organic produce. Some options on the menu during a recent visit included morale biscuits and gravy, a garlicky tempeh Ruben, roast vegetable salad and a homemade oat and veggie burger.

CENTRAL COAST

Too often forgotten or dismissed as 'fly-over' country between San Francisco and LA, this idyllic stretch of California coast is packed with wild Pacific beaches, misty redwood forests where hot springs hide, and rolling golden hills of fertile vineyards and farm fields.

Pescadero

A foggy speck of coastside crossroads between the cities of San Francisco and Santa Cruz, 150-year-old Pescadero is a close-knit rural town of sugar-lending neighbors and community pancake breakfasts. But on weekends the tiny downtown strains its seams with long-distance cyclists panting for carbohydrates and day trippers dive-bombing in from the oceanfront highway. With its cornucopia of tide-pool coves and parks of sky-blotting redwood canopy, city dwellers come here to slow down and smell the sea breeze wafting over fields of bushy artichokes.

Sights & Activities

A number of pretty sand beaches speckle the coast, though one of the most interesting places to stop is **Pebble Beach**, a tide-pool jewel a mile and a half south of Pescadero Creek Rd. As the name implies, the shore is awash in bite-sized eye candy of agate, jade and carnelians, and sandstone troughs are pockmarked by groovy honeycombed formations called tafoni.

Pigeon Point Light Station Lighthouse

(☎650-879-2120; www.parks.ca.gov/?page_id=533) Five miles south along the coast, the 115ft Light Station is one of the tallest lighthouses on the West Coast. The 1872 landmark had to close access to the upper tower when chunks of its cornice began to rain from the sky (restoration is in progress), but the beam still flashes brightly and the bluff is a prime though blustery spot to scan for breaching gray whales. The hostel here is one of the best in the state.

 Sleeping & Eating

HI Pigeon Point Lighthouse Hostel Hostel $

(☎650-879-0633; www.norcalhostels.org/pigeon; 210 Pigeon Point Rd; dm $26-27, r/t/6-bed $75/101/162, all with shared bath; @ 📶) Not your workaday HI outpost, this highly coveted coastside hostel is all about location. Check in early to snag a spot in the outdoor hot tub, and contemplate roaring waves as the lighthouse beacon races through a starburst sky.

Pescadero Creek Inn B&B Inn $$

(☎888-307-1898; www.pescaderocreekinn.com; 393 Stage Rd; r $155-225; 📶) Unwind in the private two-room cottage or one of the spotless Victorian rooms in a restored 100-year-old farmhouse with a tranquil creekside garden.

Duarte's Tavern American $$

(☎650-879-0464; www.duartestavern.com; 202 Stage Rd; mains $11-45; ⏰7am-9pm) You'll rub shoulders with fancy-pants foodies, spandex-swathed cyclists and dusty cowboys at this casual, surprisingly unpretentious fourth-generation family restaurant. Duarte's is the culinary magnet of Pescadero – for many the town and eatery are synonymous. Feast on crab cioppino and a half-and-half split of the cream of artichoke and green chili soups, and bring it home with a wedge of olallieberry pie.

Año Nuevo State Park

More raucous than a full-moon beach rave, thousands of boisterous elephant seals party down year-round on the dunes of Año Nuevo point, their squeals and barks reaching fever pitch during the winter pupping season. The beach is 5 miles south of Pigeon Point and 27 miles north of Santa Cruz.

In the midwinter peak season, during the mating and birthing time from December 15 to the end of March, you must plan well ahead if you want to visit the reserve, because visitors are only permitted access through heavily booked guided tours. For the busiest period, mid-January to mid-February, it's recommended you

Elephant seals, Año Nuevo State Park

MINT IMAGES - FRANS LANTING / GETTY IMAGES ©

book eight weeks ahead. If you haven't booked, bad weather can sometimes lead to last-minute cancellations.

The rest of the year, advance reservations aren't necessary, but visitor permits from the entrance station are required; arrive before 3pm from September through November and by 3:30pm from April through August.

Although the **park office** (**650-879-2025, recorded information 650-879-0227; www.parks.ca.gov/?page_id=523**) can answer general questions, high-season tour bookings must be made at 800-444-4445 or http://anonuevo.reserveamerica.com. When required, these tours cost $7, and parking is $10 per car year-round. From the ranger station it's a 3- to 5-mile round-trip hike on sand, and a visit takes two to three hours. No dogs are allowed on-site, and visitors aren't permitted for the first two weeks of December.

There's another more convenient and free viewing site further south along the Central Coast near Point Piedras Blancas.

Santa Cruz

Santa Cruz has marched to its own beat since long before the Beat Generation. It's counterculture central, a touchy-feely, new-agey city famous for its leftie-liberal politics and live-and-let-live ideology.

On the waterfront is the famous beach boardwalk, and in the hills redwood groves embrace the University of California, Santa Cruz (UCSC) campus.

Sights

One of the best things to do in Santa Cruz is simply stroll, shop and people-watch along **Pacific Ave** downtown. A 15-minute walk away is the beach and the **Municipal Wharf**, where seafood restaurants, gift shops and barking sea lions compete for attention. Ocean-view **West Cliff Dr** follows the waterfront southwest of the wharf, paralleled by a paved recreational path.

Sun-kissed Santa Cruz has warmer beaches than often-foggy Monterey. *Baywatch* it isn't, but 29 miles of coastline reveal a few Hawaii-worthy beaches, craggy coves, some primo surf spots and big sandy stretches where your kids will have a blast. Too bad fog ruins many a summer morning; it often burns off by the afternoon.

Santa Cruz Beach Boardwalk — Amusement Park

(**831-423-5590; www.beachboardwalk.com; 400 Beach St; per ride $3-6, all-day pass $32-40; daily Apr-early Sep, seasonal hours vary;**) The West Coast's oldest beachfront amusement park, this 1907 boardwalk has a glorious old-school Americana vibe. The smell of cotton candy mixes with the salt air, punctuated by the squeals of kids hanging upside down on carnival rides. Famous thrills include the Giant Dipper, a 1924 wooden roller coaster, and the 1911 Looff carousel, both National Historic Landmarks. During summer, catch free mid-week movies and Friday night concerts by rock veterans you may have thought were already dead.

Seymour Marine Discovery Center — Museum

(**831-459-3800; http://seymourcenter.ucsc.edu; 100 Shaffer Rd; adult/child 3-16yr $8/6; 10am-5pm Tue-Sun year-round, also 10am-5pm Mon Jul & Aug;**) By Natural Bridges State Beach, this kids' educational center is part of UCSC's Long Marine Laboratory. Interactive natural-science exhibits include tidal touch pools and aquariums, while outside you can gawk at the world's largest blue-whale skeleton. Guided one-hour tours happen at 1pm, 2pm and 3pm daily, with a special 30-minute tour for families with younger children at 11am; sign up for tours in person an hour in advance (no reservations).

Sanctuary Exploration Center — Museum

(**831-421-9993; www.montereybay.noaa.gov; 35 Pacific Ave; 10am-5pm Wed-Sun;**) FREE Operated by the Monterey Bay National Marine Sanctuary, this educational museum near the beach boardwalk is an interactive multimedia experience that teaches kids and adults about the bay's marine treasures, watershed conservation and high-tech underwater exploration for scientific research.

Below: Santa Cruz Municipal Wharf (p173); **Right:** Sea Swings, Santa Cruz Beach Boardwalk (p173)

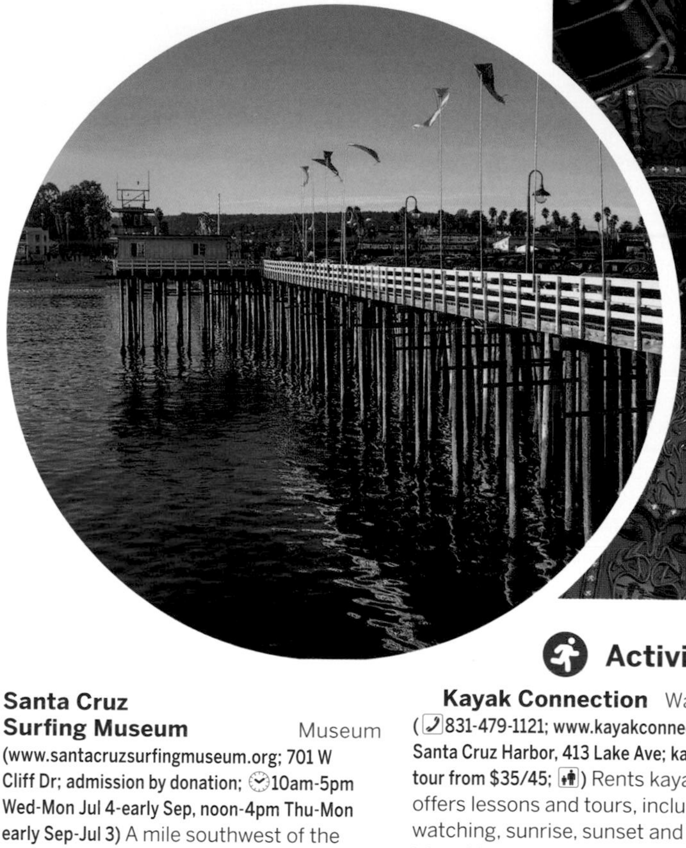

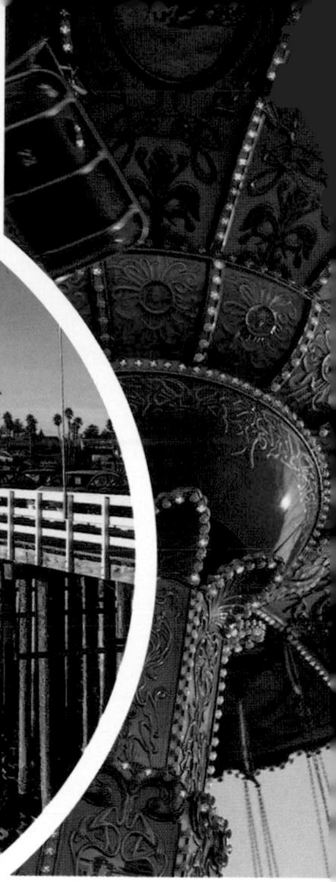

Santa Cruz Surfing Museum Museum

(www.santacruzsurfingmuseum.org; 701 W Cliff Dr; admission by donation; ⏲10am-5pm Wed-Mon Jul 4-early Sep, noon-4pm Thu-Mon early Sep-Jul 3) A mile southwest of the wharf along the coast, this tiny museum inside an old lighthouse is packed with memorabilia, including vintage redwood surfboards. Fittingly, Lighthouse Point overlooks two popular surf breaks.

Big Basin Redwoods State Park Park

(☎831-338-8860; www.bigbasin.org; 21600 Big Basin Way, Boulder Creek; entry per car $10, campsites $35; ⏲sunrise-sunset) A 45-minute drive north of Santa Cruz into the mountains via Hwys 9 and 236, this state park protects over 18,000 acres of redwood forest and 80 miles of trails, one of which drops to the Pacific.

Activities

Kayak Connection Water Sports

(☎831-479-1121; www.kayakconnection.com; Santa Cruz Harbor, 413 Lake Ave; kayak rental/tour from $35/45; 👪) Rents kayaks and offers lessons and tours, including whale-watching, sunrise, sunset and full-moon trips. Also rents stand-up paddle boarding (SUP) sets (from $25), wetsuits ($10) and boogie boards ($10).

Santa Cruz Surf School Surfing

(☎831-345-8875, 831-426-7072; www.santacruzsurfschool.com; 131 Center St; 2hr group/1hr private lesson $90/120; 👪) Wanna learn to surf? Near the wharf, friendly male and female instructors will have you standing and surfing on your first day out.

Sleeping

HI Santa Cruz Hostel Hostel $

(☎831-423-8304; www.hi-santacruz.org; 321 Main St; dm $26-29, r $60-110, all with

shared bath; check-in 5-10pm; @) Budget overnighters dig this cute hostel at the century-old Carmelita Cottages surrounded by flowering gardens, just two blocks from the beach. Cons: midnight curfew, daytime lockout (10am to 5pm) and three-night maximum stay. Reservations are essential. Street parking costs $2.

Adobe on Green B&B B&B **$$**
(831-469-9866; www.adobeongreen.com; 103 Green St; r incl breakfast $169-219;) Peace and quiet are the mantras at this place, a short walk from Pacific Ave. The hosts are practically invisible, but their thoughtful touches are everywhere, from boutique-hotel amenities in spacious, stylish and solar-powered rooms to breakfast spreads from their organic gardens.

Dream Inn Hotel **$$$**
(866-774-7735, 831-426-4330; www.dreaminnsantacruz.com; 175 W Cliff Dr; r $249-479; @) Overlooking the wharf from a spectacular hillside perch, this chic boutique hotel is as stylish as Santa Cruz gets. Rooms have all mod cons, while the beach is just steps away. Don't miss happy hour at Aquarius restaurant's ocean-view bar. Parking is $25.

Eating

Penny Ice Creamery Ice Cream **$**
(www.thepennyicecreamery.com; 913 Cedar St; snacks $2-4; noon-11pm;) With a cult following, this artisan ice-cream shop crafts zany flavors such as bourbon candied ginger, lemon verbena blueberry and ricotta apricot all from scratch using local, organic and wild-harvested ingredients. Even plain old vanilla is special: it's made using Thomas Jefferson's original recipe. Also at a **downtown kiosk** (1520 Pacific Ave; noon-6pm Sun-Thu, to 9pm Fri & Sat;) and near **Pleasure Point** (820 41st Ave; noon-9pm Sun-Thu, to 11pm Fri & Sat;).

Soif Bistro **$$$**
(831-423-2020; www.soifwine.com; 105 Walnut Ave; small plates $5-17, mains $19-25; 5-9pm Sun-Thu, to 10pm Fri & Sat) Bon vivants

Mystery Spot

A kitschy, old-fashioned tourist trap, Santa Cruz's **Mystery Spot** (☎831-423-8897; www.mysteryspot.com; 465 Mystery Spot Rd; admission $6; ⏰10am-4pm Mon-Fri, to 5pm Sat & Sun Sep-May, 10am-6pm Mon-Fri, 9am-7pm Sat & Sun Jun-Aug) has scarcely changed since it opened in 1940. On a steeply sloping hillside, compasses seem to point crazily, mysterious forces push you around and buildings lean at odd angles. Make reservations, or risk being stuck waiting for a tour. It's about 4 miles northeast of downtown, up into the hills on Branciforte Dr. Parking costs $5.

swoon over a heady selection of three dozen international wines by the glass, paired with a sophisticated, seasonally driven Euro-Cal menu. Expect tastebud-ticklers like roasted beet salad with fava beans and maple vinaigrette or squid-ink linguini with spicy chorizo.

Laili Afghani **$$$**
(☎831-423-4545; www.lailirestaurant.com; 101b Cooper St; mains $13-28; ⏰11:30am-2:30pm Tue-Sun, 5-9pm Tue-Thu & Sun, to 10pm Fri & Sat) A chic downtown dining oasis, family-owned Laili invites diners in with an elegant high-ceilinged dining room and garden patio. Share apricot-chicken flatbread, tart pomegranate eggplant, roasted cauliflower with saffron, succulent lamb kebabs and more. Service is spotty. Reservations advised.

Monterey

Working-class Monterey is all about the sea. What draws many tourists is the world-class aquarium, overlooking Monterey Bay National Marine Sanctuary, which protects dense kelp forests and a sublime variety of marine life, including seals and sea lions, dolphins and whales. The city possesses the best-preserved historical evidence of California's Spanish and Mexican periods, with many restored adobe buildings. An afternoon's wander through downtown's historic quarter promises to be more edifying than time spent in the tourist ghettos of Fisherman's Wharf and Cannery Row.

Sights

Cannery Row Historic Site
(👪) John Steinbeck's novel *Cannery Row* immortalized the sardine-canning business that was Monterey's lifeblood for the first half of the 20th century. A bronze **bust** of the Pulitzer Prize–winning writer sits at the bottom of Prescott Ave, just steps from the unabashedly touristy experience that the famous row has devolved into. The historical **Cannery Workers Shacks** at the base of flowery Bruce Ariss Way provide a sobering reminder of the hard lives led by Filipino, Japanese, Spanish and other immigrant laborers.

Monterey State Historic Park Historic Site
(☎audio tour 831-998-9458, info 831-649-7118; www.parks.ca.gov) FREE Old Monterey is home to an extraordinary assemblage of 19th-century brick and adobe buildings, administered as Monterey State Historic Park, all found along a 2-mile self-guided walking tour portentously called the 'Path of History.' You can inspect dozens of buildings, many with charming gardens; expect some to be open while others aren't, according to a capricious schedule dictated by unfortunate state-park budget cutbacks.

Pacific House Museum
(☎831-649-7118; www.parks.ca.gov; 20 Custom House Plaza; admission incl Custom House $3, incl walking tour $5; ⏰10am-4pm Fri-Sun) Find out what's currently open at Monterey

State Historic Park, grab a free map and buy tickets for guided walking tours inside this 1847 adobe building, where fascinatingly in-depth exhibits covering the state's early Spanish, Mexican and American eras.

Nearby are some of the state park's historical highlights, including an **old whaling station** and **California's first theater**. A 10-minute walk south is the **old Monterey jail** featured in John Steinbeck's novel *Tortilla Flat*.

Museum of Monterey Museum
(831-372-2608; www.museumofmonterey.org; 5 Custom House Plaza; adult/child under 13yr $8/free, free 1st Wed of each month; 10am-7pm Tue-Sat & noon-5pm Sun late May-early Sep, 10am-5pm Wed-Sat & noon-5pm Sun early Sep-late May;) Near the waterfront, this voluminous modern exhibition hall illuminates Monterey's salty past, from early Spanish explorers to the roller-coaster–like rise and fall of the local sardine industry that brought Cannery Row to life in the mid-20th century. Highlights include a ship-in-a-bottle collection and the historic Fresnel lens from Point Sur's lighthouse.

Activities

WHALE-WATCHING

You can spot whales off the coast of Monterey Bay year-round. The season for blue and humpback whales runs from April to early December, while gray whales pass by from mid-December through March. Tour boats depart from downtown's Fisherman's Wharf and also Moss Landing. Reserve trips at least a day in advance; be prepared for a bumpy, cold ride.

Sanctuary Cruises Whale-Watching
(831-917-1042; www.sanctuarycruises.com; 7881 Sandholdt Rd; adult/child 12yr & under $50/40;) Departing from Moss Landing, 20 miles north of Monterey, this biodiesel boat runs recommended whale-watching and dolphin-spotting tours (reservations essential).

Monterey Whale Watching Boat Tour
(831-205-2370, 888-223-9153; www.montereywhalewatching.com; 96 Fisherman's Wharf; 2½hr tour adult/child 5-11yr $45/35;) Several daily departures; no children under age five or pregnant women allowed.

Monterey Bay Whale Watch Boat Tour
(831-375-4658; www.montereybaywhalewatch.com; 84 Fisherman's Wharf; 3hr tour adult/child 4-12yr from $40/27;) Morning and afternoon departures; young children are welcome on board.

Cannery Row

Monterey Peninsula

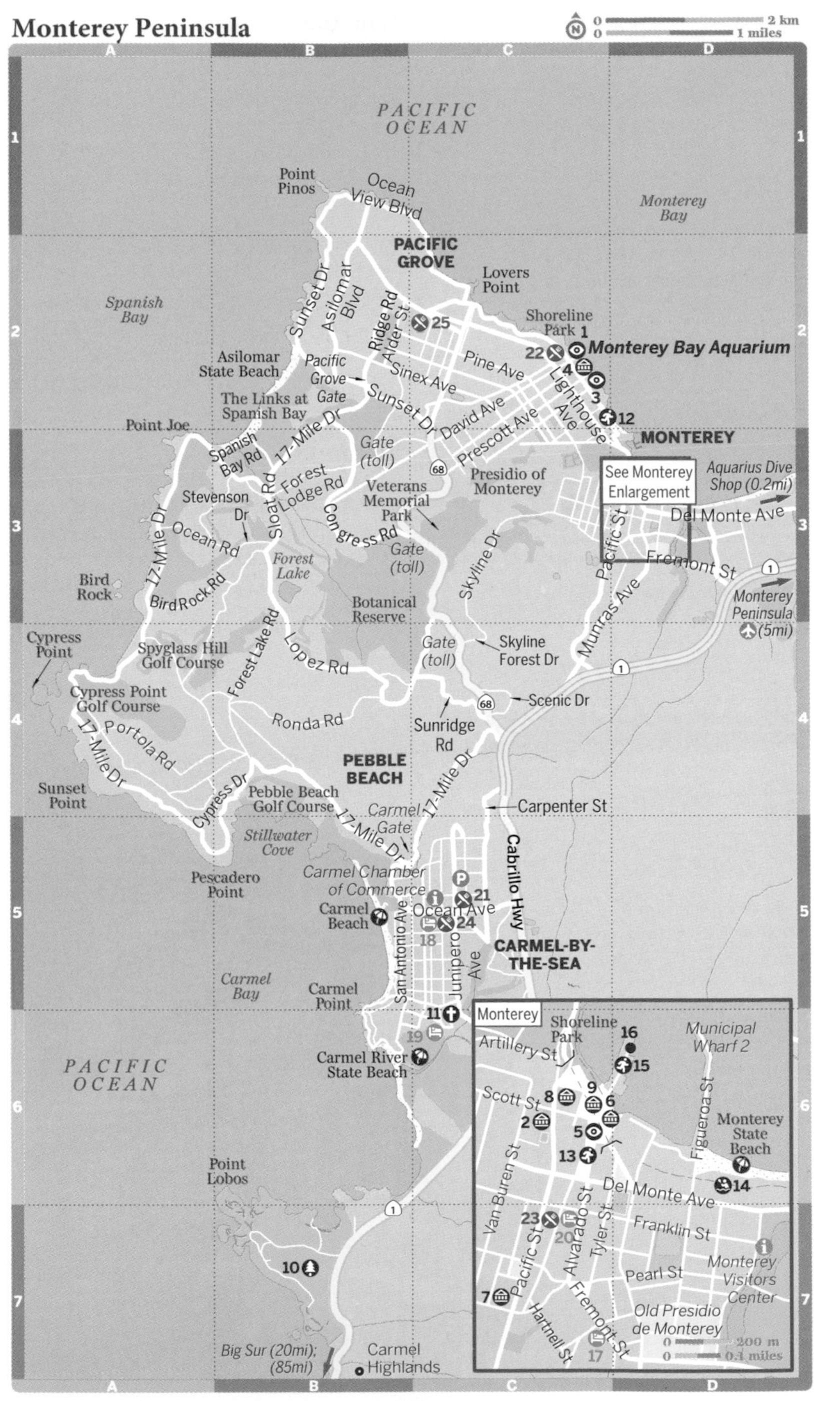

PACIFIC OCEAN
Point Pinos
Ocean View Blvd
Monterey Bay
PACIFIC GROVE
Lovers Point
Spanish Bay
Sunset Dr
Asilomar Blvd
Ridge Rd
Alder St
25
Shoreline Park
1
22
Monterey Bay Aquarium
Asilomar State Beach
Pacific Grove Gate
Sinex Ave
Pine Ave
4
3
The Links at Spanish Bay
Sunset Dr
Lighthouse Ave
David Ave
Point Joe
17-Mile Dr
Prescott Ave
12
MONTEREY
Spanish Bay Rd
Gate (toll)
Presidio of Monterey
See Monterey Enlargement
Aquarius Dive Shop (0.2mi)
Stevenson Dr
Sloat Rd
Forest Lodge Rd
Veterans Memorial Park
Del Monte Ave
17-Mile Dr
Ocean Rd
Congress Rd
Gate (toll)
Skyline Dr
Pacific St
Fremont St
Forest Lake
Bird Rock
Bird Rock Rd
Botanical Reserve
Munras Ave
Monterey Peninsula (5mi)
Cypress Point
Spyglass Hill Golf Course
Forest Lake Rd
Lopez Rd
Gate (toll)
Skyline Forest Dr
Cypress Point Golf Course
Scenic Dr
Ronda Rd
Sunridge Rd
Portola Rd
17-Mile Dr
PEBBLE BEACH
Sunset Point
Cypress Dr
Pebble Beach Golf Course
Carmel Gate
17-Mile Dr
Carpenter St
Stillwater Cove
Cabrillo Hwy
Pescadero Point
Carmel Chamber of Commerce
21
Carmel Beach
Ocean Ave
24
18
San Antonio Ave
Junipero Ave
CARMEL-BY-THE-SEA
Carmel Bay
Carmel Point
11
19
Carmel River State Beach
PACIFIC OCEAN
Point Lobos
10
Big Sur (20mi); (85mi)
Carmel Highlands
Monterey
Shoreline Park
16
Municipal Wharf 2
Artillery St
15
Scott St
8
9
6
2
5
Figueroa St
Monterey State Beach
13
Van Buren St
Del Monte Ave
14
23
20
Alvarado St
Tyler St
Franklin St
Pacific St
Pearl St
Monterey Visitors Center
7
Hartnell St
Fremont St
Old Presidio de Monterey
17
0 200 m
0 0.1 miles
0 2 km
0 1 miles

Monterey Peninsula

DIVING & SNORKELING

Monterey Bay offers world-renowned diving and snorkeling, including off **Lovers Point** in Pacific Grove and at **Point Lobos State Natural Reserve** near Carmel-by-the-Sea. You'll want a wet suit year-round.

Aquarius Dive Shop Diving
(831-375-1933; www.aquariusdivers.com; 2040 Del Monte Ave; snorkel/scuba-gear rental $35/65, dive tours from $65) Talk to this five-star PADI operation for gear rentals, classes and guided dives into Monterey Bay.

KAYAKING & CYCLING

Monterey Bay Kayaks Kayaking
(831-373-5357, 800-649-5357; www.montereybaykayaks.com; 693 Del Monte Ave; kayak or SUP set rental per day from $30, tours from $55) Rents kayaks and SUP equipment, offers paddling lessons and leads guided tours of Monterey Bay, including full-moon and sunrise trips.

Adventures by the Sea Cycling, Kayaking
(831-372-1807; www.adventuresbythesea.com; 299 Cannery Row; rental per day kayak or bicycle $30, SUP set $50, tours from $60;) Beach cruisers, electric bike and water-sports gear rentals and tours available at multiple locations on Cannery Row and **downtown** (831-372-1807; www.adventures-bythesea.com; 210 Alvarado St;).

Sleeping

Casa Munras Boutique Hotel **$$**
(800-222-2446, 831-375-2411; www.hotelcasamunras.com; 700 Munras Ave; r from $120;) Built around an adobe hacienda once owned by a 19th-century Spanish colonial don, chic modern rooms come with lofty beds and some gas fireplaces, all inside two-story motel-esque buildings. Splash in a heated outdoor pool, unwind at the tapas bar or take a sea-salt scrub in the tiny spa. Pet fee $50.

Monterey Hotel Historic Hotel **$$**
(800-966-6490, 831-375-3184; www.montereyhotel.com; 406 Alvarado St; r $80-220;) In the heart of downtown and a short walk from Fisherman's Wharf, this 1904 edifice harbors five-dozen small, somewhat noisy, but freshly renovated rooms with Victorian-styled furniture and plantation shutters. No elevator. Parking $17.

Eating

First Awakenings American **$$**
(www.firstawakenings.net; American Tin Cannery, 125 Oceanview Blvd; mains $8-12; 7am-2pm Mon-Fri, to 2:30pm Sat & Sun;) Sweet and savory, all-American breakfasts and lunches and bottomless pitchers of coffee merrily weigh down outdoor tables at this cafe uphill from the aquarium. Try the unusual 'bluegerm' pancakes or a spicy Sonoran fritatta.

Passionfish Seafood **$$$**
(831-655-3311; www.passionfish.net; 701 Lighthouse Ave, Pacific Grove; mains $16-32;

5-9pm Sun-Thu, to 10pm Fri & Sat) Fresh, sustainable seafood is artfully presented in any number of inventive ways, and a seasonally inspired menu also carries slow-cooked meats and vegetarian dishes spotlighting local farms. The earth-tone decor is spare, with tables squeezed conversationally close together. An ambitious world-ranging wine list is priced near retail, and there are twice as many Chinese teas as wines by the glass.

Montrio Bistro Californian **$$$**
(831-648-8880; www.montrio.com; 414 Calle Principal; mains $17-29; 5-10pm Sun-Thu, to 11pm Fri & Sat;) Inside a 1910 firehouse, Montrio looks dolled up with leather walls and iron trellises, but the tables have butcher paper and crayons for kids. The eclectic seasonal menu mixes local, organic fare with Californian, Asian and European flair, including tapas-style small bites and mini desserts.

Information

Monterey Visitors Center (877-666-8373, 831-657-6400; www.seemonterey.com; 401 Camino El Estero; 9am-6pm Mon-Sat, to 5pm Sun, closing 1hr earlier Nov-Mar) Free tourist brochures; ask for a *Monterey County Literary & Film Map*.

Carmel-by-the-Sea

Quaint Carmel-by-the-Sea has the well-manicured feel of a country club. Fairy-tale Comstock cottages, with their characteristic stone chimneys and pitched gable roofs, dot the town.

Founded as a seaside resort in the 1880s – fairly odd, given that its beach is often blanketed in fog – Carmel quickly attracted famous artists and writers, such as Sinclair Lewis and Jack London, and their hangers-on. An artistic flavor survives in the more than 100 galleries that line the town's immaculate streets.

Sights

San Carlos Borroméo de Carmelo Mission Church
(www.carmelmission.org; 3080 Rio Rd; adult/child 7-17yr $6.50/2; 9:30am-7pm) Monterey's original mission was established by Franciscan friar Junípero Serra in 1770, but poor soil and the corrupting influence of Spanish soldiers forced the move to Carmel two years later. Today this is one of California's most strikingly beautiful missions, an oasis of solemnity bathed in flowering gardens. The mission's adobe chapel was later replaced with an arched basilica made of stone quarried in the Santa Lucia Mountains. Museum exhibits are scattered throughout the meditative complex.

Activities

Not always sunny, **Carmel Beach** is a gorgeous white-sand crescent, where pampered pups excitedly run off-leash.

Point Lobos State Natural Reserve Park
(831-624-4909; www.pointlobos.org; Hwy 1; per car $10; 8am-7pm, closes 30min after sunset early Nov–mid-Mar;) They bark, they bathe and they're fun to watch – sea lions are the stars here at Punta de los Lobos Marinos (Point of the Sea Wolves), almost 4 miles south of Carmel, where a dramatically rocky coastline offers excellent tide-pooling. The full perimeter hike is 6 miles, but shorter walks take in wild scenery too, including Bird Island, shady cypress groves, the historical Whaler's Cabin and Devil's Cauldron, a whirlpool that gets splashy at high tide.

Sleeping

Cypress Inn Boutique Hotel **$$$**
(831-624-3871, 800-443-7443; www.cypress-inn.com; Lincoln St, at 7th Ave; r incl breakfast from $245;) Done up in Spanish Colonial style, this 1929 inn is co-owned by movie star Doris Day. Airy terra-cotta hallways with colorful tiles give it a

JOHN ELK / GETTY IMAGES ©

Don't Miss
Monterey Bay Aquarium

Monterey's most mesmerizing experience is its enormous aquarium, built on the former site of the city's largest sardine cannery. All kinds of aquatic creatures are on proud display, from kid-tolerant sea stars and slimy sea slugs to animated sea otters and surprisingly nimble 800lb tuna. The aquarium is much more than an impressive collection of glass tanks – thoughtful placards underscore the bay's cultural and historical contexts.

Every minute, upwards of 2000 gallons of seawater are pumped into the three-story **kelp forest**, re-creating as closely as possible the natural conditions you see out the windows to the east. The large fish of prey are at their charismatic best during mealtimes; divers hand-feed at 11:30am and 4pm. More entertaining are the sea otters, which may be seen basking in the **Great Tide Pool** outside the aquarium, where they are readied for reintroduction to the wild.

Even new-agey music and the occasional infinity-mirror illusion don't detract from the astounding beauty of jellyfish in the **Jellies Gallery**. To see marine creatures – including hammerhead sharks and green sea turtles – that outweigh kids many times over, ponder the awesome **Open Sea** tank. Upstairs and downstairs you'll find **touch pools**, where you can get close to sea cucumbers, bat rays and tidepool creatures. Younger kids will love the interactive, bilingual **Splash Zone**, with penguin feedings at 10:30am and 3pm.

NEED TO KNOW

info 831-648-4800, tickets 866-963-9645; www.montereybayaquarium.org; 886 Cannery Row; adult/child 3-12yr/youth 13-17yr $40/25/30; 9:30am-6pm daily Jun, to 6pm Mon-Fri, to 8pm Sat & Sun Jul-Aug, 10am-5pm or 6pm daily Sep-May;

Mediterranean feel, while sunny rooms face the courtyard. Pet fee $30.

Mission Ranch Inn **$$$**
(☎800-538-8221, 831-624-6436; www.missionranchcarmel.com; 26270 Dolores St; r incl breakfast $135-300; 📶) If woolly sheep grazing on green fields by the beach doesn't convince you to stay here, maybe knowing Hollywood icon Clint Eastwood restored this historic ranch will. Accommodations are shabby-chic, even a tad rustic.

Eating

Bruno's Market & Deli Deli, Market **$**
(www.brunosmarket.com; cnr 6th & Junípero Aves; sandwiches $6-9; ⏲7am-8pm) Small supermarket deli counter makes a saucy sandwich of oakwood-grilled tri-tip beef and stocks all the accoutrements for a beach picnic, including Sparkys root beer from Pacific Grove.

Mundaka Spanish, Tapas **$$**
(☎831-624-7400; www.mundakacarmel.com; San Carlos St, btwn Ocean & 7th Aves; small plates $6-25; ⏲5:30-10pm Sun-Wed, to 11pm Thu-Sat) This stone courtyard hideaway is a svelte escape from Carmel's stuffy 'newly wed and nearly dead' crowd. Taste Spanish tapas and house-made sangria while world beats spin.

Information

Downtown buildings have no street numbers, so addresses specify the street and nearest intersection only.

Carmel Chamber of Commerce (☎800-550-4333, 831-624-2522; www.carmelcalifornia.org; San Carlos St, btwn 5th & 6th Aves; ⏲10am-5pm) Free maps and brochures, including local art gallery guides.

Getting There & Around

Carmel is 5 miles south of Monterey via Hwy 1. Find free unlimited parking in a **municipal lot** (cnr 3rd & Junípero Aves) behind the Vista Lobos building.

Big Sur

Big Sur is more a state of mind than a place you can pinpoint on a map. There are no traffic lights, banks or strip malls, and when the sun goes down, the moon and the stars are the only streetlights – if summer's dense fog hasn't extinguished them, that is. Much ink has been spilled extolling the raw beauty and energy of this precious piece of land shoehorned between the Santa Lucia Range and the Pacific Ocean, but nothing quite prepares you for your first glimpse of the craggy, unspoiled coastline.

San Carlos Borroméo de Carmelo Mission (p180)

Scenic Drive: 17-Mile Drive

WHAT TO SEE

Pacific Grove and Carmel are linked by the spectacularly scenic, if overhyped **17-Mile Drive**, which meanders through Pebble Beach, a wealthy private resort. It's no chore staying within the 25mph limit – every curve in the road reveals another postcard vista, especially when wildflowers bloom. Cycling the route is enormously popular, but try to do it during the week, when traffic isn't as heavy, and ride with the flow of traffic, from north to south.

Using the self-guided touring map provided upon entry, you can easily pick out landmarks such as **Spanish Bay**, where explorer Gaspar de Portolá dropped anchor in 1769; treacherously rocky **Point Joe**, which in the past was often mistaken for the entrance to Monterey Bay and thus became the site of several shipwrecks; and **Bird Rock**, also a haven for harbor seals and sea lions. The ostensible pièce de résistance is the trademark **Lone Cypress**, which has perched on a seaward rock for more than 250 years.

Besides the coastal scenery, star attractions at Pebble Beach include world-famous **golf courses**, where a celebrity and pro tournament happens every February.

THE ROUTE

Operated as a toll road by the Pebble Beach Company, the **17-Mile Drive** (www.pebblebeach.com; per car/bicycle $10/free) is open from sunrise to sunset.

TIME & MILEAGE

There are five separate gates for the 17-Mile Drive; how far you drive and how long you take is up to you. For the most scenery, enter at Pacific Grove (off Sunset Dr) and exit at Carmel.

In the 1950s and '60s, Big Sur – so named by Spanish settlers living on the Monterey Peninsula, who referred to the wilderness as *el país grande del sur* ('the big country to the south') – became a retreat for artists and writers, including Henry Miller and Beat Generation visionaries such as Lawrence Ferlinghetti. Today Big Sur attracts self-proclaimed artists, new-age mystics, latter-day hippies and city slickers seeking to unplug and reflect more deeply on this emerald-green edge of the continent.

Sights & Activities

The following sights are listed in geographical order from north to south, to aid navigation. At state parks, your parking fee ($10) receipt is valid for same-day entry to all except Limekiln; don't skip paying the entry fee by parking illegally outside along Hwy 1.

Bixby Bridge Landmark

Less than 15 miles south of Carmel, this landmark spanning Rainbow Canyon is one of the world's highest single-span bridges. Completed in 1932, it was built by prisoners eager to lop time off their sentences. There's a perfect photo-op pull-off on the bridge's north side. Before Bixby Bridge was constructed, travelers had to trek inland on what's now called the **Old Coast Rd**, a rough dirt route that reconnects after 11 miles with Hwy 1 near Andrew Molera State Park.

Driving Hwy 1

Driving this narrow two-lane highway through Big Sur and beyond is very slow going. Allow about three hours to cover the distance between the Monterey Peninsula and San Luis Obispo, much more if you want to explore the coast. Traveling after dark can be risky and more to the point, it's futile, since you'll miss out on the seascapes. Watch out for cyclists and always use signposted roadside pullouts to let faster-moving traffic pass.

Point Sur State Historic Park Lighthouse

(**831-625-4419; www.pointsur.org; off Hwy 1; adult/child 6-17yr from $12/5; tours usually at 1pm Wed, 10am Sat & Sun Nov-Mar, 10am & 2pm Wed & Sat, 10am Sun Apr-Oct, also 10am Thu Jul & Aug**) A little over 6 miles south of Bixby Bridge, Point Sur rises like a velvety green fortress out of the sea. It looks like an island, but is actually connected to land by a sandbar. Atop the volcanic rock sits an 1889 stone lightstation, which was staffed until 1974. During three-hour guided tours, ocean views and tales of the lighthouse keepers' family lives are engrossing. Meet your tour guide at the locked farm gate ¼-mile north of Point Sur Naval Facility.

Andrew Molera State Park Park

(**831-667-2315; www.parks.ca.gov; Hwy 1; per car $10; 30min before sunrise-30min after sunset;**) Named after the farmer who first planted artichokes in California, this oft-overlooked park is a trail-laced pastiche of grassy meadows, ocean bluffs and rugged sandy beaches offering excellent wildlife watching. Look for the entrance just over 8 miles south of Bixby Bridge.

South of the parking lot, you can learn all about endangered California condors inside the **Big Sur Discovery Center** (**831-624-1202; www.ventanaws.org/discovery_center/; 10am-4pm Sat & Sun late May-early Sep;**) FREE. At the bird-banding lab inside a small shed, naturalists carry out long-term species monitoring programs.

Pfeiffer Big Sur State Park Park

(**831-667-2315; www.parks.ca.gov; 47225 Hwy 1; per car $10; 30min before sunrise-30min after sunset;**) Named after Big Sur's first European settlers who arrived in 1869, this is Big Sur's largest state park, where hiking trails loop through stately redwood groves. The most popular hike – to 60ft-high **Pfeiffer Falls**, a delicate cascade hidden in the forest, which usually runs from December to May – is a 2-mile round-trip. Built in the 1930s by the Civilian Conservation Corps (CCC), rustic Big Sur Lodge stands near the park entrance, about 13 miles south of Bixby Bridge.

Pfeiffer Beach Beach

(**www.fs.usda.gov/lpnf; end of Sycamore Canyon Rd; per car $10; 9am-8pm;**) This phenomenal, crescent-shaped and dog-friendly beach is known for its huge double rock formation, through which waves crash with life-affirming power. It's often windy, and the surf is too dangerous for swimming. But dig down into the wet sand – it's purple! That's because manganese garnet washes down from the craggy hillsides above. To get here from Hwy 1, make a sharp right onto Sycamore Canyon Rd, marked by a small yellow sign that says 'narrow road' at the top.

Henry Miller Memorial Library Arts Center

(**831-667-2574; www.henrymiller.org; 48603 Hwy 1; 11am-6pm**) 'It was here in Big Sur I first learned to say Amen!' wrote novelist Henry Miller, a Big Sur denizen from 1944 to 1962. More of a beatnik memorial, alt-cultural venue and bookshop, this community gathering spot was never Miller's home. The house belonged to Miller's friend, painter Emil White, until his death and is now run by a nonprofit group. Stop by to browse and hang out on the front deck. It's about 0.4 miles south of Nepenthe restaurant.

Julia Pfeiffer Burns State Park — Park

(☎831-667-2315; www.parks.ca.gov; Hwy 1; per car $10; ⏰30min before sunrise-30min after sunset; 👪) If you're chasing waterfalls, swing into this state park named for a Big Sur pioneer. From the parking lot, the 1.3-mile round-trip Overlook Trail rushes downhill toward the ocean, passing through a tunnel underneath Hwy 1. Everyone comes to photograph 80ft-high **McWay Falls**, which tumbles year-round over granite cliffs and freefalls into the sea – or the beach, depending on the tide. The park entrance is on the east side of Hwy 1, about 8 miles south of Nepenthe restaurant.

Sleeping

With few exceptions, Big Sur's lodgings do not have TVs and rarely have telephones. There aren't a lot of rooms overall, so demand often exceeds supply and prices can be outrageous. Reservations are essential everywhere.

Pfeiffer Big Sur State Park Campground — Campground $

(☎reservations 800-444-7275; www.reserveamerica.com; 47225 Hwy 1; tent & RV sites $35-50; 🐾) Best for novice campers and families with young kids, here over 200 campsites nestle in a redwood-shaded valley. Facilities include drinking water, fire pits and coin-op hot showers and laundry.

Deetjen's Big Sur Inn — Lodge $$

(☎831-667-2377; www.deetjens.com; 48865 Hwy 1; d $90-260) Nestled among redwoods and wisteria, this creekside conglomeration of rustic, thin-walled rooms and cottages was built by Norwegian immigrant Helmuth Deetjen in the 1930s. Some antiques-furnished rooms are warmed by wood-burning fireplaces, while cheaper

Bixby Bridge (p183)

ones share bathrooms. This timeless escape isn't for everyone.

Glen Oaks Motel Motel, Cabin **$$$**
(☎831-667-2105; www.glenoaksbigsur.com; 47080 Hwy 1; d $225-390;) At this 1950s redwood-and-adobe motor lodge, rustic rooms and cabins seem effortlessly chic. Dramatically transformed by eco-conscious design, snug romantic hideaway rooms all have gas fireplaces. Woodsy cabins in a redwood grove have kitchenettes and share outdoor fire pits, or retreat to the one-bedroom house with a full kitchen.

Treebones Resort Lodge **$$$**
(☎805-927-2390, 877-424-4787; www.treebonesresort.com; 71895 Hwy 1; d with shared bath incl breakfast from $215;) Don't let the word 'resort' throw you. Yes, it's got an ocean-view hot tub, heated pool and massage treatments. But a unique woven 'human nest' and canvas-sided yurts with polished pine floors, quilt-covered beds, sink vanities and redwood decks are more like glamping, with little privacy. Communal bathrooms and showers are a short stroll away. Wi-fi in main lodge only.

Post Ranch Inn Resort **$$$**
(☎831-667-2200; www.postranchinn.com; 47900 Hwy 1; d incl breakfast from $675;) The last word in luxurious coastal getaways, the exclusive Post Ranch pampers demanding guests with slate spa tubs, wood-burning fireplaces, private decks and walking sticks for coastal hikes. Ocean-view rooms celebrate the sea, while treehouses lack views and have a bit of sway. Paddle around the clifftop infinity pool after a shamanic-healing session or yoga class in the spa. No children allowed.

Eating & Drinking

Nepenthe Californian **$$$**
(☎831-667-2345; www.nepenthebigsur.com; 48510 Hwy 1; mains $15-42; ⏲11:30am-4:30pm & 5-10pm) Nepenthe comes from a Greek word meaning 'isle of no sorrow,' and indeed, it's hard to feel blue while sitting by the fire pit on this aerial terrace. Just-okay California cuisine (try the renowned Ambrosia burger) takes a backseat to the views and Nepenthe's history – Orson Welles and Rita Hayworth briefly owned a cabin here in the 1940s. Reservations essential.

Mission San Luis Obispo de Tolosa (p188)

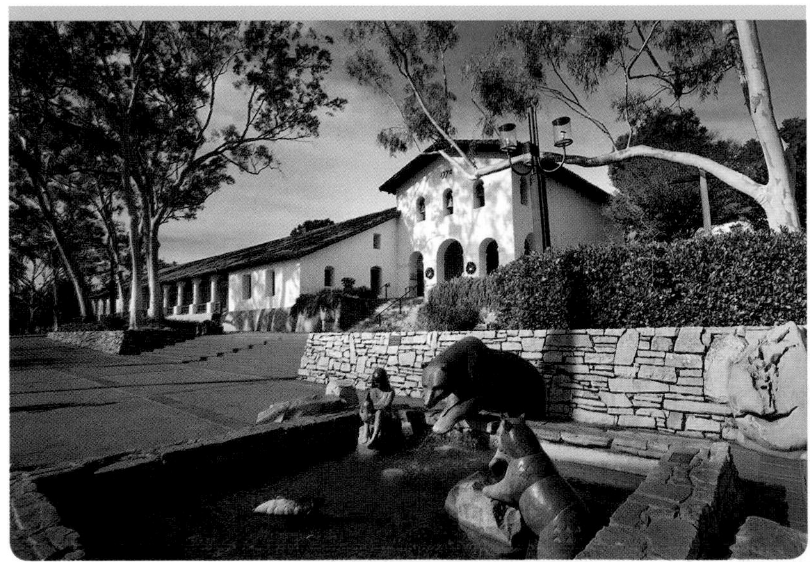

GERI LAVROV / GETTY IMAGES ©

Big Sur Roadhouse Californian, Cajun **$$$**
(☎831-667-2370; www.bigsurroadhouse.com; 47080 Hwy 1; mains breakfast & lunch $6-12, dinner $19-30; ⏰7:30am-9pm) This Southern-spiced roadhouse glows with color-splashed artwork and an outdoor fire pit. At riverside tables, fork into a New Orleans-born chef's hearty fried chicken, white grits with serrano peppers, po' boy sandwiches and blackened locally caught fish with a dollop of fresh herb aioli. Reservations advised for dinner, or just stop by for drinks and small bites such as buttermilk biscuits.

Big Sur Taphouse Bar
(www.bigsurtaphouse.com; 47520 Hwy 1; ⏰noon-10pm Mon-Thu, to midnight Fri & Sat, 10am-10pm Sun; 📶) Down California craft beers and regional wines on the back deck or by the fireplace inside this high-ceilinged wooden bar with board games, sports TVs and pub grub from the next-door deli.

Information

Visitors often wander into businesses along Hwy 1 and ask, 'How much further to Big Sur?' In fact, there is no town of Big Sur as such, though you may see the name on maps. Cellphone reception is spotty to non-existent.

Big Sur Chamber of Commerce (☎831-667-2100; www.bigsurcalifornia.org; ⏰9am-1pm Mon, Wed & Fri) Pick up the free *Big Sur Guide* newspaper at local businesses; it's also available online as a free PDF download.

Point Piedras Blancas

Many lighthouses still stand along California's coast, but few offer such a historically evocative seascape. Federally designated an outstanding natural area, the jutting, windblown grounds of this 1875 **light station** (☎805-927-7361; www.piedrasblancas.gov; tours adult/child 6-17yr $10/5; ⏰tours usually 9:45am Mon-Sat mid-Jun–Aug, 9:45am Tue, Thu & Sat Sep–mid-Jun) – one of the tallest on the West Coast – have been laboriously replanted with native flora. Picturesquely, everything looks much the way it did when the first lighthouse keepers helped ships find safe harbor at the whaling station at San Simeon Bay. Guided tours currently meet at 9:45am on Tuesdays, Thursdays and Saturdays at the old Piedras Blancas Motel, about 1.5 miles north of the lightstation.

At a signposted vista point, around 4.5 miles north of Hearst Castle, you can observe a colony of northern elephant seals bigger than the one at Año Nuevo State Park near Santa Cruz. During peak winter season, about 18,000 seals seek shelter in the coves and beaches along this stretch of coast. Interpretative panels along a beach boardwalk and blue-jacketed **Friends of the Elephant Seal** (www.elephantseal.org) guides demystify the behavior of these giant beasts.

San Luis Obispo

Almost halfway between LA and San Francisco, San Luis Obispo (SLO) is the classic stopover point for road trippers. With no must-see attractions, SLO might not seem to warrant much of your time. That said, this lively yet low-key town has an enviably high quality of life – in fact, it has been named America's happiest city. Nestled at the base of the Santa Lucia foothills, SLO is just a grape's throw from thriving Edna Valley wineries.

Sights

San Luis Obispo Creek, once used to irrigate mission orchards, flows through downtown. Uphill from Higuera St, **Mission Plaza** is a shady oasis with restored adobe buildings and fountains overlooking the creek. Look for the **Moon Tree**, a coast redwood grown from a seed that journeyed onboard Apollo 14's lunar mission.

Madonna Inn

'Oh, my!' is one of the more printable exclamations overheard from visitors at the **Madonna Inn** (**805-543-3000, 800-543-9666; www.madonnainn.com; 100 Madonna Rd, San Luis Obispo; r $189-309;**), a garish confection visible from Hwy 101. You'd expect outrageous kitsch like this in Las Vegas, not San Luis Obispo, but here it is, in all its campy extravagance. Japanese tourists, vacationing Midwesterners and hipster, irony-loving urbanites all adore the 110 themed rooms – including Yosemite Rock, Caveman and hot-pink Floral Fantasy. Check out photos of the different rooms online, or wander the halls and spy into the ones being cleaned. The urinal in the men's room is a bizarre waterfall. But the most irresistible reason to stop here? Old-fashioned cookies from the storybook-esque bakery.

Mission San Luis Obispo de Tolosa — Church

(**805-543-6850; www.missionsanluisobispo.org; 751 Palm St; donation $2; 9am-5pm late-Mar–Oct, to 4pm Nov–mid-Mar**) Those satisfyingly reverberatory bells heard around downtown emanate from this active parish dating from 1772. The fifth California mission founded by Junípero Serra, it was named for a 13th-century French saint. The modest church has an unusual L-shape and whitewashed walls decorated with Stations of the Cross. An adjacent building contains an old-fashioned museum about daily life during the Chumash tribal and Spanish colonial periods.

Activities

Montaña de Oro State Park — Park

(**805-772-7434; www.parks.ca.gov; 3550 Pecho Valley Rd, Los Osos; 6am-10pm**) FREE In spring the hillsides are blanketed by bright California poppies and other wildflowers, giving this park its Spanish name, meaning 'mountain of gold.' Wind-tossed coastal bluffs with wild, wide-open sea views make it a favorite spot with hikers and mountain bikers. The northern half of the park features sand dunes and an ancient marine terrace visible due to seismic uplifting.

The park is about 20 miles west of San Luis Obispo via Los Osos Valley Rd.

Sleeping

Peach Tree Inn — Motel $$

(**800-227-6396, 805-543-3170; www.peachtreeinn.com; 2001 Monterey St; r incl breakfast $89-140; office 7am-11pm;**) The folksy, nothing-fancy motel rooms here are inviting, especially those right by the creek or with rocking chairs on wooden porches overlooking grassy lawns, eucalyptus trees and rose gardens. Continental breakfast features homemade breads.

Petit Soleil — Inn $$$

(**800-676-1588, 805-549-0321; www.petitsoleilslo.com; 1473 Monterey St; d incl breakfast $169-299; office 7am-10pm;**) This French-themed, gay-friendly 'bed et breakfast' is a mostly charming retrofit of a courtyard motel. Each room is tastefully decorated with Provençal flair, and breakfast is a gourmet feast. The front rooms catch some street noise. Pet fee $25.

Eating

San Luis Obispo Farmers Market — Market $

(**www.downtownslo.com; 6-9pm Thu**) The county's biggest and best weekly farmers market turns downtown SLO's Higuera St into a giant street party, with smokin' barbecues, overflowing fruit and veggie stands, live music and free sidewalk entertainment, from salvation peddlers to wackadoodle political activists. Rain cancels it.

DOUG STEAKLEY / GETTY IMAGES ©

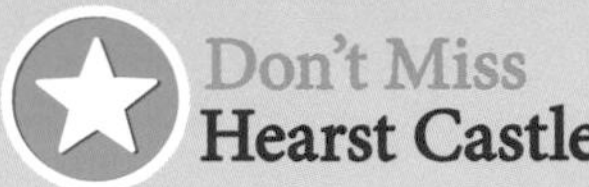

Don't Miss Hearst Castle

Built for William Randolph Hearst (1863–1951), Hearst Castle is a wondrous, historic, over-the-top homage to material excess, perched high on a hill. From the 1920s into the '40s, Hearst and Marion Davies, his longtime mistress, entertained a steady stream of the era's biggest movers and shakers. Invitations were highly coveted, but Hearst had his quirks – he despised drunkenness, and guests were forbidden to speak of death.

Architect Julia Morgan based the main building, Casa Grande, on the design of a Spanish cathedral, and over decades catered to Hearst's every design whim, deftly integrating the spoils of his fabled European shopping sprees. The estate sprawls across acres of lushly landscaped gardens, accentuated by shimmering pools and fountains, statues from ancient Greece and Moorish Spain, and the ruins of what was in Hearst's day the world's largest private zoo (drivers along Hwy 1 can sometimes still spot the zebras). The indoor Roman Pool (pictured above) echoes ancient splendor.

Much like Hearst's construction budget, the castle will devour as much of your time and money as you let it. To see anything of this state historic monument, you have to take a tour. In peak summer months, show up early enough and you might be able to get a same-day ticket for later that afternoon. For special holiday and evening tours, book at least two weeks in advance.

The center's five-story-high theater shows a 40-minute historical film (admission included with most tour tickets) about the castle and Hearst family.

NEED TO KNOW

info 805-927-2020, reservations 800-444-4445; www.hearstcastle.org; 750 Hearst Castle Rd, San Simeon; tours adult/child 5-12yr from $25/12; from 9am daily except Thanksgiving, Christmas & New Year's Day, closing time varies

Below: Statues, Mission Santa Barbara; **Right:** Mural room, Santa Barbara County Courthouse
(BELOW) WITOLD SKRYPCZAK / GETTY IMAGES ©; (RIGHT) FOTOSEARCH / GETTY IMAGES ©

Firestone Grill Barbecue **$**
(www.firestonegrill.com; 1001 Higuera St; dishes $4-10; 11am-10pm Sun-Wed, to 11pm Thu-Sat;) If you can stomach huge lines, long waits for a table, and sports-bar-style service, you'll get to sink your teeth into an authentic Santa Maria–style tri-tip steak sandwich on a toasted garlic roll and a basket of super-crispy fries.

Big Sky Café Californian **$$**
(www.bigskycafe.com; 1121 Broad St; dinner mains $11-22; 7am-9pm Mon-Thu, to 10pm Fri, 8am-10pm Sat, to 9pm Sun;) Big Sky is a big room, and still the wait can be long – its tagline is 'analog food for a digital world.' Vegetarians have almost as many options as carnivores, and many of the ingredients are sourced locally. Big-plate dinners can be a bit bland, but breakfast (served until 1pm daily) gets top marks.

Luna Red Fusion **$$$**
(805-540-5243; www.lunaredslo.com; 1023 Chorro St; shared plates $6-20, mains $20-39; 11am-9pm Mon-Wed, to 11:30pm Thu-Fri, 9:30am-11:30pm Sat, to 9pm Sun;) Local bounty from the land and sea, artisan cheeses and farmers-market produce pervade the chef's Californian, Asian and Mediterranean small-plates menu. Cocktails and glowing lanterns enhance a sophisticated ambience indoors, or linger over brunch on the mission-view garden patio. Reservations recommended.

SANTA BARBARA

Frankly put, this area is damn pleasant to putter around. Just a 90-minute drive northwest of Los Angeles, tucked between mountains and the Pacific, Santa Barbara basks smugly in its near-perfection. Founded by a Spanish mission, the city's signature red-tile roofs, white stucco buildings and Mediterranean vibe have long given credence to its claim to the title of the 'American Riviera.' Santa Barbara is blessed with almost freakishly good weather, and no one can deny the appeal of those beautiful beaches that line the city tip to toe either. Just ignore those pesky oil derricks out to sea.

Sights

Mission Santa Barbara Church

(www.santabarbaramission.org; 2201 Laguna St; adult/child 5-15yr $6/1; 9am-4:30pm Apr-Oct, to 4:15pm Nov-Mar; P) California's 'Queen of the Missions' reigns above the city on a hilltop perch over a mile northwest of downtown. Its imposing Doric facade, an architectural homage to an ancient Roman chapel, is topped by an unusual twin bell tower. Inside the mission's 1820 stone church, notice the striking Chumash artwork. Outside is an eerie cemetery – skull carvings hang over the door leading outside – with 4000 Chumash graves and the elaborate mausoleums of early California settlers.

Santa Barbara County Courthouse Historic Site

(805-962-6464; www.courthouselegacyfoundation.org; 1100 Anacapa St; 8:30am-4:45pm Mon-Fri, 10am-4:15pm Sat & Sun) FREE Built in Spanish-Moorish Revival style in 1929, the courthouse features hand-painted ceilings, wrought-iron chandeliers, and tiles from Tunisia and Spain. Step inside the hushed mural room depicting Spanish-colonial history on the 2nd floor, then climb El Mirador, the 85ft clock tower, for arch-framed panoramas of the city, ocean and mountains. You're free to explore on your own, but you'll get a lot more out of a free docent-guided tour, usually at 2pm daily and 10:30am on weekdays (except Thursday).

Downtown Santa Barbara

Santa Barbara Maritime Museum Museum

(☎805-962-8404; www.sbmm.org; 113 Harbor Way; adult/child 6-17yr $7/4, all free 3rd Thu of each month; ⏰10am-5pm, to 6pm late May–early Sep; P 👪) On the harborfront, this jam-packed, two-story exhibition hall celebrates the town's briny history with nautical artifacts, memorabilia and hands-on exhibits, including a big-game fishing chair from which you can 'reel in' a trophy marlin. Take a virtual trip through the Santa Barbara Channel, stand on a surfboard or watch deep-sea diving documentaries in the theater. There's 90 minutes of free parking in the public lot or take the Lil' Toot water taxi from Stearns Wharf.

Stearns Wharf Historic Site

(www.stearnswharf.org; P) FREE The southern end of State St gives way onto Stearns Wharf, a rough wooden pier lined with souvenir shops, snack stands and seafood shacks. Built in 1872, it's the oldest continuously operating wharf on the

Downtown Santa Barbara

Sights
1 Chase Palm Park....D5
2 Santa Barbara County Courthouse....C1
3 Santa Barbara Maritime Museum....A5
4 Santa Barbara Museum of Natural History Sea Center....C5
5 Stearns Wharf....B5

Activities, Courses & Tours
6 Los Baños del Mar....A4
7 Paddle Sports Center....A5
8 Santa Barbara Sailing Center....A5
9 Wheel Fun Rentals....C4
10 Wheel Fun Rentals....B4

Sleeping
11 Harbor House Inn....B4

Eating
12 Lark....C4
13 Lilly's Taquería....B3
14 Santa Barbara Shellfish Company....B5

Drinking & Nightlife
Figueroa Mountain Brewing Co.... (see 12)

West Coast, although the actual structure has been rebuilt more than once. During the 1940s it was co-owned by tough-guy actor Jimmy Cagney and his brothers. If you've got kids, tow them inside the **Santa Barbara Museum of Natural History Sea Center** (☎805-962-2526; www.sbnature.org; 211 Stearns Wharf; adult/child 2-12yr/youth 13-17yr $10/7/8; ⏰10am-5pm; P 👪).

The long, sandy stretch between Stearns Wharf and Montecito is **East Beach**, Santa Barbara's largest and most crowded. At its far end, near the Biltmore hotel, Armani swimsuits and Gucci sunglasses abound at chic, but narrow **Butterfly Beach**.

Between Stearns Wharf and the harbor, **West Beach** is popular with tourists. There **Los Baños del Mar** (☎805-966-6110; www.friendsoflosbanos.org; 401 Shoreline Dr; admission $6; ⏰call for public swim schedules; 👪), a municipal heated outdoor pool complex, is good for recreational and lap swimming, plus a kids' wading pool (open summer only). West of the harbor, **Leadbetter Beach** is the spot for beginning surfers and windsurfers. Climbing the stairs on the west end takes you to **Shoreline Park**, with picnic tables and awesome kite-flying conditions.

Further west, near the junction of Cliff Dr and Las Positas Rd, family-friendly **Arroyo Burro Beach County Park**, nicknamed Hendry's, has free parking and a restaurant and bar. Above the beach is the **Douglas Family Preserve**, offering cliffside romps for dogs.

Outside town off Hwy 101 you'll find even more spacious, family-friendly state

Ship's wheel, Santa Barbara Maritime Museum

beaches, including **Carpinteria State Beach**, about 12 miles southeast of Santa Barbara, and **Refugio & El Capitán State Beaches**, over 20 miles west past Goleta.

Activities

A paved recreational path stretches for 3 miles along the waterfront between Leadbetter Beach and Andrée Clark Bird Refuge, passing Stearns Wharf. **Bike Santa Barbara County** (www.bike-santabarbara.org) offers free cycling tour maps online.

Wheel Fun Rentals Cycling
(805-966-2282; www.wheelfunrentals.com) Cabrillo Blvd (23 E Cabrillo Blvd; 8am-8pm Mar-Oct, to 6pm Nov-Feb;); **State St** (22 State St; 8am-8pm Mar-Oct, to 6pm Nov-Feb;) Hourly rentals of beach cruisers ($10), mountain bikes ($11) and two-/four-person surreys ($29/39), with discounted half-day and full-day rates.

Paddle Sports Center Kayaking
(805-617-3425; www.channelislandso.com; 117b Harbor Way; single/double kayak rental per hour $25/40, per day $50/65; usually 8am-6pm) Long-established Channel Islands outfitter also guides harbor and coastal kayaking tours ($75 to $95) for beginner to advanced paddlers. Kayak rentals are available year-round at the harbor and Goleta Beach, and from late May through early September on West Beach. Book ahead online or by phone.

Santa Barbara Sailing Center Cruise, Sailing
(805-962-2826; www.sbsail.com; off Harbor Way; cruises $15-65;) Climb aboard the *Double Dolphin*, a 50ft sailing catamaran, for a two-hour coastal or sunset cruise. Seasonal whale-watching trips and quick one-hour spins around the harbor to view sea lions are also kid friendly. If you want to learn to pilot your own sailboat, sign up for a 20-hour instructional course.

Sleeping

Prepare for sticker shock: basic motel rooms by the beach command over $200 in summer. Don't show up without reservations, especially on weekends. Cheaper motels and hotels cluster along upper State St and Hwy 101 between Goleta and Carpinteria.

Santa Barbara Auto Camp Campground $$
(888-405-7553; www.autocamp.com/sb; 2717 De La Vina St; d $175-215; P) Bed down with vintage style in one of five shiny metal Airstream trailers parked near upper State St, north of downtown. All five architect-designed trailers have unique perks, such as a clawfoot tub or extra twin-size beds for kiddos, as well as a full kitchen and complimentary cruiser bikes to borrow. Book ahead; two-night minimum may apply. Pet fee $25.

Harbor House Inn Motel $$
(888-474-6789, 805-962-9745; www.harborhouseinn.com; 104 Bath St; r from $180; P) Down by the harbor, this converted motel offers brightly lit studios with hardwood floors and a beachy design scheme. A few have full kitchens and fireplaces, but there's no air-con. Rates include a welcome basket of breakfast goodies (with a two-night minimum stay) and beach towels, chairs and umbrellas and three-speed bicycles to borrow. Pet fee $20.

El Encanto Luxury Hotel $$$
(805-845-5800, 800-393-5315; www.elencanto.com; 800 Alvarado Pl; d from $475; P@) Triumphantly reborn, this 1920s icon of Santa Barbara style is a hilltop hideaway for travelers who demand the very best of everything. An infinity pool gazes out at the Pacific, while flower-filled gardens, fireplace lounges, a full-service spa and private bungalows with sun-drenched patios concoct the glamorous atmosphere perfectly fitted to SoCal socialites. Grab sunset drinks on the ocean-view terrace. Parking $35.

Santa Barbara for Children

Santa Barbara Museum of Natural History (805-682-4711; www.sbnature.org; 2559 Puesta del Sol; adult/child 2-12yr/youth 13-17yr $11/7/8, incl planetarium show $15/11/12; 10am-5pm; P) Stuffed wildlife mounts, glittering gems and a pitch-dark planetarium captivate kids' imaginations.

Arroyo Burro Beach County Park (Hendry's; www.countyofsb.org/parks/; Cliff Dr at Las Positas Rd; 8am-sunset; P) Wide sandy beach, away from the tourist crowds, popular with local families.

Santa Barbara Museum of Natural History Sea Center (p193) Gawk at a gray-whale skeleton, touch tide-pool critters and crawl through a 1500-gallon surge tank.

Santa Barbara Maritime Museum (p192) Peer through a periscope, reel in a virtual fish or check out the gorgeous model ships.

Chase Palm Park (323 E Cabrillo Blvd;) Antique carousel rides and a shipwreck-themed playground with a miniature lighthouse.

Eating

Lilly's Taquería Mexican $

(www.lillystacos.com; 310 Chapala St; items from $1.60; 10:30am-9pm Sun-Mon & Wed-Thu, to 10pm Fri & Sat) There's almost always a line roping around this downtown taco shack at lunchtime. But it goes fast, so you'd best be snappy with your order – the *adobada* (marinated pork) and *lengua* (beef tongue) are stand-out choices. Second location in Goleta west of the airport, off Hwy 101.

Santa Barbara Shellfish Company Seafood $$

(www.sbfishhouse.com; 230 Stearns Wharf; dishes $4-19; 11am-9pm; P) 'From sea to skillet to plate' sums up this end-of-the-wharf seafood shack that's more of a buzzing counter joint than a sit-down restaurant. Chase away the seagulls as you chow down on garlic-baked clams, crab cakes and coconut-fried shrimp at wooden picnic tables outside. Awesome lobster bisque, ocean views and the same location for over 25 years.

Lark Californian $$$

(805-284-0370; www.thelarksb.com; 131 Anacapa St; shared plates $5-32, mains $24-38; 5-10pm Tue-Sun, bar till midnight) There's no better place in Santa Barbara County to taste the bountiful farm and fishing goodness of this stretch of SoCal coast. Named after an antique Pullman railway car, this chef-run restaurant in the Funk Zone morphs its menu with the seasons, presenting unique flavor combinations like fried olives with chorizo aioli and chile-spiced mussels in lemongrass-lime broth. Make reservations.

Drinking & Nightlife

Figueroa Mountain Brewing Co Bar

(www.figmtnbrew.com; 137 Anacapa St; 11am-11pm) Father and son brewers have brought their gold medal-winning hoppy IPA, Danish red lager, and double IPA from Santa Barbara's Wine Country to the Funk Zone. Clink pint glasses on the taproom's open-air patio while acoustic acts play. Enter on Yanonali St.

DAVID EPPERSON / GETTY IMAGES ©

Don't Miss
Santa Barbara Wine Country

Oak-dotted hillsides, winding country lanes, rows of sweetly heavy grapevines stretching as far as the eye can see – it's hard not to gush about the Santa Maria and Santa Ynez Valleys.

With more than 100 wineries spread out across the landscape, it can seem daunting at first. But the wine country's five small towns – Buellton, Solvang, Santa Ynez, Ballard and Los Olivos – are all clustered within 10 miles of one another, so it's easy to stop, shop and eat whenever and wherever you happen to feel like it.

The pastoral **Foxen Canyon Wine Trail** (www.foxencanyonwinetrail.com) runs north from Hwy 154, just west of Los Olivos, into the rural Santa Maria Valley. The **Santa Rita Hills Wine Trail** (www.santaritahillswinetrail.com) shines brightly when it comes to ecoconscious farming practices. Country tasting rooms line a scenic loop west of Hwy 101 via Santa Rosa Rd and Hwy 246. In the **Santa Ynez Valley** you'll find dozens of wineries inside the triangle of Hwys 154, 246 and 101, including in downtown Los Olivos and Solvang.

No wheels to head up to Santa Barbara's wine country? No problem. Ramble between over a dozen wine-tasting rooms downtown and in the Funk Zone near the beach on Santa Barbara's **Urban Wine Trail** (www.urbanwinetrailsb.com).

Shopping

Downtown's **State St** is packed with shops, from vintage clothing to brand-name boutiques; cheapskates stick to lower State St, while trust-fund babies head uptown. For indie shops, dive into the **Funk Zone**, east of State St, just south of Hwy 101.

Information

Santa Barbara Visitors Center (805-568-1811, 805-965-3021; www.santabarbaraca.com; 1 Garden St; 9am-5pm Mon-Sat & 10am-5pm Sun Feb-Oct; 9am-4pm Mon-Sat Nov-Jan) Pick up maps and brochures while consulting with the helpful, but busy staff. The website offers free downloadable DIY touring maps and itineraries, from famous movie locations to wine trails, art galleries and outdoors fun. Self-pay metered parking lot nearby.

Getting There & Away

If you use public transportation to get to Santa Barbara, you can get valuable hotel discounts, plus get a nice swag bag of coupons for various activities and attractions, all courtesy of **Santa Barbara Car Free** (www.santabarbaracarfree.org).

Amtrak (800-872-7245; www.amtrak.com; 209 State St) Trains run south to LA ($31, three hours) and north to San Luis Obispo ($27, 2¾ hours).

Napa & Sonoma Wine Country

America's premier viticulture region has earned its reputation as being among the world's best. Despite the hype about Wine Country style, it is from the land that all Wine Country lore springs. Rolling hills, dotted with century-old oaks, turn the color of lion's fur under the summer sun. Swaths of vineyards carpet hillsides as far as the eye can see. Where they end, lush redwood forests follow serpentine rivers to the ocean.

There are over 600 wineries in Napa and Sonoma Counties, but it's quality, not quantity, that sets the region apart – especially in Napa, which competes with France and doubles as an outpost of San Francisco's top-end culinary scene. Sonoma prides itself on agricultural diversity, with goat-cheese farms, you-pick-'em orchards and roadside fruit stands – plan to get lost on back roads. As you picnic atop sun-dappled hillsides, grab a hunk of earth and appreciate firsthand Wine Country's *raison d'être*.

Sonoma Valley vineyards

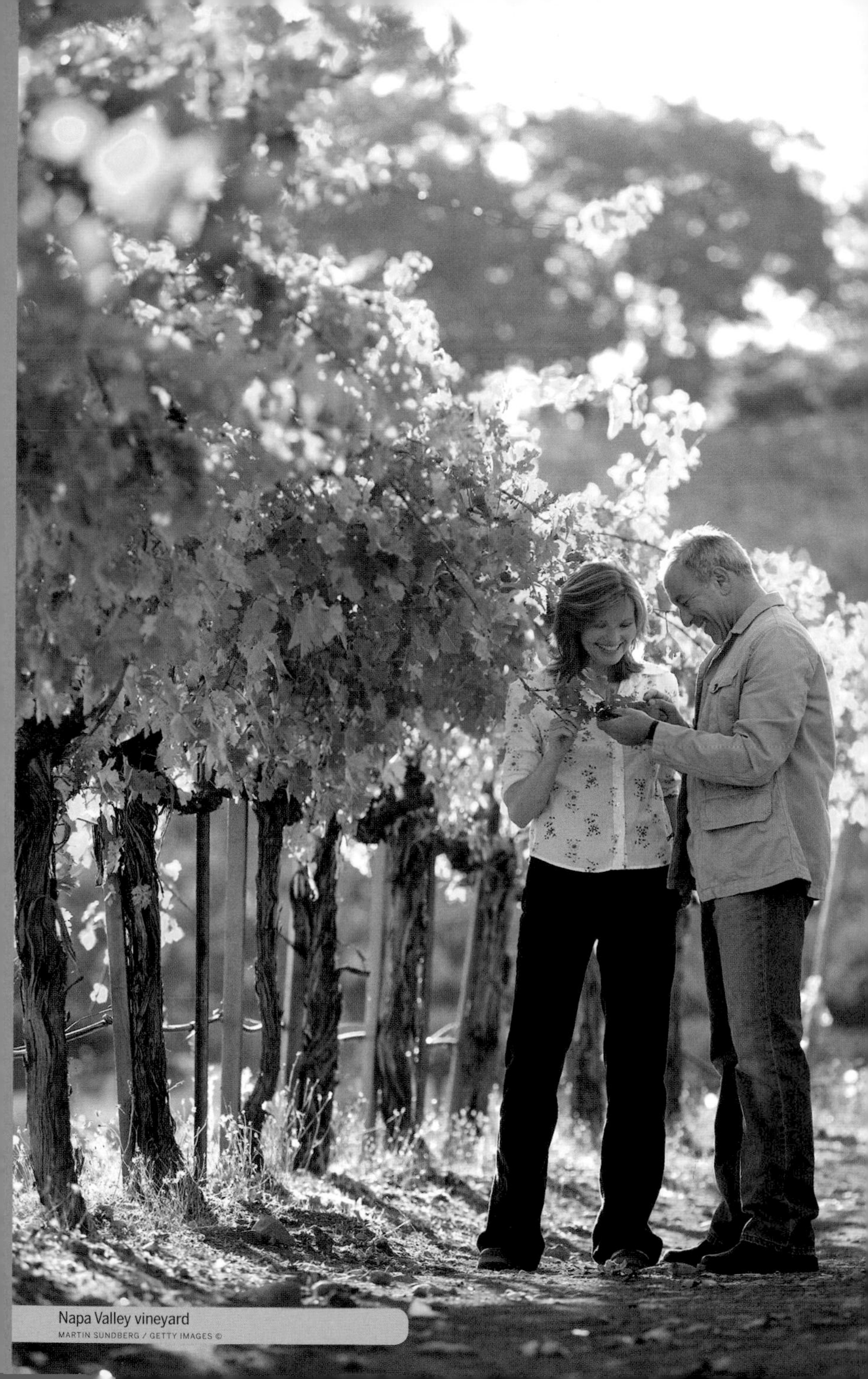

Napa Valley vineyard
MARTIN SUNDBERG / GETTY IMAGES ©

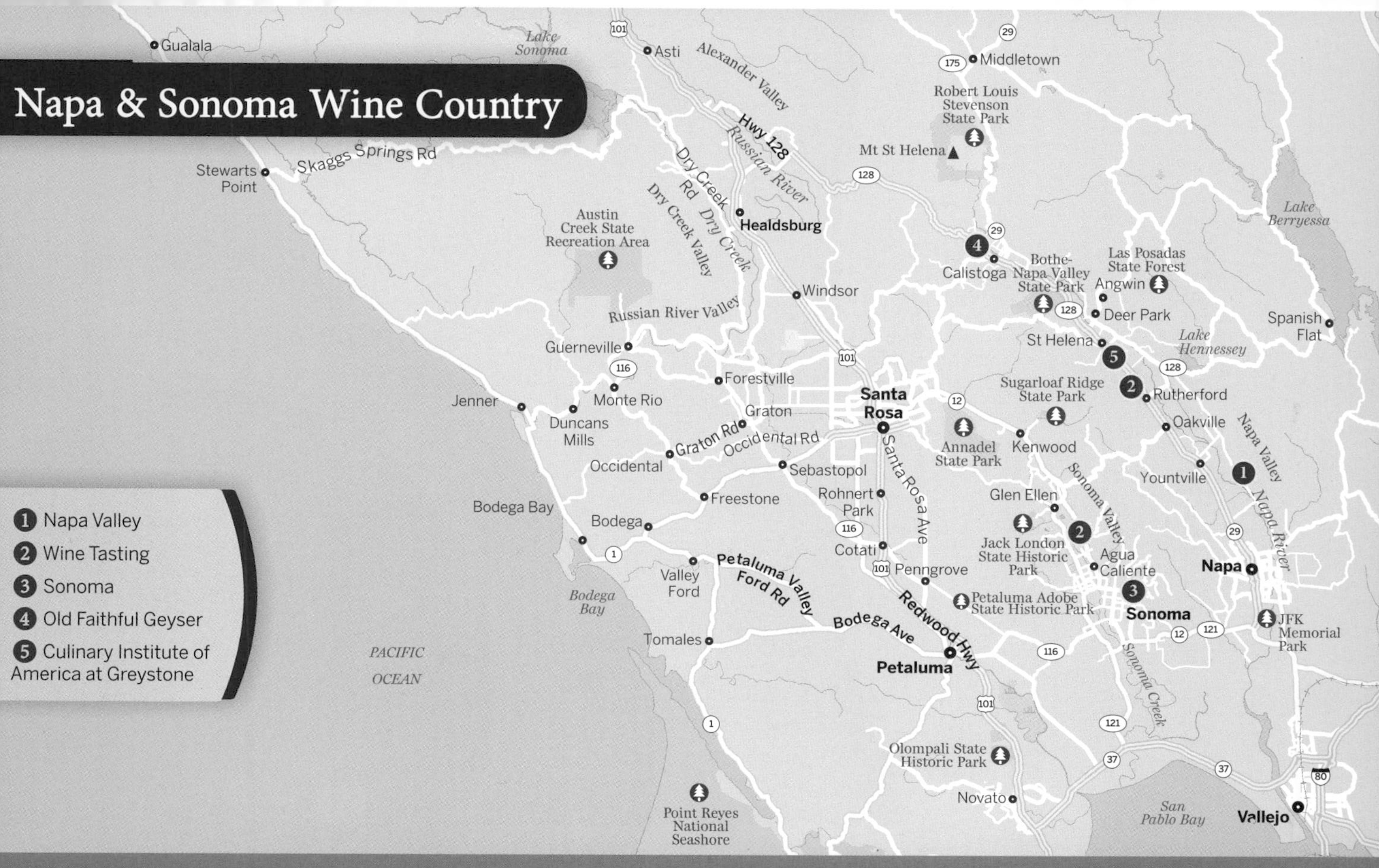

Napa & Sonoma Wine Country
1 Napa Valley
2 Wine Tasting
3 Sonoma
4 Old Faithful Geyser
5 Culinary Institute of America at Greystone
Gualala
Lake Sonoma
Asti
Alexander Valley
Middletown
Robert Louis Stevenson State Park
Mt St Helena
Hwy 128
Russian River
Stewarts Point
Skaggs Springs Rd
Dry Creek Rd
Dry Creek
Dry Creek Valley
Healdsburg
Austin Creek State Recreation Area
Windsor
Calistoga
Bothe-Napa Valley State Park
Las Posadas State Forest
Angwin
Deer Park
Lake Berryessa
Spanish Flat
Lake Hennessey
St Helena
Russian River Valley
Guerneville
Forestville
Monte Rio
Jenner
Duncans Mills
Graton
Graton Rd
Occidental Rd
Occidental
Santa Rosa
Santa Rosa Ave
Sugarloaf Ridge State Park
Rutherford
Oakville
Napa Valley
Annadel State Park
Kenwood
Sebastopol
Yountville
Napa River
Freestone
Rohnert Park
Glen Ellen
Sonoma Valley
Bodega Bay
Bodega
Cotati
Jack London State Historic Park
Agua Caliente
Napa
Valley Ford
Petaluma Valley Ford Rd
Penngrove
Bodega Bay
Petaluma Adobe State Historic Park
Sonoma
JFK Memorial Park
Redwood Hwy
Bodega Ave
Tomales
PACIFIC OCEAN
Petaluma
Sonoma Creek
Olompali State Historic Park
Point Reyes National Seashore
Novato
San Pablo Bay
Vallejo

Napa & Sonoma Wine Country Highlights

Napa Valley

With world-class wineries (over 400 in total), luxurious mud-bath spas, top-tier restaurants and pastoral farmlands of precious vines, Napa Valley (p210) packs it in and flaunts it all. California's fabled *terroir* produces some of world's best bottles yet still harbors lots of natural attractions for families. The best times to visit are spring and fall. Don't leave before taking a tasty stroll through Napa's Oxbow Public Market.

1

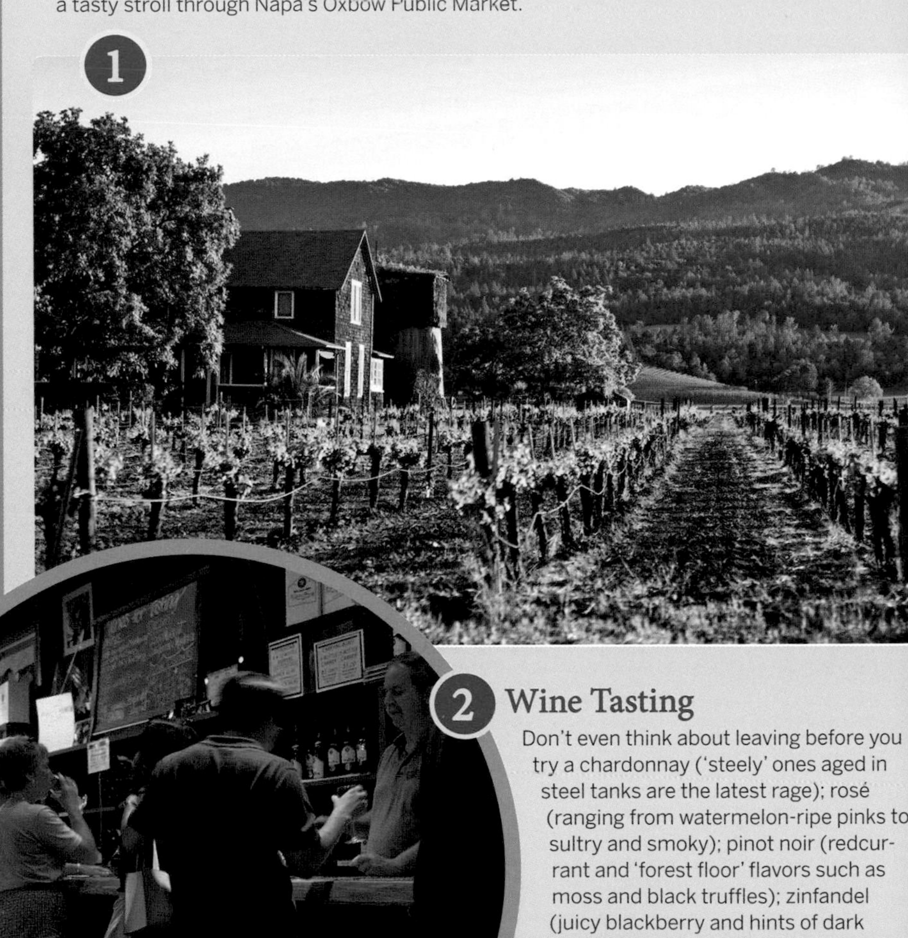

2 Wine Tasting

Don't even think about leaving before you try a chardonnay ('steely' ones aged in steel tanks are the latest rage); rosé (ranging from watermelon-ripe pinks to sultry and smoky); pinot noir (redcurrant and 'forest floor' flavors such as moss and black truffles); zinfandel (juicy blackberry and hints of dark chocolate or black pepper); and cabernet sauvignon (Napa's specialty).

GLENN VAN DER KNIJFF / GETTY IMAGES ©

Historic Sonoma

3

California history buffs should make sure to take a stroll around Sonoma Plaza (p231) and Sonoma State Historic Park (p232) for vestiges of the 1846 revolution against Mexico, when some American settlers, tanked up on liquid courage, declared independence in the town of Sonoma. Tour the military barracks, now a museum, as well as the Mission San Francisco de Solano.

Right: Sonoma City Hall, Sonoma Plaza (p231)

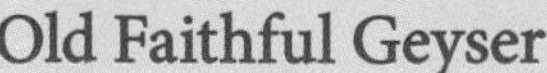

JOHN ELK / GETTY IMAGES ©

4

Old Faithful Geyser

Calistoga's hot-spring resorts may have tapped the earth's subterranean flow, but there's nothing like seeing a furious jolt of boiling water burst 60ft to the sky. Bring the whole family to witness this twice-an-hour spectacle (p226), a very visible demonstration of geothermal power. Just missed the frothy show? While away your time at the on-site petting zoo until the next eruption.

5

Culinary Institute of America at Greystone

A must-see for foodies, the CIA (p221) will boggle your mind with tasty options beyond its celebrated Wine Spectator Greystone Restaurant. Not only does it offer cooking demonstrations, but also wine-flight lessons, olive-oil tastings, multiday boot camps and chocolate sampling. Home chefs should budget time to ogle the more than 1000 cookbook titles at its shop.

Napa & Sonoma Wine Country's Best...

Winery Picnic Spots

- **Bartholomew Park Winery** 19th-century vineyards and valley-view hiking trails. (p228)
- **Casa Nuestra** Relax beneath weeping willows. (p213)
- **Gundlach-Bundschu Winery** One of Sonoma Valley's oldest and loveliest estate vineyards. (p229)
- **Tres Sabores** Make an appointment for a tour and then linger under the olive trees. (p212)
- **Kaz** Kids love the Play-Doh, playground and grape juice (p228)

Car-Free Transportation

- **Balloon** Soar above the rolling hills and vineyard valleys. (p210)
- **Bicycle** Explore quiet roads and wineries using your own pedal power. (p209)
- **Ferry** Cruise in via Vallejo from San Francisco. (p209)
- **Napa Valley Wine Train** Coast the countryside in a vintage Pullman dining car. (p209)
- **Hiking** Hike the volcanic cone of Mt St Helena at Robert Louis Stevenson State Park. (p227)

Places for Kids

- **Safari West** Take an expedition through a free-roaming exotic animal reserve. (p227)
- **Traintown** Steam-engine rides, a carousel and a Ferris wheel. (p232)
- **Old Faithful Geyser** Hourly water jets to the sky, plus a fun petting zoo. (p226)
- **Indian Springs Resort** An old-school resort with a toasty spring-fed swimming pool and outdoor games. (p225)
- **Benziger** Open-air tram ride and peacocks. (p231)

Romantic Wine Country

- **Poetry Inn** Private balconies, wood-burning fireplaces and indoor-outdoor showers. (p218)
- **Spa treatments** Spoil yourselves with a couples massage or delicious mud bath for two. (p224)
- **Madrona Manor** Victorian mansion inn and restaurant with a garden-view veranda. (p219)
- **Carneros Inn** Chic cottages with fireplaces, giant tubs and alfresco showers, plus a hilltop pool. (p214)

Left: Balloon over Napa Valley vineyards; **bove:** Tour group, Safari West (p227), Calistoga

(LEFT) GERALD FRENCH / GETTY IMAGES ©; (ABOVE) JUDY BELLAH / GETTY IMAGES ©

Need to Know

ADVANCE PLANNING

- **Two months before** Try to book a table at French Laundry or at another revered restaurant.
- **From several weeks to a few days before** Make tasting appointments at wineries that require them.

RESOURCES

- **Napa Valley** (www.legendarynapavalley.com) Napa Valley tourism information, spa deals and wine-tasting passes.
- **Sonoma Valley** (www.sonomavalley.com) Travel deals, special events and free downloadable winery maps.
- **Russian River Valley Winegrowers** (http://rrvw.og) Vineyard driving tours and winery events.
- **Healdsburg** (www.healdsburg.com) For wine enthusiasts, locavore foodies and outdoor nuts.
- **Outlet Shopping** (www.premiumoutlets.com) Max out your credit cards in Napa and Petaluma.

GETTING AROUND

- **Car** Needed for extensive winery-hopping, unless you stay in major hub towns such as Napa or Sonoma, or book a private limousine.
- **Bicycle** Visit wineries via quiet back roads, independently or on guided group tours.
- **Bus** Napa Valley Transit, Sonoma County Transit and Golden Gate Transit buses connect some towns, but won't help you go vineyard hoppping.
- **Airport shuttle** Shuttles run from the San Francisco and Oakland Airports to Napa, and connect to the Santa Rosa airport.

BE FOREWARNED

- **Visiting wineries** Some wineries accept visitors only by appointment.
- **Traffic** Expect heavy traffic on summer weekends.
- **Don't drink and drive** The curvy roads are dangerous, and police watch like hawks for traffic violators, especially on Napa's Hwy 29.
- **The 'crush'** Lodging prices skyrocket during the fall harvest.

Napa & Sonoma Wine Country Itineraries

California's top wine country features rolling hills, farm-to-table restaurants and plush spas and resorts. And there are hundreds of tasting rooms ensconced in million-dollar estates and quirky barnyards.

3 DAYS

CALISTOGA TO NAPA
OF WINE & WATER

Base yourself in the classic Napa Valley resort town of ❶ **Calistoga** (p224) for a bit of pampering and stress reduction. Book a mud treatment, and spend the rest of the day lazing around a hot-springs-fed swimming pool. If you prune quickly, set off to witness ❷ **Old Faithful Geyser** (p226), which shoots 60ft to 100ft into the sky a bit short of every hour; the kids can go wild in a petting zoo as you await the next scheduled eruption.

The following day, prepare your taste buds for the epicurean ambrosia to come with a wine-tasting class at the Culinary Institute of America at Greystone in ❸ **St Helena** (p220), and spruce up last season's wardrobe with a few items from the town's many boutiques. Book an afternoon limo tour to some well-chosen Napa Valley wineries then, for your evening meal, partake of the excellent local French cuisine as you dine in gourmet-thick ❹ **Yountville** (p218).

In the morning, depart for ❺ **Napa** (p214) to sample the Oxbow Public Market's foodie delights and to tour the sculpture garden just west of town at di Rosa Art + Nature Preserve or ride the Napa Valley Wine Train.

SONOMA TO HEALDSBURG
ROOTED IN HISTORY

Bear west and book two nights in or nearby the town of ❶ **Sonoma** (p231). Laid out by Mexican General Vallejo in 1834, the plaza contains colonial-era buildings and remains the heart of a lively downtown lined with hotels, restaurants and shops. Have a gander at the madcap works in the town's avant-garde landscape garden. Pull together a picnic including local cheeses and pass the next day touring wineries throughout the ❷ **Sonoma Valley** (p227). Literary buffs should make a stop at the ❸ **Jack London State Historic Park** (p234), which contains the final resting spot for the creator of *The Call of the Wild.*

Spend the following two nights in ❹ **Healdsburg** (p238), taking a cooking class and then sampling some of the gourmet highlights in the gastronomic capital of Sonoma County. Sign up for a bicycle tour and set off on another wine-tasting hurrah through the ❺ **Dry Creek Valley** (p237), working off last night's dinner by pedaling the pretty country lanes. On your final day, head north to the ❻ **Alexander Valley** (p235) or dip your paddles in for a refreshing canoe trip down the Russian River.

Bardessono hotel (p218), Yountville
STEPHEN SAKS / GETTY IMAGES ©

Discover Napa & Sonoma Wine Country

At a Glance

- **Napa Valley** (p210) Awash in cabernet, upscale shopping and top-end restaurants.
- **Calistoga** (p224) Napa Valley's renowned spa town has hot springs and mud baths.
- **Sonoma Valley** (p227) The folksier side of Wine Country boasts wineries and 19th-century historical sights.
- **Healdsburg & the Russian River** (p235) The gastronomic capital of Sonoma County.

Spa resort, Calistoga (p224)

PLUSH STUDIOS / GETTY IMAGES ©

Getting There & Away

From San Francisco, public transportation gets you to the valleys, but it's insufficient for vineyard hopping. For public-transit information, dial ☎511 from Bay Area telephones, or look online at www.transit.511.org.

Both valleys are 90 minutes' drive from San Francisco. Napa has over 400 wineries and attracts the most visitors (expect heavy traffic on summer weekends). Sonoma County has 260 wineries, 40 in Sonoma Valley, which is less commercial and less congested than Napa. If you have time to visit only one, for ease choose Sonoma.

Bus

Evans Transportation (**☎707-255-1559; www.evanstransportation.com**) Shuttles ($29) to Napa from San Francisco and Oakland Airports.

Golden Gate Transit (**☎415-923-2000; www.goldengate.org**) Bus 70/80 from San Francisco to Petaluma ($10.25) and Santa Rosa ($11.25); board at 1st and Mission Sts. Connects with Sonoma County Transit buses.

Greyhound Buses (**☎800-231-2222; www.greyhound.com**) San Francisco to Santa Rosa ($22 to $30); transfer to local buses.

Napa Valley Vine (**☎707-251-2800, 800-696-6443; www.nctpa.net**) Operates local bus 10 daily from downtown Napa to Calistoga ($1.50); express bus 29 Monday to Friday from the Vallejo Ferry Terminal ($3.25) and El Cerrito del Norte BART station ($5.50), via Napa, to Calistoga; and local bus 11 daily from the Vallejo Ferry Terminal to downtown Napa ($1.50)

Sonoma County Airport Express (**☎707-837-8700, 800-327-2024; www.airportexpressinc.com**) Shuttles ($34) between Sonoma County Airport (Santa Rosa) and San Francisco and Oakland Airports.

Booking Winery Appointments

Because of strict county zoning laws, many Napa wineries cannot legally receive drop-in visitors; unless you've come strictly to buy, you'll have to call ahead. This is *not* the case with all wineries. We recommend booking one appointment and planning your day around it.

Sonoma County Transit (800-345-7433, 707-576-7433; www.sctransit.com) Buses from Santa Rosa to Petaluma ($2.45, 70 minutes), Sonoma ($3.05, 1¼ hours) and western Sonoma County, including Russian River Valley towns ($3.05, 30 minutes).

Ferry

Baylink Ferry (877-643-3779; sanfranciscobayferry.com) Downtown San Francisco to Vallejo (adult/child $13/6.50, 60 minutes); connect with Napa Valley Vine bus 29 (weekdays) or bus 11 (daily).

Train

Amtrak (800-872-7245; www.amtrak.com) trains travel to Martinez (south of Vallejo), with connecting buses to Napa (45 minutes), Santa Rosa (1¼ hours) and Healdsburg (1¾ hours).

BART trains (415 989-2278; www.bart.gov) run from San Francisco to El Cerrito del Norte ($4.40, 30 minutes). Napa Valley Vine bus 29 runs weekdays from BART to Calistoga, via Napa; on Saturdays take **SolTrans** (707-648-4666; www.soltransride.com) from BART to Vallejo ($5, 30 minutes), then connect with Napa Valley Vine bus 11 to Napa and Calistoga; on Sundays, there's no connecting bus service from BART.

Getting Around

You'll need a car or bike to winery-hop. Alternatively visit tasting rooms in downtown Napa or downtown Sonoma.

Bicycle

Touring Wine Country by bicycle is unforgettable. Stick to back roads. We most love pastoral West Dry Creek Rd, northwest of Healdsburg, in Sonoma County. Through Sonoma Valley, take Arnold Dr instead of Hwy 12; through Napa Valley, take the Silverado Trail instead of Hwy 29.

Cycling between wineries isn't demanding – the valleys are mostly flat – but crossing between Napa and Sonoma Valleys is intense, particularly via steep Oakville Grade and Trinity Rd (between Oakville and Glen Ellen).

Public Transportation

Napa Valley Vine (707-251-2800, 800-696-6443; www.nctpa.net) Bus 10 runs daily from downtown Napa to Calistoga ($1.50, 1¼ hours).

Car

Summer and fall weekend traffic is unbearable, especially on Hwy 29 between Napa and St Helena. Plan accordingly. Cross-valley roads linking Silverado Trail with Hwy 29 – including Yountville, Oakville and Rutherford crossroads – are bucolic and get less traffic.

There are a number of shortcuts between the Napa and Sonoma Valleys: from Oakville, take Oakville Grade to Trinity Rd; from St Helena, take Spring Mountain Rd into Calistoga Rd; from Calistoga, take Petrified Forest Rd to Calistoga Rd.

Train

A cushy, if touristy, way to see Wine Country, the **Napa Valley Wine Train** (800-427-4124, 707-253-2111; www.winetrain.com; adult/child from $109/74) offers three-hour daily trips in vintage Pullman dining cars, from Napa to St Helena and back, with an optional winery tour. Trains depart from McKinstry St near 1st St.

Tours

BICYCLE

Guided tours start around $90 per day including bikes, tastings and lunch. Daily rentals cost $25 to $85; make reservations.

Flying & Ballooning

Wine Country is stunning from the air – a multihued tapestry of undulating hills, deep valleys and rambling vineyards. Make reservations.

The **Vintage Aircraft Company** (Map p228; ☎707-938-2444; www.vintageaircraft.com; 23982 Arnold Dr, Sonoma) flies over Sonoma in a vintage biplane with an awesome pilot who'll do loop-de-loops on request (add $50). Twenty-minute tours cost $175/260 for one/two adults.

Napa Valley's signature hot-air balloon flights leave early, around 6am or 7am, when the air is coolest; they usually include a champagne breakfast on landing. Adults pay about $200 to $250, and kids $150 to $175. Call **Balloons Above the Valley** (☎800-464-6824, 707-253-2222; www.balloonrides.com) or **Napa Valley Balloons** (☎800-253-2224, 707-944-0228; www.napavalleyballoons.com), both in Yountville.

Getaway Adventures Cycling

(☎800-499-2453, 707-568-3040; http://getawayadventures.com; tours $149) Great guided tours, some combined with kayaking, of Napa, Sonoma, Calistoga, Healdsburg and Russian River. Single- and multi-day trips.

Napa Valley Adventure Tours Cycling

(Map p216; ☎707-224-9080, 707-259-1833; www.napavalleyadventuretours.com; 1147 1st St, Napa) Guides tours between wineries, off-road trips, hiking and kayaking. Daily rentals.

Napa Valley Bike Tours Cycling

(☎707-944-2953; www.napavalleybiketours.com; 6500 Washington St, Yountville; ⏰8:30am-5pm) Daily rentals; easy and moderately difficult tours.

Wine Country Bikes Cycling

(☎707-473-0610, toll free 866-922-4537; www.winecountrybikes.com; 61 Front St, Healdsburg; rentals per day from $39, multi-day guided tours from $595; ⏰9am-5pm) Rents bikes in downtown Healdsburg and guides multi-day Sonoma County tours.

JEEP & LIMOUSINE

Note that some wineries do not allow limousines, and limousine companies have set itineraries with little flexibility (ie, you'll have few choices about which wineries you visit).

Wine Country Jeep Tours Jeep Tour

(☎800-539-5337, 707-546-1822; www.jeeptours.com; 3hr tour $75) Tour Wine Country's back roads and boutique wineries by Jeep, year-round at 10am and 1pm. Also operates tours of Sonoma Coast.

Magnum Tours Limousine Tour

(☎707-753-0088; www.magnumwinetours.com) Sedans and specialty limousines from $65 to $125 per hour (four-hour minimum, five hours Saturdays). Exceptional service.

Antique Tours Limousine Limousine Tour

(☎707-761-3949; www.antiquetours.net) Drive in style in a 1947 Packard convertible; tours cost $120 to $170 per hour.

NAPA VALLEY

The birthplace of modern-day Wine Country is famous for regal cabernet sauvignons, château-like wineries and fabulous food. Napa Valley attracts more than four million visitors a year, each expecting to be wined, dined, soaked in hot-springs spas and tucked between crisp linens.

Napa Valley South

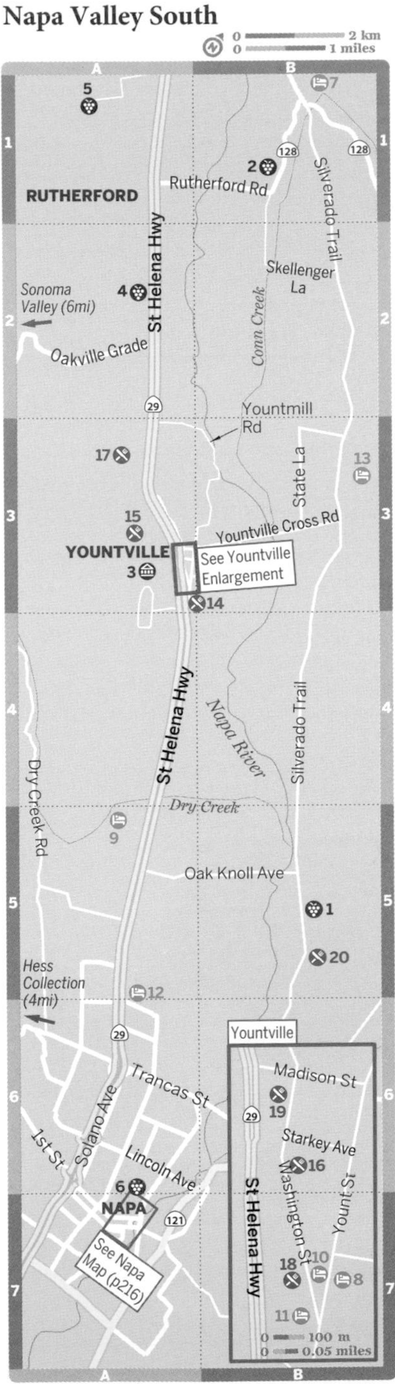

Napa Valley South

Sights

1 Darioush ... B5
2 Frog's Leap ... B1
3 Napa Valley Museum ... A3
4 Robert Mondavi ... A2
5 Tres Sabores ... A1
6 Twenty Rows ... A6

Sleeping

7 Auberge du Soleil ... B1
8 Bardessono ... B7
9 Cottages of Napa Valley ... A5
10 Maison Fleurie ... B7
11 Napa Valley Railway Inn ... B7
12 Napa Winery Inn ... A5
13 Poetry Inn ... B3

Eating

14 Ad Hoc ... B3
Bouchon ... (see 10)
Bouchon Bakery ... (see 10)
15 Étoile ... A3
16 French Laundry ... B6
17 Mustards Grill ... A3
18 Napa Style Paninoteca ... B7
19 Redd Wood ... B6
20 Soda Canyon Store ... B5

Napa Valley Wineries

Cab is king in Napa. No varietal captures imaginations like the fruit of the cabernet sauvignon vine – Bordeaux is the French equivalent – and no wine fetches a higher price. Other heat-loving varietals, such as sangiovese and merlot, also thrive here.

Hess Collection Winery, Gallery

(**707-255-1144; www.hesscollection.com; 4411 Redwood Rd, Napa; tasting $15; gallery free; 10am-5:30pm**) Art lovers: don't miss **Hess Collection**, whose galleries display mixed-media and large-canvas works, including pieces by Francis Bacon and Louis Soutter. In the cave-like tasting room, find well-known cabernet and chardonnay, but also try the viognier. Hess overlooks the valley: be prepared to drive a winding road. Reservations recommended. Bottles: $20 to $60. (NB: Don't confuse Hess Collection with Hess Select, the grocery-store brand.)

Darioush Winery

(**Map p211; 707-257-2345; www.darioush.com; 4240 Silverado Trail, Napa; tasting $18-40;**

10:30am-5pm) Like a modern-day Persian palace, Darioush ranks high on the fabulosity scale, with towering columns, Le Corbusier furniture, Persian rugs and travertine walls. Though known for cabernet, Darioush also bottles chardonnay, merlot and shiraz, all made with 100% of their respective varietals. Call about wine-and-cheese pairings. Bottles cost $40 to $95.

Tres Sabores — Winery

(Map p211; 707-967-8027; www.tressabores.com; 1620 South Whitehall Lane, St Helena; tour & tasting $20; by appointment;) At the valley's westernmost edge, where sloping vineyards meet wooded hillsides, Tres Sabores is a portal to old Napa – no fancy tasting room, no snobbery, just great wine in a spectacular setting. Bucking the cabernet custom, Tres Sabores crafts elegantly structured, Burgundian-style zinfandel, and spritely sauvignon blanc, which the *New York Times* dubbed a Top 10 of its kind in California. Reservations essential.

Guinea fowl and sheep control pests on the 35-acre estate, while golden labs chase butterflies through gnarled old vines. After your tour, linger at olive-shaded picnic tables and drink in gorgeous valley views. Bottles cost $22 to $80.

Hall — Winery

(Map p222; 707-967-2626; www.hallwines.com; 401 St Helena Hwy, St Helena; tasting $30, tour $50; 10am-5:30pm;) Owned by Bill Clinton's former ambassador to Austria, Hall specializes in sauvignon blanc, merlot and cabernet sauvignon, crafted in big-fruit California style. Its dramatic tasting room has a stand-up bar with 180-degree views of vineyards and mountains through floor-to-ceiling glass, and the glorious art collection includes a giant chrome rabbit leaping over the vines. Bottles cost $22 to $80.

Frog's Leap — Winery

(Map p211; 707-963-4704; www.frogsleap.com; 8815 Conn Creek Rd, Rutherford; tasting $15, incl tour $20; by appointment;) Meandering paths wind through magical gardens and fruit-bearing orchards – pick peaches in July – surrounding an 1884 barn and farmstead with cats and chickens. The vibe is casual and down-to-earth, with a major emphasis on *fun*. Sauvignon blanc is its best-known wine, but the merlot merits attention. There's also a dry, restrained cabernet, atypical of Napa.

Sculpture Meadow, di Rosa Art + Nature Preserve (p214; foreground artwork by Viola Frey; background artwork by Mark Di Suvero)

FAITH ECHTERMEYER, COURTESY DI ROSA, NAPA ©

All are organic. Appointments required. Bottles cost $22 to $42.

Schramsberg Winery
(Map p222; ☎707-942-2414; www.schramsberg.com; 1400 Schramsberg Rd, off Peterson Dr; tour & tasting $50; ⏲by appointment 10am, 11:30am, 12:30pm, 1:30pm & 2:30pm) Napa's second-oldest winery, Schramsberg makes some of California's best brut sparkling wines, and in 1972 was the first domestic wine served at the White House. Blanc de blancs is the signature. The appointment-only tasting and tour (book well ahead) is expensive, but you'll sample all the *tête de cuvées*, not just the low-end wines. Tours include a walk through the caves; bring a sweater. Bottles cost $22 to $100.

Castello di Amorosa Winery, Castle
(Map p222; ☎707-967-6272; www.castellodiamorosa.com; 4045 Hwy 29, Calistoga; admission & tasting $19-29, incl guided tour $34-75; ⏲9:30am-6pm, to 5pm Nov-Feb) It took 14 years to build this perfectly replicated, 12th-century Italian castle, complete with moat, hand-cut stone walls, ceiling frescoes by Italian artisans, Roman-style cross-vault brick catacombs, and a torture chamber with period equipment. You can taste without an appointment, but this is one tour worth taking. Oh, the wine? Some respectable Italian varietals, including a velvety Tuscan blend, and a merlot blend that goes great with pizza. Bottles are $20 to $125.

Robert Mondavi Winery
(Map p211; ☎888-766 6328; www.robertmondaviwinery.com; 7801 Hwy 29, Oakville; tasting & tour $20-55; ⏲10am-5pm; 👪) Tour buses flock to this corporate-owned winery, but if you know nothing about wine and can cope with crowds, the worthwhile tours provide excellent insight into winemaking. Otherwise, skip it unless you're considering one of its glorious outdoor summer **concerts**; call for schedules. Bottles cost $25 to $150.

If You Like... Sustainable Napa Valley Wines

If you like the sustainable practices at Frog's Leap, we think you'll want to visit these other green-leaning Napa Valley wineries.

1 **CASA NUESTRA**
(Map p222; ☎866-844-9463; www.casanuestra.com; 3451 Silverado Trail North, St Helena; tasting $10; ⏲by appointment) A peace flag and portrait of Elvis greet you at this old-school, mom-and-pop winery, which produces unusual blends and interesting varietals (including good chenin blanc) and 100% cabernet franc. Vineyards are all-organic; the sun provides power. Picnic free (call ahead and buy a bottle), beneath weeping willows shading happy goats. Bottles are $20 to $60.

2 **CADE**
(Map p222; ☎707-965-2746; www.cadewinery.com; 360 Howell Mountain Rd S, Angwin; tasting $40-70; ⏲by appointment) Ascend Mt Veeder for drop-dead vistas, 1800ft above the valley, at Napa's oh-so-swank, first-ever organically farmed, LEED gold-certified winery, partly owned by former San Francisco mayor Gavin Newsom. Hawks ride thermals at eye level as you sample bright sauvignon blanc and luscious cabernet sauvignon that's more Bordelaise in style than Californian. Reservations required. Bottles cost $44 to $80.

Artesa Vineyards & Winery Winery
(☎707-254-2126; www.artesawinery.com; 1345 Henry Rd, Napa; glass $12; tasting $15-20, incl tour $30; ⏲10am-4:30pm) Begin or end the day with a glass of bubbly or pinot at Artesa, southwest of Napa. Built into a mountainside, the ultramodern Barcelona-style architecture is stunning, and you can't beat the top-of-the-world vistas over San Pablo Bay. Tours run at 11am and 2pm. Bottles cost $20 to $60.

Napa

The city of Napa anchors the valley, but the real work happens up-valley in the prettier towns of St Helena, Yountville and Calistoga – the latter more famous for water than wine.

Sights

di Rosa Art + Nature Preserve Gallery, Gardens
(**707-226-5991; www.dirosaart.org; 5200 Hwy 121; admission $5, tours $12-15; 10am-4pm Wed-Sun**) West of downtown, scrap-metal sheep graze Carneros vineyards at 217-acre di Rosa Preserve, a stunning collection of Northern California art, displayed indoors in galleries and outdoors in sculpture gardens. Reservations recommended for tours.

Twenty Rows Winery
(**Map p211; 707-265-7750; www.twenty-rows.com; 880 Vallejo St, Napa; tasting $10; 11am-5pm Tue-Sat, by appointment Sun & Mon**) Downtown Napa's only working winery crafts light-on-the-palate cabernet sauvignon for just $20 a bottle. Taste in a chilly garage, on plastic furniture, with fun dudes who know their wines. Good sauvignon blanc, too.

Sleeping

Carneros Inn Resort **$$$**
(**707-299-4900; www.thecarnerosinn.com; 4048 Sonoma Hwy; r Mon-Fri $485-570, Sat & Sun $650-900;**) Carneros Inn's contemporary aesthetic and retro, small-town agricultural theme shatter the predictable Wine Country mold. The semi-detached, corrugated-metal cottages look like itinerant housing, but inside they're snappy and chic, with cherry-wood floors, ultrasuede headboards, wood-burning fireplaces, heated-tile bathroom floors, giant tubs and indoor-outdoor showers. Linger by day at the hilltop pool, by night at the outdoor fireplaces. Two excellent on-site restaurants.

Left: Castello di Amorosa (p213); **Below:** Wine cellar, Napa Valley
(LEFT) EMILY RIDDELL / GETTY IMAGES ©; (BELOW) WES WALKER / GETTY IMAGES ©

Cottages of Napa Valley Bungalow **$$$**
(Map p211; ☎707-252-7810; www.napacottages.com; 1012 Darns Lane; d $395-500, q $475-575; ❄📶) Eight pristine cottages of quality construction – made for romantic hideaways, with extra-long soaking tubs, indoor gas fireplaces and outdoor campfire pits – surround a big garden shaded by towering pines. Cottages 4 and 8 have private porches and swinging chairs. The only drawback is while noise from traffic, but interiors are silent.

Napa Winery Inn Hotel **$$$**
(Map p211; ☎800-522-8999, 707-257-7220; www.napawineryinn.com; 1998 Trower Ave; r incl breakfast Mon-Fri $179-279, Sat & Sun $229-339; ❄@📶🏊🐾) Request a remodeled room at this good-value hotel, north of downtown, decorated with generic Colonial-style furniture. Hot tub, good service.

Eating

Alexis Baking Co Cafe **$**
(Map p216; ☎707-258-1827; www.alexisbakingcompany.com; 1517 3rd St; dishes $7-13; ⏰7am-3pm Mon-Fri, 7:30am-3pm Sat, 8am-2pm Sun; 🥕👪) Our fave spot for quality scrambles, granola, focaccia sandwiches, big cups of joe and boxed lunches to go.

Soda Canyon Store Deli **$**
(Map p211; ☎707-252-0285; www.sodacanyonstore.com; 4006 Silverado Trail; ⏰6am-5:30pm Mon-Sat, 7:30am-5pm Sun) This roadside deli, with shaded picnic area, makes an easy stop while winery-hopping north of town.

Oenotri Italian **$$**
(Map p216; ☎707-252-1022; www.oenotri.com; 1425 1st St; mains lunch $13-15, dinner $17-29; ⏰11:30am-2:30pm & 5:30-9pm Sun-Thu, to 10pm Fri & Sat) 🌿 House-made salumi and pastas, and wood-fired Naples-style pizzas are the stars at always-busy Oenotri,

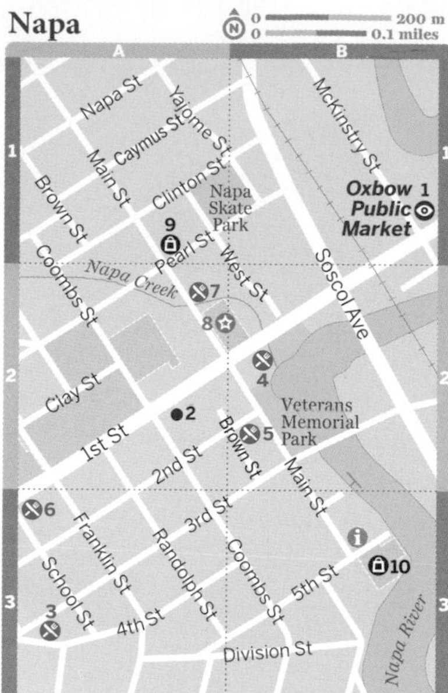

Napa

Don't Miss Sights
1 Oxbow Public Market B1

Activities, Courses & Tours
2 Napa Valley Adventure Tours A2

Eating
3 Alexis Baking Co A3
4 Bounty Hunter Wine Bar & Smokin' BBQ B2
5 Carpe Diem Wine Bar B2
6 Oenotri A3
Oxbow Public Market .... (see 1)
7 Torc A2

Entertainment
8 City Winery at Napa Valley Opera House A2

Shopping
9 Betty's Girl A1
10 Napa General Store B3

which draws crowds for daily-changing, locally sourced, rustic-Italian cooking, served in a cavernous brick-walled space.

Carpe Diem Wine Bar Californian **$$**
(Map p216; ☎707-224-0800; www.carpediemwinebar.com; 1001 2nd St; mains $17-19; ⏰4-9pm Mon-Thu, to 10pm Fri & Sat) This busy storefront wine bar and restaurant makes inventive, flavorful small plates, from simple skewers and flatbreads, to elaborate ostrich burgers, salumi platters and – wait for it – duck confit 'quack and cheese.'

Bounty Hunter Wine Bar & Smokin' BBQ Barbecue **$$**
(Map p216; ☎707-226-3976; www.bountyhunterwinebar.com; 975 1st St; mains $13-24; ⏰11am-10pm Sun-Thu, to midnight Fri & Sat; 👪) Inside an 1888 grocery store, Bounty Hunter has an Old West vibe and superb barbecue, made with house-smoked meats. The standout whole chicken is roasted over a can of Tecate. Ten local beers and 40 wines by the glass.

Torc Californian **$$$**
(Map p216; ☎707-252-3292; www.torcnapa.com; 1140 Main St; mains $26-29; ⏰5-9:30pm daily, 10:30am-2:30pm Sat & Sun) Wildly popular Torc plays off the seasons with dynamic combinations of farm-fresh ingredients, such as springtime white asparagus with black-truffle toasts, and squab with artichoke and licorice. Well-arranged for people-watching, the big stone dining room has an open-truss ceiling, and exposed pinewood tables that downplay formality. Reservations essential.

Drinking & Entertainment

City Winery at Napa Valley Opera House Theater
(Map p216; ☎707-260-1600; www.citywinery.com/napa; 1030 Main St) Napa's vintage-1880s opera theater houses a happening wine bar and restaurant downstairs, and 300-seat cabaret upstairs, hosting acts like Ginger Baker and Graham Nash. Opening hours vary, though it's usually open Thursday to Sunday evenings.

Shopping

Betty's Girl Women's Clothing, Vintage
(Map p216; ☎707-254-7560; www.bettysgirlnapa.com; 968 Pearl St; ⏰11am-6pm Thu & Fri, 10am-2pm Sat) Expert couturier Kim Northrup fits women with fabulous vintage cocktail dresses and custom-

WALTER BIBIKOW / ROBERT HARDING ©

Don't Miss
Oxbow Public Market

Graze your way through this gourmet market and plug into the Northern California food scene. Showcasing all things culinary – produce stalls (pictured above), kitchen shops, and everywhere something to taste – Oxbow is foodie central, with emphasis on seasonal eating and sustainability. Come hungry. Look for Hog Island oysters; comfort cooking at celeb-chef Todd Humphries' Kitchen Door; Venezuelan cornbread sandwiches at Pica Pica; standout Cal-Mexican at C Casa; pastries at Ca'Momi; and Three Twins certified-organic ice cream. Tuesday is locals night, with many discounts. Tuesday and Saturday mornings, there's a farmers market. Some stalls remain open till 9:30pm, even on Sundays, but many close earlier.

NEED TO KNOW

Map p216; ☎707-226-6529; www.oxbowpublicmarket.com; 610 1st St; ⏰9am-7pm Mon, Wed & Thu, to 8pm Tue, Fri & Sat, 10am-6pm Sun; 👪

made designs, altering and shipping for no additional charge. Open extra hours by appointment.

Napa General Store Gifts
(Map p216; ☎707-259-0762; www.napageneralstore.com; 540 Main St; ⏰8am-6pm) Finally, cutesy Wine Country souvenirs reasonably priced. The on-site wine bar is convenient for non-shopping spouses.

Information

Napa Valley Welcome Center (Map p216; ☎707-251-5895, lodging assistance 707-251-9188, toll free 855-847-6272; www.visitnapavalley.com; 600 Main St; ⏰9am-5pm; 👪) Lodging assistance, wine-tasting passes, spa deals and comprehensive winery maps.

Yountville

This one-time stagecoach stop, 9 miles north of Napa, is now a major foodie destination, with more Michelin stars per capita than any other American town. There are some good inns here, but it's deathly boring at night. You stay in Yountville to drink with dinner without having to drive afterward – town is walkable. Most businesses are on Washington St.

Sights

Napa Valley Museum Museum

(Map p211; ☎707-944-0500; www.napavalley-museum.org; 55 Presidents Circle, off California Drive; adult/child $5/2.50; ⏰10am-5pm Wed-Mon) Yountville's modernist 40,000-sq-ft museum chronicles cultural history and showcases local paintings. Good picnicking outside. From town, it's across Hwy 29.

Sleeping

Napa Valley Railway Inn Inn **$$**

(Map p211; ☎707-944-2000; www.napavalley-railwayinn.com; 6523 Washington St; r $125-260; ❄@📶🏊) Sleep in a converted railroad car, part of two short trains parked at a central platform. They've little privacy, but come moderately priced. Bring earplugs.

Bardessono Luxury Hotel **$$$**

(Map p211; ☎877-932-5333, 707-204-6000; www.bardessono.com; 6524 Yount St; r $600-800, ste from $800; ❄@📶🏊) 🍃 The outdoors flows indoors at California's first-ever (for what it's worth) LEED-platinum-certified green hotel, made of recycled everything, styled in Japanese-led austerity, with neutral tones and hard angles that are exceptionally urban for farm country. Glam pool deck and onsite spa. Tops for a splurge.

Poetry Inn Inn **$$$**

(Map p211; ☎707-944-0646; www.poetryinn.com; 6380 Silverado Trail; r incl breakfast $650-1400; ❄📶🏊) There's no better valley view than from this contemporary three-room inn, high on the hills east of Yountville. Decorated with posh restraint, rooms have private balconies, wood-burning fireplaces, 1000-thread-count linens and enormous baths with indoor-outdoor showers. Bring a ring.

Napa Valley Museum

Splurge-Worthy Restaurants

If you like the culinary delights of French Laundry, make reservations at these top tables in Wine Country.

Restaurant at Meadowood (Map p222; ☎707-967-1205; www.meadowood.com; 900 Meadowood Lane; 9-course menu $225; ⊙5:30-10pm Mon-Sat) If you couldn't score reservations at French Laundry, fear not: Meadowood – the valley's only other Michelin-three-star restaurant – has a slightly more sensibly priced menu, elegantly unfussy dining room, and lavish haute cuisine that's not too esoteric. **Auberge** (Map p211; ☎800-348-5406, 707-963-1211; www.aubergedusoleil.com; 180 Rutherford Hill Rd, Rutherford) has better views, but Meadowood's food and service far surpass it.

Madrona Manor (☎800-258-4003, 707-433-4231; www.madronamanor.com; 1001 Westside Rd, Healdsburg; 6-/11-course menu $106/$129; ⊙6-9pm Wed-Sun) You'd be hard-pressed to find a lovelier place to propose than this retro-formal Victorian mansion's garden-view verandah – though there's nothing old-fashioned about the artful haute cuisine: the kitchen churns its own butter, each course comes with a different variety of just-baked bread, lamb and cheese originate down the road, and desserts include ice cream flash-frozen tableside. Reserve a pre-sunset table on the verandah.

Solbar (Map p222; ☎707-226-0850; www.solagecalistoga.com; 755 Silverado Trail; lunch mains $17-20, dinner $24-34; ⊙7am-11am, 11:30am-3pm & 5:30-9pm) We like the warm, relaxed vibe of this Michelin-starred resort restaurant, whose menu maximizes seasonal produce in elegant dishes, playfully composed. And this being a spa (p224), too, the menu is split for calorie-counters into light and hearty dishes. Reservations essential.

Maison Fleurie B&B $$$

(Map p211; ☎800-788-0369, 707-944-2056; www.maisonfleurienapa.com; 6529 Yount St; r incl breakfast $160-295; ❄@🛜≋) Rooms at this ivy-covered country inn are in a century-old home and carriage house, decorated in French-provincial style. Big breakfasts, afternoon wine and *hors d'oeuvres*, hot tub.

Eating

Make reservations (or you might not eat).

Bouchon Bakery Bakery $

(Map p211; ☎707-944-2253; http://bouchonbakery.com; 6528 Washington St; items from $3; ⊙7am-7pm) Bouchon makes as-good-as-in-Paris French pastries and strong coffee. There's always a line and rarely a seat: get it to go.

Napa Style Paninoteca Cafe $

(Map p211; ☎707-945-1229; www.napastyle.com; 6525 Washington St; dishes $8-10; ⊙11am-3pm) TV-chef Michael Chiarello's cafe (inside his store, Napa Style) makes camera-ready salads and paninos – try the slow-roasted pork – that pair nicely with his organic wines.

Redd Wood Italian $$

(Map p211; ☎707-299-5030; www.redd-wood.com; 6755 Washington St; pizzas $12-16, mains $24-28; ⊙11:30am-3pm & 5-10pm, to 11pm Fri & Sat) Celeb-chef Richard Reddington's casual Italian trattoria serves outstanding homemade pastas, salumi, and tender-to-the-tooth pizzas from a wood-fired oven.

French Laundry Californian $$$

(Map p211; ☎707-944-2380; www.frenchlaundry.com; 6640 Washington St; prix-fixe dinner $295; ⊙seatings 11am-1pm Fri-Sun, 5:30-9:15pm daily)

The pinnacle of California dining, Thomas Keller's French Laundry is epic, a high-wattage culinary experience on par with the world's best. Book two months ahead at 10am sharp, or log onto www.opentable.com precisely at midnight. Avoid tables before 7pm; first-service seating moves a touch quickly. This is the meal you can brag about the rest of your life.

Ad Hoc Californian **$$$**

(Map p211; ☎707-944-2487; www.adhocrestaurant.com; 6476 Washington St; prix-fixe dinner from $52; ⏰5-10pm Thu-Sat & Mon, 10am-1pm & 5-10pm Sun) A winning formula by Yountville's culinary patriarch, Thomas Keller, Ad Hoc serves the master's favorite American home cooking in four-course family-style menus, with no variations (dietary restrictions notwithstanding). Monday is fried-chicken night, which you can also sample weekend lunchtime, take-out only, behind the restaurant at Keller's latest venture, **Addendum** (open 11am to 2pm Thursday to Saturday), which serves to-go boxed-lunch barbecue (order ahead to ensure availability).

Bouchon French **$$$**

(Map p211; ☎707-944-8037; www.bouchonbistro.com; 6354 Washington St; mains $19-45; ⏰11am-midnight Mon-Fri, from 10am Sat & Sun) Details at celeb-chef Thomas Keller's French brasserie are so impeccable – zinc bar to white-aproned waiters – you'd swear you were in Paris. Only the Bermuda-shorts-clad Americans look out of place. On the menu: oysters, onion soup, roasted chicken, leg of lamb, trout with almonds, runny cheeses and perfect profiteroles.

Étoile Californian **$$$**

(Map p211; ☎707-944-8844; www.chandon.com; 1 California Dr, Chandon Winery; lunch mains $28-36, dinner mains $29-39; ⏰11:30am-2:30pm & 6-9pm Thu-Mon) At Chandon winery, Étoile is perfect for a top-shelf white-tablecloth lunch, an ideal one-stop destination when you want to visit a winery, eat a good meal, and minimize driving.

Mustards Grill Californian **$$$**

(Map p211; ☎707-944-2424; www.mustardsgrill.com; 7399 St Helena Hwy; mains $25-30; ⏰11:30am-9pm, to 10pm Fri & Sat; 👪) The valley's original and always-packed roadhouse makes platters of crowd-pleasing, wood-fired, California comfort food – roasted meats, lamb shanks, pork chops, hearty salads and sandwiches.

St Helena

You'll know you're arriving when traffic halts. St Helena (ha-*lee*-na) is the Rodeo Dr of Napa, with fancy boutiques lining Main St (Hwy 29). The historic downtown is good for a stroll, with great window-shopping, but parking is next-to-impossible on summer weekends.

Culinary Institute of America at Greystone

STEPHEN SAKS / GETTY IMAGES ©

Sights & Activities

Silverado Museum Museum

(Map p222; 707-963-3757; www.silveradomuseum.org; 1490 Library Lane; noon-4pm Tue-Sat) FREE Contains a fascinating collection of Robert Louis Stevenson memorabilia. In 1880, the author – then sick, penniless and unknown – stayed in an abandoned bunkhouse at the old Silverado Mine on Mt St Helena with his wife, Fanny Osbourne; his novel *The Silverado Squatters* is based on his time there. Turn east off Hwy 29 at the Adams St traffic light and cross the railroad tracks.

Culinary Institute of America at Greystone Cooking Course

(Map p222; 707-967-2320; www.ciachef.edu/california; 2555 Main St; mains $25-29, cooking demonstration $20; restaurant 11:30am-9pm, cooking demonstrations 1:30pm Sat & Sun) Inside an 1889 stone chateau, now a cooking school, there's a gadget- and cookbook-filled **culinary shop**; fine **restaurant**; weekend **cooking demonstrations**; and **wine-tasting classes** by luminaries including Karen MacNeil, author of *The Wine Bible.*

Sleeping

El Bonita Motel $$

(Map p222; 707-963-3216; www.elbonita.com; 195 Main St; r $169-239;) Book in advance to secure this sought-after motel, with up-to-date rooms (quietest are in back), attractive grounds, hot tub and sauna.

Meadowood Resort $$$

(Map p222; 800-458-8080, 707-963-3646; www.meadowood.com; 900 Meadowood Lane; r from $600;) Hidden in a wooded dell with towering pines and miles of hiking, Napa's grandest resort has cottages and rooms in satellite buildings surrounding a croquet lawn. We most like the hillside fireplace cottages; lawn-view rooms lack privacy but are good for families. The vibe is Republican country club: wear linen and play *Great Gatsby.* Kids love the mammoth pool.

Wydown Hotel Boutique Hotel $$$

(Map p222; 707-963-5100; www.wydownhotel.com; 1424 Main St; r Mon-Fri $269-380, Sat & Sun $379-475;) Opened 2012, this fashion-forward boutique hotel, with

Silverado Museum

JOHN ELK / GETTY IMAGES ©

Napa Valley North

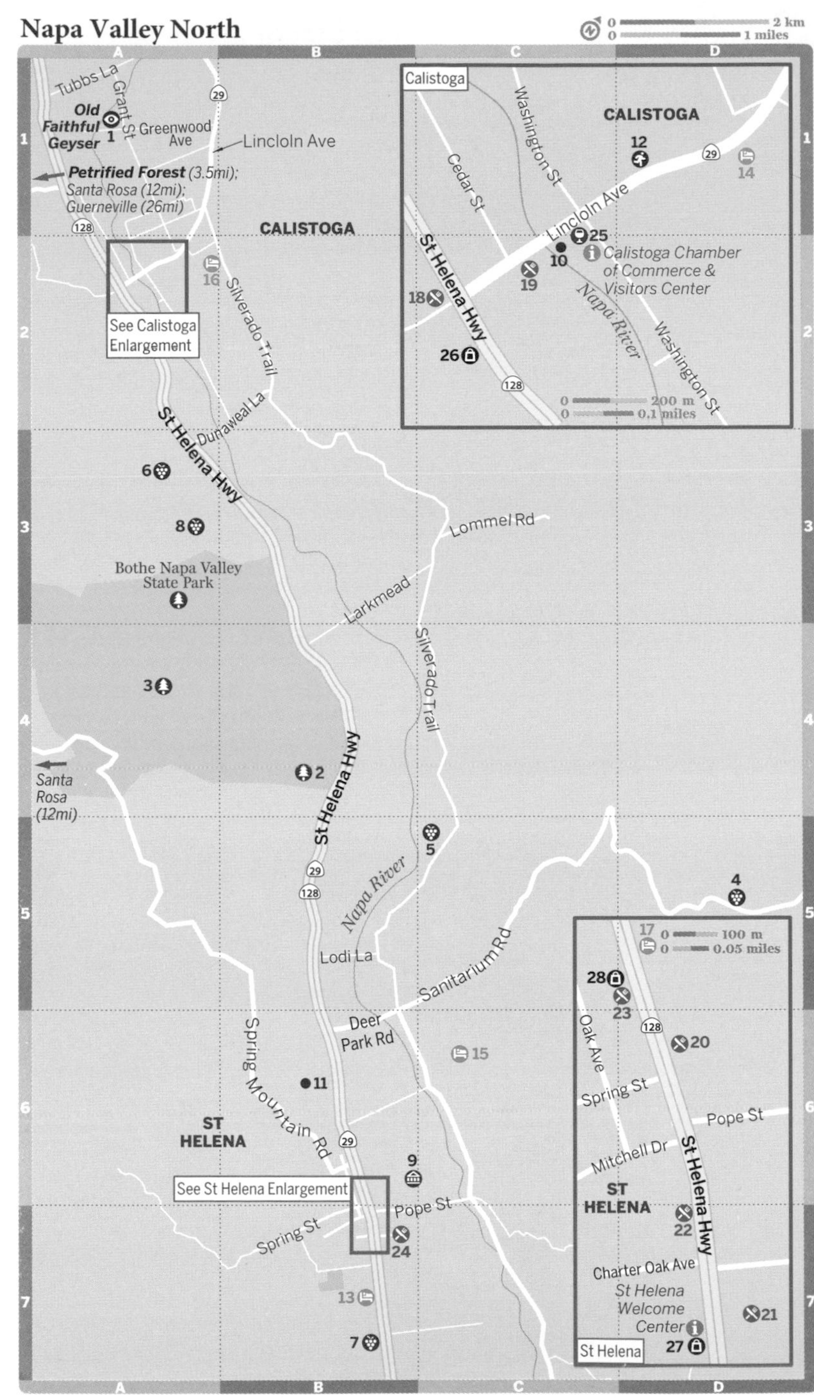

Napa Valley North

Don't Miss Sights

1 Old Faithful Geyser ... A1

Sights

2 Bale Grist Mill State Historic Park ... B4
3 Bothe-Napa Valley State Park ... A4
4 Cade ... D5
5 Casa Nuestra ... C5
6 Castello di Amorosa ... A3
7 Hall ... B7
8 Schramsberg ... A3
9 Silverado Museum ... B6

Activities, Courses & Tours

10 Calistoga Bike Shop ... C2
11 Culinary Institute of America at Greystone ... B6
12 Dr Wilkinson's Hot Springs Resort ... D1
Indian Springs Spa ... (see 14)
Spa Solage ... (see 16)

Sleeping

Bothe-Napa Valley State Park Campground ... (see 3)
Dr Wilkinson's Motel & Hideaway Cottages ... (see 12)
13 El Bonita ... B7
14 Indian Springs Resort ... D1
15 Meadowood ... C6
16 Solage ... A2
17 Wydown Hotel ... D5

Eating

18 Buster's Southern BBQ ... C2
19 Calistoga Inn & Brewery ... C2
20 Cook ... D6
21 Farmstead ... D7
22 Gott's Roadside ... D7
23 Model Bakery ... D5
24 Napa Valley Olive Oil Mfg Co ... B7
Restaurant at Meadowood ... (see 15)
Solbar ... (see 16)

Drinking & Nightlife

25 Brannan's Grill ... C2
Solbar ... (see 16)

Shopping

26 Calistoga Pottery ... C2
27 Napa Soap Company ... D7
28 Woodhouse Chocolates ... C5

good service, sits smack downtown, its 12 oversized rooms smartly decorated with tufted-velvet, distressed leather, subway-tile baths, and California-king beds with white-on-white high-thread-count linens.

Eating

Make reservations where possible.

Napa Valley Olive Oil Mfg Co Market $
(Map p222; ☎707-963-4173; www.oliveoilsainthe-lena.com; 835 Charter Oak Ave; ⏰8am-5:30pm) Before the advent of fancy-food stores, this ramshackle market introduced Napa to Italian delicacies – real prosciutto and salami, meaty olives, fresh bread, nutty cheeses and, of course, olive oil. Ask nicely and the owner will lend you a knife and a board to picnic at the rickety tables in the grass outside. Cash only.

Model Bakery Cafe $
(Map p222; ☎707-963-8192; www.themodelbak-ery.com; 1357 Main St; items $5-10; ⏰6:30am-6pm Mon-Sat, 7am-5pm Sun) Good bakery with scones, muffins, salads, pizzas, sandwiches and exceptional coffee.

Gott's Roadside American $$
(Map p222; ☎707-963-3486; http://gotts.com; 933 Main St; mains $10-15; ⏰7am-9pm, to 10pm May-Sep; 👪) Wiggle your toes in the grass and feast on quality burgers – of beef or ahi tuna – plus Cobb salads and fish tacos at this classic roadside drive-in, whose original name, 'Taylor's Auto Refresher,' remains on the sign. Avoid weekend waits by phoning ahead or ordering online. There's another at **Oxbow Public Market (Map p216; ☎707-226-6529; www.oxbowpublicmarket.com; 644 1st St; items from $3; ⏰9am-7pm Mon & Wed-Sat, to 8pm Tue, 10am-5pm Sun)**.

Cook Cal-Italian $$
(Map p222; ☎707-963-7088; www.cooksthelena.com; 1310 Main St; lunch $14-23, dinner $16-28; ⏰11:30am-10pm Mon-Sat, 10am-9pm Sun) Locals crowd this tiny storefront bistro, beloved for its earthy Cal-Italian cooking – homemade pasta and risotto, melt-off-the-bone ribs and simple-delicious burgers. Expect a wait, even with reservations.

Farmstead New American $$$
(Map p222; ☎707-963-9181; www.farmsteadna-pa.com; 738 Main St; mains $16-27; ⏰11:30am-9pm) An enormous open-truss barn

with big leather booths and rocking-chair porch, Farmstead draws a youthful crowd and grows many of its own ingredients – including grass-fed beef – for an earthy menu highlighting wood-fired cooking.

 Shopping

Main St is lined with high-end boutiques (think $100 socks), but some mom-and-pop shops remain.

Woodhouse Chocolates Food
(Map p222; www.woodhousechocolate.com; 1367 Main St; 10:30am-5:30pm) Woodhouse looks more like Tiffany than a candy shop, with housemade chocolates similarly priced, but their quality is beyond reproach.

Napa Soap Company Beauty
(Map p222; www.napasoap.com; 651 Main St; 10am-5:30pm) Eco-friendly bath products, locally produced.

 Information

St Helena Welcome Center Visitors Center
(Map p222; 707-963-4456; www.sthelena.com; 657 Main St; 9am-5pm Mon-Fri, plus 10am-4pm Sat-Sun May-Nov) The visitor center has information and lodging assistance.

Calistoga

The least gentrified town in Napa Valley feels refreshingly simple, with an old-fashioned main street lined with shops, not boutiques, and diverse characters wandering the sidewalks.

Calistoga is synonymous with the mineral water bearing its name, bottled here since 1924. Its springs and geysers have earned it the nickname the 'hot springs of the West.'

Sights & Activities

Calistoga is famous for hot-spring spas and mud-bath emporiums, where you're buried in hot mud and emerge feeling supple, detoxified and enlivened. (The mud is made with volcanic ash and peat; the higher the ash content, the better the bath.)

Packages take 60 to 90 minutes and cost $70 to $90. You start semi-submerged in hot mud, then soak in hot mineral water. A steam bath and blanket-wrap follow. The treatment can be extended with a massage, increasing the cost to $130 and up.

Baths can be taken solo or, at some spas, as couples. Variations include thin, painted-on clay-mud wraps (called 'fango' baths, good for those uncomfortable sitting in mud), herbal wraps, seaweed baths and various massage treatments. Discount coupons are sometimes available from the visitors center. Book ahead, especially on summer weekends. Reservations essential at all spas.

Indian Springs Spa Spa
(Map p222; 707-942-4913; www.indianspringscalistoga.com; 1712 Lincoln Ave; by appointment 9am-8pm) California's longest continually operating spa, and original Calistoga resort, has concrete mud tubs and mines its own ash. Treatments include use of the huge, hot-spring-fed pool. Great cucumber body lotion.

Spa Solage Spa
(Map p222; 707-226-0825; www.solagecalistoga.com/spa; 755 Silverado Trail; by appointment 8am-8pm) Chichi, austere, top-end spa, with couples' rooms and a fango-mud bar for DIY paint-on treatments. Also has zero-gravity chairs for blanket wraps, and a clothing-optional pool.

Dr Wilkinson's Hot Springs Resort Spa
(Map p222; 707-942-4102; www.drwilkinson.com; 1507 Lincoln Ave; by appointment 10am-3:30pm) Fifty years running; 'the doc' uses more peat in its mud.

Calistoga Bike Shop Cycling
(Map p222; 707-942-9687; www.calistogabikeshop.com; 1318 Lincoln Ave, Calistoga; 10am-6pm) Wine-tour rental package ($90) includes wine pickup.

Sleeping

Mountain Home Ranch Resort **$$**
(707-942-6616; www.mountainhomeranch.com; 3400 Mountain Home Ranch Rd; r $111-121, cabins $71-156;) In continuous operation since 1913, this 340-acre homestead outside town is a flashback to old California. Doubling as a retreat center, the ranch has simple lodge rooms and rustic freestanding cabins, some with kitchens and fireplaces, ideal for families, but you may be here during someone else's family reunion or spiritual quest.

Dr Wilkinson's Motel & Hideaway Cottages Motel, Cottages **$$**
(Map p222; 707-942-4102; www.drwilkinson.com; 1507 Lincoln Ave; r $149-255, cottages $165-270; ) This good-value vintage-1950s motel has well-kept rooms facing a swimming-pool courtyard with hot tub, three pools (one indoors), and mud baths. Also rents simple, great-value stand-alone cottages with kitchens, at the affiliated Hideaway Cottages, also with pool and hot tub.

Indian Springs Resort Resort **$$$**
(Map p222; 707-942-4913; www.indianspringscalistoga.com; 1712 Lincoln Ave; lodge r $229-359, cottage $259-429, 2-bedroom cottage $359-499;) The definitive old-school Calistoga resort, Indian Springs has cottages facing a central lawn with palm trees, shuffleboard, bocce, hammocks and Weber grills – not unlike a vintage Florida resort. Some sleep six. There are also top-end, motel-style lodge rooms (adults only). Huge hot-springs-fed swimming pool.

Solage Resort **$$$**
(Map p222; 866-942-7442, 707-226-0800; www.solagecalistoga.com; 755 Silverado Trail; r $530-675;) Calistoga's top spa-hotel ups the style factor, with Cali-chic semidetached cottages and a glam palm-tree-lined pool. Rooms are austere, with vaulted ceilings, zillion-thread-count linens and pebble-floor showers. Cruiser bikes included.

Eating

Buster's Southern BBQ Barbecue **$**
(Map p222; 707-942-5605; www.busterssouthernbbq.com; 1207 Foothill Blvd; dishes $8-12; 10am-7:30pm Mon-Sat, 10:30am-6pm Sun;)

Hot tub at a Calistoga resort

PLUSH STUDIOS / GETTY IMAGES ©

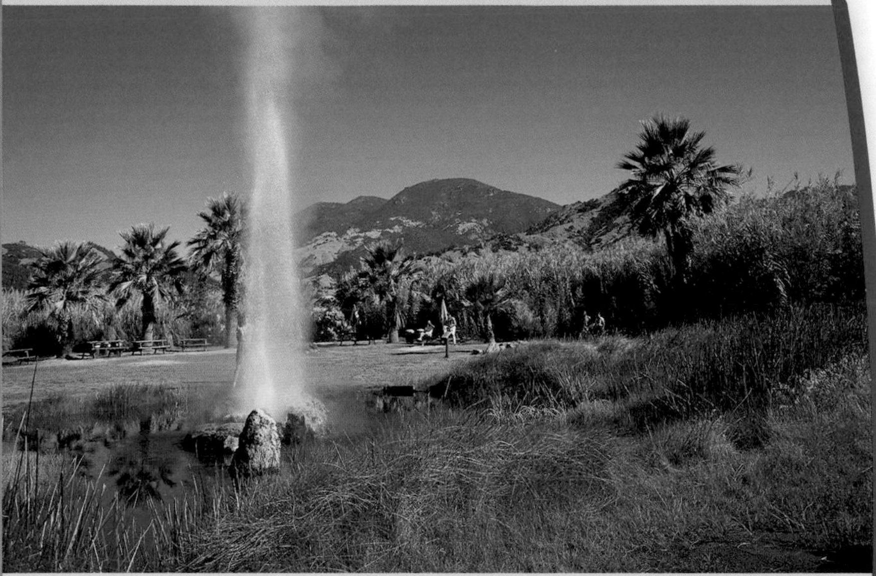

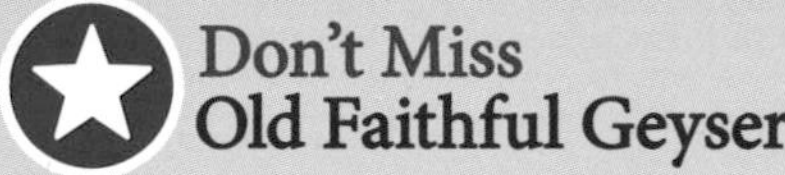

Don't Miss Old Faithful Geyser

Calistoga's mini version of Yellowstone's Old Faithful shoots boiling water 60ft to 100ft into the air, every 30 minutes. The vibe is pure roadside Americana, with folksy hand-painted interpretive exhibits, picnicking and a little petting zoo, where you can come nose-to-nose with llamas. It's 2 miles north of town, off Silverado Trail. Find discount coupons online.

NEED TO KNOW

Map p222; ☎707-942-6463; www.oldfaithfulgeyser.com; 1299 Tubbs Lane; adult/child/under 5yr $14/8/free; ⏲9am-6pm, to 5pm Nov-Mar; 👪

The sheriff dines at this indoor-outdoor barbecue joint, which serves smoky ribs, chicken, tri-tip steak and burgers, but closes early at dinnertime. Beer and wine.

Calistoga Inn & Brewery — American $$

(Map p222; ☎707-942-4101; www.calistogainn.com; 1250 Lincoln Ave; mains lunch $11-15, dinner $15-30; ⏲11:30am-3pm & 5:30-9pm) Locals crowd the outdoor beer garden Sundays. Midweek we prefer the country dining room's big oakwood tables – a homey spot for simple American cooking. Live music summer weekends.

Drinking

Solbar — Bar

(Map p222; ☎707-226-0850; www.solagecalistoga.com; 755 Silverado Trail; ⏲11am-9pm) Sip craft cocktails beside outdoor fireplaces and palm-lined pool at this Napa-swank resort bar.

Brannan's Grill — Bar

(Map p222; ☎707-942-2233; www.brannanscalistoga.com; 1374 Lincoln Ave; ⏲11am-11pm) The mahogany bar at Calistoga's handsomest restaurant is great for martinis and microbrews, especially weekends when jazz combos play.

Shopping

Calistoga Pottery Ceramics
(Map p222; 707-942-0216; www.calistoga-pottery.com; 1001 Foothill Blvd; 9am-5pm) Artisanal pottery, hand-thrown on-site.

Information

Calistoga Chamber of Commerce & Visitors Center (Map p222; 707-942-6333, 866-306-5588; www.calistogavisitors.com; 1133 Washington St; 9am-5pm)

Around Calistoga

Bale Grist Mill & Bothe-Napa Valley State Parks Historic Park
(707-942-4575; parks.ca.gov;) Both these parks have picnic areas and admission to one includes the other. **Bale Grist Mill State Historic Park** (Map p222; 707-963-2236; adult/child $5/2;) features a 36ft-high **water-powered mill wheel** dating to 1846 – the largest still operating in North America; Saturdays and Sundays (and sometimes Fridays and Mondays) from 10am to 4pm, it grinds flour. A mile-long trail leads to adjacent **Bothe-Napa Valley State Park** (Map p222; 707-942-4575; parking $8; 8am-sunset;), where there's a **swimming pool** ($5), and **camping** (Map p222; 800-444-7275; www.reserveamerica.com; 3801 Hwy 128; camping & RV sites $35;), plus hiking through redwood groves.

Robert Louis Stevenson State Park Park
(707-942-4575; www.parks.ca.gov; Hwy 29; sunrise-sunset) FREE At this undeveloped state park 8 miles north of Calistoga, the long-extinct volcanic cone of Mt St Helena marks Napa Valley's end and often gets snow in winter. It's a strenuous 5-mile climb to the peak's 4343ft summit, but what a view – 200 miles on a clear winter's day. Check conditions before setting out. Also consider 2.2-mile one-way **Table Rock Trail** (go south from the summit parking area) for drop-dead valley views.

Safari West Wildlife Reserve
(707-579-2551; www.safariwest.com; 3115 Porter Creek Rd; adult $70-80, child 3-12yr $32;) Giraffes in Wine Country? Whadya know. Safari West sprawls over 400 acres and protects zebras, cheetahs and other exotic animals, which mostly roam free. See them on a guided two-and-a-half-hour safari in open-sided jeeps; reservations required, no kids under three. If you're feeling adventurous, stay overnight in nifty canvas-sided **tent cabins** (cabin including breakfast $225 to $305) inside the preserve.

SONOMA VALLEY

We have a soft spot for Sonoma's folksy ways. Unlike in fancy Napa, nobody cares if you drive a clunker and vote Green. Locals call it 'Slow-noma.' Anchoring the bucolic 17-mile-long Sonoma Valley, the town of Sonoma makes a great jumping-off point for exploring Wine Country – it's only an hour from San Francisco – and has a marvelous sense of place, with storied 19th-century historical sights surrounding the state's largest town square. If you have more than a day, explore Sonoma's quiet, rustic side along the Russian River Valley and work your way to the sea.

Sonoma Valley Wineries

Rolling grass-covered hills rise from 17-mile-long Sonoma Valley. Its 40-some wineries get less attention than Napa's, but many are equally good. If you love zinfandel and syrah, you're in for a treat.

Picnicking is allowed at Sonoma wineries. Get maps and discount coupons in the town of Sonoma or, if you're approaching from the south, the Sonoma Valley Visitors Bureau (p234) at Cornerstone Gardens.

Bartholomew Park Winery Winery
(707-939-3026; www.bartpark.com; 1000 Vineyard Lane, Sonoma; tasting $10, incl tour $20; 11am-4:30pm) A great bike-to winery, Bartholomew Park occupies a 375-acre preserve, with oak-shaded picnicking and

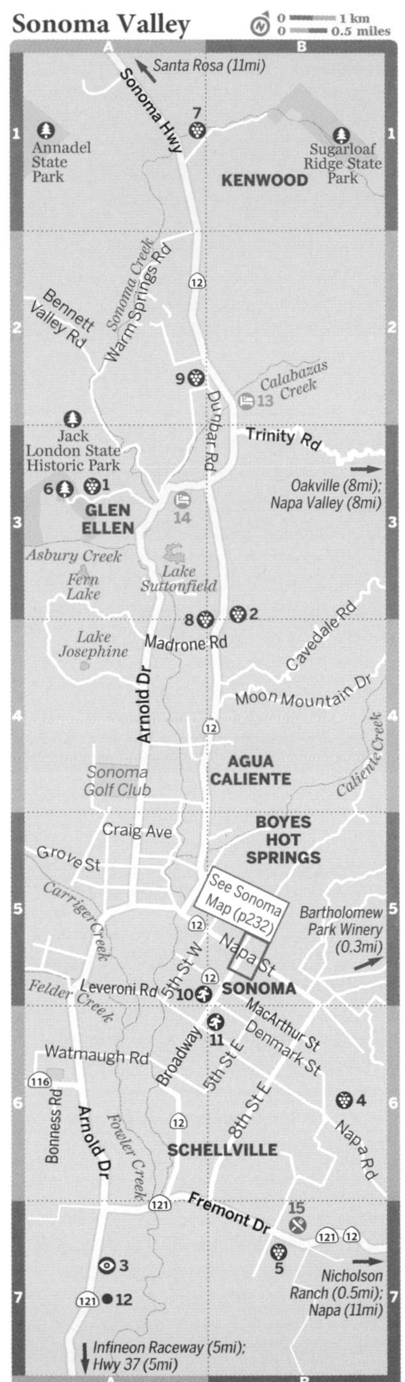

Sonoma Valley

Sights

1 Benziger ... A3
2 BR Cohn ... B3
3 Cornerstone Sonoma ... A7
4 Gundlach-Bundschu Winery ... B6
5 Homewood ... B7
6 Jack London State Historic Park ... A3
7 Kaz ... A1
8 Little Vineyards ... A4
9 Wellington ... A2

Activities, Courses & Tours

10 Sonoma Valley Cyclery ... A5
11 Traintown ... B6
12 Vintage Aircraft Company ... A7

Sleeping

13 Beltane Ranch ... B2
14 Gaige House Inn ... A3

Eating

15 Fremont Diner ... B7

valley-view hiking. The vineyards were originally cultivated in 1857 and now yield certified-organic, citrusy sauvignon blanc, cabernet sauvignon softer in style than Napa, and lush zinfandel. Tours (reservations required) are available Friday to Sunday. Bottles are $22 to $45.

Kaz Winery

(Map p228; ☎707-833-2536; www.kazwinery.com; 233 Adobe Canyon Rd, Kenwood; tasting $5; ⊙11am-5pm Fri-Mon;) Sonoma's cult favorite, supercool Kaz is about blends: whatever's in the organic vineyards goes into the wine – and they're blended at crush, not during fermentation. Expect lesser-known varietals like Alicante Bouschet and Lenoir, and a worthwhile cabernet-merlot blend. Kids can sample grape juice, then run around the playground outside. Bottles cost $20 to $48.

Gundlach-Bundschu Winery Winery

(Map p228; ☎707-939-3015; www.gunbun.com; 2000 Denmark St, Sonoma; tasting $10-15, incl tour $20-50; ⊙11am-4:30pm, to 5:30pm Jun–mid-Oct;) California's oldest family-run winery looks like a castle, but has a down-to-earth vibe. Founded 1858 by a Bavarian immigrant, its signatures are gewürztraminer and pinot noir, but 'Gun-Bun' was the first American winery

ANDREA LYNN / GETTY IMAGES ©

Don't Miss Petrified Forest

Three million years ago, a volcanic eruption at nearby Mt St Helena blew down a stand of redwoods between Calistoga and Santa Rosa. The trees fell in the same direction, away from the blast, and were covered in ash and mud. Over the millennia, the mighty giants' trunks turned to stone; gradually the overlay eroded, exposing them. The first stumps were discovered in 1870. A monument marks Robert Louis Stevenson's 1880 visit. He describes it in *The Silverado Squatters.*

It's 5 miles northwest of town, off Hwy 128.

NEED TO KNOW

☎707-942-6667; www.petrifiedforest.org; 4100 Petrified Forest Rd; adult/child $10/5; ⏲9am-7pm summer, to 5pm winter

to produce 100% merlot. Down a winding lane, it's a terrific bike-to winery, with picnicking, hiking and a lake. Tour the 2000-barrel cave ($20) by reservation only. Bottles are $22 to $45.

Homewood Winery
(Map p228; ☎707-996-6353; www.homewood-winery.com; 23120 Burndale Rd, at Hwy 121/12; tasting $5; ⏲10am-4pm; 🐾) Barn cats dart about at this down-home winery, where the tasting room is a garage, and the winemaker crafts standout ports and Rhône-style grenache, mourvèdre and syrah – 'Da redder, da better' – plus some late-harvest dessert wines, including excellent viognier and albariño. Bottles are $22 to $42, the tasting fee is waived with a purchase.

BR Cohn Winery
(Map p228; ☎800-330-4064, 707-938-4064; www.brcohn.com; 15000 Sonoma Hwy, Glen Ellen; tasting $10; ⏲10am-5pm) Picnic like a rock star at always-busy BR Cohn, whose founder managed '70s-superband the Doobie Brothers before moving on to

Below: Sonoma Valley vineyard; Right: Historic building on Sonoma Plaza
(BELOW) TRAVELER1116 / GETTY IMAGES ©; (RIGHT) RICHARD CUMMINS / GETTY IMAGES ©

make outstanding organic olive oils and fine wines – including excellent cabernet sauvignon, atypical in Sonoma. The little gourmet shop offers lots to taste, plus limited picnic supplies. In autumn, benefit concerts showcase bands like Skynyrd and the Doobies. Bottles are $16 to $56.

Little Vineyards Winery

(Map p228; 707-996-2750; www.littlevineyards.com; 15188 Sonoma Hwy, Glen Ellen; tasting $15; 11am-4:30pm Thu-Mon;) The name fits at this family-owned small-scale winery surrounded by grapes, with a lazy dog to greet you and a weathered, cigarette-burned tasting bar, at which Jack London formerly drank (before it came here). The big reds include Syrah, petite sirah, zin, cab and several delish blends. Good picnicking on the vineyard-view terrace. Also rents a cottage in the vines. Bottles cost $20 to $45.

Benziger Winery

(Map p228; 707-935-4527, 888-490-2739; www.benziger.com; 1883 London Ranch Rd, Glen Ellen; tasting $15-20, tram tour adult/under 21yr $25/10; 10am-5pm, tram tours 11:30am-3:30pm;) If you're new to wine, make Benziger your first stop for Sonoma's best crash course in winemaking. The worthwhile, non-reservable tour includes an open-air tram ride (weather permitting) through biodynamic vineyards, and a five-wine tasting. Great picnicking, plus a playground, make it tops for families. The large-production wine's OK (head for the reserves); the tour's the thing. Bottles are $15 to $80.

Wellington Winery

(Map p228; 800-816-9463; www.wellingtonvineyards.com; 11600 Dunbar Rd, Glen Ellen; tasting $10; 10:30am-4:30pm) Known for port (including a white) and meaty reds, Wellington makes great zinfandel, one from vines planted in 1892 – wow, what

color! The noir de noir is a cult favorite. Alas, servers have vineyard views, while you face the warehouse. Bottles are $15 to $30 and the tasting fee is refundable with a purchase.

Sonoma & Around

Fancy boutiques may lately be replacing hardware stores, but Sonoma still retains an old-fashioned charm, thanks to the plaza – California's largest town square – and its surrounding frozen-in-time historic buildings. You can legally drink on the plaza – a rarity in California parks – but only between 11:30am and sunset.

Sights & Activities

Sonoma Plaza Square
(Map p232; btwn Napa, Spain & 1st Sts) Smack in the center of the plaza, the Mission-revival-style **city hall**, built 1906–08, has identical facades on four sides, reportedly because plaza businesses all demanded City Hall face their direction. At the plaza's northeast corner, the **Bear Flag Monument** marks Sonoma's moment of revolutionary glory. The weekly **farmers market** (5:30pm to 8pm Tuesday, April to October) showcases Sonoma's incredible produce.

Sonoma State Historic Park Historic Site
(707-938-9560; www.parks.ca.gov; adult/child $3/2; 10am-5pm) The park is comprised of multiple sites, most side-by-side. The 1823 Mission San Francisco Solano de Sonoma anchors the plaza, and was the final California mission. Sonoma Barracks houses exhibits on 19th-cenutry life. The 1886 Toscano Hotel lobby is beautifully preserved – peek inside. The 1852 Vallejo Home lies a half-mile northwest. One ticket allows admission to all, including **Petaluma Adobe** (**707-762-4871; www.petalumaadobe.com; 3325 Adobe Rd, Petaluma; 10am-5pm Sat & Sun**), Vallejo's ranch, 15 miles away.

Sonoma

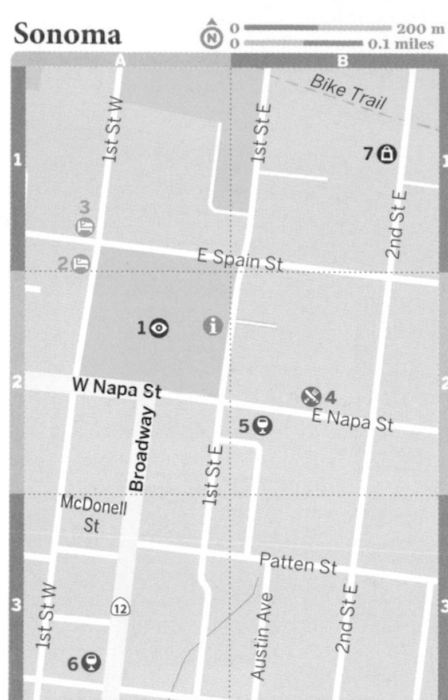

Sonoma

Sights

1 Sonoma Plaza A2

Sleeping

2 El Dorado Hotel A1
3 Sonoma Hotel A1

Eating

4 Cafe La Haye B2
El Dorado Kitchen .... (see 2)

Drinking & Nightlife

5 Enoteca Della Santina B2
6 Hopmonk Tavern A3

Shopping

7 Vella Cheese Co B1

Cornerstone Sonoma Gardens
(Map p228; ☎707-933-3010; www.cornerstonegardens.com; 23570 Arnold Dr, Hwy 121; ⏰10am-4pm; 👪) FREE There's nothing traditional about Cornerstone Gardens, which showcases 25 walk-through gardens by renowned avant-garde landscape designers who explore the intersection of art and nature. Let the kids run free while you explore top-notch garden shops, taste wine, and gather information from the onsite Sonoma Valley Visitors Bureau (p234); there's also a good, if pricy, on-site cafe. Look for the enormous blue Adirondack chair at road's edge.

Sonoma Valley Cyclery Bicycle Rental
(Map p228; ☎707-935-3377; www.sonomacyclery.com; 20091 Broadway/Hwy 12; bikes per day from $30; ⏰10am-6pm Mon-Sat, to 4pm Sun; 👪) Sonoma is ideal for cycling – not too hilly – with multiple wineries near downtown. Book ahead for weekends.

Traintown Amusement Park
(Map p228; ☎707-938-3912; www.traintown.com; 20264 Broadway; ⏰10am-5pm daily late May–mid-Sep, Fri-Sun mid-Sep–late May; 👪) Little kids adore Traintown, 1 mile south of the plaza. A miniature steam engine makes 20-minute loops ($5.75), and six other vintage amusement-park rides ($2.75 per ride) include a carousel and Ferris wheel.

Sleeping

Off-season rates plummet. Reserve ahead.

Sonoma Hotel Historic Hotel **$$**
(Map p232; ☎800-468-6016, 707-996-2996; www.sonomahotel.com; 110 W Spain St; r incl breakfast $170-200, ste $250; ❄📶) Long on charm, this good-value, vintage-1880s hotel, decorated with country-style willow-wood furnishings, sits right on the plaza. Double-pane glass blocks the noise, but there's no elevator or parking lot.

Beltane Ranch B&B **$$$**
(Map p228; ☎707-996-6501; www.beltaneranch.com; 11775 Hwy 12, Glen Ellen; d incl breakfast $160-285; 📶) 🍃 Surrounded by horse pastures and vineyards, Beltane is a throwback to 19th-century Sonoma. The cheerful, lemon-yellow, 1890s ranch house has double porches, lined with swinging chairs and white wicker. Though it's technically a B&B, each country-Americana-style room has a private entrance. No phones or TVs mean zero distraction from pastoral bliss.

El Dorado Hotel Boutique Hotel **$$$**
(Map p232; ☎707-996-3220; www.eldoradosonoma.com; 405 1st St W; r Mon-Fri $165-265, Sat & Sun $245-325; P❄📶🏊) Stylish touches,

such as high-end linens, justify rates and compensate for the rooms' compact size, as do private balconies, which overlook the plaza or rear courtyard (we prefer the plaza view, despite noise). No elevator.

Gaige House Inn B&B **$$$**
(Map p228; 707-935-0237, 800-935-0237; www.gaige.com; 13540 Arnold Dr, Glen Ellen; d incl breakfast from $275, ste from $425; **)** Among the valley's most chic inns, Gaige has 23 rooms, five inside an 1890 house decked out in Euro-Asian style. Best are the Japanese-style 'Zen suites,' with requisite high-end bells and whistles, including freestanding tubs made from hollowed-out granite boulders. Fabulous.

Eating

Fremont Diner American **$$**
(Map p228; 707-938-7370; http://thefremontdiner.com; 2698 Fremont Dr; mains $10-16; 8am-3pm Mon-Wed, to 9pm Thu-Sun;) Lines snake out the door peak times at this farm-to-table roadside diner. We prefer the indoor tables, but will happily accept a picnic table in the big outdoor tent to feast on ricotta pancakes with real maple syrup, chicken and waffles, oyster po' boys, finger-licking barbecue and skillet-baked cornbread. Arrive early, or late, to beat queues.

Cafe La Haye Californian **$$$**
(Map p232; 707-935-5994; www.cafelahaye.com; 140 E Napa St; mains $20-32; 5:30-9pm Tue-Sat) One of Sonoma's top tables for earthy New American cooking, La Haye only uses produce sourced from within 60 miles. Its dining room gets packed cheek-by-jowl and service can border on perfunctory, but the clean simplicity and flavor-packed cooking make it many foodies' first choice. Reserve well ahead.

El Dorado Kitchen Californian **$$$**
(Map p232; 707-996-3030; www.eldoradosonoma.com; 405 1st St W; lunch mains $12-17, dinner $24-31; 8-11am, 11:30am-2:30pm & 5:30-9:30pm) The swank plaza-side choice for modern California-Mediterranean cooking, El Dorado showcases seasonal-regional ingredients in dishes like duck-confit salad and housemade ravioli, served in a see-and-be-seen dining room with a big community table at its center. The happening lounge serves good small plates ($9 to $15) and craft cocktails. Make reservations.

Drinking

Hopmonk Tavern Brewery
(Map p232; 707-935-9100; www.hopmonk.com; 691 Broadway; 11:30am-10pm) This happening gastro-pub (mains $10 to $20) and beer garden takes its brews seriously, with

Mission San Francisco Solano de Sonoma (p231)

16 on tap, served in type-appropriate glassware. Live music Friday through Sunday.

Enoteca Della Santina Wine Bar
(Map p232; www.enotecadellasantina.com; 127 E Napa St; 4-10pm Mon-Thu, to 11pm Fri, 2-11pm Sat, to 10pm Sun) Thirty global vintages by the glass let you compare what you're tasting in California with the rest of the world's wines.

Shopping

Vella Cheese Co Food
(Map p232; 707-938-3232; www.vellacheese.com; 315 2nd St E; 9:30am-6pm Mon-Sat) Known for its dry-jack cheeses (made here since the 1930s), Vella also makes good Mezzo Secco with cocoa powder–dusted rind. Staff will vacuum-pack for shipping.

Information

Sonoma Valley Visitors Bureau (Map p232; 707-996-1090; www.sonomavalley.com; 453 1st E; 9am-5pm Mon-Sat, 10am-5pm Sun) Arranges accommodations; has a good walking-tour pamphlet and events information. There's another at Cornerstone Gardens.

Jack London State Historic Park

Napa has Robert Louis Stevenson, but Sonoma's got Jack London. This 1400-acre **park (Map p228; 707-938-5216; www.jacklondonpark.com; 2400 London Ranch Rd, Glen Ellen; per car $10, tour adult/child $4/2; 9:30am-5pm)** traces the last years of the author's life.

Changing occupations from Oakland fisherman to Alaska gold prospector to Pacific yachtsman – and novelist on the side – London (1876–1916) ultimately took up farming. He bought 'Beauty Ranch' in 1905 and moved there in 1910. With his second wife, Charmian, he lived and wrote in a small cottage while his mansion, **Wolf House**, was under construction. On the eve of its completion in 1913, it burned down. The disaster devastated London, and although he toyed with rebuilding, he died before construction got underway.

His widow, Charmian, built the **House of Happy Walls**, which has been preserved as a museum. It's a half-mile walk from there to the remains of Wolf House, passing London's grave along

Cottage, Jack London State Historic Park

A Wine Country Primer

When people talk about Sonoma, they're referring to the *whole* county, which unlike Napa is huge. It extends all the way from the coast, up the Russian River Valley, into Sonoma Valley and eastward to Napa Valley; in the south it stretches from San Pablo Bay (an extension of San Francisco Bay) to Healdsburg in the north. It's essential to break Sonoma down by district.

West County refers to everything west of Hwy 101 and includes the **Russian River Valley** and the coast. **Sonoma Valley** stretches north–south along Hwy 12. In northern Sonoma County, **Alexander Valley** lies east of Healdsburg, and **Dry Creek Valley** lies north of Healdsburg. In the south, **Carneros** straddles the Sonoma–Napa border, north of San Pablo Bay. Each region has its own particular wines; what grows where depends upon the weather.

Inland valleys get hot; coastal regions stay cool. In West County and Carneros, nighttime fog blankets the vineyards. Burgundy-style wines do best, particularly pinot noir and chardonnay. Further inland, Alexander, Sonoma and much of Dry Creek Valleys (as well as Napa Valley) are fog-protected. Here, Bordeaux-style wines thrive, especially cabernet sauvignon, sauvignon blanc, merlot and other heat-loving varieties. For California's famous cabernets, head to Napa. Zinfandel and Rhône-style varieties, such as syrah and viognier, grow in both regions, warm and cool. In cooler climes, resultant wines are lighter, more elegant; in warmer areas they are heavier and more rustic. As you explore, notice the bases of grapevines: the fatter they are, the older. 'Old vine' grapes yield color and complexity not found in grapes from younger vines.

the way. Other paths wind around the farm to the cottage where he lived and worked. Miles of hiking trails (some open to mountain bikes) weave through oak-dotted woodlands, between 600ft and 2300ft elevation. Watch for poison oak.

HEALDSBURG & THE RUSSIAN RIVER

Lesser known West Sonoma County was formerly famous for its apple farms and vacation cottages. But vineyards have been replacing the orchards, and the Russian River has now taken its place among California's important wine appellations for superb pinot noir.

'The River,' as locals call it, has long been a summertime weekend destination for Northern Californians, who come to canoe, wander country lanes, taste wine, hike redwood forests and live at a lazy pace. In winter the river floods, and nobody's here.

The Russian River begins in the mountains north of Ukiah, in Mendocino County, but the most famous sections lie southwest of Healdsburg, where it cuts a serpentine course toward the sea.

Russian River Area Wineries

Nighttime coastal fog drifts up the Russian River Valley, then usually clears by midday. Pinot noir does beautifully, as does chardonnay, which also grows in hotter regions, but prefers the longer 'hang time' of cooler climes.

RUSSIAN RIVER VALLEY

The highest concentration of wineries is along **Westside Rd**, between Guerneville and Healdsburg.

Iron Horse Vineyards Winery
(☎707-887-1507; www.ironhorsevineyards.com; 9786 Ross Station Rd, Sebastopol; tasting $20;

Charles M Schulz Museum

Charles Schulz, creator of *Peanuts* cartoons, was a long-term Santa Rosa resident. Born in 1922, he published his first drawing in 1937, introduced the world to Snoopy and Charlie Brown in 1950, and produced *Peanuts* cartoons until just before his death in 2000. This modern **museum** (707-579-4452; www.schulzmuseum.org; 2301 Hardies Lane; adult/child $10/5; 11am-5pm Mon & Wed-Fri, 10am-5pm Sat & Sun;) honors his legacy with a Snoopy labyrinth, Peanuts-related art, and a recreation of Schulz's studio. Skip Snoopy's Gallery gift shop; the museum has the good stuff.

10am-4:30pm) Atop a hill with drop-dead views over the county, Iron Horse is known for pinot noir and sparkling wines, which the White House often pours. The outdoor tasting room is refreshingly unfussy; when you're done with your wine, pour it in the grass. Sunday noon to 4pm, April to October, they serve oysters ($3). Located off Hwy 116. Bottles cost $27 to $85.

Porter Creek Winery
(707-433-6321; www.portercreekvineyards.com; 8735 Westside Rd, Healdsburg; 10:30am-4:30pm;) FREE Inside a vintage-1920s garage, Porter Creek's tasting bar is a former bowling-alley lane, plunked atop barrels. Porter is old-school Northern California, an early pioneer in biodynamic farming. High-acid, food-friendly pinot noir and chardonnay are specialties, but there's silky zinfandel and other Burgundian- and Rhône-style wines, too. Check out the aviary. Bottles cost $20 to $72 and tastings are free.

De La Montanya Winery
(707-433-3711; www.dlmwine.com; 999 Foreman Lane, Healdsburg; tasting $10; by

Farmers market, Healdsburg

ROBERTO SONCIN GEROMETTA / GETTY IMAGES ©

S. GREG PANOSIAN / GETTY IMAGES ©

Don't Miss
Dry Creek Valley

Hemmed in by 2000ft-high mountains, Dry Creek Valley is relatively warm, ideal for sauvignon blanc and zinfandel, and in some places cabernet sauvignon. It's west of Hwy 101, between Healdsburg and Lake Sonoma. Parallel-running **West Dry Creek Rd** is an undulating country lane with no center stripe – one of Sonoma's great back roads, ideal for cycling.

Bella Vineyards (707-473-9171; www.bellawinery.com; 9711 West Dry Creek Rd; tasting $10; 11am-4:30pm) Atop the valley's north end, always-fun Bella has caves built into the hillside.

Preston Vineyards (www.prestonvineyards.com; 9282 West Dry Creek Rd; tasting $5; 11am-4:30pm;) An early leader in organics, Lou Preston's 19th-century farm feels like old Sonoma.

Quivira (707-431-8333; www.quivirawine.com; 4900 West Dry Creek Rd; tasting $10; 11am-5pm;) Sunflowers, lavender and crowing roosters greet your arrival at this winery and biodynamic farm.

Unti Vineyards (707-433-5590; www.untivineyards.com; 4202 Dry Creek Rd; tasting $5; by appointment 10am-4pm;) Inside a vineyard-view tasting room, Unti pours all estate-grown reds. If you love small-batch wines, don't miss it.

appointment Mon-Thu, 11am-4:30pm Fri-Sun;) This tiny winery, tucked amid vineyards, is known for 17 small-batch varieties made with estate-grown fruit. Viognier, primitivo, pinot and cabernet are signatures; the 'summer white' and gewürztraminer are great back-porch wines. Apple-shaded picnic area, bocce ball and horseshoes add to the fun. Bottles are $20 to $60 and the tasting fee is refundable with a purchase.

Healdsburg

Once a sleepy ag town best known for its Future Farmers of America parade, Healdsburg has emerged as northern Sonoma County's culinary capital. Foodie-scenester restaurants and cafes, wine-tasting rooms and fancy boutiques line Healdsburg Plaza, the town's sun-dappled central square (bordered by Healdsburg Ave and Center, Matheson and Plaza Sts). It's best visited on weekdays – stroll tree-lined streets, sample locavore cooking and savor NorCal flavor.

Tasting rooms surround the plaza.

Activities

Russian River Adventures Canoeing
(**☎707-433-5599; russianriveradventures.com; 20 Healdsburg Ave, Healdsburg; adult/child $50/25;**) Paddle a secluded stretch of river, in quiet inflatable canoes, stopping for rope swings, swimming holes, beaches and bird-watching. This ecotourism outfit points you in the right direction and shuttles you back at day's end. Or staff will guide your kids downriver while you go wine tasting (guides $125 per day). Reservations required.

River's Edge Kayak & Canoe Trips Boating
(**☎707-433-7247; www.riversedgekayakandcanoe.com; 13840 Healdsburg Ave, Healdsburg)** Rents hard-sided canoes ($90/110 per half/full day) and kayaks ($40/55). Self-guided rentals include shuttle.

Sleeping

Geyserville Inn Motel **$$**
(**☎877-857-4343, 707-857-4343; www.geyservilleinn.com; 21714 Geyserville Ave, Geyserville; r Mon-Fri $129-169, Sat & Sun $269-289;**) Eight miles north of Healdsburg, this immaculately kept upmarket motel is surrounded by vineyards. Rooms have unexpectedly smart furnishings and quality extras, like feather pillows. Request a remodeled room. Hot tub.

H2 Hotel Hotel **$$$**
(**☎707-431-2202, 707-922-5251; www.h2hotel.com; 219 Healdsburg Ave, Healdsburg; r incl breakfast Mon-Fri $289-389, Sat & Sun $409-509;**) Little sister to Hotel Healdsburg, H2 has the same angular concrete style, but was built LEED-gold-certified from the ground up, with a living roof, reclaimed everything, and fresh-looking rooms with cush organic linens. Tiny pool, free bikes.

Eating

Healdsburg is the gastronomic capital of Sonoma County. Reservations essential.

Shed Cafe, Market **$**
(**☎707-431-7433; healdsburgshed.com; 25 North St, Healdsburg; dishes $3-15; ⏰8am-7pm Wed-Mon;**) At the vanguard of

Streetscape, Healdsburg
YINYANG / GETTY IMAGES ©

locavore eating, the Shed integrates food at all stages of production, milling its own locally sourced flours and olive oils, fermenting vinegars and kombucha from local fruit, and growing its own produce. It comprises a cafe with wood-fired dishes, fermentation bar with housemade shrubs, coffee bar with stellar pastries, and a market with prepared to-go foods.

Dry Creek General Store Deli **$**
(707-433-4171; www.drycreekgeneral-store1881.com; 3495 Dry Creek Rd, Healdsburg; sandwiches $8-10; 6:30am-6pm) Before wine-tasting in Dry Creek Valley, stop at this vintage general store, where locals and bicyclists gather for coffee on the creaky front porch. Perfect picnic supplies include Toscano-salami-and-manchego sandwiches on chewy-dense ciabatta.

Scopa Italian **$$**
(707-433-5282; www.scopahealdsburg.com; 109A Plaza St, Healdsburg; mains $15-24; 5:30-10pm Tue-Sun) Space is tight inside this converted barbershop, but it's worth cramming in for perfect thin-crust pizza and rustic Italian home cooking, like Nonna's slow-braised chicken, with sautéed greens, melting into toasty polenta. A lively crowd and good wine prices create a convivial atmosphere.

Drinking & Entertainment

Flying Goat Coffee Cafe
(www.flyinggoatcoffee.com; 324 Center St, Healdsburg; 7am-7pm) See ya later, Starbucks. Flying Goat is what coffee should be – fair-trade and house-roasted – and locals line up for it every morning.

Bear Republic Brewing Company Brewery
(707-433-2337; www.bearrepublic.com; 345 Healdsburg Ave, Healdsburg; 11am-9:30pm Sun-Thu, to 11pm Fri & Sat) Bear Republic features handcrafted award-winning ales, non-award-winning pub grub, and live music weekends.

Information

Healdsburg Chamber of Commerce & Visitors Bureau (707-433-6935, 800-648-9922; www.healdsburg.com; 217 Healdsburg Ave, Healdsburg; 9am-5pm Mon-Fri, to 3pm Sat, 10am-2pm Sun) A block south of the plaza. Has winery maps and information on ballooning, golf, tennis, spas and nearby farms (get the *Farm Trails* brochure); 24-hour walk-up booth.

Yosemite & the Sierra Nevada

An outdoor adventurer's wonderland, the Sierra Nevada is a year-round pageant of snow sports, white-water rafting, hiking, biking, backpacking and rock climbing. Skiers and snowboarders blaze hushed pine-tree slopes, and wilderness-seekers get away from the stresses of modern civilization. With granite mountains watching over high-altitude lakes, the eastern spine of California is a formidable topographical barrier embracing magnificent natural landscapes. And interspersed between its river canyons and 14,000ft peaks are the ghost towns left behind by California's pioneer settlers, and bubbling hot-springs pools. In the foothills, Gold Rush sites take you back to the days of the '49ers.

In the majestic national parks of Yosemite, Sequoia and Kings Canyon, visitors will be humbled by the enduring groves of solemn giant sequoias, the ancient rock formations and valleys, and the omnipresent opportunity to see bears and other wildlife.

Yosemite Valley (p259)

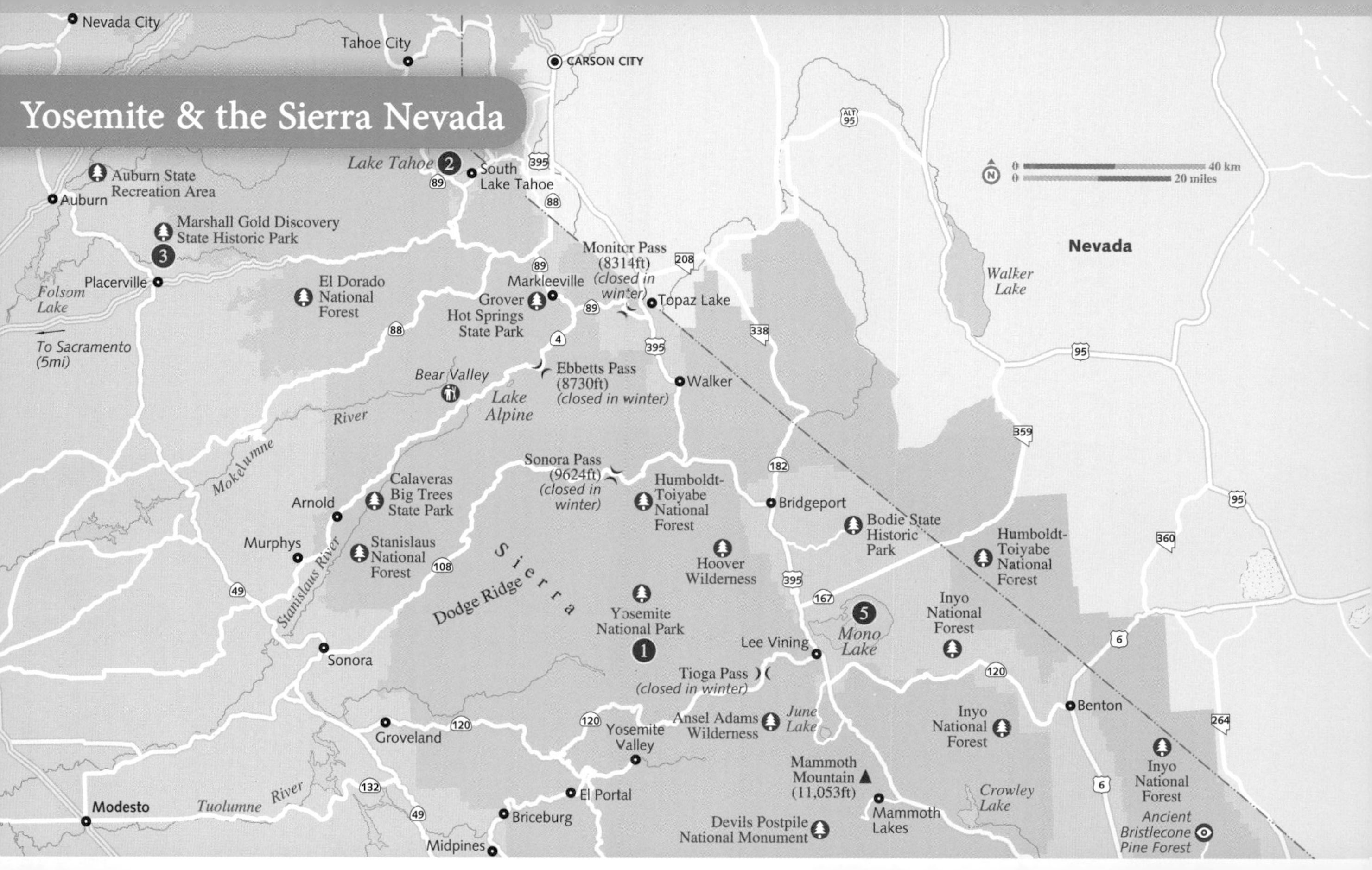

Yosemite & the Sierra Nevada
Nevada City
Tahoe City
CARSON CITY
Lake Tahoe
2
South Lake Tahoe
Auburn State Recreation Area
Auburn
Marshall Gold Discovery State Historic Park
3
Placerville
Folsom Lake
To Sacramento (5mi)
El Dorado National Forest
Monitor Pass (8314ft) (closed in winter)
Markleeville
Grover Hot Springs State Park
Topaz Lake
Ebbetts Pass (8730ft) (closed in winter)
Walker
Bear Valley
Lake Alpine
River
Mokelumne
Sonora Pass (9624ft) (closed in winter)
Calaveras Big Trees State Park
Arnold
Murphys
Stanislaus National Forest
Stanislaus River
Humboldt-Toiyabe National Forest
Bridgeport
Bodie State Historic Park
Hoover Wilderness
Sierra
Dodge Ridge
Yosemite National Park
1
Sonora
Lee Vining
5
Mono Lake
Tioga Pass (closed in winter)
Groveland
Yosemite Valley
Ansel Adams Wilderness
June Lake
Mammoth Mountain (11,053ft)
Mammoth Lakes
El Portal
Briceburg
Midpines
Modesto
Tuolumne River
Devils Postpile National Monument
Crowley Lake
Nevada
Walker Lake
40 km
20 miles
Inyo National Forest
Benton
Ancient Bristlecone Pine Forest

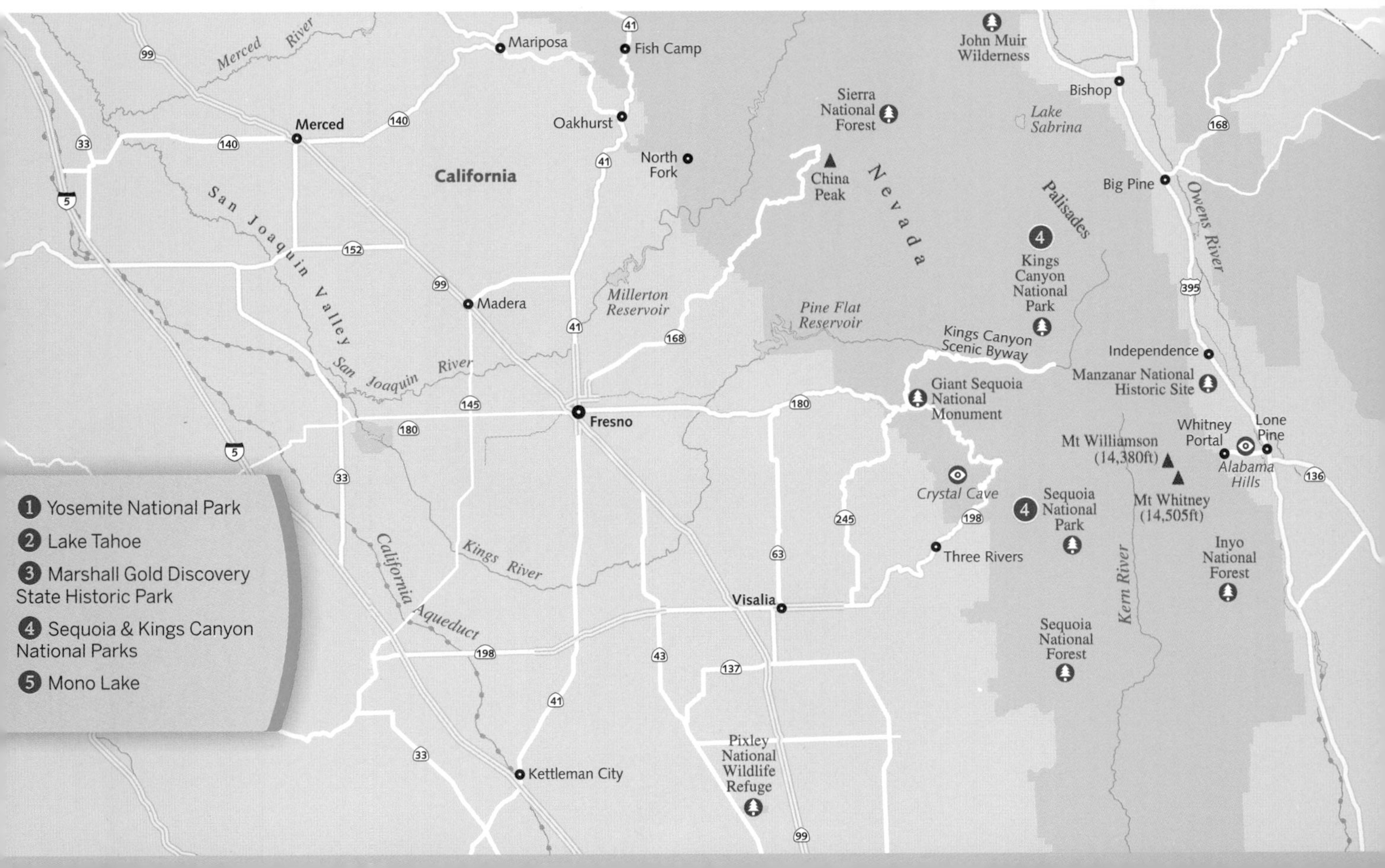

1 Yosemite National Park
2 Lake Tahoe
3 Marshall Gold Discovery State Historic Park
4 Sequoia & Kings Canyon National Parks
5 Mono Lake
Mariposa
Fish Camp
John Muir Wilderness
Bishop
Merced River
Merced
Oakhurst
Sierra National Forest
Lake Sabrina
California
North Fork
China Peak
Sierra Nevada
Palisades
Big Pine
Owens River
San Joaquin Valley
Kings Canyon National Park
Madera
Millerton Reservoir
Pine Flat Reservoir
Kings Canyon Scenic Byway
Independence
San Joaquin River
Manzanar National Historic Site
Giant Sequoia National Monument
Fresno
Lone Pine
Whitney Portal
Mt Williamson (14,380ft)
Alabama Hills
Crystal Cave
Sequoia National Park
Mt Whitney (14,505ft)
Three Rivers
Inyo National Forest
Kings River
California Aqueduct
Visalia
Kern River
Sequoia National Forest
Pixley National Wildlife Refuge
Kettleman City

Yosemite & the Sierra Nevada Highlights

Yosemite National Park

Yosemite (p258) has a way with humans. Its beauty – which can be utterly overwhelming – inspired writers and artists such as John Muir and Ansel Adams to produce some of their finest work. It's one of those rare places that touches you, and makes you want to slow down and hurry back. Peak waterfall viewing is in May and June.

1

2 Playtime in Lake Tahoe

Seen from the summit of a powdery white mountain or from a kayak streaming through placid waters, the peak-ringed idyll of Lake Tahoe (p250) rejuvenates and inspires. The largest alpine lake in North America, 'Big Blue' is a year-round outdoor playground that beckons you to experience it on foot, bike or skis, or by boat or car.

YVETTE CARDOZO / GETTY IMAGES ©

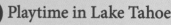

RICHARD CUMMINS / GETTY IMAGES ©

Hunting for Gold

3

So what if it's been over 160 years: maybe there's still an unearthed jackpot to be discovered near the Marshall Gold Discovery State Historic Park (p277). Visit the now-quiet epicenter of the Gold Rush days – where prospectors swarmed from across the country and around the world to make their fortunes – and try your own luck panning for gold.

Right: Wagon, Marshall Gold Discovery State Historic Park

CAROL POLICH PHOTO WORKSHOPS / GETTY IMAGES ©

TOMAS KASPAR / GETTY IMAGES ©

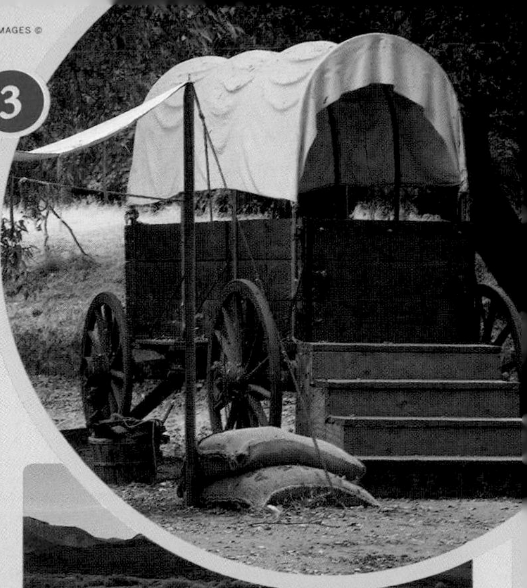

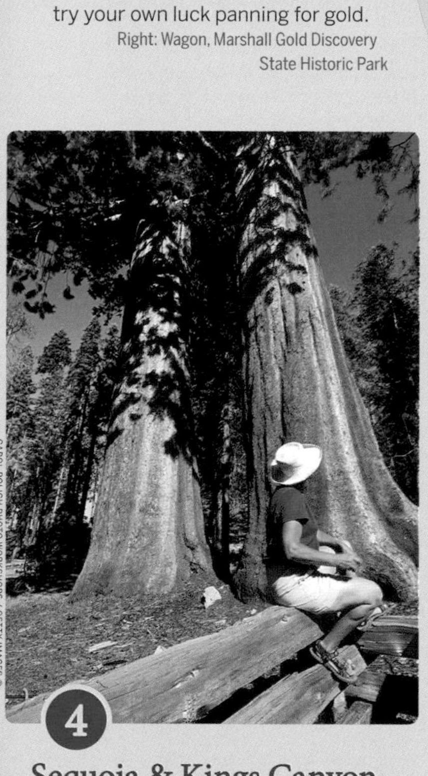

4

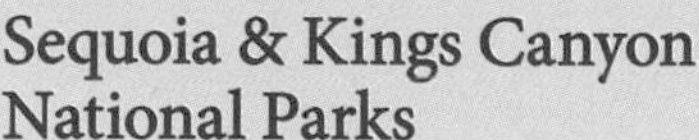

Sequoia & Kings Canyon National Parks

Often eclipsed by the supernova of Yosemite, these parks (p268) encapsulate the best of the Sierra Nevada. Crane your neck between divine granite peaks and North America's deepest canyons, and explore river caves and a never-ending supply of alpine meadows and lakes. Let your jaw hang slack at the shaggy forests of giant sequoias, the biggest trees on earth. Above: Sequoia National Park (p271)

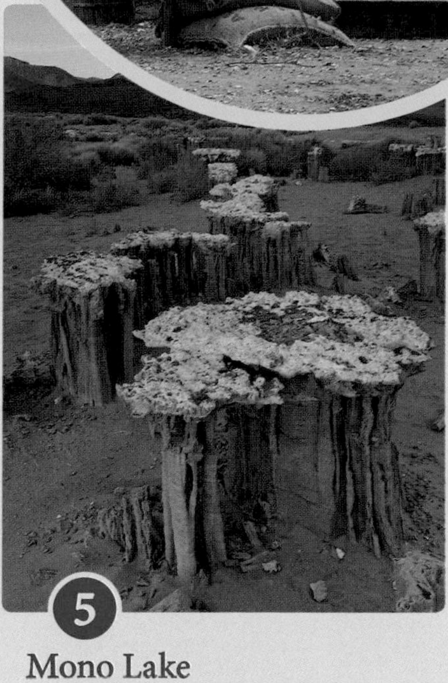

5

Mono Lake

Saved from extinction by local conservationists, this enormous basin (p271) – the second-oldest lake in North America – is truly a sight to ponder. Salty tufa castles rise from subterranean springs, standing watch where mountains meet the desert. Migrating birds feast on clouds of lake flies once relished by local Native American tribes, and bubbly volcanic craters and deep rock fissures buffer the vast blue bowl. Above: Tufa castles, Mono Lake

Yosemite & the Sierra Nevada's Best...

Ski Resorts

- **Squaw Valley** The north shore's biggest and most luxurious resort complex. (p250)
- **Mammoth Mountain** Lots of sunshine and dramatic surrounding peaks, plus the longest season in the state. (p274)
- **Heavenly** Shred the slopes in both California and Nevada. (p251)
- **Northstar California** Another big player on the north shore, and recently revamped. (p251)

Time Warps

- **Bodie State Historic Park** A well-preserved high-desert ghost town. (p278)
- **Vikingsholm Castle** Hike in to a 1920s Scandinavian-style mansion on the bay. (p255)
- **Manzanar National Historic Site** A memorial to one of the darkest events in US history. (p276)
- **Sutter's Fort State Historic Park** Sacramento's first pioneer settlement. (p279)

Flora & Fauna

- **Mariposa Grove** Towering redwoods in Yosemite National Park. (p261)
- **Giant Forest** The largest living trees on earth, in Sequoia National Park. (p271)
- **Tuolumne Meadows** Summer wildflowers bring dazzling contrast to Yosemite's verdant landscape. (p261)
- **Mono Lake** Migratory birds roost on the lake's islands in spring and summer. (p271)
- **Stream Profile Chamber** Explore underwater wildlife in South Lake Tahoe. (p251)

Scenic Drives

- **Hwy 395** Be wowed by snowy Eastern Sierra mountain views. (p271)
- **Kings Canyon Scenic Byway** A jaw-dropping descent into a deep rock canyon. (p268)
- **Tioga Road** View Yosemite's pristine high-country along Hwy 120. (p260)
- **Lake Tahoe** Take a loop around the shore of this blue jewel, ringed by snow-dusted mountains. (p250)

Left: Statue of mammoth, Mammoth Mountain (p274); **Above:** Bodie State Historic Park (p278)

(LEFT) JOHN ELK / GETTY IMAGES ©; (ABOVE) MITCH DIAMOND / GETTY IMAGES ©

Need to Know

ADVANCE PLANNING

- **Five months before** Reserve a campsite in Yosemite National Park.
- **One week before** Buy ski-lift tickets online for discounts at Mammoth Mountain and Heavenly.
- **Two days before** If you didn't score a Half Dome hiking permit in the preseason lottery, try your luck again.

RESOURCES

- **California Department of Transportation** (www.dot.ca.gov) For up-to-date highway conditions in California.
- **@YosemiteNPS** (www.twitter.com/yosemitenps) Yosemite's official tweets.
- **Roadside Heritage** (www.roadsideheritage.org) Free audio downloads about the history and sights along Hwy 395.
- **Yosemite Online** (www.yosemite.ca.us) By folks who know Yosemite.
- **Sacramento Bee** (www.sacbee.com) Sacramento's daily newspaper.
- **Sierra Web** (www.thesierraweb.com) Area events and links to local visitor information in the Eastern Sierra.

GETTING AROUND

- **Air** Larger airports in Sacramento and Reno, Nevada; limited service to Fresno and Mammoth Lakes.
- **Train** Amtrak runs from the Bay Area to Sacramento, Lake Tahoe and Reno, Nevada; connections available to Yosemite.
- **Car** The best way to explore off-the-beaten-track destinations.
- **Bus** Some local and regional transportation options, including free shuttles within Yosemite.

BE FOREWARNED

- **Road closures** Hwy 120 (across Yosemite) shuts down from about November through May, and heavy snow sometimes closes Hwy 89 near Emerald Bay at Lake Tahoe.
- **Snow chains** Roads are plowed in winter, but snow chains may be required.
- **Half Dome permits** This grueling, iconic hike now requires a permit, obtainable online.

Yosemite & the Sierra Nevada Itineraries

Outdoor lovers, this is where you recharge your batteries. Brace yourself for the oxygen-scarce mountain peaks and thundering waterfalls that comprise some of the most stunning natural attractions in the state.

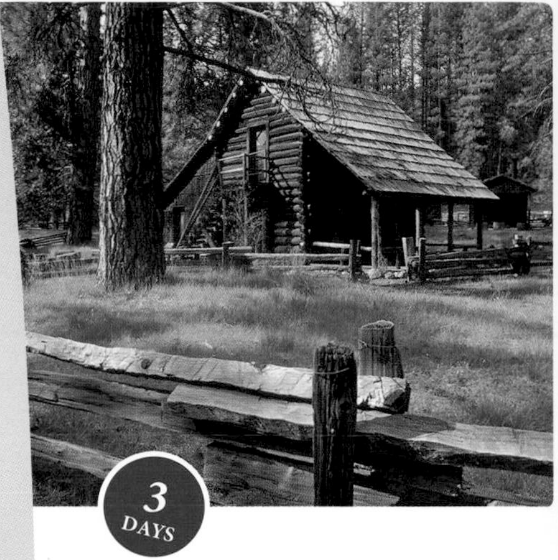

3 DAYS

YOSEMITE VALLEY TO TUOLUMNE MEADOWS

WEEKEND IN YOSEMITE

Kick off a taste of Yosemite National Park with a stop at the ❶**Tunnel View** lookout (p259). Try to keep the superlatives from tumbling through your lips as you gaze at daredevil waterfalls and ageless monoliths that form the crown jewel of ❷**Yosemite Valley** (p259). Climbing out of the Valley, lace up your boots and head out to conquer the ❸**Mist Trail** (p263), giving yourself time and lots of scenic breather stops along the way. The following day, drive south to ❹**Wawona** (p261), stopping for breakfast at the historic Wawona Hotel and then taking the shuttle for a gander at the giant sequoias of Mariposa Grove. Then motor up to ❺**Glacier Point** (p261), stopping en route for a hike to Dewey Point. Save lunch for when you get to road's end, in full view of Half Dome and the frothy ribbons of white water at Vernal and Nevada Falls. On the third day, head to the high country via Tioga Rd (Hwy 120). Stop at the moonscape overlook of ❻**Olmsted Point** (p261), finishing the journey with a ramble through the summertime wildflower carpet at ❼**Tuolumne Meadows** (p261) or out to a glistening high-country lake.

Top Left: Pioneer Yosemite History Center (p261), Wawona; **Top Right:** Alabama Hills (p276), Sierra Nevada

MONO LAKE TO ALABAMA HILLS

AWESOME EASTERN SIERRA

From Tuolumne Meadows, continue east over Tioga Pass to explore the splendor along scenic Hwy 395. A divine apparition of tufa formations poke out of saline 1 **Mono Lake** (p271), where you can kayak or canoe around eerie islands and discreetly spy on nesting birds. Spend a day wandering the high-desert ghost town of 2 **Bodie State Historic Park** (p278), an abandoned Wild West settlement that looks ready for its next gunfight. Drive south along the snowcapped Sierra crest to the high-altitude resort town of 3 **Mammoth Lakes** (p274), and take your pick of outdoor adventures, including hikes to granite-rimmed lakes or careening down its summer mountain-bike park. Don't leave town without a stroll out to witness the curious basalt rock columns of 4 **Devils Postpile National Monument** (p273). Continuing south, tour the reconstructed remnants and excellent interpretive museum at 5 **Manzanar National Historic Site** (p276), a desolate WWII-era Japanese American detention center. End your journey watching the sunset glow off the iconic orange landscape of the 6 **Alabama Hills** (p276), the setting for countless Western movies.

Discover Yosemite & the Sierra Nevada

At a Glance

- **Lake Tahoe** (p250) Year-round outdoor recreation and snow-sports paradise.
- **Yosemite National Park** (p258) A jaw-dropping valley and one of the country's most iconic parks.
- **Eastern Sierra** (p271) Fierce mountains, oodles of lakes and dramatic wilderness.
- **Gold Country** (p277) Relive the Gold Rush in these historical settlements.

Skiers, Squaw Valley

LAKE TAHOE

Shimmering in myriad shades of blue and green, Lake Tahoe is the USA's second-deepest lake and, at 6255ft high, it's also one of the highest-elevation lakes in the country. Driving around the lake's spellbinding 72-mile scenic shoreline will give you quite a workout behind the wheel.

The horned peaks surrounding the lake, which straddles the California–Nevada state line, are year-round destinations. Winter brings bundles of snow, perfect for those of all ages to hit the slopes at Tahoe's top-tier ski and snowboard resorts.

Tahoe Ski & Snowboard Resorts

Squaw Valley Skiing, Snowboarding (530-452-4331; www.squaw.com; 1960 Squaw Valley Rd, off Hwy 89, Olympic Valley; adult/youth 13-22yr/child under 13yr $114/94/66;) Few ski hounds can resist the siren call of this mega-sized, world-class, see-and-be-seen resort that hosted the 1960 Winter Olympic Games. Hardcore skiers thrill to white-knuckle cornices, chutes and bowls, while beginners practice their turns in a separate area on the upper mountain.

Northstar California Skiing, Snowboarding (530-562-1010; www.northstarcalifornia.com; 5001 Northstar Dr, off Hwy 267, Truckee; adult/youth 13-22yr/child 5-12yr $116/96/69; 8:30am-4pm;) An easy 7 miles south of I-80, this hugely popular resort has great intermediate terrain. Northstar's relatively sheltered location makes it the second-best choice

The Doomed Donner Party

In the 19th century, tens of thousands of people migrated west along the Overland Trail with dreams of a better life in California. Among them was the ill-fated Donner Party.

By the time the party reached the eastern foot of the Sierra Nevada, near present-day Reno, morale and food supplies were running dangerously low. To restore their livestock's energy and reprovision, the emigrants decided to rest here for a few days. But an exceptionally fierce winter came early, quickly rendering what later came to be called Donner Pass impassable and forcing the pioneers to build basic shelter near today's Donner Lake. Snow fell for weeks, reaching a depth of 22ft.

By the time the first rescue party arrived in late February, the trapped pioneers were still surviving – barely – on boiled ox hides. But when the second rescue party, led by James Reed, who had earlier been banished by the group, made it through in March, evidence of cannibalism was rife. Reports tell of 'half-crazed people living in filth, with naked, half-eaten bodies strewn about the cabins.'

after Homewood when it's snowing, and the seven terrain parks and pipes are top-ranked. Advanced and expert skiers can look for tree-skiing challenges on the back of the mountain.

Heavenly Skiing, Snowboarding
(**☎775-586-7000; www.skiheavenly.com; 3860 Saddle Rd, South Lake Tahoe; adult/youth 13-18yr/child 5-12yr $99/89/59; ⏰9am-4pm Mon-Fri, 8:30am-4pm Sat, Sun & holidays;** 👪) The 'mother' of all Tahoe mountains boasts the most acreage, the longest run (5.5 miles) and the biggest vertical drop around. Follow the sun by skiing on the Nevada side in the morning, moving to the California side in the afternoon. Views of the lake and the high desert are heavenly indeed.

South Lake Tahoe & Stateline

Highly congested and arguably overdeveloped, South Lake Tahoe is a chock-a-block commercial strip bordering the lake, framed by picture-perfect alpine mountains. At the foot of the world-class Heavenly mountain resort and buzzing from the gambling tables in the casinos just across the border in Stateline, Nevada, Lake Tahoe's south shore draws visitors with a cornucopia of activities and lodging and restaurant options, especially for summer beach access and tons of powdery winter snow.

Sights & Activities

Heavenly Gondola Cable Car
(**www.skiheavenly.com; Heavenly Village; adult/child 5-12yr/youth 13-18yr from $45/27/37; ⏰10am-5pm Jun-Aug, reduced off-season hours;** 👪) Soar to the top of the world as you ride this gondola, which sweeps you some 2.4 miles from Heavenly Village up the mountain in just 12 minutes. From the observation deck at 9123ft, get gobstopping panoramic views of the entire Tahoe Basin, the Desolation Wilderness and Carson Valley.

Stream Profile Chamber Outdoors
(**☎530-543-2674; www.tahoeheritage.org; trailhead at USFS Taylor Creek Visitor Center, off Hwy 89; ⏰8am-5pm late May-Sep, 8am-4pm Oct) FREE** Along a family-friendly hiking trail, this submerged glass structure in a teeming creek lets you check out what plants and fish live below the waterline. The best time to visit is in October during

Lake Tahoe

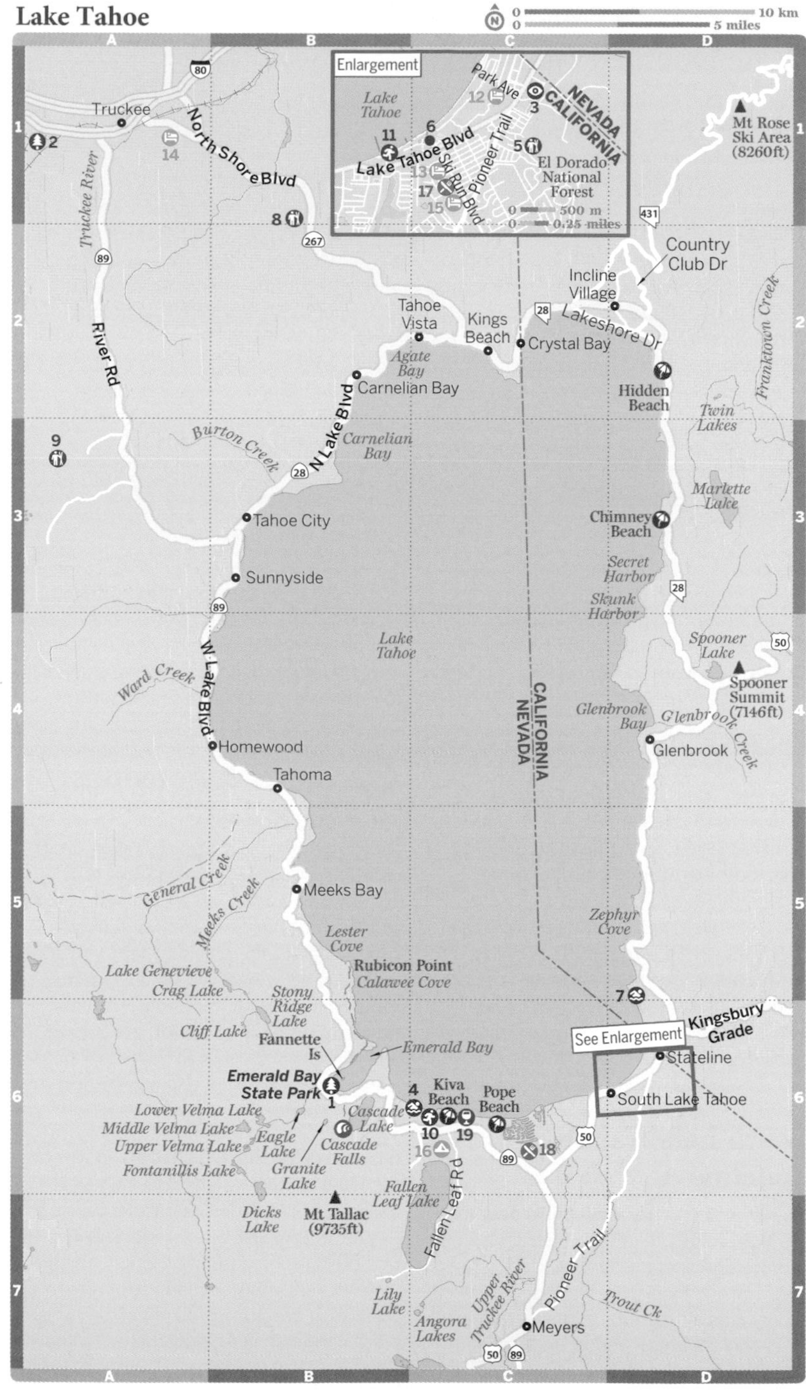

0 10 km
0 5 miles
Enlargement
Lake Tahoe
Park Ave
NEVADA
CALIFORNIA
Lake Tahoe Blvd
Ski Run Blvd
Pioneer Trail
El Dorado National Forest
0 500 m
0 0.25 miles
Truckee
North Shore Blvd
Truckee River
Mt Rose Ski Area (8260ft)
Country Club Dr
Incline Village
Tahoe Vista
Kings Beach
Crystal Bay
Lakeshore Dr
Agate Bay
Carnelian Bay
N Lake Blvd
Hidden Beach
Twin Lakes
Franktown Creek
River Rd
Burton Creek
Marlette Lake
Tahoe City
Chimney Beach
Secret Harbor
Sunnyside
Skunk Harbor
Lake Tahoe
Spooner Lake
Spooner Summit (7146ft)
Ward Creek
W Lake Blvd
Glenbrook Bay
Glenbrook Creek
Homewood
Glenbrook
Tahoma
General Creek
Meeks Creek
Meeks Bay
Zephyr Cove
Lester Cove
Rubicon Point
Calawee Cove
Lake Genevieve
Crag Lake
Stony Ridge Lake
Cliff Lake
Fannette Is
Emerald Bay
Kingsbury Grade
See Enlargement
Stateline
Emerald Bay State Park
Kiva Beach
Pope Beach
South Lake Tahoe
Lower Velma Lake
Middle Velma Lake
Upper Velma Lake
Eagle Lake
Cascade Lake
Cascade Falls
Fontanillis Lake
Granite Lake
Fallen Leaf Lake
Fallen Leaf Rd
Dicks Lake
Mt Tallac (9735ft)
Pioneer Trail
Lily Lake
Upper Truckee River
Trout Ck
Angora Lakes
Meyers

Lake Tahoe

Don't Miss Sights
1 Emerald Bay State Park....................B6

Sights
2 Donner Memorial State Park..............A1
3 Heavenly Gondola..............................C1
Vikingsholm Castle.....................(see 1)

Activities, Courses & Tours
4 Baldwin Beach..................................C6
5 Heavenly C1
6 Lake Tahoe Cruises...........................C1
7 Nevada Beach...................................D5
8 Northstar California..........................B1
9 Squaw Valley....................................A3
10 Stream Profile Chamber...................C6
11 Timber Cove Marina.........................B1

Sleeping
12 968 Park Hotel C1
13 Alder Inn..C1
14 Cedar House Sport Hotel A1
15 Deerfield Lodge at Heavenly.............C1
16 Fallen Leaf Campground C6

Eating
17 Blue Angel Cafe................................C1
18 Burger Lounge C6

Drinking & Nightlife
19 Beacon Bar & Grill............................C6

the Kokanee salmon run, when the brilliant red beauties arrive to spawn. See the website for scheduled activities.

Kayak Tahoe Kayaking, Water Sports
(530-544-2011; www.kayaktahoe.com; kayak single/double 1hr $20/32, 1 day $65/85, lessons & tours from $40; 10am-5pm Sat & Sun Jun-Sep) Rent a kayak or stand-up paddleboard (SUP), take a lesson or sign up for a guided tour, including sunset cove paddles, trips to Emerald Bay and explorations of the Upper Truckee River estuary and the eastern shore. Five seasonal locations at **Timber Cove Marina**, Vikingsholm (Emerald Bay) and Baldwin, Pope and Nevada Beaches.

BEACHES & SWIMMING

On the Californian side, the nicest strands are **Pope Beach** (per car $7), **Kiva Beach** and **Baldwin Beach** (per car $7). They're all found along Emerald Bay Rd (Hwy 89), running west and east of Tallac Historic Site.

Many folks prefer to head over to Stateline and keep driving north 2 miles to pretty **Nevada Beach** (per car $7), where the wind really picks up in the afternoons, or always-busy **Zephyr Cove** (www.zephyrcove.com; 760 Hwy 50; per car $8), which has rustic resort and marina facilities along its sandy mile-long shoreline.

MOUNTAIN BIKING

For expert mountain bikers, the classic **Mr Toad's Wild Ride**, with its steep downhill sections and banked turns reminiscent of a Disneyland theme-park ride, should prove sufficiently challenging. Usually open from June until October, the one-way trail along Saxon Creek starts off Hwy 89 south of town near Grass Lake and Luther Pass.

Sleeping

Fallen Leaf Campground Campground $
(530-544-0426, reservations 877-444-6777; www.recreation.gov; Fallen Leaf Lake Rd; tent & RV sites $32-34, yurts $84; mid-May–mid-Oct;) Near the north shore of stunning Fallen Leaf Lake, this is one of the biggest and most popular campgrounds on the south shore, with pay showers and approximately 200 wooded sites and six canvas-sided yurts that can sleep a family of five (bring your own sleeping bags).

Alder Inn Inn $$
(530-544-4485; www.thealderinn.com; 1072 Ski Run Blvd; r $99-150;) Even better than staying at your best friend's house by the lake, this hospitable inn on the Heavenly ski-shuttle route charms with color schemes that really pop, pillow-top mattresses, organic bath goodies, mini-fridges, microwaves and flat-screen TVs. Dip your toes in the kidney-shaped pool in summer. Continental breakfast included on weekends.

968 Park Hotel Boutique Hotel $$
(530-544-0968; www.968parkhotel.com; 968 Park Ave; r $109-309; @) A refashioned motel with serious hipster edge, recycled, rescued and re-envisioned building materials have made this

LEED-certified property an aesthetically pleasing ecohaven near the lake. A new lobby bar offers free wine tastings on Friday evenings, and in summer, unwind in a cabana by the sunny pool or in the zen garden before sinking into your dreamy Sterling bed.

Deerfield Lodge at Heavenly Boutique Hotel **$$$**
(**530-544-3337; www.tahoedeerfieldlodge.com; 1200 Ski Run Blvd; r/ste incl breakfast from $179/229;**) A small boutique hotel close to Heavenly ski resort, Deerfield has a dozen intimate rooms and spacious suites that each have a patio or balcony facing the green courtyard, along with a whirlpool tub, flickering gas fireplace and amusing coat racks crafted from skis and snowboards. Pet fee $25.

Eating

Burger Lounge Fast Food **$**
(**530-542-2010; www.burgerloungeintahoe.com; 717 Emerald Bay Rd; burgers $6-8; 10am-8pm daily Jun-Sep, 11am-7pm Wed-Sun Oct-May;**) You can't miss that giant beer mug standing outside a shingled cabin. Step inside for the south shore's tastiest burgers, including the crazy 'Jiffy burger' (with peanut butter and cheddar cheese), the zingy pesto fries or the knockout ice-cream shakes.

Blue Angel Cafe Californian **$$**
(**530-544-6544; www.theblueangelcafe.com; 1132 Ski Run Blvd; mains lunch $11-16, dinner $12-25; 11am-9pm;**) Inside a cute wooden house on the way uphill to ski at Heavenly, this modern international-inspired kitchen churns out seafood, club sandwiches, elaborate salads, pastas and flank steaks to stuff your belly. Turn up for happy hour or the rotating lunch and dinner specials.

Drinking & Entertainment

Beacon Bar & Grill Bar
(**www.camprichardson.com; Camp Richardson Resort, 1900 Jameson Beach Rd; 11am-10pm**) Imagine all of Lake Tahoe is your very own front yard when you and your buddies sprawl across this big wraparound wooden deck. If you want to get schnockered, order the signature Rum Runner cocktail. Bands rock here in summer.

Western Shore

Lake Tahoe's densely forested western shore, between Emerald Bay and Tahoe City, is idyllic. Hwy 89 sinuously wends past gorgeous state parks with swimming beaches, hiking trails, pine-shaded campgrounds and historic mansions.

Sleeping & Eating

Tahoma Meadows B&B Cottages Cabin **$$**
(**530-525-1553; www.tahomameadows.com; 6821 W Lake Blvd, Tahoma; cottages incl breakfast $99-389;**) North of Meeks Bay, Tahoma Meadows B&B Cottages rents darling country cabins (pet fee $20) and offers evening wine & cheese hours and fresh country breakfasts.

Fire Sign Cafe American **$**
(**www.firesigncafe.com; 1785 W Lake Blvd; mains $7-13; 7am-3pm;**) For breakfast, everyone heads to the friendly Fire Sign for down-home omelets, blueberry pancakes, eggs Benedict with smoked salmon, fresh made-from-scratch pastries and other carbo-loading bombs, plus organic coffee. In summer, hit the outdoor patio. Lines are usually very long, so get there early.

Tahoe City

The north shore's commercial hub, Tahoe City straddles the junction of Hwys 89 and 28, making it almost inevitable that you'll find yourself breezing through here at least once during your 'round-the-lake sojourn.

Sleeping

Mother Nature's Inn Inn **$$**
(**530-581-4278; www.mothernaturesinn.com; 551 N Lake Blvd; r $80-125;**) Right in town behind Cabin Fever knickknack boutique, this good-value option offers

ANDREW LIPOVSKY / GETTY IMAGES ©

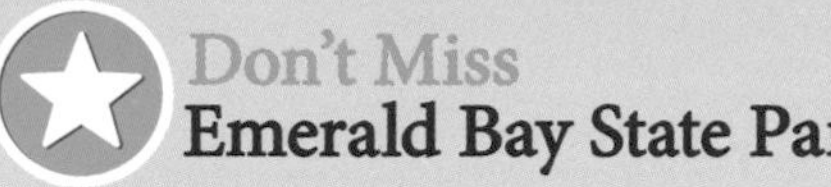

Don't Miss
Emerald Bay State Park

Sheer granite cliffs and a jagged shoreline hem in glacier-carved Emerald Bay, a teardrop cove that will have you digging for your camera. Its most captivating aspect is the water, which changes from cloverleaf green to light jade depending on the angle of the sun.

You'll spy panoramic pullouts all along Hwy 89, including at **Inspiration Point**, opposite Bayview Campground. Just south, the road shoulder evaporates on both sides of a steep drop-off, revealing a postcard-perfect view of Emerald Bay to the north and Cascade Lake to the south.

The mesmerizing blue-green waters of the bay frame **Fannette Island**. This uninhabited granite speck, Lake Tahoe's only island, holds the vandalized remains of a tiny 1920s teahouse belonging to heiress Lora Knight, who would occasionally motorboat guests to the island from **Vikingsholm Castle** (tour adult/child $10/8; 11am-4pm late May–Sep), her ancient Scandinavian-style mansion on the bay. Completed in 1929, the mansion has trippy design elements aplenty, including sod-covered roofs that sprout wildflowers in late spring.

NEED TO KNOW

530-541-6498; www.parks.ca.gov; per car $10; late May–Sep

quiet motel-style rooms with a tidy country look, fridges and coffeemaker, eclectic furniture and comfy pillow-top mattresses. It's within walking distance of Commons Beach. Pet fee $15.

Eating & Drinking

Dockside 700 Wine Bar & Grill American **$$**

(530-581-0303; www.dockside700.com; 700

N Lake Blvd; mains lunch $10-17, dinner $14-32; ⏲11:30am-8pm Mon-Thu, to 9pm Fri-Sun; 👪🐾) On a lazy summer afternoon, grab a table on the back deck that overlooks the boats bobbing at Tahoe City Marina. Barbecue chicken, ribs and steak light a fire under dinner (reservations advised), alongside seafood pastas and pizzas.

Tahoe Mountain Brewing Co. Brewery
(www.tahoebrewing.com; 475 N Lake Blvd; ⏲11:30am-10pm) Brewed in nearby Truckee, the Sugar Pine Porter, barrel-aged sours and award-winning Paddleboard Pale Ale here pair splendidly with sweet potato fries, burgers and other pub grub on the outdoor lake-facing patio.

Truckee & Donner Lake

Cradled by mountains and the Tahoe National Forest, Truckee is a thriving town steeped in Old West history. Today tourism fills much of the city's coffers, thanks to a well-preserved historical downtown and its proximity to Lake Tahoe and no fewer than six downhill and four cross-country ski resorts.

Sights

Donner Memorial State Park Park
(www.parks.ca.gov; Donner Pass Rd; per car $8; ⏲museum 10am-5pm, closed Tue & Wed Sep-May; 👪) At the eastern end of Donner Lake, this state-run park occupies one of the sites where the doomed Donner Party got trapped during the fateful winter of 1846–47 (see boxed text, p251). Though its history is gruesome, the park is gorgeous and has a sandy beach, picnic tables, hiking trails and wintertime cross-country skiing and snowshoeing. The entry fee includes admission to the excellent **Emigrant Trail Museum**, which has fascinating, if admittedly macabre historical exhibits

Left: Donner Lake; **Below:** Downtown Truckee
(LEFT) SHERYL GRIFFIN / GETTY IMAGES ©; (BELOW) STEPHEN SAKS / GETTY IMAGES ©

and a 25-minute film re-enacting the Donner Party's horrific plight.

Sleeping

Clair Tappaan Lodge Hostel **$**

(530-426-3632; www.sierraclub.org; 19940 Donner Pass Rd, Norden; dm incl meals adult/child from $65/45) About a mile west of Sugar Bowl, this cozy Sierra Club–owned rustic mountain lodge puts you near major ski resorts and sleeps up to 140 people in dorms and family rooms. Rates include family-style meals, but you're expected to do small chores and bring your own sleeping bag, towel and swimsuit (for the hot tub!).

Cedar House Sport Hotel Boutique Hotel **$$$**

(530-582-5655; www.cedarhousesporthotel.com; 10918 Brockway Rd; r incl breakfast $180-280; @) This chic, environmentally conscious contemporary lodge aims at getting folks out into nature. It boasts countertops made from recycled paper, 'rain chains' that redistribute water from the green roof garden, low-flow plumbing and in-room recycling. However, it doesn't skimp on plush robes, sexy platform beds with pillow-top mattresses, flat-screen TVs or the outdoor hot tub. Pet fee $75.

Eating & Drinking

Squeeze In Diner **$$**

(www.squeezein.com; 10060 Donner Pass Rd; mains $8-15; 7am-2pm;) Across from the Amtrak station, this snug locals' favorite dishes up breakfasts big enough to feed a lumberjack. Over 60 varieties of humungous omelets – along with burgers, burritos and big salads – are dished up in this funky place crammed with silly tchotchkes and colorful handwritten notes plastered on the walls.

Moody's Bistro & Lounge Californian **$$$**
(☎530-587-8688; www.moodysbistro.com; 10007 Bridge St; lunch mains $12-18, dinner mains $13-32; ⏰11:30am-9:30pm) With its sophisticated supper-club looks and live jazz (Thursday to Saturday evenings), this gourmet restaurant in the Truckee Hotel oozes urbane flair. Only fresh, organic and locally grown ingredients make it into the chef's perfectly pitched concoctions like pork loin with peach barbecue sauce, roasted beets with shaved fennel or pan-roasted Arctic char.

YOSEMITE NATIONAL PARK

The jaw-dropping head-turner of America's national parks, and a Unesco World Heritage site, Yosemite (yo-*sem*-it-ee) garners the devotion of all who enter. From the waterfall-striped granite walls buttressing emerald-green Yosemite Valley to the skyscraping giant sequoias catapulting into the air at Mariposa Grove, the place inspires a sense of awe and reverence – four million visitors wend their way to the country's third-oldest national park annually. But lift your eyes above the crowds and you'll feel your heart instantly moved by unrivalled splendors: the haughty profile of Half Dome, the hulking presence of El Capitan, the drenching

Yosemite Valley

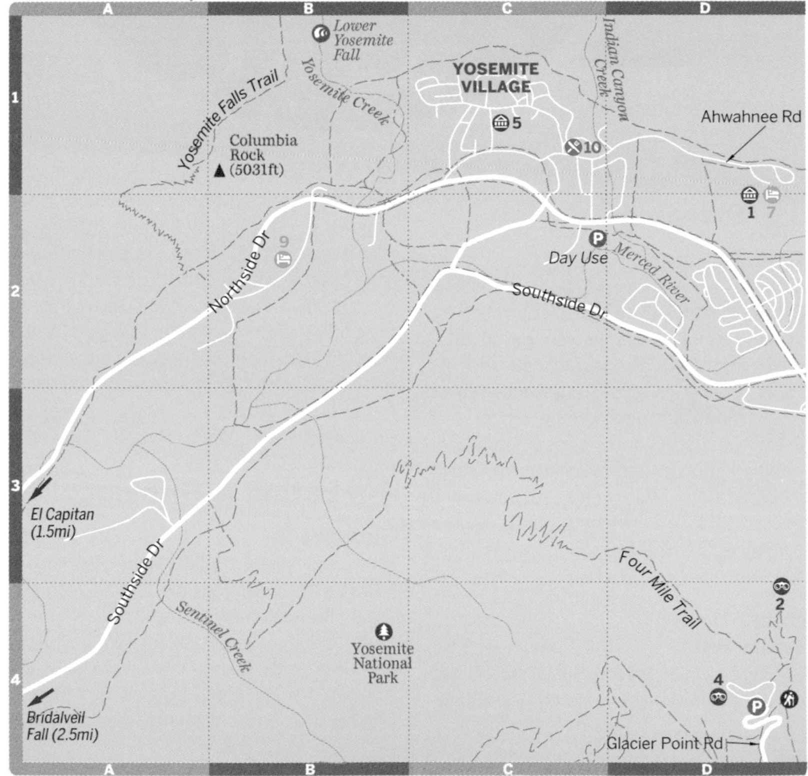

mists of Yosemite Falls, the gemstone lakes of the high country's subalpine wilderness and Hetch Hetchy's pristine pathways.

HISTORY

The Ahwahneechee, a group of Miwok and Paiute peoples, lived in the Yosemite area for around 4000 years before a group of pioneers, most likely led by legendary explorer Joseph Rutherford Walker, came through in 1833. During the Gold Rush era, conflict between the miners and indigenous tribes escalated to the point where a military expedition (the Mariposa Battalion) was dispatched in 1851 to punish the Ahwahneechee, eventually forcing the capitulation of Chief Tenaya and his tribe.

In 1864 President Abraham Lincoln signed the Yosemite Grant, which eventually ceded Yosemite Valley and the Mariposa Grove of Giant Sequoias to California as a state park. This landmark decision paved the way for a national park system, of which Yosemite became a part in 1890, thanks to efforts led by pioneering conservationist John Muir.

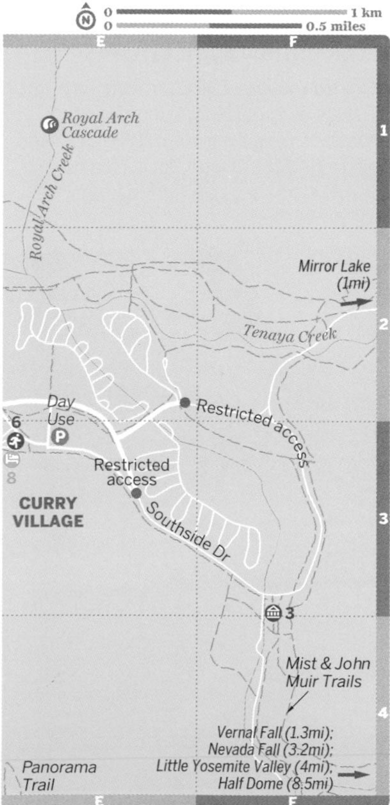

Sights

YOSEMITE VALLEY

The park's crown jewel, spectacular meadow-carpeted Yosemite Valley stretches 7 miles long, bisected by the rippling Merced River and hemmed in by some of the most majestic chunks of granite anywhere on earth. The most famous are, of course, the monumental 7569ft **El Capitan** (El Cap), one of the world's largest monoliths and a magnet for rock climbers, and 8842ft **Half Dome**, the park's spiritual centerpiece – its rounded granite pate forms an unmistakable silhouette. You'll have great views of both from **Valley View** on the valley floor, but for the classic photo op head up Hwy 41 to **Tunnel View**, which boasts a new viewing area.

Yosemite Valley

Sights
1 Ahwahnee Hotel D2
2 Glacier Point D4
3 Nature Center at Happy Isles F3
4 Sentinel Dome D4
5 Yosemite Museum C1

Activities, Courses & Tours
6 Curry Village Ice Rink E3
Raft Rentals .... (see 6)

Sleeping
7 Ahwahnee Hotel D2
8 Curry Village E3
9 Yosemite Lodge at the Falls B2

Eating
Ahwahnee Dining Room .... (see 7)
10 Degnan's Deli C1
Mountain Room Restaurant .... (see 9)

Drinking & Nightlife
Ahwahnee Bar .... (see 7)
Mountain Room Lounge .... (see 9)

Yosemite's waterfalls mesmerize even the most jaded traveler, especially when the spring runoff turns them into thunderous cataracts. Most are reduced to a mere trickle by late summer. **Yosemite Falls** is considered the tallest in North America, dropping 2425ft in three tiers. A slick wheelchair-accessible trail leads to the bottom of this cascade or, if you prefer solitude and different perspectives, you can also clamber up the **Yosemite Falls Trail**, which puts you atop the falls after a grueling 3.4 miles. No less impressive is nearby **Bridalveil Fall** and others scattered throughout the valley.

Any aspiring Ansel Adams should lug their camera gear along the 1-mile paved trail to **Mirror Lake** early or late in the day to catch the ever-shifting reflection of Half Dome in the still waters. The lake all but dries up by late summer.

Yosemite Museum — Museum

(Map p258; ☎209-372-0200; ⏰9am-5pm, often closed noon-1pm) FREE This museum has Miwok and Paiute artifacts, including woven baskets, beaded buckskin dresses and dance capes made from feathers. There's also an **art gallery** with paintings and photographs from the museum's permanent collection. Behind the museum, a self-guided interpretive trail winds past a reconstructed c 1870 **Indian village** with pounding stones, an acorn granary, a ceremonial roundhouse and a conical bark house.

Nature Center at Happy Isles — Museum

(Map p258; ⏰9:30am-5pm late May-Sep; 👪) A great hands-on nature museum, the Nature Center displays explain the differences between the park's various pinecones, rocks, animal tracks and (everyone's favorite subject) scat. Out back, don't miss an exhibit on the 1996 rock fall, when an 80,000-ton rock slab plunged 2000ft to the nearby valley floor, killing a man and felling about 1000 trees.

TIOGA ROAD & TUOLUMNE MEADOWS

Tioga Rd (or Hwy 120 E) travels through 56 miles of superb high country at elevations ranging from 6200ft at Crane Flat to 9945ft at Tioga Pass. Heavy

Mirror Lake, Yosemite National Park

snowfall keeps it closed from about November until May. Beautiful views await after many a bend in the road, the most impressive being **Olmsted Point**, where you can gawp all the way down Tenaya Canyon to Half Dome. Above the canyon's east side looms the aptly named 9926ft **Clouds Rest**. Continuing east on Tioga Rd soon drops you at **Tenaya Lake**, a placid blue basin framed by pines and granite cliffs.

Beyond here, about 55 miles from Yosemite Valley, 8600ft **Tuolumne Meadows** is the largest subalpine meadow in the Sierra. It provides a dazzling contrast to the valley, with its lush open fields, clear blue lakes, ragged granite peaks and domes, and cooler temperatures. If you come during July or August, you'll find a painter's palette of wildflowers decorating the shaggy meadows.

WAWONA

Wawona, about 27 miles south of Yosemite Valley, is the park's historical center.

Mariposa Grove Forest

(Map p262) The main lure here is the biggest, most impressive cluster of giant sequoias in Yosemite. The star of the show – and what everyone comes to see – is the **Grizzly Giant**, a behemoth that sprang to life some 1800 years ago. You can't miss it – it's a half-mile walk along a well-worn path starting near the parking lot. Beyond here, crowds thin out a bit, although for more solitude, arrive early in the morning or after 6pm.

Pioneer Yosemite History Center Museum

(Map p262; rides adult/child $5/4; 24hr, rides Wed-Sun Jun-Sep) FREE In Wawona itself, about 6 miles north of the grove, take in the manicured grounds of the elegant Wawona Hotel and cross a covered bridge to this rustic center, where some of the park's oldest buildings were relocated. It also features stagecoaches that brought early tourists to Yosemite, and offers short **rides**.

Glacier Point

A lofty 3200ft above the valley floor, 7214ft **Glacier Point** (Map p258) presents one of the park's most eye-popping vistas and practically puts you at eye level with Half Dome. To the left of Half Dome lies U-shaped, glacially carved Tenaya Canyon, while below you'll see Vernal and Nevada Falls. Glacier Point is about an hour's drive from Yosemite Valley via Glacier Point Rd off Hwy 41. Along the road, hiking trails lead to other spectacular viewpoints, such as **Dewey Point** and **Sentinel Dome** (Map p258).

HETCH HETCHY

In the park's northwestern corner, Hetch Hetchy, which is Miwok for 'place of tall grass,' gets the least amount of traffic yet sports waterfalls and granite cliffs that rival its famous counterparts in Yosemite Valley. The main difference is that Hetch Hetchy Valley is now filled with water, following a long political and environmental battle in the early 20th century.

The 8-mile long **Hetch Hetchy Reservoir**, its placid surface reflecting clouds and cliffs, stretches behind O'Shaughnessy Dam, site of a parking lot and trailheads. An easy 5.4-mile (round-trip) trail leads to the spectacular **Tueeulala** (*twee*-lala) and **Wapama Falls**, which each plummet more than 1000ft over fractured granite walls on the north shore of the reservoir.

Activities

HIKING

Over 800 miles of hiking trails cater to hikers of all abilities. Take an easy half-mile stroll on the valley floor; venture out all day on a quest for viewpoints, waterfalls and lakes; or go camping in the remote outer reaches of the backcountry.

Yosemite National Park

A B C D

1 2 3 4 5 6 7

Stanislaus National Forest
Emigrant Lake
Pacific Crest Trail
Falls Creek
Tilden Lake
Stubblefield Canyon
Spotted Fawn Lake
Kibbie Lake
Piute Mtn (10,541ft)
Matterhorn Canyon
Rancheria Creek
Benson Lake
Benson Pass
Cherry Lake
Lake Eleanor
Hetch Hetchy Dome (6197ft)
O'Shaughnessy Dam
Hetch Hetchy Rd
Hetch Hetchy Reservoir
Tuolumne River
Harden Lake
Mather
5
Pothole Dome (8766ft)
Mt Hoffmann (10,850ft)
May Lake
Evergreen Rd
(open summer only)
Tioga Rd
120
Groveland (25mi)
Tenaya Lake
John Muir Trail
Yosemite National Park
Big Oak Flat Rd
Clouds Rest (9926ft)
See Yosemite Valley Map (p258)
Half Dome (8842ft)
El Capitan (7569ft)
Little Yosemite Valley
Merced Lake
Sentinel Dome (8122ft)
Mt Clark (11,522ft)
El Portal
Glacier Point Rd
140
3
4
Illilouette Creek
Merced Peak (11,726ft)
S Fork Merced River
Wawona Rd
Chilnualna Creek
Buena Vista Peak (9709ft)
Sierra National Forest
2
Wawona
6
1
Fish Camp
41

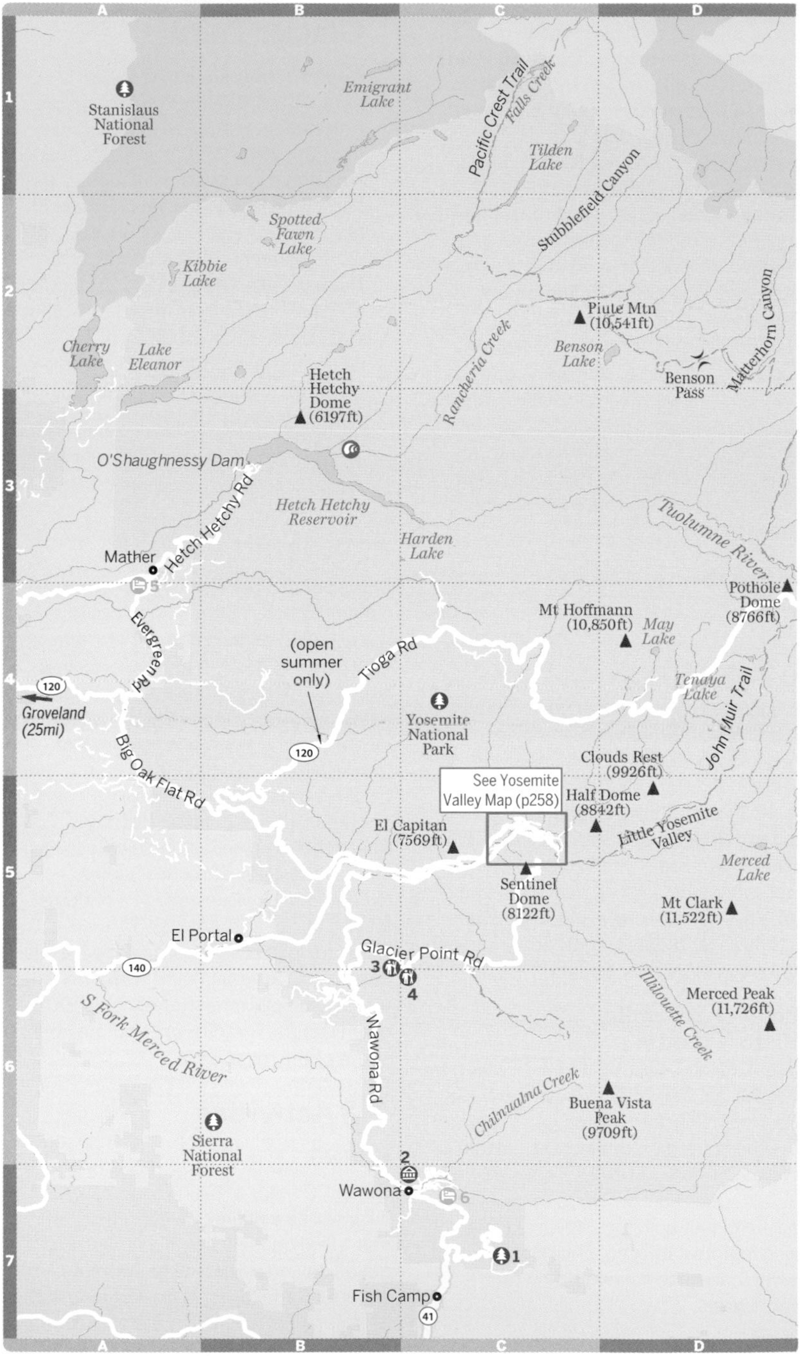

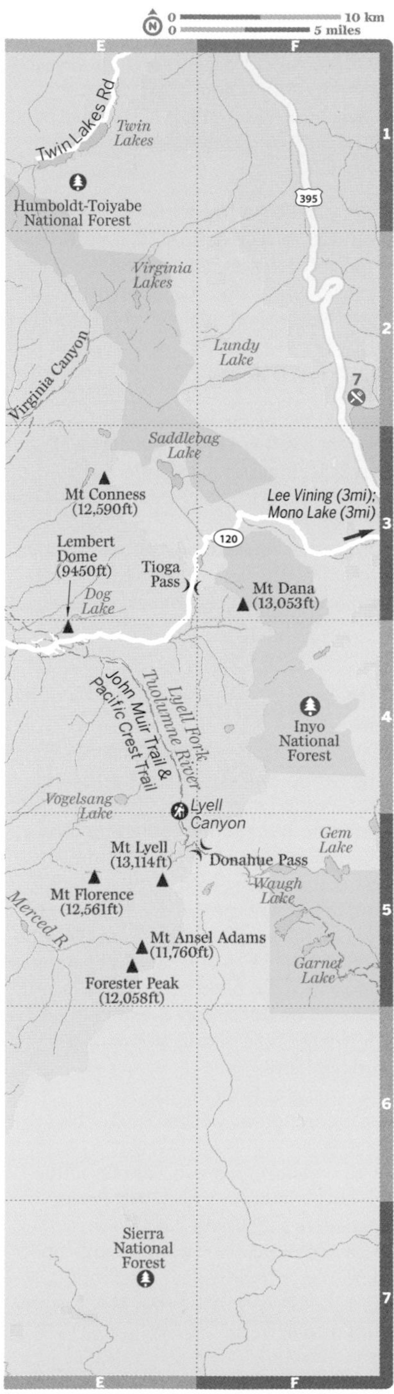

Yosemite National Park

Sights

1 Mariposa Grove....................................C7
2 Pioneer Yosemite History Center.......C7

Activities, Courses & Tours

3 Badger Pass B5
4 Yosemite Ski School............................ C6

Sleeping

5 Evergreen Lodge Resort.......................A4
6 Wawona Hotel C7

Eating

7 Historic Mono Inn F2
Wawona Hotel Dining Room........(see 6)

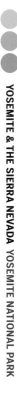

Some of the park's most popular hikes start right in Yosemite Valley, including to the top of **Half Dome** (17-mile round-trip), the most famous of all. It follows a section of the **John Muir Trail** and is strenuous, difficult and best tackled in two days with an overnight in Little Yosemite Valley. Reaching the top can only be done after rangers have installed fixed cables. Depending on snow conditions, this may occur as early as late May or as late as July, and the cables usually come down in mid-October. To whittle down the cables' notorious human logjams, the park now requires permits for day hikers, but the route is still nerve-wracking as hikers must 'share the road.' The less ambitious or physically fit will still have a ball following the **Mist Trail** as far as **Vernal Fall** (2.6-mile round-trip), the top of **Nevada Fall** (6.5-mile round-trip) or idyllic **Little Yosemite Valley** (8-mile round-trip). The **Four Mile Trail** (9.2-mile round-trip) to Glacier Point is a strenuous but satisfying climb to a glorious viewpoint.

ROCK CLIMBING

With its sheer spires, polished domes and soaring monoliths, Yosemite is rock-climbing nirvana. The main climbing season runs from April to October.

SWIMMING

On a hot summer day, nothing beats a dip in the gentle Merced River, though if chilly

Mandatory Half Dome Permits

To stem lengthy lines (and increasingly dangerous conditions) on the vertiginous cables of Half Dome, the park now requires that all-day hikers obtain an advance permit to climb the cables. Consult www.nps.gov/yose/planyourvisit/hdpermits.htm for the latest information. Rangers check permits at the base of the cables.

water doesn't float your boat, you can always pay to play in the outdoor swimming pools at Curry Village and Yosemite Lodge at the Falls (adult/child $5/4).

RAFTING

From around late May to July, floating the Merced River from Stoneman Meadow, near Curry Village, to Sentinel Bridge is a leisurely way to soak up Yosemite Valley views. Four-person **raft rentals** (Map p258; ☎209-372-4386; per person $31) for the 3-mile trip are available from the concessionaire in Curry Village and include equipment and a shuttle ride back to the rental kiosk.

WINTER SPORTS

The white coat of winter opens up a different set of things to do, as the valley becomes a quiet, frosty world of snow-draped evergreens, ice-coated lakes and vivid vistas of gleaming white mountains sparkling against blue skies.

Badger Pass Snow Sports
(Map p262; ☎209-372-8430; www.badgerpass.com; lift ticket adult/child $49/25; ⏲9am-4pm mid-Dec–Mar) Most of the action converges on one of California's oldest ski resorts. The gentle slopes are perfect for families and beginner skiers and snowboarders. It's about 22 miles from the valley on Glacier Point Rd. There are five chairlifts, 800 vertical feet and 10 runs, a full-service lodge, equipment rental ($27 to $37 for a full set of gear) and the excellent **Yosemite Ski School** (Map p262), where generations of novices have learned how to get down a hill safely (group lessons from $47).

Curry Village Ice Rink Skating
(Map p258; adult/child $10/9.50, skate rental $4) A delightful winter activity is taking a spin on the outdoor rink, where you'll be skating under the watchful eye of Half Dome.

Tours

First-timers often appreciate the two-hour **Valley Floor Tour** (per adult/child $25/13; ⏲year-round) run by DNC Parks & Resorts, which covers the valley highlights.

For other tour options stop at the tour and activity desks at Yosemite Lodge at the Falls, Curry Village or Yosemite Village, call ☎209-372-4386 or check www.yosemitepark.com.

Sleeping

Competition for campsites is fierce from May to September, when arriving without a reservation and hoping for the best is tantamount to getting someone to lug your Barcalounger up Half Dome. Even first-come, first-served campgrounds tend to fill by noon, especially on weekends and around holidays. **Reservations** (☎877-444-6777, 518-885-3639; www.recreation.gov) become available from 7am PST on the 15th of every month in one-month blocks, and often sell out within minutes.

Opening dates for seasonal campgrounds vary according to the weather.

All noncamping reservations within the park are handled by **DNC Parks & Resorts** (☎801-559-4884; www.yosemitepark.com) and can be made up to 366 days in advance; reservations are absolutely critical from May to early September.

YOSEMITE VALLEY

Curry Village Cabins **$$**
(Map p258; tent cabin $123-128, cabin without/with bath $146/195;) Founded in 1899 as a summer camp, Curry has hundreds of units squished tightly together beneath towering evergreens. The canvas cabins are basically glorified tents, so for more comfort, quiet and privacy get one of the cozy wood cabins, which have bedspreads, drapes and vintage posters. There are also 18 attractive motel-style rooms in the **Stoneman House** (r $198), including a loft suite sleeping up to six.

Ahwahnee Hotel Historic Hotel **$$$**
(Map p258; r from $470; @) The crème de la crème of Yosemite's lodging, this sumptuous historic property dazzles with soaring ceilings, Turkish kilims lining the hallways and atmospheric lounges with mammoth stone fireplaces. It's the gold standard for upscale lodges, though if you're not blessed with bullion, you can still soak up the ambience during afternoon tea, a drink in the bar or a gourmet meal.

Yosemite Lodge at the Falls Motel **$$$**
(Map p258; r from $199; @) Situated a short walk from Yosemite Falls, this multibuilding complex contains a wide range of eateries, a lively bar, big pool and other handy amenities. Delightful rooms, thanks to a recent eco-conscious renovation, now feel properly lodge-like, with rustic wooden furniture and striking nature photography. All have cable TV, telephone, fridge and coffeemaker, and great patio or balcony panoramas.

WAWONA

Wawona Hotel Historic Hotel **$$$**
(Map p262; r without/with bath incl breakfast $153/226; mid-Mar–Dec;) This National Historic Landmark, dating from 1879, is a collection of six graceful, whitewashed New England–style buildings flanked by wide porches. The 104 rooms – with no phone or TV – come with Victorian–style furniture and other period items, and about half the rooms share bathrooms, with nice robes provided for the walk there.

HETCH HETCHY

Evergreen Lodge Resort Cabins, Campground **$$$**
(Map p262; 209-379-2606; www.evergreen-lodge.com; 33160 Evergreen Rd; tents $85-120, cabins $180-415; @) Outside the park near the entrance to Hetch Hetchy, this classic 90-year-old resort lets roughing-it guests cheat with comfy, prefurnished tents and rustic to deluxe mountain cabins with private porches but no phone or TV. Outdoor recreational

Tueeulala Falls (p261)
JOHN MOCK / GETTY IMAGES ©

Below: Kings Canyon National Park (p269); **Right:** Wawona Hotel (p265)
(BELOW) WWW.SIERRALARA.COM / GETTY IMAGES ©; (RIGHT) JOHN ELK / GETTY IMAGES ©

activities abound, many of them family-oriented, with equipment rentals available.

There's a general store, tavern with a pool table and a fantastic restaurant serving three hearty meals every day.

Eating

Degnan's Deli — Deli $

(Map p258; Yosemite Village; sandwiches $7-8; 7am-5pm;) Excellent made-to-order sandwiches, breakfast items and snack foods.

Mountain Room Restaurant — American $$$

(Map p258; 209-372-1403; www.yosemitepark.com; Yosemite Lodge; mains $21-35; 5:30-9:30pm;) With a killer view of Yosemite Falls, the window tables at this casual and elegant contemporary steakhouse are a hot commodity. The chefs whip up the best meals in the park, with flat-iron steak and locally caught mountain trout wooing diners under a rotating display of nature photographs. Reservations accepted only for groups larger than eight; casual dress is okay.

Ahwahnee Dining Room — Californian $$$

(Map p258; 209-372-1489; Ahwahnee Hotel; mains breakfast $7-22, lunch $16-22, dinner $28-46; 7-10am, 11:30am-3pm & 5:30-9pm;) The formal ambience (mind your manners) may not be for everybody, but few would not be awed by the sumptuous decor, soaring beamed ceiling and palatial chandeliers. The menu is constantly in flux, but most dishes have perfect pitch and are beautifully presented. There's a dress code at dinner, but otherwise shorts and sneakers are okay.

Wawona Hotel Dining Room — American $$$

(Map p262; Wawona Hotel; breakfast & lunch $11-15, dinner $22-30; 7:30-10am, 11:30am-1:30pm & 5:30-9pm Easter-Dec;)

Beautiful sequoia-painted lamps light this old-fashioned white-tablecloth dining room, and the Victorian detail makes it an enchanting place to have an upscale (though somewhat overpriced) meal. 'Tasteful, casual attire' is the rule for dinner dress, and there's a barbecue on the lawn every Saturday during summer.

Drinking

Mountain Room Lounge Bar

(Map p258; Yosemite Lodge, Yosemite Valley; noon-11pm Sat & Sun, 4:30-11pm Mon-Fri) Catch up on the latest sports news while knocking back draft brews at this large bar that buzzes in wintertime. Order a s'mores kit (graham crackers, chocolate squares and marshmallows) to roast in the open-pit fireplace. Kids welcome until 10pm.

Ahwahnee Bar Bar

(Map p258; Ahwahnee Hotel, Yosemite Valley; 11:30am-11pm) Settle in for a drink at this cozy bar, complete with pianist – the perfect way to experience the Ahwahnee without dipping too deep into your pockets. Appetizers and light meals ($10 to $25) provide sustenance.

Information

Yosemite's entrance fee is $20 per vehicle or $10 for those on bicycle or foot and is valid for seven consecutive days.

For recorded park information, campground availability, and road and weather conditions, call 209-372-0200.

Yosemite National Park **(www.nps.gov/yose)** Official Yosemite National Park Service site with the most comprehensive and current information. News and road closures/openings are often posted first on its Facebook page (www.facebook.com/YosemiteNPS).

Yosemite Valley Visitor Center **(209-372-0299; Yosemite Village; 9am-6pm summer, shorter hours year-round)** The main office, with exhibits and free film screenings in the theater.

Scenic Drive: Kings Canyon Scenic Byway (Highway 180)

The 31-mile rollercoaster road connecting Grant Grove and Cedar Grove ranks among the most dazzling in all of California.

The road soon begins its jaw-dropping descent into the canyon, snaking past chiseled rock walls, some tinged by green moss and red iron minerals, others decorated by waterfalls. Turnouts provide superb views, especially at **Junction View**.

Eventually the road runs parallel with the gushing Kings River, its thunderous roar ricocheting off granite cliffs soaring as high as 8000ft, making Kings Canyon even deeper than the Grand Canyon. Stop at **Boyden Cavern** (www.caverntours.com/BoydenRt.htm; Hwy 180; tours adult/child from $14.50/8.50; May–mid-Nov;) for a tour of its whimsical formations. About 5 miles further east, **Grizzly Falls** can be torrential or drizzly, depending on the time of year.

On your return trip, consider a detour via **Hume Lake**, created in 1908 as a dam for logging operations and now offering boating, swimming and fishing.

Getting There & Away

Yosemite is one of the few national parks that can be easily reached by public transportation. Greyhound buses and Amtrak trains serve Merced, west of the park, where they are met by buses operated by Yosemite Area Regional Transportation System (YARTS; 877-989-2787; www.yarts.com), and you can buy Amtrak tickets that include the YARTS segment all the way into the park.

In summer, another YARTS route runs from Mammoth Lakes along Hwy 395 to Yosemite Valley via Hwy 120.

Getting Around

Bicycle

Bicycling is an ideal way to take in Yosemite Valley. You can rent a wide-handled cruiser (per hour/day $11.50/32) or a bike with an attached child trailer (per hour/day $19/59) at Yosemite Lodge at the Falls or Curry Village.

Car

Roadside signs with red bears mark the many spots where bears have been hit by motorists, so think before you hit the accelerator, and follow the pokey posted speed limits. Glacier Point and Tioga Rds are closed in winter.

Public Transportation

The free, air-conditioned **Yosemite Valley Shuttle Bus** is a comfortable and efficient way of traveling around the park. Buses operate year-round at frequent intervals and stop at 21 numbered locations, including parking lots, campgrounds, trailheads and lodges.

Free buses also operate between Wawona and the Mariposa Grove (spring to fall), and Yosemite Valley and Badger Pass (winter only). The **Tuolumne Meadows Shuttle** runs between Tuolumne Lodge and Olmsted Point in Tuolumne Meadows (usually mid-June to early September).

SEQUOIA & KINGS CANYON

The twin parks of Sequoia and Kings Canyon dazzle with superlatives, though they're often overshadowed by Yosemite, their smaller neighbor to the north (a three-hour drive away). With towering forests of giant sequoias containing some of the largest trees in the world, and the mighty Kings River careening through the depths of Kings Canyon, one of the deepest chasms in the country, the parks are lesser-visited jewels where it's easier to find quiet and solitude. Throw in opportunities for cave spelunking, rock climbing and backcountry hiking through granite-carved Sierra landscapes, and backdoor access to Mt Whitney – the tallest peak in the lower 48 states – and you have all the ingredients for two of the best parks in the country.

The two parks, though distinct, are operated as one unit with a single admission (valid for seven consecutive days) of $20 per carload. For 24-hour recorded information, including road conditions, call ☎559-565-3341 or visit www.nps.gov/seki, the parks' comprehensive website.

Kings Canyon National Park

With a dramatic cleft deeper than the Grand Canyon, Kings Canyon offers true adventure to those who crave seemingly endless trails, rushing streams and gargantuan rock formations.

Sights & Activities

GENERAL GRANT GROVE

This sequoia grove is nothing short of magnificent. The paved half-mile **General Grant Tree Trail** is an interpretive walk that visits a number of mature sequoias, including the 27-story **General Grant Tree**. This giant holds triple honors as the world's third-largest living tree, a memorial to US soldiers killed in war, and as the nation's Christmas tree. The nearby **Fallen Monarch**, a massive, fire-hollowed trunk that you can walk through, has been a cabin, hotel, saloon and stables for US Cavalry horses.

CEDAR GROVE & ROAD'S END

Pretty spots around here include **Roaring River Falls**, where water whips down a sculpted rock channel before tumbling into a churning pool, and the 1.5-mile **Zumwalt Meadow Loop**, an easy nature trail around a verdant green meadow bordered by river and granite canyon.

Sleeping & Eating

John Muir Lodge Lodge **$$$**
(☎877-436-9615, 559-335-5500; www.visitsequoia.com; Hwy 180; r $202-212; wifi) An atmospheric wooden building hung with historical black-and-white photographs, this year-round hotel is a place to lay your head and still feel like you're in the forest. Wide porches have wooden rocking chairs, and homespun rooms contain rough-hewn wood furniture and patchwork bedspreads. Cozy up to the big stone fireplace on chilly nights with a board game.

Kings Canyon National Park

DAVID CLAPP / GETTY IMAGES ©

Don't Miss Crystal Cave

Discovered in 1918 by two fishermen, Crystal Cave was carved by an underground river and has formations estimated to be 10,000 years old. Stalactites hang like daggers from the ceiling, and milky white marble formations take the shape of ethereal curtains, domes, columns and shields.

Tickets are *only* sold at the Lodgepole and Foothills visitor centers and *not* at the cave. Allow about one hour to get to the cave entrance, which is a half-mile walk from the parking lot at the end of a twisty 7-mile road; the turnoff is about 3 miles south of the Giant Forest. Bring a sweater or light jacket, as it's a huddle-for-warmth 48°F inside.

NEED TO KNOW

559-565-3759; www.sequoiahistory.org; Crystal Cave Rd; tours adult/child from $15/8; mid-May–Nov;

Grant Grove Restaurant American **$$**

(Hwy 180; mains $9-18; 7-10pm late May-early Sep, reduced hours early Sep-late May;) The only place to chow down in Grant Grove Village, its building will be torn down and rebuilt in 2015/2016, with plans for a temporary food area during construction. A new menu highlights seasonal dishes with rainbow trout or free-range chicken, but doesn't leave out comfort foods like pizza or fresh baked apple pie.

Information

Kings Canyon Visitor Center **(559-565-4307; 8am-5pm, shorter winter hours)** In Grant Grove Village. Has exhibits, maps and wilderness permits.

Getting There & Around

The road to Cedar Grove Village is only open from around April or May until the first snowfall.

Sequoia National Park

Picture unzipping your tent flap and crawling out into a 'front yard' of trees as high as a 20-story building and as old as the Bible. Brew some coffee as you plan your day in this extraordinary park with its soul-sustaining forests and gigantic peaks soaring above 12,000ft.

Sights & Activities

GIANT FOREST

Named by John Muir in 1875, this area is the top destination in the parks, and about 2 miles south of Lodgepole Village. By volume the largest living tree on earth, the massive **General Sherman Tree** rockets 275ft to the sky. Pay your respects via a short descent from the Wolverton Rd parking lot, or join the **Congress Trail**, a paved 2-mile pathway that takes in General Sherman and other notable named trees, including the **Washington Tree**, the world's second-biggest sequoia, and the see-through **Telescope Tree**.

Giant Forest Museum Museum
(559-565-4480; Generals Hwy; 9am-4:30pm or 6pm mid-May–mid-Oct;) FREE For a primer on the intriguing ecology, fire cycle and history of the 'big trees,' drop in at this excellent museum, then follow up your visit with a spin around the paved (and wheelchair-accessible) 1.2-mile interpretive **Big Trees Trail**, which starts from the museum parking lot.

Sleeping & Eating

Wuksachi Lodge Lodge **$$$**
(866-807-3598, 559-565-4070; www.visitsequoia.com; 64740 Wuksachi Way, off Generals Hwy; r from $225;) Built in 1999, the Wuksachi Lodge is the park's most upscale lodging and dining option. But don't get too excited – the wood-paneled atrium lobby has an inviting stone fireplace and forest views, but charmless motel-style kitchenette rooms with oak furniture and thin walls have an institutional feel. The lodge's location, however, just north of Lodgepole Village, can't be beat.

Lodgepole Village Market **$**
(Generals Hwy; mains $6-10; market & snack bar 9am-6pm mid-Apr–late May & early Sep–mid-Oct, 8am-8pm late May-early Sep, deli 11am-6pm mid-Apr–mid-Oct;) The park's most extensive market sells all kinds of groceries, camping supplies and snacks. Inside, a fast-food snack bar slings burgers and grilled sandwiches and dishes up breakfast. The adjacent deli is a tad more upscale and healthy, with focaccia sandwiches, veggie wraps and picnic salads.

Information

Lodgepole Visitor Center (559-565-4436; 9am-4:30pm or 6pm daily, shorter winter hours) Maps, information, exhibits, Crystal Cave tickets and wilderness permits.

EASTERN SIERRA

Cloud-dappled hills and sun-streaked mountaintops dabbed with snow typify the landscape of the Eastern Sierra, where slashing peaks – many over 14,000ft – rush abruptly upward from the arid expanses of the Great Basin and Mojave deserts. It's a dramatic juxtaposition that makes for a potent cocktail of scenery. Pine forests, lush meadows, ice-blue lakes, simmering hot springs and glacier-gouged canyons are some of the beautiful sights you'll find.

The Eastern Sierra Scenic Byway, officially known as Hwy 395, runs the entire length of the range. Note that in winter, when traffic thins, many facilities are closed.

Mono Lake

North America's second-oldest lake is a quiet and mysterious expanse of deep blue water, whose glassy surface reflects jagged Sierra peaks, young volcanic

If You Like... Aquatic Fun

If you like exploring Mono Lake's waters, you might enjoy these other aquatic adventures.

1 **LAKE TAHOE CRUISES**
(800-238-2463; www.zephyrcove.com; adult/child from $49/15) Two paddle wheelers ply Lake Tahoe's 'big blue' year-round with a variety of sightseeing, drinking, dining and dancing cruises, including a narrated two-hour daytime trip to Emerald Bay. The *Tahoe Queen* leaves from Ski Run Marina (summer parking fee $8) in town, while the MS *Dixie II* is based at Zephyr Cove Marina on the eastern shore in Nevada.

2 **AUBURN STATE RECREATION AREA**
(530-885-4527; www.parks.ca.gov; per car $10; 8am-sunset) This is a park of deep gorges cut by the rushing waters of the North and Middle Forks of the American River that converge below a bridge on Hwy 49, about 4 miles south of Auburn. In the early spring, when waters are high, this is immensely popular for white-water rafting, as the rivers are Class II to V runs. Late summer, calmer waters allow for sunning and swimming, especially around the confluence. Numerous trails are shared by hikers, mountain-bikers and horses.

3 **MUIR ROCK**
On excursions to Kings Canyon, John Muir would allegedly give talks on this large flat river boulder, a short walk from the Road's End parking lot and a mile past Zumwalt Meadow. A sandy river beach here is taken over by gleeful swimmers in midsummer. Don't jump in when raging waters, swollen with snowmelt, are dangerous. Ask at the Road's End ranger station if conditions are calm enough for a dip.

cones and the unearthly tufa (*too*-fah) towers that make the lake so distinctive. Jutting from the water like drip sand castles, tufas form when calcium bubbles up from subterranean springs and combines with carbonate in the alkaline lake waters.

The brackish water teems with buzzing alkali flies and brine shrimp, both considered delicacies by dozens of migratory bird species that return here year after year, including about 85% of the state's nesting population of California gulls, which takes over the lake's volcanic islands from April to August.

Sights & Activities

South Tufa Nature Reserve
(entry adult/child $3/free) Tufa spires ring the lake, but the biggest grove is on the south rim with a mile-long interpretive trail. Ask about ranger-led tours at the Mono Basin Scenic Area Visitor Center. To get to the reserve, head south from Lee Vining on Hwy 395 for 6 miles, then east on Hwy 120 for 5 miles to the dirt road leading to a parking lot.

Navy Beach Beach
The best place for swimming is at Navy Beach, just east of the South Tufa reserve. It's also the best place to put in canoes or kayaks. From late June to early September, the **Mono Lake Committee** (760-647-6595; www.monolake.org/visit/canoe; tours $25; 8am, 9:30am & 11am Sat & Sun) operates one-hour canoe tours around the tufas. Half-day kayak tours along the shore or out to Paoha Island are also offered by **Caldera Kayaks** (760-934-1691; www.calderakayak.com; tours $75; mid-May–mid-Oct). Both require reservations.

Sleeping & Eating

Yosemite Gateway Motel Motel **$$**
(760-647-6467; www.yosemitegatewaymotel.com; Hwy 395; r $119-159;) Think vistas. This is the only motel on the east side of the highway, and the views from some of the rooms are phenomenal. Recently remodeled, its boutique-style rooms have comfortable beds with thick duvets and swank new bathrooms.

Historic Mono Inn Californian **$$**
(Map p262; 760-647-6581; www.monoinn.com; 55620 Hwy 395; mains $10-28; 5-9pm Apr–mid-Nov) A restored 1922 lodge owned by the family of photographer Ansel

Devils Postpile

The surreal volcanic formation of **Devils Postpile National Monument** (📞760-934-2289; www.nps.gov/depo; shuttle day pass adult/child $7/4; ⏰late May-Oct) is a fascinating attraction. The 60ft curtains of near-vertical, six-sided basalt columns formed when rivers of molten lava slowed, cooled and cracked with perplexing symmetry. This honeycomb design is best appreciated from atop the columns, reached by a short trail. The columns are an easy, half-mile hike from the Devils Postpile Ranger Station.

The road here is only accessible from about June until September, weather permitting, but is closed to private vehicles unless you are camping, have lodge reservations or are disabled (in which case you must pay a $10 per car fee). Otherwise you must use a mandatory **shuttle bus** (per adult/child $7/4).

Adams, this is now an elegant lakefront restaurant with outstanding California comfort food, fabulous wine and views to match. Browse the 1000-volume cookbook collection upstairs, and stop in for the occasional live band on the creekside terrace. It's located about 5 miles north of Lee Vining. Reservations recommended.

Whoa Nellie Deli Californian **$$**
(📞760-647-1088; www.whoanelliedeli.com; Tioga Gas Mart, Hwys 120 & 395; mains $10-20; ⏰6:30am-9pm late Apr-early Nov; 👪) After putting this unexpected gas station restaurant on the map, its famed chef has moved on to Mammoth, but locals think the food is still damn good. Stop in for delicious fish tacos, wild buffalo meatloaf and other tasty morsels, and live bands two nights a week.

Information

Mono Basin Scenic Area Visitor Center (📞760-647-3044; www.fs.usda.gov/inyo; ⏰8am-5pm Apr-Nov) Half a mile north of Lee Vining, this center has maps, interpretive displays, Inyo National Forest wilderness permits, bear-canister rentals, a bookstore and a 20-minute movie about Mono Lake.

Devils Postpile National Monument

Mammoth Lakes

This is a small mountain resort town endowed with larger-than-life scenery – active outdoorsy folks worship at the base of its dizzying 11,053ft Mammoth Mountain. Thick powder clings to these slopes, and when the snow finally fades, the area's an outdoor wonderland of mountain-bike trails, excellent fishing, endless alpine hiking and blissful hidden spots for hot-spring soaking.

Activities

Mammoth Mountain Skiing, Snowboarding

(**760-934-2571, 800-626-6684, 24hr snow report 888-766-9778; www.mammothmountain.com; lift tickets adult/senior/youth 13-18/child 7-12 $99/84/77/35)** A skiers' and snowboarders' dream resort, where sunny skies, a reliably long season (usually November to June) and over 3500 acres of fantastic tree-line and open-bowl skiing are a potent cocktail. At the top you'll be dealing with some gnarly, nearly vertical chutes. The other stats are just as impressive: 3100 vertical feet, 150 trails, 29 lifts (including 10 quads).

Mammoth Mountain Bike Park Mountain Biking

(**800-626-6684; www.mammothmountain.com; day pass adult/child 7-12 $49/23; 9am-4:30pm Jun-Sep)** Come summer, Mammoth Mountain morphs into the massive Mammoth Mountain Bike Park, with more than 80 miles of well-kept single-track trails. Several other trails traverse the surrounding forest. In general, Mammoth-style riding translates into plenty of hills and soft, sandy shoulders, which are best navigated with big knobby tires.

HIKING

Mammoth Lakes rubs up against the Ansel Adams Wilderness and John Muir Wilderness areas, both laced with fabulous trails leading to shimmering lakes, rugged peaks and hidden canyons. Major trailheads leave from the Mam-

Left: Manzanar National Historic Site (p276); **Below:** California State Capitol (p279), Sacramento

(LEFT) DANITA DELIMONT / GETTY IMAGES ©; (BELOW) GARY LAVROV / GETTY IMAGES ©

moth Lakes Basin, Reds Meadow and Agnew Meadows; the latter two are accessible only by shuttle.

Sleeping

Tamarack Lodge Lodge, Cabins **$$**
(800-626-6684, 760-934-2442; www.tamaracklodge.com; 163 Twin Lakes Rd; r incl breakfast with/without bath $189/139, cabins from $229; @) In business since 1924, this charming year-round resort on Lower Twin Lake has a cozy fireplace lodge, a bar and excellent restaurant, 11 rustic-style rooms and 35 cabins. The cabins range from very simple to simply deluxe, and come with full kitchen, private bathroom, porch and wood-burning stove. Some can sleep up to 10 people. Daily resort fee $20.

Austria Hof Lodge Lodge **$$**
(760-934-2764; www.austriahof.com; 924 Canyon Blvd; r incl breakfast $109-215;) Close to Canyon Lodge, rooms here have modern knotty pine furniture, thick down duvets and DVD players. Ski lockers and a sundeck hot tub make winter stays here even sweeter. The lodge restaurant (dinner mains $25 to $40) serves meaty gourmet German fare in a muraled cellar dining room.

Eating

Good Life Café Californian **$**
(www.mammothgoodlifecafe.com; 126 Old Mammoth Rd; mains $9-15; 6:30am-3pm, to 9pm Thu-Mon in winter) Healthy food, generously filled veggie wraps and big bowls of salad make this a perennially popular place. The front patio is blissful for a long brunch on a warm day.

Toomey's New American **$$**
(www.toomeyscatering.com; 6085 Minaret Rd, The Village; mains $13-30; 7am-9pm;) The legendary chef from Whoa Nellie Deli in

Lee Vining has decamped here, along with his eclectic menu of wild-buffalo meatloaf, seafood jambalaya and lobster taquitos with mango salsa – plus a lifetime's worth of baseball paraphernalia. The central location's perfect for grabbing a to-go breakfast or a sit-down dinner near the Village gondola or Mammoth Mountain bike-park shuttle.

 Information

The **Mammoth Lakes Welcome Center** (**☎760-924-5500, 888-466-2666; www.visitmammoth.com; ⏰8am-5pm**) and **Mammoth Lakes Ranger Station** (**☎760-924-5500; www.fs.fed.us/r5/inyo; ⏰8am-5pm**) share a building on the north side of Hwy 203.

Manzanar National Historic Site

A stark wooden guard tower alerts drivers to one of the darkest chapters in US history, which unfolded on a barren and windy sweep of land some 5 miles south of Independence. Little remains of the infamous war concentration camp, a dusty square mile where more than 10,000 people of Japanese ancestry were corralled during WWII following the attack on Pearl Harbor. The camp's lone remaining building, the former high-school auditorium, houses a superb free **interpretive center** (**☎760-878-2194; www.nps.gov/manz; ⏰9am-4:30pm Nov-Mar, to 5:30pm Apr-Oct; 👪**).

Watch the 20-minute documentary, then explore the thought-provoking exhibits chronicling the stories of the families that languished here yet built a vibrant community. Afterwards, take a self-guided 3.2-mile driving tour around the grounds, which includes a recreated mess hall and barracks, vestiges of buildings and gardens, as well as the haunting camp cemetery.

Alabama Hills

In Lone Pine, the warm colors and rounded contours of the Alabama Hills stand in contrast to the jagged snowy Sierras just behind. The setting for countless ride-'em-out movies and the popular *Lone Ranger* TV series, the stunning orange rock formations are a beautiful place to experience sunrise or sunset. A

Cannon, Sutter's Fort State Historic Park (p279)

Calaveras Big Trees State Park

This **park** (☎209-795-2334; www.parks.ca.gov; per car $10; ⊙sunrise-sunset) is home to giant sequoia redwood trees. Reaching as high as 325ft and with trunk diameters up to 33ft, these leftovers from the Mesozoic era are thought to weigh upwards of 3000 tons, or close to 20 blue whales.

The redwood giants are distributed in two large groves, one of which is easily seen from the **North Grove Big Trees Trail**, a 1.7-mile self-guided loop, near the entrance, where the air is fresh with pine and rich soil. The **River Canyon Trail**, a challenging 8-mile hike out and back, climbs out of the North Grove, crosses a ridge and descends 1000ft to the Stanislaus River. Pack enough water for the return trip back up.

number of graceful rock arches are within easy hiking distance of the roads. Head west on Whitney Portal Rd and either turn left at Tuttle Creek Rd, after a half-mile, or north on Movie Rd, after about 3 miles.

GOLD COUNTRY

Gold Country is where it all began – the drowsy hill towns and oak-lined byways of today's quiet road trip belie the wild chaos of California's founding. Shortly after a sparkle caught James Marshall's eye in 1848, the rush for gold brought a stampede of 300,000 '49ers to the Sierra foothills. Today, fading historical markers tell tales of bloodlust and banditry, while the surviving boomtowns survive on antiques, ice cream, wine and Gold Rush ephemera.

Nevada City

Maybe it's all those prayer flags, or new-agey Zen goodies that clutter the sandalwood-scented gift shops, but, like a yogi in the lotus position, Nevada City is all about *balance*. The city has the requisite Victorian Gold Rush tourist attractions – an elegantly restored town center, an informative local history museum, girlishly decorated bed-and-breakfasts by the dozen – and a proud contemporary identity, with a small but thriving independent arts and culture scene.

Sleeping & Eating

Outside Inn Motel, Cabin **$$**
(☎530-265-2233; www.outsideinn.com; 575 E Broad St; r $79-104, ste $129-145, cottage $155-200; ❄📶🏊🐾**)** The best option for active explorers, this is an unusually friendly and fun motel, with 12 rooms and three cottages maintained by staff that loves the outdoors and has excellent information about area hiking. Some rooms have a patio overlooking a small creek; all have nice quilts and access to BBQ grills. It's a 10-minute walk from downtown.

New Moon Café Californian **$$$**
(www.thenewmooncafe.com; 203 York St; mains $21-29.50; ⊙11:30-2pm Tue-Fri, 5-8:30pm Tue-Sun) 🌿 Pure elegance, Peter Selaya's organic and local ingredient menu changes with the seasons. If you visit during the peak of the summer, go for the line-caught fish or their housemade, moon-shaped fresh ravioli.

Marshall Gold Discovery State Historic Park

Compared to the stampede of gun-toting, hill-blasting, hell-raising settlers that populate tall tales along Hwy 49, **Marshall Gold Discovery State Historic Park (☎530-622-3470; marshallgold.org; per car $8; ⊙park 8am-5pm, to 7pm late May-early Sep, museum 10am-5pm;** 👪**)** is a place of bucolic tranquillity, with two

Don't Miss
Bodie State Historic Park

For a time warp back to the Gold Rush era, swing by Bodie, one of the West's most authentic and best preserved ghost towns. Gold was first discovered here in 1859, and within 20 years the place grew from a rough mining camp to an even rougher boomtown with a population of 10,000 and a reputation for unbridled lawlessness. Fights and murders took place almost daily, the violence no doubt fueled by liquor dispensed in the town's 65 saloons, some of which did double duty as brothels, gambling halls or opium dens. The hills disgorged some $35 million worth of gold and silver in the 1870s and '80s, but when production plummeted, so did the population, and eventually the town was abandoned to the elements.

About 200 weather-beaten buildings still sit frozen in time in this cold, barren and windswept valley heaped with tailing piles. The former Miners' Union Hall now houses a **museum** and **visitor center** (9am-one hour before park closes). Rangers conduct free general tours.

Bodie is about 13 miles east of Hwy 395 via Rte 270; the last 3 miles are unpaved. Although the park is open year-round, the road is usually closed in winter and early spring, so you'd have to don snowshoes or cross-country skis to get there.

NEED TO KNOW

760-647-6445; www.parks.ca.gov/bodie; Hwy 270; adult/child $5/3; 9am-6pm mid-May–Oct, to 4pm Nov–mid-May

tragic heroes in John Sutter and James Marshall. Sutter, who had a fort in Sacramento, partnered with Marshall to build a sawmill on a swift stretch of the American River in 1847. It was Marshall who discovered gold here on January 24, 1848, and though the men tried to keep their findings secret, it eventually brought a chaotic rush of prospectors from around the world. In one of the great tragic ironies of the Gold Rush, the men who made this discovery died nearly penniless.

The park's quiet charms are mostly experienced outdoors, strolling past the carefully reconstructed mill and taking in the grounds. There's also a **Visitor Information Center & Museum** (☎530-622-3470; 310 Back St, Coloma; tours adults/child $3/2; ⏰10am-5pm Mar-Nov, to 4pm Dec-Feb, guided tours 11am & 1pm year round) with a tidy shop where you can buy kitsch from the frontier days.

Panning for gold is popular – you can pay $7 to pan for a quick training session and 45 minutes of gold panning, or pan for free if you have your own.

Sacramento

Square in the middle of the sweltering valley, Sacramento's downtown is couched by the confluence of two cool rivers – the American and the Sacramento – and its streets are shushed by the leaves of huge oaks.

Sights

California State Railroad Museum Museum
(www.csrmf.org; 125 I St; adult/child $10/5, incl train ride $20/10; ⏰10am-5pm; 👪) At Old Sac's north end is this impressive collection of railcars and locomotives from miniature to true scale. While the candy-coated recounting of the struggles of those who laid the track is unsettling, the fully outfitted Pullman sleeper and vintage diner cars will thrill rail fans. Board a restored passenger train (adult/child $10/5) from the Sacramento Southern Railroad ticket office, across the plaza on Front St, for a 40-minute jaunt along the river. Train rides run hourly on weekends from April to September.

California State Capitol Historic Building
(capitolmuseum.ca.gov; 1315 10th St; ⏰8am-5pm Mon-Fri, from 9am Sat & Sun) FREE The gleaming dome of the California State Capitol is Sacramento's most recognizable structure. A painting of the Terminator in a suit hangs in the west wing with the other governors' portraits. Some will find **Capitol Park**, the 40 acres of gardens and memorials surrounding the building, more interesting than what's inside. Tours run hourly until 4pm.

Sutter's Fort State Historic Park Historic Site
(www.suttersfort.org; 2701 L St; adult/child $5/3; ⏰10am-5pm) Originally built by John Sutter, this park was once the only trace of white settlement for hundreds of miles. Reserve a couple of hours to stroll within its walls, where furniture, medical equipment and a blacksmith shop are straight out of the 1850s.

Sleeping & Eating

HI Sacramento Hostel Hostel $
(☎916-443-1691; http://norcalhostels.org/sac; 925 H St; dm $29-33, r with shared/private bath from $58/99; ⏰check-in 2-10pm; @📶) In a grand Victorian mansion, this hostel offers impressive trimmings at rock-bottom prices. It's within walking distance of the capitol, Old Sac and the train station and has a piano in the parlor and large dining room. It attracts an international crowd often open to sharing a ride to San Francisco or Lake Tahoe.

Citizen Hotel Boutique Hotel $$$
(☎916-492-4460; www.jdvhotels.com; 926 J St; r/ste $169/269; ❄@📶🐾) With an elegant, ultra-hip upgrade by the Joie de Vivre group, the long-vacant Citizen has suddenly become one of the coolest stays in these parts. Rooms are sleek, with lux linen and bold-patterned decor. The front desk has loaner bikes. There's an upscale farm-to-fork **restaurant** (mains from $28) on the ground floor.

La Bonne Soupe Cafe Deli $
(☎916-492-9506; 920 8th St; items $5-8; ⏰11am-3pm Mon-Wed, to 8pm Thu & Fri) Divine soup and sandwiches assembled with such care that the line of downtown lunchers snakes out the door. If you're in a hurry, skip it. This humble lunch counter is focused on quality that predates drive-through haste.

WM. PENN HOTE
ELSEVIER
PENN
HOTE
OLÉ MA
ONE WAY
Welcome
RIMS
2008

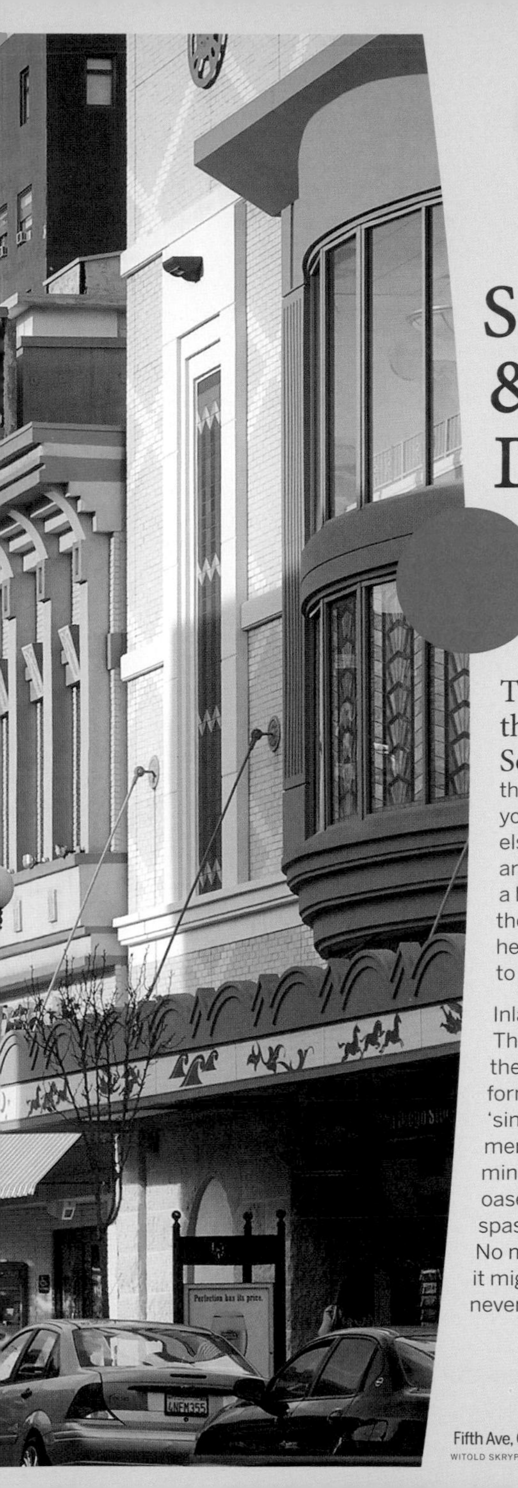

San Diego & the Deserts

There's a certain arrogance that comes with living on the SoCal coast. It's a breezy confidence that springs from the assumption that your life is just, well, *better* than everyone else's. But as far as snobs go, San Diegans are the ones we like the most. Whether it's a battle-tested docent sharing stories on the USS *Midway* or a no-worries surf diva helping you catch a wave, folks are willing to share the good life.

Inland, a different kind of beauty beckons. There's something undeniably artistic in the way the landscape unfolds in the California desert: weathered volcanic peaks, 'singing' sand dunes, mountains shimmering in rainbow hues, and hot, natural, mineral water spurting forth to feed palm oases and soothe aching muscles in stylish spas. Through it all threads iconic Route 66. No matter what your trail through the desert, it might creep into your consciousness and never fully leave.

Fifth Ave, Gaslamp Quarter (p290), San Diego

San Diego & the Deserts

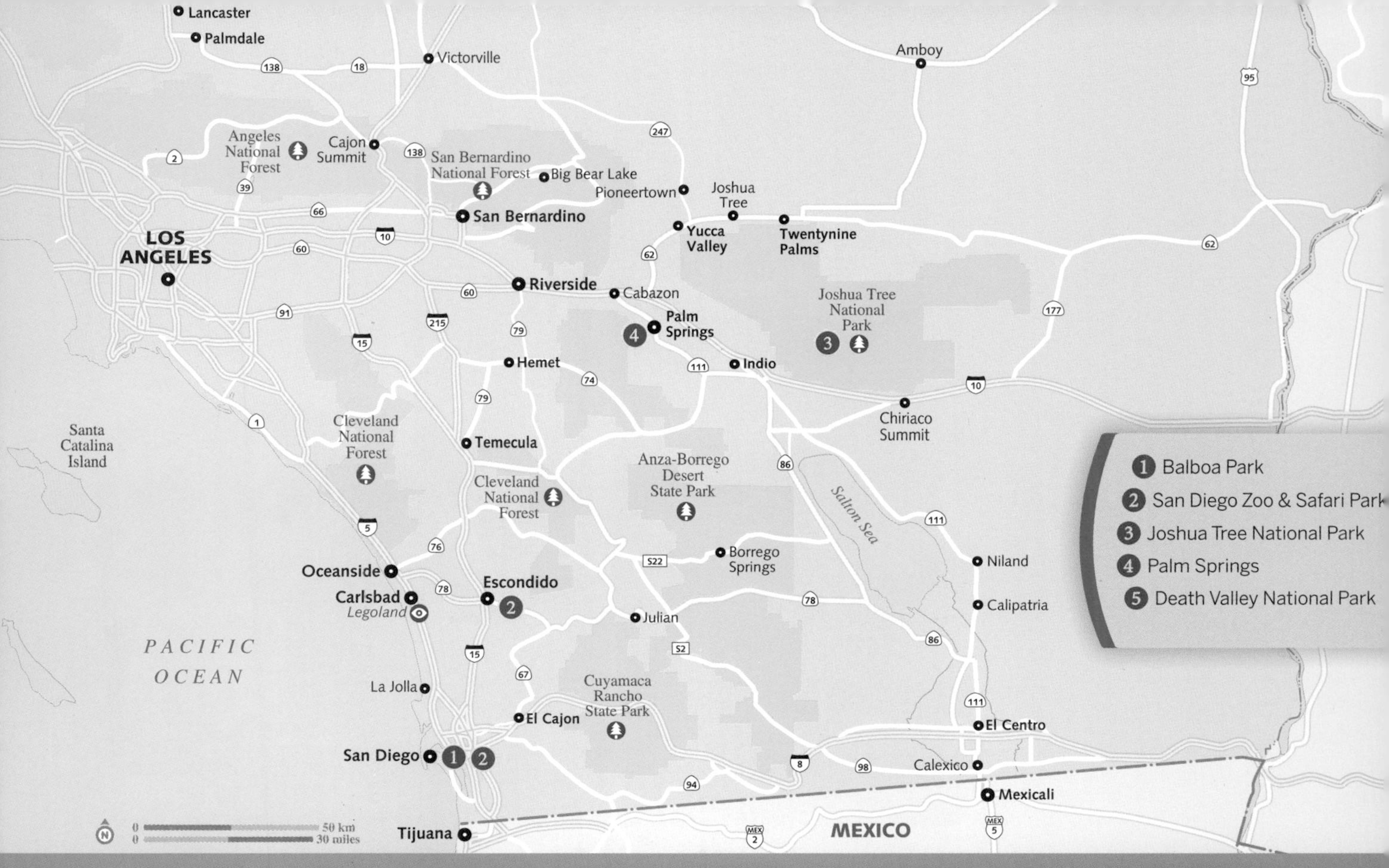
1 Balboa Park
2 San Diego Zoo & Safari Park
3 Joshua Tree National Park
4 Palm Springs
5 Death Valley National Park
Lancaster
Palmdale
Victorville
Amboy
Angeles National Forest
Cajon Summit
San Bernardino National Forest
Big Bear Lake
Pioneertown
Joshua Tree
San Bernardino
LOS ANGELES
Yucca Valley
Twentynine Palms
Riverside
Cabazon
Joshua Tree National Park
Palm Springs
Hemet
Indio
Chiriaco Summit
Santa Catalina Island
Cleveland National Forest
Temecula
Cleveland National Forest
Anza-Borrego Desert State Park
Salton Sea
Borrego Springs
Niland
Oceanside
Escondido
Carlsbad
Legoland
Julian
Calipatria
PACIFIC OCEAN
La Jolla
Cuyamaca Rancho State Park
El Cajon
El Centro
San Diego
Calexico
Mexicali
Tijuana
MEXICO
0 50 km
0 30 miles

San Diego & the Deserts Highlights

Balboa Park

The rumors are true: Balboa Park (p293) is the largest urban cultural park in the US. It's famous for its picturesque El Prado promenade, lined with theaters, museums and formal gardens. The 1200-acre park is also an ideal place to watch San Diegans at play. Beware that mornings are busy with school groups and some museums close on Mondays.

1

2 San Diego Zoo & Safari Park

Explore the animal kingdom at the world-famous San Diego Zoo (p299; pictured left), set on 100 beautifully landscaped acres in northern Balboa Park. It's home to more than 3000 finned, furry and feathered creatures – more than 800 species are represented. At the affiliated Safari Park (p291), a 1800-acre open-range zoo just outside the city, herds of giraffes, zebras, rhinos and other animals roam the valley floor.

SERGIO PITAMITZ / ROBERT HARDING ©

Joshua Tree National Park

3

Straddling the transition zone between the Colorado Desert and the higher, cooler Mojave Desert, Joshua Tree National Park (p318) is known for its stunning wildflowers, varied cacti (such as ocotillos, whose octopus-like tentacles shoot out crimson flowers in spring), and, of course, its famous Joshua trees. The park's mystical desert vistas and lush oases charm hikers and mountain-bikers throughout the year.

4

Palm Springs

In the 1950s and '60s, Palm Springs (p311) was the swinging getaway of Sinatra, Elvis and dozens of other stars who partied the night away. Today, you can rub shoulders with the local hipsters and elderly folk, hike palm-oasis canyons, soak in hot springs and shop for modern art. A ride on the Palm Springs Aerial Tramway is a great way to take it all in.

Above: Palm Springs Aerial Tramway (p311)

5

Death Valley National Park

The largest national park in the continental USA, Death Valley National Park (p322) spans more than 5000 sq miles. Though the name is foreboding, this crazy-quilted geological playground is full of life – you'll find giant sand dunes, mosaic marbled canyons, extinct volcanic craters, palm-shaded oases and dozens of rare wildlife species that exist nowhere else in the world.

San Diego & the Deserts' Best...

Sandy Landscapes

- **Death Valley National Park** Famous for 'singing' sand dunes and surreal desert vistas. (p322)
- **Coronado** Go barefoot on the white, powder-soft sand in front of the Hotel del Coronado. (p301)
- **Palm Springs** Natural hot springs and a retro-cool resort town in the middle of a hot desert. (p311)
- **La Jolla** This picturesque shoreline is dotted with sunbathing sea lions. (p302)

Scenic Vistas

- **Cabrillo National Monument** Sweeping panoramas of San Diego Bay. (p301)
- **Dante's View** Above Death Valley's colorful badlands. (p323)
- **Palm Springs Aerial Tramway** A head-spinning ride with 360° views. (p311)
- **Keys View** Spy on the Salton Sea, or even Mexico. (p318)
- **Aguereberry Point** Lofty lookout high above Death Valley. (p323)

Historic Sites

- **Old Town State Historic Park** San Diego's original settlement. (p298)
- **Mission Basilica San Diego de Alcalá** Founded in 1774 by Padre Junípero Serra. (p298)
- **Hotel del Coronado** *Some Like It Hot* was filmed here in 1959. (p301)
- **Desert Queen Ranch** Pioneering homestead in Joshua Tree. (p318)
- **Whaley House** The Victorian house is 'officially' haunted. (p298)

Hikes

- **Tahquitz Canyon** Trails go past waterfalls and rock art. (p313)
- **Indian Canyons** Cuts through the Agua Caliente Indian Reservation. (p313)
- **Mosaic Canyon** Multicolored rock walls delight hikers. (p323)
- **Kelso Dunes** The Mojave's famous 'singing' sand dunes. (p321)
- **Telescope Peak** Death Valley's most challenging summit. (p324)

Left: Cabrillo National Monument (p301); **Above:** Sea lions, La Jolla (p302)

Need to Know

ADVANCE PLANNING

- **Two months before** Look up festivals and events around the areas you're visiting; some may be worth planning your stay around.
- **One month before** Look online for discount tickets and promotions to expensive attractions such as SeaWorld San Diego and the San Diego Zoo Safari Park.
- **Two weeks before** Break in your boots for all of the hiking you'll do around Death Valley and Joshua Tree.

RESOURCES

- **www.sandiego.org** The official San Diego traveler's resource.
- **www.visitpalmsprings.com** Online visitor's guide to the Palm Springs area.
- **www.nps.gov/deva** Death Valley resources and information.
- **visit29.org** Joshua Tree area tourism.

GETTING AROUND

- **Car** The obvious choice for Route 66, Death Valley and Joshua Tree.
- **Train** Amtrak's Pacific Surfliner trains run north from San Diego to LA; much of the oceanside ride is wonderfully scenic.
- **Walking** Downtown San Diego and downtown Palm Springs are very walkable.
- **Bus** Public transportation is easy in central San Diego, less so to outlying beach towns.

BE FOREWARNED

- **Deathly temperatures** It's way too hot to hike in Death Valley National Park during summer; don't even think about it.
- **Driving** Southern California is very much a driver's destination. Allow extra time for traffic jams in metro areas, especially on the I-5 and I-10 Fwys.
- **In-demand campsites** If you're dying to camp in any of California's national parks, especially popular ones such as Joshua Tree, try to reserve a site well in advance.

San Diego & the Deserts Itineraries

Don't miss Death Valley and Joshua Tree; Palm Springs serves as a midtrip oasis. In San Diego, the most appealing attractions – wild animals, beach paths and science centers – aren't just for kids.

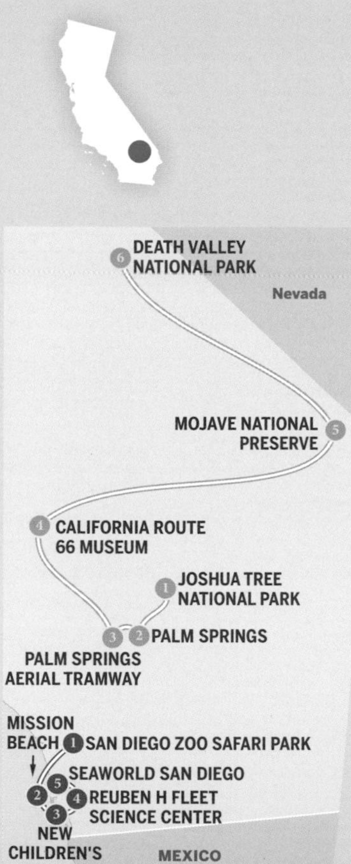

3 DAYS

SAN DIEGO ZOO SAFARI PARK TO SEAWORLD

SAN DIEGO FUN

The southern quarter of California is a dream for youngsters. A must-see for kids (and adults) is the ❶**San Diego Zoo Safari Park** (p291), a game-changer on the zoo market, where the animals roam free and the people are fenced off. For a relaxing late afternoon or sunset, get some fresh air at ❷**Mission Beach** (p300), where younger kids will beg for a ride on the antique roller coaster at Belmont Park and older kids will enjoy cycling or in-line skating on the beach paths.

Alternate the wild-animal activity and exercise with a quieter day by stopping at the ❸**New Children's Museum** (p291), where parents will dig the modern-art vibe, and the nap-time-and-apple-juice-set will love the hands-on exhibits. In the afternoon, head to the ❹**Reuben H Fleet Science Center** (p295) in Balboa Park. The interactive science center, with a new IMAX theater, is as fun for parents as it is for children. Get a good night's sleep before venturing on to the pièce de résistance, ❺**SeaWorld San Diego** (p300), where trained orcas, splashy water rides, marine-animal shows and cotton candy make for a child's dream day.

Top Left: SeaWorld San Diego (p300); **Top Right:** Mojave National Preserve (p321)

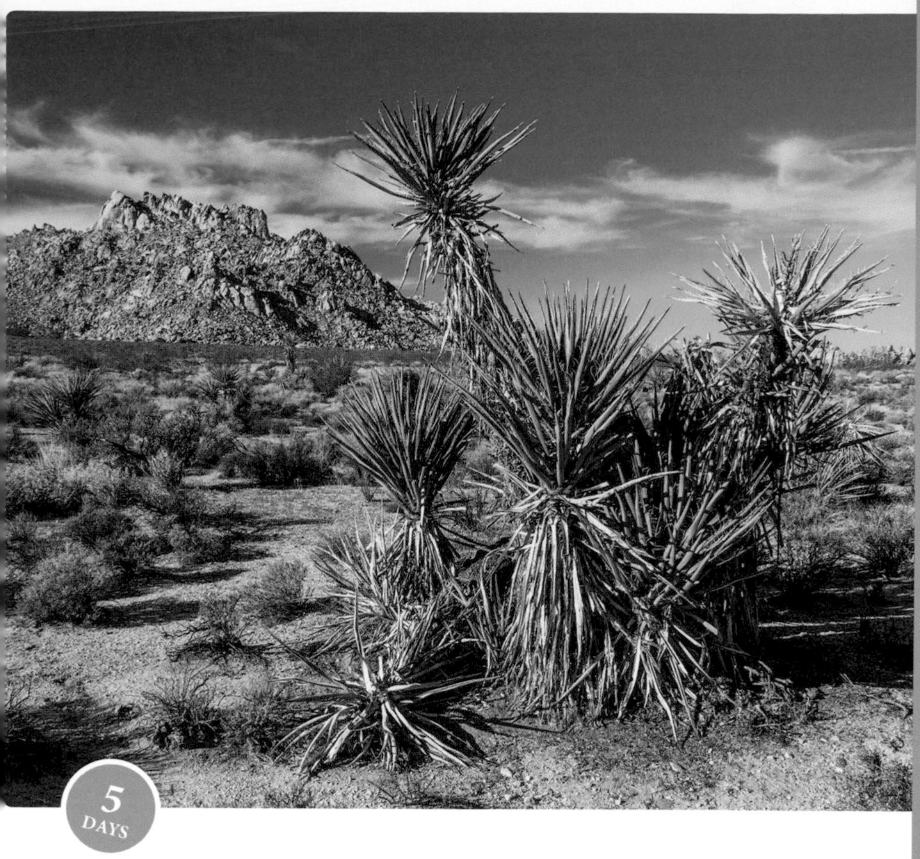

5 DAYS

JOSHUA TREE TO DEATH VALLEY

DESERT ROAD TRIP

There's no reason you have to rough it for a week just because you're visiting a pair of national parks – just make Palm Springs your glamorous pit stop. Begin in ❶ **Joshua Tree National Park** (p318), where you can hop around smooth, big-shouldered boulders in Hidden Valley and take artistic photographs of the legendary trees. Shake the dirt off your hiking boots and head west to ❷ **Palm Springs** (p311) for a day and night of art-gallery hopping, cocktails and shopping. Don't miss a ride aboard the ❸ **Palm Springs Aerial Tramway** (p311) – it's a rare opportunity to ascend through five distinct life zones in fewer than 15 minutes.

Fill up your tank and grab a large cup of coffee: your drive north to Death Valley will take half a day. If you're not in a particular hurry, detour to Victorville's ❹ **California Route 66 Museum** (p321) to revel in the Mother Road or head east at Barstow to the spectacular volcanic cinder cones, desert tortoises, jackrabbits and coyotes of the ❺ **Mojave National Preserve** (p321). Finish your trip amid the eerie desert landscapes and Old West–style ghost towns of ❻ **Death Valley National Park** (p322).

Discover San Diego & the Deserts

At a Glance

- **San Diego** (p290) Laid-back SoCal capital features museums and beaches.
- **Palm Springs** (p311) Desert oasis for hot springs, galleries and shopping.
- **Joshua Tree National Park** (p318) Boulder-strewn landscape of legendary trees.
- **Route 66** (p320) Famous highway uncovers classic Americana.
- **Death Valley National Park** (p322) Trippy geology and awe-inspiring, colorful panoramas.

Downtown San Diego

SAN DIEGO

Sights

California's second-largest city and America's eighth largest, San Diego doesn't seduce like San Francisco or thrill like LA, but life here is so persistently pleasant, what with 70 miles of coastline and the nation's most enviable climate, you won't care much. Small wonder that San Diegans promote their hometown as 'America's Finest City.'

The area around 5th Ave, once known as the Stingaree, used to be a notorious red-light district. These days, the Gaslamp Quarter is enjoying a second, post-Petco wave of revitalization and growth. Restored buildings (built between the 1870s and the 1920s) have become home to restaurants, bars, galleries, shops and theaters. The 16-acre area south of Broadway between 4th and 6th Aves is designated a National Historic District.

DOWNTOWN

Just south of Broadway, running along 5th Ave, is the historic **Gaslamp Quarter**, the primary hub for shopping, dining and entertainment.

Museum of Contemporary Art Museum
(MCASD Downtown; Map p292; ☎858-454-3541; www.mcasd.org; 1001 Kettner Blvd; adult/child under 25yr/senior $10/free/$5, free 5-7pm 3rd Thu each month; ⏰11am-5pm Thu-Tue, to 7pm 3rd Thu each month) This Financial District museum has brought an ever-changing variety of innovative artwork to San Diegans since the 1960s here in the downtown location and La Jolla branch (p303); check the website for exhibits. Across from the main building, a slickly renovated section of San Diego's train

DAVID KILPATRICK / ALAMY ©

Don't Miss San Diego Zoo Safari Park

How close can you get to the animals at this 1800-acre open-range zoo just 30 miles northeast of Downtown? Consider this sign in the Gorilla Forest: 'In gorilla society prolonged eye contact is not only impolite, but it's considered a threat. Please respect the social signals of our gorillas and do not stare at them directly.' Seems we're so close we need to be reminded of our manners. But the sign is indicative of the experience here, where protecting and preserving wild animals and their habitats – while educating guests in a soft-handed manner – is the primary goal.

For a minisafari, hop aboard the biodiesel Africa Tram for a drive through the world's second-largest continent. Sit on the left-hand side for slightly better views of the rhinos, giraffes, ostriches and other herbivores (by law, predators can't share space with prey). The park is in Escondido. Take the I-15 Fwy north to the Via Rancho Parkway exit, turn right and continue to San Pasqual Rd. Turn right and follow signs to the park. Parking costs $10.

NEED TO KNOW

Off Map p291; ☎760-747-8702; www.sdzsafaripark.org; 15500 San Pasqual Valley Rd; adult/child from $44/34, 2-day ticket incl San Diego Zoo $79/61; ⏰9am-7pm late Jun–mid-Aug, to 5pm or 6pm mid-Aug–late Jun; P 👪

station houses permanent works by Jenny Holzer and Richard Serra. Tickets are valid for seven days in all locations.

New Children's Museum Museum

(Map p292; www.thinkplaycreate.org; 200 W Island Ave; admission $10; ⏰noon-4pm Sun, 1am-4pm Mon & Wed-Sat; 👪) This interactive children's museum is new both chronologically (opened 2008) and conceptually, in that it's interactive art meant for kids. Installations are designed by artists, so tykes can learn principles of movement and physics while simultaneously being

Downtown San Diego

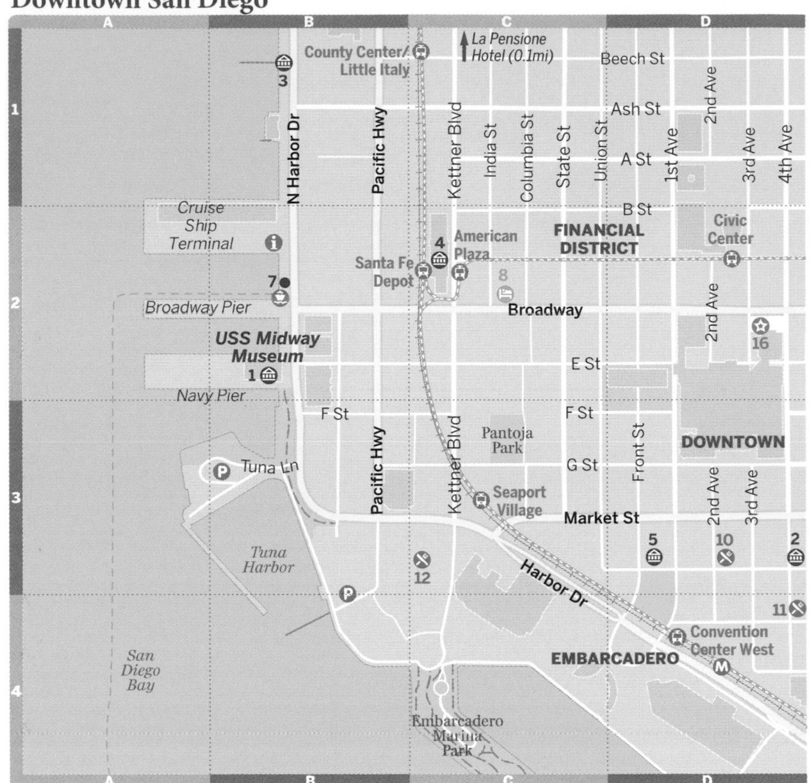

exposed to art and working out the ants in their pants. Exhibits change every 18 months or so, so there's always something new.

Petco Park Stadium

(Map p292; 619-795-5011; www.padres.com; 100 Park Blvd; tours adult/child/senior $12/8/9; 10:30am & 12:30pm Sun-Fri, 10:30am, 12:30pm & 3pm off season;) A quick stroll southeast of the Gaslamp is one of the newest stadiums in baseball, home of the **San Diego Padres (Map p292; www.padres.com; Petco Park, 100 Park Blvd; tickets $11-91; season Apr-early Oct)**. It's also one of the most beautiful, with brick construction and skyscraper views over the outfield. If you can't attend a game, take an 80-minute behind-the-scenes tour which might include bullpen, press box and luxury suite. Call for tour schedules in season (April to early October).

Gaslamp Museum & William Heath Davis House Museum

(Map p292; www.gaslampquarter.org; 410 Island Ave; adult/senior & student $5/4, walking tour $10/8; 10am-6pm Tue-Sat, 9am-3pm Sun, walking tour 11am Sat) This house, a pre-fab affair brought from Maine in 1850, contains a small museum with 19th-century furnishings. From here, the Gaslamp Quarter Historical Foundation leads a weekly, two-hour **walking tour** of the neighborhood, which includes admission to the house.

EMBARCADERO

USS Midway Museum Museum

(Map p292; 619-544-9600; www.midway.org; 910 N Harbor Dr; adult/child $20/10; 10am-5pm, last entry 4pm; P) The giant aircraft

Downtown San Diego

Don't Miss Sights

1 USS Midway Museum B2

Sights

2 Gaslamp Museum & William Heath Davis House D3
3 Maritime Museum B1
4 Museum of Contemporary Art C2
5 New Children's Museum D3
6 Petco Park E4

Activities, Courses & Tours

7 Flagship Cruises B2

Sleeping

8 500 West Hotel C2
9 Hotel Solamar E4

Eating

10 Café 222 .... D3
11 Oceanaire D4
12 Puesto at the Headquarters C3

Drinking & Nightlife

13 Bang Bang E3
14 Noble Experiment E3

Entertainment

15 4th & B E2
16 Arts Tix D2
San Diego Padres .... (see 6)

carrier USS *Midway* was one of the navy's flagships from 1945 to 1991, last playing a combat role in the first Gulf War. On the flight deck of the hulking vessel, walk right up to some 25 restored aircraft including an F-14 Tomcat and F-4 Phantom jet fighter. Admission includes an audio tour, along the narrow confines of the upper decks to the bridge, admiral's war room, brig and 'pri-fly' (primary flight control; the carrier's equivalent of a control tower).

Maritime Museum Museum

(Map p292; ☎619-234-9153; www.sdmaritime.org; 1492 N Harbor Dr; adult/child $16/8; ⏰9am-9pm late May-early Sep, to 8pm early Sep-late May; 👪) This museum is easy to find: look for the 100ft-high masts of the iron-hulled square-rigger *Star of India*. Built on the Isle of Man and launched in 1863, the tall ship plied the England–India trade route, carried immigrants to New Zealand, became a trading ship based in Hawaii and, finally, ferried cargo in Alaska. It's a handsome vessel, but don't expect anything romantic or glamorous on board.

LITTLE ITALY

Little Italy was settled in the mid-19th century by Italian immigrants, mostly fishermen and their families, who lived off a booming fish industry and whiskey trade. Over the last few years, the Italian community been joined by exciting contemporary architecture, galleries, gourmet restaurants and fun bars, making this one of San Diego's hippest neighborhoods.

You'll find the busiest patio tables along **India Street**, a prime spot for a glass of Chianti.

BALBOA PARK

The park stretches over an impressive 1200 acres, preening on prime real estate just minutes from Hillcrest, Downtown, the beaches and Mission Valley.

Metropolitan San Diego

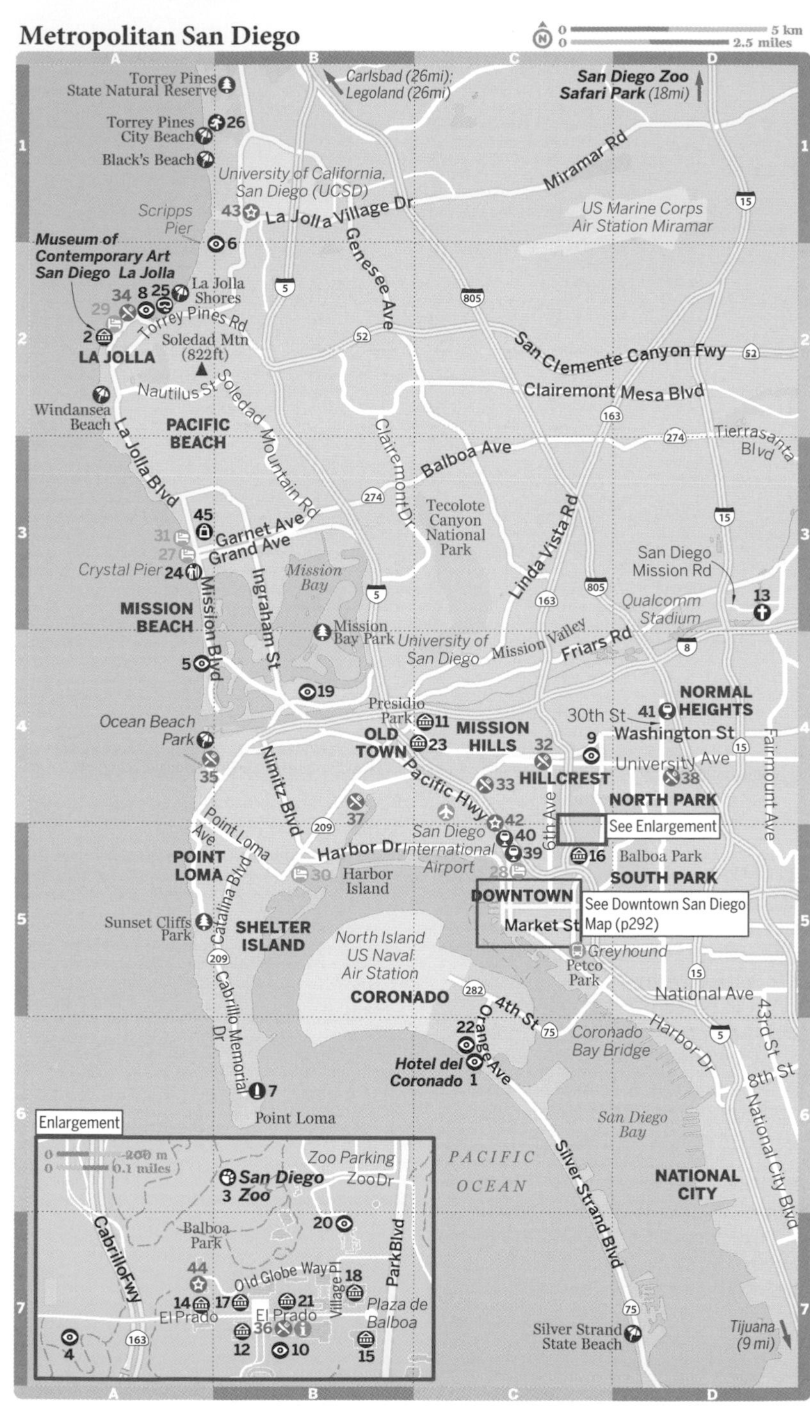

Metropolitan San Diego

Don't Miss Sights

1 Hotel del Coronado ... C6
2 Museum of Contemporary Art San Diego – La Jolla ... A2
3 San Diego Zoo ... B6

Sights

4 Balboa Park Gardens ... A7
5 Belmont Park ... A4
6 Birch Aquarium at Scripps ... B2
7 Cabrillo National Monument ... B6
8 Cave Store ... A2
Coronado Museum of History and Art ... (see 22)
9 Hillcrest Farmers Market ... C4
10 Japanese Friendship Garden ... B7
11 Junípero Serra Museum ... C4
12 Mingei International Museum ... B7
13 Mission Basilica San Diego de Alcalá ... D3
14 Museum of Man ... A7
15 Reuben H Fleet Science Center ... B7
16 San Diego Air & Space Museum ... C5
17 San Diego Museum of Art ... B7
18 San Diego Natural History Museum ... B7
19 SeaWorld San Diego ... B4
20 Spanish Village Art Center Artist Colony ... B7
21 Timken Museum of Art ... B7
22 Visitor Center ... C6
23 Whaley House ... C4

Activities, Courses & Tours

24 Pacific Beach Surf Shop ... A3
25 San Diego-La Jolla Underwater Park ... A2
26 Torrey Pines Gliderport ... B1

Sleeping

27 Crystal Pier Hotel & Cottages ... A3
Hotel del Coronado ... (see 1)
28 La Pensione Hotel ... C5
29 La Valencia ... A2
30 Pearl ... B5
31 Tower 23 ... A3

Eating

1500 Ocean ... (see 1)
32 Bread & Cie ... C4
33 El Indio ... C4
34 George's at the Cove ... A2
35 Hodad's ... A4
JRDN ... (see 31)
36 Prado ... B7
37 Stone Brewing World Bistro & Gardens ... B4
38 Waypoint Public ... D4

Drinking & Nightlife

39 Ballast Point Tasting Room & Kitchen ... C5
40 El Camino ... C5
41 Polite Provisions ... D4

Entertainment

42 Casbah ... C4
43 La Jolla Playhouse ... B1
44 Old Globe Theaters ... A7

Shopping

45 Pangaea Outpost ... A3

El Prado is the park's main pedestrian thoroughfare, surrounded on both sides by romantic Spanish Colonial Revival-style buildings originally constructed for the 1915–16 Panama-California Exposition.

For a good park map, stop by the **Balboa Park Visitors Center (Map p294; 619-239-0512; www.balboapark.org; 1549 El Prado; 9:30am-4:30pm)** in the House of Hospitality. Helpful staff here sell discount passes for the museums and the zoo.

Museum of Man — Museum

(Map p294; 619-239-2001; www.museumofman.org; Plaza de California, 1350 El Prado; adult/student/child $12.50/8/5; 10am-5pm) This is the county's only anthropological museum, with exhibits spanning ancient Egypt, the Mayans and local native Kumeyaay people, human evolution and the human life cycle. Recent temporary exhibits have covered everything from women's empowerment to beer. The basket and pottery collections are especially fine. The museum shop sells handicrafts from Central America and elsewhere.

Reuben H Fleet Science Center — Museum

(Map p294; 619-238-1233; www.rhfleet.org; 1875 El Prado; adult/child $13/11, incl Giant Dome Theater $17/14; 10am-5pm Mon-Thu, to 6pm Fri-Sun;) One of Balboa Park's most popular venues, this hands-on science museum features interactive displays and a toddler room. Look out for opportunities to build gigantic structures with Keva planks and visit the **Gallery of Illusions and Perceptions**. The biggest drawcard is the **Giant Dome Theater** ($7 if purchased separately), which screens several different films each day. The hemispherical,

wraparound screen and 152-speaker state-of-the-art sound system create sensations ranging from pretty cool to mind-blowing.

San Diego Natural History Museum Museum
(Map p294; ☎619-232-3821; www.sdnhm.org; 1788 El Prado; adult/child $17/11; ⏲10am-5pm; 👪) The 'Nat' houses 7.5 million specimens, including rocks, fossils and taxidermied animals, as well as an impressive dinosaur skeleton and a California fault-line exhibit, all in beautiful spaces. Kids love the movies about the natural world in the giant-screen cinema; the selections change frequently. Children's programs are held most weekends. Special exhibits (some with an extra charge) span pirates to King Tut. The museum also arranges field trips and nature walks in Balboa Park and further afield.

San Diego Air & Space Museum Museum
(Map p294; ☎619-234-8291; www.sandiegoairandspace.org; 2001 Pan American Plaza; adult/child $18/7; ⏲10am-5:30pm Jun-Aug, to 4:30pm Sep-May; 👪) The round building at the southern end of the plaza houses an excellent museum with extensive displays of aircraft throughout history – originals, replicas, models – plus memorabilia from legendary aviators including Charles Lindbergh and astronaut John Glenn. Catch films in the new 3D/4D theater.

San Diego Museum of Art Museum
(SDMA; Map p294; ☎619-232-7931; www.sdmart.org; 1450 El Prado; adult/child $12/4.50; ⏲10am-5pm Mon-Tue & Thu-Sat, from noon Sun, also 5-9pm Thu Jun-Sep) The SDMA is the city's largest art museum. The permanent collection has works by a number of European masters from the renaissance to the modernist eras (though no renowned pieces), American landscape paintings and several fantastic pieces in the Asian galleries, and there are often important traveling exhibits. The **Sculpture Garden** has works by Alexander Calder and Henry Moore.

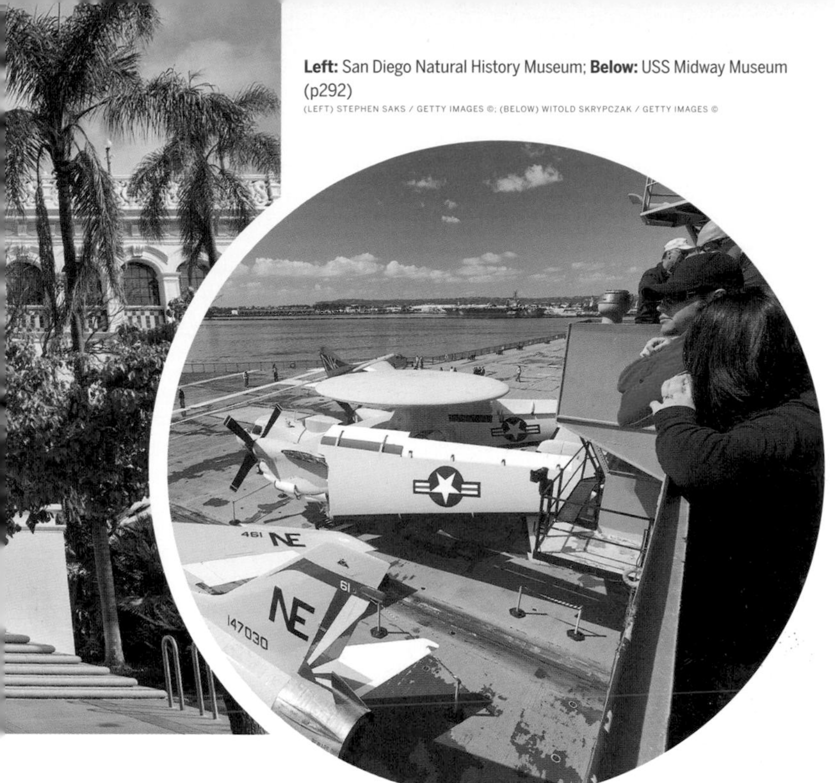

Left: San Diego Natural History Museum; **Below:** USS Midway Museum (p292)

(LEFT) STEPHEN SAKS / GETTY IMAGES ©; (BELOW) WITOLD SKRYPCZAK / GETTY IMAGES ©

Timken Museum of Art Museum

(Map p294; ☎619-239-5548; www.timkenmuseum.org; 1500 El Prado; ⌚10am-4:30pm Tue-Sat, from 1:30pm Sun) FREE Don't skip the Timken, home of the Putnam collection, a small but impressive group of paintings, including works by Rembrandt, Rubens, El Greco, Cézanne and Pissarro, plus a wonderful selection of Russian icons. Built in 1965, the building stands out for *not* being in imitation Spanish style.

Mingei International Museum Museum

(Map p294; ☎619-239-0003; www.mingei.org; 1439 El Prado; adult/child $8/5; ⌚10am-5pm Tue-Sun; 👪) A rare New Zealand kauri tree (a fragrant evergreen with flat leaves) marks the entrance to this diverse collection of folk art, costumes, toys, jewelry, utensils and other handmade objects from traditional cultures from around the world, plus changing exhibitions covering beads to surfboards. Check the website to find out what's on.

Balboa Park Gardens Gardens

(Map p294) Balboa Park includes a number of gardens, reflecting different horticultural styles and environments, including **Alcazar Garden**, a formal, Spanish-style garden; **Palm Canyon**, with more than 50 species of palms; **Japanese Friendship Garden (Map p294; www.niwa.org; adult/senior/child under 6yr $6/4/free; ⌚10am-4:30pm except major holidays)**; **Australian Garden**; **Rose Garden**; and **Desert Garden** (best in spring). **Florida Canyon** gives an idea of the San Diego landscape before Spanish settlement. Free weekly **Offshoot tours (www.balboapark.org/info/tours.php; ⌚10am Sat mid-Jan–Thanksgiving)** depart the Balboa Park visitors center (p295) and cover a rotating selection of themes including history and botany.

Spanish Village Art Center Artist Colony Artist Colony
(Map p294; 11am-4pm) FREE Behind the Natural History Museum is a grassy square with a magnificent Moreton Bay fig tree (sorry, climbing is prohibited). Opposite the square stand there's an enclave of small tiled cottages (billed by park authorities as 'an authentic reproduction of an ancient village in Spain') that are rented out as artists' studios, where you can watch potters, jewelers, glass blowers, painters and sculptors churn out their crafts.

OLD TOWN & AROUND

In 1769 Padre Junípero Serra and Gaspar de Portola established the first Spanish settlement in California on Presidio Hill, overlooking the valley of the San Diego River.

Today, this area below Presidio Hill is called Old Town, and it presents life as it was between 1821 and 1872. Although it is neither very old (most of the buildings are reconstructions), nor exactly a town (more like a leafy suburb), it's a more-or-less faithful copy of San Diego's original nucleus, offering a pedestrian plaza surrounded by historic buildings, shops, a number of restaurants and cafes, and a good opportunity to explore San Diego's early days.

Whaley House Historic Building
(Map p294; 619-297-7511; www.whaleyhouse.org; 2476 San Diego Ave; adult/child before 5pm $6/4, after 5pm $10/5; 10am-10pm late May-early Sep, to 5pm Mon-Tue, to 10pm Thu-Sat early Sep-late May) Two blocks from the Old Town perimeter sits the city's oldest brick building (circa 1856), officially certified as haunted by the US Department of Commerce. Check out the collection of period furniture and clothing from when the house served as a courthouse, theater and private residence. After 5pm, admission is by tour only.

Junípero Serra Museum Museum
(Map p294; 619-297-3258; www.sandiegohistory.org; 2727 Presidio Dr; adult/child $6/3; 10am-4pm Sat & Sun mid-Sep–mid-May, to 5pm Sat & Sun mid-May–mid-Sep; P) Located in one of the most important historical buildings in the city, this small but interesting collection of artifacts and pictures is from the Mission and rancho periods, and it gives a good sense of the earliest days of European settlement up to 1929 when the museum was founded.

Mission Basilica San Diego de Alcalá Church
(Map p294; 619-281-8449; www.missionsandiego.com; 10818 San Diego Mission Rd; adult/child $3/1; 9am-4:30pm; P) Although the site of the first California mission (1769) was on Presidio Hill by present-day Old Town, in 1774 Padre Junípero Serra moved it about

Spanish Village Art Center Artist Colony
RICHARD CUMMINS / GETTY IMAGES ©

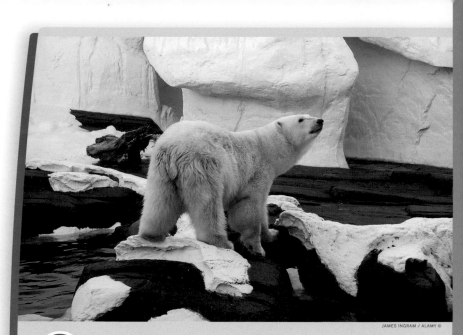

JAMES INGRAM / ALAMY ©

Don't Miss
San Diego Zoo

If it slithers, crawls, stomps, swims, leaps or flies, chances are you'll find it in this world-famous zoo in northern Balboa Park. Since its opening in 1916, the zoo has also pioneered ways to house and display animals that mimic their natural habitat, leading to a revolution in zoo design and, so the argument goes, to happier animals.

Today, the zoo is home to thousands of animals representing 800-plus species in a beautifully landscaped setting. Perennial favorite **Polar Bear Plunge** wows crowds with up-close, underwater views of the bears through thick glass walls. Other hot spots are **Elephant Odyssey** and **Panda Canyon**, where a live narrator shares facts about pandas at the outdoor viewing area here and, more importantly, keeps the line moving.

Arboreal orangutans and siamangs peacefully coexist in the **Lost Forest**. Don't miss the vast **Scripps Aviary** and **Rainforest Aviary**, where carefully placed feeders (and remarkably fearless birds) allow for close-up viewing. The koalas in the **Aussie Outback** have proved so popular that Australians may be surprised to find them an unofficial symbol of San Diego. At **Discovery Outpost**, youngsters can pet small critters and watch animal shows.

Arrive early, when the animals are most active. There's a large, free parking lot off Park Blvd that starts filling fast right at opening time. Bus 7 will get you there from downtown.

NEED TO KNOW

Map p294; ☎619-231-1515; www.sandiegozoo.org; 2920 Zoo Dr; 1-day pass adult/child from $46/36; 2-visit pass to Zoo and/or Safari Park adult/child $82/64; ⏰9am-9pm mid-Jun–early Sep, to 5pm or 6pm early Sep–mid-Jun; P 👪

San Diego Beach Towns

If you feel at home among the surfers and sun-worshippers of La Jolla and Coronado, kick off your flip-flops at a few of San Diego's other beachfront neighborhoods.

MISSION BEACH

Home since 1925 to the retro, family-style amusement park **Belmont Park** (Map p294; ☎858-458-1549; www.belmontpark.com; 3146 Mission Blvd; per ride $2-6, all-day pass adult/child $27/16; ⏲from 11am daily, closing time varies; P). The classic wooden **Giant Dipper** roller coaster might just shake the teeth right out of your mouth. Continue onto Pacific Beach (PB) via the beachfront boardwalk, **Ocean Front Walk**.

PACIFIC BEACH

Along **Garnet Ave**, hordes of twentysomethings toss back brews and gobble cheap tacos. At the ocean end, **Crystal Pier** is worth a look. Built in the 1920s, it's home to San Diego's quirkiest hotel, the Crystal Pier Hotel, which consists of a cluster of Cape Cod–style cottages built out over the waves.

OCEAN BEACH

In bohemian Ocean Beach you can get tattooed, shop for antiques and walk into a restaurant barefoot. Newport Ave is the main drag, filled with surf shops, bars, music stores, java joints and used-clothing stores. The street ends a block from the half-mile-long **Ocean Beach Pier**; just north is the central beach scene, with volleyball courts and sunset barbecues.

7 miles upriver, closer to water and more arable land, now the Mission Basilica San Diego de Alcalá. In 1784 missionaries built a solid adobe-and-timber church, which was destroyed by an earthquake in 1803. The church was promptly rebuilt, and at least some of it still stands on a slope overlooking Mission Valley.

SeaWorld San Diego Theme Park
(Map p294; ☎800-257-4268; www.seaworldsandiego.com; 500 SeaWorld Dr; adult/child 3-9yr $84/78; ⏲daily; P 👪) SeaWorld opened in San Diego in 1964 and remains one of California's most popular theme parks. Many visitors spend the whole day here, shuttling between shows, rides and exhibits – you can pick up a map at the entrance to plan your day around scheduled events.

The attraction is best known for the live shows featuring trained dolphins, sea lions and killer whales. **One Ocean** is the most visually impressive, a 30-minute show featuring the famous Shamu and other killer whales gliding through the water while interacting with each other, their trainers and the audience.

HILLCREST

Just up from the northwestern corner of Balboa Park, you hit **Hillcrest**, the heart of Uptown. It's San Diego's most bohemian district, with a decidedly urban feel, despite the suburban visuals. It's also the headquarters of the city's gay and lesbian community.

For a tour, begin at the **Hillcrest Gateway**, which arches over University Ave at 5th Ave. East on University Ave at No 535, look for the 1928 **Kahn Building**, an original commercial building with architectural elements that border on kitsch. Then head south on 5th Ave to find a variety of cafes, friendly gay bars, vintage clothing shops and independent bookstores.

CORONADO

In February 1888, the Hotel del Coronado (at the time the largest hotel west of the Mississippi) welcomed its very first guests. Today, the hotel and its stunning surroundings are the primary reasons to visit this well-manicured community.

The city of Coronado is now connected to the mainland by the graceful 2.12-mile-long **Coronado Bay Bridge** (opened in 1969), as well as by a narrow spit of sand known as the **Silver Strand**, which runs south to Imperial Beach and connects Coronado to the mainland.

Hotel del Coronado — Hotel

(Map p294; ☎800-582-2595, 619-435-6611; www.hoteldel.com; 1500 Orange Ave; 👪) Few hotels in the world are as easily recognized or as much loved as the 'The Del.' The world's largest resort (p305) when it was built, the all-timber, whitewashed main building offers conical towers, cupolas, turrets, balconies, dormer windows and cavernous public spaces typical of their designers, railroad-depot architects James and Merritt Reed. Acres of polished wood give the interior a warm, old-fashioned feel that conjures daydreams of Panama hats and linen suits.

Coronado Visitors Center — Art & Tours

(☎866-599-7242, 619-437-8788; www.coronadovisitorcenter.com; 1100 Orange Ave; walking tour $15; ⏰9am-5pm Mon-Fri, 10am-5pm Sat & Sun, walking tours 10:30am Mon, Wed & Fri, 2pm Sat & Sun) Coronado's visitors center doubles as the **Coronado Museum of History and Art** FREE and offers 90-minute historical **walking tours**.

POINT LOMA

Cabrillo National Monument — Monument

(Map p294; ☎619-557-5450; www.nps.gov/cabr; 1800 Cabrillo Memorial Dr; per car/person walk-in $5/3, good for 7 days; ⏰9am-5pm; P) Atop a steep hill at the tip of the peninsula, this is San Diego's finest locale for history, views and nature walks. It's also the best place in town to see the gray-whale migration

Giant Dipper roller coaster, Belmont Park, Mission Beach

RICHARD CUMMINS / GETTY IMAGES ©

Below: Old Point Loma Lighthouse; **Right:** La Jolla Cove
(BELOW) RON AND PATTY THOMAS PHOTOGRAPHY / GETTY IMAGES ©; (RIGHT) TERRY HEALY / GETTY IMAGES ©

(January to March) from land.
You may forget you're in a major metropolitan area.

The **visitors center** has a comprehensive, old-school presentation on Portuguese explorer Juan Rodríguez Cabrillo's 1542 voyage up the California coast, plus good exhibits on native inhabitants and the area's natural history.

The 1854 **Old Point Loma Lighthouse**, atop the point, is furnished with late-19th-century period furniture, including lamps and picture frames hand-covered with hundreds of shells – testimony to the long, lonely nights endured by lighthouse keepers. The 1.8 mile **Bayside Trail** has about a 300ft elevation and interpretive signs about local plant life. On the ocean side, drive the steep mile down to the **tide pools** to look for anemones, starfish, crabs, limpets and dead man's fingers (thin, tubular seaweed), best seen in low tide in winter.

If you're not driving, the monument can be reached by the hourly bus 84 from Old Town Transit Center (p311).

LA JOLLA VILLAGE & THE COAST

For a camera-worthy stroll, take the half-mile bluff-top path that winds above the shoreline a few blocks west of the Village. Near the path's western end is the **Children's Pool**, off Coast Dr near Jenner Blvd. Originally intended to give La Jolla's youth a safe place to frolic, the Children's Pool beach is now populated by sea lions, which you can view up close as they lounge on the shore.

A short walk north leads to picnic tables and grills plus views of **La Jolla Cove** just below the path. This gem of a beach provides access to some of the

best snorkeling around; it's also popular with rough-water swimmers.

Museum of Contemporary Art San Diego – La Jolla Art Museum

(MCASD; Map p294; ☎858-454-3541; www.mcasd.org; 700 Prospect St, La Jolla; adult/child $10/free, 3rd Thu each month 5-7pm free; ⏲11am-5pm Thu-Tue, to 7pm 3rd Thu each month) La Jolla's branch of this museum gets changing, world-class exhibitions. Originally designed by Irving Gill in 1916 as the home of newspaper heiress **Ellen Browning Scripps**, who basically created modern La Jolla circa 1897, the building was renovated by aPhiladelphia's post-modern architect Robert Venturi and has an Andy Goldsworthy sculpture out the front; tickets are good for one week at all three of the museum's locations (p290).

San Diego-La Jolla Underwater Park Snorkeling, Diving

(Map p294) Some of California's best and most accessible diving is in this reserve, accessible from La Jolla Cove. With an average depth of 20ft, the 6000 acres of look-but-don't-touch underwater real estate is great for snorkeling, too. Ever-present are the spectacular, bright orange Garibaldi fish – California's official state fish and a protected species (there's a $500 fine for poaching one). Further out you'll see forests of giant California kelp (which can increase its length by up to 3ft per day) and the 100ft-deep **La Jolla Canyon**.

A number of commercial outfits conduct scuba-diving courses, sell or rent equipment, fill tanks, and conduct boat trips to nearby wrecks and islands. The **Cave Store (Map p294; ☎858-459-0746; www.cavestore.com; 1325 Coast Rd; adult/child $4/3; ⏲10am-5pm; 👪)** and other outfitters rent snorkel and fin sets (about $20 for two hours).

LA JOLLA SHORES

Called 'the Shores,' this area northeast of La Jolla Cove is where La Jolla's cliffs meet the wide, sandy beaches that stretch north to Del Mar.

Birch Aquarium at Scripps Aquarium

(Map p294; ☎858-534-3474; www.aquarium.ucsd.edu; 2300 Exhibition Way, La Jolla; adult/child $17/12.50; ⏰9am-5pm; P 👪) Marine scientists were working at the Birch Aquarium at Scripps Institution of Oceanography (SIO) as early as 1910 and, helped by donations from the ever-generous Scripps family, the institute has grown to be one of the world's largest marine research institutions. It is now a part of UCSD. Off N Torrey Pines Rd, the aquarium has brilliant displays. The **Hall of Fishes** has more than 30 fish tanks, simulating marine environments from the Pacific Northwest to tropical seas.

Torrey Pines State Natural Reserve Park

(☎858-755-2063; www.torreypine.org; 12600 N Torrey Pines Rd, La Jolla; ⏰7:15am-dusk, visitor center 10am-4pm Oct-Apr, 9am-6pm May-Sep; P) Between N Torrey Pines Rd and the ocean, and from the **Torrey Pines Gliderport (Map p294; ☎858-452-9858; www.flytorrey.com; 2800 Torrey Pines Scenic Dr; 20min paragliding $150, hang gliding tandem flight per person $200)** to Del Mar, this reserve preserves the last mainland stands of the Torrey pine *(Pinus torreyana)*, a species adapted to sparse rainfall and sandy, stony soils. Steep sandstone gullies have eroded into wonderfully textured surfaces, and the views over the ocean and north, including whale-watching, are superb. Rangers lead nature walks on weekends and holidays. Several walking trails wind through the reserve and down to the beach. Parking fees per car vary from $4 per hour to $15 per day.

Activities

Pacific Beach Surf Shop Surfing

(Map p294; ☎858-373-1138; www.pbsurfshop.com; 4150 Mission Blvd; ⏰store 9am-7pm, lessons hourly until 4pm) This shop provides instruction through its Pacific Beach Surf School. It has friendly service, and also rents wetsuits and both soft (foam) and hard (fiberglass) boards. Call ahead for lessons.

Family Kayak Kayak Rental

(☎619-282-3520; www.familykayak.com; adult/child from $44/18; 👪) Offer guided tours and lessons. Inquire about longer tours. Locations vary, so check the website.

Tours

Old Town Trolley Tours & Seal Tours Trolley Tour

(☎888-910-8687; www.trolleytours.com; adult/child $39/19) Not to be confused with the municipal San Diego Trolley, this outfit operates hop-on-hop-off, open-air buses decorated like old-style streetcars, looping around the main attractions of Downtown and Coronado in about two hours, every 30 minutes or so. The main trolley stand is in Old

Sandstone slopes, Torrey Pines State Natural Reserve

BRYAN MULLENNIX / GETTY IMAGES ©

Detour: Legoland

In the North County beach town of Carlsbad, this theme park is a fantasy environment built largely of those little colored plastic blocks from Denmark. Many rides and attractions are targeted to elementary schoolers: a junior 'driving school', a jungle cruise lined with Lego animals, wacky 'sky cruiser' pedal cars on a track, and fairytale, princess, pirate, adventurer and dino-themed escapades.

Just adjacent are the Sea Life Aquarium (in which real sea creatures swim among Lego creations) and Legoland Water Park. The new **Legoland Hotel** (877-534-6526, 760-918-5346; california.legoland.com/legoland-hotel; 5885 the Crossings Dr; r incl breakfast from $369;) is tailor-made for little ones, from kid-size bunk beds and junior-level peepholes in the door, to bedtime stories in the lobby and bin after bin of the bricks to play with.

From the I-5 Fwy, take the Legoland/Cannon Rd exit and follow the signs. Parking is $15.

Town, but you can start or stop at any of the well-marked trolley-tour stops.

Flagship Cruises Boat Tour
(Map p292; 619-234-4111; www.flagshipsd.com; 990 N Harbor Dr; tours adult/child from $23/11.50;) Harbor tours and seasonal whale-watching cruises from the Embarcadero, from one to several hours long.

Sleeping

DOWNTOWN

500 West Hotel Hotel $
(Map p292; 619-234-5252, 866-500-7533; www.500westhotelsd.com; 500 W Broadway; s/d with shared bath from $59/79;) Rooms are shoebox-sized and many bathrooms are down the hallway in this updated 1920s YMCA building, but hipsters on a budget love the bright decor, tiny flat-screen TVs, communal kitchen (or diner-style restaurant), gym at the Y ($10) and easy access to trolleys and long-distance buses. No air-con.

Hotel Solamar Boutique, Contemporary $$
(Map p292; 619-531-8740, 877-230-0300; www.hotelsolamar.com; 435 6th Ave; r $169-299;) A great compromise in the Gaslamp: hip style that needn't break the bank. Lounge beats animate your view of skyscrapers from the pool deck and bar, and rooms have sleek lines and nautical blue and neo-rococo accents for a touch of fun. There's a fitness center, in-room yoga kit, loaner bikes and a nightly complimentary wine hour. Parking costs $41.

La Pensione Hotel Boutique Hotel $$
(Map p294; www.lapensionehotel.com; 606 W Date St; r $110-159; ; 5, Pacific Hwy & W Cedar St) Despite the name, Little Italy's la Pensione isn't a pension but an intimate, friendly, recently renovated hotel of 68 rooms with queen-size beds and private bathrooms. It's set around a frescoed courtyard and it's just steps to the neighborhood's dining, cafes and galleries, and walking distance to most Downtown attractions. There's an attractive cafe downstairs. Parking is $15.

CORONADO

Hotel del Coronado Luxury Hotel $$$
(Hotel Del; Map p294; 800-468-3533, 619-435-6611; www.hoteldel.com; 1500 Orange Ave; r from $289;) San Diego's iconic hotel provides the essential Coronado experience: over a century of history (p301), a pool, full-service spa,

shops, restaurants, manicured grounds, a white-sand beach and an ice-skating rink in winter. Even the basic rooms have luxurious marbled bathrooms. Note: half the accommodations are not in the main Victorian-era hotel (368 rooms) but in an adjacent seven-story building constructed in the 1970s. For a sense of place, book a room in the original hotel. Parking is $37.

POINT LOMA

Pearl Motel **$$**
(Map p294; 877-732-7574, 619-226-6100; www.thepearlsd.com; 1410 Rosecrans St; r $129-169; P) The midcentury modern Pearl feels more Palm Springs than San Diego. The 23 rooms in its 1959 shell have soothing blue hues, trippy surf motifs and bettas in fishbowls. There's a lively pool scene (including 'dive-in' movies on Wednesday nights), or play Jenga or Parcheesi in the groovy, shag-carpeted lobby. Light sleepers: request a room away from busy street traffic. On-site parking is limited and costs $10.

PACIFIC BEACH

Crystal Pier Hotel & Cottages Cottage **$$$**
(Map p294; 858-483-6983, 800-748-5894; www.crystalpier.com; 4500 Ocean Blvd; d $185-525; P) Charming, wonderful and unlike anyplace else in San Diego, Crystal Pier has cottages built right on the pier above the water. Almost all 29 cottages have full ocean views and kitchens; most date from 1936. Newer, larger cottages sleep up to six. Book eight to 11 months in advance for summer reservations. Minimum-stay requirements vary by season. No air-con. Rates include parking.

Tower 23 Boutique Hotel **$$$**
(Map p294; 858-270-2323, 866-869-3723; www.t23hotel.com; 723 Felspar St, Pacific Beach; r from $249; P) If you like your oceanfront stay with contemporary cool style, this modernist show place has an awesome location, minimalist decor, lots of teals and mint blues, water features and a sense of humor. There's no pool, but dude, you're right on the beach. Parking is $20.

LA JOLLA

La Valencia Historic Hotel **$$$**
(Map p294; 800-451-0772, 858-454-0771; www.lavalencia.com; 1132 Prospect St; r from $385; P) Publicity stills of Lon Cheney, Lillian Gish and Greta Garbo line the hallways of this 1926 landmark: pink-walled, Mediterranean-style and designed by William Templeton Johnson. Among its 112 rooms, those in the main building are rather compact, but villas are spacious, and in any case the property wins for Old Hollywood romance.

Eating

DOWNTOWN & EMBARCADERO

Café 222 Breakfast **$**
(Map p292; 619-236-9902; www.cafe222.com; 222 Island Ave; mains $7-11; 7am-1:30pm) Downtown's favorite breakfast place serves renowned peanut butter and banana French toast; buttermilk, orange-pecan or granola pancakes; and eggs in scrambles or benedicts. It also sells lunchtime sandwiches and salads, but we always go for breakfast (available until closing).

Puesto at the Headquarters Mexican **$$**
(Map p292; 610-233-8800; www.eatpuesto.com; 789 W Harbor Dr, The Headquarters; mains $11-19; 11am-10pm) This upscale eatery serves Mexican street food that knocked our *zapatos* off: innovative takes on traditional tacos such as chicken (with hibiscus, chipotle, pineapple and avocado) and some out-there fillings including potato-soy chorizo. Other highlights: crab guacamole, *barbacoa* short ribs (braised in chile sauce) and Mexican street bowl (tropical fruits with chili, sea salt and lime).

Oceanaire Seafood **$$$**
(Map p292; 619-858-2277; www.theoceanaire.com; 400 J St; mains $23-52; 5-10pm Sun-Thu, to 11pm Fri & Sat) The look is art-deco ocean liner, and the service is just as elegant, with an oyster bar and creations such as Maryland blue-crab cakes and horseradish-crusted Alaskan halibut. If

you don't feel like a total splurge, happy hour features bargain-priced oysters and fish tacos in the bar (times vary).

BALBOA PARK

Prado — Californian $$$

(Map p294; ☎619-557-9441; www.pradobalboa.com; House of Hospitality, 1549 El Prado; lunch mains $12-21, dinner mains $22-35; ⏰11:30am-3pm Mon-Fri, from 11am Sat & Sun, 5-9pm Sun & Tue-Thu, to 10pm Fri & Sat) In one of San Diego's most beautiful dining rooms, feast on Cal-eclectic cooking by one of San Diego's most renowned chefs: bakery sandwiches, chicken and *orecchiette* pasta, and pork prime rib. Go for a civilized lunch on the verandah or for afternoon cocktails and appetizers in the bar.

HILLCREST & AROUND

Check out the **Hillcrest Farmers Market (Map p294; cnr Normal St & Lincoln Ave; ⏰9am-1pm Sun)** if you're here on a Sunday.

Bread & Cie — Bakery, Cafe $

(Map p294; www.breadandcie.com; 350 University Ave, Hillcrest; mains $6-11; ⏰7am-7pm Mon-Fri, to 6pm Sat, 8am-6pm Sun; P) Aside from crafting some of San Diego's best breads (including anise and fig, kalamata black olive and three-raisin), this wide-open bakery-deli makes fabulous sandwiches with fillings such as curried-chicken salad and Black Forest ham. Boxed lunches cost $11. Great pastries, too.

El Indio — Mexican $

(Map p294; ☎619-299-0333; www.el-indio.com; 3695 India St; mains $3-9; ⏰8am-9pm; P 👪) Counter-service shop famous since 1940 for its taquitos, *mordiditas* (tiny taquitos), tamales and excellent breakfast burritos. Eat in a rudimentary dining room or at picnic tables under metal umbrellas across the street.

Waypoint Public — Gastropub $$

(☎619-255-8778; www.waypointpublic.com; 3794 30th St, North Park; mains $9-21; ⏰4pm-1am Mon-Fri, from 10am Sat & Sun; 🐾) Chef-driven Waypoint's comfort food menu is meant to pair craft beers with dishes from smoked tomato minestrone with grilled cheese to a burger with mozzarella, pulled pork, tomatillo salsa, fried egg and spicy pickled vegetables. Walls are attractively done up in reclaimed wood, and glass garage doors roll up to the outside, all the better for hipster-watching in busy North Park.

HMS *Surprise*, Maritime Museum (p293), San Diego

CORONADO

1500 Ocean Californian **$$$**

(☎619-435-6611; www.hoteldel.com/1500-ocean; Hotel del Coronado, 1500 Orange Ave; mains $33-45; ⌚5:30-10pm Tue-Sat, plus Sun summer; P) It's hard to beat the romance of supping at the Hotel del Coronado, especially at a table overlooking the sea from the verandah of its 1st-class dining room, where silver service and coastal cuisine with local ingredients set the perfect tone for popping the question or fêting an important anniversary.

OCEAN BEACH & POINT LOMA

Hodad's Burgers **$**

(Map p294; ☎619-224-4623; www.hodadies.com; 5010 Newport Ave, Ocean Beach; mains $4-13; ⌚11am-9pm Sun-Thu, to 10pm Fri & Sat) Since the flower-power days of 1969, OB's legendary burger joint has served great shakes, massive baskets of onion rings and succulent hamburgers wrapped in paper. The walls are covered in license plates, grunge/surf-rock plays (loud!) and your bearded, tattooed server might sidle in to your booth to take your order. No shirt, no shoes, no problem, dude.

Stone Brewing World Bistro & Gardens Beer Hall **$$**

(www.stonelibertystation.com; Liberty Station, 2816 Historic Decatur Rd #116; lunch mains $14-21, dinner mains $15-29; ⌚11:30am-10pm Mon-Sat, 11am-9pm Sun; P) Local brewer Stone has transformed the former mess hall of the naval training center at Liberty Station into a temple to local craft beer. Tuck into standard-setting, spin-the-globe dishes (yellowfin *poke* tacos, chicken schnitzel, beef *ssambap* – Korean-style lettuce cups – etc) at long tables or comfy booths under its tall beamed ceiling, or beneath twinkling lights in its courtyard.

PACIFIC BEACH

JRDN California **$$$**

(Jordan; Map p294; ☎858-270-5736; Tower 23 Hotel, 723 Felspar St; breakfast & lunch mains $9-14, dinner mains $26-46; ⌚9am-9pm Sun-Thu, to 9:30pm Sat & Sun) A big heaping dose of chic amid PB's congenital laid-back feel. There's both an ocean view and a futuristic interior (and most excellent bar scene). Sustainably farmed meats and seafood join local veggies to create festivals on the plate. Try the lobster BLT,

Equestrian statue, Museum of Man (p295), San Diego

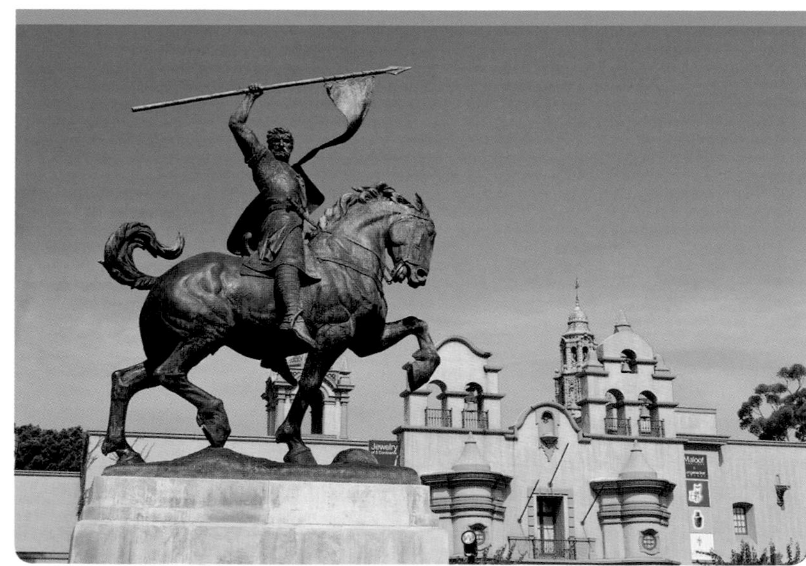

San Diego Microbreweries

San Diegans take their craft beers seriously – even at a dive bar, you might overhear local guys talking about hops and cask conditioning. Various microbreweries on the city outskirts specialize in India Pale Ale (IPA) and Belgian-style brews. At one beer-enthusiast favorite, **Stone Brewing Company** (760-471-4999; www.stonebrew.com; 1999 Citracado Pkwy, Escondido; tours noon-6pm daily), you can take a free tour before a guided tasting of Oaked Arrogant Bastard Ale and Stone Barley Wine. To leave the driving to others, book with **Brewery Tours of San Diego** (619-961-7999; www.brewerytoursofsandiego.com; per person $65-95).

or 'build your own' steak with green onion 'creamers' (aka mashed potatoes).

LA JOLLA

George's at the Cove Californian **$$$**
(Map p294; 858-454-4244; www.georgesatthecove.com; 1250 Prospect St, La Jolla; mains $13-50; 11am-10pm Mon-Thu, to 11pm Fri-Sun) If you've got the urge to splurge, the Euro-Cal cooking is as dramatic as the oceanfront location thanks to the bottomless imagination of chef Trey Foshée. George's has graced just about every list of top restaurants in California, and indeed the USA. Three venues allow you to enjoy it at different price points: Ocean Terrace, George's Bar and George's California Modern.

Drinking

Bang Bang Bar
(Map p292; www.bangbangsd.com; 526 Market St; closed Mon) Beneath lantern-light, the Gaslamp's hottest new spot gigs in local and world-known DJs and serves sushi and Asian small plates including dumplings and panko-crusted shrimp to nurse the imaginative cocktails (some in giant goblets meant for sharing with your posse). Plus, the bathrooms are shrines to Ryan Gosling and Hello Kitty: in a word, awesome.

Noble Experiment Bar
(Map p292; 619-888-4713; http://nobleexperimentsd.com; 777 G St; 7pm-2am Tue-Sun) This place is literally a find. Open a secret door and enter a contemporary speakeasy with miniature gold skulls on the walls, classical paintings on the ceilings and some 400 cocktails on the list (from $12). The hard part: getting in. Text for a reservation, and staff will tell you if your requested time is available and how to find it.

Ballast Point Tasting Room & Kitchen Pub
(Map p294; 619-255-7213; www.ballastpoint.com; 2215 India St; 11am-11pm Mon-Sat, to 9pm Sun) Opened in 2013, this is the newest and funnest location from this San Diego–based brewery, and it does a lot of R&D for the rest of the company. Three 4oz tasters of itsbeers for just $5 is the best deal in town. Enjoy them with a full menu (mains $7 to $14) including housemade pretzels, beer-steamed mussels, salads and grilled dishes.

Polite Provisions Cocktail Bar
(www.politeprovisions.com; 4696 30th St, North Park; 11:30am-1:30am) A mile north of central North Park, this swanky new cocktail bar is special from its glass ceiling to wood-paneled walls and tiled floors. It makes its own syrups, sodas and infusions and pour a daily-changing selection of wine, cocktails and beers from taps. For vittles, the 'soda and swine' menu features meatballs and dozens of ways to eat them.

El Camino Lounge
(Map p294; 2400 India St) We're not sure what it means that this buzzy watering

hole has a Dia de los Muertos (Mexican Day of the Dead holiday) theme in the flight path of San Diego Airport – watch planes land from the outdoor patio – but whatever, dude. The clientele is cool, design mod, the drinks strong and the Mexican vittles *fabuloso*.

 Entertainment

Tabloid-sized magazines, **CityBeat** (www.sdcitybeat.com) and **San Diego Reader** (www.sdreader.com), cover the active music, art and theater scenes. Find them in shops and cafes. **Arts Tix (Map p292; ☎858-381-5595; www.sdartstix.com; Lyceum Theatre, 79 Horton Plaza)**, in a kiosk near Westfield Horton Plaza, has half-price tickets for many shows.

4th & B Live Music
(Map p292; www.4thandB.com; 345 B St) This midsized venue has music lovers head-bobbing with performances from an eclectic mix of talent and club nights, from unsigned hopefuls to the Psychedelic Furs, Snoop Dogg and the Last Comic Standing tour. Rest your feet – and eardrums – in the lounge. There's often a cover charge.

Old Globe Theaters Theater
(Map p294; www.theoldglobe.org; Balboa Park) Balboa Park's Old Globe Theaters date from the 1935 Exposition, and in the 1970s the main stage was rebuilt in the style of the original 17th-century Globe in England, where Shakespeare's works were originally performed. Between the three stages here – **Old Globe**, **Cassius Carter Stage** and the outdoor **Lowell Davies Festival Theater** – there are performances most days, including non-Shakespearean works.

La Jolla Playhouse Theater
(Map p294; ☎858-550-1010; www.lajollaplayhouse.org; 2910 La Jolla Village Dr) Inside the Mandell Weiss Center for the Performing Arts, this theater has sent dozens of productions to Broadway including *Jersey Boys, Peter and the Starcatcher* and 2010 Tony winner *Memphis*.

Casbah Live Music
(Map p294; ☎619-232-4355; www.casbahmusic.com; 2501 Kettner Blvd; tickets $5-45) Bands from Smashing Pumpkins to Death Cab for Cutie all rocked the Casbah on their way up the charts and it's still a good place to catch tomorrow's headliners.

 Shopping

Local fashionistas head to La Jolla. Shoppers in search of colorful housewares such as the museum stores at Balboa Park and the Mexican artisan stands of Old Town. Hipsters hit the secondhand clothing racks in Hillcrest, Ocean Beach

Alcazar Garden (p297), Balboa Park, San Diego
BARRY WINIKER / GETTY IMAGES ©

and Pacific Beach. Surf shops and bikini boutiques dot the coast.

Pangaea Outpost Fashion
(Map p294; 909 Garnet Ave, Pacific Beach) Like a mini-world unto themselves, the 70-plus merchants here offer a supremely eclectic selection of clothing, jewelry, wraps, handbags and semi-precious stones (just for starters!) from all around the world.

Information

International Visitor Information Center (Map p292; ☎619-236-1212; www.sandiego.org; 1140 N Harbor Dr; ⊙9am-5pm Jun-Sep, to 4pm Oct-May) Across from the B St Cruise Ship Terminal, helpful staff offer very detailed neighborhood maps, sell discounted tickets to attractions and maintain a hotel reservation hotline.

Getting There & Away

Air

San Diego International Airport (Map p294; www.san.org; 3325 N Harbor Dr) Just 4 miles from downtown San Diego.

Bus

Greyhound (Map p294; ☎619-515-1100, 800-231-2222; www.greyhound.com; 1313 National Ave)

Train

Amtrak (☎800-872-7245; www.amtrak.com)

Getting Around

To/From the Airport

Bus 992 ('the Flyer,' $2.25) operates at 10- to 15-minute intervals between the airport and Downtown, with stops along Broadway. A taxi fare to Downtown from the airport is $10 to $16.

Boat & Bicycle

Coronado Ferry (Map p292; ☎619-234-4111; www.flagshipsd.com; tickets $4.25; ⊙9am-10pm) Hourly ferry shuttles between the Broadway Pier on the Embarcadero to the Coronado Ferry Landing at the foot of First Street, where **Bikes & Beyond (☎619-435-7180; www.bikes-and-beyond.com; 1201 1st St, Coronado; per hr/day from $8/30; ⊙9am-sunset)** rents bicycles.

Bus

MTS (www.sdmts.com) covers most of the metropolitan area; the one-way fare is usually $2.25. It's most convenient if you're based Downtown and not staying out late.

Trolley

Blue Line trolleys head south to San Ysidro (last stop, just before Tijuana, Mexico) and north to **Old Town Transit Center (4009 Taylor St)**. The Green Line runs from Old Town east through Mission Valley to Mission Basilica San Diego de Alcalá. The Orange Line connects the Convention Center and Seaport Village with Downtown.

Fares are $2.50 per ride; buy tickets at vending machines on station platforms.

PALM SPRINGS

In the 1950s and '60s, Palm Springs (PS), some 100 miles east of LA, was the swinging getaway of Sinatra, Elvis and dozens of other stars, partying the night away in Mid-Century Modern estate homes. In today's PS, elderly denizens mix amicably with younger hipsters and an active gay and lesbian community.

The best evening to be in Palm Springs is Thursday, when Palm Canyon Dr morphs into a fun street fair with farmers market, food vendors, live music and arts and handicrafts booths. Called **Villagefest**, the weekly partly brings out locals and visitors in droves.

Sights

Palm Springs Aerial Tramway Cable Car
(☎888-515-8726; www.pstramway.com; 1 Tram Way; adult/child $24/17; ⊙from 10am Mon-Fri, 8am Sat & Sun, last tram up 8pm, last tram down 9:45pm daily) North of downtown, this rotating cable car is a highlight of any Palm Springs trip. It climbs nearly 6000 vertical feet through five different vegetation zones, from the Sonoran desert floor to the San Jacinto Mountains, in less than 15 minutes. The 2.5-mile ascent is said to be the temperature equivalent of driving from Mexico to Canada. It's 30°F to 40°F (up to 22°C) cooler as you step out into

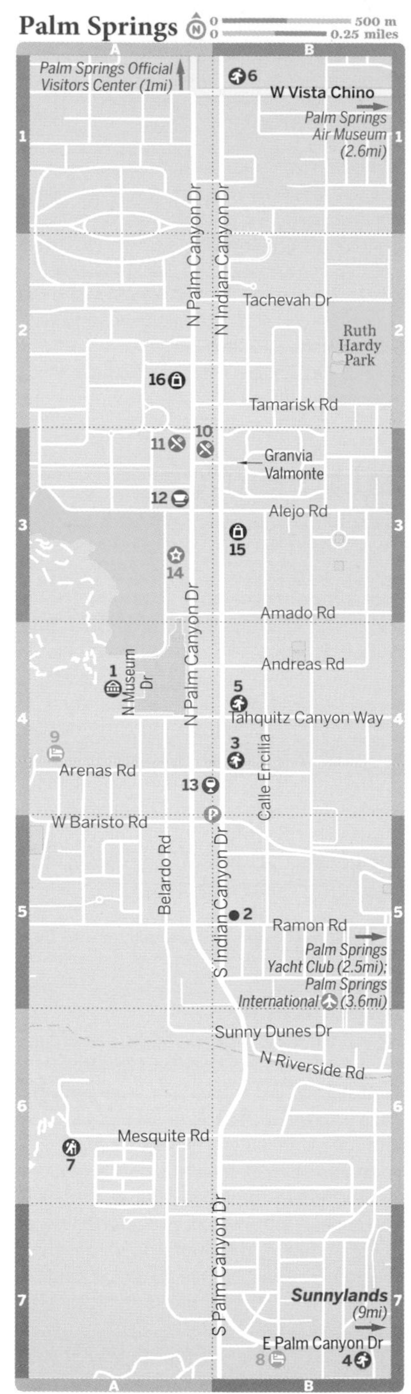

Palm Springs

Sights

1 Palm Springs Art Museum A4

Activities, Courses & Tours

2 Best of the Best Tours B5
3 Bike Palm Springs B4
4 Feel Good Spa at Ace Hotel & Swim Club B7
5 Spa Resort Casino B4
6 Spa Terre at Riviera Palm Springs B1
7 Tahquitz Canyon A6

Sleeping

8 Caliente Tropics B7
9 Orbit In A4
Riviera Palm Springs .... (see 6)

Eating

10 Cheeky's A3
11 Trio A3

Drinking & Nightlife

Birba .... (see 10)
12 Koffi A3
13 Shanghai Red's A4

Entertainment

14 Azul A3

Shopping

15 Angel View B3
16 Trina Turk A2

pine forests at the top, so bring warm clothing.

Palm Springs Art Museum — Museum

(☎760-322-4800; www.psmuseum.org; 101 Museum Dr; adult/child $12.50/free, 4-8pm Thu free; ⏰10am-5pm Tue-Wed & Fri-Sun, noon-8pm Thu) See the evolution of American painting, sculpture, photography and glass art over the past century. Alongside well-curated temporary exhibitions, the permanent collection is especially strong in modern painting and sculpture, with works by Henry Moore, Ed Ruscha, Mark di Suvero and other heavy hitters. There's also stunning glass art by Dale Chihuly and William Morris and a collection of pre-Columbian figurines.

Living Desert Zoo & Gardens — Zoo

(☎760-346-5694; www.livingdesert.org; 47900 Portola Ave, Palm Desert, off Hwy 111; adult/child $17.25/8.75; ⏰9am-5pm Oct-May, 8am-1:30pm

Jun-Sep; 👪) This amazing zoo exhibits a variety of desert plants and animals, alongside exhibits on desert geology and Native American culture. Highlights include a walk-through wildlife hospital and an African-themed village with a fair-trade market and storytelling grove. Camel rides, a spin on the endangered species carousel, and a hop-on, hop-off shuttle cost extra. It's educational fun and worth the 30-minute (15 mile) drive down-valley.

Palm Springs Air Museum Museum
(☎760-778-6262; www.palmspringsairmuseum.org; 745 N Gene Autry Trail; adult/child $15/8; ⏲10am-5pm) Adjacent to the airport, this museum has an exceptional collection of WWII aircraft and flight memorabilia, a movie theater and occasional flight demonstrations.

Activities

Tahquitz Canyon Hiking
(☎760-416-7044; www.tahquitzcanyon.com; 500 W Mesquite Ave; adult/child $12.50/6; ⏲7:30am-5pm Oct-Jun, Fri-Sun only Jul-Sep) A historic and sacred centerpiece for the Agua Caliente people, this canyon featured in the 1937 Frank Capra movie *Lost Horizon*. In the 1960s it was taken over by teenage squatters and soon became a point of contention between tribespeople, law-enforcement agencies and squatters in its rock alcoves and caves. After the squatters were booted out, it took the tribe years to haul out trash, erase graffiti and restore the canyon to its natural state.

Indian Canyons Hiking
(☎760-323-6018; www.indian-canyons.com; 38520 S Palm Canyon Dr; adult/child $9/5, 90min guided hike $3/2; ⏲8am-5pm Oct-Jun, Fri-Sun only Jul-Sep) Streams flowing from the San Jacinto Mountains sustain a rich variety of plants in oases around Palm Springs. Home to Native American communities for hundreds of years and now part of the Agua Caliente Indian Reservation, these canyons, shaded by fan palms and surrounded by towering cliffs, are a delight for hikers.

Smoke Tree Stables Horseback Riding
(☎760-327-1372; www.smoketreestables.com; 2500 S Toledo Ave; 1-/2hr guided ride $50/100) Near the Indian Canyons, this outfit arranges trail rides ranging from one-hour outings to all-day treks, for both novice and experienced riders. Reservations required.

Palm Springs' Top Spas

Get your stressed-out self to these pampering shrines to work out the kinks and turn your body into a glowing lump of tranquility.

Feel Good Spa at Ace Hotel & Swim Club (☎760-329-8791; www.acehotel.com/palmsprings/spa; 701 E Palm Canyon Dr) At Palm Springs' newest hipster spa you can get a treatment inside a yurt.

Spa Resort Casino (☎760-778-1772; www.sparesortcasino.com; 100 N Indian Canyon Dr) Try a five-step 'taking of the waters' course through the valley's original hot springs.

Spa Terre at Riviera Palm Springs (p315) The ultimate in swanky pampering, with Watsu pool and exotic spa rituals.

Palm Springs Yacht Club (☎760-770-5000; www.theparkerpalmsprings.com/spa; Parker Palm Springs, 4200 E Palm Canyon Dr) This newly renovated spa is again the ritzy, glitzy fave of celebs and society ladies.

Below: Hiker, Indian Canyons (p313); **Right:** WWII fighter aircraft, Palm Springs Air Museum (p313)
(BELOW) MICHAEL DEFREITAS / GETTY IMAGES ©; (RIGHT) STEPHEN SAKS / GETTY IMAGES ©

Tours

The visitors center has brochures for self-guided tours, including public art and historic sites (free), modernism ($5) and stars' homes ($5).

Best of the Best Tours General Interest
(**760-320-1365; www.thebestofthebesttours.com; 490 S Indian Canyon Dr; tours from $35**) Extensive program includes windmill tours and bus tours of celebrity homes.

Desert Adventures 4WD
(**760-340-2345; www.red-jeep.com; tours $59-135**) Four-wheel-drive tours cover a diverse lineup from gay icons of Palm Springs to an eco-tour to canyons of the San Andreas Fault.

Historic Walking Tours Walking
(**760-323-8297; www.pshistoricalsociety.org; tours $15**) Just what it says: a variety of tours covering architecture, Hollywood stars and more. Organized by the Palm Springs Historical Society.

Sleeping

Caliente Tropics Motel **$**
(**760-327-1391, 800-658-6034; www.calientetropics.com; 411 E Palm Canyon Dr; r weekday/weekend from $54/109;**) Elvis once frolicked poolside at this premier budget pick, a nicely kept 1964 tiki-style motor lodge. Drift off to dreamland on quality mattresses in rooms that are spacious and dressed in warm colors.

Orbit In Boutique Hotel **$$**
(**760-323-3585, 877-966-7248; www.orbitin.com; 562 W Arenas Rd; r incl breakfast from $149;**) Swing back to the '50s – pinkie raised and all – during the 'Orbitini' happy hour at this fabulously retro property, with high-end mid-century modern furniture (Eames, Noguchi et

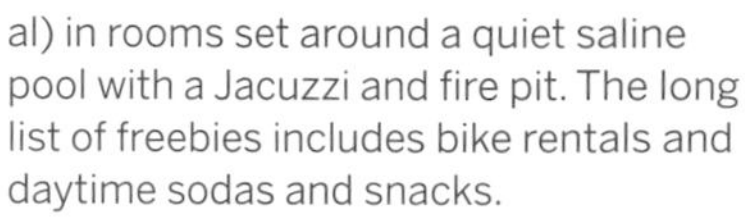

al) in rooms set around a quiet saline pool with a Jacuzzi and fire pit. The long list of freebies includes bike rentals and daytime sodas and snacks.

Riviera Palm Springs Luxury Hotel **$$$**
(☎760-327-8311; www.psriviera.com; 1600 Indian Canyon Dr; r $240-260, ste $290-540; P ⊜ ❄ @ ᯤ ≋ 🐾) This Rat Pack playground now sparkles brighter than ever. Expect the full range of fancy mod-cons amid luscious gardens, three amoeba-shaped pools, 17 (count 'em) fire pits, the **Spa Terre** (☎760-778-6690), and '60s accents such as shag rugs, classy-campy crystal chandeliers and Warhol art. **Circa 59** indoor-outdoor restaurant and lounge makes you and your sweetie look good.

Eating

Cheeky's Californian **$$**
(☎760-327-7595; www.cheekysps.com; 622 N Palm Canyon Dr; mains $8-13; ⏰8am-2pm Wed-Mon, last seating 1:30pm) Waits can be long and service only so-so, but the farm-to-table menu dazzles with witty inventiveness. Dishes change weekly, but custardy scrambled eggs, arugula pesto frittata and bacon bar 'flights' keep making appearances.

Trio Californian **$$$**
(☎760-864-8746; www.triopalmsprings.com; 707 N Palm Canyon Dr; lunch mains $11-26, dinner mains $14-29; ⏰11am-10pm Sun-Thu, until 11pm Fri & Sat) The winning formula in this '60s modernist space: updated American comfort food (awesome Yankee pot roast!), eye-catching artwork and picture windows. The $19 prix-fixe three-course dinner (served until 6pm) is a steal.

Drinking

Birba Bar
(www.birbaps.com; 622 N Palm Canyon Dr; ⏰5-11pm Sun & Wed-Thu, to midnight Fri & Sat) It's cocktails and pizza at this fabulous indoor-outdoor space where floor-to-ceiling sliding glass doors separate the

long marble bar from a hedge-fringed patio with sunken fire pits.

Koffi Coffee Shop
(www.kofficoffee.com; 515 N Palm Canyon Dr; snacks & drinks $3-6; 5:30am-7pm;) Tucked among the art galleries on N Palm Canyon Dr, this coolly minimalist, indie java bar serves strong organic coffee. There's a second Palm Springs location at 1700 S Camino Real, near the Ace Hotel.

Shanghai Red's Bar
(www.fishermans.com; 235 S Indian Canyon Dr; 4pm-late Mon-Sat, from noon Sun) This joint has a busy courtyard, an inter-generational crowd and live blues on Friday and Saturday nights.

Entertainment

Azul Music
(760-325-5533; www.azultapaslounge.com; 369 N Palm Canyon Dr; Judy Show incl dinner $35; 11am-late) Popular with gays and their friends, the Azul restaurant has almost nightly entertainment in its piano bar, plus the wickedly funny **Judy Show** (www.thejudyshow.com) on Sundays, starring impersonator Michael Holmes as Judy Garland, Mae West and other campy legends of yore. Mains $11 to $24.

Shopping

Trina Turk Clothing, Homewares
(760-416-2856; www.trinaturk.com; 891 N Palm Canyon Dr; 10am-5pm Mon-Fri, to 6pm Sat, noon-5pm Sun) Trina makes form-flattering 'California-chic' fashions that are beautifully presented amid shag carpeting and floral foil wallpaper in her original boutique in a 1960s Albert Frey building. Her Mr Turk menswear line is also available here.

Angel View Thrift Shop
(760-320-1733; www.angelview.org; 462 N Indian Canyon Dr; 9am-6pm Mon-Sat, 10am-5pm Sun) At this well-established thrift store, today's hipsters can shop for clothes and accessories as cool as when they were first worn a generation or two ago.

Information

Palm Springs Official Visitors Center (760-778-8418; www.visitpalmsprings.com; 2901 N

Downtown Palm Springs

DAVID LITSCHEL / ALAMY ©

Don't Miss Sunnylands

Sunnylands is the retro-glam, mid-century modern estate of Walter and Leonore Annenberg, one of America's 'first families'. Walter (1908–2002) was an American publisher, ambassador and philanthropist, and 'Lee' (1918–2009) was Chief of Protocol under President Ronald Reagan. At their winter estate in Rancho Mirage, designed by A Quincy Jones and surrounded by grounds incorporating a nine-hole golf course, the Annenbergs entertained seven US presidents, royalty, and Hollywood and international celebrities. These days Sunnylands is nicknamed the 'West Coast Camp David' for summits between President Obama and world leaders including Chinese president Xi Jinping and King Abdullah of Jordan.

Now the rest of us can visit too. A new visitor center and museum screen a film and show changing exhibits about the estate. Just beyond is a magnificent desert garden. Reserve as early as possible for tours of the stunning house with its art collection, architecture and furniture. Tickets go on sale online on the 1st and 15th of each month for the period beginning two weeks onward.

NEED TO KNOW

760-328-2829; www.sunnylands.org; 37977 Bob Hope Dr, Rancho Mirage; admission free, house tour $35; 9am-4pm Thu-Sun, closed Jul & Aug

Palm Canyon Dr; 9am-5pm) Well-stocked and well-staffed visitors center 3 miles north of downtown, in a 1965 Albert Frey–designed gas station at the tramway turnoff.

Getting There & Away

Air

A 10-minute drive northeast of downtown is Palm Springs International Airport (p397).

Car & Motorcycle

From LA, the trip to Palm Springs and the Coachella Valley takes about two to three hours via I-10.

 Getting Around

To/From the Airport

Many area hotels provide free airport transfers. Otherwise a taxi to downtown Palm Springs costs about $12 to $15.

Bicycle

Bike Palm Springs (**☎760-832-8912; www.bikepsrentals.com; 194 S Indian Canyon Dr; standard/kids/electric/tandem bikes half-day from $20/12/30/40, full day $25/15/50/50)** Great for tooling around central Palm Springs.

Car & Motorcycle

Though you can walk to most sights in downtown Palm Springs, you'll need a car to get around the valley. Major rental-car companies have airport desks.

JOSHUA TREE NATIONAL PARK

Taking a page from a Dr Seuss book, the whimsical Joshua trees (actually tree-sized yuccas) welcome visitors to this 794,000-acre **park (☎760-367-5500; www.nps.gov/jotr; 7-day entry per car $15)** at the convergence of the Colorado and Mojave Deserts.

Hikers seek out hidden, shady, desert-fan-palm oases fed by natural springs and small streams, while mountain bikers are hypnotized by the desert vistas seen from dirt 4WD roads.

The mystical quality of this stark, boulder-strewn landscape has inspired many artists, most famously the band U2, which named its 1987 album *The Joshua Tree.*

 Sights & Activities

Keys View Lookout

From Park Blvd, it's an easy 20-minute drive up to Keys View (5185ft), where breathtaking views take in the entire Coachella Valley and extend as far as the Salton Sea and – on a good day – Mexico. Looming in front of you are Mt San Jacinto (10,834ft) and Mt San Gorgonio (11,500ft), two of Southern California's highest peaks, while down below you can spot a section of the San Andreas Fault.

Desert Queen Ranch Historic Site

(☎reservations 760-367-5555; tour adult/child $5/2.50; ⏰tours 10am & 1pm daily year-round, 7pm Tue & Thu-Sat Oct-May) Anyone interested in local history and lore should take the 90-minute guided tour of this ranch that's also known as Keys Ranch after its builder, Russian immigrant William Keys. He built a homestead here on 160 acres in 1917 and over the next 60 years turned it into a full working ranch, school, store and workshop. The buildings stand much as they did when Keys died in 1969.

HIKING

Staff at the visitors centers can help you match your time and fitness level to the perfect trail. Distances given are round-trip.

49 Palms Oasis Trail Hiking

Escape the crowds on this 3-mile, up-and-down trail starting near **Indian Cove**.

Barker Dam Trail Hiking

A 1.1-mile loop that passes a little lake and a rock incised with Native American petroglyphs; starts at Barker Dam parking lot.

Lost Horse Mine Trail Hiking

A strenuous 4-mile climb that visits the remains of an authentic Old West silver and gold mine, in operation until 1931.

Lost Palms Oasis Trail Hiking

Reach this remote canyon filled with desert fan palms on a fairly flat 7.2-mile hike starting from Cottonwood Spring.

CYCLING

Popular riding routes include challenging **Pinkham Canyon Rd**, starting from the Cottonwood visitor center, and the long-distance **Black Eagle Mine Rd**, which starts 6.5 miles further north. Cycling is only permitted on paved and dirt public roads; bikes are not allowed on hiking trails.

ROCK CLIMBING

JT's rocks are famous for their rough, high-friction surfaces, and from boulders to cracks to multipitch faces, there are more than 8000 established routes, many right off the main road.

Shops catering to climbers with quality gear, advice and tours include the following:

Nomad Ventures Rock Climbing
(760-366-4684; www.nomadventures.com; 61795 Twentynine Palms Hwy, Joshua Tree; 8am-6pm Mon-Thu, to 8pm Fri & Sat, to 7pm Sun Oct-Apr, 9am-7pm daily May-Sep)

Coyote Corner Rock Climbing
(760-366-9683; www.joshuatreevillage.com/546/546.htm; 6535 Park Blvd, Joshua Tree; 9am-7pm)

Sleeping

Inside the park there are only campgrounds but there are plenty of lodging options along Hwy 62.

Hicksville Trailer Palace Motel **$$**
(310-584-1086; www.hicksville.com; d $100-250;) Fancy sleeping among glowing wigs, in a haunted house, or in a horse stall? Check in at Hicksville, where 'rooms' are eight outlandishly decorated vintage trailers set around a kidney-shaped, saltwater swimming pool. The vision of LA writer and director Morgan Higby Night, each offers a journey into a unique, surreal and slightly wicked world. All but two share facilities. To keep out looky-loos, you'll only be given directions after making reservations.

Eating

Pie for the People Pizza **$$**
(760-366-0400; www.pieforthepeople.com; 61740 Hwy 62, Joshua Tree; pizzas $11-25; 11am-9pm Mon-Thu, to 10pm Fri & Sat, to 8pm Sun;) Thin-crust pizzas for takeout and delivery. Flavors span standards to the David Bowie: white pizza with mozzarella, Guinness caramelized onions, jalapenos, pineapple, bacon, and sweet plum sauce. Enjoy yours under the exposed rafters in the wood and corrugated metal dining room, or under the tree on the back patio.

Rock climber, Joshua Tree National Park

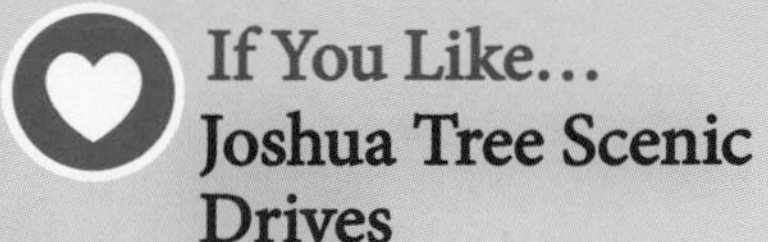

If You Like... Joshua Tree Scenic Drives

If you catch your thrills by hitting the open road across dramatic desertscapes and motoring up to Keys View, fill up your tank and try one of these unforgettable car journeys:

1 **GEOLOGY TOUR RD**
East of Hidden Valley, travelers with 4WD vehicles or mountain bikes can take this 18-mile field trip down into and around Pleasant Valley, where the forces of erosion, earthquakes and ancient volcanoes have played out in stunning splendor.

2 **COVINGTON FLATS**
Joshua trees grow throughout the northern park, including right along Park Blvd, but some of the biggest trees are found in this area accessed via La Contenta Rd, south off Hwy 62 between the towns of Yucca Valley and Joshua Tree. For photogenic views, follow the dirt road 3.8 miles up the Eureka Peak (5516ft) from the picnic area.

3 **PINTO BASIN RD**
To see the natural transition from the high Mojave Desert to the low Colorado Desert, wind along down to Cottonwood Spring, a 30-mile drive from Hidden Valley. Stop at **Cholla Cactus Garden**, where a quarter-mile loop leads around waving ocotillo plants and jumping 'teddy bear' cholla.

Information

Joshua Tree National Park is flanked by I-10 in the south and by Hwy 62 (Twentynine Palms Hwy) in the north. Entry permits ($15 per vehicle) are valid for seven days and come with a map and the seasonally updated *Joshua Tree Guide*.

Tourist Information

Cottonwood Visitor Center (**Cottonwood Springs, 8 miles north of I-10 Fwy; 9am-3pm**) National Park visitor center, just inside the park's south entrance.

Joshua Tree National Park Visitor Center (**6554 Park Blvd, Joshua Tree; 8am-5pm**) Just south of Hwy 62.

Oasis Park Visitor Center (**National Park Blvd, at Utah Trail, Twentynine Palms; 8am-5pm**) Outside the north entrance.

Getting There & Around

Rent a car in Palm Springs or LA. From LA, the trip takes about 2½ to three hours via I-10 and Hwy 62. From Palm Springs it takes about an hour to reach the park's west (preferable) or south entrances.

ROUTE 66

Completed in 1926, iconic Route 66 connected Chicago and Los Angeles across the heartland of America. What novelist John Steinbeck called the 'Mother Road' came into its own during the Depression, when thousands of migrants escaped the Dust Bowl by slogging westward in beat-up old jalopies painted with 'California or Bust' signs, *Grapes of Wrath*-style.

Los Angeles to Barstow

Route 66 kicks off in Santa Monica, at the intersection of Ocean Ave and Santa Monica Blvd. Follow the latter through Beverly Hills and West Hollywood, turn right on Sunset Blvd and pick up the 110 Fwy north to Pasadena. Take exit 31B and drive south on Fair Oaks Ave for an egg cream at **Fair Oaks Pharmacy** (**626-799-1414; www.fairoakspharmacy.net; 1526 Mission St; mains $4-8; 9am-9pm Mon-Fri, to 10pm Sat, 10am-7pm Sun;**), a nostalgic soda fountain from 1915.

Continue east on Colorado Blvd to Colorado Pl and **Santa Anita Park** (**tickets 626-574-6366; www.santaanita.com; 285 W Huntington Dr, Arcadia; admission general $5, clubhouse $10, under 17yr free; racing season Christmas–mid-Apr, late Sep–early Nov, tram tours 8:30am & 9:45am Sat & Sun**), where the Marx Brothers' *A Day at the Races* was filmed and legendary thoroughbred Seabiscuit ran.

Colorado Pl turns into Huntington Dr E, which you'll follow to 2nd Ave, where you turn north, then east on Foothill Blvd. This older alignment of Route 66 follows Foothill Blvd through Monrovia, where the 1925 Mayan Revival–style architecture of the allegedly haunted **Aztec Hotel** (626-358-3231; 311 W Foothill Blvd, Monrovia) is worth a look.

Continue east on W Foothill Blvd, then jog south on S Myrtle Ave and hook a left on E Huntington Dr through Duarte, which puts on a **Route 66 parade** (http://duarteroute66parade.com) every September, with boisterous marching bands, old-fashioned carnival games and a classic-car show.

Cruising on through Fontana, birthplace of the notorious Hells Angels biker club, you'll see the now-boarded-up **Giant Orange** (15395 Foothill Blvd, Fontana; no public entry), a 1920s juice stand of the kind that was once a fixture alongside SoCal's citrus groves.

Foothill Blvd continues on to Rialto where you'll find the **Wigwam Motel** (909-875-3005; www.wigwammotel.com; 2728 W Foothill Blvd, Rialto; r $65-80;), whose kooky concrete faux tipis date from 1949. Pick up the I-15 Fwy northbound and drive up to the Cajon Pass. At the top, take the Oak Hill Rd exit (No 138) to the **Summit Inn Cafe** (760-949-8688; 5960 Mariposa Rd, Hesperia; mains $5-10; 6am-8pm Mon-Thu, to 9pm Fri & Sat), a 1950s roadside diner with antique gas pumps, a retro jukebox and a lunch counter that serves ostrich burgers and date shakes.

Get back on I-15 and drive downhill to Victorville, exiting at 7th St and driving past the San Bernardino County Fairgrounds, home of the Route 66 Raceway. Follow 7th St to D St and turn left for the excellent **California Route 66 Museum** (760-951-0436; www.califrt66museum.org; 16825 D St, Victorville; donations welcome; 10am-4pm Thu-Sat & Mon, 11am-3pm Sun), inside the old Red Rooster Cafe opposite the Greyhound bus station.

Mojave National Preserve

If you're on a quest for the 'middle of nowhere,' you'll find it in the wilderness of the **Mojave National Preserve** (760-252-6100; www.nps.gov/moja) FREE, a 1.6-million-acre jumble of sand dunes, Joshua trees, volcanic cinder cones and habitats for bighorn sheep, desert tortoises, jackrabbits and coyotes.

Hole-in-the-Wall, Mojave National Preserve

Follow South D St north under I-15 where it turns into the National Trails Hwy. Beloved by Harley bikers, this rural stretch to Barstow is like a scavenger hunt for Mother Road ruins, such as antique filling stations and tumbledown motor courts.

Pulling into Barstow, detour across the train tracks to the **Route 66 'Mother Road' Museum** (☎760-255-1890; www.route66museum.org; 681 N 1st St; ⌚10am-4pm Fri & Sat, 11am-4pm Sun, or by appointment) FREE, inside the beautifully restored 1911 Casa del Desierto, and the **Western America Railroad Museum** (www.barstowrailmuseum.org; 685 N 1st St; ⌚11am-4pm Fri-Sun) FREE next door.

DEATH VALLEY NATIONAL PARK

The name itself evokes all that is harsh, hot and hellish – a punishing, barren and lifeless place of Old Testament severity. Yet closer inspection reveals that in Death Valley nature is putting on a truly spectacular show: singing sand dunes, water-sculpted canyons, boulders moving across the desert floor, extinct volcanic craters, palm-shaded oases and plenty of endemic wildlife. This is a land of superlatives, holding the US records for hottest temperature (134°F, or 57°C), lowest point (Badwater, 282ft below sea level) and largest national park outside Alaska (over 5000 sq miles).

Sights

FURNACE CREEK

Furnace Creek is Death Valley's commercial hub, with a general store, park visitor center, gas station, post office, ATM, internet access, golf course, lodging and restaurants.

The **Borax Museum** (☎760-786-2345; ⌚9am-9pm Oct-May, variable in summer) FREE is great for finding out what all the fuss about borax was about. It also has a great collection of pioneer-era stagecoaches and wagons out back. A short drive north, an interpretive trail follows in the footsteps of late-19th-century Chinese laborers and through the adobe ruins of **Harmony Borax Works**, where you can take a side trip through twisting **Mustard Canyon**.

Zabriskie Point, Death Valley National Park

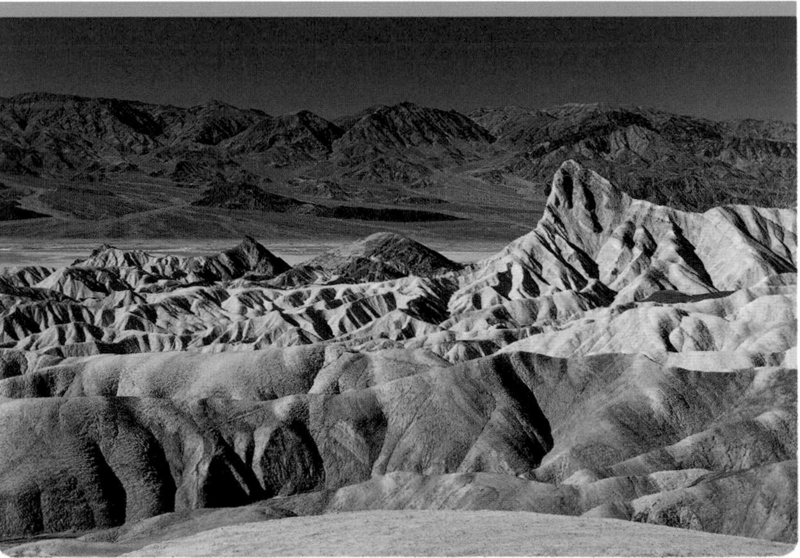

PHIL / GETTY IMAGES ©

SOUTH OF FURNACE CREEK

If possible start out early in the morning to drive up to **Zabriskie Point** for spectacular valley views across golden badlands eroded into waves, pleats and gullies. Escape the heat by continuing on to **Dante's View** at 5475ft, where you can simultaneously see the highest (Mt Whitney) and lowest (Badwater) points in the contiguous USA. The drive there takes about 1½ to two hours round-trip.

Badwater itself, a foreboding landscape of crinkly salt flats, is a 17-mile drive south of Furnace Creek. Here you can walk out onto a boardwalk above a constantly evaporating bed of salty, mineralized water that's otherworldly in its beauty. Along the way, you may want to check out narrow **Golden Canyon**, easily explored on a 2-mile round-trip walk, and **Devil's Golf Course**, where salt has piled up into saw-toothed miniature mountains. A 9-mile one-way scenic loop along **Artists Drive** is best done in the late afternoon when exposed minerals and volcanic ash make the hills erupt in fireworks of color.

STOVEPIPE WELLS & AROUND

Stovepipe Wells, about 26 miles northwest of Furnace Creek, was Death Valley's original 1920s tourist resort. Today it has a small store, gas station, ATM, motel, campground and bar. En route, look for the roadside pull-off where you can walk out onto the powdery, Sahara-like **Mesquite Flat sand dunes**. Across the road, look for the **Devil's Cornfield**, full of arrow weed clumps. Some 2.5 miles southwest of Stovepipe Wells, a 3-mile gravel side road leads to **Mosaic Canyon**, where you can hike and scramble along the smooth multi-hued rock walls. Colors are sharpest at midday.

ALONG EMIGRANT CANYON RD

Some 6 miles southwest of Stovepipe Wells, Emigrant Canyon Rd veers off Hwy 190 and travels south to the park's higher elevations. En route you'll pass the turnoff to **Skidoo**, a mining ghost town where the silent movie *Greed* was filmed in 1923. It's an 8-mile trip on a graded gravel road suitable only for high-clearance vehicles to get to the ruins and jaw-dropping Sierra Nevada views.

Further south Emigrant Canyon Rd passes the turnoff for the 7-mile dirt road leading past the **Eureka Mines** to the vertiginous **Aguereberry Point** (high-clearance vehicles only), where you'll have fantastic views into the valley and out to the colorful Funeral Mountains from a lofty 6433ft. The best time to visit is in the late afternoon.

Emigrant Canyon Rd now climbs steeply over Emigrant Pass and through Wildrose Canyon to reach the **charcoal kilns**, a lineup of large, stone, beehive-shaped structures historically used by miners to make fuel for smelting silver and lead ore. The landscape is subalpine, with forests of piñon pine and juniper; it can be covered with snow, even in spring.

SCOTTY'S CASTLE

About 55 miles north of Furnace Creek, **Scotty's Castle** is named for Walter E Scott, alias 'Death Valley Scotty,' a gifted tall-tale teller who captivated people with his fanciful stories of gold. Restored to its 1930s glory, the historic house has sheepskin drapes, carved California redwood, handmade tiles, elaborately wrought iron, woven Shoshone baskets and a bellowing pipe organ. Advance tickets are recommended at least one day before your visit. On tour days, tickets are sold on a first-come, first-served basis at the **visitor center** (☎760-786-2392, ext 231; North Hwy; ⏲8:45am-4:30pm May-Oct, 8:30am-5:30pm Nov-Apr).

Activities

Farabee's Jeep Rentals Driving Tour (☎760-786-9872; www.farrabeesjeeprentals.com; 2-/4-door Jeep incl 200 miles $195/235; ⏲mid-Sep–late May) If you don't have a 4WD but would like to explore the park's backcountry, rent a Jeep from this outfit. You must be over 25 years old, have a valid driver's license, credit card and proof of insurance. Rates include water

and supplies such as GPS in case of emergency. It's next to **Inn at Furnace Creek** (800-236-7916, 760-786-2345; www.furnacecreekresort.com; Hwy 190; r/ste from $345/450; mid-Oct–mid-May; P).

Furnace Creek Bike Rentals — Mountain Biking

(760-786-3371; bike hire 1/24hr $15/49, Hells Gate Downhill Bike Tour $49; year-round, Hells Gate Downhill Bike Tour 10am & 2pm) The general store at the Ranch at Furnace Creek rents mountain bikes. Cycling is allowed on all established paved and dirt roads, but never on hiking trails. On demand, staff also organize the 2½-hour **Hells Gate Downhill Bike Tour**, which transports you up to a 2200ft elevation for a 10-mile downhill ride back to the valley floor.

Furnace Creek Golf Course — Golf

(760-786-3373; www.furnacecreekresort.com/activities/golfing; Hwy 190, Furnace Creek; greens fees summer/winter $30/60; year-round) For novelty's sake, play a round at the world's lowest-elevation golf course (214ft below sea level, 18 holes, par 70), redesigned by Perry Dye in 1997. It's also been certified by the Audubon Society for its environmentally friendly management.

HIKING

Avoid hiking in summer, except on higher-elevation mountain trails, which may be snowed in during winter.

On Hwy 190, just north of Beatty Cutoff Rd, is the half-mile **Salt Creek Interpretive Trail**. A few miles south of Furnace Creek is **Golden Canyon**, where a self-guided interpretive trail winds for a mile up to the now-oxidized iron cliffs of **Red Cathedral**. Before reaching Badwater, stretch your legs with a 1-mile round-trip walk to the **Natural Bridge**.

The park's most demanding summit is **Telescope Peak** (11,049ft), with views that plummet down to the desert floor, which is as far below as two Grand Canyons deep! The 14-mile round-trip climbs 3000ft above Mahogany Flat, off upper Wildrose Canyon Rd.

Sleeping

In-park lodging is pricey and often booked solid in springtime but there are several gateway towns with cheaper lodging. Of the park's nine campgrounds, only **Furnace Creek** (877-444-6777; www.recreation.gov) accepts reservations and only from mid-April to mid-October.

Stovepipe Wells Village — Motel $$

(760-786-2387; www.escapetodeathvalley.com; Hwy 190, Stovepipe Wells; RV sites $33, r $117-176; P) The 83 rooms at this sea-level tourist village are newly spruced-up and have quality linens beneath Death Valley–themed artwork, cheerful Native American–patterned bedspreads, coffeemakers and TVs. The small pool is cool and the cowboy-style **Toll Road restaurant** (Stovepipe Wells Village, Hwy 190; breakfast buffet $13, lunch $10-17, dinner $13-26; 7am-10am, 11:30am-2pm & 6-10pm) serves three squares a day.

Ranch at Furnace Creek — Resort $$

(760-786-2345; www.furnacecreekresort.com; Hwy 190, Furnace Creek; cabins $130-162, r $162-213; P) Tailor-made for families, this rambling resort with multiple, motel-style buildings has received a vigorous facelift, resulting in spiffy rooms swathed in desert colors, updated bathrooms and French doors leading to porches with comfortable patio furniture. The grounds encompass a playground, spring-fed swimming pool, tennis courts, restaurants, shops and the **Borax Museum**.

Eating & Drinking

Furnace Creek and Stovepipe Wells have general stores stocking basic groceries and camping supplies.

Inn at Furnace Creek — International $$$

(760-786-2345; lunch mains $13-17, dinner mains $18-45; 7:30-10:30am, noon-2:30pm & 5:30-9:30pm mid-Oct–mid-May) Views of the Panamint Mountains are stellar from this formal dining room with a dress code (no shorts or T-shirts, jeans ok), where the

Inn at Furnace Creek, Death Valley National Park

THOMAS DRESSLER / GETTY IMAGES ©

menu draws inspiration from Continental, Southwestern and Mexican cuisine. Afternoon tea in the lobby lounge and Sunday brunch are hoity-toity affairs. At least have a cocktail on the stone terrace as the sun sets beyond the mountains (and the parking lot, but who's complaining?).

Information

Entry permits ($20 per vehicle) are valid for seven days and sold at self-service pay stations throughout the park. For a free map and newspaper, show your receipt at the visitor center.

Furnace Creek Visitor Center (**760-786-3200760-786-3200; www.nps.gov/deva; 8am-5pm**) The park's recently renovated main visitors center has fabulous exhibits on the local ecosystem and the native Timbasha and Shoshone peoples. The gorgeously shot movie *Seeing Death Valley* screens here. Fill up water bottles, and check schedules for ranger-led activities.

Getting There & Away

Gas is expensive in the park, so fill up your tank beforehand.

Furnace Creek can be reached via Baker (115 miles, two to 2½ hours), Beatty (45 miles, one to 1½ hours), Las Vegas (via Hwy 160, 120 miles, 2½ to three hours), Lone Pine (105 miles, two hours), Los Angeles (300 miles, five to 5½ hours) and Ridgecrest (via Trona, 120 miles, 2½ to three hours).

Disneyland & Orange County

Once upon a time, long before the *Real Housewives* threw lavish pool parties and the rich teens of MTV's *Laguna Beach* screamed at each other on our TV screens, Orange County's public image was defined by an innocent animated mouse. Even in his wildest imagination, Walt Disney couldn't have known that Mickey would one day share the spotlight with Botoxed socialites and rich kids driving Porsches along the sunny Pacific Coast Hwy. But Walt might have imagined the bigger picture – those same catfighting teens are now adults and will be bringing their little ones to Disneyland soon.

These seemingly conflicting cultures, plus a growing population of Vietnamese and Latino immigrants seeking the American dream, form the county's diverse population of more than three million. And while there's truth to the televised stereotypes, look closer – there are also deep pockets of individuality and open-mindedness keeping the OC real.

Crescent Bay, Laguna Beach (p349)

Disneyland & Orange County

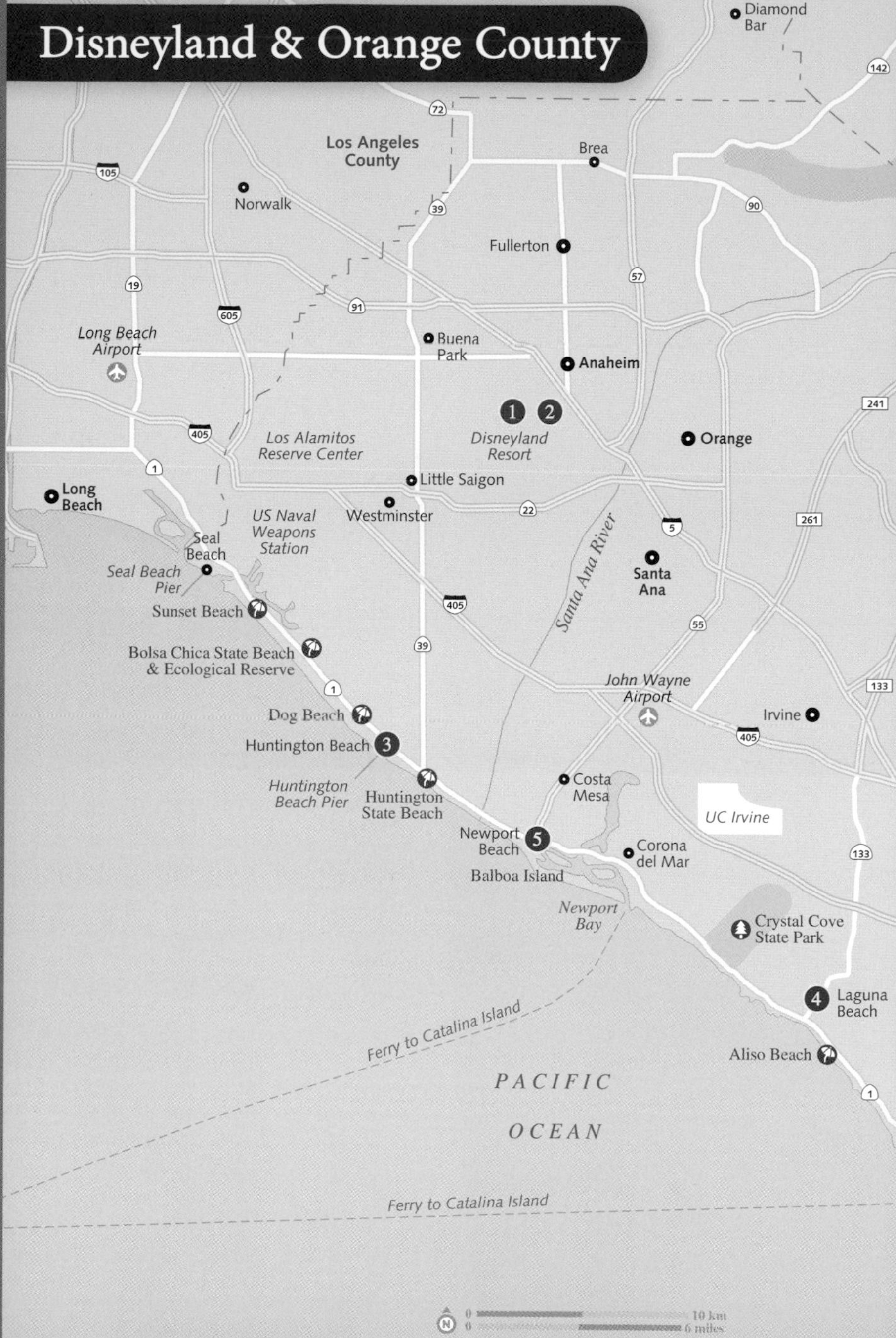

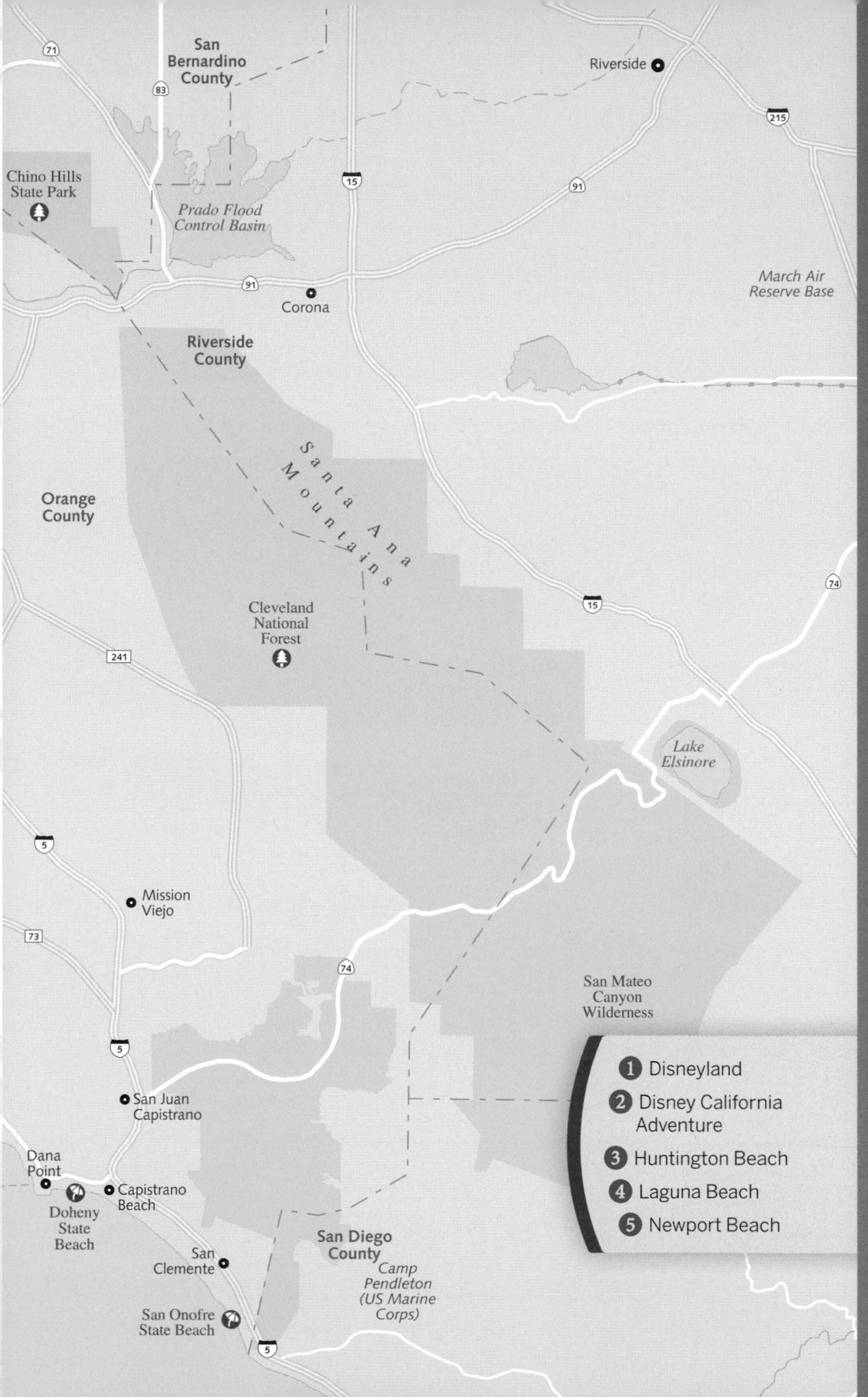
San Bernardino County
Riverside
Chino Hills State Park
Prado Flood Control Basin
Corona
March Air Reserve Base
Riverside County
Santa Ana Mountains
Orange County
Cleveland National Forest
Lake Elsinore
Mission Viejo
San Mateo Canyon Wilderness
San Juan Capistrano
Dana Point
Doheny State Beach
Capistrano Beach
San Clemente
San Onofre State Beach
San Diego County
Camp Pendleton (US Marine Corps)
71
83
15
91
215
74
241
5
73
1 Disneyland
2 Disney California Adventure
3 Huntington Beach
4 Laguna Beach
5 Newport Beach

Disneyland & Orange County Highlights

Laguna Beach

If you've ever wanted to step into a painting, a sunset stroll through Laguna Beach (p349) might be the next best thing. The hidden coves, romantic cliffs, azure waves and waterfront parks aren't the only draw. Arts festivals and gallery nights imbue the city with an artistic sensibility you won't find elsewhere in SoCal. The locals, though wealthy, are live-and-let-live – there's a palpable artistic *joie de vivre* in the air. Below: Laguna Beach

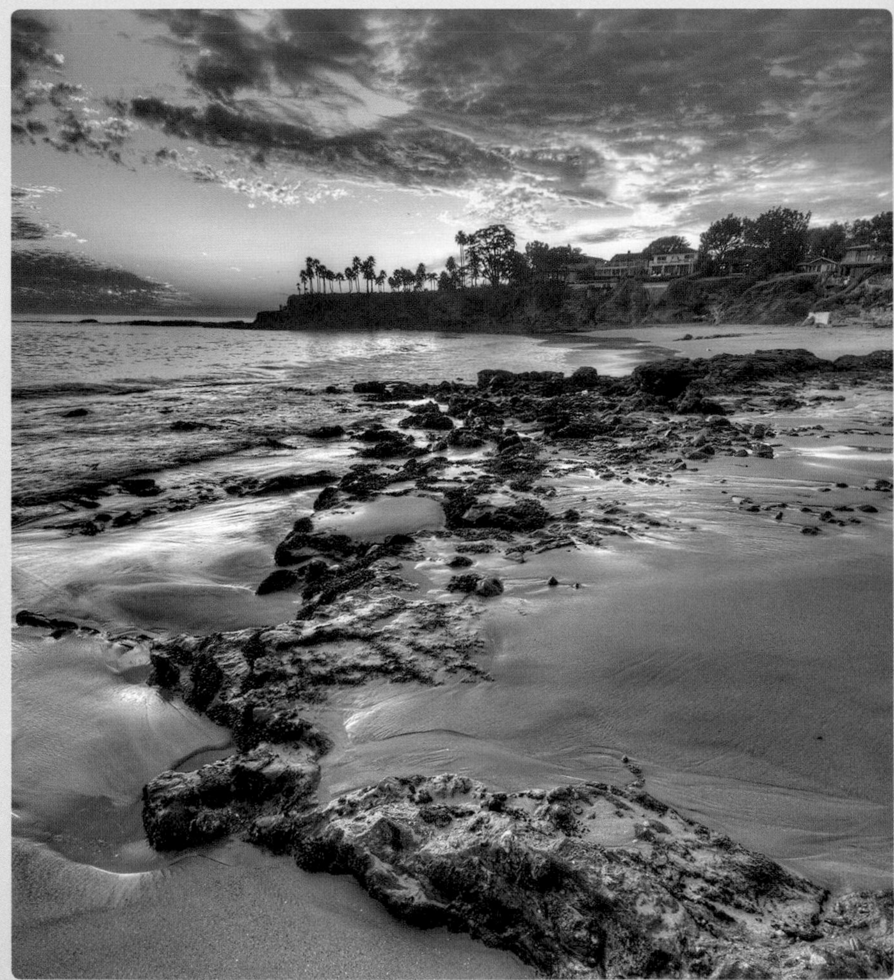

Huntington Beach

In Surf City, USA (a name taken from Jan and Dean's 1963 pop hit by the same name), the classic SoCal pastime is big business – buyers from major retailers come here to see what surfers are wearing so they can market the look. Just look around at the skateboarders, dog walkers, cyclists, beach-volleyball enthusiasts, and party animals – Huntington Beach (p345) is the quintessential place to celebrate the coastal lifestyle. Top right: Huntington Beach

Disneyland

Disneyland (p336), also known as 'the Happiest Place on Earth' is Walt's original theme park. Inside this 'imagineered' hyperreality, the streets are always clean, the employees – called Cast Members – are always upbeat, and there's a parade every day of the year. For the more than 14 million kids, grandparents, honeymooners and international tourists who visit every year, Disneyland remains a magical experience.

Disney California Adventure

'The other park,' Disney California Adventure (DCA; p338), opened in 2001, is an ode to Californian geography, history and culture – or at least a sanitized, G-rated version of it. DCA covers more acres than Disneyland, features more modern rides and attractions, and is usually less crowded than the original park. Downtown Disney, an open-air pedestrian mall, is sandwiched between the two parks.

Newport Beach

Orange County's ritziest beach community is known for beautiful, moneyed people and a particularly lovely environment: Newport Beach (p347) surrounds a pretty natural harbor that's one of the largest for pleasure craft in the US. At almost any hour of the day, you'll see a steady stream of cyclists, joggers and skaters on paved beach paths that extend as far as the eye can see. Bottom right: Newport Beach

Disneyland & Orange County's Best...

Theme Park Attractions

- **Indiana Jones™ Adventure** An exciting archaeological adventure at Disneyland. (p337)
- **Space Mountain** Disneyland's thrillingly futuristic in-the-dark roller coaster. (p337)
- **Twilight Zone Tower of Terror** Drop 13 stories down an elevator chute at DCA. (p339)
- **Pirates of the Caribbean** An eerie 17-minute-long cruise past pirate ships and cannon fights. (p337)

Fun Food & Drinks

- **Blue Bayou** Southern spice at Disneyland's New Orleans Square. (p342)
- **Trader Sam's Enchanted Tiki Lounge** Disneyland Resort's little faux-grass shack. (p343)
- **Duke's** Clink beer bottles while overlooking the surf at Huntington Beach. (p347)
- **Bear Flag Fish Company** Superbly fresh seafood and picnic tables with palm-tree views. (p348)

Vintage Landmarks

- **Balboa Fun Zone** The postcard-pretty Ferris wheel dates from 1936. (p347)
- **Main Street, USA** Walt modeled Disneyland's entryway on his childhood town. (p336)
- **Ruby's Crystal Cove Shake Shack** Retro fast-food stand with ocean views. (p348)
- **Huntington Pier** The All-American wooden pier, built in 1904, is on the US National Register of Historic Places. (p345)

Beach Moments

- **Watch the surfers** Spy on professional surfers from Huntington Beach's pier. (p345)
- **Explore hidden coves** Find your own patch of sand off Hwy 1 around Laguna Beach. (p349)
- **Check out the Wedge** Marvel at giant waves – and brave knee-boarders and bodysurfers – at Newport Beach. (p347)
- **Bike along the beach** Rental stands are everywhere on the Balboa Peninsula. (p345)

Left: Ruby's Crystal Cove Shake Shack (p348); **Above:** Huntington Pier (p345)

Need to Know

ADVANCE PLANNING

For Disneyland Resort:

- **One month before** Make area hotel reservations or book a Disneyland vacation package.
- **One week before** Check the theme parks' opening hours and entertainment schedules online. Make dining reservations for sit-down restaurants. Print out your tickets or passes at home to avoid lines at the park.
- **The night before** Pack sunscreen, sunglasses, a jacket, and extra batteries and memory cards for digital and video cameras. Make sure your electronic devices (including cameras and phones) are fully charged.

RESOURCES

- **Mouse Wait** (www.mousewait.com) This free mobile app offers up-to-the-minute info on ride wait times and what's happening in the parks.
- **Mouse Planet** (www.mouseplanet.com) One-stop fansite for all things Disney, with news updates, podcasts, reviews and discussion boards.
- **The OC Forever Summer** (www.visittheoc.com) Orange County's official tourism website.

BE FOREWARNED

- **Chilly waters** Don't let the sunshine fool you – the Pacific is cold. Surfers often wear wet suits even in summer.
- **Limited attractions** If you visit off-season, some of Disneyland's attractions, shows and fireworks may not be running – check the website to avoid disappointment.
- **Necessary reservations** If you show up without reservations to any of Disney's sit-down restaurants, you might not be able to get a table.
- **Trouble in paradise** Some kids' rides – including Mr Toad's Wild Ride – can be surprisingly scary. Tell your kids that if they get lost, they should contact the nearest Disney staff, who will escort them to a 'lost children' center (on Disneyland's Main Street, USA or at DCA's Pacific Wharf).

Disneyland & Orange County Itineraries

To see both Disney parks, plan for three full days, allowing short breaks to avoid Mickey overload. With a few more days, combine a trip to Disneyland with visits to a few of Orange County's idyllic beaches.

3 DAYS

DISNEYLAND TO DISNEY CALIFORNIA ADVENTURE
BEST OF DISNEYLAND

Three days is about the right amount of time to fully appreciate both parks: Disneyland and the adjacent Disney California Adventure. On day one, arrive at ❶ **Disneyland** (p336) as early as possible. Stroll down Main Street, USA, stopping for coffee and pastries while taking in views of Sleeping Beauty Castle. Enter Tomorrowland and get in line to ride Space Mountain. Traveling with kids? Head to Fantasyland for the classic "it's a small world," then race down the Matterhorn Bobsleds or take tots to Mickey's Toontown. Head back to the hotel for a break during the park's busiest afternoon hours.

Later, or on day two, grab a Fastpass for Indiana Jones™ Adventure and Pirates of the Caribbean before dining in New Orleans Square. Plummet down Splash Mountain, then visit the Haunted Mansion before the fireworks and Fantasmic! shows begin.

At ❷ **Disney California Adventure** (p338), take a virtual hang-gliding ride on Soarin' Over California before having fun at Paradise Pier, with its roller coaster, Ferris wheel and carnival games. Watch the Pixar Play Parade, then explore Cars Land. After dark, drop by the Twilight Zone Tower of Terror and catch the World of Color show.

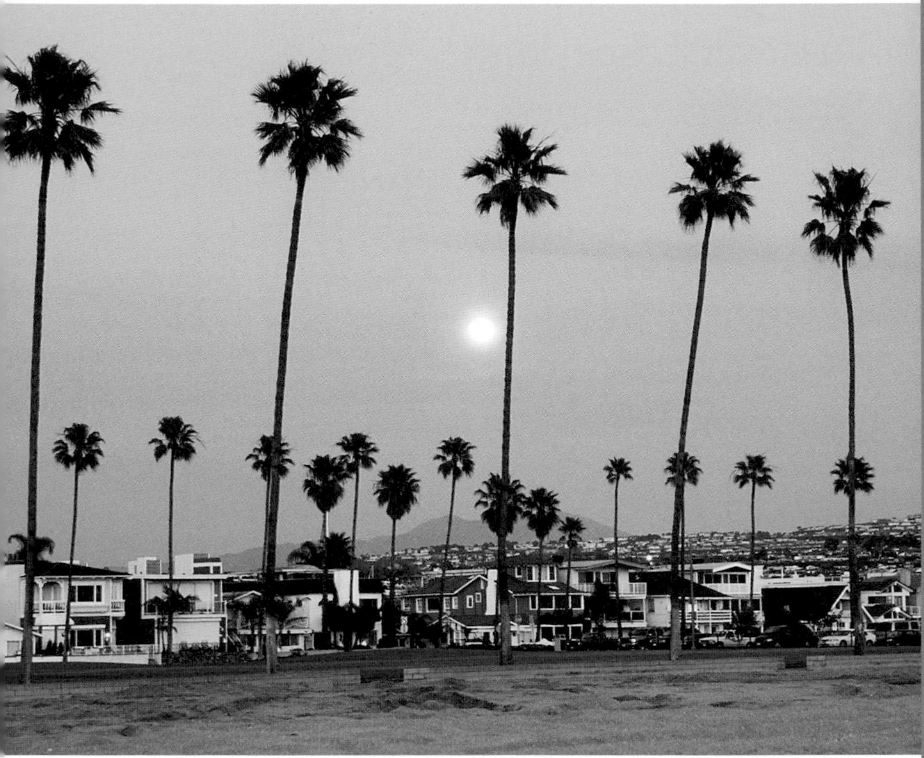

DISNEYLAND TO LAGUNA BEACH
5 DAYS DISNEY MEETS THE BEACH

You can get your Disney fix and still have time to revel in the relaxed SoCal beach scene. Start with a day or two at ❶ **Disneyland** (p336). After wandering down Main Street, USA, stop for a classic photo op at Sleeping Beauty Castle. Don't miss a ride on thrilling Space Mountain. You'll need a Fastpass – or a good deal of patience waiting in line – to get onto Indiana Jones Adventure and Pirates of the Caribbean. Other essential attractions include the classic It's a Small World, and the eerie – but not too scary for kids – Haunted Mansion. Catch the fireworks at the day's end.

Next, head for the beach, starting with nearby Surf City, USA – ❷ **Huntington Beach** (p345). Catch a surf competition, go for fish tacos and margaritas at happy hour on Main St, or just rent a bike and pedal along the beach paths. Continue south to ritzy ❸ **Newport Beach** (p347). Take the ferry to ❹ **Balboa Island** (p347) for boutique shopping, ice cream and pretty views. In the artsy beach 'village' of ❺ **Laguna Beach** (p349), go gallery hopping and explore hidden beach coves. Finish by touring historic Mission San Juan Capistrano (p349).

Beachfront houses, Balboa Island (p347)
RICHARD CUMMINS / GETTY IMAGES ©

Discover Disneyland & Orange County

At a Glance

- **Disneyland** (p336) & **Disney California Adventure** (p338) 'The happiest place on earth' – Walt's original theme park.
- **Huntington Beach** (p345) Otherwise known as Surf City, USA.
- **Newport Beach** (p347) Glamorous yachts and beautiful beaches.
- **Laguna Beach** (p349) Bohemian-chic art enclave by the sea.

Discovery Science Center (p340)
SUPERSTOCK / ALAMY ©

DISNEYLAND & ANAHEIM

Sights & Activities

You can see either **Disneyland** (714-781-4400, 714-781-4565; www.disneyland.com; 1313 Harbor Blvd, Anaheim; 1-day pass Disneyland Park or DCA adult/child 3-9yr $96/90, both parks $150/144;) or **Disney California Adventure** (DCA; 714-781-4565, 714-781-4400; www.disneyland.com; 1313 Harbor Blvd, Anaheim; 1-day pass Disneyland Park or DCA adult/child 3-9yr $96/90, both parks $150/144;) in a day, but going on all the rides requires at least two days (three if visiting both parks), as waits for top attractions can be an hour or more.

DISNEYLAND

Main Street, U.S.A. Rides, Attractions
Fashioned after Walt's hometown of Marceline, Missouri, bustling Main St, U.S.A. resembles the classic turn-of-the-20th-century, all-American town. It's an idyllic, relentlessly upbeat representation, complete with barbershop quartet, penny arcades, ice-cream shops and a steam train. The music playing in the background is from American musicals, and there's a flag-retreat ceremony every afternoon.

Tomorrowland Rides, Attractions
How did 1950s imagineers envision the future? As a galaxy-minded community filled with monorails, rockets and Googie-style architecture, apparently. In 1998 this 'land' was revamped to honor three timeless futurists – Jules Verne, HG Wells, and Leonardo da Vinci – while major corporations

such as Microsoft, Honda, Siemens and HP sponsor futuristic robot shows and interactive exhibits in the **Innoventions** pavilion.

The retro high-tech **monorail** glides to a stop in Tomorrowland, its rubber tires traveling a 13-minute, 2.5-mile round-trip route to Downtown Disney. Just outside Tomorrowland station, kiddies will want to shoot laser beams on **Buzz Lightyear's Astro Blaster** adventure and drive their own miniature cars in the classic **Autopia** ride (don't worry, they're on tracks – drive too slowly, and you may get bumped from behind!). Then jump aboard the **Finding Nemo Submarine Voyage** to look for the world's most famous clownfish from within a refurbished submarine and rumble through an underwater volcanic eruption.

Star Tours – The Adventure Continues clamps you into a Starspeeder shuttle for a wild and bumpy 3D ride through the desert canyons of Tatooine on a space mission with several alternate storylines, so you can ride it again and again. **Space Mountain**, Tomorrowland's signature attraction and one of the USA's best roller coasters, hurtles you into complete darkness at frightening speed. Another classic is **Captain EO**, a special-effects tribute film, starring none other than Michael Jackson.

Fantasyland Rides, Attractions

Fantasyland is filled with the characters of classic children's stories. If you only see one attraction in Fantasyland, visit **"it's a small world"**, a boat ride past hundreds of creepy Audio-Animatronics children from different cultures all singing the annoying theme song in an astounding variety of languages, now joined by Disney characters.

Frontierland Rides, Attractions

Arrgh matey! Captain Jack Sparrow and his pirate crew have hijacked an American classic. Frontierland's Tom Sawyer Island – the only attraction in the park personally designed by Uncle Walt – has been reimagined in the wake of the *Pirates of the Caribbean* movies. Renamed the **Pirate's Lair on Tom Sawyer Island**, the island now honors Tom in name only.

Is It a Small World After All?

Pay attention to the cool optical illusion along Main Street, USA. As you look from the entrance up the street toward Sleeping Beauty Castle, everything seems far away and larger-than-life. When you're at the castle looking back, everything seems closer and smaller. This technique is known as forced perspective, a trick used on Hollywood sets where buildings are constructed at a decreasing scale to create an illusion of height or depth. Welcome to Disneyland.

Adventureland Rides, Attractions

Loosely deriving its jungle theme from Southeast Asia and Africa, Adventureland has a number of attractions, but the hands-down highlight is the safari-style **Indiana Jones™ Adventure** in which enormous Humvee-type vehicles lurch and jerk their way through the wild for spine-tingling encounters with creepy crawlies and scary skulls in re-creations of stunts from the famous films.

New Orleans Square Rides, Attractions

New Orleans Square has all the charm of the eponymous city's French Quarter but none of the marauding drunks. New Orleans was Walt's and his wife Lillian's favorite city, and he paid tribute to it by building this stunning square.

Pirates of the Caribbean is the longest ride in Disneyland (17 minutes) and provided 'inspiration' for the popular movies. You'll float through the subterranean haunts of tawdry pirates, where dead buccaneers perch atop their mounds of booty and Jack Sparrow pops up occasionally. Over at the **Haunted Mansion**, 999 'happy haunts' – spirits, goblins, shades and ghosts – appear and evanesce while you ride in a cocoon-like

Disneyland Resort

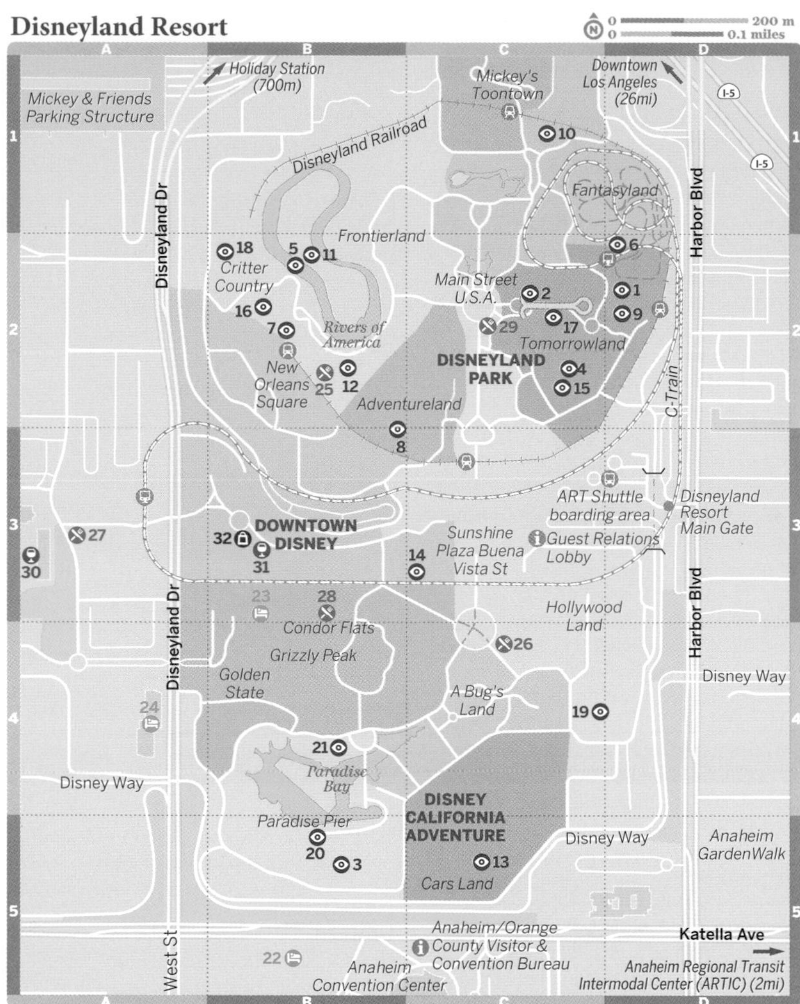

'Doom Buggy' through web-covered graveyards of dancing skeletons.

Critter Country Rides, Attractions

Critter Country's main attraction is **Splash Mountain**, a flume ride through the story of Brer Rabbit and Brer Bear, based on the controversial 1946 film *Song of the South*. Right at the big drop, a camera snaps your picture. Some visitors lift their shirts, earning the ride the nickname 'Flash Mountain,' though R-rated pics are destroyed. Just past Splash Mountain, hop in a mobile beehive on **The Many Adventures of Winnie the Pooh**. Nearby on the Rivers of America, you can paddle **Davy Crockett's Explorer Canoes** on summer weekends.

DISNEY CALIFORNIA ADVENTURE

Hollywood Land Rides, Attractions

California's biggest factory of dreams is presented here in miniature, with soundstages, movable props, and –

Disneyland Resort

Sights

1 Autopia D2
2 Buzz Lightyear's Astro Blaster C2
3 California Screamin' B5
4 Captain EO C2
5 Davy Crockett's Explorer Canoes B2
6 Finding Nemo Submarine Voyage D2
7 Haunted Mansion B2
8 Indiana Jones Adventure B3
9 Innoventions D2
10 it's a small world C1
11 Pirate's Lair on Tom Sawyer Island B2
12 Pirates of the Caribbean B2
13 Radiator Springs Racers C5
14 Soarin' Over California C3
15 Space Mountain C2
16 Splash Mountain B2
17 Star Tours - The Adventure Continues C2
18 The Many Adventures of Winnie the Pooh B2
19 The Twilight Zone Tower of Terror C4
20 Toy Story Midway Mania! B5
21 World of Color B4

Sleeping

22 Anabella B5
23 Disney's Grand Californian Hotel & Spa B3
24 Paradise Pier Hotel A4

Eating

25 Blue Bayou B2
26 Carthay Circle C4
27 Earl of Sandwich A3
28 Napa Rose B3
29 Plaza Inn C2

Drinking & Nightlife

30 Trader Sam's Enchanted Tiki Lounge A3
31 Uva Bar B3

Shopping

32 Disney Vault 28 .... B3

of course – a studio store. The big attraction is **The Twilight Zone Tower of Terror,** a 13-story drop down an elevator chute situated in a haunted hotel – one eerily resembling the historic **Hollywood Roosevelt Hotel** (www.hollywoodroosevelt.com; 7000 Hollywood Blvd; 24hr; P) FREE in Los Angeles. From the upper floors of the tower, you'll have views of the Santa Ana mountains, if only for a few heart-pounding seconds.

Golden State Rides, Attractions

Golden State is broken into sections highlighting California's natural and human achievements. Its main attraction, **Soarin' Over California**, is a virtual hang-gliding ride using Omnimax technology that 'flies' you over landmarks such as the Golden Gate Bridge, Yosemite Falls, Lake Tahoe, Malibu and, of course, Disneyland itself. Enjoy the light breeze as you soar, keeping your nostrils open for the smell of the sea, orange groves and pine forests blowing in the wind.

Paradise Pier Rides, Attractions

If you like carnival rides, you'll love Paradise Pier, designed to look like a combination of all the beachside amusement piers in California. The state-of-the-art **California Screamin'** roller coaster resembles an old wooden coaster, but it's got a smooth-as-silk steel track: it feels like you're being shot out of a cannon. Just as popular is **Toy Story Midway Mania!**, a 4D ride where you earn points by shooting at targets while your carnival car swivels and careens through an oversize, old-fashioned game arcade.

Cars Land Rides, Attractions

DCA's newest arrival, based on the popular Disney Pixar movie *Cars*, opened in 2012 and became an instant hit. Top billing goes to the wacky **Radiator Springs Racers**, a race-car ride that bumps and jumps around a track painstakingly decked out like the Great American West.

Sleeping

For the full Disney experience, splurge and stay right at the **resort** (800-225-2024, reservations 714-956-6425; www.disneyland.com).

Anabella Hotel $$

(800-863-4888, 714-905-1050; www.anabellahotel.com; 1030 W Katella Ave; r $89-199, ste $109-199; P @) Formerly three separate motels, this 7-acre complex has the feel of a laid-back country club, complete with trams that carry guests effortlessly from the lobby to their buildings. Large rooms have wooden floors and a whisper of Spanish Colonial style, with extras like mini-fridges and TV entertainment systems. Bunk-bedded kids' suites have Disney-inspired decor.

Disney's Grand Californian Hotel & Spa Luxury Hotel **$$$**
(info 714-635-2300, reservations 714-956-6425; disneyland.disney.go.com/grand-californian-hotel; 1600 S Disneyland Dr; d from $360; P ❄ @ ≋) Soaring timber beams rise above the cathedral-like lobby of the six-story Grand Californian, Disney's homage to the Arts and Crafts architectural movement. Cushy rooms have triple-sheeted beds, down pillows, bathrobes and all-custom furnishings. Outside there's a faux-redwood waterslide into the pool. At night, kids wind down with bedtime stories by the lobby's giant stone hearth. For a little adult pampering, your coconut rub and milk ritual wrap awaits at the Mandara Spa. Even if you're not staying here, a brief respite in the astounding lobby is a must (and totally acceptable). Enter from DCA or Downtown Disney.

Paradise Pier Hotel Hotel **$$$**
(info 714-999-0990, reservations 714-956-6425; http://disneyland.disney.go.com/paradise-pier-hotel; 1717 S Disneyland Dr; d from $240; P ❄ @ ≋) Sunbursts, surfboards and a giant superslide are all on deck at the Paradise Pier Hotel, the smallest (472 rooms), cheapest and maybe the most fun of the Disney hotel trio. Kids will love the beachy decor and game arcade, not to mention the roof deck pool and the tiny-tot video room filled with mini Adirondack chairs.

Eating

There are dozens of dining options inside the theme parks; it's part of the fun to hit the walk-up food stands for treats like huge turkey legs and Mickey-shaped pretzels.

Kid-Friendly Attractions

If you (or ahem, your kids) can't get enough of the wholesome, family-oriented attractions at Disneyland, pile the family into the car and try out a few of these.

Knott's Berry Farm (714-220-5200; www.knotts.com; 8039 Beach Blvd, Buena Park; adult/child $62/33; from 10am, closing time varies 6-11pm) Old West-themed Knott's Berry Farm often teems with packs of speed-crazed adolescents testing their mettle on an intense line-up of thrill rides. Gut-wrenchers include the wooden Ghost Rider and the '50s-themed Xcelerator, while the single-digit-aged find tamer action at Camp Snoopy.

ExplorOcean (949-675-8915; www.explorocean.org; 600 E Bay Ave, Balboa Fun Zone; adult/child 4-12yr $5/3; 11am-3:30pm Mon-Thu, to 6pm Fri & Sat, to 5pm Sun) In the Balboa Fun Zone (p347), this newly refurbished museum calls itself an 'ocean literacy center' with critter-filled touch tanks, remotely operated vehicles, the rowboat used by adventurer Roz Savage on her five-year, round-the-world solo voyage, and an innovation lab.

Discovery Science Center (714-542-2823; www.discoverycube.org; 2500 N Main St, Santa Ana; adult/child 3-14yr & senior $16/13, 4D movies $2 extra; 10am-5pm) More than 100 interactive displays await in exhibit areas with names such as Discovery Theater (playing 4-D movies), Dino Quest and more. Step into the eye of a hurricane – your hair will get mussed – or grab a seat in the Shake Shack to virtually experience a magnitude 6.4 quake. Special science-themed exhibits, like 'Grossology' or adventures in archaeology inspired by Indiana Jones, are fun too. It's about 5 miles southeast of Disneyland via the I-5.

Don't Miss Disney Fireworks & Parades

The fireworks spectacular above Sleeping Beauty Castle, **Remember – Dreams Come True**, happens nightly around 9:25pm in summer. (In winter, artificial snow falls on Main Street, USA after the fireworks.) In **Mickey's Soundsational Parade**, floats glide down Main Street, USA with bands playing a variety of music from Latin to Bollywood, accompanying costumed characters.

The outdoor extravaganza on Disneyland's Rivers of America, **Fantasmic!**, may be the best show of all, with its full-size ships, lasers and pyrotechnics, pink elephants, princesses and an evil queen. Arrive early to scope a spot – the best are down front by the water – or reserve balcony seats in New Orleans Square. Book reserved seating (☎714-781-7469, adult/child $60/50) up to 30 days in advance.

DCA's premier show is **World of Color**, a dazzling nighttime display of lasers, lights and animation projected over Paradise Bay. It's so popular, you'll need a Fastpass ticket. Otherwise, reserved seating (☎714-781-4400, per person $15) includes a picnic meal; make reservations up to 30 days in advance.

During the day, don't miss the **Pixar Play Parade**, led by race car Lightning McQueen from *Cars* and featuring energetic appearances by characters from other animated movies such as *Monsters, Inc, The Incredibles, Ratatouille, Finding Nemo* and *Toy Story*. Be prepared to get squirted by aliens wielding water hoses.

DISNEYLAND

Plaza Inn American **$$**
(Main Street, U.S.A.; breakfast buffet adult/child 3-9yr $27/13, mains $12-17; ⏲breakfast, lunch & dinner) Finger-lickin' good fried chicken platter and pot roast come with mashed potatoes, buttermilk biscuits and veggies at this 1950s original. There's a fun breakfast buffet with Disney characters. The rest of the day, if you can snag an outdoor table you'll also get great people

Balboa Island Ferry (p347)

KEVIN STEELE/GETTY IMAGES ©

watching here, at the crossroads of Main Street, U.S.A.

Blue Bayou Southern **$$$**
(**☎714-781-3463; New Orleans Sq; lunch mains $26-40, dinner mains $30-46; ⏲lunch & dinner)** Surrounded by the 'bayou' inside the Pirates of the Caribbean attraction, this is the top choice for sit-down dining in Disneyland Park and is famous for its Creole and Cajun specialties at dinner. Order fresh-baked pecan pie topped by a piratey souvenir for dessert.

DISNEY CALIFORNIA ADVENTURE

Carthay Circle American **$$**
(Buena Vista St; lunch mains $20-30, dinner mains $25-44; ⏲lunch & dinner) Decked out like a Hollywood country club, new Carthay Circle is the best dining in either park, with steaks, seafood, pasta, smart service and a good wine list. We highly recommend at least one order of fried biscuits, stuffed with white cheddar, bacon, and jalapeño and served with apricot honey butter.

Inquire about special packages including dinner and the **World of Color** show.

Napa Rose Californian **$$$**
(☎714-300-7170; Grand Californian Hotel & Spa; mains $39-45, 4-course prix-fixe dinner from $90; ⏲5:30-10pm; 👪) Soaring windows, high-back Arts and Crafts–style chairs, leaded-glass windows and towering ceilings befit the Disneyland Resort's top-drawer restaurant. On the plate, seasonal 'California Wine Country' (read: NorCal) cuisine is as impeccably crafted as Sleeping Beauty Castle. Kids' menu available. Reservations essential. Enter the hotel from DCA or Downtown Disney.

DOWNTOWN DISNEY

Earl of Sandwich Sandwiches **$**
(☎714-817-7476; Downtown Disney; mains $4-7; ⏲8am-11pm Sun-Thu, 8am-midnight Fri & Sat) This counter-service spot near the Disneyland Hotel serves grilled sandwiches that are both kid- and adult-friendly. The 'original 1762' is roast beef, cheddar and horseradish, or look for chipotle chicken

Left: Crystal Cove State Park (p347); **Below:** Independence Hall Museum, Knott's Berry Farm (p340)
(LEFT) ROBERT POSTMA / GETTY IMAGES ©; (BELOW) RICHARD CUMMINS / GETTY IMAGES ©

with avocado or holiday turkey. There are also pizza, salad and breakfast options.

Drinking & Entertainment

You can't buy any alcohol in Disneyland, but you can at DCA, Downtown Disney and Disney's trio of resort hotels. Downtown Disney offers bars, live music, a 12-screen cinema and more.

Trader Sam's Enchanted Tiki Lounge Tiki Bar
(**1150 Magic Way, Disneyland Hotel**) It's tiki to the max and good, clean fun inside this faux-grass shack in the Disneyland Hotel's courtyard. Look for strong, sweet cocktails such as the Shrunken Zombie Head and Hippopotamai-tai served with ice cubes that light up. Order the right drink, and the walls might start moving. No, really.

Uva Bar Wine Bar
(**www.patinagroup.com; Downtown Disney**) *Uva* is Italian for grape, and this bar resembling a Paris Metro station is Downtown Disney's best outdoor spot to tipple wine, nibble Cal-Mediterranean tapas and people-watch. There are 40 wines available by the glass. Come for happy hour.

Shopping

Every theme park 'land' has its own shopping options tailored to its own particular theme – Davy Crockett, New Orleans, the Old West, Route 66 or a seaside amusement park. The biggest theme-park stores – Disneyland's **Emporium** (**Main Street, U.S.A.**) and DCA's **Greetings from California** – have a mind-boggling variety of souvenirs, clothing and Disneyana, from T-shirts to mouse ears.

Anaheim Packing District

With all the hype of the Mouse House, it's sometimes easy to forget that there's a whole other Anaheim outside the gates. New developments are changing that. Case in point: the **Anaheim Packing District** (http://anaheimpackingdistrict.com; S Anaheim Bl), around a long shuttered 1925 car dealership and 1919 orange-packing house a couple miles from Disneyland, near the city's actual downtown. It relaunched in 2013–14 with chic new restaurants such as **Umami Burger** (714-991-8626; www.umamiburger.com; 338 S Anaheim Blvd; mains $11-15; 11am-11pm Sun-Thu, to midnight Fri & Sat), the **Anaheim Brewery** (www.anaheimbrew.com; 336 S Anaheim Blvd; 5-9pm Tue-Thu, 4-9pm Fri, 11am-9pm Sat, to 6pm Sun), an evolving collection of shops and a park for events.

Disney Vault 28 Clothing, Gifts

(Downtown Disney) From distressed T-shirts with edgy Cinderella prints to black tank tops patterned with white skulls, the hipster inventory is discombobulating. They stock a few familiar brands including Harajuku Lovers and Betsey Johnson, but it's the Disney-only boutique lines – such as Disney Couture, by top designers – that really intrigue.

Information

For more help and up-to-date information about the parks, contact the Disneyland Resort (live assistance 714-781-7290, recorded info 714-781-4565 ; www.disneyland.com).

FASTPASS

With a bit of preplanning, you can significantly cut your wait time for popular attractions. One option is using the FASTPASS system. At the FASTPASS ticket machine (located near the entrance to the ride) insert your ticket. You'll receive a slip of paper showing a window of time for boarding the ride. Show up within that window and join the FASTPASS line.

Tickets & Opening Hours

Both parks are open 365 days a year, but park hours depend on the marketing department's projected attendance numbers. You can access the current calendar by phone or online.

One-day admission to *either* Disneyland or DCA currently costs $96 for adults and $90 for children aged three to nine. To visit *both* parks in one day costs $150/144 per adult/child on a 'Park Hopper' ticket. Multiday 'Park Hopper' tickets cost $217/211 for two days up to $305/299 for five days of admission within a two-week period.

Tourist Information

For information or help inside the parks, just ask any cast member or visit Disneyland's **City Hall** or DCA's guest relations lobby.

Getting There & Away

Air

Southern California Gray Line/Coach America (714-978-8855, 800-828-6699; www.graylineanaheim.com) runs the Disneyland Resort Express between LAX and Disneyland-area hotels at least hourly (one way/round-trip to LAX $35/48). It also serves John Wayne Airport (SNA) in Santa Ana ($20/35).

Bus

Frequent departures are available with Greyhound (714-999-1256, 800-231-222; www.greyhound.com; 100 W Winston Rd, Anaheim) to and from downtown LA ($12, 40 minutes) and San Diego ($18, 2¼ hours).

Car

Disneyland Resort is just off I-5 on Harbor Blvd, about 30 miles south of downtown LA.

Train

All trains stop at the newly opened Anaheim Regional Transit Intermodal Center (ARTIC) next to Angel Stadium, a quick ART shuttle or taxi ride east of Disneyland. Amtrak (714-385-1448;

www.amtrak.com; 2150 E Katella Ave) has almost a dozen daily trains to/from LA's Union Station ($15, 40 minutes) and San Diego ($28, two hours).

Getting Around

Bus

Anaheim Resort Transportation (ART; ☎714-563-5287; www.rideart.org; single ride $3, day pass adult/child $5/2) operates some 20 shuttle routes between Disneyland and area hotels, convention centers, malls, stadiums and the transit center, saving traffic jams and parking headaches.

Many hotels and motels offer their own free shuttles to Disneyland and other area attractions; ask before booking.

Car

All-day parking costs $16 ($20 for oversize vehicles). Enter the 'Mickey & Friends' parking structure from southbound Disneyland Dr, off Ball Rd. Walk outside and follow the signs to board the free tram to Downtown Disney.

Downtown Disney parking is reserved for diners, shoppers and movie-goers. It has a different rate structure, with the first three hours free.

Monorail

With an admission ticket to Disneyland, you can ride the monorail between Tomorrowland and the far end of Downtown Disney, near the Disneyland Hotel.

ORANGE COUNTY BEACHES

Huntington Beach

In June 2011, the mayor of Huntington Beach (HB) presented the 'key to the city' to surfing legend Kelly Slater – an event that tells you everything you need to know about this beach community.

California towhee, Bolsa Chica Ecological Reserve (p346)
DAVID TIPLING / GETTY IMAGES ©

In late July and early August, the city hosts the **US Open of Surfing** (www.usopenofsurfing.com), a six-star competition drawing more than 600 surfers, 400,000 spectators and a minivillage of concerts, motocross demos and skater jams.

Sights & Activities

Surfing in Huntington Beach is competitive; control your longboard or draw the ire of territorial locals. Surf north of the pier. If you just want to watch surfers in action, walk down to **Huntington City Beach** at the foot of the **pier** (⏰5am-midnight). In the evening, volleyball games give way to beach bonfires. Romp with your dog in the surf at **Dog Beach**, between Goldenwest St and Seapoint Ave, north of Huntington City Beach.

International Surfing Museum Museum
(www.surfingmuseum.org; 411 Olive Ave; donations welcome; ⏰noon-5pm Mon-Fri, 11am-6pm Sat & Sun) One of the few of its kind in

Carousel, Balboa Fun Zone

RICHARD CUMMINS / GETTY IMAGES ©

California, this small museum is an entertaining stop for surf-culture enthusiasts. Exhibits chronicle the sport's history with photos, vintage surfboards, movie memorabilia and surf music. For the best historical tidbits, spend a minute chatting with the all-volunteer staff.

Bolsa Chica Ecological Reserve Nature Preserve

(http://bolsachica.org; sunrise-sunset) You'd be forgiven for overlooking Bolsa Chica, at least on first glance. Against a backdrop of nodding oil derricks, this flat expanse of wetlands doesn't exactly promise the unspoilt splendors of nature. However, more than 200 bird species aren't so aesthetically prejudiced, either making the wetlands their home throughout the year, or dropping by mid-migration.

Sleeping

Shorebreak Hotel Boutique Hotel **$$$**

(714-861-4470; www.shorebreakhotel.com; 500 Pacific Coast Hwy, Huntington Beach; r $189-495; P ❄ @ ☕ 🐾) Stow your surfboard (lockers provided) as you head inside HB's hippest hotel, a stone's throw from the pier. The Shorebreak has a surf concierge, a fitness center and yoga studio, bean-bag chairs in the lobby and rattan and hardwood furniture in geometric-patterned air-con rooms (some pet-friendly). Have sunset cocktails on the upstairs deck at Zimzala restaurant. Parking is $27.

Eating & Drinking

Sugar Shack Cafe **$**

(www.hbsugarshack.com; 213 1/2 Main St; mains $4-10; 6am-4pm Mon-Tue & Thu, to 8pm Wed, to 5pm Fri-Sun; 👪**)** Expect a wait at this HB institution, or get here early to see surfer dudes don their wet suits. Breakfast is served all day on the bustling Main St patio and inside, where you can grab a spot at the counter or a two-top. Photos of surf legends plastering the walls raise this place almost to shrine status.

Sancho's Tacos Mexican **$**

(714-536-8226; www.sanchostacos.com; 602 Pacific Coast Hwy; mains $3-10; 8am-9pm Mon-Sat, to 8pm Sun) There's no shortage of taco stands in HB, but locals are fiercely dedicated to Sancho's, across from the beach. This two-room shack with patio grills flounder, shrimp and tri-tip to order. Trippy Mexican-meets-skater art.

Duke's Seafood, Hawaiian **$$**
(☎714-374-6446; www.dukeshuntington.com; 317 Pacific Coast Hwy; lunch mains $7-16, dinner mains $19-32; ⏰11:30am-2:30pm Tue-Fri, 10am-2pm Sun, 5-9pm Tue-Sun) It may be touristy, but this Hawaiian-themed restaurant – named after surfing legend Duke Kahanamoku – is a kick. With unbeatable views of the beach, a long list of fresh fish and a healthy selection of sassy cocktails, it's a primo spot to relax and show off your tan. For just drinks and appetizers, step into the Barefoot Bar (open from 3:30pm daily).

Information

Visit Huntington Beach (☎714-969-3492; www.surfcityusa.com; 2nd fl, 301 Main St; ⏰9am-5pm) provides tourist maps and other information, but the **Pier Plaza (www.surfcityusa.com; Pier Plaza; ⏰11am-7pm)** booth is more convenient.

Newport Beach & Around

The upscale suburb of Newport is as famous for its ritzy homes ($15 million, anyone?) as it is for its surprisingly relaxed beach. The 4-mile-long Balboa Peninsula has two piers – **Newport Pier** and **Balboa Pier** – stretches of white sandy beach and a renowned body surfing spot at the end: the **Wedge**.

Sights & Activities

Balboa Fun Zone Amusement Park
(www.thebalboafunzone.com; 600 E Bay Ave; ⏰Ferris wheel 11am-8pm Sun-Thu, to 9pm Fri, to 10pm Sat) On the harbor side of Balboa Peninsula, the Fun Zone has delighted locals and visitors since 1936. There's a small Ferris wheel ($4 per ride, where Ryan and Marissa shared their first kiss on *The OC*), arcade games, touristy shops and restaurants, and frozen banana stands (just like the one in the TV sit-com *Arrested Development*). Nearby the landmark 1905 **Balboa Pavilion** is beautifully illuminated at night. The Fun Zone is also the place to catch a harbor cruise, fishing of whale-watching expedition, or the **ferry to Balboa Island** just across the channel.

Balboa Island Island
(www.balboa-island.net) In the middle of the harbor sits the island that time forgot. Its streets are still largely lined with tightly clustered cottages built in the 1920s and '30s when this was a summer getaway from LA. The 1.5-mile promenade that circles the island makes a terrific car-free stroll or jog. The ferry lands at Agate Ave, about 11 blocks west of Marine Ave, which is lined with swimwear boutiques, Italian trattorias and cocktail bars. Near the Ferris wheel on the harbor side, the **Balboa Island Ferry (www.balboaislandferry.com; 410 S Bay Front; adult/child $1/50¢, car incl driver $2; ⏰6:30am-midnight Sun-Thu, to 2am Fri & Sat)** shuttles passengers across the bay.

Crystal Cove State Park Beach
(☎949-494-3539; www.parks.ca.gov; 8471 N Coast Hwy; per car $15, campsites $25-75) A few miles of open beach and 2000 acres of undeveloped woodland at this state beach let you forget you're in a crowded metropolitan area, at least once you get past the parking lots and stake out a place on the sand.

Orange County Museum of Art Museum
(☎949-759-1122; www.ocma.net; 850 San Clemente Dr; adult/student/child under 12yr $10/8/free; ⏰11am-5pm Wed-Sun, to 8pm Thu) Less than a half mile from Fashion Island, this engaging museum highlights California art and cutting-edge contemporary artists, with exhibitions rotating through two large spaces. Recent exhibitions have included 'Birth of the Cool: Art, Design and Culture at Midcentury' and '15 Minutes of Fame: Portraits from Ansel Adams to Andy Warhol.' There's also a sculpture garden, eclectic gift shop and a theater screening classic, foreign and art-related films.

Sleeping

Crystal Cove Beach Cottages Cabin **$$**
(☎reservations 800-444-7275; www.crystalcovebeachcottages.com; 35 Crystal Cove, Newport Beach; r with shared bath $42-127, cottages $162-249; ⏰check-in 4-9pm) To snag these historic oceanfront cottages, book on the

first day of the month six months before your intended stay – or pray for last-minute cancellations.

Newport Channel Inn Motel **$$**

(**800-255-8614, 949-642-3030; www.newportchannelinn.com; 6030 W Coast Hwy; r $129-199;**) The ocean is just across PCH from this spotless 30-room, two-story 1960s-era motel. Other perks include large rooms with microwaves and mini-fridges, a big common sundeck, beach equipment for loan and genuinely friendly owners with lots of local knowledge. Enjoy a vacation-lodge vibe under the A-frame roof of room 219, which sleeps up to seven.

Eating

Ruby's Crystal Cove Shake Shack Diner **$**

(**www.rubys.com; 7703 E Coast Hwy; shakes $5; 6:30am-9pm, to 10pm Fri & Sat**) South Carolina has South of the Border, South Dakota has Wall Drug and SoCal has Ruby's Crystal Cove Shake Shack. Although this been-here-forever wooden shake stand is now owned by the Ruby's Diner chain, at least the ocean views are as good as ever. Don't fear the date shake, it's delish. The shack is just east of the Crystal Cove/Los Trancos entrance to the state park's historic district.

Bear Flag Fish Company Seafood **$$**

(**949-673-3434; www.bearflagfishco.com; 407 31st St, Newport Beach; mains $8-15; 11am-9pm Tue-Sat, to 8pm Sun & Mon;**) This squat glass box is *the* place for generously sized, grilled and panko-breaded fish tacos, ahi burritos, spankin' fresh ceviche and oysters. Pick out what you want from the ice-cold display cases, then grab a picnic-table seat. About the only way this seafood could be any fresher is if you caught and hauled it off the boat yourself!

Eat Chow Californian **$$**

(**949-423-7080; www.eatchownow.com; 211 62nd St; mains $8-15; 8am-9pm Mon-Thu, to 10pm Fri, 7am-10pm Sat, to 9pm Sun**) Hidden a block off of W Coast Hwy, the crowd is equal parts tatted hipsters and ladies who lunch, which makes it very Newport indeed. They all queue happily for big salads such as ribeye Thai beef salad, grilled salmon tacos with curry slaw, and bodacious burgers including the Chow BBQ burger with homemade barbecue sauce, smoked gouda, crispy onions and more. Groovy indie-rock soundtrack.

Getting Around

OCTA (**714-560-6282; www.octa.net**) bus 1 connects Newport Beach and Fashion Island mall with the OC's other beach towns, including Corona del Mar just east, every 30 minutes to one hour. From the intersection of Newport Blvd

Serra Chapel, Mission San Juan Capistrano
STEPHEN SAKS / GETTY IMAGES ©

Detour: Mission San Juan Capistrano

Famous for its swallows that fly back to town every year on March 19 (though sometimes they're just a bit early), San Juan Capistrano is also home to the 'jewel of the California missions.' It's a little town, about 11 miles south and inland of Laguna Beach. Plan on spending at least an hour poking around the sprawling **mission** (949-234-1300; www.missionsjc.com; 26801 Ortega Hwy, San Juan Capistrano; adult/child $9/6; 9am-5pm), with its tiled roofs, covered arches, lush gardens, fountains and courtyards – including the padre's quarters, soldiers' barracks and the cemetery. The **Serra Chapel** – whitewashed outside with restored frescoes inside – is believed to be the oldest existing building in California (1778).

and PCH, bus 71 heads south along the Balboa Peninsula to Main Ave every hour or so. On all routes, the one-way fare is $2 (exact change).

Laguna Beach

Orange County's most relaxed beach town has just about everything you'd want in a casual seaside vacation – great shopping, cliff-top restaurants, myriad art galleries, romantic inns and palm trees.

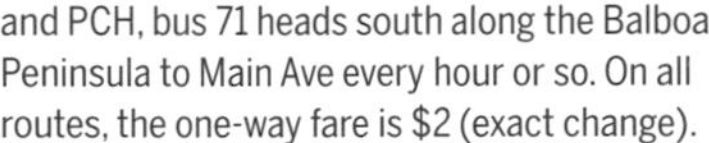

Sights & Activities

At the western end of Broadway, **Main Beach** has benches, tables, restrooms and volleyball and basketball courts. It's also the best beach for swimming.

Just northwest of Main Beach, follow the path to the grassy, bluff-top **Heisler Park** for sweeping views of the craggy coves and deep blue sea. Drop down below the park to **Divers Cove**, a deep, protected inlet popular with snorkelers and, of course, divers.

Laguna Art Museum Museum
(949-494-8971; www.lagunaartmuseum.org; 307 Cliff Dr; adult/student & senior/child $7/5/free, 1st Thu of month free; 11am-5pm Fri-Tue, to 9pm Thu) This breezy museum has changing exhibitions featuring contemporary Californian artists, and a permanent collection heavy on Californian landscapes, vintage photographs and works by early Laguna bohemians. Free guided tours are usually given at 11am Tuesday, Thursday and Saturday, and there's a unique gift shop. Hours may be extended during some exhibitions.

La Vida Laguna Water Sports
(949-275-7544; www.lavidalaguna.com; 1257 S Coast Hwy; 2hr guided tour $95) Take a guided kayaking tour of the craggy coves of Laguna's coast and you might just see a colony of sea lions. Make reservations at least a day in advance.

Sleeping

Inn at Laguna Beach Hotel **$$$**
(800-544-4479, 949-497-9722; www.innatlagunabeach.com; 211 N Coast Hwy; r $210-600; P) Pride of place goes to this three-story white concrete hotel, at the north end of Main Beach. Its 70 keen rooms were recently renovated with rattan furniture, blond woods, marble, French blinds and thick featherbeds. Some have balconies overlooking the water. Extras include DVD and CD players, bathrobes, beach gear to borrow and nightly ocean-view wine and beer reception. Parking costs $29.

Eating

Taco Loco Mexican **$**
(http://tacoloco.net; 640 S Coast Hwy; mains $3-14; 11am-midnight Sun-Thu, to 2am Fri & Sat;) Throw back Coronas with the surfers

If You Like... Small Towns

If the relaxed vibe and slow pace of 'the Village' in Laguna Beach is your thing, check out these picturesque SoCal towns.

1 ORANGE

(www.cityoforange.org) For a pleasant dose of small-town life complete with a wide selection of family-owned restaurants and shops, head to Old Towne Orange. Built around a pretty plaza at the intersection of Chapman Ave and Glassell Sts, it has the most concentrated collection of antiques shops in Orange County. It's located east of Anaheim and the I-5 Fwy.

2 SEAL BEACH

(www.sealbeachca.gov) In the pageant for charming small towns, Seal Beach enjoys unfair advantages over the competition: 1.5 miles of pristine beach glittering like a crown, plus a three-block Main St lined with mom-and-pop restaurants and indie shops. It's northwest of Huntington Beach on Hwy 1.

3 CORONA DEL MAR

(www.visitnewportbeach.com) This ritzy bedroom community, perched on the privileged eastern bluffs of the Newport Channel, has some of the best coastal views in SoCal. It also includes a high-end stretch of Pacific Coast Hwy, with trendy shops and restaurants, and the lovely **Corona del Mar State Beach** (Corona del Mar State Beach; ☎949-644-3151; ⌚6am-10pm; P).

while watching the passersby on PCH at this Mexican sidewalk cafe. Taco, quesadilla and nacho options seem endless: blackened calamari or tofu, swordfish, veggie (potato, mushroom, tofu) and shrimp to name a few. For dessert: hemp brownies. Order at the counter, dude.

Zinc Cafe & Market Cafe **$**

(www.zinccafe.com; 350 Ocean Ave, Laguna Beach; mains $6-11; ⌚market 7am-6pm, cafe to 4pm; 🍴) Ground zero for Laguna's see-and-be-seen vegetarians, this gourmet market has a hedge-enclosed patio where you can munch on tasty vegetarian and vegan meals such as garden-fresh salads and pizzas. If you've been hesitant to order oatmeal at a restaurant, resist no more: Zinc's fresh fruit-covered version is delish. Strong espresso too.

House of Big Fish & Cold Beer Seafood **$$**

(☎949-715-4500; www.houseofbigfish.com; 540 S Coast Hwy; mains $7-15; ⌚11:30am-10:30pm) The name says it all (what else do you need?): Hawaii-style *poke* (marinated raw fish), Baja-style fish tacos, coconut shrimp and the fresh catch o' the day. Fish are sustainably raised, and there are dozens of beers including about one-third from California. Make reservations, or wait, like, forever.

242 Cafe Fusion Sushi Japanese **$$$**

(www.fusionart.us; 242 N Coast Hwy; mains $18-45; ⌚4:30-10pm Sun-Thu, to 10:30pm Fri & Sat) One of the only female sushi chefs in Orange County, Miki Izumisawa slices and rolls organic rice into Laguna's best sushi, artfully presented. The place seats maybe two dozen people at a time, so expect a wait or come early. The 'sexy' handroll – spicy ahi and scallops with mint, cilantro, avocado and crispy potato – is date-enhancing.

Drinking

Rooftop Lounge Bar

(www.rooftoplagunabeach.com; 1289 S Coast Hwy) Perched atop **La Casa del Camino** (☎855-634-5736, 949-497-2446; www.lacasadelcamino.com; r from $159; P🚭❄@📶), this bar, with 270-degree coastal views and a friendly vibe, has locals singing hallelujahs. Follow the fashionable crowds through the hotel's lobby and take the elevator to the top. Mango and wild berry mojitos add some spice to the cocktail menu, and you can snack on plates such as meatballs in guava barbecue sauce.

Koffee Klatsch Coffeehouse

(1440 S Coast Hwy; ⌚7am-11pm Sun-Thu, to midnight Fri & Sat) About a mile south of

Pier, Seal Beach

JUAN CAMILO BERNAL PHOTOGRAPHER / GETTY IMAGES ©

downtown, this cozy coffee shop draws a mixed gay/straight/hipster crowd for coffees, breakfasts, salads and ginormous cakes.

Information

Visit Laguna Beach Visitors Center (949-497-9229; www.lagunabeachinfo.com; 381 Forest Ave; 10am-5pm;) Helpful staff, bus schedules, restaurant menus and free brochures on everything from hiking trails to self-guided walking tours.

Getting There & Around

To reach Laguna Beach from the I-405, take Hwy 133 (Laguna Canyon Rd) southwest. Laguna is served by **OCTA** (714-560-6282; www.octa.net) bus 1, which runs along the coast from Long Beach to San Clemente.

Laguna Beach Transit (www.lagunabeachcity.net; 375 Broadway) has its central bus depot on Broadway, just north of the visitors center in the heart of the Village. For tourists, the most important route is the one that runs along PCH.

California
In Focus

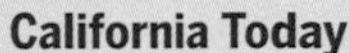

Vineyard, Napa Valley (p210)

California Today

> *California is not a finished work. Today the thorniest issues revolve around growth.*

belief systems
(% of population)

if California were 100 people

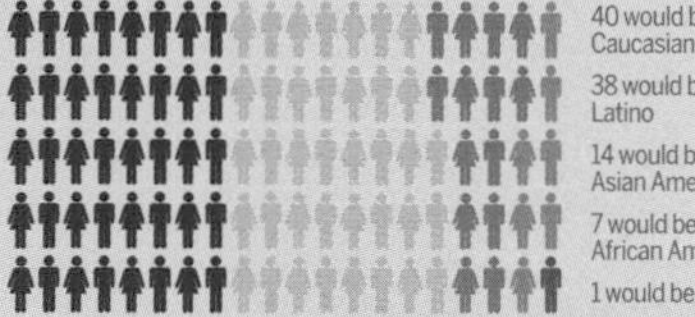

population per sq mile

Huntington Beach (p345)

California Dreams vs Reality

Even if you've seen it in movies or on TV, California still comes as a shock to the system. Venice Beach skateboarders, Santa Cruz hippies, Rodeo Drive–pillaging trophy wives and Silicon Valley billionaires aren't on different channels; they all live here, where tolerance for other people's beliefs, be they conservative, liberal or just plain wacky, is the social glue.

California is not a finished work, however. Today the thorniest issues revolve around growth. In a state that has an economy bigger than Canada's and is the headquarters for cutting-edge tech companies, from space probes to social media, how to manage a burgeoning human population – with accompanying traffic gridlock, housing shortages and a sky-high cost of living – is challenging.

MATTHEW MICAH WRIGHT / GETTY IMAGES ©

Environmental Roots

There's no denying California's culture of conspicuous consumption, exported via Hollywood flicks and reality TV. But Californians have also trailblazed another 'greener' way by choosing more sustainable foods and low-impact lifestyles, preserving old-growth forests with tree-sitting activism, declaring nuclear-free zones, pushing for environmentally progressive legislation and establishing the USA's biggest market for hybrid vehicles. Over 60% of Californians admit that yes, they've hugged a tree.

It was Californians who helped kick-start the world's conservation movement in the midst of the 19th-century industrial revolution, with laws curbing industrial dumping, setting aside swaths of prime real estate for parks and protecting wilderness. That said, the state's current long-term drought has resulted in a suspension of some key environmental legal protections.

Fast Companies, Slow Food

California's technological innovations need no introduction by anyone. Perhaps you've heard of PCs, iPods, Google and the internet? The home of Silicon Valley and a burgeoning biotech industry, NorCal is giving SoCal's gargantuan movie, TV and entertainment industry a run for its money as the state's main economic engine.

Meanwhile, although less than 10% of Californians live in rural areas, they're still responsible for one of the state's other powerhouse industries: agriculture. With over 80,000 farms statewide raising $42 billion worth of food for the rest of the country and the world each year, it's obvious why climate change and ongoing drought are of such concern.

You may notice Californians tend to proselytize about their food and idolize homegrown chefs like rock stars. After a few bites, you may begin to understand their obsession. It's no accident that the term 'locavore' – people who eat food grown locally – was born here.

New World Religions

Despite their proportionately small numbers, California's alternative religions and utopian communities dominate the popular imagination. California made national headlines in the 1960s with gurus from India, in the 1970s with Jim Jones' People's Temple and Erhard Seminars Training (EST) and in the 1990s with the Heaven's Gate doomsday UFO cult in San Diego. The controversial Church of Scientology is still seeking acceptance with celebrity proponents from movie-star Tom Cruise to musician Beck.

History

Mastodon diorama, Page Museum & La Brea Tar Pits (p68)

LONELY PLANET / GETTY IMAGES

Beckoning from the edge of the continent, California has witnessed a steady stream of people drawn to its natural resources and culture of cutting-edge ideas. Successively inhabited and developed by Native American tribes, European explorers and missionaries, white land-hungry settlers and frenzied gold miners, the Golden State is also the birthplace of the 1960s countercultural movement and ground zero for computer technology and innovation.

The First Peoples

Immigration is hardly a new phenomenon here, since people have been migrating to California for millennia. Archaeological sites indicate this geographic region was first inhabited soon after people migrated across the long-gone land bridge from Asia during an ice age at least 20,000 years ago. Many archaeological sites have yielded evidence, from large middens of

25,000–10,000 BC

Earliest known humans cross over the Bering Strait from Asia.

seashells along the beaches to campfire sites on the Channel Islands, that people have been living along this coast for around 13,000 years.

Archaeological evidence paints a clear picture of the diversity of indigenous peoples living here at the time of first European contact. Native peoples spoke around 100 different languages and numbered as many as 300,000. They mostly lived in small groups, often migrating with the seasons from the coast into the mountains. Acorn meal was their dietary staple, supplemented by small, wild game and seafood.

The Best... Places for Ancient History

1 La Brea Tar Pits (p68)

2 Redwood trees (p149)

3 Petroglyphs at Lava Beds National Monument (p168)

4 Petrified Forest (p229)

5 Devils Postpile National Monument (p273)

A New World for Europeans

Following the conquest of Mexico in the early 16th century, the Spanish turned their attention toward exploring the edges of their new empire. In 1542 the Spanish crown engaged Juan Rodríguez Cabrillo, a Portuguese explorer and retired conquistador, to lead an expedition up the West Coast to find the fabled golden land beyond Mexico's west coast.

When Cabrillo sailed into San Diego Bay in 1542, he and his crew became the first Europeans to see mainland California. Staring back at them from shore were the Kumeyaay – to learn more about this coastal tribe, visit San Diego's Museum of Man. Cabrillo's ships sat out a storm in the harbor, then sailed northward. They made a stop at the Channel Islands where, in 1543, Cabrillo fell ill, died and was buried. The expedition continued as far as Oregon, but returned with no evidence of a sea route to the Atlantic, a city of gold or islands of spice. The unimpressed Spanish authorities forgot about California for the next 60 years.

The English privateer Sir Francis Drake sailed up the California coast in 1579. He missed the entrance to San Francisco Bay, but pulled in near what is now called Point Reyes to repair his ship, which was bursting with the weight of plundered Spanish silver. He claimed the land for Queen Elizabeth, named it Nova Albion (New England) and left for other adventures, starting with journeying north up the Pacific Coast to Alaska.

6000 BC
Date of earliest petroglyphs (rock art) found at Lava Beds National Monument near Mt Shasta.

1542
Juan Rodríguez Cabrillo becomes the first European to 'discover' California.

1579
English explorer Sir Francis Drake stops by Marin County.

IN FOCUS HISTORY

The Mission Period

Around the 1760s, as Russian ships came to California's coast in search of sea-otter pelts, and British trappers and explorers spread throughout the West, King Carlos III of Spain grew worried that these other newcomers might pose a threat to Spain's claim. Conveniently for the king, the Catholic Church was anxious to start missionary work among the indigenous peoples, so church and state combined forces to found missions beside presidios (military posts).

Ostensibly, the presidios' purpose was to protect the missions and deter foreign intruders. The idea was to have Native American converts live inside the missions, learn trade and agricultural skills, and ultimately establish pueblos (small towns). But these garrisons created more threats than they deterred, as the soldiers aroused local hostility by raiding Native American camps to sexually assault and kidnap women. Not only were the presidios militarily weak, but their weaknesses were well known to Russia and Britain, and didn't strengthen Spain's claims to California.

Ultimately, the mission period was pretty much a failure. The Spanish population remained small; the missions achieved little more than mere survival; foreign intruders were not greatly deterred; and more Native Americans died than were converted. Most of California's missions are still standing today, though a few are in ruins. Of California's original chain of 21 missions, the earliest were founded by peripatetic Franciscan priest Junípero Serra.

From Mexico to Manifest Destiny

When Mexico gained independence from Spain in 1821, many of the new nation's people looked to California to satisfy their thirst for private land. By the mid-1830s the Spanish missions had been secularized, with a series of Mexican governors doling out hundreds of free land grants, or ranchos, that were largely given over to rearing livestock to supply a profitable trade in hide and tallow. The new landowners, called rancheros or Californios, quickly prospered and became the social, cultural and political heavyweights of Alta (Upper) California.

American explorers, trappers, traders, whalers, settlers and opportunists showed increasing interest in California, seizing on prospects that the rancheros ignored. Some of the Americans who started businesses converted to Catholicism, married locals and assimilated into Californio society. Impressed by California's potential wealth and hoping to fulfill the promise of Manifest Destiny (the USA's imperialist doctrine to extend its borders from coast to coast), US President Andrew Jackson sent an emissary to offer the financially strapped Mexican government $500,000 for California in 1835. Though American settlers were by then showing up by the hundreds, especially in Northern California, Jackson's emissary was tersely rejected.

In 1836 Texas had seceded from Mexico and declared itself an independent republic. On May 11, 1846, the US declared war on Mexico, following disputes over the former's annexation of Texas. By July, US naval units occupied every port on the California

1769

Padre Junípero Serra establishes the first of 21 missions along the 650-mile El Camino Real. Street sign, El Camino Real, Monterey

STEPHEN SAKS / GETTY IMAGES ©

1821

Mexico wins independence from Spain, taking over rule of Alta (Upper) California after Spain's 52-year reign.

coast, including Monterey, the capital of Alta California. When US troops captured Mexico City in September 1847, ending the war, the Mexican government had little choice but to cede much of its northern territory to the US. The Treaty of Guadalupe Hidalgo, signed on February 2, 1848, turned over what is now California, Nevada, Utah and parts of Arizona, New Mexico, Colorado and Wyoming to the US. Two years later, California was admitted as the 31st state of the USA.

The Best... California Mission Buildings

1 Mission Santa Barbara (p191)

2 Mission San Juan Capistrano (p349)

3 Mission Dolores (p108)

4 Mission Basilica San Diego de Alcalá (p298)

There's Gold in Them Thar Hills

By remarkable coincidence, gold was discovered at Sutter's Creek, about 120 miles northeast of San Francisco, little more than a week before the signing of the Treaty of Guadalupe Hidalgo that ended the Mexican–American War. By 1849, surging rivers of wagon trains were creaking into California filled with miners, pioneers, savvy entrepreneurs, outlaws and prostitutes, all seeking their fortunes.

Population growth and overnight wealth stimulated every aspect of California life, from agriculture and banking to construction and journalism. But mining damaged the land: hills were stripped bare, erosion wiped out vegetation, streams silted up and mercury washed down rivers into San Francisco Bay. San Francisco became a hotbed of gambling, prostitution, drink and chicanery, giving rise to its moniker 'the Barbary Coast,' whose last vestiges live on today in the strip joints in the North Beach neighborhood.

Development, Discrimination & Natural Resources

Opening the floodgates to massive migration into the West, the transcontinental railroad drastically shortened the trip from New York to San Francisco from two months to less than four days, profitably linking markets on both coasts. Los Angeles was not connected to the transcontinental railroad until 1876, when Southern Pacific Railroad laid tracks from San Francisco south to the fledgling city.

By this time, rampant speculation had raised land prices in California to levels no farmer or immigrant could afford; the railroad brought in products that undersold goods made in California; and some 12,000 Chinese laborers – no longer needed for railroad construction – flooded the labor market. A period of unrest ensued, which culminated in anti-Chinese discrimination and the federal 1882 Chinese Exclusion Act, banning Chinese immigration. The act was not repealed until 1943.

1840s

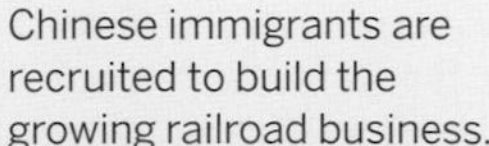

Chinese immigrants are recruited to build the growing railroad business.

1846

The Mexican–American War begins; drunk Californians in Sonoma declare independence, which lasts for 22 days.

1849

The Gold Rush continues; San Francisco gains 10 times the population and 100 times the bars.

The Best... Places to Experience the Gold Rush

1 Bodie State Historic Park (p278)

2 Sonoma (p231)

3 Marshall Gold Discovery State Historic Park (p277)

4 Nevada City (p277)

5 Sutter's Fort State Historic Park (p279)

Much of the land granted to the railroads was sold in big lots to speculators who also acquired, with the help of corrupt politicians and administrators, a lot of the farmland intended for new settlers. A major share of the state's agricultural land thus became consolidated as large holdings in the hands of a few city-based landlords, establishing the pattern (which continues to this day) of industrial-scale 'agribusiness' rather than small family farms. These big businesses were well placed to provide the substantial investment and the political connections required to bring irrigation water to the farmland. They also solidified an ongoing need for cheap farm labor.

In the absence of coal, iron ore or abundant water, heavy industry developed slowly in California, though the 1892 discovery of oil in central Los Angeles by Edward Doheny stimulated the development of petroleum processing and chemical industries. By the year 1900, California was producing 4 million barrels of oil per year and the population of LA had doubled to over 100,000 people.

While bucolic Southern California was urbanizing, Northern Californians who had witnessed devastation from mining and logging firsthand were forming the nation's first conservation movement. Naturalist John Muir founded the Sierra Club in 1892 and campaigned for the federal government to establish the first national park in Yosemite. However, dams and pipelines continued to be built to support communities in SoCal deserts and coastal cities – including the Hetch Hetchy Reservoir in Yosemite, which supplies the Bay Area with water today, and aqueducts from the Eastern Sierra to slake the thirst of Los Angeles. In drought-prone California, tensions still regularly come to a boil between developers and conservationists, and NorCal drinking-water hoarders and SoCal lawn-water splurgers.

Growing into the 20th Century

The population, wealth and importance of California increased dramatically throughout the 20th century. The great San Francisco earthquake and fire of 1906 decimated the city, but it was barely a hiccup in the state's development. The revolutionary years in Mexico, from 1910 to 1921, caused a huge influx of immigrants from south of the border, reestablishing Latino communities that had been smothered by Anglo dominance. Meanwhile, SoCal's oil industry boomed in the 1920s and Hollywood entered its so-called 'Golden Age,' which lasted through the 1950s.

1892

John Muir founds the Sierra Club after helping establish Yosemite as a national park.

1906

A 7.8 earthquake and resulting fire destroys much of San Francisco.

1928

The Jazz Singer is released as the first feature-length 'talkie'; worldwide demand for films grows Hollywood.

The Great Depression saw another wave of immigrants, this time from the impoverished Great Plains states of the Dust Bowl. Outbreaks of social and labor unrest led to the rapid growth of the Democratic Party in California, as well as trade unions for blue-collar workers. Many of the Depression-era public works projects sponsored by the federal government had lasting benefits, from San Francisco's Bay Bridge to the restoration of historic missions statewide, notably Mission La Purísima Concepción near Santa Barbara.

WWII had a major impact on California. Women were co-opted into wartime factory work and proved themselves in a range of traditionally male jobs. Anti-Asian sentiments resurfaced, many Japanese Americans were interned and more Mexicans crossed the border to fill labor shortages. Some military servicepeople who passed through California liked the place so much that they returned to settle after the war. In the postwar decade, the state's population jumped by 40%, reaching 13 million by 1955.

Radicals, Trendsetters & Technology

Unconstrained by tradition, Californians have long been leaders in new attitudes and social movements. During the affluent postwar years of the 1950s, the Beat movement

Exhibit, Marshall Gold Discovery State Historic Park (p277)

1939
Hewlett-Packard is formed in Dave Packard's garage in Palo Alto.

1962
César Chávez organizes migrant laborers into what will eventually become the United Farm Workers.

1967
San Francisco's Summer of Love kicks off the hippie movement.

The Best... History Museums

1 California State Railroad Museum (p279)

2 San Diego Natural History Museum (p296)

3 Emigrant Trail Museum (p256)

4 Monterey State Historic Park (p176)

5 La Plaza de Cultura y Artes (p61)

6 Manzanar National Historic Site (p276)

in San Francisco's North Beach railed against the banality and conformity of suburban life, instead choosing bohemian coffeehouses for jazz, poetry and pot.

When the postwar baby boomers came of age, many took up where the Beat generation left off, heeding 1960s countercultural icon Timothy Leary's counsel to 'turn on, tune in and drop out.' Their revolt climaxed in San Francisco's Haight-Ashbury during the 1967 'Summer of Love.' Sex, drugs and rock 'n' roll ruled the day. With the foundation for social revolution already laid, gay liberation exploded in San Francisco in the '70s. Today San Francisco remains one of the world's most exuberantly gay cities – just take a stroll through the Castro.

In the 1980s and '90s, California catapulted to the forefront of the healthy lifestyle, with more aerobics classes and self-actualization workshops than you could shake a shaman's stick at. In-line skating, snowboarding and mountain-biking rose to fame here first.

Geeking Out

As digital technology continually reinvents our world view, California has also led the world in developing computer technology. In the 1950s, Stanford University needed to raise money to finance postwar growth, so it built an industrial park and leased space to high-tech companies like Hewlett-Packard, which formed the nucleus of Northern California's Silicon Valley.

When Silicon Valley introduced the first personal computer in 1968, advertisements breathlessly gushed that Hewlett-Packard's 'light' (40lb) machine could 'take on roots of a fifth-degree polynomial, Bessel functions, elliptic integrals and regression analysis' – all for just $4900 (about $33,000 today). Consumers didn't know quite what to do with computers, but in his 1969 *Whole Earth Catalog*, author (and former CIA LSD tester) Stewart Brand explained that the technology governments used to run countries could empower ordinary people. Hoping to bring computer power to the people, 21-year-old Steve Jobs and 26-year-old Steve Wozniak introduced the Apple II, with unfathomable memory (4KB of RAM) and microprocessor speed (1MHz), at the 1977 West Coast Computer Faire. But the question remained: what would ordinary people do with all that computing power?

1978

San Francisco elects the nation's first openly gay politician, Harvey Milk (assassinated later that year).

1989

The Bay Area is hit by the 6.9 Loma Prieta earthquake during the World Series. San Francisco earthquake damage, 1989

By the mid-1990s, an entire dot-com industry of online start-ups boomed in Silicon Valley, and suddenly people were getting their mail, news, politics, pet food and, yes, sex online. In the fat years of the late 1990s, companies nationwide jumped on the dot-com bandwagon following the exponential growth of the web, and many reaped huge overnight profits.

Booms, Bankruptcy & Beyond

When dot-com profits weren't forthcoming, venture funding dried up and fortunes in stock options disappeared on one nasty Nasdaq-plummeting day: March 10, 2000. No place in America was more affected by the demise of the dot-coms in 2000 than California. Overnight, 26-year-old vice-presidents and Bay Area service-sector employees alike found themselves jobless. But as online users continued to look for useful information, and for one another, in those billions of web pages, search engines and social media boomed.

Meanwhile, California's biotech industry had already taken off. In 1976 an upstart company called Genentech was founded in the San Francisco Bay Area, and quickly got to work cloning human insulin and introducing the hepatitis B vaccine. In 2004 California voters approved a $3 billion bond measure for stem-cell research, and by 2008 California had become the USA's biggest funder of stem-cell research, as well as the focus of NASDAQ's new Biotechnology Index.

But even these high-tech industries weren't enough to salvage the state's economy when, in 2008, the unraveling subprime mortgage-lending crisis triggered a US stock-market crash and caused the entire nation to sink into a recession. Massive unemployment devastated California, once the world's sixth-largest economy. By 2009 the state was so broke that it issued IOU slips to creditors. Struggling to make ends meet, California began a series of vilified cost-cutting measures that included steep tuition hikes at public universities and severe cutbacks to social services and other public programs, including many of California's 275-plus state parks. More recently, Governor Jerry Brown (Democrat) and state legislators have reversed such austerity measures as the economy bounces back.

2004
The most anticipated IPO in history, Google shares start at $85 (eventually peaking above $1000).

2008
Californians pass Proposition 8, against same-sex marriage. Courts ruled it unconstitutional.

2013
The Bay Bridge's eastern span opens. It's the costliest public works project in California history.

Family Travel

Monterey Bay Aquarium (p181)

California is a tailor-made destination for traveling with kids. In addition to Southern California's theme parks, there are thousands of places to explore. Sunny skies lend themselves to outdoor activities including swimming, snorkeling, bicycling, kayaking, hiking and horseback riding. In winter, when it's cold and rainy or snowing outside, or even during summer when fog hugs the coast, you'll find museums and indoor entertainment galore.

California with Kids

Children's discounts are widely available for everything from museum admission and movie tickets to bus fares and motel stays. The definition of a 'child' varies – in some places anyone under 18 is eligible while at others the cutoff is age six. At amusement parks, some rides may have minimum-height requirements, so let younger kids know about this in advance to avoid disappointment and tears.

It's perfectly fine to bring kids, even toddlers, along to casual restaurants, which often have high chairs. Many diners and family restaurants break out paper place mats and crayons for drawing. Ask about cheaper children's menus too. At theme parks, pack a cooler in the car and have a picnic in the parking lot to avoid ballpark prices. On the road, many larger supermarkets have wholesome, ready-to-eat takeout dishes.

Baby food, infant formula, soy and cow's milk, disposable diapers (nappies) and other necessities are widely available in drugstores and supermarkets. Most women are discreet about breastfeeding in public. Many public toilets have a baby-changing table and gender-neutral private 'family' bathrooms may be available at airports, museums etc.

Children's Highlights

It's easy to keep kids entertained no matter where you travel in California. Throughout this book, look for family attractions and other fun activities, all marked with the child-friendly icon (). At national and state parks, be sure to ask at visitor centers about ranger-led activities and self-guided 'Junior Ranger' programs, in which kids earn themselves a badge after completing an activity.

Theme Parks

- **Disneyland & Disney California Adventure** All ages of kids, even teens and the eternally young at heart, adore the 'Magic Kingdom.'
- **Knott's Berry Farm** SoCal's original thrills-a-minute theme park.
- **Universal Studios Hollywood** Movie-themed action rides, special-effects shows and a tram tour of a working studio backlot.
- **Legoland** In San Diego's North County, this fantasyland of building blocks is made for tots and youngsters.

Aquariums & Zoos

- **Monterey Bay Aquarium** Get acquainted with the denizens of the deep next door to the Central Coast's biggest marine sanctuary.
- **San Diego Zoo & Safari Park** Journey around the world and go on safari outdoors at California's best and biggest zoo.
- **Aquarium of the Pacific** Long Beach's high-tech aquarium houses critters from balmy Baja California to the chilly north Pacific, including a shark lagoon.

Need to Know

- **Changing facilities** Available in most public locations, such as malls and rest stops.
- **Cots** Many hotels offer cots for kids for a fee or occasionally at no cost.
- **Diapers (nappies)** Readily available at grocery stores and even most convenience stores.
- **Health** California retains a very high standard of health and clean facilities.
- **High chairs & kids menus** Almost ubiquitous in casual restaurants; call ahead at upscale places.
- **Strollers** Available to rent at Disneyland and some other theme parks.
- **Transportation** On buses, parents hold children on laps. Car seats are required for children under six or those who weigh less than 60lb.

Beaches

- **Los Angeles** Carnival fun at Santa Monica Pier, Manhattan Beach's waterfront volleyball courts or Malibu's perfect beaches just beyond.
- **Orange County** Newport Beach with its kiddie-sized Balboa Pier rides, Laguna Beach's miles of million-dollar sands, Huntington Beach (aka Surf City, USA) and old-fashioned Seal Beach.
- **San Diego** Head over to Coronado's idyllic Silver Strand, play in Mission Bay by SeaWorld, lap up La Jolla and kick back in surf-style North County beach towns.
- **Central Coast** Laze on Santa Barbara's unmatched beaches, then roll all the way north to Santa Cruz's famous boardwalk and pier.
- **Lake Tahoe** In summer, it's California's favorite high-altitude beach escape: a sparkling diamond tucked in the craggy Sierra Nevada mountains.

Parks

- **Yosemite National Park** Get a juicy slice of Sierra Nevada scenery, with gushing waterfalls, alpine lakes, and glacier-carved valleys and peaks.
- **Redwood National and State Parks** On the misty North Coast, a string of nature preserves protect magnificent wildlife, beaches and the planet's tallest trees.
- **Lassen Volcanic National Park** Off-the-beaten-path destination in the Northern Mountains, with otherworldly volcanic scenery, and lakeside camping and cabins.
- **Griffith Park** Bigger than NYC's Central Park, this LA green space has tons of fun for younger kids, from miniature train rides and a merry-go-round to planetarium shows.

Museums

- **San Francisco** The Bay Area is a mind-bending classroom for kids, especially at the hands-on Exploratorium and ecofriendly California Academy of Sciences.
- **Los Angeles** See stars (the real ones) at the Griffith Observatory, and dinosaur bones at the Page Museum & La Brea Tar Pits.
- **San Diego** Balboa Park is jam-packed with museums like the Reuben H Fleet Science Center (and a world-famous zoo, too), or take younger kids downtown to the engaging New Children's Museum.

Planning

Accommodations

Motels and hotels typically have rooms with two beds or an extra sofa bed, ideal for families. They also may have rollaway beds or cots that can be brought into the room, typically for a surcharge. Some offer 'kids stay free' promotions, although this may apply only if no extra bedding is required. Some B&Bs don't allow children; ask when booking.

Resorts may have drop-off day camps for kids or on-call babysitting services. At other hotels, the front-desk staff or concierge might help you make arrangements. Be sure to ask whether babysitters are licensed and bonded, what they charge per hour per child, whether there's a minimum fee and if they charge extra for transportation and meals.

Transportation

Airlines usually allow infants (up to age two) to fly for free. Children receive substantial discounts on most trains and buses. In cars, any child under age six or weighing less than 60lb must be buckled up in the back seat in a child or infant safety seat. Most car-rental agencies rent these seats for about $10 per day, but you must specifically book them in advance. Rest stops on freeways are few and far between, and gas stations and fast-food bathrooms are frequently icky. However, you're not usually too far from a shopping mall, which generally has well-kept restrooms.

The Best... Attractions for Kids

1 Exploratorium (p106)

2 Monterey Bay Aquarium (p181)

3 Disneyland (p336)

4 San Diego Zoo (p299)

5 Yosemite National Park (p258)

6 Santa Cruz Beach Boardwalk (p173)

What to Pack

Sunscreen. Lots of sunscreen.

And bringing sunscreen will remind you to bring hats, bathing suits, flip-flops and goggles. If you like beach umbrellas and sand chairs, pails and shovels, you'll probably want to bring or buy your own at local supermarkets and drugstores. At many beaches, you can rent bicycles and all kinds of water-sports gear (eg snorkel sets).

For outdoor vacations, bring broken-in hiking shoes and your own camping equipment. Outdoor gear can be purchased or sometimes rented from outdoor outfitters and specialty shops.

If you forget some critical piece of equipment, Traveling Baby Company (www.travelbaby.com) and Baby's Away (www.babysaway.com) rent cribs, strollers, car seats, high chairs, backpacks, beach gear and more.

The Arts

Urban Light by Chris Burden, outside Los Angeles County Museum of Art (LACMA; p62)

California supports thriving music and arts scenes that aren't afraid to be completely independent, even outlandish at times. And thanks to the movie industry, perhaps no other city can claim the pop-cultural influence that Los Angeles exerts worldwide. Meanwhile, writers and musicians have been seeking inspiration in gritty LA and bohemian San Francisco for decades. Southern California in particular has proved to be fertile ground for new architectural styles.

Film & TV

California's major export – film – is a powerful presence in the lives of not only Americans but people around the world. Images of California are distributed far beyond its borders, ultimately reflecting back upon the state itself. With increasing regularity, Hollywood films feature California as both a setting and a topic and, in some cases, almost as a character.

Today, the high cost of filming in LA has sent location scouts beyond the San Fernando Valley (where most movie and TV studios are found) and north of the border to Canada, where they're welcomed with open arms in 'Hollywood North.' A few production companies are still based in the Bay Area, including Pixar Animation Studios, Francis Ford Coppola's American Zoetrope and George

Lucas' Industrial Light & Magic, made up of high-tech gurus who produce computer-generated special effects for Hollywood blockbusters.

The first TV station began broadcasting in Los Angeles in 1931. Through the next decades, iconic images of LA were beamed into living rooms across the US in shows such as *Dragnet* (1950s); *The Beverly Hillbillies* (1960s); *The Brady Bunch* (1970s); *LA Law* (1980s); *Baywatch, Melrose Place* and *The Fresh Prince of Bel-Air* (1990s); and teen 'dramedies' (drama-comedies) *Beverly Hills, 90210* (1990s), which made that LA zip code into a status symbol, and *The OC* (2000s), set in Newport Beach, Orange County. If you're a fan of reality TV, you'll spot Southern California starring in everything from *Top Chef* to *The Real Housewives of Orange County* and MTV's drama-reality hybrids *Laguna Beach* and *The Hills*, about rich, gorgeous twentysomethings cavorting in SoCal. Get a sneak peek of new TV shows by joining a live studio audience in LA.

Literature

Californians read more than movie scripts: they make up the largest market for books in the US, and they read more than the national average. Skewing the curve is bookish San Francisco, with more writers, playwrights and book purchases per capita than any other US city.

The West Coast has long drawn artists and writers, and today California's resident literary community is as strong as ever with such talent as Alice Walker, Pulitzer Prize–winning author of *The Color Purple* (1982); Chilean American novelist Isabel Allende, who wrote *The House of the Spirits* (1982); Amy Tan, author of such popular fiction as *The Joy Luck Club* (1989); Maxine Hong Kingston, coeditor of the landmark anthology *The Literature of California* (2000); Dave Eggers, the hipster behind *McSweeney's* quarterly literary journal; and Michael Chabon, author of the Pulitzer Prize–winning *The Amazing Adventures of Kavalier and Clay* (2000).

Few writers nail California culture as well as Joan Didion. She's best known for her collection of essays, *Slouching Towards Bethlehem* (1968), which takes a caustic look at 1960s flower power and Haight-Ashbury. Tom Wolfe also put '60s San Francisco in perspective with *The Electric Kool-Aid Acid Test* (1968), which follows Ken Kesey's band of Merry Pranksters, who began their acid-laced 'magic bus' journey near Santa Cruz. Charles Bukowski's semiautobiographical novel *Post Office* (1971) captures LA's

Classic California on Celluloid

Here are our top picks for classic California flicks:

- *The Maltese Falcon* (1941) John Huston directs Humphrey Bogart as Sam Spade, the classic San Francisco private eye.
- *Sunset Boulevard* (1950) Billy Wilder's classic stars Gloria Swanson and William Holden in a bonfire of Hollywood vanities.
- *Vertigo* (1958) The Golden Gate Bridge dazzles and dizzies in Alfred Hitchcock's noir thriller starring Jimmy Stewart and Kim Novak.
- *Chinatown* (1974) Roman Polanski's gripping version of the early-20th-century water wars that made and nearly broke LA.
- *LA Story* (1991) Steve Martin lovingly wrote this hilarious, though dated, parody of nearly every aspect of LA life, from enemas to earthquakes.

The Best... Big-City Art Museums

1 Los Angeles County Museum of Art (LACMA; p62)

2 Getty Center, West LA (p69)

3 MH de Young Museum, San Francisco (p107)

4 Asian Art Museum, San Francisco (p100)

5 Museum of Contemporary Art, San Diego (p290)

down-and-out Downtown. Richard Vasquez' *Chicano* (1971) takes a dramatic look at LA's Latino barrio.

Back in the 1930s, San Francisco and LA became the capitals of pulp detective novels, which were often made into classic noir films. Dashiell Hammett (*The Maltese Falcon*, 1930) made San Francisco's fog a sinister character. The king of hard-boiled crime writers was Raymond Chandler (*The Big Sleep*, 1939), who thinly disguised Santa Monica as shadowy Bay City. A renaissance of noir crime fiction has been masterminded by James Ellroy (*LA Confidential*, 1990) and Walter Mosley (*Devil in a Blue Dress*, 1990), whose Easy Rawlins detective novels are set in LA's South Central district.

Music

From smoky jazz clubs that once filled San Francisco's North Beach to hard-edged West Coast rap and hip-hop born in South Central LA, California music has rocked the world. Much of the US recording industry is based in Los Angeles, and SoCal's film and TV industries have proven powerful talent incubators. But today's troubled pop princesses and airbrushed boy bands are only here thanks to the tuneful revolutions of the decades of innovation that came before, from country folk to urban rap.

In the 1960s, Jim Morrison and The Doors busted onto the Sunset Strip, and San Francisco launched the psychedelic-rock revolution with big-name acts such as the Grateful Dead and Janis Joplin. The late '70s and early '80s saw the birth of California's own brand of punk, including the LA-based bands X and Black Flag, and the Dead Kennedys in San Francisco. In the 1980s, the funk-punk sound of the Red Hot Chili Peppers exploded out of LA and avant-garde rocker Frank Zappa's 1982 single *Valley Girl* taught the rest of America to say 'Omigo-o-od!' like an LA teenager.

By the 1990s alternative rock acts like Beck and Weezer had gained national presence. Los Lobos was king of the Latino bands, an honor that has since passed to Ozomatli. Another key '90s band was the ska-punk-alt-rock No Doubt, of Orange County. Berkeley revived punk in the '90s with Grammy Award–winning Green Day. In the late 1990s, the Bay Area birthed underground artists like E-40 and the 'hyphy movement,' a reaction against the increasing commercialization of hip-hop. LA today is still the hotbed for West Coast rap and hip-hop.

Architecture

California's architecture, a fruitful jumble of styles, is as diverse as the state's population. The late-18th and early-19th centuries saw the construction of Spanish colonial missions built with materials that were on hand: adobe, limestone and grass. During the mid-19th-century Gold Rush, California's nouveau riche started constructing grand mansions. Victorian architecture, especially the showy Queen Anne style, is most prevalent in NorCal cities such as San Francisco.

Simplicity was the hallmark of the early-20th-century Arts and Crafts style, a reaction against the mass production of the industrial revolution. Mid-century modernism had characteristics such as boxlike building shapes, open floor plans, plain facades and abundant glass, and was adapted to residential houses that reflected SoCal's see-and-be-seen culture. More recently, postmodernism has sought to reemphasize the structural form of the building and the space around it; examples in LA include Richard Meier's Getty Center and Frank Gehry's Walt Disney Concert Hall.

Visual Arts

With the invention of photography, the improbable truth of California's landscape and its inhabitants was revealed. San Francisco native Ansel Adams' sublime photographs documented the majesty of Yosemite, and Berkeley-based Dorothea Lange turned her unflinching lens on the plight of California migrant workers in the Great Depression and Japanese Americans forced to enter internment camps in WWII.

After WWII, poolside SoCal aesthetics competed with San Francisco's love of rough-and-readymade 1950s Beat collage, 1960s psychedelic Fillmore posters, earthy '70s funk and beautiful-mess punk, and '80s graffiti and skate culture.

Today, the California contemporary art scene brings all these influences together with muralist-led social commentary, cutting-edge technology and an obsessive dedication to craft. To see California art at its most exciting and experimental, don't miss the alternative gallery scene in Culver City and the converted warehouses of Downtown LA. In San Francisco, check out the indie art spaces in the Mission District and laboratory-like galleries and museums in the Yerba Buena arts district.

California Cuisine

Californian summer buffet

AMY NEUNSINGER / GETTY IMAGES ©

If you don't kiss the ground when you set foot in California, you might once you've tried the food. As you graze the Golden State from surfer-worthy fish tacos to foraged-ingredient tasting menus, you'll often have cause to compliment the chef – but they're quick to share the compliment with local producers. What's come to represent California cuisine need not be fancy. It's all about the ingredients.

If not for the hundreds of cultures and nationalities that have immigrated to California over the past 200 years, Californians might never eat. Fusion dominates menus these days, from kimchi tacos to vegan soul food. Like actors' credits in a film, you'll find that California menus often list by name the many cheesemakers, wineries, farms, ranches and fisheries that provide the stellar ingredients.

Regional Cuisine

Los Angeles

Most of California's produce is grown in the hot, irrigated Central Valley, south of the Bay Area, but road-tripping foodies tend to bolt through this sunny stretch lined with fast-food speed traps to reach Los Angeles in time for dinner. Authenticity-trippers know exactly where to go, however: directly to Koreatown for tender *kalbi* (marinated barbecued beef short ribs) and strong *soju* (Korean vodka), East LA for tacos *al pastor* (tacos with marinated fried pork) and margaritas on the rocks, and Little Tokyo for sashimi faceted like diamonds and palate-purifying *junmai* sake.

San Francisco

When San Francisco ballooned into a Gold Rush boomtown of 25,000 in 1850 there was only one woman per 100 men – but there were hundreds of eateries, ranging from ubiquitous Chinese noodle shops to struck-it-rich French fine dining. The first Italian restaurant in the USA opened in San Francisco's North Beach in 1886, serving the ever-popular cioppino (seafood stew).

More than 150 years after that boom went bust, there's still one restaurant for every 466 San Franciscans – that's more than any other North American city. All that competition keeps chefs innovating and prices may be higher than you'd find for equivalent dining experiences elsewhere. Chinese, Mexican, French and Italian restaurants remain perennial local favorites, along with more recent crazes for pho (Vietnamese noodles), fusion food trucks and, yes, even artisanal toast. San Francisco has more award-winning chefs per capita than any other US city (sorry, New York). Today the busiest SF tourist attraction is no longer the Golden Gate Bridge, but the local, sustainable, seasonal bounty at the San Francisco Ferry Plaza Farmers Market.

The Best... Farmers Markets

1 LA's Original Farmers Market (p79)

2 Oxbow Public Market, Napa (p217)

3 Ferry Plaza Farmers Market, San Francisco (p100)

4 Santa Monica Farmers Markets (p80)

5 San Luis Obispo Farmers Market (p188)

The Bay Area & Northern California

Just as influential as (or more so than) San Francisco, the greater Bay Area and Northern California have changed the way the world looks at food. California cuisine was perfected in Berkeley at Alice Waters' iconic Chez Panisse. World-renowned food writer and expert Michael Pollan is a journalism professor at nearby UC Berkeley.

Scratch any food trend's surface and you'll likely find it happening in the Bay Area and Northern California. Marin County, one of the wealthiest in the USA, can afford to make sustainable and organic food a priority.

Napa & Sonoma Wine Country

George Yount (of Yountville fame) was the first Napa resident to plant a few grapevines in the 1830s, and before the arrival of the 20th century, there were already almost 150 wineries in the region. The climate and soil were a perfect mix for agriculture, and the natural hot springs around Calistoga brought tourists in from San Francisco. Even before Prohibition, Northern California's Wine Country was cemented as a destination for folks with a taste for the good life. By the 1930s Sonoma was supplying some excellent Jack cheese to accompany the local wine.

Local chefs have kept the food scene evolving. Chef Thomas Keller transformed Yountville's saloon-turned-restaurant French Laundry into an international foodie landmark in 1994, showcasing local produce and casual elegance in multicourse feasts. Other chefs eager to make their names and fortunes among free-spending wine tasters flocked to the area. If you'd like to learn a thing or two about cooking, you can sign up for day or weekend courses, or a full-time chef training program at the Culinary Institute of America at Greystone in St Helena.

Drinks

Powerful drink explains a lot about California. Mission vineyards planted in the 18th century gave Californians a taste for wine, which led settlers to declare an independent

'Bear Flag Republic' in the Mexican settlement of Sonoma one drunken night in 1846 (it lasted less than a month). The Gold Rush brought a rush on the bar: by 1850, San Francisco had 500 saloons shilling hooch. Today California's traditions of wine, beer and cocktails are converging in saloon revivals, cult winemakers, and microbrewery and microdistillery booms –and for the morning after, specialty coffee roasters.

Wine

Up until the 1830s, mission communion wine was considered fine for Sundays and minor revolutions, but by this time, Californians were importing premium varietals. When imported French wine was slow to arrive via Australia during the Gold Rush, three brothers from Bohemia named Korbel started making their own bubbly in 1882, and today their winery is the biggest US producer of sparkling wines. Drinkers began switching to the local stuff from Sonoma and Napa Valleys, and by the end of the century, vintages from California Wine Country were quietly winning medals at Paris expositions. Some California vines survived federal scrutiny during Prohibition (1920–33), on the grounds that the grapes were needed for sacramental wines back east – a bootlegging bonanza that kept West Coast speakeasies well supplied, and saved old vinestock from being torn out by authorities.

California had an established reputation for mass-market plonk and bottled wine spritzers by 1976, when upstart wineries in Napa Valley and the Santa Cruz Mountains suddenly gained international status. Stag's Leap Wine Cellars Cabernet Sauvignon, Chateau Montelena Chardonnay, and Ridge Monte Bello Cabernet Sauvignon beat venerable French wines to take top honors at a landmark blind tasting by international critics now known as the Judgment of Paris. The tasting was repeated 30 years later, with Stag's Leap and Ridge again taking top honors (Chateau Montelena had sold out its original vintage).

Sonoma, Napa and the Santa Cruz Mountains today continue to produce the state's most illustrious vintages. With an exceptional combination of coastal fog, sunny valleys, rocky hillsides and volcanic soils, the Napa and Sonoma Valleys together mimic wine-growing regions across France and Italy. Precious bottom-land sells for up to $20,000 an acre in skinny, 30-mile-long Napa, where many wineries understandably stick to established, marketable chardonnay and cabernet sauvignon. Neighboring Sonoma County has complex microclimates, with morning fog cover to protect the thin-skinned, prized pinot noir grape.

But California's risk-taking attitude prevails even on prestigious Napa and Sonoma turf, with unconventional red blends and freak-factor pinots with 'forest floor' flavors claiming top honors in the industry.

Today, sustainable winemaking processes have become widespread across California, following the Lodi Rules for green winemaking (see www.lodiwine.com) and pursuing

Food Trucks

Weekday lunches may last only 30 minutes for Californians, and every minute counts. Californians torn between gourmet sit-down meals and enjoying sunshine outdoors no longer have to make a choice: food trucks deliver gourmet options to office hubs, from rotisserie chicken salads to clamshell buns packed with roast duck and fresh mango.

To find out when trucks are coming to a curb near you, search for 'food truck' and your location on **Twitter**. Come prepared with cash and sunblock: most trucks are cash only, and queues for popular trucks can take 10 to 20 minutes. Look for prominently displayed permits as your guarantee of proper food preparation, refrigeration and regulated working conditions.

Demeter certification for biodynamic wines (http://demeter-usa.org). California's renegade winemakers are now experimenting with natural-process winemaking methods such as wild-yeast fermentation, bringing the thrill of the unexpected to tasting rooms across the state. While you're visiting, you may notice owl boxes for pest management, sheep for weed control, and solar panels atop LEED-certified winery buildings – all increasingly standard features of California's 'green' wineries.

The Best... California Brews

1 Anderson Valley Brewery (Mendocino) Boont Amber Ale

2 Stone Brewing Co (San Diego) Arrogant Bastard Ale

3 Anchor Steam (San Francisco) Christmas Ale

4 Bear Republic (Healdsburg) Racer 5 IPA

5 Sierra Nevada (Chico) Pale Ale

Beer

Drinking snobbery is often reversed in California: wine drinkers are always game for a glass of something local and tasty, while beer drinkers fuss over their monk-brewed triple Belgians and debate relative hoppiness levels. California beer-drinkers are spoiled for choice: according to the Brewers' Association, California has almost 400 breweries, more than any other state. You won't get attitude for ordering beer with fancy food here – many California sommeliers are happy to suggest beer pairings with your meal, and some NorCal brewpubs offer tasting plates specifically to accompany beer.

For quality small-batch brews you won't find elsewhere, seek out microbreweries – any self-respecting Californian city has at least one craft brewery or brewpub of note. But for instant relief on scorching summer days, craft beers are widely available at California corner stores in bottles and cans, in six-packs and singles. California's craft breweries are increasingly canning craft beer to make their beer cheaper, greener, and more widely distributed across California, while preserving the classic satisfaction of popping the tab on a cold one outdoors on a hot day.

Spirits

Tonight you're gonna party like it's 1899. Before picking up their shakers at night, local bartenders have spent days dusting off 19th-century recipes. The highest honorific for a California bartender these days isn't mixologist (too technical) or artisan (too medieval), but 'drink historian.' Gone are the mad-scientist's mixology beakers of a decade ago: California bartenders are now judged by their absinthe fountains and displays of swizzle sticks from long-defunct ocean liners. Just don't be surprised if your anachronistic cocktail comes served in a cordial glass, punch bowl or Mason jar, instead of a tumbler, highball or martini glass. All that authenticity-tripping over happy hour may sound self-conscious, but after strong pours at California's vintage saloons and revived speakeasies, consciousness is hardly an issue.

Coffee

When California couples break up, the thorniest issue is: who gets to keep the cafe? Californians are fiercely loyal to specific roasts and baristas, and most first internet dates meet on neutral coffee grounds. Berkeley's Peet's Coffee kicked off this specialty coffee craze for espresso drinks made with single-origin beans in 1966, and in 1971 supplied beans to an upstart competitor known as Starbucks. Santa Cruz was another early adopter of specialty coffee roasting and drinking in 1978 – like Berkeley, it's a college town – and Santa Cruz Coffee Roasting became one of the first US roasters and cafes to offer certified fair-trade coffee beans.

Beaches & Outdoor Activities

Cyclist, Tioga Pass, Yosemite National Park (p260)

KYLE SPARKS / GETTY IMAGES ©

Californians know they're spoiled silly with spectacular natural riches, so they express their gratitude by taking every chance to hit the trails, hop onto the saddle or grab a paddle. Now it's your turn: go kayaking under sea arches and along rocky coastlines, spot a whale breaching off the bow of your boat or make your California dreamin' come true with a surfing lesson.

Swimming

If lazing on the beach and taking quick dips in the Pacific is what you've got in mind, look to Southern California (SoCal). With miles and miles of wide, sandy beaches, you won't find it hard to get wet and wild, especially between Santa Barbara and San Diego. Once you get far enough south, let's say Santa Barbara, the beaches become golden and sandy, and the weather and the waters turn balmy. By the time you hit Los Angeles, Orange County (aka 'the OC') and San Diego, you'll find SoCal beach culture in full swing – at least during summer. SoCal beaches can be chilly and too stormy for swimming in winter. Ocean temperatures become tolerable by May or June, peaking in July and August.

Northern California waters are unbearably cold year-round, with a dangerously high swell in places and rocky beaches that often make swimming uninviting. Diehards should bring or rent a wetsuit!

The biggest hazards along the coast are riptides and dangerous ocean currents. Popular beaches have lifeguards, but can still be dangerous places to swim. Obey all posted warning signs and ask about local conditions before venturing out. If you get caught in a riptide, which pulls you away from shore, don't fight it or you'll get exhausted and drown. Instead, swim parallel to the shoreline and, once the current stops pulling you out, swim back to shore.

Surfing

Surf's up! Are you down? Even if you never set foot on a board – and we, like, totally recommend that you do, dude – there's no denying the influence of surfing on every aspect of Californian beach life. Invented by Pacific Islanders, surfing first washed ashore in 1914, when business tycoon Henry Huntington invited Irish Hawaiian surfer George Freeth to LA to help promote real-estate developments – California has never been the same since.

The state has plenty of easily accessible world-class surf spots, with the lion's share in SoCal. You won't find many killer spots north of the San Francisco Bay Area. Famous surf spots southbound include Mavericks, past Half Moon Bay, south of San Francisco; Steamer Lane in Santa Cruz; Rincon Point, outside Santa Barbara; Surfrider in Malibu; and Trestles, south of San Clemente in the OC. All are point breaks, known for their consistently clean, glassy, big waves.

Generally speaking, the most powerful swells arrive in winter (especially at Mavericks, world-famous for its big-wave surfing competition), while early summer sees the flattest conditions (except at Trestles, which still goes off then) but also warmer waters. Bring or rent a wet suit.

Scuba Diving & Snorkeling

All along the coast, rocky reefs, shipwrecks and kelp forests teem with sea creatures ready for their close-up. Santa Catalina Island and Channel Islands National Park are hot spots for diving and snorkeling. Thanks to the Monterey Bay National Marine Sanctuary, Monterey Bay offers year-round, world-renowned diving and snorkeling, though you'll need to don a wet suit. Nearby Point Lobos State Natural Reserve is another diving gem. North of San Francisco, dive boats depart from windy Bodega Bay.

Move Your Bod

If you don't have the time or inclination to master the art of surfing, there are other ways to catch your 'dream wave' at many SoCal beaches. Bodysurfing and body boarding (or boogie boarding) can extend your ride on the waves, sometimes as much as 100ft (30.5m) or more. Both sports benefit from the use of flippers to increase speed and control. If you're not sure how to do it, watch others or strike up a watery kinship and simply ask for pointers. But it's really pretty easy, and you'll be howling with glee once you catch that first wave.

Windsurfing & Kitesurfing

Experienced windsurfers tear up the waves up and down the coast, while newbies (or those who want a mellower ride) skim along calm bays and protected beaches. There's almost always a breeze, with the best winds springing up from September through November, but the water is cold year-round and, unless you're a polar bear, a wet suit is a necessity. Any place that has good windsurfing usually has good kitesurfing. Look for surfers doing aerial acrobatics while parachute-like kites propel them over the waves.

Kayaking

Few water sports are as accessible or as much fun for the whole family as kayaking. Prior experience is rarely necessary. Lots of rental outfitters can be found along the Central Coast, for example in Morro Bay, whose waters are protected by a gorgeous 4-mile sand spit, and from Monterey north to Santa Cruz, especially around Elkhorn Slough. Sausalito in Marin County is a mere paddle's-length away from San Francisco's skyline, while sheltered Tomales Bay at Point Reyes National Seashore and Bodega Bay are also popular spots.

As you head further up the chilly north coast, various small towns offer challenging put-in points for experienced sea kayakers. On the Redwood Coast, you can take a scenic spin around Humboldt Bay, Trinidad Cove or Humboldt Lagoons State Park, with outfitters in Eureka and Arcata. Meanwhile, SoCal's warmer waters beckon sea kayakers to Santa Catalina Island and Channel Islands National Park offshore, and San Diego's Mission Bay and La Jolla.

Whale-Watching

During summer, majestic gray whales feed in the Arctic waters between Alaska and Siberia, and every fall they start moving south down the Pacific Coast to the sheltered lagoons of the Gulf of California in Mexico's Baja California. While there, pregnant whales give birth to calves weighing up to 1500lb (680kg; which go on to live up to 60 years, grow to 50ft in length and weigh up to 40 tons). In early spring, these whales turn around and head back to the Arctic. Luckily for us, during their 12,000-mile round-trip, these whales pass just off the California coast between December and April.

Mothers tend to keep newborn calves closer to shore for safety, so your best chances of catching a glimpse may be during the whales' northbound migration. You can try your luck from shore (free, but you're less likely to see anything and are more removed from the action) or by taking a boat cruise. A few of the best dockside spots from which to point your binoculars include Point Reyes Lighthouse, Bodega Head on the North Coast, and Cabrillo National Monument at San Diego's Point Loma.

Hiking

California is perfect for exploring on foot, whether you've got your heart set on peak-bagging in the Sierra Nevada, trekking to desert palm-tree oases, rambling among the world's tallest, largest or most ancient trees, or simply heading for a coastal walk accompanied by booming surf. The best trails are generally found among the jaw-dropping scenery in national and state parks, national forests and wilderness areas. You can choose from an infinite variety of routes, from easy, interpretive nature walks negotiable by wheelchairs and baby strollers to multiday backpacking routes through rugged wilderness. Parks and forests almost always have a visitors center or ranger station with clued-in staff to offer route suggestions, trail-specific tips and weather forecasts. The most popular backcountry trails may be subject to daily quotas and require wilderness permits for overnight backpacking or occasionally day hikes.

Camping

All across California, campers are absolutely spoiled for choice. You can pitch a tent beside alpine lakes and streams with views of snaggle-toothed Sierra Nevada peaks, along gorgeous strands of Southern California sand or on the wilder, windswept beaches of the north coast. Take shelter underneath redwoods, the tallest trees on earth, from south of San Francisco north to the Oregon border. Inland, deserts are magical places to camp, especially next to sand dunes on full-moon nights. If you don't have your own tent, you can rent or buy camping gear in most cities and some towns.

The Best... Places to Swim

1 San Diego: La Jolla, Coronado

2 Orange County: Newport Beach, Laguna Beach

3 Los Angeles: Santa Monica, South Bay

4 Central Coast: Carpinteria, Santa Barbara

Rock Climbing

Rock hounds can test their mettle on world-class climbs on the big walls and granite domes of Yosemite National Park, where the climbing season runs from April through October. In the warmest summer months, climbers move camp from the Yosemite Valley to Tuolumne Meadows, off Tioga Rd, which also has good bouldering. In SoCal, Joshua Tree National Park is another climbing mecca, with over 8000 established routes ranging from boulders and cracks to multipitch faces; the climbing season runs year-round, but beware of blistering summer heat. Both of these national parks are excellent places to try the sport for the first time, and outdoor outfitters offer guided climbs and instruction. Other prime spots for bouldering and rock climbing include Bishop in the Eastern Sierra and Sequoia and Kings Canyon National Parks, south of Yosemite.

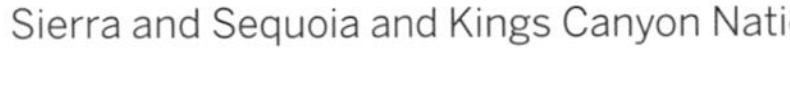

Cycling & Mountain Biking

Top up those tires and strap on that helmet! California is outstanding cycling territory, whether you're off for a leisurely spin by the beach, an adrenaline-fueled mountain ride or a multiday cycling tour along the Pacific Coast Hwy.

With few exceptions, mountain biking is not allowed in wilderness areas or on trails in national or state parks, but you can usually cycle on paved or dirt roads that are open to vehicles. Mountain bikers are allowed on single-track trails in national forests and Bureau of Land Management (BLM) areas, but must yield to hikers and stock animals.

Snow Sports

High-speed modern ski lifts, mountains of fresh powder, a cornucopia of trails from easy-peasy 'Sesame Street' to black-diamond 'Death Wish,' skyscraping alpine scenery, luxury mountain cabins – they're all hallmarks of a vacation in the snow in California. The Sierra Nevada offers the best slopes and trails for skiers and snowboarders, although conditions have been less reliable in recent years due to lack of snowfall.

Over a dozen downhill skiing and snowboarding resorts ring Lake Tahoe, and the season at Mammoth Mountain in the Eastern Sierra usually lasts into May. For family-friendly sno-parks that offer sledding and snow play, visit http://ohv.parks.ca.gov/?page_id=1233 online.

White-Water Rafting

California has scads of mind-blowing rivers, and feeling their surging power is like taking a thrilling ride on nature's roller coaster. Sure, there are serene floats suitable for picnics with grandma and the kiddies, but then there are others. White-water giants swelled by the snowmelt rip through sheer canyons, and roaring cataracts hurtle you through chutes where gushing water compresses through a 10ft gap between menacing boulders. Pour-overs, voracious hydraulics, endless Class III-IV standing waves wrench at your shoulders as you scream and punch on through to the next onslaught. Paddling these giant white-water rapids, your thoughts are reduced to just two simple words: 'survive' and 'damn!' Too much for you? Between the two extremes run myriad others suited to the abilities of any wannabe river rat.

Rafters, Kern River, Sierra Nevada
WITOLD SKRYPCZAK / GETTY IMAGES ©

Land & Wildlife

Bear footprint, Yosemite National Park (p258)

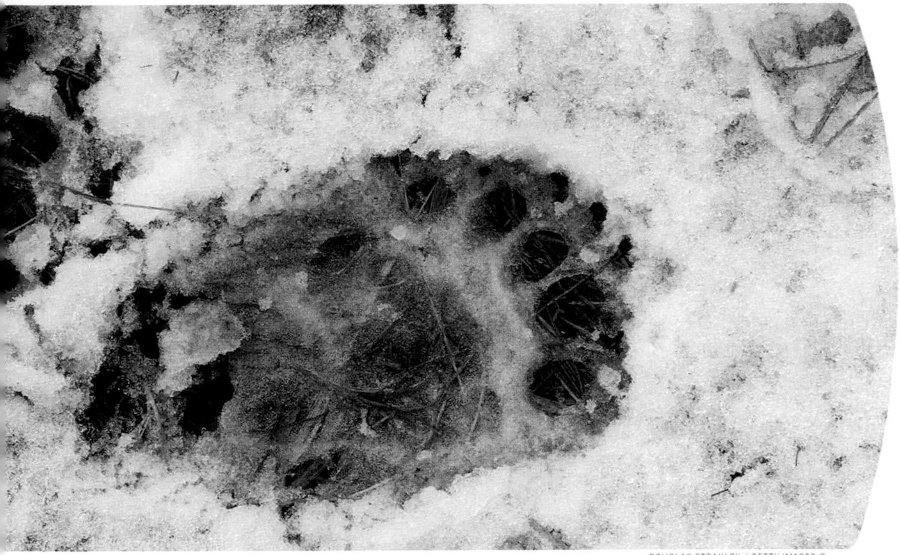

DOUGLAS STEAKLEY / GETTY IMAGES ©

From soaring snowcapped peaks, to scorching deserts and dense forests, California is home to a bewildering variety of ecosystems and animals. The state not only has the highest biodiversity in North America, it has more types of climate and more types of soils than nearly any location in the world. Much of coastal California has a Mediterranean climate, characterized by dry summers and mild wet winters.

The Land

The third-largest US state after Alaska and Texas, California covers more than 155,000 sq miles and is larger than the UK. It is bordered to the north by Oregon, to the south by Mexico, with Nevada and Arizona on its eastern border, and 840 miles of glorious Pacific shoreline on the west. Its cool northern border stands at the same latitude as Rome, Italy, while the arid southern border is at the same latitude as Tel Aviv, Israel.

Geology & Earthquakes

California has a complex geologic landscape formed from fragments of rock and earth crust scraped together as the North American continent drifted westward over hundreds of millions of years. Crumpled coast ranges, the downward-bowing Central Valley and the still-rising Sierra Nevada all provide evidence of gigantic forces exerted as the continental and ocean plates crushed together.

Everything changed about 25 million years ago, when the ocean plates stopped colliding and instead started sliding against each other, creating the massive San Andreas Fault. Because this contact zone doesn't slide smoothly, but catches and slips irregularly, it rattles California with an ongoing succession of tremors and earthquakes.

The state's most famous earthquake in 1906 measured 7.8 on the Richter scale and demolished San Francisco, leaving more than 3000 people dead. The Bay Area made headlines again in 1989 when the Loma Prieta earthquake (6.9) caused a section of the Bay Bridge to collapse. Los Angeles' last 'big one' was in 1994, when the Northridge quake (6.7) caused parts of the Santa Monica Fwy to fall down, making it the most costly quake in US history – so far.

Mountains & Valleys

Much of the California coast is fronted by rugged, little-explored coastal mountains that capture winter's water-laden storms. San Francisco divides the coastal ranges roughly in half: the foggy North Coast remains sparsely populated, while the Central and southern coasts have a balmy climate, sandy beaches and lots of people.

On their eastern flanks, the coastal ranges subside into gently rolling hills that give way to the sprawling Central Valley. Further east looms California's most prominent topographic feature, the world-famous Sierra Nevada. At 400 miles long and 70 miles wide, it's one of the largest mountain ranges in the world and a vast wilderness areas with 13 peaks over 14,000ft (4267m).

Deserts

All lands east of the Sierra Nevada crest are dry and desertlike, receiving less than 10in of rain a year. Areas in the northern half of the state, especially on the elevated Modoc Plateau of northeastern California, are a cold desert blanketed with hardy sagebrush shrubs and pockets of juniper trees. Temperatures increase to the south, with a prominent transition occurring when you descend from Mammoth to Bishop and the Owens Valley. This hot desert (the Mojave Desert) includes Death Valley, one of the hottest places on earth.

Southern California is a hodgepodge of small mountain ranges and desert basins. Mountains on the eastern border of the Los Angeles Basin continue southward past San Diego and down the spine of northern Baja California, while the Mojave Desert of the southern Sierra Nevada morphs into the Colorado Desert around the Salton Sea. This entire region is dry and rocky, and mostly devoid of vegetation except for pockets of desert-adapted shrubs, cacti and Joshua trees.

National & State Parks

The majority of Californians rank outdoor recreation as vital to their quality of life, and the amount of preserved lands has steadily grown due to important pieces of legislation passed since the 1960s, including the landmark 1976 California Coastal Act, which saved the coastline from further development. Today, California State Parks protect nearly one-third of the state's coastline, along with redwood forests, mountain lakes, desert canyons, waterfalls, wildlife preserves and historical sites.

In recent years, both federal and state budget shortfalls and chronic underfunding have been partly responsible for widespread park closures, more limited visitor services and steadily rising park-entry and outdoor recreation fees. And unfortunately, some of California's parks are also being loved to death. Overcrowding severely impacts the environment, and it's increasingly difficult to balance public access with conservation. Try to visit big-name parks such as Yosemite in the shoulder seasons (ie not summer) to avoid the biggest crowds. Alternatively, lesser-known parks, especially in the northern mountains and Southern California deserts, may go relatively untouched most of the year.

Wildlife

Much of California is a biological island cut off from the rest of North America by the soaring heights of the Sierra Nevada and, as on other 'islands' in the world, evolution creates unique plants and animals under these conditions. As a result, California ranks first in the nation for its number of endemic plants, amphibians, reptiles, freshwater fish and mammals. Even more impressive, 30% of all the plant species, 50% of all the bird species and 50% of all the mammal species found in the USA exist in California.

Animals

Many types of birds, including ducks and geese, either pass through California or linger through the winter, making the state one of the top destinations in North America for bird-watchers. Year-round, the best places to see birds are the state's beaches, estuaries and bays, where herons, cormorants, shorebirds and gulls gather.

The black bear is one of the most magnificent animal species found in California. This burly omnivore feeds on berries, nuts, roots, grasses, insects, eggs, small mammals and fish, but can become a nuisance around camping grounds and mountain cabins where food is not properly stored.

The Best... Impressive Peaks

1 Mt Whitney (14,505ft)

2 Mt Shasta (14,162ft)

3 Telescope Peak, Death Valley (11,049ft)

4 Mammoth Mountain, Mammoth Lakes (11,053ft)

5 Half Dome, Yosemite National Park (8842ft)

Mountain lions hunt throughout the mountains and forests of California, especially in areas teeming with deer. Solitary lions, which can grow 8ft in length and weigh 175lb, are formidable predators. The few attacks on humans occur mostly where encroachment has pushed hungry lions to their limits – for example, at the boundaries between wilderness and rapidly developing suburbs.

The coast of California is blessed with a fantastic assortment of marine mammals, including one of the few whale migration routes in the world that can be easily viewed from land or near-shore boats (see p380). It also offers many chances to see sleek seals, bulky sea lions and mammoth elephant seals weighing more than 6000lb.

Plants

When it comes to plants, California is a land of superlatives: the tallest (coastal redwoods approaching 380ft), the largest (giant sequoias of the Sierra Nevada exceeding 36ft across at the base) and the oldest (bristlecone pines of the White Mountains that are almost 5000 years old). The giant sequoia, which is unique to California, survives in isolated groves scattered on the Sierra Nevada's western slopes, including in Yosemite, Sequoia and Kings Canyon National Parks.

Water is an overriding issue for many of California's plants because there is almost no rain during the prime growing season. Desert areas begin their peak blooming in February, with other lowland areas of the state producing abundant wildflowers through April.

Environmental Issues

California has the largest human population of any US state and one of the highest projected growth rates in the nation, putting a tremendous strain on California's many precious resources. Although California is in many ways a success story, development and growth have come at great environmental cost.

Elephant Seals

Northern elephant seals follow a precise calendar. In November and December, adult male 'bull seals' return to their colony's favorite Californian beaches and start the ritual struggles to assert superiority; only the largest, strongest and most aggressive 'alpha' males gather a harem. In January and February, adult females, already pregnant from last year's beach antics, give birth to their pups and soon mate with the dominant males, who promptly depart on their next feeding migration.

Female seals leave the beach in March, abandoning their offspring. For up to two months the young seals, now known as 'weaners,' lounge around in groups, gradually learning to swim, first in tidal pools, then in the sea. Then they, too, depart by May.

Between June and October, elephant seals of all ages and both sexes return in smaller numbers to the beaches to molt.

Water, or the lack thereof, has always been at the heart of California's epic environmental struggles and catastrophes. Despite campaigning by California's greatest environmental champion, John Muir, in the 1920s the Tuolumne River was dammed at Hetch Hetchy (inside Yosemite National Park) so that San Francisco could have drinking water. Likewise, the diversion of water to the Los Angeles area has contributed to the destruction of Owens Lake and its fertile wetlands, and the degradation of Mono Lake.

Although air quality in California has improved markedly over the past two decades, auto exhaust and industrial emissions continue to produce smog, making sunny days in Los Angeles and the Central Valley look hazy.

Survival Guide

Cyclists, Santa Barbara Wine Country (p196)
ED FREEMAN / GETTY IMAGES ©

Directory

Sleeping Price Ranges

The following price ranges refer to a private room with bath during high season, unless otherwise specified. Taxes and breakfast are not normally included in the price.

- **$** less than $100
- **$$** $100 to $200
- **$$$** more than $200

Accommodations

Amenities

- Budget-conscious accommodations include campgrounds, hostels and motels. Because midrange properties generally offer better value for money, most of our accommodations fall into this category.
- At midrange motels and hotels, expect clean, comfortable and decent-sized rooms with at least a private bathroom, and standard amenities such as cable TV, direct-dial telephone, a coffeemaker, and perhaps a microwave and mini fridge.
- Top-end lodgings offer top-notch amenities and perhaps a scenic location, high design or historical ambience. Pools, fitness rooms, business centers, full-service restaurants and bars and other convenient facilities are all standard.
- In Southern California, nearly all lodgings have air-conditioning, but in Northern California, where it rarely gets hot the opposite is true. In coastal areas as far south as Santa Barbara, only fans may be provided.
- Accommodations offering online computer terminals for guests are designated with the internet icon. A fee may apply (eg at full-service business centers inside hotels).
- There may be a fee for wireless internet, especially for in-room access. Look for free wi-fi hot spots in hotel public areas (eg lobby, poolside).
- Many lodgings are now exclusively nonsmoking. Where they still exist, smoking rooms are often left unrenovated and in less desirable locations. Expect a hefty 'cleaning fee' ($100 or more) if you light up in designated nonsmoking rooms.

Rates & Reservations

- Generally, midweek rates are lower except at urban hotels geared toward business travelers, which lure leisure travelers with weekend deals.
- Discount membership cards (eg AAA, AARP) may get you about 10% off standard rates at participating hotels and motels.
- Look for freebie ad magazines packed with hotel and motel discount coupons at gas stations, highway rest areas, tourist offices and online at **HotelCoupons** (http://hotelcoupons.com).
- High season is from June to August everywhere, except the deserts and mountain ski areas, where December through April are the busiest months.
- Demand and prices spike even higher around major holidays and for festivals, when some properties may impose multiday minimum stays.
- Reservations are recommended for weekend and holiday travel year-round, and every day of the week during high season.

Book Your Stay Online

For more accommodations reviews by Lonely Planet authors, check out http://hotels.lonelyplanet.com. You'll find independent reviews, as well as recommendations on the best places to stay. Best of all, you can book online.

- Bargaining may be possible for walk-in guests without reservations, especially at off-peak times.

B&Bs & Vacation Rentals

If you want an atmospheric or perhaps romantic alternative to impersonal motels and hotels, bed-and-breakfast inns typically inhabit fine old Victorian houses or other heritage buildings, bedecked with floral wallpaper and antique furnishings. Travelers who prefer privacy may find B&Bs too intimate.

Rates often include breakfast, but occasionally do not (never mind what the name 'B&B' suggests). Amenities vary widely, but rooms with TV and telephone are the exception; the cheapest units share bathrooms. Standards are high at places certified by the **California Association of Boutique & Breakfast Inns** (www.cabbi.com). Quality varies wildly at hosted and DIY-style vacation rental properties listed with **Airbnb** (www.airbnb.com) and **Vacation Rentals By Owner** (www.vrbo.com).

Most B&Bs require advance reservations; only a few will accommodate drop-in guests. Smoking is generally prohibited and children are usually not welcome. Multiple-night minimum stays may be required, especially on weekends and during high season.

Climate

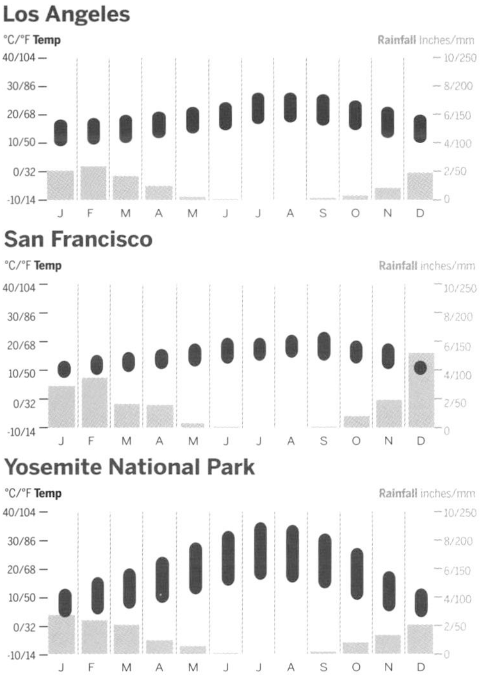

Los Angeles

°C/°F **Temp** — **Rainfall** Inches/mm

40/104, 30/86, 20/68, 10/50, 0/32, -10/14 — 10/250, 8/200, 6/150, 4/100, 2/50, 0

J F M A M J J A S O N D

San Francisco

°C/°F **Temp** — **Rainfall** inches/mm

40/104, 30/86, 20/68, 10/50, 0/32, -10/14 — 10/250, 8/200, 6/150, 4/100, 2/50, 0

J F M A M J J A S O N D

Yosemite National Park

°C/°F **Temp** — **Rainfall** inches/mm

40/104, 30/86, 20/68, 10/50, 0/32, -10/14 — 10/250, 8/200, 6/150, 4/100, 2/50, 0

J F M A M J J A S O N D

Customs Regulations

Currently, non-US citizens and permanent residents may import:

- 1L of alcohol (if you're over 21 years old)
- 200 cigarettes (one carton) or 100 non-Cuban cigars (if you're over 18 years old)
- $100 worth of gifts

Amounts higher than $10,000 in cash, traveler's checks, money orders and other cash equivalents must be declared. Don't even think about bringing in illegal drugs. For more complete, up-to-date information, check the **US Customs and Border Protection website** (www.cbp.gov).

Discount Cards

'America the Beautiful' Annual Pass (http://store.usgs.gov/pass; 12-month pass $80) Admits four adults and all children under 16 years for free to all national parks and federal recreational lands (eg USFS, BLM) for 12 months from the date of purchase. US citizens and permanent residents aged 62 years and older are eligible for a lifetime Senior Pass ($10), which grants free entry and 50% off some recreational-use fees such as camping.

American Association of Retired Persons (AARP; 800-566-0242; www.aarp.org; annual membership $16) This advocacy group for Americans 50 years and older offers member discounts (usually 10%) on hotels, car rentals and more.

American Automobile Association (AAA; 877-428-2277; www.aaa.com; annual membership from $57) Members of AAA and its foreign affiliates (eg CAA) qualify for small discounts (usually 10%) on Amtrak trains, car rentals, motels and hotels, chain restaurants and shopping, tours and theme parks.

Go Los Angeles, San Diego & San Francisco Cards (www.smarterdestinations.com; 1-day pass adult/child from $58/50) The Go LA Card and pricier Go San Diego Card include admission to major SoCal theme parks (but not Disneyland). The cheaper Go San Francisco Card covers museums, bicycle rental and a bay cruise. You've got to do a lot of sightseeing over multiple days to make passes even come close to paying off. For discounts, buy online.

Southern California CityPass (www.citypass.com/southern-california; adult/child from $328/284) If you're visiting SoCal theme parks, CityPass covers three-day admission to Disneyland and Disney California Adventure and one-day admission each to Universal Studios and SeaWorld, with add-ons available for Legoland and the San Diego Zoo or Safari Park. Passes are valid for 14 days from the first day of use. It's cheapest to buy them online in advance.

Electricity

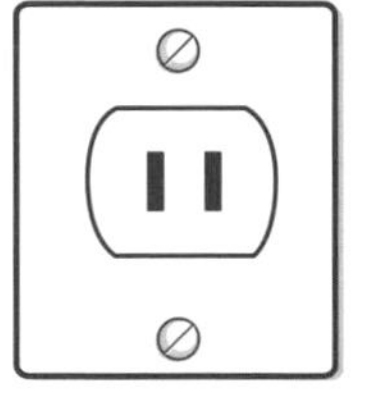

120V/60Hz

Food

- Lunch is generally served between 11:30am and 2:30pm, and dinner between 5pm and 9pm daily, though some restaurants stay open later, especially on Friday and Saturday nights.
- If breakfast is served, it's usually between 7:30am and 10:30am. Some diners and cafes keep serving breakfast into the afternoon, or all day. Weekend brunch is a laid-back affair, usually available from 11am until 3pm on Saturdays and Sundays.
- Like all things Californian, restaurant etiquette tends to be informal. Only a handful of restaurants require more than a dressy shirt, slacks and a decent pair of shoes; most places require far less.
- Tipping 18% to 20% is expected anywhere you receive table service.
- Smoking is illegal indoors. Some restaurants have patios or sidewalk tables where smoking is tolerated (ask first, or look around for ashtrays), but don't expect your neighbors to be happy about secondhand smoke.
- You can bring your own wine to most restaurants; a 'corkage' fee of $15 to $30 usually applies. Lunches rarely include booze, though a glass of wine or beer, while not common everywhere, is socially acceptable.

Eating Price Ranges

The following price ranges refer to an average main course at dinner, unless otherwise stated. These prices don't include taxes or tip. Note the same dishes at lunch will usually be cheaper, even half-price.

- **$** less than $10
- **$$** $10 to $20
- **$$$** more than $20

- If you ask the kitchen to divide a plate between two (or more) people, there may be a small split-plate surcharge.
- Vegetarians, vegans and travelers with food allergies or restrictions are in luck – many restaurants are used to catering to specific dietary needs.

Gay & Lesbian Travelers

California is a magnet for LGBTQ travelers. Hot spots include the Castro in San Francisco, West Hollywood (WeHo), Silver Lake and Long Beach in LA, San Diego's Hillcrest neighborhood, the desert resort of Palm Springs, Guerneville in the Russian River Valley and Calistoga in Napa Valley. Some scenes are predominantly male-oriented, but women usually won't feel too left out.

Same-sex marriage is legal in California. Despite widespread tolerance, homophobic bigotry still exists. In small towns, especially away from the coast, tolerance often comes down to a 'don't ask, don't tell' policy.

Helpful Resources

Advocate (www.advocate.com/travel) Online news, gay travel features and destination guides.

Damron (www.damron.com) Classic, advertiser-driven gay travel guides and 'Gay Scout' mobile app.

GayCities (www.gaycities.com) Local events, activities, tours, lodging, shopping, restaurants, bars and nightlife in a dozen California cities.

Gay.net Travel (www.gay.net/travel) City guides, travel news and pride events.

Gay & Lesbian National Hotline (☎ 888-843-4564; www.glnh.org; ⌚ 1-9pm Mon-Fri, 9am-2pm Sat) For counseling and referrals of any kind.

Out Traveler (www.outtraveler.com) Free online magazine with travel tips, destination guides and hotel reviews.

Purple Roofs (www.purpleroofs.com) Online directory of LGBTQ accommodations.

Health

Healthcare & Insurance

- Medical treatment in the USA is of the highest caliber, but the expense could kill you. Many health-care professionals demand payment at the time of service, especially from out-of-towners or international visitors.
- Except for medical emergencies (in which case call ☎ 911 or go to the nearest 24-hour hospital emergency room, or ER), phone around to find a doctor who will accept your insurance.
- Keep all receipts and documentation for billing and insurance claims, and reimbursement purposes.
- Some health-insurance policies require you to get pre-authorization for medical treatment before seeking help.

Practicalities

- **DVDs** Coded for region 1 (USA and Canada only)
- **Electricity** 110/120V AC, 50/60Hz
- **Newspapers** *Los Angeles Times* (www.latimes.com), *San Francisco Chronicle* (www.sfchronicle.com), *San Jose Mercury News* (www.mercurynews.com), *Sacramento Bee* (www.sacbee.com)
- **Radio** National Public Radio (NPR), lower end of FM dial
- **Time** California is on Pacific Standard Time (UTC-8). Clocks are set one hour ahead during Daylight Saving Time (DST), from the second Sunday in March until the first Sunday in November.
- **TV** PBS (public broadcasting); cable: CNN (news), ESPN (sports), HBO (movies), Weather Channel
- **Weights & Measures** Imperial (except 1 US gallon = 0.83 gallons)

- Overseas visitors with travel-health-insurance policies may need to contact a call center for an assessment by phone before getting medical treatment.

Insurance

Getting travel insurance to cover theft, loss and medical problems is highly recommended. Some policies do not cover 'risky' activities such as scuba diving, motorcycling and skiing so read the fine print. Make sure the policy at least covers hospital stays and an emergency flight home.

Paying for your airline ticket or rental car with a credit card may provide limited travel accident insurance. If you already have private US health insurance or a homeowners or renters policy, find out what those policies cover and only get supplemental insurance. If you have prepaid a large portion of your vacation, trip cancellation insurance may be a worthwhile expense.

Worldwide travel insurance is available at www.lonelyplanet.com/travel-insurance. You can buy, extend and claim online anytime – even if you're already on the road.

Internet Access

- Cybercafes typically charge $6 to $12 per hour for online access.
- With branches in most cities and towns, **FedEx Office** (**☎800-463-3339; www.fedex.com/us/office**) offers internet access at self-service computer workstations (30¢ to 40¢ per minute) and sometimes free wi-fi, plus digital-photo printing and CD-burning stations.
- Accommodations, cafes, restaurants, bars etc that provide guest computer terminals for going online are identified by the internet icon; the wi-fi icon indicates that wireless access is available. There may be a charge for either service.
- Free or fee-based wi-fi hot spots can be found at major airports; many hotels, motels and coffee shops (eg Starbucks); and some tourist information centers, campgrounds (eg KOA), stores (eg Apple), bars and restaurants (including fast-food chains such as McDonald's).
- Free public wi-fi is proliferating (for a list, visit www.ca.gov/WiFi) and even some state parks are now wi-fi–enabled (get details at www.parks.ca.gov).
- Public libraries have internet terminals (online time may be limited, advance sign-up required and a nominal fee charged for out-of-network visitors) and, increasingly, free wi-fi.

Legal Matters

Drugs & Alcohol

- Possession of less than 1oz of marijuana is a misdemeanor in California. Possession of any other drug or an ounce or more of weed is a felony punishable by lengthy jail time. For foreigners, conviction of any drug offense is grounds for deportation.
- Police can give roadside sobriety checks to assess if you've been drinking or using drugs. If you fail, they'll require you to take a breath, urine or blood test to determine if your blood-alcohol level is over the legal limit (0.08%). Refusing to be tested is treated the same as if you had taken and failed the test.
- Penalties for driving under the influence (DUI) of drugs or alcohol range from license suspension and fines to jail time.
- It's illegal to carry open containers of alcohol inside a vehicle, even if they're empty. Unless they're full and still sealed, store them in the trunk.
- Consuming alcohol anywhere other than at a private residence or licensed premises is a no-no, which puts most parks and beaches off-limits (although many campgrounds allow it).
- Bars, clubs and liquor stores often ask for photo ID to prove you are of legal drinking age (21 years old). Being 'carded' is standard practice, so don't take it personally.

Police & Security

- For police, fire and ambulance emergencies, dial 911. For nonemergency police assistance, contact the nearest local police station (dial 411 for directory assistance).
- If you are stopped by the police, be courteous. Don't get out of the car unless asked.

Keep your hands where the officer can see them (eg on the steering wheel) at all times.

- There is no system of paying fines on the spot. Attempting to pay the fine to the officer may lead to a charge of attempted bribery.
- For traffic violations the ticketing officer will explain your options. There is usually a 30-day period to pay a fine; most matters can be handled by mail or online.
- If you are arrested, you have the right to remain silent and are presumed innocent until proven guilty. Everyone has the right to make one phone call. If you don't have a lawyer, one will be appointed to you free of charge. Foreign travelers who don't have a lawyer, friends or family to help should call their embassy or consulate; the police can provide the number upon request.
- Due to security concerns about terrorism, never leave your bags unattended, especially not at airports or bus and train stations.
- Carrying mace or cayenne-pepper spray is legal in California, as long as the spray bottle contains no more than 2.5oz of active product. Federal law prohibits it from being carried on planes.
- In cases of sexual assault, rape crisis center and hospital staff can advocate on your behalf and act as a liaison to community services, including the police. Telephone books have listings of local crisis centers, or call the 24-hour **National Sexual Assault Hotline** (800-656-4673; www.rainn.org).

Smoking

- Smoking is generally prohibited inside all public buildings, including airports, shopping malls and train and bus stations.
- There is no smoking allowed inside restaurants, although lighting up may be tolerated at outdoor patio or sidewalk tables (ask first).
- At hotels, you must specifically request a smoking room, but note some properties are entirely nonsmoking by law.
- In some cities and towns, smoking outdoors within a certain distance of any public business is illegal.

Money

ATMs

- ATMs are available 24/7 at most banks, shopping malls, airports and grocery and convenience stores.
- Expect a minimum surcharge of around $3 per transaction, in addition to any fees charged by your home bank.
- Most ATMs are connected to international networks and offer decent foreign-exchange rates.
- Withdrawing cash from an ATM using a credit card usually incurs a hefty fee and high interest rates; contact your credit-card company for details and a PIN number.

Cash

- Most people do not carry large amounts of cash for everyday use, relying instead on credit and debit cards. Some businesses refuse to accept bills over $20.

Credit Cards

- Major credit cards are almost universally accepted. In fact, it's almost impossible to rent a car, book a hotel room or buy tickets over the phone without one. A credit card may also be vital in emergencies.
- Visa, MasterCard and American Express are the most widely accepted.

Moneychangers

- You can exchange money at major airports, some banks and all currency-exchange offices such as **American Express** (www.americanexpress.com) or **Travelex** (www.travelex.com). Always enquire about rates and fees.
- Outside big cities, exchanging money may be a problem, so make sure you have a credit card and sufficient cash on hand.

Taxes

- California state sales tax (7.5%) is added to the retail price of most goods and services (gasoline is an exception).
- Local and city sales taxes may tack on up to an additional 2.5%.
- Tourist lodging taxes vary statewide, but currently average 12% or more.

Traveler's Checks

- Traveler's checks have pretty much fallen out of use.

- Big-city restaurants, hotels and department stores will often accept traveler's checks (in US dollars only), but small businesses, markets and fast-food chains may refuse them.
- Visa and American Express are the most widely accepted issuers of traveler's checks.

Opening Hours

Standard opening hours are as follows.

Banks 9am–5pm Monday–Friday, to 6pm Friday, some 9am–1:30pm Saturday

Bars 5pm–2am daily

Business hours (general) 9am–5pm Monday–Friday

Nightclubs 10pm–4am Thursday–Saturday

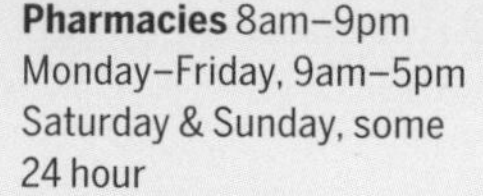

Pharmacies 8am–9pm Monday–Friday, 9am–5pm Saturday & Sunday, some 24 hour

Post offices 8:30am–4:30pm Monday–Friday, some 9am–noon Saturday

Restaurants 7:30am–10:30am, 11:30am–2:30pm & 5.30–9pm daily, some later Friday & Saturday

Shops 10am–6pm Monday–Saturday, noon–5pm Sunday (malls open later)

Supermarkets 8am–9pm or 10pm daily, some 24 hour

Public Holidays

On the following national holidays, banks, schools and government offices (including post offices) are closed, and transportation, museums and other services operate on a Sunday schedule. Holidays falling on a weekend are usually observed the following Monday.

New Year's Day January 1

Martin Luther King Jr Day Third Monday in January

Presidents' Day Third Monday in February

Good Friday Friday before Easter in March/April

Memorial Day Last Monday in May

Independence Day July 4

Labor Day First Monday in September

Columbus Day Second Monday in October

Veterans Day November 11

Thanksgiving Day Fourth Thursday in November

Christmas Day December 25

School Holidays

- Colleges take a one- or two-week 'spring break' around Easter, sometime in March or April. Some hotels and resorts, especially along the coast, near SoCal's theme parks and in the deserts, raise their rates during this time.
- School summer vacations run from mid-June until mid-August, making July and August the busiest travel months.

Tipping

Tipping is *not* optional. Only withhold tips in cases of outrageously bad service.

Airport skycaps & hotel bellhops	$2 per bag, minimum $5 per cart
Bartenders	15% per round, minimum $1 per drink
Concierges	Nothing for simple information, up to $10 for securing last-minute restaurant reservations, sold-out show tickets etc
Housekeeping staff	$2 to $4 daily, left under the card provided; more if you're messy
Parking valets	At least $2 when handed back your car keys
Restaurant servers & room service	18% to 20%, unless a gratuity is already charged (common for groups of six or more)
Taxi drivers	10% to 15% of metered fare, rounded up to the next dollar

Safe Travel

Despite its seemingly apocalyptic list of dangers – guns, violent crime, riots, earthquakes – California is a reasonably safe place to visit. The greatest danger is posed by car accidents (buckle up – it's the law), while the biggest annoyances are metro-area traffic and crowds. Wildlife poses some small threats, and of course there is the dramatic, albeit unlikely, possibility of a natural disaster.

Earthquakes

Earthquakes happen all the time but most are so tiny they are detectable only by sensitive seismological instruments. If you're caught in a serious shaker:

- If indoors, get under a desk or table or stand in a doorway.
- Protect your head and stay clear of windows, mirrors or anything that might fall.
- Don't head for elevators or go running into the street.
- If you're in a shopping mall or large public building, expect the alarm and/or sprinkler systems to come on.
- If outdoors, get away from buildings, trees and power lines.
- If you're driving, pull over to the side of the road away from bridges, overpasses and power lines. Stay inside the car until the shaking stops.
- If you're on a sidewalk near buildings, duck into a doorway to protect yourself from falling bricks, glass and debris.
- Prepare for aftershocks.
- Turn on the radio and listen for bulletins.
- Use the telephone only if absolutely necessary.

Wildlife

- Never feed or approach any wild animal, not even harmless-looking critters – it causes them to lose their innate fear of humans, which in turn makes them dangerously aggressive. Many birds and mammals, including deer and rodents such as squirrels, carry serious diseases that can be transmitted to humans through biting.
- Disturbing or harassing protected species, including many marine mammals such as whales, dolphins and seals, is a crime, subject to enormous fines.
- Black bears are often attracted to campgrounds, where they may find food, trash and any other scented items left out on picnic tables or stashed in tents and cars. Always use bear-proof containers where they are provided. For more bear-country travel tips, visit the **SierraWild website** (www.sierrawild.gov/bears).
- If you encounter a black bear in the wild, don't run. Stay together, keeping small children next to you and picking up little ones. Keep back at least 100yds. If the bear starts moving toward you, back away slowly off-trail and let it pass by, being careful not to block any of the bear's escape routes or to get caught between a mother and her cubs. Sometimes a black bear will 'bluff charge' to test your dominance. Stand your ground by making yourself look as big as possible (eg waving your arms above your head) and shouting menacingly.
- Mountain lion attacks on humans are rare, but can be deadly. If you encounter a mountain lion stay calm, pick up small children, face the animal and retreat slowly. Make yourself appear larger by raising your arms or grabbing a stick. If the lion becomes menacing, shout or throw rocks at it. If attacked, fight back aggressively.
- Snakes and spiders are common throughout California, not just in wilderness areas. Always look inside your shoes before putting them back on outdoors, especially when camping. Snake bites are rare, but occur most often when a snake is stepped on or provoked (eg picked up or poked with a stick). Antivenom is available at most hospitals.

Telephone

Cell (Mobile) Phones

- You'll need a multiband GSM phone to make calls in the USA. Popping in a US prepaid rechargeable SIM card is usually cheaper than using your network.
- SIM cards are sold at telecommunications and electronics stores. These stores also sell inexpensive prepaid phones, including some airtime.
- You can rent a cell phone at Los Angeles (LAX) and San Francisco (SFO) International Airports from **TripTel** (☎877-

874-7835; www.triptel.com); pricing plans vary, but typically are expensive.

Dialing Codes

- US phone numbers consist of a three-letter area code followed by a seven-digit local number.
- When dialing a number within the same area code, use the seven-digit number (if that doesn't work, try all 10 digits).
- For long-distance calls, dial ☎1 plus the area code plus the local number.
- Toll-free numbers begin with 800, 855, 866, 877 or 888 and must be preceded by 1.
- For direct international calls, dial ☎011 plus the country code plus the area code (usually without the initial '0') plus the local phone number.
- If you're calling from abroad, the country code for the US is 1 (the same as Canada, but beware international rates apply between the two countries).

Payphones & Phonecards

Where payphones still exist, they are usually coin-operated, although some may only accept credit cards (eg in national parks). Local calls usually cost 50¢ minimum. For long-distance calls, you're usually better off buying a prepaid phonecard, sold at supermarkets, pharmacies, newsstands and electronics and convenience stores.

Tourist Information

- For pretrip planning, peruse the information-packed website of the **California Travel and Tourism Commission** (www.visitcalifornia.com).
- The same government agency operates nearly 20 statewide **California Welcome Centers** (www.visitcwc.com), where staff dispense maps and brochures and may be able to help find accommodations.
- Almost every city and town has a local visitor center or a chamber of commerce where you can pick up maps, brochures and information.

Travelers with Disabilities

Much of California is reasonably well-equipped for travelers with disabilities, especially in metro areas and popular tourist spots.

Accessibility

- Most traffic intersections have dropped curbs and sometimes audible crossing signals.
- The Americans with Disabilities Act (ADA) requires public buildings built after 1993 to be wheelchair-accessible, including restrooms.
- Motels and hotels built after 1993 must have at least one ADA–compliant accessible room; state your specific needs when making reservations.
- For nonpublic buildings built prior to 1993, including hotels, restaurants, museums and theaters, there are no accessibility guarantees; call ahead to find out what to expect.
- Most national and many state parks and some other outdoor recreation areas offer paved or boardwalk-style nature trails accessible by wheelchairs.
- Many theme parks go out of their way to be accessible to wheelchairs and guests with mobility limitations and various disabilities.
- US citizens and permanent residents with a permanent

Important Numbers

All phone numbers have a three-digit area code followed by a seven-digit local number. For long-distance and toll-free calls, dial ☎1 plus all 10 digits.

Country code ☎1

International dialing code ☎011

Operator ☎0

Emergency (ambulance, fire & police) ☎911

Directory assistance (local) ☎411

disability quality for a free lifetime **'America the Beautiful' Access Pass** (http://store.usgs.gov/pass/access.html), which waives entry fees to all national parks and federal recreational lands and offers 50% discounts on some recreation fees (eg camping).

- California State Parks' disabled discount pass ($3.50) entitles those with permanent disabilities to 50% off day-use parking and camping fees; for an application, click to www.parks.ca.gov.

Communications

- Telephone companies provide relay operators (☎711) for the hearing impaired.
- Many banks provide ATM instructions in Braille.

Helpful Resources

A Wheelchair Rider's Guide to the California Coast (www.wheelingcalscoast.org) Free accessibility information covering beaches, parks and trails, plus downloadable PDF guides to the San Francisco Bay Area and Los Angeles and Orange County coasts.

Access Northern California (www.accessnca.com) Extensive links to accessible-travel resources, publications, tours and transportation, including outdoor recreation opportunities, plus a searchable lodgings database and an events calendar.

Accessible San Diego (www.access-sandiego.org) Free online city guide (downloadable/print version $4/5) that's updated annually.

California State Parks (http://access.parks.ca.gov) Searchable online map and database of accessible features at state parks.

Flying Wheels Travel (☎507-451-5005; www.flyingwheelstravel.com; 143 W Bridge St, Owatonna, MN 55060) Full-service travel agency for travelers with disabilities, mobility issues and chronic illness.

Los Angeles for Disabled Visitors (www.discoverlosangeles.com/search/site/disabled) Tips for accessible sightseeing, entertainment, museums and transportation.

San Francisco Access Guide (www.sanfrancisco.travel/accessibility/san-francisco-access-guide.html) Free downloadable accessible travel info – dated, but useful.

Santa Cruz County Access Guide (www.scaccessguide.com) Dated but still-handy bilingual (English/Spanish) accessible travel guide (US shipping $3).

Theme Park Access Guide (www.mouseplanet.com/tag) An insider's view of Disneyland and other SoCal theme parks 'on wheels.'

Yosemite National Park Accessibility (www.nps.gov/yose/planyourvisit/accessibility.htm) Detailed, downloadable accessibility information for Yosemite National Park, including American Sign Language (ASL) interpretation.

Wheelchair Traveling (www.wheelchairtraveling.com) Travel tips, lodging and helpful California destination info.

Transportation

- All major airlines, Greyhound buses and Amtrak trains can accommodate people with disabilities, usually with 48 hours of advance notice required.
- Major car-rental agencies offer hand-controlled vehicles and vans with wheelchair lifts at no extra charge, but you must reserve these well in advance.
- For wheelchair-accessible van rentals, also try **Wheelchair Getaways** (☎800-642-2042; www.wheelchairgetaways.com) in LA and San Francisco or **Mobility Works** (☎877-275-4915; www.mobilityworks.com) in LA, San Francisco, Oakland, San Jose, Sacramento, Fresno and Chico.
- Local buses, trains and subway lines usually have wheelchair lifts.
- Seeing-eye dogs are permitted to accompany passengers on public transportation.
- Taxi companies have at least one wheelchair-accessible van, but you'll usually need to call and then wait for one.

Visas

- Visa information is highly subject to change. Depending on your country of origin, the rules for entering the USA keep changing. Double-check current visa requirements *before* coming to the USA.

- Currently, under the US Visa Waiver Program (VWP), visas are not required for citizens of 38 countries for stays up to 90 days (no extensions) as long as you have a machine-readable passport (MRP) that meets current US standards and is valid for six months beyond your intended stay.
- Citizens of VWP countries must still register with the Electronic System for Travel Authorization (ESTA) online (https://esta.cbp.dhs.gov) at least 72 hours before travel. Once approved, ESTA registration ($14) is valid for up to two years or until your passport expires, whichever comes first.
- Citizens from all other countries or whose passports don't meet US standards need to apply for a visa in their home country. The process costs a nonrefundable fee (minimum $160), involves a personal interview and can take several weeks, so apply as early as possible.
- For up-to-date information about entry requirements and eligibility, check the visa section of the **US Department of State website** (www.travel.state.gov) or contact the nearest USA embassy or consulate in your home country (for a complete list, visit www.usembassy.gov).

Transport

Getting There & Away

Getting to California by air or overland by bus, car or train is easy, although it's not always cheap. Flights, cars and tours can be booked online at www.lonelyplanet.com/bookings.

Entering the Region

California is an important agricultural state. To prevent the spread of pests and diseases, certain food items (including meats, fresh fruit and vegetables) may not be brought into the state. Bakery items, chocolates and hard-cured cheeses are admissible. If you drive into California across the border from Mexico or from the neighboring states of Oregon, Nevada or Arizona, you may have to stop for a quick questioning and inspection by **California Department of Food and Agriculture** (www.cdfa.ca.gov) agents.

Passports

- Under the Western Hemisphere Travel Initiative (WHTI), all travelers must have a valid machine-readable passport (MRP) when entering the USA by air, land or sea.
- The only exceptions are for some US, Canadian and Mexican citizens traveling *by land* who can present other WHTI-compliant documents (eg preapproved 'trusted traveler' cards). A regular driver's license is *not* sufficient.
- All foreign passports must meet current US standards and be valid for at least six months longer than your intended stay.
- MRPs issued or renewed after October 26, 2006, must be e-passports (ie have a digital photo and integrated chip with biometric data).
- For more information, consult www.cbp.gov/travel.

 Air

- To get through airport security checkpoints (30-minute wait times are standard), you'll need a boarding pass and photo ID.
- Some travelers may be required to undergo a secondary screening, involving hand pat-downs and carry-on bag searches.
- Airport security measures restrict many common items (eg pocket knives, scissors) from being carried on planes. Check current restrictions with the **Transportation Security Administration** (TSA; ☎866-289-9673; www.tsa.gov).
- Currently, TSA requires that all carry-on liquids and gels be stored in 3oz or smaller bottles placed inside a quart-sized clear plastic zip-top

bag. Exceptions, which must be declared to checkpoint security officers, include medications.

- All checked luggage is screened for explosives. TSA may open your suitcase for visual confirmation, breaking the lock if necessary. Leave your bags unlocked or use a TSA-approved lock.

Airports

California's major international airports are in Los Angeles and San Francisco. Smaller regional airports are served primarily by domestic US carriers.

Los Angeles International Airport (LAX; www.lawa.org/lax; 1 World Way) California's largest and busiest airport, 20 miles southwest of Downtown LA, near the beaches.

Mineta San José International Airport (www.flysanjose.com; 1701 Airport Blvd, San Jose) Forty-five miles south of San Francisco, near Silicon Valley.

Oakland International Airport (OAK; www.oaklandairport.com; 1 Airport Dr) Nationwide domestic service, plus some international flights. The cheapest way to reach downtown San Francisco (15 miles west) from Oakland Airport is via AirBART trams ($6), which connect to the Coliseum station, where you catch BART to downtown SF ($4.05, 25 minutes).

Palm Springs International Airport (PSP; www.palmspringsairport.com; 3400 E Tahquitz Canyon Way) In the desert, east of LA.

San Diego International Airport (Map p294; www.san.org; 3325 N Harbor Dr) Just 4 miles from downtown San Diego.

San Francisco International Airport (www.flysfo.com; S McDonnell Rd) Northern California's major hub, 14 miles south of downtown San Francisco.

Land

Train

Amtrak (☎ 800-872-7245; www.amtrak.com) operates a fairly extensive rail system throughout the USA. Trains are comfortable, if a bit slow, and are equipped with dining and lounge cars on long-distance routes. Fares vary according to the type of train and seating (eg coach or business class, sleeping compartments).

Amtrak's major long-distance routes to/from California:

California Zephyr Daily service between Chicago and Emeryville (from $163, 52 hours), near San Francisco, via Denver, Salt Lake City, Reno, Truckee and Sacramento.

Coast Starlight Travels the West Coast daily from Seattle to LA (from $92, 35 hours) via Portland, Sacramento, Oakland and Santa Barbara.

Southwest Chief Daily departures from Chicago and LA (from $135, 43 hours) via Kansas City, Albuquerque, Flagstaff and Barstow.

Sunset Limited Thrice-weekly service between New Orleans and LA (from $130, 47 hours) via Houston, San Antonio, El Paso, Tucson and Palm Springs.

Train Passes

Amtrak's USA Rail Pass is valid for coach-class train travel only (and not Thruway buses) for 15 ($449), 30 ($679) or 45 ($879) days; children aged two to 15 pay half-price. Travel is limited to eight, 12 or 18 one-way 'segments,' respectively. A segment is not the same as a

Climate Change & Travel

Every form of transport that relies on carbon-based fuel generates CO_2, the main cause of human-induced climate change. Modern travel is dependent on airplanes, which might use less fuel per kilometer per person than most cars but travel much greater distances. The altitude at which aircraft emit gases (including CO_2) and particles also contributes to their climate change impact. Many websites offer 'carbon calculators' that allow people to estimate the carbon emissions generated by their journey and, for those who wish to do so, to offset the impact of the greenhouse gases emitted with contributions to portfolios of climate-friendly initiatives throughout the world. Lonely Planet offsets the carbon footprint of all staff and author travel.

one-way trip; if reaching your destination requires riding more than one train, you'll use multiple pass segments. Purchase passes online, then make advance reservations for each trip segment.

Getting Around

Most people drive around California, although you can also fly (if time is limited, but your budget isn't) or save money by taking buses or often scenic trains.

Air

Several major US carriers fly within California. Flights are often operated by their regional subsidiaries, such as American Eagle, Delta Connection and United Express. Alaska Airlines, Frontier Airlines and Horizon Air serve many regional airports, as do low-cost airlines Southwest and Spirit. Virgin America currently flies out of Los Angeles, San Francisco, San Diego and Palm Springs. JetBlue serves LA County, the San Francisco Bay Area, San Diego and Sacramento.

Bicycle

Although cycling around California is a nonpolluting 'green' way to travel, the distances involved demand a high level of fitness and make it hard to cover much ground. Forget about the deserts in summer and the mountains in winter.

Adventure Cycling Association (www.adventurecycling.org) Online resource for purchasing bicycle-friendly maps and long-distance route guides.

California Bicycle Coalition (http://calbike.org) Links to cycling route maps, events, safety tips, laws, bike-sharing programs and community nonprofit bicycle shops.

Better World Club (☎866-238-1137; www.betterworldclub.com) Annual membership (from $40) gets you two 24-hour emergency roadside pickups and transport within a 30-mile radius.

Road Rules

- Cycling is allowed on all roads and highways – even along freeways if there's no suitable alternative, such as a smaller parallel road; all mandatory exits are marked.
- Some cities have designated bicycle lanes, but make sure you have your wits about you in traffic.
- Cyclists must follow the same rules of the road as vehicles. Don't expect drivers to always respect your right of way.
- Wearing a bicycle helmet is mandatory for riders under 18 years old.
- Ensure you have proper lights and reflective gear, especially if you're pedaling at night or in fog.

Rental & Purchase

- You can rent bikes by the hour, day or week in most cities and tourist towns.
- Rentals start around $10 per day for beach cruisers up to $45 or more for mountain bikes; ask about multiday and weekly discounts.
- Most rental companies require a large security deposit using a credit-card.
- Buy new models from specialty bike shops and sporting-goods stores, or used from notice boards at hostels, cafes, etc.
- To buy or sell used bikes online, check **Craigslist** (www.craigslist.org).

Transporting Bicycles

- Greyhound transports bicycles as luggage (surcharge typically $30 to $40), provided the bicycle is disassembled and placed in a rigid container ($10 box available at some terminals).
- Amtrak's *Cascades*, *Pacific Surfliner*, and *San Joaquin* trains have onboard racks where you can secure your bike unboxed; try to reserve a spot when making your ticket reservation ($5 surcharge may apply).
- On Amtrak trains without racks, bikes must be put in a box ($15 at most staffed terminals) then checked as luggage (fee $10). Not all stations or trains offer checked-baggage service.

Boat

Boats won't get you around California, although there are a few offshore routes, notably to Catalina Island off the coast of Los Angeles and Orange County, and to Channel Islands National Park from Ventura or Oxnard, north of LA toward Santa Barbara. On San Francisco Bay, regular ferries operate between San

Francisco and Sausalito, Larkspur, Tiburon, Angel Island, Oakland, Alameda and Vallejo.

Car, Motorcycle & RV

California's love affair with cars runs deep for at least one practical reason: the state is so big, public transportation can't cover it. For flexibility and convenience, you'll probably want a car, but rental rates and gas prices can eat up a good chunk of your trip budget.

Automobile Associations

For 24-hour emergency roadside assistance, free maps and discounts on lodging, attractions, entertainment, car rentals and more, consider joining an auto club.

American Automobile Association (AAA; ☎ 877-428-2277; www.aaa.com) Walk-in offices throughout California, add-on coverage for RVs and motorcycles, and reciprocal agreements with some international auto clubs (eg CAA in Canada, AA in the UK) – bring your membership card from home.

Better World Club (☎ 866-238-1137; www.betterworldclub.com) Ecofriendly alternative auto club that supports environmental causes and offers optional emergency roadside assistance for cyclists.

Driver's Licenses

- Visitors may legally drive a car in California for up to 12 months with their home driver's license.
- If you're from overseas, an International Driving Permit (IDP) will have more credibility with traffic police and simplify the car-rental process, especially if your license doesn't have a photo or isn't written in English.
- To drive a motorcycle, you'll need a valid US state motorcycle license or a specially endorsed IDP.
- International automobile associations can issue IDPs, valid for one year, for a fee. Always carry your home license together with the IDP.

Fuel

- Gas stations in California, nearly all of which are self-service, are ubiquitous, except in national parks and some sparsely populated desert and mountain areas.
- Gas is sold in gallons (one US gallon equals 3.78L). At press time, the average cost for mid-grade fuel was more than $4.

Insurance

California law requires liability insurance for all vehicles. When renting a car, check your auto-insurance policy from home or your travel insurance policy to see if you're already covered. If not, expect to pay about $20 per day.

Insurance against damage to the car itself, called Collision Damage Waiver (CDW) or Loss Damage Waiver (LDW), costs another $10 to $20 or more per day. The deductible may require you to pay the first $100 to $500 for any repairs.

Some credit cards will cover CDW/LDW, provided you charge the entire cost of the car rental to the card. If there's an accident you may have to pay the rental-car company first, then seek reimbursement from the credit-card company.

Parking

- Parking is usually plentiful and free in small towns and rural areas, but often scarce and/or expensive in cities.
- When parking on the street, read all posted regulations and restrictions (eg street-cleaning hours, permit-only residential areas) and pay attention to colored curbs, or you may be ticketed and towed.
- You can pay municipal parking meters and sidewalk pay stations with coins (eg quarters) and sometimes credit or debit cards.
- Expect to pay $30 to $50 for overnight parking in a city lot or garage.
- Flat-fee valet parking at hotels, restaurants, nightclubs etc is common in major cities, especially LA and Las Vegas, NV.

Rental

CARS

To rent your own wheels, you'll typically need to be at least 25 years old, hold a valid driver's license and have a major credit card, *not* a check or debit card. A few companies may rent to drivers under 25 but over 21 for a hefty surcharge. If you don't have a credit card, occasionally you may be able to make a large cash deposit instead.

With advance reservations, you can often get an economy-size vehicle from around $30 per day, plus insurance, taxes and fees.

Weekend and weekly rates are usually the most economical. Airport rental locations may offer lower rates, but have higher fees; if you buy a fly-drive package, local taxes may be extra. City-center branches sometimes offer free pickups and drop-offs.

Rates generally include unlimited mileage, but expect surcharges for additional drivers and one-way rentals. Some rental companies let you pre-pay for your last tank of gas; this is rarely a good deal, as prices are higher than at gas stations and you'd need to bring the car back almost on empty. Child or infant safety seats are legally required; reserve them when booking for about $10 per day.

If you'd like to minimize your contribution to California's polluted air, some major car-rental companies now offer 'green' fleets of hybrid or bio-fueled rental cars, but they're in short supply. Expect to pay significantly more for these models and reserve them well in advance.

To find and compare independent car-rental companies, as well as to search for cheaper long-term rentals, try **Car Rental Express** (www.carrentalexpress.com).

Alamo (☎ 877-222-9075; www.alamo.com)

Avis (☎ 800-633-3469; www.avis.com)

Budget (☎ 800-218-7992; www.budget.com)

Dollar (☎ 800-800-4000; www.dollar.com)

Enterprise (☎ 800-261-7331; www.enterprise.com)

Fox (☎ 800-225-4369; www.foxrentacar.com) Locations near LA, Burbank, San Diego, Orange County and San Francisco Bay Area airports.

Hertz (☎ 800-654-3131; www.hertz.com)

National (☎ 877-222-9058; www.nationalcar.com)

Rent-a-Wreck (☎ 877-877-0700; www.rentawreck.com) Minimum rental age and under-25 driver surcharges vary at a dozen locations, mostly around LA and the San Francisco Bay Area.

Simply Hybrid (☎ 888-359-0055, 323-653-0011; www.simplyhybrid.com) Rents hybrid, electric and flex-fuel vehicles in LA; ask about free delivery and pickup.

Thrifty (☎ 800-847-4389; www.thrifty.com)

Zipcar (☎ 866-494-7227; www.zipcar.com) Currently available in the San Francisco Bay Area, LA, San Diego, Sacramento, Santa Barbara and Santa Cruz, this car-sharing club charges usage fees (per hour or day), including free gas, insurance (a damage fee of up to $750 may apply) and limited mileage. Apply online (foreign drivers accepted); application fee $25, annual membership from $60.

MOTORCYCLES

Motorcycle rentals and insurance are not cheap, especially if you've got your eye on a Harley. Depending on the model, renting a motorcycle costs $100 to $250 per day plus taxes and fees, including helmets, unlimited miles and liability insurance; one-way rentals and collision insurance (CDW) cost extra. Discounts may be available for multi-day and weekly rentals. Security deposits range up to $2000 (credit card required).

California Motorcycle Adventures (☎ 650-969-6198; www.californiamotorcycleadventures.com; 2554 W Middlefield Rd, Mountain View; ⌚ 9am-6pm Mon-Fri, to 5pm Sat, 10am-5pm Sun) Harley-Davidson rentals in Silicon Valley.

Dubbelju (☎ 415-495-2774, 866-495-2774; www.dubbelju.com; 689a Bryant St, San Francisco; ⌚ 9am-6pm Mon-Sat) Rents Harley-Davidson, BMW and Japanese and Italian imported motorcycles, as well as scooters.

Eagle Rider (☎ 310-536-6777, 888-900-9901; www.eaglerider.com) Nationwide company with 10 locations in California, as well as Las Vegas, NV.

Route 66 Riders (☎ 888-434-4473, 310-578-0112; www.route66riders.com; 4161 Lincoln Blvd, Marina del Rey; ⌚ 10am-6pm Tue-Sat, 11am-5pm Sun) Harley-Davidson rentals in LA's South Bay.

RECREATIONAL VEHICLES

It's easy to find campgrounds throughout California with electricity and water hookups for RVs, but in big cities RVs are a nuisance, since there are few places to park or plug them in. RVs are cumbersome

Road Distances (miles)

	Anaheim	Arcata	Bakersfield	Death Valley	Las Vegas	Los Angeles	Monterey	Napa	Palm Springs	Redding	Sacramento	San Diego	San Francisco	San Luis Obispo	Santa Barbara	Sth Lake Tahoe
Arcata	680															
Bakersfield	135	555														
Death Valley	285	705	235													
Las Vegas	265	840	285	140												
Los Angeles	25	650	110	290	270											
Monterey	370	395	250	495	535	345										
Napa	425	265	300	545	590	400	150									
Palm Springs	95	760	220	300	280	110	450	505								
Redding	570	140	440	565	725	545	315	190	650							
Sacramento	410	300	280	435	565	385	185	60	490	160						
San Diego	95	770	230	350	330	120	465	520	140	665	505					
San Francisco	405	280	285	530	570	380	120	50	490	215	85	500				
San Luis Obispo	225	505	120	365	405	200	145	265	310	430	290	320	230			
Santa Barbara	120	610	145	350	360	95	250	370	205	535	395	215	335	105		
Sth Lake Tahoe	505	400	375	345	460	480	285	160	485	260	100	600	185	390	495	
Yosemite	335	465	200	300	415	310	200	190	415	325	160	430	190	230	345	190

to drive and they burn fuel at an alarming rate. That said, they do solve transportation, accommodation and cooking needs in one fell swoop. Even so, there are many places in national and state parks and in the mountains that RVs can't go.

Book RV rentals as far in advance as possible. Rental costs vary by size and model, but you can expect to pay over $100 per day. Rates often don't include mileage, taxes, vehicle prep fees and bedding or kitchen kits. If pets are even allowed, a surcharge may apply.

Cruise America (480-464-7300, 800-671-8042; www.cruiseamerica.com) Nationwide RV rental company with almost two dozen locations statewide.

El Monte (562-483-4956, 888-337-2214; www.elmonterv.com) With 15 locations across California, this national RV rental agency offers AAA discounts.

Escape Campervans (310-672-9909, 877-270-8267; www.escapecampervans.com) Awesomely painted campervans at economical rates in LA and San Francisco.

Happy Travel Campers (855-754-6555, 310-929-5666; www.camperusa.com) Campervan rentals in the San Francisco Bay Area, LA and Las Vegas, NV.

Jucy Rentals (800-650-4180; www.jucyrentals.com) Campervan rentals in San Francisco, LA and Las Vegas, NV.

Vintage Surfari Wagons (714-585-7565, 949-716-3135; www.vwsurfari.com) VW campervan rentals in Orange County.

Road Conditions & Hazards

For up-to-date highway conditions in California, including road closures and construction updates, dial 800-427-7623 or visit www.dot.ca.gov. For Nevada highways, call 877-687-6237 or check www.nvroads.com.

In places where winter driving is an issue, snow tires and tire chains may be required in mountain areas. Ideally, carry your own chains and learn how to use them before you hit the road. Otherwise, chains can usually be bought (but not cheaply) on the highway, at gas stations or in the nearest town. Most car-rental companies don't permit the use of chains and also prohibit driving off-road or on dirt roads.

In rural areas, livestock sometimes graze next to unfenced roads. These areas are typically signed as 'Open Range,' with the silhouette of a steer. Where deer and other wild animals frequently appear roadside, you'll see signs with the silhouette of a leaping deer. Take these signs seriously, particularly at night.

In coastal areas thick fog may impede driving – slow down and if it's too soupy, get off the road. Along coastal cliffs and in the mountains, watch out for falling rocks, mudslides and avalanches that could damage or disable your car if struck.

Road Rules

- Drive on the right-hand side of the road.
- Talking or texting on a cell phone without a hands-free device while driving is illegal.
- The use of seat belts is required for drivers, front-seat passengers and children under age 16.
- Infant and child safety seats are required for children under six years old or weighing less than 60lb.
- All motorcyclists must wear a helmet. Scooters are not allowed on freeways.
- High-occupancy (HOV) lanes marked with a diamond symbol are reserved for cars with multiple occupants, sometimes only during signposted hours.
- Unless otherwise posted, the speed limit is 65mph on freeways, 55mph on two-lane undivided highways, 35mph on major city streets and 25mph in business and residential districts and near schools.
- Except where indicated, turning right at a red stoplight after coming to a full stop is permitted, although intersecting traffic still has the right of way.
- At four-way stop signs, cars proceed in the order in which they arrived. If two cars arrive simultaneously, the one on the right has the right of way. When in doubt, politely wave the other driver ahead.
- When emergency vehicles (ie police, fire or ambulance) approach from either direction, carefully pull over to the side of the road.
- California has strict anti-littering laws; throwing trash from a vehicle may incur a $1000 fine.
- Driving under the influence of alcohol or drugs is illegal. It's also illegal to carry open containers of alcohol, even empty ones, inside a vehicle. Store them in the trunk.

Local Transportation

Except in cities, public transit is rarely the most convenient option, and coverage to outlying towns and suburbs can be sparse. However, it's usually cheap, safe and reliable.

Bicycle

- Cycling is a feasible way of getting around smaller cities and towns, but it's not much fun in traffic-dense areas like LA.
- San Francisco, Calistoga, Arcata, Sacramento, Santa Cruz, San Luis Obispo, Santa Barbara, Santa Monica and Coronado are among California's most bike-friendly communities, as rated by the **League of American Bicyclists** (www.bikeleague.org).
- Bicycles may be transported on many local buses and trains, sometimes during off-peak, non-commuter hours only.

Bus, Cable Car, Streetcar & Trolley

- Almost all cities and larger towns have reliable local bus systems (average $1 to $3 per ride). Outside of major metro areas, they may provide only limited evening and weekend service.
- San Francisco's extensive Municipal Railway (MUNI) network includes not only buses and trains, but also historic streetcars and those famous cable cars.
- San Diego runs trolleys around some neighborhoods and to the Mexican border.

Train

- LA's Metro is a combined, ever-expanding network of subway and light-rail. Metrolink commuter trains connect LA with surrounding counties.
- San Diego's *Coaster* commuter trains run from downtown and Old Town to Carlsbad, Encinitas, Solana Beach and Oceanside in the North County.
- To get around the San Francisco Bay Area, hop aboard

Bay Area Rapid Transit (BART) or Caltrain.

Taxi

- Taxis are metered, with flag-fall fees of $2.50 to $3.50 to start, plus around $2 to $3 per mile. Credit cards may be accepted, but bring cash just in case.
- Taxis may charge extra for baggage and airport pickups.
- Drivers expect a 10% to 15% tip, rounded up to the next dollar.
- Taxis cruise the streets of the busiest areas in large cities, but elsewhere you may need to call a cab company.

Tours

Green Tortoise (☎ 800-867-8647, 415-956-7500; www.greentortoise.com) Youthful budget-backpacker trips utilize converted sleeping-bunk buses for adventure tours of California's national parks, northern redwood forests, southern deserts and Pacific Coast.

Road Scholar (☎ 800-454-5768; www.roadscholar.org) Formerly Elderhostel, this nonprofit organization offers educational trips – including bus and walking tours and outdoor activities like hiking and birding – for older adults.

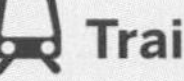

Train

Amtrak (p397) runs comfortable, if occasionally tardy, trains to major California cities and limited towns. At some stations Thruway buses provide onward connections. Smoking is prohibited on board trains and buses.

Costs

Purchase tickets at train stations, by phone or online (in advance for the cheapest prices). Fares depend on the day of travel, the route, the type of seating, etc. Fares may be slightly higher during peak travel times (eg summer). Round-trip tickets typically cost the same as two one-way tickets.

Usually seniors over 62 years and students with an ISIC or Student Advantage Card receive a 15% discount, while up to two children aged two to 15 who are accompanied by an adult get 50% off. AAA members save 10%. Special promotions can become available anytime, so check the website or ask when making reservations.

Reservations

Amtrak reservations can be made up to 11 months prior to departure. In summer and around holidays, trains sell out quickly, so book tickets as early as possible. The cheapest coach fares are usually for unreserved seats; business-class fares come with guaranteed seats.

Travelers with disabilities who need special assistance, wheelchair space, transfer seats or accessible accommodations should call ☎ 800-872-7245 (TDD/TTY ☎ 800-523-6590), and also inquire about discounted fares when booking.

Train Passes

Amtrak's California Rail Pass costs $159 ($80 for children aged two to 15) and is valid on all trains (except certain long-distance routes) and most connecting Thruway buses for seven days of travel within a 21-day period. Passholders must reserve each leg of travel in advance and obtain hard-copy tickets prior to boarding.

Behind the Scenes

Author Thanks

Sara Benson

Thanks to Suki Gear, Cliff Wilkinson, Alison Lyall and the entire Lonely Planet team, including my co-authors. Family and friends all over California generously gave me insider tips, good company on road trips and most importantly, spare rooms to crash in. Special thanks to my Golden Gate Bridge running partners Beth Kohn (also my Sierra Nevada trail guru) and Derek Wolfgram (expert advisor on Bay Area craft beer).

Acknowledgments

Climate map data adapted from Peel MC, Finlayson BL & McMahon TA (2007) 'Updated World Map of the Köppen-Geiger Climate Classification', Hydrology and Earth System Sciences, 11, 1633¬44.

Cover photographs
Front: Yosemite National Park, Jeff Hunter/Getty
Back: Lone Cypress, 17-Mile Drive, Big Sur, Pietro Canali/4Corners

This Book

This 3rd edition of Lonely Planet's *Discover California* was written by Sara Benson, Andrew Bender, Alison Bing, Celeste Brash, Tienlon Ho, Beth Kohn, Adam Skolnick & John A Vlahides. The previous edition was written by Beth Kohn, Andrew Bender, Sara Benson, Alison Bing and John A Vlahides, along with Bridget Gleeson, Nate Cavalieri and Andrea Schulte-Peevers.
This guidebook was produced by the following:
Destination Editor Clifton Wilkinson
Product Editors Elizabeth Jones, Anne Mason
Senior Cartographer Alison Lyall
Book Designers Wibowo Rusli
Assisting Editor Jeanette Wall
Cover Researcher Naomi Parker
Thanks to Sasha Baskett, Kate Chapman, Penny Cordner, Victoria Crookes, Brendan Dempsey, Chris Espinosa, Ryan Evans, Larissa Frost, Anna Harris, Chris Love, Virginia Moreno, Jennifer Mullins, Katie O'Connell, Jessica Rose, Samantha Russell-Tulip, Lyahna Spencer, Saralinda Turner, Amanda Williamson.

SEND US YOUR FEEDBACK

We love to hear from travelers – your comments keep us on our toes and help make our books better. Our well-traveled team reads every word on what you loved or loathed about this book. Although we cannot reply individually to your submissions, we always guarantee that your feedback goes straight to the appropriate authors, in time for the next edition. Each person who sends us information is thanked in the next edition, the most useful submissions are rewarded with a selection of digital PDF chapters.

Visit **lonelyplanet.com/contact** to submit your updates and suggestions or to ask for help. Our award-winning website also features inspirational travel stories, news and discussions.

Note: We may edit, reproduce and incorporate your comments in Lonely Planet products such as guidebooks, websites and digital products, so let us know if you don't want your comments reproduced or your name acknowledged. For a copy of our privacy policy visit lonelyplanet.com/privacy.

Index

000 Map pages

D

000 Map pages

E

F

G

H

I

J

K

L

M

000 Map pages

N

O

P

000 Map pages

Q

R

S

T

U

000 Map pages

How to Use This Book

These symbols give you the vital information for each listing:

- Telephone Numbers
- Opening Hours
- Parking
- Nonsmoking
- Air-Conditioning
- Internet Access
- Wi-Fi Access
- Swimming Pool
- Vegetarian Selection
- English-Language Menu
- Family-Friendly
- Pet-Friendly
- Bus
- Ferry
- Metro
- Subway
- Tram
- BART

All reviews are ordered in our authors' preference, starting with their most preferred option. Additionally:

Sights are arranged in the geographic order that we suggest you visit them, and within this order, by author preference.

Eating and Sleeping reviews are ordered by price range (budget, mid-range, top end) and within these ranges, by author preference.

Look out for these icons:

FREE No payment required

A green or sustainable option

Our authors have nominated these places as demonstrating a strong commitment to sustainability – for example by supporting local communities and producers, operating in an environmentally friendly way, or supporting conservation projects.

Map Legend

Note: Not all symbols displayed appear on the maps in this book

Sights

- Beach
- Bird Sanctuary
- Buddhist
- Castle/Palace
- Christian
- Confucian
- Hindu
- Islamic
- Jain
- Jewish
- Monument
- Museum/Gallery/Historic Building
- Ruin
- Shinto
- Sikh
- Taoist
- Winery/Vineyard
- Zoo/Wildlife Sanctuary
- Other Sight

Activities, Courses & Tours

- Bodysurfing
- Diving
- Canoeing/Kayaking
- Course/Tour
- Sento Hot Baths/Onsen
- Skiing
- Snorkeling
- Surfing
- Swimming/Pool
- Walking
- Windsurfing
- Other Activity

Sleeping

- Sleeping
- Camping

Eating

- Eating

Drinking & Nightlife

- Drinking & Nightlife
- Cafe

Entertainment

- Entertainment

Shopping

- Shopping

Transport

- Airport
- BART station
- Border crossing
- Boston T station
- Bus
- Cable car/Funicular
- Cycling
- Ferry
- Metro station
- Monorail
- Parking
- Petrol station
- Subway/SkyTrain station
- Taxi
- Train station/Railway
- Tram
- Underground station
- Other Transport

Information

- Bank
- Embassy/Consulate
- Hospital/Medical
- Internet
- Police
- Post Office
- Telephone
- Toilet
- Tourist Information
- Other Information

Geographic

- Beach
- Lighthouse
- Lookout
- Mountain/Volcano
- Oasis
- Park
- Pass
- Picnic Area
- Waterfall

Population

- Capital (National)
- Capital (State/Province)
- City/Large Town
- Town/Village

Boundaries

- International
- State/Province
- Disputed
- Regional/Suburb
- Marine Park
- Cliff; Wall

Routes

- Tollway
- Freeway
- Primary
- Secondary
- Tertiary
- Lane
- Unsealed road
- Plaza/Mall
- Steps
- Tunnel
- Pedestrian overpass
- Walking Tour
- Walking Tour detour
- Path/Walking Trail

Hydrography

- River, Creek
- Intermittent River
- Canal
- Water
- Dry/Salt Lake
- Reef

Areas

- Airport/Runway
- Beach/Desert
- Cemetery (Christian)
- Cemetery (Other)
- Glacier
- Mudflat
- Park/Forest
- Sight (Building)
- Sportsground
- Swamp

TIENLON HO

Gold Country An Ohioan by birth but a Californian at stomach, Tienlon Ho has walked, run, climbed, crawled, tumbled, fished, swam, and eaten her way around the state enough times to say California is huge – and spectacular. Besides authoring guides and books for Lonely Planet, she writes about food, environment and technology for a number of publications. Follow her travels and more at tienlon.com and @tienlonho.

BETH KOHN

Northern California & Central Coast, Yosemite & the Sierra Nevada A lucky long-time resident of San Francisco, Beth lives to be playing outside or splashing in big puddles of water. For this guidebook, she hiked and biked Bay Area byways, backpacked Yosemite and Lake Tahoe in winter and soaked in myriad mountain-view hot springs. She is an author of Lonely Planet's *Yosemite, Sequoia & Kings Canyon National Parks* and *Mexico* guides, and you can see more of her work at www.bethkohn.com.

ADAM SKOLNICK

Los Angeles Adam Skolnick has written about travel, culture, health, sports, human rights and the environment for Lonely Planet, *The New York Times*, *Outside*, *Men's Health*, *Travel & Leisure*, Salon.com, BBC.com and ESPN.com. He has authored or co-authored 25 Lonely Planet guidebooks. Find him on Twitter and Instagram (@adamskolnick).

JOHN A VLAHIDES

Napa & Sonoma Wine Country John A Vlahides co-hosts the TV series *Lonely Planet: Roads Less Travelled,* screening on National Geographic Channels International. John studied cooking in Paris, with the same chefs who trained Julia Child, and is a former luxury-hotel concierge and member of Les Clefs d'Or, the international union of the world's elite concierges. He lives in San Francisco, where he sings tenor with the San Francisco Symphony, and spends free time skiing the Sierra Nevada. For more, see JohnVlahides.com and @JohnVlahides on Twitter.

Read more about John at:
lonelyplanet.com/members/johnvlahides

Our Story

A beat-up old car, a few dollars in the pocket and a sense of adventure. In 1972 that's all Tony and Maureen Wheeler needed for the trip of a lifetime – across Europe and Asia overland to Australia. It took several months, and at the end – broke but inspired – they sat at their kitchen table writing and stapling together their first travel guide, *Across Asia on the Cheap*. Within a week they'd sold 1500 copies. Lonely Planet was born.

Today, Lonely Planet has offices in Franklin, London, Melbourne, Oakland, Beijing and Delhi, with more than 600 staff and writers. We share Tony's belief that 'a great guidebook should do three things: inform, educate and amuse'.

Our Writers

SARA BENSON

Coordinating Author, Santa Barbara County, Central Coast Following her graduation from college, Sara jumped on a plane to California with just one suitcase and $100 in her pocket. After driving tens of thousands of miles to every corner of this state, she settled in a little beach town halfway between San Francisco and LA. She's an avid hiker, backpacker, cyclist and all-seasons outdoor enthusiast who has worked for the National Park Service in the Sierra Nevada Mountains. The author of more than 65 travel and nonfiction books, Sara is the lead writer for Lonely Planet's *California*, *California's Best Trips*, *Coastal California* and *Los Angeles, San Diego & Southern California* guidebooks. Follow her latest adventures online at www.indietraveler.blogspot.com, www.indietraveler.net, @indie_traveler on Twitter and indietraveler on Instagram.

Read more about Sara at:
lonelyplanet.com/members/Sara_Benson

ANDREW BENDER

Los Angeles Andy is a true Angeleno, not because he was born in Los Angeles but because he's made it his own. This native New Englander drove cross-country to work in film production, and eventually realized that the joy was in the journey (and writing about it). He writes the Seat 1A travel site for Forbes, and his writing has also appeared in the *Los Angeles Times*, in-flight magazines and over three dozen Lonely Planet titles. Current obsessions: discovering SoCal's next great ethnic enclave, and photographing winter sunsets over the Pacific.

ALISON BING

San Francisco Over 10 guidebooks and 20 years in San Francisco, author Alison Bing has spent more time in Alcatraz than some inmates, become an aficionado of drag and burritos, and wilfully ignored Muni signs warning that 'safety requires avoiding unnecessary conversation.'

CELESTE BRASH

North Coast & the Redwoods, Northern Mountains Celeste's ancestors moved to Northern California in 1906 and this is the region she will always consider home. After 15 years in French Polynesia she now lives in the Pacific Northwest and was thrilled to head south to explore and imbibe the treasures of her old stomping grounds, hike snowy peaks, find petroglyphs in caves, be awed by redwoods and seduced by the wild coast. Find out more about Celeste at www.celestebrash.com.

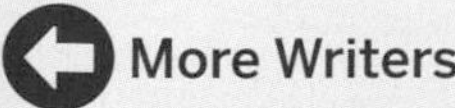

More Writers

Published by Lonely Planet Publications Pty Ltd
ABN 36 005 607 983
3rd edition – April 2015
ISBN 978 1 74220 624 0

10 9 8 7 6 5 4 3 2 1
Printed in China